CULTURAL
ANTHROPOLOGY

BERING
SEA

ALEUTIANS

U.S. STATE OF
ALASKA

GREENLAND
(Denmark)

ICELAND

UNIT
KINGI

IRELAND

BELC

FRANC

CANADA

HUDSON
BAY

NORTH PACIFIC OCEAN

*NORTH
ATLANTIC OCEAN*

PORTUGAL SPAI

UNITED STATES

AZORES (Port.)
MADEIRA (Port.)

U.S. STATE OF
HAWAII

BERMUDA (Br.)

CANARY I. (Sp.)

MOROCCO

MEXICO

BAHAMAS

CUBA

HAITI

DOMINICAN REPUBLIC
PUERTO RICO (U.S.)
GUADELOUPE (Fr.)
MARTINIQUE (Fr.)
ST. LUCIA (Br.)
BARBADOS
TRINIDAD & TOBAGO

ALO

CAPE
VERDE MAURITANIA

MALI

BELIZE
HONDURAS JAMAICA

GUATEMALA
EL SALVADOR NICARAGUA GRENADA

COSTA RICA

SENEGAL
GAMBIA

GUINEA

BURKIN
FASO

PANAMA VENEZUELA
GUYANA
SURINAME
FRENCH GUIANA

GUINEA BISSAU

SIERRA LEONE

LIBERIA

IVORY COAST

GHANA

TOGO

BEN

GALAPAGOS I. (Ec.)

COLOMBIA

WESTERN SAMOA

ECUADOR

SÃO TOMÉ & PRINC

MARQUESAS I. (Fr.)

PERU

SOCIETY I. (Fr.)
TONGA

BRAZIL

ASCENSION I. (Br.)

TUAMOTU I. (Fr.)

COOK I. (Br.)

BOLIVIA

PARAGUAY

*SOUTH
ATLANTIC OCEAN*

CHILE

URUGUAY

CAPE O'

ARGENTINA

SOUTH PACIFIC OCEAN

FALKLAND I. (Br.)

CAPE HORN

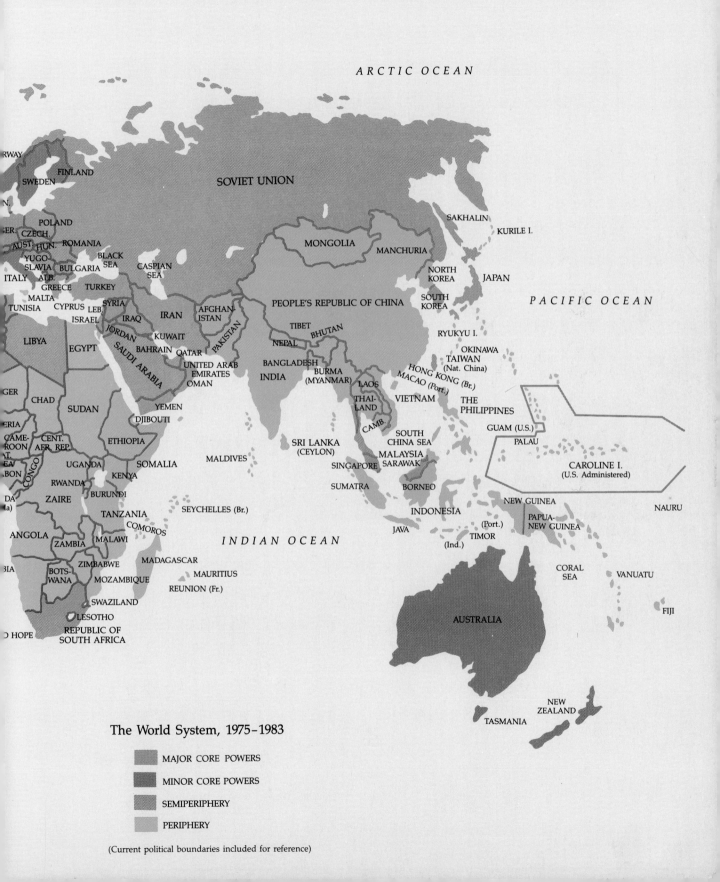

ARCTIC OCEAN

SWEDEN
FINLAND
N.
POLAND
GER
CZECH
SOVIET UNION
AUST HUN.
ROMANIA
BLACK
SEA
YUGO-
SLAVIA BULGARIA
CASPIAN
SEA
ITALY ALB.
GREECE TURKEY
MALTA
TUNISIA CYPRUS LEB.
SYRIA
ISRAEL
IRAQ
IRAN
JORDAN KUWAIT
LIBYA
EGYPT
SAUDI ARABIA
BAHRAIN
QATAR
UNITED ARAB
EMIRATES
OMAN
GER
CHAD
SUDAN
YEMEN
DJIBOUTI
ERIA
CAME-
ROON
T.
EA
CENT.
AFR. REP
ETHIOPIA
BON
CONGO
UGANDA
RWANDA
KENYA
DA
a)
ZAIRE
BURUNDI
TANZANIA
COMOROS
ANGOLA
ZAMBIA
MALAWI
BIA
ZIMBABWE
BOTS-
WANA
MOZAMBIQUE
MADAGASCAR
MAURITIUS
REUNION (Fr.)
SWAZILAND
LESOTHO
HOPE
REPUBLIC OF
SOUTH AFRICA

MONGOLIA
MANCHURIA
SAKHALIN
KURILE I.
NORTH
KOREA
JAPAN
PEOPLE'S REPUBLIC OF CHINA
SOUTH
KOREA
PACIFIC OCEAN
AFGHAN-
ISTAN
TIBET
BHUTAN
PAKISTAN
NEPAL
RYUKYU I.
OKINAWA
TAIWAN
(Nat. China)
BANGLADESH
BURMA
(MYANMAR)
HONG KONG (Br.)
MACAO (Port.)
INDIA
LAOS
VIETNAM
THAI-
LAND
THE
PHILIPPINES
GUAM (U.S.)
PALAU
CAMB.
SRI LANKA
(CEYLON)
SOUTH
CHINA SEA
MALDIVES
SINGAPORE
MALAYSIA
SARAWAK
CAROLINE I.
(U.S. Administered)
SUMATRA
BORNEO
NEW GUINEA
SEYCHELLES (Br.)
NAURU
INDONESIA
PAPUA-
NEW GUINEA
JAVA
(Port.)
TIMOR
(Ind.)
INDIAN OCEAN
CORAL
SEA
VANUATU
FIJI
AUSTRALIA

NEW
ZEALAND
TASMANIA

The World System, 1975–1983

MAJOR CORE POWERS

MINOR CORE POWERS

SEMIPERIPHERY

PERIPHERY

(Current political boundaries included for reference)

FIFTH EDITION

CULTURAL ANTHROPOLOGY

Conrad Phillip Kottak

McGRAW-HILL, INC.

New York   St. Louis   San Francisco   Auckland   Bogotá
Caracas   Hamburg   Lisbon   London   Madrid   Mexico   Milan   Montreal
New Delhi   Paris   San Juan   São Paulo   Singapore   Sydney   Tokyo   Toronto

This book was set in Palatino by Waldman Graphics, Inc.
The editors were Phillip A. Butcher,
Lori Pearson, and Bob Greiner;
the designer was Joan E. O'Connor;
the production supervisor was Richard A. Ausburn.
The photo editor was Barbara Salz.
Von Hoffmann Press, Inc., was printer and binder.

Cover: Rice Planting, Japan. Grant V. Faint/The Image Bank.

CULTURAL ANTHROPOLOGY

2 3 4 5 6 7 8 9 0   VNH   VNH   9 5 4 3 2 1

ISBN 0-07-035615-7

Library of Congress Cataloging-in-Publication Data is
available: LC Card #20434.

ABOUT THE AUTHOR

Conrad Phillip Kottak received his Ph.D. from Columbia University in 1966 and is professor of anthropology at the University of Michigan, where he has taught since 1968. He is currently chair of the general anthropology division of the American Anthropological Association.

Kottak has done field work in cultural anthropology in Brazil (since 1962), in Madagascar (since 1966), and in the United States. His general area of interest includes the processes by which local cultures are incorporated into larger systems; this interest links his earlier work on ecology and state formation in Africa and Madagascar to his more recent research on global change, economic development, national and international culture, and the mass media.

Professor Kottak's highly readable book *Assault on Paradise: Social Change in a Brazilian Village* was published in 1983 by Random House. Kottak's most recent research project blended ethnography and survey research in studying "Television's Behavioral Effects in Brazil." Kottak and his associates studied six field sites in different regions of Brazil, with support from the National Science Foundation, the National Institute of Mental Health, and the Wenner-Gren Foundation for Anthropological Research. That research is the basis for Kottak's latest book, *Prime-Time Society: An Anthropological Analysis of Television and Culture* (Wadsworth, 1990)—a comparative study of the nature and impact of television in Brazil and the United States.

Kottak's other books include *The Past in the Present: History, Ecology and Cultural Variation in Highland Madagascar* and *Researching American Culture: A Guide for Student Anthropologists* (both University of Michigan Press), as well as *Madagascar: Society and History* (Carolina Academic Press). Kottak's articles have appeared in academic journals, including *American Anthropologist, Journal of Anthropological Research, American Ethnologist, Ethnology,* and *Luso-Brazilian Review,* and in more popular journals including *Transaction/SOCIETY, Natural History,* and *Psychology Today.*

Kottak is currently directing research projects investigating ecological awareness and risk perception in Brazil; the social context of urban waste water use for irrigation in Natal, Brazil; and developing a remote sensing approach to the human context and impact of deforestation in Madagascar.

To my mother,
Mariana Kottak Roberts

CONTENTS IN BRIEF

CONTENTS

CHAPTER 3 **CULTURE** 35

CHAPTER 4 **BIOLOGICAL DIVERSITY AND RACE** 49

CHAPTER 14   **RELIGION**   239

PREFACE

Having done a major revision for the fourth edition of *Cultural Anthropology*, I hadn't planned to change much for the fifth. However, as I began considering what to revise, I discovered that cultural anthropology had been changing faster than I had realized. Also, a very thorough set of reviews (see list of reviewers) generally complimented the stylistic and content changes I made in the last edition but also suggested improvements I hadn't planned. Organization and updating were among the most important components of the revision this time. I tried to retain the features, including the livelier writing style, that most users of the fourth edition liked.

Instructors, students, and reviewers especially liked certain chapters and sections introduced in the fourth edition. I've updated and strengthened these, which include the chapters on Field Methods (Chapter 2), Culture (Chapter 3), The Future (Chapter 19), and the section on careers in anthropology in Chapter 17. I originally wrote that section, which many reviewers said they found particularly useful, because my own students so often ask me, "What can I do with an anthropology major?" or "How will anthropology help me get a job?"

I've added some new **profiles** and boxes to the fourth edition's popular **issues boxes**. The fifth edition now has one or more of these in each chapter. These boxes provide students with an oppor-

tunity to consider anthropology's relevance to today's world and to their own lives. Some boxes examine current events or debates. Others are personal accounts of field experiences, which add human feeling to the presentation of anthropology's subject matter. Many boxes illustrate a point by bringing in an example familiar to students from their enculturation or everyday experience.

As with the fourth edition, the entire book was typed into a computer, allowing me to scrutinize every word, sentence, paragraph, and caption—to attend to style, content, and organization. I was able to respond to hundreds of suggestions from users and reviewers. The result, I hope, is a well-organized, interesting, and "user-friendly" introduction to cultural anthropology.

What about **content** revision? In addition to **updating** all chapters, I have added two new chapters: Biological Diversity and Race (Chapter 4) and The World System, Industrialism, and Stratification (Chapter 9). Many chapters have **new sections**—responses to users' and reviewers' suggestions and to my recent teaching experience.

The book now has an obvious **unifying world system theme**, which builds on my previous emphasis on cultural ecology, political economy, and social change. This theme is introduced in Chapter 1 and is developed throughout the book, most obviously in the new Chapter 9.

Chapters have been **reorganized**. The new organization focuses on the themes of political economy, ecological adaptation, change, variation, and diversity—**unifying anthropology's subdisciplines**. (However, other approaches are also discussed and respected.)

I have added new **environmental issues**, content, and themes and new discussions of ecocide, ethnocide, genocide, tribal resistance and cultural survival (especially in Chapters 9 and 18). These topics and issues tie in nicely with the clearer organizational emphasis on adaptation and socioeconomic change within social systems of increasing scale—for example, the rise of the state, the modern world system.

Given the focus on **diversity** in today's curriculum, I believe that the discussion of **race**, **stratification**, and **gender** should be an important part of a cultural anthropology course. Anthropology has a special contribution to make to understanding these topics. Accordingly, the first new chapter (4) discusses the race concept in biology and society, shows how race is socially constructed, and counters arguments that connect race and intelligence. The other new chapter (9) discusses key features of modern stratification systems.

Since the last edition I have also been an active participant in the important **Gender in the Curriculum** Project of the American Anthropological Association. Cooperating with the project organizer Sandra Morgen, I was paired with Yolanda Moses, who commented extensively on, and met with me to discuss, the treatment of gender issues in the fourth edition. In response to Dr. Moses's very useful comments, **gender issues now receive expanded attention in most chapters**. The old sex roles chapter is now a **modern gender chapter** (11), taking account of the many gender studies done by anthropologists during the 1980s.

The following is an **annotated outline**, by chapter, of the main changes in *Cultural Anthropology*:

1. The Scope of Anthropology (major revision contains new overview and statement of the book's **unifying themes—the world system and cultural ecology**; expanded discussion of adaptation and of each subdiscipline; new Mead profile).
2. Field Methods (revised version changes places with the culture chapter, contains new profile-box on Malinowski and issues in **re-**

flexive anthropology, interpretive anthropology, and **writing ethnography**).
3. Culture (revised chapter changes places with chapter on field methods).
4. Biological Diversity and **Race** chapter is new.
5. The Primates (updated version has expanded discussion of **sociobiology** and **gender** issues).
6. Cultural Evolution and Adaptive Strategies is a revised chapter.

The following is the **reorganized core of the book** (Chapters 7 to 11). Earlier discussion of **political economy** issues—**power, stratification, modes of production,** and **gender**—makes the organization of the fifth edition much tighter.

7. Bands and Tribes (major revision includes new discussion of **warfare and tribal peoples** within the modern world system).
8. Chiefdoms and Nonindustrial States (major revision has expanded discussion of **stratification—including gender stratification** and Marx and Weber—and contains useful new chart correlating mode of production, stratification system, and sociopolitical type).
9. The World System, Industrialization, and Stratification are in a **key new chapter**. Core topics are the emergence of the world capitalist economy; industrialism and stratification; why the industrial revolution began in England; colonialism; core, semiperiphery, and periphery. Two new boxes cover the contemporary U.S. periphery (rural Tennessee) and industrialization and gender in Malaysia.

These organizational changes and the new chapters prepare the reader for the examples and case material from bands, tribes, chiefdoms, nonindustrial states, industrial nations, and the world system in each of the following chapters:

10. Economic Systems (revised chapter now compares North Pacific potlatching with cargo-fiesta system in Latin America, within the context of political economy, the world system, and colonialism).
11. Gender Roles (major revision of old sex roles chapter takes studies of the 1980s into account, has new box).

12. Kinship and Descent (revised and updated).
13. Marriage (revised and updated).
14. Religion (revised and updated).
15. Personality and Worldview (all new discussion of **cognitive anthropology** and schema theory are included; discussions of the culture of poverty, limited good, and the Protestant ethic are all linked to political economy and world system theory).
16. Language (revised and updated chapter has new discussions of **language and power**—the political economy of language in the modern world system).

Former Chapters 16 and 17 have been reversed and reorganized. The discussion of applied anthropology (including American examples) now precedes the chapter on contemporary global change and development.

17. Applied Anthropology (major revision covers anthropology and **colonialism,** ethical issues, urban, medical, business and media anthropology, **careers** in anthropology with discussion aimed at undergraduates, particularly prospective majors).
18. Social Change and Development (major revision includes expansion of the world system, acculturation, syncretisms, **media impact, ethnocide, ecocide, genocide, tribal resistance and cultural survival; development anthropology, interventionist philosophy,** development fallacies—the fallacies of overinnovation and underdifferentiation, **culturally appropriate innovation;** with a new box).
19. The Future (updated chapter has new material on the **culture of consumption, the global economy** and **conservation issues,** poverty and the income gap, race, ethnicity, and homelessness—all in world system perspective).

The **appendix** on contemporary American culture has been expanded and updated and new cases have been added.

What about **design, pedagogy, and study aids**? The McGraw-Hill staff and I have taken suggestions by users and reviewers seriously in planning the illustrations. We've increased the number of illustrations, choosing almost all new photos. Most photos and art are now in **color.**

We've retained the pedagogical devices at the end of each chapter that were introduced in the fourth edition: **summary, study questions,** a **glossary** defining terms boldfaced in the chapter, and a short list of **suggested reading.** In addition, a complete **bibliography** appears at the end of the book.

The new **instructor's manual** contains a list of **free rental films** for adopters, organized by topic. Placement of orders can be made through McGraw-Hill sales representatives. The instructor's manual also contains a huge selection of multiple-choice, true-or-false, and essay questions. These are also available on diskette for use with the **computerized test-maker,** allowing instructors to generate entirely new tests from questions included on the diskette.

Available for the first time with the fifth edition is a useful new **Study Guide** for students written by Emanuel Polioudakis, who has worked with me for several years teaching introductory anthropology at the University of Michigan. In the Fall of 1990, Dr. Polioudakis became assistant professor of anthropology at Ohio University.

ACKNOWLEDGMENTS

I owe thanks to many colleagues at McGraw-Hill. It's been a real pleasure getting to know and working with Phil Butcher, the executive editor in charge of anthropology. Phil and senior associate editor Sylvia Shepard helped me immeasurably in planning and accomplishing this revision. Sylvia read draft after draft of several chapters and offered numerous detailed suggestions for improvements. I also enjoyed renewing my long-time friendship with Barry Fetterolf. Barry, who has been associated with this book since its first edition, now heads McGraw-Hill's social sciences publishing.

Jennifer Sutherland did her usual conscientious and efficient work as editing supervisor. Without her I might not have met my deadlines. Bob Greiner took over as editing supervisor after most of the manuscript was in production; he has been an able replacement for Jennifer as the galleys and page proofs arrive. Elise Pattison, editorial assistant, diligently checked all stages of proof. It has been a pleasure to work again with Barbara Salz, photo researcher, and Kathy Bendo, photo manager. I also thank Eric Lowenkron, for his excellent copyediting; Joan O'Connor, for conceiving and executing the attractive new design; Rich Ausburn, for shepherding the manuscript through production; Lori Pearson, marketing manager (and new anthropology editor); Sally Constable, marketing manager, and the McGraw-Hill sales representatives for making sure that instructors get to sample *Cultural Anthropology*.

Thanks are also due to reviewers of the fifth edition: Thomas W. Collins, Memphis State University; William G. Davis, University of California–Davis; Chantal Ferraro, City University of New York–Flushing; Brian L. Foster, Arizona State University; Luther Gerlach, University of Minnesota; Robert Bates Graber, Northeast Missouri State University; Barbara K. Larson, University of New Hampshire; Richard H. Moore, The Ohio State University; John Alan Ross, Eastern Washington University; Mary J. Schneider, University of Arkansas; and Andrei Simic, University of Southern California—especially to Yolanda Moses, who worked with me in the Gender in the Curriculum Project—and to my colleagues in anthropology who use the book and send me comments, corrections, and suggestions.

As always, my wife, children, and mother offered support and inspiration during my work, which lasted more than a year. I renew my dedication of this book to Mariana Kottak Roberts, for kindling my interest in the human condition, for reading and commenting on what I write, and for the insights about people and society she continues to provide.

After three decades in anthropology and over twenty years of teaching, I have benefitted from the knowledge, help, and advice of so many friends, colleagues, teaching assistants, and students that I can no longer fit all their names into a short preface. I hope they know who they are and accept my thanks.

Annually since 1968 I've taught Anthropology 101 to a class of 500 to 600 students, with the help of 8 to 12 teaching assistants each time. Feedback from students and teaching assistants keeps me up-to-date on the interests, needs, and perceptions of the people for whom this book is written. I continue to believe that effective textbooks must be based in enthusiasm and in practice—in the enjoyment of one's own teaching experience. I hope that this product of my experience will be helpful to others.

Conrad Phillip Kottak

CULTURAL
ANTHROPOLOGY

CHAPTER 1

THE SCOPE OF ANTHROPOLOGY

That's just human nature." "People are pretty much the same all over the world." Such opinions, which we hear in conversations, in the mass media, and in a hundred scenes in daily life, promote the erroneous idea that people in other countries have the same desires, feelings, and aspirations that we do. Such statements proclaim that because people are the same, they are eager to receive the values, practices, and products of an expansive American culture. Often this assumption turns out to be wrong.

Anthropology offers a broader perspective. Most people think that anthropologists study fossils and nonindustrial cultures, and they do. My research has taken me to remote villages in Brazil and Madagascar, a large island off the southeast coast of Africa. In Brazil I sailed with fishermen in simple sailboats on Atlantic waters. Among Madagascar's Betsileo people I worked in rice fields and took part in ceremonies in which I entered tombs to rewrap the corpses of decaying ancestors.

However, anthropology is much more than the study of nonindustrial peoples. It is a comparative science that examines all societies, ancient and modern, simple and complex. Most of the other social sciences tend to focus on a single society, usually the United States. Anthropology, however, offers a distinctive cross-cultural perspective, comparing the customs of one society with those of others. Exemplifying cross-cultural comparison and anthropology's increasing focus on modern society is my own most recent research project—a study of the social and cultural context and impact of commercial television in the United States and Brazil (Kottak 1990).

To become a cultural anthropologist, one normally does ethnographic field work. This entails spending a year or more in another culture, living with the natives and learning about their customs. No matter how much the anthropologist learns about that culture, he or she remains an alien there. That experience of alienation has a profound impact. Having learned to respect other customs and beliefs, anthropologists can never forget that there is a wider world. There are normal ways of thinking and acting other than our own.

ADAPTATION, VARIATION, AND CHANGE

Humans are the most adaptable animals in the world. In the Andes of South America, people awaken in villages 17,500 feet above sea level and then trek 1,500 feet higher to work in tin mines. Tribes in the Australian desert worship animals and discuss philosophy. People survive malaria in the tropics. Men have walked on the moon. The model of the *Starship Enterprise* in Washington's Smithsonian Institution symbolizes the desire to seek out new life and civilizations, to boldly go where no one has gone before. Wishes to know the unknown, control the uncontrollable, and bring order to chaos find expression among all peoples. Flexibility and adaptability are basic human attributes, and human diversity is the subject matter of anthropology.

Students are often surprised by the breadth of anthropology, which is a uniquely **holistic** science. It studies the whole of the human condition: past, present, and future; biology, society, language, and culture. People share **society**—organized life in groups—with other animals. Culture, however, is distinctly human. **Cultures** are traditions and customs, transmitted through learning, that govern the beliefs and behavior of the people exposed to them. Children *learn* these traditions by growing up in a particular society.

Cultural traditions include customs and opinions, developed over the generations, about proper and improper behavior. Cultural traditions answer such questions as: How do we do things? How do we interpret the world? How do we tell right from wrong? A culture produces consistencies in behavior and thought in a given society.

The most critical element of cultural traditions is their transmission through learning rather than biological inheritance. Culture is not itself biological, but it rests on hominid biology. (**Hominids** are members of the zoological family that includes fossil and living humans.) For more than a million years, hominids have had at least some of the biological capacities on which culture depends. These abilities are to learn, to think symbolically, to use language, and to employ tools and other cultural features in organizing their lives and adapting to their environments.

Bound neither by time nor by space, anthropology ponders and confronts major questions of human existence. By examining ancient bones and tools, anthropologists solve the mysteries of hominid origins. When did our own ancestors separate from those remote great-aunts and great-uncles whose descendants are the apes? Where and when did *Homo sapiens* originate? How has our species changed? What are we now and where are we going? How have changes in culture and society influenced biological change? Our genus, *Homo,* has been changing for more than 1 million years. Cultural and biological adaptation and evolution have been interrelated and complementary, and humans continue to adapt both biologically and culturally.

Human **adaptation** (the process by which organisms cope with environmental stresses) involves an interplay between culture, heredity, and biological plasticity. As an illustration, consider four different ways in which humans may cope with low oxygen pressure. Pressurized airplane cabins equipped with oxygen masks illustrate *cultural* (technological) adaptation. Natives of highland Peru seem to have certain *genetic* advantages for life at very high altitudes, where air pressure is low. However, human adaptation to high altitudes is not limited to culture and genes.

People who have grown up at a high altitude are physiologically more efficient there than are genetically similar people who have not. Human biological plasticity (the ability to change) permits such *long-term physiological* adaptation during growth and development. We also have the capacity for *immediate physiological* adaptation. Thus, lowlanders arriving in the highlands immediately increase their breathing rate, often doubling their usual rate at sea level. Hyperventilation increases the oxygen in their arteries and lungs, and, as the pulse also increases, blood reaches their tissues more rapidly. All these varied adaptive responses—cultural and biological, voluntary and involuntary, conscious and unconscious—are directed at a single goal: increasing the supply of oxygen in the human organism.

Much of the diversity we see in cultures, as in nature, reflects adaptation to varied environments and circumstances. People creatively manipulate their environment; they are not just determined by it. Recognizing this, John Bennett (1969, p. 19) has defined cultural adaptation as "the problem-solving, creative or coping element in human behavior" as people get and use resources and solve the immediate problems confronting them. This is the first dimension of adaptive behavior: It involves "goal-satisfaction: if coping is successful, the people realize their objectives" (Bennett 1969, p. 13). In a modern market economy these objectives include production, income, and consumption wants or needs.

Besides satisfaction of *individual* goals, a second and equally important dimension of cultural adaptation is conservation of resources. "An economy that realizes economic gain but does so at the cost of exhausting or abusing its resources may be adapting in one dimension (the first) but can be said to be *maladaptive* [emphasis added] along the other." In other words, behavior that benefits individuals may harm the environment and threaten the group's long-term survival. Societies "must attempt to balance conservation of resources against economic success if they hope for a permanent or indefinite settlement [of their environment]" (Bennett 1969, p. 13).

As hominid history has unfolded, social and cultural means of adaptation have become increasingly important. In this process, humans have devised a plethora of strategies for coping with the range of environments and social systems (local, regional, national, and global) they have occupied in time and space. The rate of cultural change has accelerated, particularly during the past 10,000 years. For millions of years, hunting and gathering of nature's bounty—*foraging*—was the sole basis of hominid subsistence. However, it took only a few thousand years for **food production** (cultivation of plants and domestication of animals), which originated in the Middle East 12,000 to 10,000 years ago, to supplant foraging in most areas. People started producing their own food, planting crops and stockbreeding animals, rather than simply taking what nature had to offer.

EVEN ANTHROPOLOGISTS GET CULTURE SHOCK

I first lived in Arembepe (Brazil) during the (North American) summer of 1962. That was between my junior and senior years at New York City's Columbia College, where I was majoring in anthropology. I went to Arembepe as a participant in a now defunct program designed to provide undergraduates with experience doing ethnography—firsthand study of an alien society's culture and social life.

Brought up in one culture, intensely curious about others, anthropologists nevertheless experience culture shock, particularly on the first field trip. *Culture shock* refers to the whole set of feelings about being in an alien setting, and the ensuing reactions. It is a chilly, creepy feeling of alienation, of being without some of the most ordinary, trivial (and therefore basic) cues of one's culture of origin.

As I planned my departure for Brazil in 1962 I could not know just how naked I would feel without the cloak of my own language and culture. My sojourn in Arembepe would be my first trip outside the United States. I was an urban boy who had grown up in Atlanta, Georgia, and New York City. I had little experience with rural life in my own country, none with Latin America, and I had received only minimal training in the Portuguese language.

New York City direct to Salvador, Bahia, Brazil. Just a brief stopover in Rio de Janeiro; a longer visit would be a reward at the end of field work. As our propjet approached tropical Salvador, I couldn't believe the whiteness of the sand. "That's not snow, is it?" I remarked to a fellow field team member. . . .

My first impressions of Bahia were of smells—alien odors of ripe and decaying mangoes, bananas, and passion fruit—and of swatting ubiquitous fruit flies I had never seen before, although I had read extensively about their reproductive behavior in genetics classes. There were strange concoctions of rice, black beans, and gelatinous gobs of unidentifiable meats and floating pieces of skin. Coffee was strong and sugar crude, and every tabletop had containers for toothpicks and manioc (cassava) flour, to sprinkle, like Parmesan cheese, on anything one might eat. I remember oatmeal soup and a slimy stew of beef tongue in tomatoes. At one meal a disintegrating fish head, eyes still attached, but barely, stared up at me as the rest of its body floated in a bowl of bright orange palm oil. . . .

I only vaguely remember my first day in Arembepe. Unlike ethnographers who have studied remote tribes in the tropical forests of interior South America or the highlands of Papua–New Guinea, I did not have to hike or ride a canoe for days to arrive at my field site. Arembepe was not isolated relative to such places, only relative to every other place *I* had ever been. . . .

I do recall what happened when we arrived. There was no formal road into the village. Entering through southern Arembepe, vehicles simply threaded their way around coconut trees, following tracks left by automobiles that had passed previously. A crowd of children had heard us coming, and they pursued our car through the village streets until we parked in front of our house, near the central square. Our first few days in Arembepe were spent with children following us everywhere. For weeks we had few moments of privacy. Children watched our every move through our living room window. Occasion-

Between 6000 and 5000 B.P. (before the present), the first civilizations arose in the Middle East. (**Civilizations, nation-states,** or, most simply, **states** are complex societies with a central government and social classes.) Much more recently, industrial production has profoundly influenced people throughout the world. Today's global economy and communications link all contemporary people, directly or indirectly, in the modern world system. People in local settings must cope with forces generated by progressively larger systems—region, nation, and world. The study of such contemporary adaptations generates new challenges for anthropology: "The cultures of world peoples need to be constantly *re*discovered as these people reinvent them in changing historical circumstances" (Marcus and Fischer 1986, p. 24).

Over the course of human history, major innovations have spread at the expense of earlier ones. Each economic revolution has had social and cultural repercussions. This book will examine behavior and institutions, beliefs, customs, and practices

An ethnographer at work. During a 1980 visit, the author, Conrad Kottak, catches up on the news in Arembepe, a coastal community in Bahia state, northeastern Brazil, that he has been studying since 1962.

ally one made an incomprehensible remark. Usually they just stood there. Sometimes they would groom one another's hair, eating the lice they found. . . .

The sounds, sensations, sights, smells, and tastes of life in northeastern Brazil, and in Arembepe, slowly grew familiar. I gradually accepted the fact that the only toilet tissue available at a reasonable price had almost the texture of sandpaper. I grew accustomed to this world without Kleenex, in which

globs of mucus habitually drooped from the noses of village children whenever a cold passed through Arembepe. A world where, seemingly without effort, women with gracefully swaying hips carried 18-liter kerosene cans of water on their heads, where boys sailed kites and sported at catching houseflies in their bare hands, where old women smoked pipes, storekeepers offered *cachaça* (common rum) at nine in the morning, and men played dominoes on lazy afternoons when there

was no fishing. I was visiting a world where human life was oriented toward water—the sea, where men fished, and the lagoon, where women communally washed clothing, dishes, and their own bodies.

This description is adapted from my ethnographic study *Assault on Paradise: Social Change in a Brazilian Village* (New York: McGraw-Hill, 1983).

associated with several economic systems: foraging, food production, industrialism, and the modern world system.

GENERAL ANTHROPOLOGY

The academic discipline of anthropology, also known as **general anthropology,** includes four main subdisciplines: sociocultural, archeological, biological, and linguistic anthropology. (From here on, I will use the shorter term *cultural anthropology* as a synonym for sociocultural anthropology.) Most American anthropologists, myself included, specialize in cultural anthropology. However, most are also familiar with the basics of the other subdisciplines. Major departments of anthropology usually include representatives of each.

There are historical reasons for the inclusion of four subdisciplines in a single field. American anthropology arose a century ago out of concern for the history and cultures of the native populations

Industrial production has profoundly influenced people throughout the world. Today's global economy and communications link all contemporary people, directly or indirectly, in the modern world system. Here children in rural Niger are fascinated by a solar-powered TV.

of North America ("American Indians"). Interest in the origins and diversity of Native Americans brought together studies of customs, social life, language, and physical traits. (Such a unified anthropology did not develop in Europe, where the subdisciplines tend to exist separately.)

There are also logical reasons for the unity of American anthropology. Each subdiscipline considers variations in time and space (that is, in different geographic areas). Cultural and archeological anthropologists study (among many other topics) changes in social life and customs. Biological anthropologists examine changes in physical form. Linguistic anthropologists may reconstruct the basics of ancient languages by studying modern ones. This concern with variation in time may be stated differently: An interest in **evolution** unifies anthropology's subdisciplines. Defined simply, evolution is change in form over generations. Charles Darwin called it "descent with modification."

The subdisciplines influence each other as an-

American anthropology arose a century ago out of concern for the history and cultures of the native populations of North America. Anthropologist James Mooney took this historic photo at Walpi Pueblo in 1893. A group of Hopi Indians are enacting their traditional bean-planting ceremony.

Cross-cultural comparison shows that many differences between the sexes arise from cultural training rather than biology. Here men in Kenya do the laundry in the river.

thropologists talk, read professional books and journals, and associate in professional organizations. General anthropology explores the basics of human biology, psychology, society, and culture and considers their interrelationships. Anthropologists share certain key assumptions. One is that sound conclusions about "human nature" can't be drawn from a single cultural tradition.

We often hear "nature-nurture" and "genetics-environment" questions. For example, consider gender differences. Do male and female capacities, attitudes, and behavior reflect biological or cultural variation? Are there universal emotional and intellectual contrasts between the sexes? Are females less aggressive than males? Is male dominance a human universal? By examining diverse cultures, anthropology shows that many contrasts between men and women arise from cultural training rather than from biology.

Anthropologists also use their knowledge of biological and cultural diversity to evaluate assertions about intellectual differences. They have found no evidence for biologically determined contrasts in intelligence between rich and poor, black and white, or men and women.

Anthropology is not a science of the exotic carried on by scholars in ivory towers but a discipline with a lot to tell the public. One of its contributions is its broadening, liberating role in a college education. Anthropology's foremost professional organization, the American Anthropological Association, has formally acknowledged a public service role by recognizing a fifth subdiscipline, **applied anthropology**—the application of anthropological data, perspectives, theory, and methods to identify, assess, and solve contemporary social problems. More and more anthropologists from the four main subdisciplines now work in such "applied" areas as public health, family planning, and economic development.

THE SUBDISCIPLINES OF ANTHROPOLOGY

Cultural Anthropology

Cultural anthropologists study society and culture, describing and explaining social and cultural similarities and differences. In considering diversity in time and space, anthropologists must distinguish between the universal, the generalized, and the particular. Certain biological, psychological, social, and cultural features are *universal*—shared by all human populations. Others are merely *generalized*—common to several but not all human groups. Still others are *particular*—not shared at all.

Cultural anthropology has two aspects: **ethnography** (field work) and ethnology (cross-cultural comparison). Ethnography is the data-gathering

PROFILE: MARGARET MEAD

Margaret Mead (1901–1978), the most famous anthropologist who ever lived, was one of my teachers at Columbia University. A full-time staff member at the American Museum of Natural History (also in New York City), Mead taught as an adjunct professor at Columbia for many years.

In winter 1962 I took Mead's course on the peoples and cultures of the Pacific. It was a large lecture, held at night. Mead made dramatic entrances and usually brought along an entourage of admirers. By that time Mead, a short woman with a commanding presence, had taken to walking with a shepherd's staff. Almost as tall as she, the forked rod made her resemble a mature Bo Peep.

Mead was known as a well-organized ethnographer. For example, she used a color-coded note system; into the field she took packs of large index cards of various colors. She used specific colors for notes on different topics, such as economics, religion, and social organization. Her meticulous meth-ods for field work extended to everything she did. Mead's students had to fill out 6- by 8-inch index cards and attach photos. She wanted information on their background and interests, including their previous course work in anthropology. Mead and I never knew each other well. However, she used the information from my class card to write me letters of recommendation for graduate school and fellowships.

During her entire professional life Mead was a public anthropologist. She wrote for social scientists, the educated public, and the popular press. She had a column in *Redbook* and often appeared with Johnny Carson on the *Tonight Show,* particularly before its move to the West Coast. Mead wrote several popular books about culture and personality (now usually called *psychological anthropology*). She was heavily influenced by Franz Boas (1858–1942), her mentor at Columbia and a "father" of American anthropology. Mead eventually did ethnography in the South Pacific, including Sa-moa and New Guinea. From her first field work emerged the popular book *Coming of Age in Samoa* (1928/1961).

Mead embarked for Samoa with a research topic that Boas had suggested: contrasts between female adolescence in Samoa and the United States. She shared Boas's assumption that different cultures train children and adolescents to have different personalities and behavior. Suspicious of biologically determined universals, she assumed that Samoan adolescence would differ from the same period in the United States and that this would affect adult personality. Using her Samoan ethnographic findings, Mead contrasted sexual freedom and experimentation there with repression of adolescent sexuality in the United States. Her research confirmed the Boasian view of *Homo sapiens* as a *tabula rasa* (blank slate) on which different cultures write different lessons. The anthropological moral was that culture, not biology or race, determines human behavior and personality.

part, consisting of field research in a particular culture. My ethnographic experience has been with ocean-going fishermen in northeastern Brazil and rice farmers in central Madagascar. Doing ethnography, I lived in small communities and studied native behavior, beliefs, customs, social life, economic activities, politics, and religion.

The anthropological perspective often differs radically from that of economics or political science. Those disciplines focus on national and official organizations and often on elites. However, the groups that anthropologists have traditionally studied have usually been relatively poor and powerless. Ethnographers often observe discriminatory practices directed toward such people, who experience food shortages, dietary deficiencies, and other aspects of poverty. The anthropological perspective is different—not necessarily better. Political scientists study programs that national planners develop, and anthropologists see how these programs work on the local level. Both perspectives are necessary to understand human life in the late twentieth century.

Anthropologists recognize that cultures are not isolated. As Franz Boas (1940/1966) noted many years ago, contact between neighboring tribes has always existed and has extended over enormous areas. A *world-system perspective* recognizes that many local cultural features reflect the economic and political position that a society occupies in a

Mead's later field work among the Arapesh, Mundugumor, and Tchambuli of New Guinea resulted in *Sex and Temperament in Three Primitive Societies* (1935/1950). That book documented variation in male and female personality traits and behavior across cultures. It provided additional support for the *tabula rasa* position.

Mead's reputation rested on her adventurous spirit, intellect, insight, forceful personality, writing ability, and productivity, along with the topics she chose to address. She made primitive life relevant to her time and her own society. Thus, *Coming of Age in Samoa* was subtitled "A Psychological Study of Primitive Youth *for Western Civilization* [emphasis added]." *Growing Up in New Guinea* (1930) was subtitled "A Comparative Study of Primitive Education."

The public viewed Margaret Mead as a romantic, exotic, and controversial figure. She lived an unorthodox life for her time and gender. She was an early feminist. She married three times. Her last two hus-

Margaret Mead, then Associate Curator of Ethnology at the American Museum of Natural History, holds two samples of Manus art brought back from a seven-month visit to the Manus of the Admiralty Islands. Mead helped anthropology flourish, using her research in the South Sea islands as lessons in alternative life styles.

bands, Reo Fortune and Gregory Bateson, were anthropologists. She was a small, lone, daring, and determined woman who journeyed to remote areas, lived with the natives, and survived to tell of it. Accounts of Mead's life include her autobiography, *Blackberry Winter* (1972), and a biography by her only daughter, Mary Catherine Bateson (1984).

Mead's clear, forceful, and vivid writing captured prominent themes of the Depression era. Her books fueled a revolution in the discussion of human sexuality spurred by Freudian psychology. The preoccupations of Depression-era society included issues that Americans still discuss: family breakdown, teenage sex, the "New Woman," birth control, an increasing divorce rate, and extramarital affairs. Anthropology flourished as South Sea islands offered lessons in romance, sexuality, and alternative life styles. "Free love" in Samoa and the Trobriand Islands (as described by Bronislaw Malinowski [1927, 1929*b*]) provided models for a new sexual order (Stocking 1986).

larger system. "Human populations construct their cultures in interaction with one another, and not in isolation" (Wolf 1982, p. ix). Villagers increasingly participate in regional, national, and world events.

There are many sources of exposure to external forces, including mass media, migration, and improved transportation. City and nation increasingly invade local communities in the guise of tourists, development agents, government and religious officials, and political candidates. Such **linkages,** or interconnections, are prominent components of regional, national, and international systems of politics, economics, and information. These larger systems increasingly affect the people

and places that anthropology has traditionally studied. The study of such linkages and systems is a prominent part of the subject matter of modern anthropology.

Ethnology, the other part of cultural anthropology, examines and compares the results of ethnography—the data gathered in different societies. Ethnologists try to identify and explain cultural differences and similarities, to distinguish between universality, generality, and particularity (see Chapter 3). Ethnology gets data for comparison not just from ethnography but also from the other subdisciplines, particularly from **archeological anthropology,** which reconstructs the social systems of the past.

Archeological Anthropology

Archeological anthropology (more simply, archeology) reconstructs, describes, and interprets human behavior and cultural patterns through material remains. Archeologists are best known for studying **prehistory** (the period before the invention of writing less than 6,000 years ago). However, archeologists also study historical and even living cultures. Through a research project begun in 1973 in Tucson, Arizona, for example, archeologist William Rathje has learned much about contemporary life by studying modern garbage. The value of "garbology," as Rathje calls it, is that it provides "evidence of what people did, not what they think they did, what they think they should have done, or what the interviewer thinks they should have done" (Harrison, Rathje, and Hughes 1989, p. 100). What people report can contrast strongly with their real behavior as revealed by garbology. For example, the garbologists discovered that the three Tucson neighborhoods that reported the lowest beer consumption had the highest number of discarded beer cans per household (Podolefsky and Brown 1989, p. 97).

Using material remains as primary data, and informed by ethnographic knowledge and ethnological theory, archeologists analyze cultural processes and patterns. Several kinds of remains interest archeologists. Garbage tells stories about consumption and activities. Wild and domesti-cated grains have different characteristics which allow archeologists to distinguish between gathering and cultivation. Examination of animal bones reveals the ages of slaughtered animals and provides other information useful in determining whether species were wild or domesticated.

Analyzing such data, archeologists answer several questions about ancient economies. Did the group being studied get its meat from hunting, or did it domesticate and breed animals, killing only those of a certain age and sex? Did plant food come from wild plants or from sowing, tending, and harvesting crops? At sites where people live or have lived, archeologists find **artifacts,** manufactured items. Did the residents make, trade for, or buy particular items? Were raw materials available locally? If not, where did they come from? From such information, archeologists reconstruct patterns of production, trade, and consumption.

Archeologists have spent much time studying **potsherds,** fragments of earthenware. Potsherds are more durable than many other artifacts, such as textiles and wood. The pottery types at a site can suggest its technological complexity. The quantity of pottery fragments allows estimation of population size and density. The discovery that potters used materials that were not locally available suggests systems of trade. Similarities in manufacture and decoration at different sites may be proof of cultural connections. Groups with similar

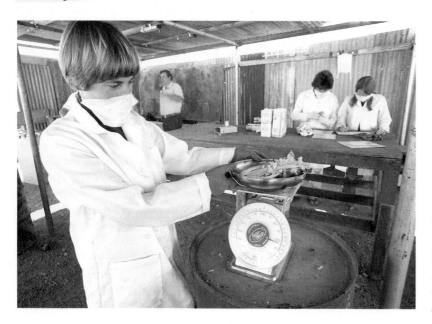

Archeological anthropology reconstructs, describes, and interprets human behavior through material remains. Besides prehistory, archeologists also study living cultures. In Tucson, University of Arizona archeologists learn about contemporary life by analyzing recent garbage.

pots may be historically related. Perhaps they shared common cultural ancestors, traded with each other, or belonged to the same political system.

Many archeologists examine paleoecology. **Ecology** is the study of interrelationships among living things in an environment. The organisms and environment together constitute an **ecosystem,** a patterned arrangement of energy flows and exchanges. Human ecology, or **cultural ecology,** studies ecosystems that include people, focusing on the ways in which human use "of nature influences and is influenced by social organization and cultural values" (Bennett 1969, pp. 10–11). **Paleoecology** looks at the ecosystems of the past. In studying either past or present societies, an ecological approach examines interrelationships among population, culturally styled needs and wants, the division of labor, technology, methods of production, and ways of dividing natural resources among those who need and use them. An ecological analysis cannot be limited to local production but must also study how local people react to informational and economic inputs from external sources.

In addition to reconstructing ecological patterns, archeologists infer cultural evolution, for example, from changes in the size and type of sites and the distance between them. A city develops in a region where only towns, villages, and hamlets existed a century earlier. The number of settlement levels (city, town, village, hamlet) is a measure of social complexity. Buildings offer clues about political and religious features. Special-purpose structures such as temples and pyramids suggest that an ancient society had a central authority capable of marshaling team labor, slave or free. The presence or absence of certain structures reveals differences in function between settlements. For example, some towns were ceremonial centers with prominent architecture. Others were burial sites; still others were farming communities.

Archeologists also document cultural patterns and processes by *excavating* (digging through a succession of levels) at particular sites. In a given area, through time, particular settlements may change in terms of form and purpose, as may the connections between settlements. Excavation can document changes in economic, social, and political activities.

Architecture provides archeologists with clues about political and religious features. Monumental buildings suggest that a society had state organization—a central government capable of marshaling team labor, slave or free. Here archeologists work to preserve the ancient Egyptian past from the flood waters of the Aswan Dam.

To learn about prehistoric populations—those with no written records—archeology is essential. Comparison of archeological sequences in different areas has enabled anthropologists to formulate laws of development. For example, certain environments or economies correlate with particular types of social groups or political systems. Comparative archeology and ethnography both contribute to the understanding of social processes.

Biological, or Physical, Anthropology

The subject matter of **biological,** or **physical, anthropology** is human biological diversity in time and space. A combination of genetic and environmental features produces much of this variation. Relevant environmental stresses include heat and cold, moisture, sunlight, altitude, and disease. The focus on human variation unites five special interests within biological anthropology:

1. Hominid evolution as revealed by the fossil record (**paleoanthropology**)
2. Human genetics
3. Human growth and development
4. Human biological plasticity (the body's ability to cope with stresses, such as heat, cold, and altitude)
5. The biology, evolution, behavior, and social life of monkeys, apes, and other nonhuman primates

These interests link physical anthropology to other fields: biology, zoology, geology, anatomy, physiology, medicine, and public health. **Osteology**—the study of bones—helps paleoanthropologists, who examine skulls, teeth, and bones, to identify hominid ancestors and chart changes in anatomy. Biological anthropologists collaborate with archeologists in reconstructing biological and cultural aspects of human evolution. Fossils and tools are often found together. Tools suggest the habits, customs, and life styles of the hominids who used them.

More than a century ago, Charles Darwin noticed that the variety that exists within any population permits some individuals (those with the favored, or adaptive, characteristics) to do better than others at surviving and reproducing. Genetics, which developed later, enlightens us about the causes and transmission of this variety. However, it isn't just genes that cause variety. During any individual's lifetime, the environment works along with heredity to develop biological features. For example, people with a genetic tendency to be tall will be shorter if they are poorly nourished during childhood. Thus biological anthropology investigates the influence of environment (nutrition, altitude, temperature, and disease) on the body as it develops. As noted earlier, human biological and cultural evolution have been interrelated and complementary, and humans continue to adapt both biologically and culturally. This is why both subdisciplines are studied within general anthropology.

Biological anthropology (along with zoology) also includes **primatology.** The **primates** include our closest relatives—apes and monkeys. Primatologists study their biology, evolution, behavior, and social life, often in their natural environments. Primatology assists paleoanthropology, because many anthropologists believe that primate behavior sheds light on early hominid behavior (and thus on our origins) and on issues of human nature and human universals.

Linguistic Anthropology

We don't know (and probably never will) when hominids began to speak. However, well-developed, grammatically complex languages have existed for thousands of years. **Linguistic anthropology,** like the other subdisciplines, examines variation in time and space. Linguists study languages of the present and make inferences about those of the past. Linguistic techniques are also useful to ethnographers because they permit the rapid learning of unwritten languages.

Descriptive linguistics studies sounds, grammar, and meaning in particular languages. *Historical* linguistics considers variation in time, such as the changes in sounds, grammar, and vocabulary between Middle English (spoken in Chaucer's time) and modern English. There is also variation among the speakers of any language at any given time. One reason for variation is geography, as in regional dialects and accents. Linguistic variation is also associated with social divisions. Examples include the bilingualism of ethnic groups and speech patterns associated with particular social classes. The study of linguistic variation in its social context is called *sociolinguistics*. Linguistic and cultural anthropologists collaborate in studying links between language and other aspects of culture.

Applied Anthropology

Because of anthropology's breadth, its techniques and perspectives have many applications. Both biological and cultural anthropologists contribute to the growing field of medical anthropology. For example, they draw on their direct knowledge of particular communities in planning and evaluating public health programs. Other applied anthropologists work for development agencies, assessing the social and cultural features that influence economic development and change. Anthropologists are experts on local cultures. As such, they often can identify specific social conditions that will influence the success or failure of development schemes. Planners in Washington or Paris often know little about, say, the labor necessary for rice cultivation in rural Madagascar. Forecasts and estimates of project success are often unrealistic if no one consults an anthropologist familiar with the rural scene. Development funds are often wasted if an anthropologist is not asked to identify the local political figures whose support for a program is critical. Such considerations have led development organizations to include anthropologists as well as agronomists, economists, veterinarians, geologists, engineers, and health specialists on planning teams.

Applied anthropologists also work in North America. Garbologists help the Environmental Protection Agency, the paper industry, and packaging and trade associations. Forensic (physical) anthropologists work with the police, medical examiners, and the courts to identify victims of crimes and accidents. From skeletal remains they determine age, sex, size, race, and number of victims. Applied physical anthropologists link injury patterns to design flaws in aircraft and vehicles.

Ethnographers have influenced social policy by showing that strong kin ties exist in city neighborhoods whose social organization was previously considered "fragmented" or "pathological." Suggestions for improvements in the education system emerge from ethnographic studies of classrooms and surrounding communities. Linguistic anthropologists show the influence of dialect differences on classroom learning. In general, applied anthropology aims to find humane and effective ways of helping the people whom anthropologists have traditionally studied.

ANTHROPOLOGY AND THE OTHER HUMAN SCIENCES

As mentioned above, the basic difference between anthropology and the other fields that study people is *holism,* anthropology's unique blend of biological, social, cultural, linguistic, historical, and contemporary perspectives. Paradoxically, while distinguishing anthropology, this breadth also links it to many other disciplines. Techniques used to date fossils and artifacts have come to anthropology from physics, chemistry, and geology. Because plant and animal remains are found with human bones and artifacts, anthropologists collaborate with zoologists, botanists, and paleontologists.

Cultural anthropology has ties to the other social sciences and the humanities. Thus contemporary sociology is experiencing an "opening to culture." Interpretive anthropology (Geertz 1973, 1983), which approaches cultures as texts whose meaning the anthropologist must unravel, links anthropology to the humanities and to history. More and more historians are interpreting historical narratives as texts, paying attention to their cultural meaning and the social context of their creation. Interdisciplinary collaboration is a hallmark of contemporary academic life, with ready borrowing of ideas and methods between disciplines (Geertz 1980). This is especially true for anthropology.

Cultural Anthropology and Sociology

Cultural anthropology and sociology share an interest in social relationships, organization, and behavior. However, important differences between these disciplines arose from the kinds of societies each traditionally studied. Initially sociologists focused on the industrial West; anthropologists, on nonindustrial societies. Different methods of data collection and analysis emerged to deal with those different kinds of societies. To study large-scale, complex nations, sociologists came to rely on questionnaires and other means of gathering masses of quantifiable data. For many years sampling and statistical techniques have been basic to sociology, whereas statistical training has been less common in anthropology (although this is changing rapidly as anthropologists increasingly work in modern nations).

Traditional ethnographers studied small, nonliterate (without writing) populations and relied on methods appropriate to that context. "Ethnography is a research process in which the anthropologist closely observes, records, and engages in the daily life of another culture—an experience labeled as the fieldwork method—and then writes accounts of this culture, emphasizing descriptive detail" (Marcus and Fischer 1986, p. 18). One key method described in this quote is **participant observation**—taking part in the events one is observing, describing, and analyzing.

With increasing interdisciplinary communication, anthropology and sociology are converging. The "opening to culture" movement is a more qualitative and interpretive approach to sociological issues and data. As the modern world system grows, sociologists pursue research topics in Third World countries and in places that were once almost exclusively within the anthropological orbit. As industrialization spreads, many anthropologists work in industrial societies, where they study diverse topics, including rural decline, inner-city life, and the role of the mass media in creating national culture patterns. Anthropologists and sociologists also share an interest in issues of race, ethnicity, social class, gender, and popular or mass culture in modern nations, including the United States.

Anthropology, Political Science, and Economics

Political science and economics developed to investigate particular domains of human behavior—as with sociology, mainly in modern nations. In the small-scale societies where ethnography grew up, politics and economics usually don't stand out as distinct activities amenable to separate analysis, as they do in a modern society. Rather, they are submerged, or *embedded,* in the general social order. Anthropologists have expanded our comparative understanding of political systems by showing, for example, that law and crime are not cultural universals and by examining such matters as the expression and resolution of conflict in societies without governments.

The subject matter of economics has been defined as economizing—the *rational* allocation of scarce means (resources) to alternative ends (uses). The goal of maximizing profit is assumed to be the force behind such rational allocation. However, the sociologist Max Weber (1904/1949), whose work has also influenced anthropology, drew an important distinction between formal rationality and substantive rationality. *Formal rationality* refers to abstract standards of rational procedure based on the profit motive. *Substantive rationality* refers

to standards of efficient procedure adjusted to cultural values. In other words, motivations vary cross-culturally and guide the kinds of decisions people make in different cultures. Following Weber's lead, anthropologists have contributed to *comparative* economics by showing that different principles propel the economy in other cultures. Through ethnography and cross-cultural comparison, the findings of economists and political scientists, usually based on research in Western nations, can be placed in a broader perspective.

Anthropology and the Humanities

The humanities study art, literature, music, dance, and other forms of creative expression. Traditionally (but this has changed—see below), they focused on highbrow "fine arts," knowledge of which was considered basic to a "cultured" person. Anthropology has always extended the definition of *cultured* beyond the elitist meaning of cultivated, sophisticated, college-educated, proper, and tasteful. For anthropologists, culture is not confined to elites or to any single social segment. Everyone acquires culture through **enculturation,** the social process by which culture is learned and transmitted across the generations. All creative expressions, therefore, are of potential interest as cultural products and documents. Growing acceptance of this view has helped broaden the study of the humanities from fine art and elite art to popular and folk art and the creative expressions of the masses.

Anthropology has influenced and is being influenced by the humanities—another example of *convergence,* the process of interdisciplinary communication and genre blurring (Geertz 1980) mentioned earlier. Adopting a characteristic anthropological view of creativity in its social and cultural context, current "postmodern" (Jameson 1984, 1988) approaches in the humanities are shifting the focus toward "lowbrow," mass, and popular culture and local creative expressions. Another area of convergence between anthropology and the humanities is the view of cultural expressions as patterned texts (Ricoeur 1971; Geertz 1973). Thus "unwritten behavior, speech, beliefs, oral tradition, and ritual" (Clifford 1988, p. 39) are approached as a corpus to be interpreted in relation to their meaning within a particular cultural context. A final link between anthropology and the humanities is the study of ethnographic accounts as a form of writing (Clifford 1988; Marcus and Fischer 1986).

Anthropology and Psychology

Like sociologists and economists, most psychologists do research in their own society. Anthropology again contributes by providing cross-cultural data. Statements about "human" psychology cannot be based solely on behavior in a single type of society. The area of culture anthropology known as psychological anthropology, or **culture and personality** (the study of variation in psychological traits and personality characteristics between cultures), links up with psychology. Margaret Mead, in her many books (1928/1961, 1930), showed that psychological traits vary widely among cultures. Societies instill different values by training children differently. Adult personalities reflect a culture's child-rearing practices.

An early contributor to the cross-cultural study of psychology was Bronislaw Malinowski, who did research among the Trobriand Islanders of the South Pacific. The Trobrianders reckon kinship matrilineally. They consider themselves related to the mother and her relatives, not to the father. The relative who disciplines the child is not the father but the mother's brother, the maternal uncle. One inherits from the uncle rather than the father. Trobrianders show a marked respect for the uncle, with whom a boy usually has a cool and distant relationship. In contrast, the Trobriand father-son relationship is friendly and affectionate.

Malinowski's work among the Trobrianders suggested modifications in Sigmund Freud's famous theory of the universality of the Oedipus complex (Malinowski 1927). According to Freud (1918/1950), boys around the age of five become sexually attracted to the mother. The Oedipus complex is resolved, in Freud's view, when the boy overcomes his sexual jealousy of, and identifies with, his father. Freud lived in patriarchal Austria dur-

An early contributor to the comparative study of psychology was Bronislaw Malinowski, who did ethnographic research among the Trobriand Islanders of the South Pacific. Here a Trobriand woman prepares dinner as her kin and neighbors watch.

ing the late nineteenth and early twentieth centuries—a social milieu in which fathers were strong authoritarian figures. The Austrian father was the child's primary authority figure and the mother's sexual partner, but in the Trobriands the father had only the sexual role.

If, as Freud contended, the Oedipus complex always creates social distance based on jealousy toward the mother's sexual partner, this would have shown up in the Trobriands. It *did not*. Malinowski concluded that the authority structure did more to influence the father-son relationship than did sexual jealousy. Like many later anthropologists, Malinowski showed that individual psychology depends on its cultural context. Anthropologists continue to provide cross-cultural perspectives on psychoanalytic propositions (Paul 1989) as well as on issues of developmental and cognitive psychology.

Anthropology and History

Convergence between history and anthropology was noted above in relation to the trend toward interdisciplinary communication. Historians increasingly interpret historical documents and accounts as texts requiring placement and interpretation within specific cultural contexts. Anthropologists and historians collaborate in the study of issues such as colonialism and the development of the modern world system (Cooper and Stoler 1989).

Despite this convergence, I think that it is useful to maintain a distinction between history (change in personnel) and evolution (change in form) as two aspects of change that involve people. In this sense *history* focuses on individuals. In a stable social system, people enter at birth and leave through death and migration. If there is true stability, people come and go but the system stays the same. There are changes in the *personnel*—in individuals—but not in the system's basic form. The second aspect of change (*evolution*) requires a larger perspective. A stable social system can become unstable. *A social system can change its structure or form.* Evolution is the study of such changes in form. (Although individual action always propels such systemic change, the focus here is on the system.)

Although there are still historians who focus on individual names and dates without much concern for process or social context, the distinction between personnel change and formal change certainly doesn't pit all, or even most, historians against anthropologists. An increasing number of historians study changes in social form—social transformations. Indeed, the growing collaboration of historians and anthropologists has been institutionalized in joint programs in history and anthropology at many universities. (I belong to the faculty of one such program at Michigan.)

SUMMARY

Anthropology, a uniquely holistic discipline, studies human biological and cultural diversity. It attempts to explain similarities and differences in time and space. Culture, which is passed on through learning rather than through biological inheritance, is a major reason for human adaptability.

Anthropology is characterized by an interest in the origins of and changes in biology and culture. The four subdisciplines of general anthropology are (socio)cultural, archeological, biological, and linguistic anthropology. All share an interest in variation in time and space and in adaptation—the process by which organisms cope with environmental stresses. All study evolution: change in form over the generations. Anthropology attempts to identify and explain universal, generalized,

and distinctive aspects of the human condition.

Cultural anthropology examines the cultural diversity of the present and the recent past. Archeology reconstructs social, economic, religious, and political patterns, usually of prehistoric populations. Biological anthropology relates biological diversity in time and space to variation in environment. It studies fossils, genetics, growth and development, bodily responses, and nonhuman primates. Linguistic anthropology documents diversity among contemporary languages. It studies ways in which speech changes in different social situations and over time. Applied anthropology uses anthropological knowledge and methods to identify and solve social problems in North America and abroad.

Concerns with past and present and with biology,

society, culture, and language link anthropology to many other fields. The main difference between cultural anthropology and sociology is that sociologists have traditionally studied urban and industrial populations whereas anthropologists have studied rural, non-Western peoples. Anthropologists bring a comparative perspective to economics and political science. Anthropologists also study art, music, and literature across cultures. However, their concern is as much with the creative expressions of common people as with art commissioned and appreciated by elites. Anthropologists

examine creators and products in their social context. Despite these traditional contrasts, interdisciplinary collaboration is a hallmark of contemporary academic life, with ready borrowing of ideas and methods between disciplines. This is especially true for anthropology because of its breadth and topical diversity.

Psychological anthropology, which relates human psychology to social and cultural variation, links anthropology and psychology. Anthropologists and historians collaborate increasingly in placing historical events in their social and cultural context.

GLOSSARY

adaptation: The process by which organisms cope with environmental stresses.

applied anthropology: The application of anthropological data, perspectives, theory, and methods to identify, assess, and solve contemporary social problems.

archeological anthropology (prehistoric archeology): The study of societies, culture patterns, and processes through their material remains.

artifacts: Manufactured items.

biological anthropology: The study of human biological variation in time and space; includes evolution, genetics, growth and development, and primatology.

civilization: A complex society with a central government and social classes; synonyms are *nation-state* and *state.*

cultural ecology: The study of ecosystems that include people, focusing on how human use of nature influences and is influenced by social organization and cultural values.

culture: Distinctly human; transmitted through learning; traditions and customs that govern behavior and beliefs.

culture and personality: A subfield of cultural anthropology; examines variation in psychological traits and personality characteristics between cultures.

ecology: The study of interrelationships among living things in an environment.

ecosystem: A patterned arrangement of energy flows and exchanges; includes organisms sharing a common environment and that environment.

enculturation: The social process by which culture is learned and transmitted across the generations.

ethnography: Field work in a particular culture.

ethnology: Cross-cultural comparison; the comparative study of ethnographic data, of society and culture.

evolution: Descent with modification; change in form over generations.

food production: Cultivation of plants and domestication (stockbreeding) of animals; first developed in the Middle East 10,000 to 12,000 years ago.

general anthropology: The field of anthropology as a whole, consisting of cultural, archeological, biological, and linguistic anthropology.

holistic: Interested in the whole of the human condition: past, present, and future; biology, society, language, and culture.

hominids: Members of the zoological family (Hominidae) that includes fossil and living humans.

linguistic anthropology: The descriptive, comparative, and historical study of language and of linguistic similarities and differences in time and space.

linkages: Interconnections between small-scale and large-scale units and systems; political, economic, informational, and other cultural links between village, region, nation, and world.

nation-state: See *civilization.*

osteology: The study of bones; useful to biological anthropologists studying the fossil record.

paleoanthropology: The study of human evolution through the fossil record.

paleoecology: The study, often by archeologists, of ecosystems of the past.

participant observation: A characteristic ethnographic technique; taking part in the events one is observing, describing, and analyzing.

potsherds: Fragments of earthenware; pottery studied by archeologists in interpreting prehistoric life styles.

prehistory: The period before the invention of writing around 5,500 years ago.

primates: Monkeys, apes, and prosimians; members of the zoological order that includes humans.

primatology: The study of the biology, behavior, and evolution of monkeys, apes, and other nonhuman primates.

society: Organized life in groups; typical of humans and other animals.

state: See *civilization.*

STUDY QUESTIONS

1. What does it mean to say that anthropology is global and holistic?
2. What are the subdisciplines of general anthropology? What unifies them into a single discipline?
3. How does cultural anthropology differ from sociology?
4. How is anthropology related to other human sciences, and what has it contributed to them?

SUGGESTED ADDITIONAL READING

BURLING, R.
   1970   *Man's Many Voices.* New York: Holt, Rinehart & Winston. Nontechnical yet comprehensive introduction to the role of language in culture and society.

CLIFFORD, J.
   1988   *The Predicament of Culture: Twentieth-Century Ethnography, Literature, and Art.* Cambridge, MA: Harvard University Press. Literary evaluation of classic and modern anthropologists and discussion of issues of ethnographic authority.

FAGAN, B. M.
   1988   *Archeology: A Brief Introduction.* 2nd ed. Glenview, IL: Scott, Foresman. Introduction to archeological theory, techniques, and approaches, including field survey, excavation, and analysis of materials.
   1989   *People of the Earth: An Introduction to World Prehistory.* 6th ed. Glenview, IL: Scott, Foresman. Introduction to the archeological study of prehistoric societies, using examples from all areas.

HARRIS, M.
   1989   *Our Kind: Who We Are, Where We Came From, Where We Are Going.* New York: Harper & Row. Fascinating popular anthropology; origins of humans, culture, and major sociopolitical institutions.

MARCUS, G. E., AND M. M. J. FISCHER
   1986   *Anthropology as Cultural Critique: An Experimental Moment in the Human Sciences.* Chicago: University of Chicago Press. Different types of ethnographic accounts as forms of writing, a vision of modern anthropology, and a consideration of anthropologists' public and professional roles.

NASH, D.
   1988   *A Little Anthropology.* Englewood Cliffs, NJ: Prentice-Hall. Short introduction to societies and cultures, with comments on developing nations and modern America.

PFEIFFER, J. E.
   1985   *The Emergence of Humankind.* 4th ed. New York: Harper & Row. Introduction to human biological evolution and the primates.

PODOLEFSKY, A., AND P. J. BROWN, EDS.
   1989   *Applying Anthropology: An Introductory Reader.* Mountain View, CA: Mayfield. Forty-one essays focusing on anthropology's relevance to contemporary life; a readable survey of the current range of activities in applied anthropology.

CHAPTER 2

FIELD METHODS

Anthropology differs from other sciences that study human beings because it is comparative, holistic, and global. Anthropologists study biology, language, and culture, past and present, in ancient and modern societies. This chapter compares the field methods of cultural anthropology with those of the other social sciences.

Anthropology started to separate from sociology around the turn of the twentieth century. Early students of society such as the French writer Émile Durkheim were among the founders of both sociology and anthropology. Comparing the organization of simple and complex societies, Durkheim studied "primitive" religions of Native Australia (Durkheim 1912/1961) and mass phenomena (such as suicide rates) in modern nations (Durkheim 1897/1951). Eventually anthropology would specialize in the former, sociology in the latter.

Anthropology emerged as a separate discipline as early anthropologists worked on Indian reservations and traveled to distant lands to study small groups of foragers and cultivators. This type of firsthand personal research in local settings is called *ethnography*. Traditionally, the process of becoming a cultural anthropologist has required firsthand experience in another society. Early ethnographers lived in small-scale, relatively isolated societies, which they called **primitive** because of their simple technologies and economies.

SURVEY RESEARCH

To the extent that anthropologists work increasingly in complex societies, they devise innovative strategies for blending ethnography and elements of survey research (see Kottak 1990). Before considering such combinations of field methods, let's focus on the differences between survey research and ethnography as traditionally practiced. Working mainly in large, populous nations, sociologists, social psychologists, political scientists, and economists have developed and refined **survey research** design, which involves sampling, impersonal data collection, and statistical analysis. Survey research usually draws a **sample** (a manageable study group) from a much larger population. By studying a properly selected and representative sample, social scientists can make accurate inferences about the larger population.

In smaller-scale societies, ethnographers get to know most of the people, but given the greater size and complexity of nations, survey research cannot help being more impersonal. Survey researchers call the people they study **respondents.** (Ethnographers work with **informants.**) Respondents are people who respond to questions during a survey. Sometimes survey researchers personally interview them. Sometimes, after an initial meeting, they ask respondents to fill out a questionnaire. In other cases researchers mail printed questionnaires to randomly selected sample members or have graduate students interview or telephone them. (In a **random sample,** all members of the population have an equal statistical chance of being chosen for inclusion. A random sample is selected by randomizing procedures, such as tables of random numbers, which are found in many statistics textbooks.)

Anyone who has grown up recently in the United States or Canada has heard of sampling. Probably the most familiar example is the polling used to predict political races. The media hire agencies to estimate outcomes and do exit polls to find out what kinds of people voted for which candidates. During sampling, researchers gather information about age, gender, religion, occupation, income, and political party preference. These characteristics (**variables**—attributes that vary among members of a sample or population) are known to influence political decisions.

We may distinguish between **predictor variables** (predictors) and **dependent variables.** Predictor variables work separately and together in influencing a dependent variable. For example, in predicting "risk of heart attack" (the dependent variable), predictors include sex, age, family history, weight, blood pressure, serum cholesterol, exercise, and cigarette smoking. Each predictor contributes separately to the risk of heart attack, and some have more impact than others. However, predictors also work together. Someone with many "risk factors" (particularly the most significant ones) has a greater risk of suffering a heart attack than does someone with few predictors.

In social science, predictor variables help us guess how people think, feel, and behave. Gen-

For research in large, populous nations, sociologists, social psychologists, and political scientists have developed and refined survey research, which is indispensable for the scientific study of such societies. A typical social survey relies on sampling, questionnaires, and statistical analysis. Survey research is also used in political polling and market research, as in this photo.

der, for instance, is a useful predictor of political party affiliation and voting behavior. More women than men claim to be Democrats, and women are more likely to vote for candidates of that party than men are. Survey research is indispensable in the study of large, populous nations, in which we must pay particular attention to variation.

Besides gender, more complex societies have role specializations based on age, profession, social class, and many other variables. The number of variables influencing social identity and behavior increases with, and can be considered a measure of, social complexity. Many more variables affect social identities, experiences, and activities in a modern nation than is the case in the small communities and local settings where ethnography grew up. In the contemporary United States or Canada hundreds of factors influence social behavior and attitudes. These social predictors include our religion; the region of the country we grew up in; whether we come from a town, suburb, or inner city; and our parents' professions, ethnic origins, and income levels.

ETHNOGRAPHY: ANTHROPOLOGY'S DISTINCTIVE STRATEGY

Ethnography emerged in societies with less social differentiation and more uniform cultural characteristics than are seen in larger, more modern societies. In such settings ethnographers have needed to consider fewer paths of enculturation to understand social life. My ethnographic field experiences illustrate some of these points. I began studying Arembepe, then a community of 750 people on the northeast coast of Brazil, in 1962. I did my first field work there as a college student and returned in 1964 and 1965 to gather data for my doctoral dissertation. I have maintained my interest in Arembepe ever since, having returned in 1973 and 1980 and almost annually since 1982. (My 1983 book *Assault on Paradise: Social Change in a Brazilian Village* tells the story of the many economic and social changes that have affected Arembepe since 1962.) It is not unusual for anthropologists to maintain a lifelong interest in the culture where they first did field work. Often they do long-term

*Linguist Francesca Merlin talks with informants near Mt. Hagen, Papua–
New Guinea. Anthropological research on language and culture requires residence,
usually lasting at least a year, with the people being studied.*

or **longitudinal research** there, spanning many
years.

Ethnographers develop personal connections,
including enduring friendships, in such communities as Arembepe and Ivato, the Betsileo village
in Madagascar I studied in 1966 and 1967. We try
to maintain contact with and revisit the people
among whom we have done field work. The people of Arembepe, for example, have told my wife
and me that unlike other outsiders who have lived
there, we always come back. Currently, Arembepe
is one of several communities being studied in a
nationwide research project under my direction,
investigating aspects of social change in modern
Brazil.

DIFFERENCES BETWEEN SURVEY RESEARCH AND ETHNOGRAPHY

There are several differences between survey research and ethnography.

1. In survey research, the object of study is usually a sample chosen (randomly or otherwise) by the researcher. Ethnographers normally study whole, functioning communities.
2. Ethnographers do firsthand field work, establishing a direct relationship with the people they study. Ethnographers strive to establish **rapport,** a good, friendly working relationship based on personal contact, with informants. Often, survey researchers have no personal contact with respondents. They may hire assistants to interview by phone or ask respondents to fill out a printed form or write answers to a questionnaire.
3. Ethnographers get to know their informants and usually take an interest in the totality of their lives. Often, a social survey focuses on a small number of variables, such as the ones that influence voting, rather than on the totality of people's lives.
4. Survey researchers normally work in modern nations, where most people are literate, per-

Ethnographers strive to establish rapport—a good, friendly relationship based on personal contact, with informants. These women in Guatemala are pleased with this anthropologist's gift—photos of themselves.

mitting respondents to fill in their own questionnaires. Ethnographers are more likely to study people who do not read and write.

5. Because survey research deals with large and diverse groups and with samples and probability, its results must be analyzed statistically. Because the societies that anthropologists traditionally study are smaller and less diverse, many ethnographers have not acquired detailed knowledge of statistics.

ETHNOGRAPHIC TECHNIQUES

The characteristic *field techniques* of the ethnographer include the following:

1. Direct, firsthand *observation* of daily behavior, including *participant observation*
2. *Conversation* with varying degrees of formality, from the daily chitchat that helps maintain rapport and provides knowledge about what

is going on to prolonged *interviews*, which can be unstructured or structured
3. *Interview schedules* to ensure that complete, comparable information is available for everyone of interest to the study
4. The *genealogical method*
5. Detailed work with *well-informed informants* about particular areas of community life
6. In-depth interviewing, often leading to the collection of *life histories* of particular people

Observation

Ethnographers must pay attention to hundreds of details of daily life, seasonal events, and unusual happenings. They must observe individual and collective behavior in varied settings. They should record what they see as they see it. Things will never seem quite as strange as they do during the first few days and weeks in the field. The ethnographer eventually gets used to, and accepts as normal, cultural patterns that were initially alien.

Many ethnographers record their impressions in a personal *diary,* which is kept separate from more formal *field notes.* Later, this record of early impressions will help point out some of the most basic aspects of cultural diversity. Such aspects include distinctive smells, noises people make, how they cover their mouths when they eat, and how they gaze at others. These patterns, which are so basic as to seem almost trivial, are part of what Bronislaw Malinowski called "the imponderabilia of native life and of typical behavior" (Malinowski 1922/1961, p. 20). These features of culture are so fundamental that natives take them for granted. They are too basic even to talk about, but the unaccustomed eye of the fledgling anthropologist perceives them. Thereafter they are submerged in familiarity and fade to the periphery of consciousness. This is why initial impressions are valuable and should be recorded. First and foremost, ethnographers should be accurate observers, recorders, and reporters of what they see in the field.

Participant Observation

Ethnographers don't study animals in laboratory cages. The experiments that psychologists do with pigeons, chickens, guinea pigs, and rats are very different from ethnographic procedure. Anthropologists don't systematically control subjects' rewards and punishments or their exposure to certain stimuli. Our subjects are not speechless animals but human beings. It is not part of ethnographic procedure to manipulate them, control their environments, or experimentally induce certain behaviors.

One of ethnography's characteristic procedures is *participant observation,* which means that we take part in community life as we study it. As human beings living among others, we cannot be totally impartial and detached observers. We must also take part in many of the events and processes we are observing and trying to comprehend. During the fourteen months I lived in Madagascar, for example, I simultaneously observed and participated in many occasions in Betsileo life. I helped out at harvest time, joining other people who climbed atop—in order to stamp down on and compact—accumulating stacks of rice stalks. One September, for a reburial ceremony, I bought a silk shroud for

a village ancestor. I entered the village tomb and watched people lovingly rewrap the bones and decaying flesh of their ancestors. I accompanied Betsileo peasants to town and to market. I observed their dealings with outsiders and sometimes offered help when problems arose.

In Arembepe, I sailed on the Atlantic in simple boats with Brazilian fishermen. I gave Jeep rides into the capital to malnourished babies, to pregnant mothers, and once to a teenage girl possessed by a spirit. All those people needed to consult specialists outside the village. I danced on Arembepe's festive occasions, drank foul-tasting libations commemorating new births, and became a godfather to a village girl. Most anthropologists have similar field experiences. The common humanity of the student and the studied, the ethnographer and the researched community, makes participant observation inevitable.

Conversation, Interviewing, and Interview Schedules

Participating in local life means that ethnographers constantly talk to people and ask questions about what they observe. As their knowledge of the native language increases, they understand more. There are several stages in learning a field language. First is the naming phase—asking name after name of the objects around us. Later we are able to pose more complex questions and understand the replies. We begin to understand simple conversations between two villagers, and if our language expertise proceeds far enough, we eventually become able to comprehend rapid-fire public discussions and group conversations. The special oratory of political events and ceremonial or ritual occasions often contains **liturgies,** set formal sequences of words and actions that we can record for later analysis with a local expert.

One data-gathering technique I have found useful in both Arembepe and Madagascar involves an ethnographic survey that includes an interview schedule. (Note that I am describing a way of combining survey research and ethnography.) In 1964, when I was a graduate student doing research for my doctoral dissertation, I attempted to complete an interview schedule in each of Arembepe's 160 households. My wife, Betty Kottak, who was also a college anthropology major, and Peter Gorlin,

RAPPORT AND PARTICIPANT OBSERVATION

I did my first field work as a member of a team of college students majoring in anthropology. I spent three months in summer 1962 in Arembepe in Bahia state in northeastern Brazil. This account of establishing rapport and participant observation is adapted from my book *Assault on Paradise: Social Change in a Brazilian Village* (Kottak 1983).

As a conscientious anthropology major, I very much wanted to put into personal practice some of the lessons I had learned in my classes. I wanted to do the kinds of things, for example, that Bronislaw Malinowski describes as the ethnographer's work in the first chapter of his well-known book *Argonauts of the Western Pacific,* which is a study of fishermen and traders in Melanesia, an island group in the South Pacific. . . .

I often compared my own experiences with Malinowski's; the settings of our field work struck me as similar. . . . Despite the fact that Arembepe is on the mainland, the phrase "South Sea island" kept running through my head. . . . As I read Malinowski's description of the moment when the ethnographer "sets foot upon a native beach, and makes his first attempts to get in touch with the natives" (Malinowski 1922/1961, p. 4), I imagined myself in his sandals. He had talked of trying to get to know the natives by observing them making things and writing down the names of tools. Like me, Malinowski initially had trouble communicating with the natives. "I was quite unable to enter any more detailed or explicit conversation with them at first. I knew well that the best remedy for this was to collect concrete data, and accordingly I took a village census, wrote down genealogies, drew up plans and collected the terms of kinship" (Malinowski 1922/1961, p. 5).

I was eager to do these things that Malinowski had done, especially to census the village. However . . . before I could hope to gather the kind of detailed and accurate data that ethnography demands, I would have to establish rapport within the community. People would have to get to know and trust me. I would have to convince them that I was not dangerous and that it would not be to their disadvantage to answer my questions. . . .

How does one establish rapport? "Get to know the men," I was told. To do this I started joining the fishermen for their evening bath in the freshwater lagoon. I developed my first doubts about the wisdom of this kind of participant observation when I accidentally swatted a floating piece of donkey dung (I like to think I identified the correct mammal) during my third bath. I abandoned lagoon bathing once and for all, however, when I heard of the lagoon system's infestation by schistosomes—liver flukes. Thereafter, I was careful to avoid the lagoon and followed the advice of public health officials to rub exposed body parts with alcohol whenever I came into contact with lagoon water. Arembepeiros found these precautions laughable: Not to worry, they said—there were small fish in the lagoon that ate the liver flukes (and germs in general) so that there was no health threat to people.

If the lagoon was now off-limits, there was still the chapel stoop, where each evening, after the fishing fleet had returned, baths had been taken, and the day's main meal consumed, men would gather to talk. This area was male territory. Only small girls and old women dared approach. Fellow field-team member David Epstein and I would sit and try to talk. My Portuguese remained rudimentary; I resented David because he spoke and seemed to understand better than I did. Still, villagers tossed questions my way. They were curious about the United States, and their questions were scintillating: "Were there camels in the United States? . . . Elephants? . . . Monkeys?" They went through a litany of animals they had seen on the lottery tickets that people brought back from Salvador [the state capital]. "Look! Up in the sky. It's a jet from the United States heading for Rio," they observed every other night, reflecting the airline's schedule. Whenever, after minutes of laborious mental rehearsal, I managed to find the proper Portuguese words to ask a question about Arembepe, I would get an incomprehensible reply, followed by some such query as "Have you ever seen a bear, Conrado?"

"Bear, bear," I parroted.

"Parrot, parrot," they guffawed.

"Yes, I have seen a bear. I have seen a bear in a zoo."

Rapport building was fascinating indeed.

Adapted from C. P. Kottak, *Assault on Paradise: Social Change in a Brazilian Village* (New York: McGraw-Hill, 1983).

another undergraduate, joined me. We entered almost every household (fewer than 5 percent refused to participate) to ask a set of questions on a printed form.

Our results provided us with a census and basic information about the village. We wrote down the name, age, and sex of each household member. We gathered data on family type, political party, religion, present and previous jobs, income, expenditures, diet, possessions, and many other items on our eight-page form.

Although we were doing a survey, our techniques differed from standard survey research. We did not select a partial sample from the total population. Instead, we tried to interview in all households in the community we were studying (that is, to have a total sample). We used an interview schedule rather than a questionnaire. With the **interview schedule,** the ethnographer talks face to face with informants, asks the questions, and writes down the answers. **Questionnaire** procedures tend to be more indirect and impersonal; the respondent often fills in the form.

Our goal of getting a total sample allowed us to meet almost everyone in the village and helped us establish rapport. Arembepeiros still talk warmly about how, almost three decades ago, we were interested enough in them to visit their homes and ask them questions. We stood in sharp contrast to the other outsiders the Arembepeiros had known, who considered them too poor and backward to be taken seriously.

Like standard survey research, however, our interview-schedule survey did gather comparable quantifiable information. It gave us a basis for assessing patterns and exceptions in village life. Our home visits also provided opportunities to do informal and follow-up interviewing. Our schedules included a core set of questions that were posed to everyone. However, some interesting side issue often came up during the interview.

We would pursue these leads into uninvestigated dimensions of village life. One woman, for instance, a midwife, became the "well-informed informant" we consulted later, when we wanted detailed information about local childbirth. Another woman had done an internship at an Afro-Brazilian cult (*candomblé*) house in the city. She still went there regularly to study, dance, and get possessed. She became our *candomblé* expert.

Thus, our interview-schedule survey provided a structure that *directed but did not confine* us as researchers. It enabled our ethnography to be both quantitative and qualitative. The quantitative part consisted of the basic information we gathered and later analyzed statistically. The qualitative dimension came from our follow-up questions, open-ended discussions, pauses for gossip, and work with well-informed informants.

In Madagascar my informants also enjoyed the structured interviews. In Arembepe we used a single schedule with many topics. In Madagascar I used a series of schedules, each about a different topic. I did these gradually, during a longer field stay among the Betsileo. The subjects included rice cultivation, secondary crops, livestock management, ceremonies, kinship and marriage, work patterns, and livestock ownership. Valuing literacy and scholarship, the Betsileo got so interested in my questions that people started coming in from surrounding villages to ensure that their histories and customs were also included in my book about the Betsileo (Kottak 1980).

The Genealogical Method

Another ethnographic technique is the **genealogical method.** Early ethnographers developed genealogical notation to deal with principles of kinship, descent, and marriage, which are the social building blocks of nonindustrial cultures. In the contemporary United States most of our contacts outside the home are with nonrelatives. However, people in nonindustrial cultures spend their lives almost exclusively with relatives. Anthropologists even classify such societies as **kin-based.** Everyone is related to, and spends most of his or her time with, everyone else, and rules of behavior attached to particular kin relationships are basic to everyday life. Marriage is also particularly crucial in organizing nonindustrial societies because strategic marriages between villages, tribes, and clans create political alliances.

Anthropologists must record genealogical data to reconstruct history and understand current relationships. In societies without a central government, these links are basic to social life and to political organization. To record genealogical data we use symbols (described in later chapters) such as triangles for males and circles for females.

Kinship and descent are important social building blocks in nonindustrial cultures. Without writing, genealogical information may be preserved in art. Here carvings on a tomb built by the Tanosy people of Ampanihy, Madagascar, depict their ancestors.

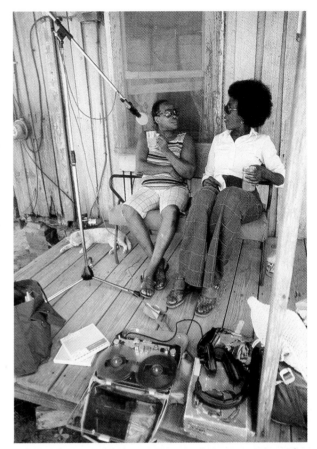

All communities have well-informed informants, natives who can provide the best information about particular areas of life. Here the researcher (right) collects folklore from a well-informed informant.

Well-Informed Informants

Every community has people who by accident, experience, or training can provide the most complete or useful information about particular aspects of life. These people are **well-informed informants.** In Ivato, the Betsileo village where I spent most of my time, a man named Rakoto was a particularly good informant about village history. However, when I asked him to work with me on a genealogy of the fifty to sixty people buried in the village tomb, he called in his cousin Tuesdaysfather, who knew more about this subject. Tuesdaysfather had survived an epidemic of Spanish influenza that ravaged Madagascar, along with much of the world, around 1919. Immune to the disease himself, Tuesdaysfather had the grim job

of burying his kin as they died. He kept track of everyone buried in the tomb. Tuesdaysfather helped me with the tomb genealogy. Rakoto joined him in telling me personal details about the deceased villagers.

Life Histories

In nonindustrial societies as in our own, individual personalities, interests, and abilities vary. Some villagers prove to be more interested in the ethnographer's work and are more helpful, interesting, and pleasant than others. Anthropologists develop likes and dislikes in the field as we do at home. Often, when we find someone unusually interesting, we collect his or her **life history.** This

Anthropologists often use life histories to show how individuals perceive, contribute, and react to changes in their communities. Marjorie Shostak (left) based her fascinating book Nisa: The Life and Words of a !Kung Woman *on the life history of a !Kung San woman living in the Kalahari Desert of southern Africa.*

recollection of a lifetime of experiences provides a more intimate and personal cultural portrait than would be possible otherwise. My book about Arembepe (Kottak 1983), for example, concludes with four accounts that show how different people have perceived, contributed to, and reacted to changes affecting their community. Life histories present community members as individuals facing common problems.

Free-Ranging, Holistic Investigation

Traditionally, ethnographers have striven to understand the whole of an alien culture (or, more realistically, as much as they can, given limitations of time and perception). To pursue this holistic goal, ethnographers adopt a free-ranging strategy for gathering information. They move from setting to setting, place to place, and subject to subject to discover the totality and interconnectedness of social life.

Ethnographers draw on varied techniques—all, however, personal and direct—to piece together a picture of otherwise alien life styles. Anthropologists usually employ several (but rarely all) of the techniques discussed here. Some ethnographers are less holistic and focus on particular topics, such as religion or economic life. Ethnography, by expanding our knowledge of the range of human diversity, provides a foundation for generaliza-

tions about human behavior and social life. Ethnographic research is basic to the comparative and holistic perspective that distinguishes anthropology.

ANTHROPOLOGICAL RESEARCH IN COMPLEX SOCIETIES

During World War I Bronislaw Malinowski spent several years studying the Trobriand Islanders. In his classic ethnographic **monograph** (a book based on ethnographic field work) *Argonauts of the Western Pacific*, Malinowski describes how an ethnographer "sets up shop" in another society. Like Malinowski's research in the Trobriands, my field work in Arembepe focused on a single community as the object of intensive study. I could get to know everyone in Arembepe because its population was small and its social system was uncomplicated. However, unlike the Trobriands, Arembepe was not a tribal society but part of a large, populous, and diverse nation. The Trobriand Islands are small enough for an ethnographer to visit every village. Malinowski might well have managed to talk with every Trobriander. I could never hope to visit every Brazilian community or meet every Brazilian.

Malinowski used his field site as a basis for describing Trobriand society as a whole. Anthropologists have been criticized for generalizing about an entire culture on the basis of research in just one community, a practice which is somewhat more defensible for small-scale, homogeneous societies than for complex nations. My study of Arembepe, a rural community in a particular region of an urbanized nation, could never encapsulate Brazil as a whole. Thus I viewed my Arembepe field study as part of a larger research program. I was just one ethnographer among many, each working separately in different Brazilian communities. Eventual comparison of those studies would help reveal the range of diversity in Brazil.

One way of using ethnography in modern nations is to do such a series of **community studies.** Field sites in different regions can be used to sample different economic adaptations, degrees of participation in the modern world, and historical trends. However, even a thousand rural communities cannot constitute an adequate sample of national diversity. We must also consider urban life and social contrasts that are absent in small communities. The range of variation encountered in any nation makes the social survey an obligatory research procedure.

Nevertheless, ethnography can be used to supplement and fine-tune survey research. Anthropologists can transfer the personal, direct, observation-based techniques of ethnography to social groups and social networks in *any setting*. A combination of survey research and ethnography can provide new perspectives on life in **complex societies** (large and populous societies with social stratification and central governments). Preliminary ethnography can also help develop relevant questions for inclusion in national surveys.

URBAN ANTHROPOLOGY

A series of community studies in a nation reveals variation in its small-town and rural life. However, there is much more to national life than small communities. One response to this problem has been **urban anthropology**—the anthropological study of cities. Particularly since the 1950s, anthropologists have systematically investigated urban problems and life styles in the United States and abroad. A common illustration of urban anthropology is the practice of having students do local field work for an anthropology course (assuming that the college is in an urban setting).

In my own courses in Ann Arbor, Michigan, undergraduates have done research on sororities, fraternities, teams, campus organizations, and the local homeless population. Other students have systematically observed behavior in public places. These include racquetball courts, restaurants, bars, football stadiums, markets, malls, and classrooms. Other "modern anthropology" projects use anthropological techniques to interpret and analyze mass media. Anthropologists have been studying American culture for decades, and anthropological research in the United States is booming today. (The Appendix, "Contemporary American Popular Culture," provides several examples.) Wherever there is patterned human behavior, there is grist for the anthropological mill.

Network Analysis

Network analysis is a technique originally developed for small-scale communities that is now used in cities. Network analysis begins by focusing on particular people in a community, neighborhood, or organization. It then investigates the extent and type of ties that each person has with others.

Each person has a particular set of relationships (economic, social, political, religious) with others—his or her **personal network.** Some people have larger networks, with more diverse types of links, than do others. Network size and extent can help an anthropologist identify community leaders, who tend to have numerous and diverse links. Ethnographers first used network analysis to study urban neighborhoods in Europe. They (Barnes 1954; Bott 1957) distinguished two types of social networks:

1. Contained, **close-knit networks,** characteristic of rural communities and nonindustrial societies, in which many of one's friends, neighbors, and relatives know one another
2. Dispersed, **loose-knit networks,** characteristic of urban and complex societies, in which people who know each other often don't know each other's friends, neighbors, and relatives.

Network analysis is a personal, socially based field method that can be used anywhere. Focusing on specific people, it considers when, why, and

THE EVOLUTION OF ETHNOGRAPHY

The great Polish anthropologist Bronislaw Malinowski (1884–1942), who spent most of his professional life in England, is generally considered the father of ethnography. Like most anthropologists of his time, Malinowski did *salvage ethnography,* in the belief that the ethnographer's job is to study and record cultural diversity threatened by westernization. Early ethnographic accounts (*ethnographies*), including Malinowski's classic *Argonauts of the Western Pacific* (1922/1961), were similar to earlier traveler and explorer accounts in describing the writer's discovery of unknown people and places. However, the *scientific* aims of ethnographies set them apart from books by explorers and amateurs.

The style that dominated "classic" ethnographies was *ethnographic realism.* The writer's goal was to present an accurate, objective, scientific account of a different way of life, written by someone who knew it firsthand. This knowledge came from an "ethnographic adventure" involving immersion in an alien language and culture. Ethnographers derived their authority—both as scientists and as voices of "the native"

or "the other"—from this personal research experience.

Malinowski wrote *functionalist* ethnographies, guided by the assumption that all aspects of culture are linked (functions of each other). A functionalist ethnography begins with *any* aspect of a culture, such as a Trobriand Islands sailing expedition. The ethnographer then follows the links between that entry point and other areas of the culture, such as magic, religion, myths, kinship, and trade. Contemporary ethnographies tend to be less inclusive, focusing on particular topics, such as kinship or religion.

According to Malinowski, a primary task of the ethnographer is "to grasp the native's point of view, his relation to life, to realize *his* vision of *his* world (1922/1961, p. 25—Malinowski's italics). Since the 1970s *interpretive anthropology* has considered the task of describing and interpreting that which is meaningful to natives. Interpretivists such as Clifford Geertz (1973) view cultures as meaningful texts which natives constantly "read" and which ethnographers must decipher. According to Geertz, anthropologists may choose anything in a culture that

interests them, fill in details, and elaborate to inform their readers about meanings in that culture. Meanings are carried by public symbolic forms, including words, rituals, and customs. In the interpretive view, cross-cultural understanding emerges through "dialogues" between natives, anthropologist, and reader, who are all parties to a conversation.

A current trend in ethnographic writing is to question traditional goals, methods, and styles, including salvage ethnography and ethnographic realism (Marcus and Cushman 1982; Clifford 1982, 1988). Marcus and Fischer argue that contemporary anthropology has reached "an experimental moment." Experimentation is needed because all people and cultures have already been "discovered" and must now be "*rediscovered* . . . in changing historical circumstances" (1986, p. 24).

These experimental anthropologists recognize that ethnographies are works of art as well as works of science. Ethnographic texts are literary creations in which the ethnographer, as mediator, communicates information from the "natives" to

how they associate with others. Eventually, personal networks can be compared and generalizations can be made about the kinds of networks that are important in particular social settings.

In the close-knit network, for example, many of one's friends, neighbors, and relatives know one another. Social life was like this throughout much of hominid history, as it still is in the small-scale societies where ethnography developed. However, in the loose-knit networks of complex societies, people who know each other often don't

know each other's friends, neighbors, and relatives. With more closely knit networks it is easier to reach agreement and put pressure on others to conform.

Practicing ethnography in a mid-sized city in the American Midwest, anthropologist Carol Stack discovered that close-knit networks also exist in contemporary urban settings. Stack's book *All Our Kin* (1975) shows the strength of expanded family networks and of close-knit kin-based relationships among modern urban African-Americans.

readers. Some recent experimental ethnographies are "dialogic," presenting ethnography as a dialogue between the anthropologist and one or more native informants (e.g., Dwyer 1982). These works draw attention to ways in which ethnographers, and by extension their readers, communicate with other cultures.

Ethnographers interpret and mediate between cultures in two ways. During field work they must interpret from native categories to their own, and in writing they must interpret for their readers. However, some dialogic ethnographies have been criticized as being too confessional, spending too much time on the anthropologist and too little on the natives and their culture.

The dialogic ethnography is one genre within a larger experimental category—*reflexive ethnography.* Here the ethnographer-writer puts his or her personal feelings and reactions to the field situation right in the text. An experimental writing strategy is prominent in reflexive accounts. The ethnographer may adopt some of the conventions of the novel, including first-person narration, conversations, dia-

logues, and humor. One example is the list of "Principal Characters" I included in my own experimental (and partially reflexive) ethnography *Assault on Paradise: Social Change in a Brazilian Village* (1983).

Marcus and Fischer (1986) caution that the desire to be personal can be overplayed to the point of exhibitionism. Nevertheless, experimental ethnographies, using new ways of showing what it means to be a Samoan or a Brazilian, may convey to the reader a richer and more complex understanding of human experience. The result may be to convince readers that culture matters more than they might otherwise have thought.

Recent ethnographic writers have also attempted to correct the deficiency of *romanticized timelessness,* which is obvious in the classics. Linked to salvage ethnography was the idea of the *ethnographic present*— the period before westernization, when the "true" native culture flourished. This notion gives classic ethnographies an eternal, timeless quality. The cultures they describe seem frozen in the ethnographic present. Providing the only jarring note in this idealized picture are oc-

casional comments by the author about traders or missionaries, suggesting that the natives were already part of the world system.

Anthropologists now recognize that the ethnographic present is a rather unrealistic and romantic construct. Cultures have been in contact—and have been changing— throughout history. At least 80 percent of native cultures had at least one major foreign encounter before any anthropologist came their way. Most of them had already been incorporated in some fashion into nation-states or colonial systems (White et al., in press).

The classic ethnographies neglected history, politics, and the world system, but contemporary ethnographies usually recognize that cultures constantly change and that an ethnographic account applies to a particular moment. A current trend in ethnography is to focus on the ways in which cultural ideas serve political and economic interests. Another trend is to describe how particular "natives" participate in broader historical, political, and economic processes (see the box in Chapter 18).

ANTHROPOLOGICAL TECHNIQUES USED IN COMPLEX SOCIETIES

Anthropologists can use field techniques such as network analysis, participant observation, and firsthand data collection in any social setting. However, for contemporary societies, anthropologists increasingly supplement traditional techniques with new procedures, many borrowed from survey research. During studies of urban life, modern anthropologists routinely gather statistical data. In any complex society, many predictor vari-

ables (*social indicators*) influence behavior and opinions. Because we must be able to detect, measure, and compare the influence of social indicators, many contemporary anthropological studies have a statistical foundation. Even in rural field work, more anthropologists now draw samples, gather quantitative data, and use statistics to interpret them. Quantifiable information may permit a more precise assessment of similarities and differences between communities. Statistical analysis can support and round out an ethnographic account of local social life.

However, in the best studies, the hallmark of ethnography remains: Anthropologists enter the community and get to know the people. They participate in local activities, networks, and associations, in the city or in the countryside. They observe and experience social conditions and problems. They watch the effects of national policies and programs on local life. I believe that the ethnographic method and the emphasis on personal relationships in social research are valuable gifts that anthropology brings to the study of a complex society.

SUMMARY

Traditionally, anthropologists worked in primitive societies; sociologists, in modern nations. Different field techniques emerged for the study of different types of societies. Sociologists and other social scientists who work in complex societies use survey research to sample variation.

There are several contrasts between survey research and ethnography. With more literate respondents, sociologists employ questionnaires, which the research subjects fill out. Anthropologists are more likely to use interview schedules, which the ethnographer fills in during a personal interview. Anthropologists do their field work in communities and study the totality of social life. Sociologists study samples to make inferences about a larger population. Sociologists are often interested in causal relationships between a limited number of variables. Anthropologists are more typically concerned with the interconnectedness of all aspects of social life.

Ethnography has several characteristic field procedures, including observation, establishing rapport, participant observation, conversation, listening to native accounts, formal and informal interviewing, the genealogical method, work with well-informed informants, and life histories. Recording the imponderabilia of daily life is particularly useful early in field work. That is when the most basic, distinctive, and alien features of another culture are most noticeable. Ethnographers do not systematically manipulate their subjects or conduct experiments. Rather, they work in natural communities and form personal relationships with informants as they study their lives.

Interview schedules are forms that ethnographers fill in by visiting many households. The schedules guide formal interviews, ensuring that the ethnographer collects comparable information from everyone. These interviews also introduce the researcher to many people. The schedule organizes the interview. However, ethnographers may also pursue additional topics in accordance with the particular interests and attributes of the interviewee.

Ethnographers work closely with well-informed informants to learn about particular areas of native life. Many ethnographers work long hours with particular informants. Life histories dramatize the fact that culture bearers are also individuals and document personal experiences with culture and culture change. The collection and analysis of genealogical information is particularly important in tribal societies, where principles of kinship, descent, and marriage organize and integrate social and political life.

Anthropologists use modified ethnographic techniques to study complex societies. The diversity of social life and subcultural variation in modern nations and cities requires social survey procedures. However, anthropologists add the intimacy and firsthand investigation characteristic of ethnography. Community studies in regions of modern nations provide firsthand, in-depth accounts of cultural variation and of regional historical and economic forces and trends. Anthropologists may use ethnographic procedures to study urban life. Network analysis focuses on individuals and the nature of their social links to, and interactions with, others. Urban networks differ from those of tribal societies. Anthropologists make greater use of statistical techniques and analysis of the mass media in their research in complex societies.

GLOSSARY

close-knit networks: Characteristic of rural communities and nonindustrial societies; many of one's friends, neighbors, and relatives know one another.

community study: Anthropological method for studying complex societies. Small communities are studied ethnographically as being (partially) representative of regional culture or particular contrasts in national life.

complex societies: Nations; large and populous, with social stratification and central governments.

dependent variables: See *predictor variables.*

genealogical method: Procedures by which ethnographers discover and record connections of kinship, descent, and marriage, using diagrams and symbols.

informants: Subjects in ethnographic research; people the ethnographer gets to know in the field, who teach him or her about their culture.

interview schedule: Ethnographic tool for structuring a formal interview. A prepared form (usually printed or mimeographed) that guides interviews with households or individuals being compared systematically. Contrasts with a *questionnaire* because the researcher has personal contact with the informants and records their answers.

kin-based: Characteristic of many nonindustrial societies. People spend their lives almost exclusively with their relatives; principles of kinship, descent, and marriage organize social life.

life history: Of an informant; provides a personal cultural portrait of existence or change in a culture.

liturgies: Set formal sequences of words and actions; common in political events and rituals or ceremonies.

longitudinal research: Long-term study of a community, society, culture, or other unit, usually based on repeated visits.

loose-knit networks: Characteristic of urban and complex societies; people who know each other often don't know each other's friends, neighbors, and relatives.

monograph: A book based on ethnographic field work.

network analysis: Technique developed by anthropologists to adapt ethnographic procedures to modern cities and nations. Focuses on types of contacts (networks of relationships) between people.

personal network: Each person's particular set of relationships (economic, social, political, religious) with all others.

predictor variables: Factors (e.g., sex, age, religion) that help predict other behavior—dependent variables (e.g., voting, occupation).

primitive: Characterized by small size and technological and economic simplicity.

questionnaire: Form (usually printed) used by sociologists to obtain comparable information from respondents. Often mailed to and filled in by research subjects rather than by the researcher.

random sample: A sample in which all members of the population have an equal statistical chance of being included.

rapport: A good, friendly working relationship between people, e.g., ethnographers and their informants.

respondents: Subjects in sociological research; the people who answer questions in questionnaires and other social surveys.

sample: A smaller study group chosen to represent a larger population.

survey research: Characteristic research procedure among social scientists other than anthropologists. Studies society through sampling, statistical analysis, and impersonal data collection.

urban anthropology: The anthropological study of cities.

variables: Attributes (e.g., sex, age, height, weight) that differ from one person or case to the next.

well-informed informant: Person who is an expert on a particular aspect of native life.

STUDY QUESTIONS

1. What is survey research design, and how does it differ from ethnography?
2. What are examples of predictor and dependent variables?
3. What are the differences between questionnaires and interview schedules?
4. What are the characteristic field techniques of the ethnographer?
5. What are the imponderabilia of daily life, and when are they most obvious to the ethnographer?
6. What is participant observation?
7. What is the genealogical method, and why did it develop in anthropology?
8. What are the advantages for ethnography of life histories and working with well-informed informants?
9. What are the problems and advantages of community study research?
10. How do social networks in cities differ from those in tribal societies?
11. What techniques do anthropologists use to study urban life?

SUGGESTED ADDITIONAL READING

AGAR, M. H.
  1980 *The Professional Stranger: An Informal Introduction to Ethnography.* New York: Academic Press. Basics of ethnography, illustrated by the author's field experiences in India and among heroin addicts in the United States.
BERNARD, H. R.
  1988 *Research Methods in Cultural Anthropology.* Newbury Park, CA: Sage. The most complete and up-to-date survey of methods of data collection, organization, and analysis in cultural anthropology.
BRIM, J. A., AND D. H. SPAIN
  1974 *Research Design in Anthropology.* New York: Holt, Rinehart & Winston. Discusses hypothesis testing and anthropological research design.
KOTTAK, C. P.
  1983 *Assault on Paradise: Social Change in a Brazilian Village.* New York: Random House. Illustrates the ethnographic field methods discussed in this chapter. The setting is a small community caught up in the modern world system.
KOTTAK, C. P., ED.
  1982 *Researching American Culture: A Guide for Student Anthropologists.* Ann Arbor: University of Michigan Press. Advice for college students doing field work in the United States. Includes papers by undergraduates and anthropologists on contemporary American culture.
PELTO, P. J., AND G. H. PELTO
  1978 *Anthropological Research: The Structure of Inquiry.* 2nd ed. New York: Cambridge University Press. Discusses data collection and analysis, including the relationship between theory and field work, hypothesis construction, sampling, and statistics.
SPRADLEY, J. P.
  1979 *The Ethnographic Interview.* New York: Holt, Rinehart & Winston. Discussion of the ethnographic method, with emphasis on discovering native viewpoints.

C H A P T E R   3

CULTURE

Humans are animals with a difference. That difference is culture, a major reason for our adaptability and success. Social and cultural means of adaptation have been crucially important in hominid evolution. *Society* is organized life in groups. Like humans, many other animals, including apes, monkeys, wolves, and ants, live in organized groups. For example, many monkeys live in social groups called **troops,** composed of multiple adult males and females and their offspring, in which dominance hierarchies, juvenile play groups, and various coordinated movements and activities regulate contacts between members. Human populations, however, are organized not only by their habitual social activities and relationships but also by exposure to a common cultural tradition. Cultural traditions or, more simply, cultures are transmitted through learning and language.

The idea of culture has long been basic to anthropology. More than a century ago, in his classic book *Primitive Culture,* British anthropologist Ed-

Many monkeys live in organized societies, in which dominance relationships and coordinated activities, such as grooming, govern their social contacts. Humans, by contrast, are organized not only by habitual social activities and relationships, but also by exposure to a common cultural tradition. Culture is transmitted through learning and through language. Contrast the West African Guinea baboons with the Tuareg boys learning Islam by studying the Koran.

ward Tylor proposed that systems of human behavior and thought are not random. Rather, they obey natural laws and therefore can be studied scientifically. Tylor's definition of culture still offers a good overview of the subject matter of anthropology and is widely quoted.

"Culture . . . is that complex whole which includes knowledge, belief, arts, morals, law, custom, and any other capabilities and habits acquired by man as a member of society" (Tylor 1871/1958, p. 1). The crucial phrase here is "acquired by man as a member of society." Tylor's definition focuses on beliefs and behavior that people acquire not through biological heredity but by growing up in a particular society where they are exposed to a specific cultural tradition. Enculturation is the process by which a child learns his or her culture.

WHAT IS CULTURE?

Culture Is All-Encompassing

For anthropologists, culture includes much more than refinement, taste, sophistication, education, and appreciation of the fine arts. Not only college graduates but all people are cultured. The most interesting and significant forces are those which affect people every day of their lives, particularly those which influence children during enculturation. *Culture,* as defined anthropologically, encompasses features that are sometimes regarded as trivial or unworthy of serious study, such as "popular" culture. To understand contemporary American culture, we must consider television, fast-food restaurants, sports, and games. As a cultural manifestation, a rock star may be as interesting as a symphony conductor, a comic book as significant as a book-award winner.

Culture Is General and Specific

All human populations have culture, which is therefore a generalized possession of the genus *Homo.* This is **Culture** (capital C) in the **general** sense, a capacity and possession shared by hominids. However, anthropologists also use the word *culture* to describe the different and varied cultural traditions of specific societies. This is **culture** in the **specific** sense (small c). Humanity shares a capac-

ity for culture, but people live in particular cultures, where they are enculturated along different lines. All people grow up in the presence of a particular set of cultural rules transmitted over the generations. These are the specific cultures or cultural traditions that anthropologists study.

Culture Is Learned

The ease with which children absorb any cultural tradition reflects the uniquely elaborated hominid capacity to learn. There are different kinds of learning, some of which we share with other animals. One kind is **individual situational learning,** which occurs when an animal learns from, and bases its future behavior on, its own experience, for example, avoiding fire after discovering that it hurts. Animals also exhibit **social situational learning,** in which they learn from other members of the social group, not necessarily through language. Wolves, for example, learn hunting strategies from other pack members. Social situational learning is particularly important among monkeys and apes, our closest relatives. Finally there is **cultural learning.** This depends on the uniquely developed human capacity to use *symbols,* signs that have no necessary or natural connection with the things for which they stand.

A critical feature in hominid evolution is dependence on cultural learning. Through culture people create, remember, and deal with ideas.

Illustrating social situational learning, a cheetah uses a hartebeest calf to teach its young how to hunt and kill.

TOUCHING, AFFECTION, LOVE, AND SEX

Comparing the United States with Brazil—or virtually any Latin nation—we can see a striking cultural contrast between a culture that discourages physical contact and demonstrations of affection and one in which the contrary is true. We can also see rampant confusion in American culture about love, sex, and affection. This stands in sharp contrast to the more realistic Brazilian separation of the three.

"Don't touch me." "Take your hands off me." These are normal statements in American culture that are virtually never heard in Brazil, the Western Hemisphere's second most populous country. Americans don't like to be touched. The world's cultures have strikingly different opinions about matters of personal space. When Americans talk, walk, and dance, they maintain a certain distance from others—their personal space. Brazilians, who maintain less physical distance, interpret this as a sign of coldness. When conversing with an American, the Brazilian characteristically moves in as the American "instinctively" retreats. In these body movements, neither Brazilian

nor American is trying consciously to be especially friendly or unfriendly. Each is merely executing a program written on the self by years of exposure to a particular cultural tradition. Because of different ideas about proper social space, cocktail parties in international meeting places such as the United Nations can resemble an elaborate insect mating ritual as diplomats from different cultures advance, withdraw, and sidestep.

One of the most obvious differences between Brazil and the United States involves kissing, hugging, and touching. Middle-class Brazilians teach their children—both boys and girls—to kiss (on the cheek, two or three times, coming and going) every adult relative they ever see. Given the size of Brazilian extended families, this can mean hundreds of people. Females continue kissing throughout their lives. They kiss male and female kin, friends, relatives of friends, friends of relatives, friends of friends, and, when it seems appropriate, more casual acquaintances. Males go on kissing their female relatives and friends. Until they are adolescents, boys also

kiss adult male relatives. Thereafter, Brazilian men greet each other with hearty handshakes and a traditional male hug (abraço). The closer the relationship, the tighter and longer-lasting the embrace. These comments apply to brothers, cousins, uncles, and friends. Many Brazilian men keep on kissing their fathers throughout their lives.

Like other Americans who spend time in a Latin culture, I miss these kisses and handshakes when I get back to the United States. After several months in Brazil, I find North Americans rather cold and impersonal. Many Brazilians share this opinion. I have heard similar feelings expressed by Italian-Americans describing Americans with different ethnic backgrounds.

Many Americans fear physical contact and confuse love and affection with sex. According to clinical psychologist David E. Klimek, who has written about intimacy and marriage, "in American society, if we go much beyond simple touching, our behavior takes on a minor sexual twist" (Slade 1984). Americans define demonstrations of affection with reference to marriage. Love

They grasp and apply specific systems of symbolic meaning. Anthropologist Clifford Geertz defines culture as ideas based on cultural learning and symbols. Cultures are sets of "control mechanisms—plans, recipes, rules, constructions, what computer engineers call programs for the governing of behavior" (Geertz 1973, p. 44). These programs are absorbed by people through enculturation in particular traditions. People gradually internalize a previously established system of meanings and symbols which they use to define their world, express their feelings, and make their judgments. Thereafter, this system helps guide

their behavior and perceptions throughout their lives.

Every person begins immediately, through a process of conscious and unconscious learning and interaction with others, to internalize, or incorporate, a cultural tradition through the process of enculturation. Sometimes culture is taught directly, as when parents tell their children to "say thank you" when someone gives them something or does them a favor.

Culture is also transmitted through observation. Children pay attention to the things that go on around them. They modify their behavior not just

The world's cultures have strikingly different opinions about personal space—how far apart people should be in normal encounters and interactions. Contrast the gap between the two American men with the closeness of the Egyptian Bedouins.

and affection are supposed to unite the married pair, and they blend into sex. When a wife asks her husband for "a little affection," she may mean, or he may think she means, sex. Listening as Americans discuss love and sex on talk shows and in other public forums, it's obvious that American culture confuses these needs and feelings.

This confusion between love, affection, and sex is clear on Valentine's Day, which used to be just for lovers. Valentines used to be sent to wives, husbands, girlfriends, and boyfriends. Now, after years of promotion by the greeting card industry, they also go to mothers, fathers, sons, daughters, aunts, and uncles. Valentine's Day "personals" in the local newspaper also illustrate this blurring of sexual and nonsexual affection, which is a source of so much confusion in contemporary American culture. In Brazil, Lovers' Day retains its autonomy. Mother, father, and children have their own separate days.

It is true, of course, that in a good marriage love and affection exist alongside sex. Nevertheless, affection does not imply sex. Brazilian culture shows that there can be rampant kissing, hugging, and touching without sex—or fears of improper sexuality. In Brazilian culture, physical demonstrations help cement several kinds of close personal relationships that have no sexual component.

because other people tell them to but as a result of their own observations and growing awareness of what their culture considers right and wrong. Culture is also absorbed unconsciously. North Americans acquire their culture's notions about how far apart people should stand when they talk not by being told to maintain a certain distance but through a gradual process of observation, experience, and conscious and unconscious behavior modification. No one tells Latins to stand closer together than North Americans do, but they learn to do so anyway as part of their cultural tradition.

Culture Is Symbolic

Symbolic thought is unique and crucial to humans and to culture. Anthropologist Leslie White defined culture as

> an extrasomatic (nongenetic, nonbodily), temporal continuum of things and events dependent upon symbolling. . . . Culture consists of tools, implements, utensils, clothing, ornaments, customs, institutions, beliefs, rituals, games, works of art, language, etc. (White 1959, p. 3)

For White, culture originated when our ancestors acquired the ability to symbol, or freely and arbitrarily to originate and bestow meaning upon a thing or event, and, correspondingly, . . . to grasp and appreciate such meaning. (White 1959, p. 3)

A **symbol** is something verbal or nonverbal, within a particular language or culture, that comes to stand for something else. There is no obvious, natural, or necessary connection between the symbol and what it symbolizes. A pet that barks is no more naturally a *dog* than a *chien, Hund,* or *mbwa,* to use the words for the animal we call "dog" in French, German, and Swahili. Language is one of the distinctive possessions of *Homo sapiens.* No other animal has developed anything approaching the complexity of language.

Symbols are usually linguistic. However, there are also nonverbal symbols, such as flags, which stand for countries, as arches do for hamburger chains. Holy water is a potent symbol in Roman Catholicism. As is true of all symbols, the association between a symbol (water) and what is symbolized (holiness) is arbitrary and conventional. Water is not intrinsically holier than milk, blood, or other liquids. Holy water is not chemically different from ordinary water. Holy water is a symbol within Roman Catholicism, which is part of an international cultural system. A natural thing has been arbitrarily associated with a particular meaning for Catholics, who share common beliefs and experiences that are based on learning and are transmitted across the generations.

For hundreds of thousands of years, people have shared the abilities on which culture rests. These abilities are to learn, to think symbolically, to manipulate language, and to use tools and other cultural products in organizing their lives and coping with their environments. Every contemporary human population has the ability to symbol and thus to create and maintain culture. Our nearest relatives—chimpanzees and gorillas—have rudimentary cultural abilities. However, no other animal has elaborated cultural abilities—to learn, to communicate, and to store, process, and use information—to the same extent as *Homo.*

Culture Seizes Nature

Culture imposes itself on nature. I once arrived at a summer camp at 5 P.M. I was hot and wanted to swim in the lake. However, I read the camp rules and learned that no swimming was permitted after five. A cultural system had seized the lake, which is part of nature. Natural lakes don't close at five, but cultural lakes do.

Culture takes the natural biological urges we share with other animals and teaches us how to express them in particular ways. People have to eat, but culture teaches us what, when, and how. In many cultures people have their main meal at noon, but Americans prefer a large dinner. English people eat fish for breakfast, but Americans prefer hot cakes and cold cereals. Brazilians put hot milk into strong coffee, whereas Americans pour cold milk into a weaker brew. Midwesterners dine at five or six, Spaniards at ten. Europeans eat with the fork in the left hand and the knife in the right. Meat cut by the knife is immediately conveyed to the mouth with the fork, which Americans switch to the right hand before eating.

For the Betsileo of Madagascar, there is no way of saying "to eat" without saying "to eat rice," their favorite and staple food. So strong is their preference for rice that they garnish it with beans, potatoes, and other starches. Eels cooked in their own grease are a delicacy for the Betsileos' honored visitors, a category in which I feared being

Human nature is appropriated by cultural systems and molded in hundreds of directions. This Japanese squid vendor makes her living by catering to food tastes that differ from those of the average American.

included because of my cultural aversion to eel meat (although I did tolerate grasshoppers cooked in peanut oil; they tasted like peanuts). In northeastern Brazil I grew to like chicken cooked in its own blood, a favorite there.

Like the lake at summer camp, human nature is appropriated by cultural systems and molded in hundreds of directions. All people must eliminate wastes from their bodies. However, some cultures teach people to defecate standing up, while others tell them to do it sitting down. Frenchmen aren't embarrassed to urinate in public, routinely stepping into barely shielded *pissoirs* in Paris streets. Peasant women in the Peruvian highlands squat in the streets and urinate into gutters. They get all the privacy they need from their massive skirts. All these habits are parts of cultural traditions that have converted natural acts into cultural customs.

Culture Is Shared

Culture is an attribute not of individuals per se but of individuals as members of *groups*. Culture is transmitted in society. We learn our culture by observing, listening, talking, and interacting with other people. Shared cultural beliefs, values, memories, expectations, and ways of thinking and acting override differences between people. Enculturation unifies people by providing us with common experiences.

Americans sometimes have trouble understanding the power of culture because of the value our culture places on the idea of the individual. Americans are fond of saying that everyone is unique and special in some way. However, in American culture individualism itself is a distinctive shared value that is transmitted through hundreds of statements and settings in our daily lives. From daytime TV's Mr. Rogers to "real-life" parents, grandparents, and teachers, our enculturative agents insist that we are all "someone special."

Today's parents were yesterday's children. If they grew up in American culture, they absorbed certain values and beliefs transmitted over the generations. People become agents in the enculturation of their children, just as their parents were for them. Although culture constantly changes, certain fundamental beliefs, values, world views, and child-rearing practices endure. Consider a simple American example of enduring shared encultura-

tion. As children, when we didn't finish a meal, our parents reminded us of starving children in some foreign country, just as our grandparents had done a generation earlier. The specific country changes (China, India, Bangladesh, Ethiopia). Still, American culture goes on transmitting the peculiar idea that by eating all our brussels sprouts and broccoli, we can somehow help a Third World child.

Culture Is Patterned

Cultures are not haphazard collections of customs and beliefs but integrated, patterned systems. Customs, institutions, beliefs, and values are interrelated; if one changes, others change as well. During the 1950s, for example, most American women expected to have domestic careers as homemakers and mothers. Today's college women expect to get jobs when they graduate.

As women enter the work force in increasing numbers, attitudes toward marriage, family, and children change. Outside work places strains on marriage and the family. Late marriage, "living together," and divorce become more common. These social changes reflect economic changes as the U.S. economy shifts from heavy goods manufacture toward services and information processing. Economic changes have produced changes in attitudes and behavior in regard to work, sex roles, marriage, and the family.

Cultures are integrated not simply by their dominant economic activities and social patterns but also by enduring themes, values, configurations, and world views. Cultures train their individual members to share certain personality traits. Separate elements of a culture can be integrated by key symbols, such as fertility or militarism. A set of characteristic central or **core values** (key, basic, or central values) integrates each culture and helps distinguish it from others. For instance, the work ethic, individualism, achievement, and self-reliance are core values that have integrated American culture for generations. Different value sets pattern other cultures.

Culture Is Adaptive and Maladaptive

To cope with or adapt to environmental stresses, humans can draw on both biological traits and

Cultures are integrated, patterned systems: when one custom, belief, or value changes, others change as well. During the 1950s most American women expected to have domestic careers. With women entering the work force in increasing numbers over the past two decades, attitudes toward work and family have changed. Most of today's college graduates plan to balance jobs and family responsibilities. Contrast the "fifties Mom" with a modern career woman—Myra McDaniel of Austin, Texas Secretary of State.

learned, symbol-based behavior patterns. Besides biological means of adaptation, human groups also employ "cultural adaptive kits" containing customary patterns, activities, and tools. Although humans continue to adapt biologically as well as culturally, reliance on social and cultural means of adaptation has increased during hominid evolution.

We saw in Chapter 1 that although adaptive behavior offers short-term benefits to individuals, it may harm the environment and threaten the group's long-term survival. Creative manipulation of the environment by men and women can foster a more secure economy, but it can also deplete strategic resources (Bennett 1969, p. 19). Thus, despite the crucial role of cultural adaptation in human evolution, cultural traits and patterns can also be **maladaptive,** threatening the group's continued existence (survival and reproduction). Many modern cultural patterns, such as policies that encourage overpopulation, inadequate food distribution systems, the nuclear arms race, and pollution, appear to be maladaptive in the long run.

Furthermore, practices that are adaptive or harmless for one culture may be maladaptive for another with which the first culture trades or which it dominates politically. Besides valuing subsistence resources, people may also esteem items (jewelry, for example) that lack subsistence or utilitarian value but are considered aesthetically pleasing or enhance social status. Given the modern world system of international trade and communication, the prestige demands of one culture can deplete the local ecosystems of others. For example, animals may be slaughtered for products that have no local value for food, dress, or ornamentation.

Many African animals are going extinct as poachers respond to the demands of collectors in other nations. Gorillas are killed, and their hands are sold to foreign collectors as ashtrays. Poachers slaughter elephants and export their ivory, which is used to make signature stamps (popular in Asia), jewelry, ornamental carvings, billiard balls, and piano keys. The main importers have been Japan and Hong Kong, which accounted for 75 percent of world ivory imports in 1988. The African elephant population declined from 1.5 million to 500,000 during the 1980s. An international ivory ban may yet save the elephant from the rapacious demands of foreign cultures. However, it may be too late for the rhinoceros, of which only a few thousand survive. Rhino horn is used for ceremonial dagger hilts in Yemen and ground up to make aphrodisiac powder in Asia (Shabecoff 1989*a* and *b*).

Levels of Culture

The destruction of resources in order to gratify cultural appetites proceeds in a world in which we may distinguish different levels of culture: national, international, and subcultural. **National culture** refers to the experiences, beliefs, learned behavior patterns, and values shared by citizens of the same nation. **International culture** is the term for cultural traditions that extend beyond national boundaries. Because culture is transmitted through learning rather than genetically, cultural traits can diffuse from one group to another. Two biological species cannot share their genetically transmitted means of adaptation. However, two cultures *can* share cultural experiences and means of adaptation through borrowing or diffusion.

Borrowing of culture traits has gone on throughout human history. **Diffusion** is direct when two cultures intermarry, wage war on, or trade with each other or when they watch the same TV program. Diffusion is indirect when products and patterns move from population A to population C via population B without any firsthand contact between A and C.

Through diffusion, migration, and multinational organizations, many culture traits and patterns have international scope. Roman Catholics in different countries share experiences, symbols, beliefs, and values transmitted by their church. Contemporary United States, Canada, Great Britain, and Australia share culture traits they have inherited from their common linguistic and cultural ancestors in Great Britain.

Cultures can also be smaller than nations. Although people in the same society or nation share a cultural tradition, all cultures also contain diversity. Individuals, families, villages, regions, classes, and other subgroups within a culture have different learning experiences as well as shared ones. **Subcultures** are different cultural symbol-based patterns and traditions associated with subgroups in the same complex society. In a complex nation such as the contemporary United States or Canada, subcultures originate in ethnicity, class, region, and religion. The religious backgrounds of Jews, Baptists, and Roman Catholics create subcultural differences between them. Although they share the same national culture, northerners and southerners exhibit differences in beliefs and customary behavior as a result of regional subcultural variation. French-speaking Canadians contrast on the subcultural level with English speakers in the same country. Italian-Americans have ethnic traditions different from those of Irish-, Polish-, and African-Americans.

Despite characteristic American notions that people should "make up their own minds" and "have a right to their opinion," little of what we think is original or unique. We share our opinions and beliefs with many other people. Illustrating the power of shared cultural background, we are most likely to agree with and feel comfortable with people who are socially, economically, and culturally similar to ourselves. This is one reason why Americans abroad tend to socialize with each other, just as French and British colonials did in their overseas empires. Birds of a feather flock together, but for people the familiar plumage is culture.

RULES, VIOLATIONS, AND RESEARCH STRATEGIES

Although cultural rules tell us what to do and how to do it, we don't always do what the rules dictate. People can learn, interpret, and manipulate the same rule in different ways. Even if they agree about what should and shouldn't be done, people don't always do as their culture directs. Many rules are violated, some very often (for example, automobile speed limits). Some anthropologists find it useful to distinguish between ideal and real culture. The *ideal culture* consists of what people say they should do and what they say they do. *Real culture* refers to their actual behavior as observed by the anthropologist. This raises the matter of different research strategies in cultural anthropology.

To study cultures, anthropologists have advocated two approaches, emic (actor-oriented) and etic (observer-oriented). An **emic** strategy investigates how natives think. How do they perceive and categorize the world? What are their shared rules for behavior and thought? What has meaning for them? How do they imagine and explain things? The anthropologist seeks the "native viewpoint" and relies on the culture bearers—the actors in a culture—to determine whether something they do, say, or think is significant.

However, natives aren't scientists. They may think that spirits cause illnesses that come from germs. They may believe political leaders who tell them that missiles are peacemakers. The **etic** (observer-oriented) approach shifts the focus of research from native categories, expressions, explanations, and interpretations to those of the anthropologist. The etic ethnographer gives more weight to what he or she (the observer) notices and considers important. As a trained scientist, the anthropologist should try to bring an objective and comprehensive viewpoint to the study of other cultures. Of course, the anthropologist, like any other scientist, is also a human being with cultural blinders that prevent complete objectivity. As in other sciences, proper training can reduce but not totally eliminate the observer's bias. Anthropologists have a greater capacity to compare behavior between different societies than natives do. The etic approach realizes that culture bearers are often too involved in what they are doing to interpret their cultures impartially.

In practice, most anthropologists combine emic and etic strategies in their field work. Native statements, perceptions, and opinions help ethnographers understand how cultures work. Native beliefs are also interesting and valuable in themselves and broaden the anthropologist's view of the world. However, natives often fail to admit, or even recognize, certain causes and consequences of their behavior. This is as true of North Americans as it is of people in any other society. To describe and interpret culture, ethnographers should recognize the biases that come from their own culture as well as those of the people being studied.

Ethnocentrism and Cultural Relativism

One of anthropology's main goals is to combat **ethnocentrism**, the tendency to apply one's own cultural values in judging the behavior and beliefs of people raised in other cultures. Ethnocentrism is a cultural universal. People everywhere think that familiar explanations, opinions, and customs are true, right, proper, and moral. They regard different behavior as strange or savage. The tribal names that appear in anthropology books often come from the native word for *people*. "What are you called?" asks the anthropologist. "Mugmug," reply informants. *Mugmug* may turn out to be synonymous with *people*, but it also may be the only word the natives have for themselves. Other tribes are not considered fully human. The not-quite-people in neighboring groups are not classified as *Mugmug*. They are given different names that symbolize their inferior humanity.

The opposite of ethnocentrism is **cultural relativism**, the argument that behavior in a particular culture should not be judged by the standards of another. This position can also present problems. At its most extreme, cultural relativism argues that there is no superior, international, or universal morality, that the moral and ethical rules of all cultures deserve equal respect. In the extreme relativist view, Nazi Germany is evaluated as nonjudgmentally as Athenian Greece.

How should anthropologists deal with ethnocentrism and cultural relativism? I believe that anthropology's main job is to present accurate accounts and explanations of cultural phenomena. The anthropologist doesn't have to approve customs such as infanticide, cannibalism, and torture to record their existence and determine their causes. However, each anthropologist has a choice about where to do field work. Some anthropologists choose not to study a particular culture because they discover in advance or early in field work that behavior they consider morally repugnant is practiced there. Anthropologists respect human diversity. Most ethnographers try to be objective, accurate, and sensitive in their accounts of other cultures. However, objectivity, sensitivity, and a cross-cultural perspective don't mean that anthropologists have to ignore international standards of justice and morality.

UNIVERSALITY, PARTICULARITY, AND GENERALITY

Anthropologists agree that cultural learning is uniquely elaborated among hominids, that culture is the major reason for human adaptability, and that the capacity for culture is shared by all humans. Anthropologists also unanimously accept a doctrine originally proposed in the nineteenth century: "the psychic unity of man." Anthropology assumes **biopsychological equality** among human

Exogamy, marriage outside one's kin group, is a cultural universal. Because it links human groups together into larger networks, exogamy has been crucial in hominid evolution. Shown here is trans-continental exogamy—the marriage of an American woman and a Colombian man.

groups. This means that although *individuals* differ in emotional and intellectual tendencies and capacities, all human *populations* have equivalent capacities for culture. Regardless of physical appearance and genetic composition, humans can learn *any* cultural tradition.

To understand this point, consider that contemporary Americans are the genetically mixed descendants of people from all over the world. Our ancestors were biologically varied, lived in different countries and continents, and participated in hundreds of cultural traditions. However, the earliest colonists, later immigrants, and their descendants have all become active participants in American life. All now share the same national culture.

To recognize biopsychological equality is not to deny differences between populations. In studying human diversity in time and space, anthropologists distinguish between the universal, the generalized, and the particular. Certain biological, psychological, social, and cultural features are **universal,** shared by all human populations in every culture. Others are merely **generalities,** common to several but not all human groups. Still other traits are **particularities,** unique to certain cultural traditions.

Universality

Universal traits are the ones that more or less distinguish *Homo sapiens* from other species. Biologically based universals include a long period of infant dependency, year-round (rather than sea-

sonal) sexuality, and a complex brain that enables us to use symbols, languages, and tools. Psychological universals arise from human biology and from experiences common to human development in all cases. These include growth in the womb, birth itself, and interaction with parents and parent substitutes.

Among the social universals is life in groups and in some kind of family. In all human societies culture organizes social life and depends on social interactions for its expression and continuation. Family living and food sharing are universals. Among the most significant cultural universals are **exogamy** and the **incest taboo** (prohibition against marrying or mating with a close relative). Humans everywhere consider some people (various cultures differ about *which* people) too closely related to mate or marry. The violation of this taboo is *incest,* which is discouraged and punished in a variety of ways in different cultures. If incest is prohibited, exogamy—marriage outside one's group—is inevitable. Because it links human groups together into larger networks, exogamy has been crucial in hominid evolution. Exogamy elaborates on tendencies observed among other primates. Recent studies of monkeys and apes show that these animals also avoid mating with close kin and often mate outside their native groups.

Particularity

Many cultural traits are widely shared because of diffusion and independent invention and as cultural universals. Nevertheless, different cultures emphasize different things. Cultures are patterned and integrated differently and display tremendous variation and diversity. Uniqueness and particularity stand at the opposite extreme from universality.

Unusual and exotic beliefs and practices lend distinctiveness to particular cultural traditions. Many cultures ritually observe such universal life-cycle events as birth, puberty, marriage, parenthood, and death. However, cultures vary in just which event merits special celebration. Americans regard expensive weddings as more socially appropriate than lavish funerals. However, the Betsileo of Madagascar, whom I have studied since 1966, take the opposite view. The marriage ceremony is a minor event that brings together just the couple and a few close relatives. However, a funeral is a measure of the deceased person's social position and lifetime achievement, and it may attract a thousand people. Why use money on a house, the Betsileo say, when one can use it on the tomb where one will spend eternity in the company of dead relatives? How different from contemporary Americans' growing preference for quick and inexpensive funerals. So important are celebrations of death in the cultures of Madagascar that the Malagasy (people of Madagascar) have been called necrophiliacs (lovers of the dead).

Cultures vary tremendously in their beliefs and practices. By focusing on and trying to explain alternative customs, anthropology forces us to reappraise our familiar ways of thinking. In a world full of cultural diversity, contemporary American culture is just one cultural variant, no more natural than the others.

Generality

Between universals and uniqueness is a middle ground that consists of cultural generalities: regularities that occur in different times and places but not in all cultures. One reason for generalities is diffusion. Societies can share the same beliefs and customs because of borrowing or through (cultural) inheritance from a common cultural ancestor. Other generalities originate in **independent invention** of the same culture trait or pattern in two or more different cultures. Similar needs and circumstances have led people in different lands to innovate in parallel ways. They have independently come up with the same cultural solution or arrangement.

One cultural generality that is present in many but not all societies is the **nuclear family,** a kinship group consisting of parents and children. Although many middle-class Americans ethnocentrically view the nuclear family as a proper and "natural" group, it is not universal. It is totally absent, for example, among the Nayars, who live on the Malabar Coast of India. The Nayars live in female-headed households, and husbands and wives do not co-reside. In many other societies, the nuclear family is submerged in larger kin groups, such as extended families, lineages, and clans. However, the nuclear family is prominent in many of the technologically simple societies that live by hunting and gathering. It is also a significant kin group among contemporary middle-class North Americans and western Europeans. Later, an explanation of the nuclear family as a basic kinship unit in specific types of society will be given.

SUMMARY

Culture, a distinctive possession of humanity, is acquired by all humans through enculturation. Culture encompasses rule-governed, shared, symbol-based learned behavior and beliefs transmitted across the generations. Everyone is cultured, not just people with elite educations. The genus *Homo* has the capacity for Culture (in a general sense), but people live in specific cultures where they are raised according to different traditions. Culture rests on the hominid capacity for cultural learning. *Culture* refers to customary beliefs and behavior and

to the rules for conduct internalized in human beings through enculturation. These rules lead people to think and act in certain consistent, distinctive, and characteristic ways.

Other animals learn, but only humans have cultural learning, which depends on symbols. Cultural learning rests on the universal human capacity to think symbolically, arbitrarily bestowing meaning on a thing or event. By convention, a symbol, which may be linguistic or nonverbal, stands for something else with which it has no necessary or natural relation. Symbols have a particular meaning and value for people in the same culture. People share experiences, memories, values, and beliefs as a result of common enculturation. People absorb cultural lessons consciously and unconsciously.

Cultural traditions seize natural phenomena, including biologically based desires and needs, and channel them in particular directions. Cultures are patterned and integrated through their dominant economic forces, social patterns, key symbols, and core values. Cultural means of adaptation have been crucial in hominid evolution, although aspects of culture can also be maladaptive.

There are different levels of cultural systems. Diffusion and migration carry the same cultural traits and patterns to different areas. These traits are shared across national boundaries. Nations include subcultural differences associated with ethnicity, region, and social class.

Cultural rules do not always dictate behavior. There

is room for flexibility and diversity within cultures. Anthropologists distinguish between what people say they do and what they actually do. Some anthropologists adopt an emic research strategy. They focus on native viewpoints and explanations and elicit natives' opinions about things that are or aren't significant in that culture. Other anthropologists pursue etic research strategies. They give less weight to informants' criteria of significance and more to those of the trained, and presumably more objective, scientific observer.

Anthropology finds no evidence that genetic differences explain cultural variation. Adopting a comparative perspective, anthropology examines biological, psychological, social, and cultural universals and generalities. It also considers unique and distinctive aspects of the human condition. In examining cultural elaborations on the fundamental biological plasticity of *Homo sapiens,* anthropology shows that American cultural traditions are no more natural than any others.

GLOSSARY

biopsychological equality: The premise that although individuals differ in emotional and intellectual capacities, all human populations have equivalent capacities for culture.

core values: Key, basic, or central values that integrate a culture and help distinguish it from others.

cultural learning: Learning based on the human capacity to think symbolically.

cultural relativism: The position that the values and standards of cultures differ and deserve respect. Extreme relativism argues that cultures should be judged solely by their own standards.

Culture, general: Spelled with a capital C; culture in the general sense as a capacity and possession shared by hominids.

culture, specific: Spelled with a small c; a culture in the specific sense, any one of the different and varied cultural traditions of specific societies.

diffusion: Borrowing between cultures either directly or through intermediaries.

emic: The research strategy that focuses on native explanations and criteria of significance.

ethnocentrism: The tendency to view one's own culture as best and to judge the behavior and beliefs of culturally different people by one's own standards.

etic: The research strategy that emphasizes the observer's rather than the natives' explanations, categories, and criteria of significance.

exogamy: Mating or marriage outside one's kin group; a cultural universal.

generality: Culture pattern or trait that exists in some but not all societies.

incest taboo: Universal prohibition against marrying or mating with a close relative.

independent invention: Development of the same culture trait or pattern in separate cultures as a result of comparable needs and circumstances.

individual situational learning: Type of learning in which animals learn from and base their future behavior on personal experience.

international culture: Cultural traditions that extend beyond national boundaries.

maladaptive: Harmful to survival and reproduction.

national culture: Cultural experiences, beliefs, learned behavior patterns, and values shared by citizens of the same nation.

nuclear family: Kinship group consisting of parents and children.

particularity: Distinctive or unique culture trait, pattern, or integration.

social situational learning: Learning from other members of the social group, not necessarily through language.

subcultures: Different cultural symbol-based traditions associated with subgroups in the same complex society.

symbol: Something, verbal or nonverbal, that arbitrarily and by convention stands for something else, with which it has no necessary or natural connection.

troop: Basic unit of social organization among nonhu-

man primates; composed of multiple adult males and females and their offspring.

universal: Something that exists in every culture.

STUDY QUESTIONS

1. What does it mean to say that culture is all-encompassing?
2. What is the difference between culture in the general sense and the specific sense?
3. What are the different kinds of learning? On which is culture based?
4. What does it mean to say that culture is symbolic?
5. What does it mean to say that culture is shared?
6. What does it mean to say that culture is patterned or integrated?
7. How is culture adaptive?
8. How are human adaptability and culture related?
9. What does it mean to say that there are levels of culture?
10. What is the distinction between emic and etic?
11. Why is that distinction important?
12. What is ethnocentrism?
13. What is cultural relativism, and what are its potential problems?
14. How does North American culture (of the United States or Canada) illustrate the idea of psychic unity?
15. What is meant by cultural universals, generalities, and particularities?
16. How is the idea of cultural particularity related to the notion of cultural patterning or integration?

SUGGESTED ADDITIONAL READING

GAMST, F.C., AND E. NORBECK, EDS.
  1976   *Ideas of Culture: Sources and Uses.* New York: Holt, Rinehart & Winston. Surveys various aspects and definitions of culture. Contains both classic and original essays.
GEERTZ, C.
  1973   *The Interpretation of Culture.* New York: Basic Books. Essays about culture viewed as a system of symbols and meaning.
HALL, E.T.
  1966   *The Hidden Dimension.* Garden City, NY: Doubleday. The intangibles of culture, particularly unconsciously transmitted ideas about personal distance and space.
HARRIS, M.
  1979   *Cultural Materialism: The Struggle for a Science of Culture.* New York: Vintage. Theories of culture, including an extended discussion of emic and etic research strategies.

  1987   *Why Nothing Works: The Anthropology of Daily Life.* New York: Simon & Schuster. Social consequences of the continuing economic shift from goods manufacture toward services and information processing.
KOTTAK, C.P.
  1990   *Prime-Time Society: An Anthropological Analysis of Television and Culture.* Belmont, CA: Wadsworth. How the content and impact of commercial television reflect cultural differences.
KROEBER, A.L., AND C. KLUCKHOLN
  1963   *Culture: A Critical Review of Concepts and Definitions.* New York: Vintage. Discusses and categorizes more than a hundred definitions of culture.
WAGNER, R.
  1981   *The Invention of Culture.* rev. ed. Chicago: University of Chicago Press. Culture, creativity, society, and the self.

CHAPTER 4

BIOLOGICAL DIVERSITY AND RACE

Humans have uniquely varied ways of adapting to environmental stresses. Chapter 3 considered adaptive (and maladaptive) aspects of *culture*. As individuals, we manipulate our artifacts and behavior in response to environmental conditions. We turn up thermostats or travel to Florida in the winter. We turn on fire hydrants, swim, or ride in air-conditioned cars from New York City to Maine to escape the summer's heat. Although such reliance on culture has increased during hominid evolution, humans have not stopped adapting biologically. As in other species, human populations adapt *genetically* in response to natural selection and individuals react *physiologically* to stresses. Thus when we work in the midday sun, sweating occurs spontaneously, cooling the skin and reducing the temperature of subsurface blood vessels.

During the eighteenth century, many scholars became interested in human origins and in our position within the classification of plants and animals. At that time the commonly accepted explanation for the origin of species came from Genesis: God had created all life during six days of Creation. According to **creationism,** biological similarities and differences originated at the Creation. Characteristics of life forms are immutable; they cannot change. Through calculations based on genealogies in the Bible, the biblical scholars James Ussher and John Lightfoot even managed to trace the Creation to a very specific date—October 23, 4004 B.C., at nine A.M.

CREATIONISM, CATASTROPHISM, AND EVOLUTION

An increasing number of fossil discoveries during the eighteenth and nineteenth centuries raised doubts about creationism. Fossils showed that different kinds of life had once existed. If all life had originated at the same time, why weren't ancient species still around. Why weren't contemporary plants and animals found in the fossil record? A modified explanation combining creationism with **catastrophism** replaced the original doctrine. In this view fires, floods, and other catastrophes, including the biblical flood involving Noah's ark, had destroyed ancient species. After each destructive event God had created again, leading to con-

temporary species. How did the catastrophists explain certain clear similarities between fossils and modern animals? They argued that some ancient species had managed to survive in isolated areas. For example, after the biblical flood, Noah's two of each kind spread throughout the world.

The alternative to creationism and catastrophism was **transformism,** also called evolution. Transformists believed that species arose from others through a long and gradual process of transformation, or descent with modification. Charles Darwin became the best known of the transformists. However, he was influenced by earlier scholars, including his own grandfather. Erasmus Darwin, in a book called *Zoonomia* published in 1794, had proclaimed the common ancestry of all animal species.

Charles Darwin was also influenced by Sir Charles Lyell, the father of geology. During Darwin's famous voyage to South America aboard the *Beagle,* he read Lyell's influential *Principles of Geology* (1837/1969), which exposed him to Lyell's principle of **uniformitarianism.** Uniformitarianism states that the present is the key to the past. Explanations for past events should be sought in the long-term operation of ordinary forces that continue to work today. Thus, natural forces (rainfall, soil deposition, and earthquakes) have gradually built geological features such as mountain ranges. The earth's physical structure has been transformed gradually through the operation of natural forces over millions of years.

Uniformitarianism was a necessary building block for evolutionary theory. It cast serious doubt on the belief that the world was only 6,000 years old. It would take much longer for such ordinary forces as rain and wind to produce major geological features. The longer time span also allowed enough time for the biological changes that the fossil discoveries were revealing. Darwin applied uniformitarianism—long-term transformation through natural forces—to living things. Like other transformists, he argued that all life forms are ultimately related. In contrast to proponents of divine creation, Darwin argued that the number of species is not immutable. It has increased with time.

Darwin offered **natural selection** as a single principle that could explain the origin of species, biological diversity, and similarities among related life forms. His major contribution was not the theory of evolution, as most people believe, but the idea that natural selection explains evolutionary change.

Darwinian natural selection is the gradual process by which nature selects the forms most fit to survive and reproduce in a given environment. For natural selection to operate on a particular population, there must be variety within that population, as there always is. Natural selection operates when there is competition for **strategic resources** (those necessary for life), such as food and space, between members of the population. Organisms whose attributes render them most fit to survive and reproduce in their environment do so in greater numbers than do others. Over the years, the less fit organisms gradually die out and the favored types survive.

This process continues as long as the relationship between the population and its environment remains the same. However, if emigration or some change in the environment occurs, natural selection will begin to select types that are favored in the new environment. This selection will continue until an equilibrium is reached. Environmental change or emigration may then occur again. Through such a gradual, branching process, involving adaptation to thousands of environments, natural selection has produced the plants and animals found in the world today.

THE BASIS OF BIOLOGICAL VARIATION

Darwin recognized that for natural selection to operate, there must be variety in the population undergoing selection. Documenting and explaining human variation is a major concern of modern biological anthropology. Genetics, a science that emerged after Darwin, helps us understand the causes of biological variation. We now know that DNA (deoxyribonucleic acid) molecules make up genes and chromosomes, which are the basic hereditary units. Biochemical changes (mutations) in DNA provide the variety on which natural selection operates. Genetic and chromosomal **recombination** produces additional variety; through bisexual reproduction, it leads to new arrangements of the hereditary units received from each parent.

Natural Selection, Genotype, and Phenotype

Natural selection is still the most powerful explanation for evolution. Essential to the modern theory of evolution through natural selection is the distinction between genotype and phenotype. **Genotype** refers to the hereditary features that control an individual's form (anatomy) and function (physiology). **Phenotype,** which includes the organism's anatomy, physiology, and behavior, is the product of a long-term interaction between genotype and environment. Organisms with different genotypes may be identical in certain features of their phenotypes. Natural selection operates only on phenotype.

Biological phenotype includes physical appearance and such internal structures as organs, tissues, and cells. Many biological reactions to diet, disease, heat, cold, sunlight, oxygen pressure, and other environmental stresses are not automatic, genetically programmed responses but plastic, or changeable. Human adaptation to environmental stresses reflects a complex and continuing interplay of heredity, culture, and biological plasticity.

However, in a given environment certain phenotypes have a better chance of surviving and reproducing than do others. Because phenotype has a genetic component, selection operating on phenotypes has genetic implications. The adaptive traits are more likely to be transmitted to later generations.

THE PROBLEMATIC CONCEPT OF RACE

Scientists have approached the study of human biological diversity from two main directions: racial classification and explanation of specific differences. Because of widespread confusion between the social and biological meanings of the term *race*, it is important to distinguish between them. In theory, a **biological race** is a discrete group whose members share certain distinctive genetic traits inherited from a common ancestor. The belief that races exist and are important is more common among the public than it is among biologists. Americans, for example, believe that our population includes one "race" called "white" or "Caucasian" and another called "black," "Ne-

Phenotype reflects the interaction of genetic potential and environment. Shown here are identical twins—genetically the same—raised in different environments. The girl on the left was raised in Puerto Rico, the one on the right in the continental United States.

groid," or "African-American." Many Americans mistakenly believe that these and other races have a biological basis.

RACE AS A SOCIAL CONSTRUCT

This section will show that the races we hear about every day are not biological but cultural, or social, categories. In Charles Wagley's terms (Wagley 1958/1968), they are **social races** (groups assumed to have a biological basis but actually perceived in a social rather than scientific context). I examine biological approaches to race below.

Many Americans believe that whites and blacks are biologically different and that each group represents a discrete racial category. Consider, however, how one gets to be "black." In American

culture, one acquires his or her racial identity at birth, but race is not based on biology or on simple ancestry. Take the case of the child of a "racially mixed" marriage or mating. We know that 50 percent of the child's genes come from one parent and 50 percent from the other. Still, American culture overlooks heredity and classifies the child as black. This rule is arbitrary. From genotype, it would be just as logical to classify the child as white.

American rules for ascribing racial status can be even more arbitrary. In some states, anyone known to have any black ancestor, no matter how remote, is classified as a member of the black race. This is a rule of **descent** (it assigns social identity on the basis of ancestry), but of a sort that is rare outside the contemporary United States. It is called **hypodescent** (Harris and Kottak 1963) (*hypo* means lower) because it automatically places the children of a union or mating between members of different socioeconomic groups in the less privileged group. Hypodescent divides American society into two groups that are unequal in their access to wealth, power, and prestige.

Very few other nations have such a cultural rule. For example, Brazil, which shares with the United States a heritage of slavery, lacks hypodescent. Beginning in the sixteenth century, Africans were brought to work as slaves on sugar plantations in northeastern Brazil. Later, Brazilians employed slave labor in gold mines and on coffee plantations. The contributions of Africans to Brazilian culture have been as great as they have been to American culture. Today, especially in areas of Brazil where slaves were most numerous, African phenotypes are obvious.

However, the system that Brazilians use to classify biological differences is very different from the American one. A Brazilian naming someone else's race might employ any one of over 500 different terms. In northeastern Brazil, I found that forty different racial terms were in use in Arembepe, a village of only 750 people (Kottak 1983). In their classification system Brazilians recognize and attempt to describe the phenotypical variation that exists in their population. The American system, in contrast, recognizes only two or three major races, blinding Americans to many phenotypical differences.

There are other differences between the social racial categories of Brazilians and Americans. In the United States one's social race does not change, but in Brazil it may—several times in a lifetime. Since phenotype is important in determining classification, a person's race may change, say, if he or she gets suntanned. In Arembepe I made it a habit to ask the same person on different days to tell me the races of others in the village. The racial term used to describe another villager could vary from week to week or even from day to day.

The American racial system is a creation of American culture rather than a reflection of biological fact. *Therefore, any statements that purport to show a relationship between American races and anything else say nothing about biology.* At most, they can only hope to show a relationship between social groupings, which Americans define arbitrarily, and other variables. Brazilians, by contrast, have developed a classification system to describe individual biological differences that is much more fluid and flexible than the one that Americans use. Unlike family members in the United States, full siblings in Brazil may, and often do, belong to different races. Brazil lacks a rule of descent like that which ascribes racial status in the contemporary United States (Harris 1964).

RACE IN BIOLOGY

The scientific validity of *race* as a biological term is questionable. Scientists have great difficulty applying it to groups of people.

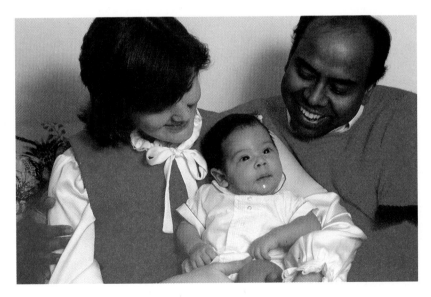

A "racially mixed" American family. Half the baby's genes come from one parent and half from the other. Still, American culture overlooks heredity (and appearance) and classifies the child as black. It would be just as logical to classify the child as white.

Classification Based on Phenotype

Early scholars attempted to define race by outward appearance. A definition framed from this viewpoint might go something like this: A race is a group of people distinguished from other groups by phenotypical differences. Several problems with this definition are immediately evident. First, which of many physical traits should be primary in assigning people who look different to different races?

European and American scientists tended to assign priority to skin color. Thus, many elementary school textbooks and encyclopedias still proclaim the existence of three great races: the white, the black, and the yellow. These terms do not accurately describe skin color. "White" people are more pink, beige, or tan than white. "Black" people are various shades of brown. "Yellow" people are more accurately tan or beige. These terms are also dignified by more scientific-sounding synonyms: Caucasoid, Negroid, and Mongoloid.

Even scientists who believe that there are three major races recognize that human populations are difficult to classify. For example, where does one put the Polynesians? **Polynesia** is a triangle of South Pacific islands formed by Hawaii to the north, Easter Island to the east, and New Zealand to the southwest. Does the "bronze" skin color of

The photos in this chapter illustrate just a small part of the range of human biological diversity. Traditional racial classification would classify this young woman from Beijing, China, as "Mongoloid."

Polynesians place them with the Caucasoids or the Mongoloids? Some scientists, recognizing this problem, enlarged the original tripartite scheme to include the Polynesian "race." Native Americans present an additional problem. Are they red or yellow? Again, some scientists add a fifth race—the red, or Amerindian—to the major racial groups.

Some of the people of southern India have dark skins, yet scientists have been reluctant to classify them with "black" Africans because of their "Caucasoid" facial features and hair form. Some, therefore, have created a separate race to accommodate these populations. What about the Australian aborigines, hunters and gatherers native to the most isolated continent? By skin color, one might place some Native Australians in the same race as tropical Africans. However, similarities to Europeans in hair color (light or reddish) and facial features have led some scientists to classify them as Caucasoids. However, there is no evidence that Australians are closer genetically or historically to either of these groups than they are to Asians. Recognizing this problem, scientists often regard Native Australians as a separate race.

Finally, consider the San ("Bushmen") of the Kalahari Desert in southern Africa. Scientists have perceived their skin color as varying from brown to yellow. Some of those who regard San skin as yellow have placed them in the same category with Asian Mongoloids. In theory, people of the same race share more recent common ancestry with each other than they do with any others. Given this assumption, the inclusion of the San in the yellow race has drawn criticism. There is no evidence for recent common ancestry between San and Asians. More reasonably, some scientists regard the San as members of the Capoid (from the Cape of Good Hope) race, which is seen as being different from other groups inhabiting Africa south of the Sahara.

Problems similar to those involved in basing racial classification on skin color emerge when any single trait is used. An attempt to base racial classification on facial features, height, weight, or any other phenotypical trait is fraught with difficulties. For example, consider the Nilotes, natives of the upper Nile region of Uganda and the Sudan. Nilotes tend to be tall and to have long, narrow noses. Certain Scandinavians are also tall and have similar noses. Given the distance between their home-

This Native Australian boy from Queensland has brown skin, light brown hair, large font teeth, and a broad nose. There is no evidence that Native Australians are genetically closer to either Europeans or Africans than to Asians.

lands, to classify them as members of the same race makes little sense. There is no reason to assume that Nilotes and Scandinavians are more closely related to each other than either is to shorter (and nearer) populations with different kinds of noses.

Would it be better to base racial classifications on a combination of physical traits? This would avoid some of the problems mentioned above, but others would arise. First, skin color, stature, skull form, and facial features (nose form, eye shape, lip thickness) do not go together as a unit. Traits determined by genes located on different chromosomes are transmitted independently to offspring. For example, people with dark skin have hair ranging from straight to very curly. Furthermore, there are dark-haired populations with light skin. The number of combinations is very large, and the amount that ancestry and genes (versus environment) contribute to such phenotypical traits is often unclear.

There is also the problem of bounding the race. In Africa, dark-skinned populations tend to live in the **tropics,** a belt extending about 23 degrees north and south of the equator, between the Tropic of Cancer and the Tropic of Capricorn. Moving north out of the tropics, skin color does not change abruptly. Rather, there is a gradual

transition—from tropical to subtropical Africa into North Africa and the Near East. The trend toward lighter skin color continues around the Mediterranean into Europe and through northern Europe. Given this gradual change in one aspect of phenotype, it is a completely arbitrary matter to say where one race ends and another begins.

There is a final objection to racial classification based on phenotypical traits. Genes and the environment work together to create phenotype. The relative contributions of genes and environment to human biological differences are often unclear. Phenotype is the changing product of a long-term interaction, particularly important during growth and development, between the organism's hereditary potential and its environment. Therefore, as the environment changes, the range of phenotypes characteristic of a given population can also change independently of genetic change. The environment's influence on the organism reflects both the nature of the stress and the individual's age when exposed. The younger the individual, the greater the impact of the environment tends to be.

There are several examples. In the early twentieth century, the anthropologist Franz Boas (1940/1966) described changes in skull form among the children of Europeans who had migrated to the United States. The reason for this was not a change in genes, for the European immigrants tended to marry among themselves. Some of their children had been born in Europe and merely raised in the United States. Something in the new environment, most probably in the diet, was producing this change.

Changes in average height and weight produced by dietary differences in a few generations are even more common. Traditional racial classifications assumed that phenotypes are stable and fixed by heredity. Like creationism, they stressed immutability. Thus the dark skin of some tropical Africans and some Native Australians was taken to indicate common ancestry. However, *phenotypes are flexible.* Much of the darkness in the skin color of the natives of southern (nontropical) Australia can be attributed to suntanning. Southern Australian natives who have left the bush are virtually indistinguishable from many southern Europeans. Furthermore, as we will see below, similar natural

This married couple, victims of Ethiopia's prolonged drought and famine, offers stark confirmation that phenotype reflects a long-term interaction between heredity and environment—particularly diet.

selective forces operating in similar tropical environments provide perfectly good explanations for dark skin color among tropical Africans, Australians, and Indians. There is no need to suppose that their shared phenotypical trait implies a recent common ancestry.

Genetic Approaches to Race

Recognizing these problems, scientists interested in race shifted their attention from phenotype to genotype. From a genetic point of view, a race came to be seen as a group with a certain frequency of a gene or cluster of genes. Again, the assumption was that the biological (here genetic) traits defining the race are stable and therefore are based on recent common ancestry. Scientists sought "neutral" genetic traits as markers of membership in the same race. They supposed that such neutral traits would persist—unaffected by natural selection—despite environmental changes. Thus

they could distinguish degrees of relationship and form the basis for racial classification.

A genetic definition of race is less arbitrary than is one based on phenotype because evaluations of gene frequencies are less impressionistic than are evaluations of such outward traits as hair type and skin color. Genotype is a less complex basis for racial classification than is phenotype, which involves both genes and the environment. However, most scientists now reject even a genetic approach to racial classification. Consider some of the reasons why.

Exogamy—mating or marriage outside one's kin group—is one of the oldest and most characteristic adaptive traits of *Homo*. Such outbreeding has linked local populations throughout hominid evolution. As one might expect, abrupt changes in gene frequencies between neighboring populations are the exception rather than the rule because of intermarriage. It is an arbitrary matter to say where one race ends and another begins.

Another problem involves selecting a specific gene as the basis for racial classification. If a cluster of genes is chosen, those genes may be located on different chromosomes, and their phenotypes may respond to different selective pressures. The larger the number of genes considered, the greater the number of combinations and the larger the number of races.

As an illustration of this point, consider human blood traits. Because the genetic determinants of blood are fairly simple and blood samples are easy to obtain, there have been many genetic studies of human blood. A sample of human blood allows the study of several genetically determined traits.

How might we construct a racial taxonomy based on blood groups? We could begin with three races whose members have high frequencies of blood groups A, B, and O. If we were then to include the Rh system, commonly recognized in the distinction between Rh-positive and Rh-negative blood, our emerging racial taxonomy based on genetically controlled blood traits would have six races characterized, respectively, by high frequencies of A positive, B positive, O positive, A negative, B negative, and O negative. Add two more genes, M and N, which determine another human blood-group system, and the number of races doubles again.

Take additional blood features, and the number

CULTURE, BIOLOGY, AND SPORTS, OR WHY JIMMY THE GREEK WAS WRONG

Culture constantly molds human biology. Culture promotes certain activities, discourages others, and sets standards of physical well-being and attractiveness. Sports activity, which is influenced by culture, helps build phenotype. American girls are encouraged to pursue—and they therefore do well in—competitive track and field, swimming, and diving. Brazilian girls, in contrast, haven't fared nearly as well in international athletic competition. Why are girls encouraged to become athletes in some nations but discouraged from physical activities in others? Why don't Brazilian women, and Latin women generally, do better in athletics?

In Brazil, fewer females swim, dive, and run than is the case in North America. This is part of a more general Brazilian pattern in which females are enculturated to avoid public activities. *Machismo* permeates Brazilian culture, which defines the public world and competition as male domains. Examples are obvious. The daily beachside joggers in Rio de Janeiro include many more men than women. Men play vigorous soccer matches on the beach, while women in string bikinis sun themselves nearby.

Cultural standards of attractiveness affect athletic activities. Americans run or swim not just to compete but to keep trim and fit. Brazil's beauty standards accept more fat, especially in female buttocks and hips. Brazilian men have had some international success in swimming and running, but Brazil rarely sends female swimmers or runners to the Olympics. One reason Brazilian women avoid competitive swimming in particular is that sport's effects on phenotype. Years of swimming sculpt a distinctive physique—an enlarged upper torso, a massive neck, and powerful shoulders and back. Successful female swimmers tend to be big, strong, and bulky. The countries that produce them are the United States, East Germany, and the Soviet Union, where this phenotype is not as stigmatized as it is in Latin countries. Dedicated swimmers develop hard bodies, but Brazilian culture says that women should be soft. A Brazilian beauty should have big hips and buttocks rather than big shoulders. Brazilian culture regards women more as reproducers than as producers, and Brazilians value the lower body because it houses the reproductive organs. Necklaces and pendants, which are beauty-enhancing tokens of male esteem, rather than medals, which are emblems of personal achievement, should adorn the necks of Brazilian beauties.

Cultural factors rather than innate biological characteristics also explain why blacks excel in certain sports and whites in others. In American schools, parks, sandlots, and city playgrounds, African-Americans have access to baseball diamonds, basketball courts, football fields, and tracks. However, because of restricted economic opportunities, many black families can't afford to buy hockey gear or ski equipment, take ski vacations, pay for tennis lessons, or belong to clubs with tennis courts and pools. In the United States mainly light-skinned boys (often in private schools) play soccer, the most popular sport in the world. In Brazil, however, soccer is the national pastime of all males—black and white, rich and poor. There is wide public access. Brazilians play soccer on the beach and in streets, squares, parks, and playgrounds. Many of Brazil's best soccer players, including the world-famous Pelé, have dark skins. When blacks have opportunities to do well in soccer, tennis, or any other sport, they are physically capable of doing as well as whites.

Why does the United States have so many black football and basketball players and so few black swimmers and hockey players? The answer lies not in biology but in cultural factors, including variable access and social stratification. Many Brazilians practice soccer, hoping to play for money for a professional club. Similarly, American blacks are well aware that certain professional sports have traditionally provided career opportunities for African-Americans. They start developing skills in those sports in childhood. The better they do, the more likely they are to persist, and the pattern continues.

The paucity of black competitive swimmers in the United States also has to do with access rather than biology. Most American swimmers begin as kids to swim competitively for clubs with membership fees. In Brazilian cities the major clubs and teams recruit talented swimmers regardless of race, and the pools are right in the city. Brazilian cities have less residential segregation than do American ones. This means that poor Brazilian children, black and white, can work out as swim-team members almost as easily as middle-class kids can. In the United States it is rare to see a black swimmer in a state championship. In Brazil, however, there are swimmers with dark skins and fast times at virtually every swimming meet. Thus, countering a claim made by TV sports commentator Jimmy the Greek Snyder a few years ago, culture—specifically differential access to sports resources—has much more to do with sports success than does "race."

of races doubles or triples with each new factor considered. By the time we consider traits conveyed by each of the twenty-three chromosome pairs of *Homo sapiens,* the number of races mounts into the millions. Thus there are great difficulties in any attempt to pigeonhole humanity into discrete categories based on either genotypical or phenotypical traits.

This leads to a very important question: What is the purpose of racial classification? On a broader level, what is the reason for any classification scheme or typology? Typologies are useful when they reveal something that we didn't know before. Racial classifications, however, merely attempt to arrange data that already exist. They say nothing about correlations and causes—associated differences and similarities among human groups and the reasons *why* people placed in different races look or behave differently. I examine and dispute certain contentions about relationships between race and behavior below.

EXPLAINING HUMAN BIOLOGICAL DIVERSITY

Although the problems involved in categorizing human beings according to race are immense, it is obvious that biological differences exist among people. Rather than try to classify humanity into artificial categories called races, anthropologists and other biologists are increasingly turning their attention toward explaining *why* specific biological differences exist. Before considering some explanations for human biological diversity, a reminder is in order: hominid evolution has involved an increasing reliance on cultural means of adaptation. Because it includes cultural means, our adaptive apparatus is much more flexible than that of any other animal. Because adaptation is not totally biological, many contemporary humans live in environments for which their biological attributes are not particularly well suited. However, they survive and reproduce because they have developed perfectly adequate cultural means of dealing with those environments.

Descendants of populations that evolved in Western Europe, for example, now live successfully in areas thousands of miles from their ancestral homelands, including Australia, New Zealand, South Africa, and North and South America. Similarly, in the United States, in the Caribbean, in Brazil, and in other parts of the New World, people whose ancestors lived in sub-Saharan Africa survive and reproduce effectively.

The movement of some human populations into their present environments has been recent compared with millions of years of hominid evolution. Given the recent occupation of certain areas, adaptive relationships between people's biological characteristics and the environments they now inhabit may be difficult to discern. With these warnings in mind, let us consider several attempts to explain biological variation among contemporary human populations.

Researchers have established links between biological traits whose genetic determinants are known (such as blood groups) and forces of natural selection (such as diseases). However, many human biological traits are not subject to simple genetic control. Genetic determination may be likely but unconfirmed, or several genes may interact to influence phenotype. In still other cases, the relative contributions of genes—whether single or multiple—and environmental conditions experienced during growth and development cannot be distinguished. For any complex biological trait, however, adult phenotype is the product of a lifetime of interaction between genetic material and environmental stress.

Certain psychological conditions have such complex causation. One such trait is schizophrenia, which affects about 1 percent of the American population at any given time and 1.5 percent at some point during the life cycle (Parachini 1988). Heredity and environment interact to cause schizophrenia. The gene responsible for at least one form of schizophrenia has been identified. However, because one identical twin may be schizophrenic while the other is not, we know that there is also environmental causation. Although identical twins have the same genotype, they never experience exactly the same environmental circumstances during their lifetimes.

Lactose Intolerance

Genes and environment also seem to work together to produce a biochemical difference between human groups: the ability to digest large amounts of milk. All milk, whatever its source, contains a complex sugar called **lactose**. The digestion of milk depends on an enzyme called **lactase**, which works in the small intestine. Among all mammals except humans and some of their pets, lactase production ceases after weaning. These mammals then lose the ability to digest milk. However, lactase production and the ability to tolerate milk after weaning vary from one human population to another. About 90 percent of northern Europeans and their descendants are lactose-tolerant; they can digest several glasses of milk with no difficulty. Similarly, about 80 percent of two African populations, the Tutsi of Uganda and the Fulani of Nigeria, produce lactase and digest milk easily. Both of these groups are herders of cattle and other dairy animals. However, such nonherding populations as the Yoruba and Ibo in Nigeria, the Ganda in Uganda, Japanese and other Asians, Israelis, Eskimos, and South American Indians cannot digest lactose (Kretchmer 1972/1975).

Variable human ability to digest milk seems to be a difference of degree rather than of kind. Some populations can tolerate very little or no milk, whereas others are able to metabolize considerably greater quantities. Studies showing that people who move from low-milk or no-milk to high-milk diets increase their lactose tolerance suggest an environmental component. We can conclude that no simple genetic trait accounts for the ability to digest milk. Lactose tolerance appears to be one of the many aspects of human biology to which both genetic and environmental factors contribute.

Skin Color

Skin color is another complex biological trait. Several genes—just how many is not known—interact with environmental conditions to produce variation in skin color among human populations. Two pigments—melanin and hemoglobin—determine human skin color. **Melanin** is a chemical substance manufactured in specialized cells in the lower layers of the epidermis, or outer skin layer. The number of these cells appears to be the same among all populations of *Homo sapiens.* However, the melanin cells of darker-skinned people produce more and larger granules of melanin than do those of lighter-skinned people. Epidermal melanin regulates the absorption of ultraviolet radiation

Before the sixteenth century, almost all the very dark-skinned populations of the world lived in the tropics. Notice the very dark skin color of this Samburu woman from Kenya.

from the sun. It thus protects people against a variety of maladies, including sunburn and skin cancer.

Before the sixteenth century, almost all the very dark-skinned populations of the world lived in the tropics. The association between dark skin color and a tropical habitat existed throughout the Old World, where hominids have lived for millions of years. The indigenous populations of southern, tropical India, for example, are darker than are the populations of northern India. Southern Australians, who live outside the tropics, are lighter than are natives of tropical northern Australia. The darkest populations of Africa evolved not in equatorial forests but in savanna, or open grassland country.

As one leaves the tropics, skin color becomes lighter. To the north there is a gradual transition from dark brown to medium brown. Progressively lighter skin color is distributed in the same gradual, continuous fashion through the Middle East, into southern Europe, through central Europe, and to the north. Similarly, south of the tropics skin color is also lighter (see Figure 4.1).

In the Americas, by contrast, tropical populations don't have especially dark skins because the settlement of the New World, by the relatively light-skinned Asian ancestors of Native Americans, was relatively recent, probably dating back no more than 30,000 years. How, aside from migrations, can we explain the geographic distribution of skin color? In the tropics, with intense ultraviolet radiation from the sun, unprotected humans face the threat of severe sunburn, which can increase susceptibility to disease. This confers a selective *dis*advantage on lighter-skinned people living in the tropics. Sunburn also impairs the body's ability to sweat. Thus light skin color, given tropical heat, can diminish the human ability to live and work in equatorial climates. Long-term exposure to high levels of ultraviolet radiation can also produce skin cancer in humans (Blum 1961). However, skin cancer is rarely fatal, and when it is, this usually occurs after the reproductive period

has ended. This casts doubt on skin cancer as a significant natural selective agent.

W. F. Loomis (1967) and others explain both light and dark skin color in terms of selective forces—the role of ultraviolet radiation in stimulating the manufacture of vitamin D by the human body. The unclothed human body can synthesize vitamin D directly from sunlight, but in an overcast environment that is also cold enough for people to clothe themselves during most of the year (such as northern Europe, where light skin color evolved), apparel impedes the manufacture of vitamin D. A shortage of vitamin D interferes with the absorption of calcium in the intestines, and a nutritional disease known as **rickets** may develop. Rickets interferes with the absorption of calcium and causes softening and deformation of the bones; in women, this deformation of the pelvis can interfere with childbirth. Thus, dark skin in northern areas can come under selective control because heavier concentrations of melanin in the skin screen out more ultraviolet radiation. Light skin color maximizes the absorption of ultraviolet radiation by the few parts of the body that are

Figure 4.1 *The distribution of human skin color c. A.D. 1400. Also shown is the average amount of ultraviolet radiation in watt-seconds per square centimeter. (Figure from* Evolution and Human Origins *by B.J. Williams. Copyright © 1979 by B.J. Williams. Reprinted by permission of Harper & Row, Publishers, Inc.)*

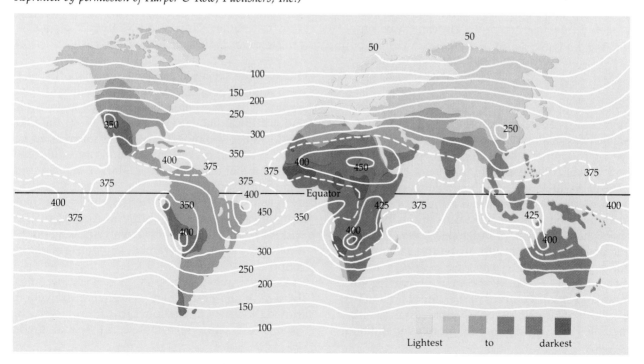

exposed to direct sunlight during northern winters. If the diet lacks vitamin D, reduced melanin is selectively favored.

Loomis has suggested that in the tropics, dark skin color protects the body against an *over*production of vitamin D by screening out ultraviolet radiation. Too much of this vitamin can lead to a potentially fatal condition in which calcium deposits build up in the body's soft tissues and the kidneys may eventually fail. In northern climates with marked seasonal variation, ultraviolet radiation is intense during the summer months. Otherwise light-skinned people adapt to this environmental stress both culturally—by wearing clothes and using lotions—and physiologically—by tanning.

As these examples show, if we attempt to *explain* particular traits rather than pigeonhole humanity into races, we learn much more about relationship between biology and adaptation. Often, populations in geographically distant parts of the world share certain biological traits. However, there is no reason to assume automatically that these similarities reflect either common ancestry or intermarriage. Instead, they may result from the operation of the same natural selective forces in different places. Similarities may also reflect similar physiological responses, founded on human biological plasticity, to similar environmental stresses, not hereditary factors. Human biology is not the immutable phenomenon assumed by the classifiers of race. Instead, it is inherently plastic, changing constantly, even without genetic change.

"RACE" AND "INTELLIGENCE"

Over the centuries groups with power have attempted to justify their privileged and dominant social positions by declaring minorities to be innately inferior. The Nazis argued for the superiority of the "Aryan race." European colonialists asserted the "white man's burden." Contemporary South Africa maintains apartheid. To justify exploitation of minorities and native peoples, those in control have proclaimed the innate inferiority of the oppressed. In the United States the supposed superiority of the white race was once standard segregationist doctrine. Belief in the biologically based inferiority of Native Americans has been an argument for their slaughter, confinement, and neglect.

The trend toward lighter skin color in more northern latitudes continues across the Mediterranean into Europe. Very light skin color, illustrated in this photo, maximizes absorption of ultraviolet radiation by those few parts of the body exposed to direct sunlight during northern winters. This helps prevent rickets.

However, anthropologists know that most of the behavioral variation among contemporary human groups rests on culture rather than biology. The cultural similarities revealed through thousands of ethnographic studies leave no doubt that capacities for cultural evolution are equal in all human populations. There is also excellent evidence that within any **stratified** (class-based) society, differences in performance between economic, social, racial, and ethnic groups reflect unequal opportunities rather than genetic makeup. (Stratified societies are those with marked differences in wealth, prestige, and power between social classes.)

However, stratification, political domination, prejudice, and ignorance continue to exist. They nurture the mistaken belief that misfortune and poverty result from lack of ability. Doctrines of innate superiority are occasionally defended by scientists, who, after all, tend to come from the favored stratum of society. Among recent examples, the best known is Jensenism, named for the educational psychologist Arthur Jensen (Jensen 1969; Herrnstein 1971), its leading proponent. Simply stated, Jensenism is the belief that genes determine intelligence. In particular, it is an interpretation of the observation that black Americans, on the average, perform less well on intelligence tests than do white Americans. Jensenism asserts that blacks are hereditarily incapable of performing as well as whites do.

However, environmental explanations for test scores are much more convincing than are the genetic tenets of Jensenism. An environmental explanation does not deny that some people may be smarter than others. In any society, for many reasons, genetic and environmental, the talents of *individuals* vary. An environmental explanation does deny, however, that these differences can be generalized to whole groups. Even when talking about individual intelligence, however, we have to decide which of several abilities is an accurate measure of intelligence.

There are some **egalitarian** societies in which hereditary differences may be completely expressed in culturally valued achievements. (Egalitarian societies are those in which there are as many positions of prestige as there are people who wish to fill them.) However, the situation is very different in stratified societies. By definition, a stratified society is not egalitarian. Some people must be better off than others. Every stratified society has mechanisms that operate to keep the underprivileged "in their place."

Working-class whites have lower average test scores than do middle-class people. Many Americans believe that success rests more on individual qualities than on social background. This belief may suggest that lower-class people have that status because of their lack of intelligence or ambition. Many Americans thus apply the same argument (genetic limitations) to class differences as to racial or ethnic differences. However, abundant evidence supports environmental rather than genetic explanations for the test performances of groups.

To determine relationships between group attributes and intelligence, it is necessary to measure intelligence. Psychologists have devised several kinds of tests, but there are problems with all of them. Early intelligence tests demanded skill in manipulating words. Such tests do not accurately measure learning ability for several reasons. For example, individuals who have learned two languages as children—bilinguals—don't do as well

on verbal intelligence tests as do people who have learned a single language. It would be absurd to suppose that children who master two languages have inferior intelligence. The explanation seems to be that because bilinguals have vocabularies, concepts, and verbal skills in both languages, their ability to manipulate either one suffers a bit. Still, this is offset by the tremendous advantage of being fluent in two languages.

Most tests are written by educated people in Europe and the United States. They reflect the experiences of the people who devise them. It is not surprising that middle- and upper-class children do better, because they are more likely to share the test makers' educational background and standards. Numerous recent studies have shown that performance on Scholastic Achievement Tests (SATs) can be improved by coaching and preparation. Parents who can afford $500 for an SAT preparation course enhance their kids' chances of getting high scores. Standardized college entrance exams are similar to IQ tests in that they purportedly measure intellectual aptitude. They may do this, but they also measure type and quality of high school education, linguistic and cultural background, and parental wealth. No test is free of class, ethnic, and cultural biases.

IQ tests often require familiarity with proverbs (for example, "Robbing Peter to pay Paul") and kinship terms used by members of the middle class. Test takers must solve problems most often encountered in middle-class settings. They are scored on their ability to define words that do not occur in certain variants of English (Kagan 1975).

Tests invariably measure particular learning histories, not the potential for learning. They use middle-class performance as a standard for determining what should be known at a given chronological age. Furthermore, tests are usually administered by middle-class white people who give instructions in a dialect or language that may not be totally familiar to the child being tested. Test performance improves when the subcultural, socioeconomic, and linguistic backgrounds of subjects and test personnel are similar. Several studies (Watson 1972) have demonstrated that the tested IQ of black schoolchildren, for example, rises an average of 6 points when the person administering the test is black.

American tests have been translated into foreign languages and given to people in other countries and cultures, whose average scores are significantly lower. Although words and phrases are translated, the concepts they test are often unfamiliar to foreigners. It would be interesting to know how well a group of middle-class Americans would do on a test composed by tribespeople from Papua–New Guinea and translated into English.

Recognizing the difficulties in devising a culture-free test, psychologists have developed several nonverbal tests, hoping to find an objective measure that is not bound to a single culture. In one such test, individuals score higher by adding body parts to a stick figure. In a maze test, subjects trace their way out of various mazes. The score increases with the speed of completion. Other tests also base scores on speed, for example, in fitting geometric objects into appropriately shaped holes. All these tests are culture-bound because American culture emphasizes speed and competition whereas most nonindustrial cultures do not.

Frequently, test performance varies in different cultures because some cultures stress cooperation and group problem solving rather than competition. In one case, a social scientist working among Australian foragers had been incorporated into the band as a fictive kinsman. When he gave the maze test to his new kinsmen, they looked up after each move for his approval. When they experienced difficulty, they asked him for help. The Australians were surprised when he refused and told other band members not to give advice either. They were accustomed to learning from others' experience and to group deliberation in decision making. However, in the United States, individual achievement and self-reliance are dominant cultural values. Dependence on others, so basic to tribal life, may be considered cheating.

Examples of cultural biases in intelligence testing abound. Biases affect performance by people in other cultures and by different groups within the same culture, such as Native Americans in the United States. Many Native Americans have grown up on reservations or under conditions of urban or rural poverty. They have suffered social, economic, political, and cultural discrimination. In one study, Native Americans scored the lowest (a mean of 81, compared with a standard of 100) of any minority group in the United States (Klineberg 1971). In a more recent comparison (Mayeske 1971), they did better than Hispanics but worse

No test is a pure measure of "native" intelligence—free of class, ethnic, or cultural biases. Standardized college entrance exams are similar to IQ tests in that they measure the type and quality of high school education, linguistic and cultural background, and parental wealth. An elite education, such as is available at this expensive private secondary school, produces higher average test scores.

than Asian-Americans (who had the highest scores), whites, and blacks.

When the environment offers experiences similar to those available to middle-class Americans, test performance tends to equalize. One study examined Native American children raised by white foster parents. Their average IQ was 102. These children were compared with their full siblings raised on the reservation, whose average IQ was 87. Another illustration of the relationship between environment and test scores comes from the Osage Indians, on whose reservation oil was discovered. Profiting from oil sales, they did not experience the stresses of poverty. They developed a good school system, and their average IQ was 104. Here the relationship between test performance and environment is particularly clear. The Osage did not settle on the reservation because they knew that oil was there. There is no reason to believe that these people were innately more intelligent than were Indians on different reservations. They were just luckier.

Similar relationships between social, economic, and educational environment and test performance show up in comparisons of American blacks and whites. At the beginning of World War I, intelligence tests were given to approximately 1 million American army recruits. Blacks from some northern states had higher average scores than did whites from some southern states. This was caused by the fact that early in this century northern blacks got a better public education than did many southern whites. Thus, their superior performance is not surprising. On the other hand, southern whites did better than southern blacks. This is also expectable, given the unequal school systems then open to whites and blacks in the South.

Some people tried to get around the environmental explanation for the superior performance of northern blacks over southern whites by suggesting selective migration—smarter blacks had moved north. However, it was possible to test this hypothesis, which turned out to be false. If smarter blacks had moved north, their superior intelligence should have been obvious in their school records while they were still living in the South. It was not. Furthermore, studies in New York, Washington, and Philadelphia showed that as length of residence increased, test scores also rose.

IQ scores do not measure innate intelligence. Rather, they test, with reference to middle-class standards, phenotypical intelligence. Consider a study (Mercer 1971) of more than 900 Mexican-American and black elementary school children which revealed a systematic relationship between social, economic, and educational attributes of the home environment and test performance. The average IQ score for both black and Mexican-American schoolchildren was 90, 10 points below the national average. However, when socioeconomic factors were considered, the influence of home environment on test performance became clear. The researchers focused on a subgroup of the black children. These children came from families that owned their homes and had five or fewer members. Household heads were married and pursued certain occupations. The mothers expected their children to get at least some education after high school. These children had an average IQ of 100, the national standard.

Studies of identical twins raised apart also illustrate the impact of environment on identical heredity. In a study of nineteen pairs of twins, IQ scores varied directly with years in school. The average

difference in IQ was only 1.5 points for the eight twin pairs with the same amount of schooling. It was 10 points for the eleven pairs with an average of five years' difference. One subject, with fourteen years more education than his twin, scored 24 points higher (Bronfenbrenner 1975). In another study (Skodak and Skeels 1949), the birth mothers of 100 foster children had an average IQ of 86; their children, an average IQ of 106. All these findings undercut claims that an average difference of 15 points in the IQ test scores of whites, compared with those of blacks or Native Americans, reflects genetic differences.

These and similar studies provide overwhelming evidence that test performance measures education and social, economic, and cultural background rather than genetically determined intelligence. During the past 500 years Europeans and their descendants extended their political and economic control over most of the world. They colonized and occupied environments that they reached in their ships and conquered with their weapons. Most people in the most powerful contemporary nations—located in North America, Europe, and Asia—have light skin color. Some people in these currently powerful countries may incorrectly believe that their world position has resulted from innate biological superiority. However, all contemporary human populations seem to have comparable learning abilities.

We are living in and interpreting the world at a particular time. In the past there were far different associations between centers of power and human physical characteristics. When Europeans were barbarians, advanced civilizations thrived in the Middle East. When Europe was in the Dark Ages, there were civilizations in West Africa, on the East African coast, in Mexico, and in Asia. Before the Industrial Revolution, the ancestors of many white Europeans and Americans were living much more like precolonial Africans than like current members of the American middle class. Their average performance on twentieth-century IQ tests would have been abominable.

SUMMARY

Influenced by earlier transformists, Charles Darwin proposed natural selection to explain the origin of species, biological diversity, and similarities encountered among

related life forms. Darwin recognized that for natural selection to operate, there must be variety within the population undergoing selection. Genetic mutations and recombination produce much of the variety essential to natural selection. The same parents can have offspring with an array of different phenotypes and genotypes.

Because of a range of problems involved in classifying humans into racial categories, contemporary biologists focus on specific biological differences and try to explain them. Most Americans believe that the "races" we recognize in the United States are biological categories. Instead, "white" and "black" designate social races—categories that are defined by American culture. American racial classification ignores both phenotype and genotype. Children of mixed unions are automatically classified with the minority-group parent. Racial classification in Brazil demonstrates that the American system is not inevitable. Brazilians recognize more than 500 racial categories. Furthermore, in contrast to the United States, race in Brazil can change during a person's lifetime, reflecting phenotypical changes. It also varies depending on who is doing the classifying.

Some scientists, recognizing the problems involved in phenotypical classification, have proposed a genetic approach to race. However, genes, like phenotypical traits, vary independently and respond to different selective forces. As the number of genetically determined traits increases, the number of races proliferates; ultimately there are as many races as people in the world.

The genetic and phenotypical diversity that exists among contemporary human populations must be explained. Biological similarities between geographically separate groups may reflect—rather than common ancestry—similar but independent genetic evolution in response to similar natural selective forces. Similarities may also be common physiological responses, founded on human biological plasticity, to similar environmental stresses.

Avoiding racial classification, modern biological anthropology attempts to explain specific aspects of human variation. Phenotype is the ever-changing product of an interaction, which begins at conception, between the organism's hereditary potentialities and its environment. Accordingly, biological anthropologists must investigate individual responses to environmental conditions during growth and development along with shorter-term physiological reactions.

Some people believe in genetically determined differences in the learning abilities of races, classes, and ethnic groups. However, environmental variables (particularly educational, economic, and social background) provide much better explanations for performance on intelligence tests by such groups. Intelligence tests reflect the cultural biases and life experiences of the people who develop and administer them. When tests devised by Americans and Europeans are translated into other languages, they retain Western cultural concepts. All tests are to some extent culture-bound. Many stress competition and speed of completion, values of a society that emphasizes time, individual achievement, and self-reliance. Equalized environmental opportunities show up in test scores.

GLOSSARY

catastrophism: Doctrine that certain ancient species were destroyed by fires, floods, and other catastrophes; thereafter, God created again, leading to contemporary species.

creationism: Doctrine that species were established at the time of the biblical Creation. Characteristics of life forms are seen as immutable; they cannot change.

descent: Rule assigning social identity on the basis of some aspect of one's ancestry.

egalitarian: Unstratified; in egalitarian societies there are as many positions of prestige as there are people who wish to fill them.

genotype: Hereditary makeup; an organism's genes and chromosomes; determines an individual's form (anatomy) and function (physiology).

hypodescent: Rule that automatically places the children of a union or mating between members of different socioeconomic groups in the less privileged group.

lactase: See *lactose.*

lactose: A complex sugar in milk; its digestion requires an enzyme called *lactase* in the small intestine. Among most mammals, lactase production ceases after weaning, and the ability to digest milk is lost.

melanin: Substance manufactured in specialized cells in the lower layers of the epidermis (outer skin layer); melanin cells in dark skin produce more melanin than do those in light skin.

natural selection: Charles Darwin's major contribution. Nature selects the forms that are fittest to survive and reproduce in a given environment; this explains evolutionary change.

phenotype: An organism's anatomy, physiology, and behavior; product of a long-term interaction between genotype and environment. Natural selection operates only on phenotype.

Polynesia: Triangle of South Pacific islands formed by Hawaii to the north, Easter Island to the east, and New Zealand to the southwest.

race, biological: Problematic concept; in theory, a biologically discrete group whose members share certain distinctive traits inherited from a common ancestor.

race, social: A group assumed to have some biological

basis but actually perceived and defined in a social context—by a particular culture rather than by scientific criteria.

recombination: New arrangements of genes and chromosomes through bisexual reproduction.

rickets: Nutritional disease caused by a shortage of vitamin D; interferes with the absorption of calcium and causes softening and deformation of the bones.

strategic resources: Those necessary for life, such as food and space.

stratified: Class-structured; stratified societies have marked differences in wealth, prestige, and power between social classes.

transformism: Synonymous with evolution; belief that species arose from others through a long and gradual process of transformation, or descent with modification.

tropics: Geographic belt extending about 23 degrees north and south of the equator, between the Tropic of Cancer (north) and the Tropic of Capricorn (south).

uniformitarianism: First stated by Charles Lyell; principle that the present is the key to the past. Explanations for past events should be sought in the long-term operation of ordinary forces (e.g., rainfall) that continue to work today.

STUDY QUESTIONS

1. How do creationism and transformism differ? Is transformism the same thing as evolution?
2. How did catastrophism supplement creationism?
3. Why was the principle of uniformitarianism important for understanding evolution through natural selection?
4. What is the difference between genotype and phenotype? On which does natural selection work, and why? Does natural selection have genetic results?
5. What is the relationship between creationism and transformism?
6. How do cultural and biological definitions of race vary?
7. What is the difference between cultural and biological racial classifications?
8. What kind of racial classification system operates in the community where you grew up or now live?

Does it differ from the racial classification system described for American culture in this chapter?

9. What is the difference between race and skin color in contemporary American culture? Are the social identities of Americans and discrimination against some Americans based on one or both of these attributes?
10. What are the main problems with racial classification based on phenotypical traits?
11. What are the main problems with racial classification based on genetic traits?
12. What explanations have been proposed for the distribution of light and dark skin color?
13. What is the basic anthropological position regarding relationships between biological and cultural determinants of intelligence?
14. What is Jensenism, and what arguments and evidence may be offered for rejecting it?

SUGGESTED ADDITIONAL READING

CROSBY, A.W., JR.
    1972 *The Columbian Exchange: Biological and Cultural Consequences of 1492.* Westport, CT: Greenwood Press. Disease, migration, slavery, and other consequences of the age of discovery.
HARRIS, M.
    1964 *Patterns of Race in the Americas.* New York: Walker. Reasons for different racial and ethnic relations in North and South America and the Caribbean.
MONTAGU, A., ED.
    1975 *Race and IQ.* New York: Oxford University Press. Scientists from several disciplines review and counter neoracist reasoning.

MORAN, E.
    1979 *Human Adaptability: An Introduction to Ecological Anthropology.* North Scituate, MA: Duxbury. Surveys many kinds of biological and cultural adaptations to various environmental stresses and conditions.
NELSON, H., AND R. JURMAIN
    1989 *Understanding Physical Anthropology and Archeology.* St. Paul: West Publishing. Basic text.
WEISS, M.L., AND A.E. MANN
    1989 *Human Biology and Behavior: An Anthropological Perspective.* 5th ed. Glenview, IL: Scott, Foresman. Basic biological anthropology textbook; includes discussions of evolutionary principles, genetics, and human variability.

CHAPTER 5

THE PRIMATES

Primatology—the study of fossil and living apes, monkeys, and prosimians, including their behavior and social life—has grown substantially since the 1950s. Following the ethnographer's example, primatologists began to study their subjects in natural settings rather than in zoos. Field studies have corrected many misleading impressions about primates derived from observations in zoos.

The study of nonhuman primates is fascinating in itself, but it also helps anthropologists make inferences about early hominid social organization and untangle issues of human nature and the origin of culture. Of particular relevance to humans are two kinds of primates:

1. Those whose ecological adaptations are similar to our own: **terrestrial** monkeys and apes, i.e., primates that live on the ground rather than in trees
2. Those that are most closely related to us: the great apes, specifically chimpanzees and gorillas

TAXONOMY AND THE PRIMATE ORDER

Similarities between humans and apes are obvious in anatomy, brain structure, genetics, and biochemistry. These resemblances are recognized in zoological **taxonomy**—the assignment of organisms to categories (*taxa*; singular, *taxon*) according to phylogenetic relationship and structural resemblance. Humans and apes belong to the same superfamily, **Hominoidea.** Monkeys are placed in two others. This means that humans and apes are more closely related to each other than either is to monkeys.

Many structural similarities between organisms reflect their common **phylogeny**—their genetic relatedness based on common ancestry. In other words, organisms share features they have inherited from the same ancestor.

Similar species belong to the same *genus* (plural, *genera*).
Similar genera make up the same *family.*
Similar families constitute the same *superfamily.*
Similar superfamilies form the same *suborder.*

Similar suborders belong to the same *order.*
Similar orders make up the same *class.*
Similar classes constitute the same *kingdom.*

The highest taxonomic division is the kingdom. At that level animals are distinguished from plants. The lowest-level taxa are species and subspecies. A **species** is a group of organisms whose members can mate and give birth to viable (capable of living) and fertile (capable of reproducing) offspring whose own offspring are viable and fertile. **Speciation** (the formation of a new species) occurs when groups that once belonged to the same species can no longer interbreed. After a sufficiently long period of reproductive isolation, two closely related species assigned to the same genus will have evolved out of one.

At the lowest level of taxonomy, a species may have subspecies. These are its more or less, but not yet totally, isolated subgroups. Subspecies can exist in time and space. For example, the Neandertals, who lived between 110,000 and 40,000 years ago, are usually assigned not to a separate species but merely to a different subspecies of *Homo sapiens.* Just one subspecies of *Homo sapiens* survives today.

The similarities used to assign organisms to the same taxon are called **homologies**, similarities they have jointly inherited from a common ancestor. Figure 5.1 shows the place of humans in zoological taxonomy and our degree of relatedness to other animals. For example, we are mammals, members of the class Mammalia. This is a major subdivision of the kingdom Animalia. Mammals share certain traits, including mammary glands, that set them apart from other taxa, such as birds, reptiles, amphibians, and insects. Mammalian homologies indicate that all mammals share more recent common ancestry with each other than they do with any bird, reptile, or insect.

At a lower taxonomic level, humans belong to the order Primates. The carnivores (dogs, cats, foxes, wolves, badgers, weasels) form another mammalian order, as do rodents (rats, mice, beavers, squirrels). Primates share structural and biochemical homologies that distinguish them from other mammals. These resemblances were inherited from their common early primate ancestors after those early primates became reproductively isolated from the ancestors of other mammals.

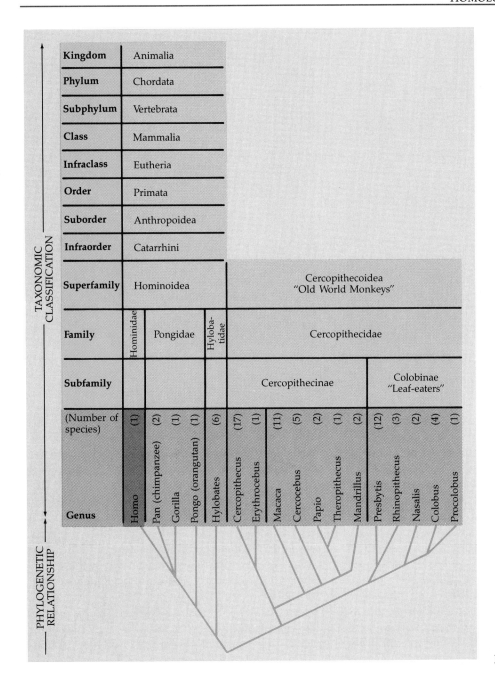

Figure 5.1 *Primate taxonomy.*

HOMOLOGIES AND ANALOGIES

Thus groups are assigned to the same higher-level taxon by homologies. For example, there are many homologies between ape and human DNA and biochemistry that confirm our common ancestry and lead to our joint classification as hominoids.

However, common ancestry is not the only reason for similarities between species. Similar traits can also arise if species experience similar selective forces to which they respond or adapt in similar ways. We call such similarities **analogies**. The process by which analogies are produced is known as **convergent evolution**. Fish and porpoises share

Similarities between humans and apes are obvious in brain structure, genetics, biochemistry, and anatomy. These resemblances are recognized in zoological taxonomy, with humans and apes assigned to the same superfamily, Hominoidea. Chimps are also highly intelligent. Compare the hairy reasoner on the left with Harry Reasoner on the right.

many analogies resulting from convergent evolution to life in the water. Like fish, porpoises, which are mammals, have fins. They are also hairless and streamlined for efficient locomotion. Analogies between birds and bats (wings, small size, light bones) illustrate convergent evolution to flying.

In theory, only homologies should be used in taxonomy. In practice, there is sometimes doubt about whether resemblances are homologies or analogies, and analogies influence classification. For example, consider the Hominoidea. Most scientists have no doubt that humans, gorillas, and chimpanzees are more closely related to each other than any of the three is to orangutans, which are Asiatic apes (Ciochon 1983). Because humans, chimps, and gorillas share a more recent ancestor with each other than they do with orangs, they should be assigned to a taxon distinct from the taxon that includes orangutans. Accordingly, some scientists assign gorillas and chimps, along with humans, to the **Hominidae** family. However, many more taxonomists still assign orangs, chimps, and gorillas to the family Pongidae on the

basis of their structural analogies. Here analogy has *improperly* influenced zoological classification.

PRIMATE TENDENCIES

No single feature distinguishes the primates from other orders. Primates are varied because they have adapted to diverse ecological niches. Some primates are active during the day; others, at night. Some eat insects; others, fruits; others, shoots, leaves, and bulk vegetation; and others, seeds or roots. Still others are omnivorous. Some primates live on the ground, others live in trees, and there are intermediate adaptations. However, because the earliest primates were tree dwellers, modern primates share homologies reflecting their common **arboreal** heritage.

Many trends in primate evolution are best exemplified by monkeys, apes, and humans. These primates constitute the suborder **Anthropoidea**. The other primate suborder, Prosimii, includes lemurs, loris, and tarsiers. These **prosimians** are more distant relatives of humans than are monkeys and apes. The primate trends—most developed in the anthropoids—can be summarized briefly. Together they constitute the anthropoid heritage that humans share with monkeys and apes.

1. Grasping.   Primates lack hooves, fins, and claws but have five-digited feet and hands which are well suited for grasping. Certain features of hands and feet that were originally adaptive for arboreal life have been transmitted to contemporary primates. Flexible hands and feet that could encircle branches were important features in the early primates' arboreal life. Thumb opposability and the resulting **precision grip** (between index finger and thumb), which is essential to tool manufacture, might have been favored by the inclusion of insects in the early primate diet. Manual dexterity makes it easier to catch insects attracted to abundant arboreal flowers and fruits. Humans and many other primates have **opposable thumbs**: The thumb can touch all other fingers. Many primates also have grasping feet, and some have opposable big toes. However, in adapting to bipedal (two-footed) locomotion, hominids eliminated most of the foot's grasping ability.

2. Smell to Sight.   Several anatomic changes reflect the shift from smell to sight as the primates' most important means of obtaining information. Monkeys, apes, and humans have excellent **stereoscopic** (ability to see in depth) and color vision. The portion of the brain devoted to vision expanded, while the area concerned with smell shrank.

3. Nose to Hand.   Sensations of touch, conveyed by tactile organs, also provide information. The tactile skin on a dog's or cat's nose transmits information. Cats' tactile hairs, or whiskers, also serve this function. In primates, however, the main touch organ is the hand, specifically the sensitive pads of the "fingerprint" region.

4. Brain Complexity.   The proportion of brain tissue concerned with memory, thought, and association has increased in primates. The primate ratio of brain size to body size exceeds that of most mammals.

5. Parental Investment.   Most primates give birth to a single offspring rather than a litter. Be-

Primates have five-digited feet and hands, well-suited for grasping. Flexible hands and feet that could encircle branches were important features in the arboreal life of early primates. In adapting to bipedal (two-footed) locomotion, hominids eliminated most of the foot's grasping ability— illustrated here by the orangutan.

cause of this, growing primates receive more attention and have more learning opportunities than do other mammals. Learned behavior is an important part of primate adaptation.

6. Sociality.   Most primates are social animals that live with others of their species. The need for longer and more attentive care of offspring places a selective value on support by a social group.

SIMILARITIES BETWEEN HUMANS AND OTHER PRIMATES

There is a large gap between primate society and fully developed human culture. However, studies of primates in varied circumstances have revealed more similarities than were once imagined. Scholars used to contend that learned (versus instinctive) behavior separates humans from other animals. We know now that monkeys and apes also rely extensively on learning. Differences between humans and other primates are quantitative rather

Learned behavior among wild chimps includes rudimentary tool making. Here, a chimpanzee uses a specially prepared stick to "fish" for termites.

than qualitative: They are differences in *degree* rather than in kind. For example, chimpanzees make tools for specific tasks, but human reliance on tools is much greater.

TOOLS

Anthropologists used to distinguish humans from other animals as tool users, and there is no doubt that *Homo* does employ tools more than any other animal does. However, tool use also turns up among several nonhuman species. For example, in the Galápagos Islands off western South America there is a "woodpecker finch" that selects twigs to dig out insects and grubs from tree bark. Sea otters use rocks to break open mollusks, which are important in their diet. Beavers are famous for dam construction.

When it became obvious that people weren't the only tool users, anthropologists started contending that only humans manufacture tools with foresight, that is, with a specific purpose in mind. Chimpanzees show that this, too, is debatable. The research of many primatologists, particularly Jane Goodall (1986), has increased our knowledge of chimp behavior in natural settings. In 1960 Goodall began observing chimps in Gombe Stream National Park in Tanzania, East Africa. More than any other primate, chimps share the human capacity for deliberate tool manufacture, although in chimps the capacity remains rudimentary. Nevertheless, wild chimps regularly make tools. To get

water from places their mouths can't reach, thirsty chimps pick leaves, chew and crumple them, and then dip them into the water. Thus, with a specific purpose in mind, they devise primitive "sponges." Chimpanzees also crumple leaves to make "toilet paper."

More impressive is "termiting." Chimps make tools to probe termite hills. They choose twigs, which they modify by removing leaves and peeling off bark to expose the sticky surface beneath. They carry the twigs to termite hills, dig holes with their fingers, and insert the twigs. Finally they pull out the twigs and dine on termites that were attracted to the sticky surface.

Termiting isn't as easy as it might seem. Learning to termite takes time, and many Gombe chimps never master it. Twigs with certain characteristics must be chosen. Furthermore, once the twig is in the termite hill and the chimp judges that termites are crawling on its surface, the chimp must quickly flip the twig as it pulls it out so that the termites are on top. Otherwise they fall off as the twig comes out of the hole. This is an elaborate skill that neither all chimps nor human observers have been able to master.

Chimps have other abilities essential to culture. When they are trained by humans, their manipulatory skills flower, as anyone who has ever seen a movie, circus, or zoo chimp knows. Wild chimps aim and throw objects. The gorilla, our other nearest relative, lacks the chimp's proclivity for tool making. However, gorillas do build nests, and they throw branches, grass, vines, and other objects. Hominids have considerably elaborated the capacity to aim and throw, which is a likely homology passed down from the common ancestor of humans and apes. Without it we would have never developed projectile technology, weaponry, and baseball.

COMMUNICATION SYSTEMS

Only humans speak. No other animal has anything approaching the complexity of language. However, evidence is accumulating that linguistic ability is also a quantitative rather than a qualitative difference between humans and other primates, especially gorillas and chimps. The natural communication systems of other primates—their **call systems**—which are composed of sounds that vary in intensity and duration, are much more complex than used to be supposed. Furthermore, although no nonhuman primate can speak, gorillas and chimpanzees can understand and manipulate *nonverbal* symbols based on human language. The African apes share with *Homo*, apparently through inheritance from our common ancestor, a tendency toward complex communication systems.

Call Systems

Wild chimps communicate through gestures and calls. Goodall (1968*a*) identified twenty-five distinct calls used by Gombe chimps. Each had a distinct meaning and was used only in particular situations. Like people, chimps also communicate through facial expressions, noises, and body movements. Other primates also use calls, which are evoked by environmental stimuli, to convey messages to other members of the group. African vervet monkeys, for example, have three slightly different calls (grunts) that they use to communicate danger from leopards, eagles, and snakes (Seyfarth, Cheney, and Marler 1980). Variation in the intensity, duration, and repetition of a call may increase the amount of information about the stimulus. Call systems require some learning; primates raised in zoos don't automatically produce all the calls used in the wild.

Calls are much less flexible than language because they are automatic and can't be combined.

When primates encounter food and danger simultaneously, they can make only one call. They can't combine the calls for food and danger into a single utterance, indicating that both are present. If by chance they did so, others would probably not understand the message. At some point in hominid evolution, however, our ancestors began to combine calls and understand the combinations. The number of calls also expanded, eventually becoming too great to be transmitted even partly through the genes. Hominid communication came to rely almost totally on learning.

Apes and Sign Language

Although wild primates use call systems, the vocal tract of apes is not suitable for speech. Until the 1960s attempts to teach spoken language to apes suggested that they lack linguistic abilities. In the 1950s a couple raised a chimpanzee, Viki, as a member of their family and systematically tried to teach her to speak. However, Viki learned only four words ("mama," "papa," "up," and "cup"). More recent experiments have shown that apes can also learn to use, if not speak, true language (Miles 1983). Several apes have learned to converse with people through means other than speech. One such communication system is American Sign Language, or **Ameslan**, which is widely used by deaf and mute Americans. Ameslan employs a limited number of basic gesture units that are

The male chimpanzee, Dar, thirteen years old in this photo by Roger Fouts, makes the sign for "smile." Dar, Washoe, and other Ameslan-using chimps are now at Central Washington State University in Ellensburg.

analogous to sounds in spoken language. These units combine to form words and larger units of meaning.

The first chimpanzee to learn Ameslan was Washoe, a female. Captured in West Africa, Washoe was acquired by R. Allen Gardner and Beatrice Gardner, scientists at the University of Nevada in Reno, in 1966, when she was a year old. Four years later she moved to Norman, Oklahoma, to a converted farm that had become the Institute for Primate Studies. Washoe's experiences in Reno revolutionized the discussion of the language-learning abilities of apes. Washoe lived in a trailer and heard no spoken language. The researchers always used Ameslan to communicate with each other in her presence. The chimp gradually acquired an expressive vocabulary of 132 signs representing English words (Gardner, Gardner, and Van Cantfort 1989). At the age of two, Washoe began to combine as many as five signs into rudimentary sentences such as "You, me go out hurry." During her first few years of learning Ameslan she varied the order of her gestures ungrammatically. She would as easily say "Tickle Washoe" as "Washoe tickle." However, work with other chimps, along with Washoe's later progress, showed that apes can distinguish between subject and object.

The second chimp to learn Ameslan was Lucy, Washoe's junior by one year. Lucy died, or was murdered by poachers, in 1986, after having been carefully introduced to "the wild" in Africa in 1979 (Carter 1988). From her second day of life until her move to Africa, Lucy lived with a family in Norman, Oklahoma. Roger Fouts, a researcher from the nearby Institute for Primate Studies, came two days a week to test and improve Lucy's knowledge of Ameslan. During the rest of the week Lucy used Ameslan to converse with her foster parents. After acquiring language, Washoe and Lucy expressed several human characteristics: swearing, joking, telling lies, and trying to teach language to others.

When irritated, Washoe called her monkey neighbors at the institute "dirty monkeys." Lucy insulted her "dirty cat." Wrestling with Roger Fouts, Washoe urinated on him and then gestured "funny." On arrival at Lucy's place, Fouts once found a pile of excrement on the floor. When he asked the chimp what it was, she replied, "dirty, dirty," her expression for feces. Asked whose "dirty, dirty" it was, Lucy named Fouts's co-worker, Sue. When Fouts refused to believe her about Sue, the chimp blamed the excrement on Fouts himself.

Cultural transmission of a communication system through learning is a fundamental attribute of language. Both Washoe and Lucy tried to teach Ameslan to other animals. Washoe has taught gestures to other institute chimps, including her son Sequoia, who died in infancy, and her adopted son Loulis, who has learned eighty signs (Fouts, Fouts, and Van Cantfort 1989). There have been other cases of cultural transmission of Ameslan from chimp to chimp.

Because of their size and strength as adults, gorillas are less likely subjects than chimps for such experiments. Lean adult male gorillas in the wild weigh 400 pounds (180 kilograms), and full-grown females can easily reach 250 pounds (110 kilograms). Because of this, psychologist Penny Patterson's work with gorillas at Stanford University seems more daring than the chimp experiments. Patterson raised her now full-grown female gorilla, Koko, in a trailer next to a Stanford museum. Koko's vocabulary surpasses that of any chimp. She regularly employs 400 Ameslan signs and has used about 700 at least once. Asking, in the evening, to get into her bedroom, Koko gestures "Penny, open key hurry bedroom." What she is saying, translated into English, is "Penny, unlock my bedroom door and be quick about it."

Koko and the chimps also show that apes share still another linguistic ability with humans—**productivity.** Speakers routinely use the rules of their language to produce entirely new expressions that are comprehensible to other native speakers. I can, for example, create "baboonlet" to refer to a baboon infant. I do this by analogy with English words in which the suffix *-let* designates the young of a species. Anyone who speaks English immediately understands the meaning of my new word. Koko, Washoe, and Lucy have shown that apes also use language productively. Lucy used gestures she already knew to create "drinkfruit" for watermelon. Washoe, seeing a swan for the first time, coined "waterbird." Koko, who knew the gestures for "finger" and "bracelet," formed "finger bracelet" when she was given a ring. Similarly, she called a mask an "eye hat."

Chimps and gorillas have at least a rudimentary

capacity for language. They may never have invented a meaningful gesture system in the wild. However, given such a system, they show many humanlike abilities in learning and using it. Of course, language use by apes is a product of human intervention and teaching. The experiments mentioned here do not suggest that apes can invent language (nor are human children ever faced with that task). However, young apes have managed to learn the basics of language. They can employ it productively and creatively, although not with the sophistication of human Ameslan users.

Apes also have the capacity for linguistic **displacement.** Absent in call systems, this is a key ingredient in language. Each call is tied to an environmental stimulus such as food. Calls are uttered only when that stimulus is present. Displacement permits humans to talk about things that are not present. We don't have to see the objects before we say the words. Human conversations are not bounded by place. We can discuss the past and future, share our experiences with others, and benefit from theirs.

Patterson has described several examples of Koko's capacity for displacement (Patterson 1978). The gorilla once expressed sorrow about having bitten Penny three days earlier. Koko has used the sign "later" to postpone doing things she doesn't want to do. Thus, she can reconstruct events, including emotional states. She imagines the future and uses language to express her thoughts.

Certain scholars still doubt the linguistic abilities of chimps and gorillas (Terrace 1979; Sebeok and Umiker-Sebeok 1980). These people contend that Koko and the chimps are comparable to circus animals and don't really have linguistic ability. However, in defense of Patterson and the other researchers, whose findings are impressive (Hill 1978; Van Cantfort and Rimpau 1982), only one of their critics has worked with an ape. This was Herbert Terrace, whose experience teaching a chimp sign language lacked the continuity and personal involvement that have contributed so much to Patterson's success with Koko.

No one denies the huge difference between human language and gorilla signs. There is a major gap between the ability to write a book or say a prayer and the few hundred gestures employed by a well-trained chimp. Apes aren't people, but

they aren't just animals either. Let Koko express it: When asked by a reporter whether she was a person or an animal, Koko chose neither. Instead, she signed "fine animal gorilla" (Patterson 1978).

The capacity to remember and combine linguistic expressions is latent in the apes (Miles 1983). In hominid evolution the same ability flowered into language. Language did not appear miraculously at a certain moment in human history. It developed over hundreds of thousands of years as our ancestors' call systems were gradually transformed. Language offered a tremendous adaptive advantage to *Homo.* Along with technology, language is a basic part of our cultural, nonbodily, or **extrasomatic,** means of adaptation. Language permits the information stored by a human society to exceed by far that of any nonhuman group. Language is a uniquely effective vehicle for learning. Because we can speak of things we have never experienced, we can anticipate responses before we encounter the stimuli. Adaptation can occur more rapidly in *Homo* than in the other primates because our adaptive means are more flexible. Humans routinely rely on biological, social, and cultural means of adaptation.

PREDATION AND HUNTING

The hominids emerged through ecological differentiation. While the ancestors of gorillas and chimps were adapting to forested and woodland environments, early hominids spent more and more time on Africa's tropical plains, or savannas. Leaving the safety of the trees behind, hominids took some of the tendencies they shared with the apes (learning, linguistic, and tool-making abilities) and perfected them to survive in open country. We can see this when we compare humans with baboons, ground-dwelling monkeys that live in the African savanna, where our ancestors evolved. In terms of numbers and geographic spread, baboons are the most successful monkeys. Likewise, humans are more successful in numbers and range than are the apes. Humans and baboons have developed different ways of surviving away from trees and forests.

Baboons have a tightly knit, hierarchical social organization and extreme **sexual dimorphism** (marked differences in male and female anatomy

In Kenya this olive baboon munches on a baby Thompson's gazelle. Like chimpanzees, baboons occasionally hunt small animals and eat their meat.

and temperament besides the contrasts in breasts and genitals). All these factors are adaptive for baboons in a terrestrial environment with predators. Human adaptation to predators, by contrast, has involved an increasing reliance on tools and weapons. Baboons might have adapted even more successfully to terrestrial life if they had developed tool manufacture as early hominids did. However, a trait does not develop merely because a group needs it.

The ancestral baboons were monkeys. As such, their characteristic locomotion was on all fours. Hominids, however, had a tendency toward upright posture, as do chimpanzees and gorillas. Upright bipedalism and the tendencies toward aimed throwing and reliance on tools were all favored in the savanna environment. These tendencies were basic to hominid survival away from the trees. Upright posture permitted the use of tools and weapons against predators. With their upright posture and tool use, early hominids could eventually become hunters of savanna animals.

Primate Hunting

Like tool making and language, hunting has been cited as a distinctive human activity that is not shared with our ape relatives. Again, however, primate research shows that what was previously thought to be a difference of kind is merely a difference of degree.

The diets of other terrestrial primates are not exclusively vegetarian, as was once thought. Baboons kill and eat young antelopes, and researchers have observed hunting by chimpanzees. Geza Teleki (1973a) has provided a detailed report based on twelve months of observing predation among chimps at Tanzania's Gombe Stream National Park. He recorded thirty cases of chimpanzee hunting, twelve of which led to a kill. About a hundred kills were recorded during a decade of research by Goodall (1968b) and her associates at Gombe.

Generally, chimps simply lunged at and seized their prey, but they also did more complex hunting. Groups of five or six sometimes patiently stalked a prey animal. Stalking was silent; vocalization occurred only when they seized the prey. Nor did the chimps use gestures to coordinate the hunt. After seizing an infant baboon, the hunter would bite or wring its neck or bash its head against the ground or a tree. Occasionally, young baboons were ripped apart when two chimps seized them simultaneously. For a few moments after the kill, chimps that had not taken part in the hunt could grab part of the carcass. Once this initial division occurred, however, meat sharing became more intricate. Chimps used a variety of gestures to request meat from their fellows. The hunters granted the requests about one-third of the time. Chimpanzee hunting is predominantly a male activity; insect eating is more common in females (McGrew 1979).

Coordinated hunting and meat sharing, previously considered exclusively human traits, have not—like linguistic ability and tool manufacture—been revealed as more generalized capacities. Hominids uniquely nurtured these abilities as they adapted to savanna life.

Predation and Resources

The potential for predation may be generalized in monkeys and apes, but its expression seems to depend on the environment. Hunting by chimpanzees might have developed in response to changes in their environment. Humans have been encroaching on their natural habitat. Something similar has happened among **gibbons** (the smallest apes, natives of Asia) in Malaysia. People are cutting down the forest homes of these slightly built tree-dwelling apes. Aggression and defense of territory by gibbons increases when there is a shortage of resources. Chimp predation also increases with environmental change and resource scarcity.

Goodall specifically linked chimpanzee predation to human encroachment. The Gombe chimps are divided into a northern group and a smaller group of southerners. Parties from the north have invaded southern territory and killed southern chimps. Infant victims were partially eaten by their assailants (Goodall 1986).

Primate behavior is not rigidly determined by the genes. It is plastic (flexible), capable of varying widely as environmental forces change. Among humans, too, aggression increases when resources are threatened or scarce. What we know about other primates makes it reasonable to assume that early hominids were neither uniformly aggressive nor consistently meek. Their aggression and predation reflected environmental variation.

BEHAVIOR AND ENVIRONMENTAL STRESS

John MacKinnon (1974) has done research among orangutans on the Indonesian islands of Borneo (Kalimantan) and Sumatra. Climatic changes, hunting by humans, and forest burning have confined orangs to these two islands, though their range once extended as far north as China. These large Asiatic apes, an endangered species, survive only in isolated, forested hilly country.

Orangs eat mainly fruits but also include acorns, shoots, leaves, bark, and wood pith in their diet. Because of extreme sexual dimorphism, female and young orangs can exploit arboreal resources much more efficiently than males can. In the wild, adult male orangutans weigh between 200 and 300 pounds (90 and 135 kilograms). Their massive size interferes with their arboreal movement, limiting orang males to the larger trunks and branches. The smaller females can feed in parts of trees that adult males cannot reach. Unlike most other primates, which live in social groups, orangutans are solitary animals. Males travel and feed alone, and females are accompanied by their offspring.

Sexual Antagonism

Orangutans have suffered as a result of human encroachment, particularly farming and timbering. On Borneo, in response to nearby human activities, orangs have developed a pattern of extreme sexual antagonism which may further endanger their survival. During MacKinnon's field work, Bornean orangs rarely had sex. Their limited sexual encounters were always brief rapes, often with screaming infants clinging to their mothers throughout the ordeal.

As MacKinnon did his field work, logging operations were forcing orangs whose territory was destroyed into his research area, swelling the population it had to support. The response to this sudden overpopulation was a drastic decline in the local orang birth rate. Primates respond in various ways to encroachment and population pressure. A change in sexual relationships that reduces the birth rate is one way of easing population pressure on resources.

DIFFERENCES BETWEEN HUMANS AND OTHER PRIMATES

The preceding sections emphasized similarities between humans and other primates. The differences discussed so far have been of degree rather than kind. Thus *Homo* has elaborated substantially on certain tendencies shared with the apes. A unique concentration and combination of characteristics makes humans distinct. However, the early hominid savanna niche also selected certain

DO WE HAVE KILLER GENES?

Notions that we are governed by forces beyond our control probably have been more common during human history than has been the belief in free will. Many religions tell us that our destinies are set. Scientists say that economic conditions, psychological drives, or genes determine or limit human action. However, flexibility is as strong a theme as determinism in anthropology. Hominid success rests on plasticity. Faced with environmental change, humans don't have to wait for a biological response. They can adapt by altering their customs.

Naturists argue that a genetically transmitted human nature controls us. *Nurturists* seek environmental causes for human behavior. Like most social scientists and almost all anthropologists, I am a nurturist. Naturists usually offer genetic explanations for *universal* behavior. However, some naturists believe that human behavioral *differences* also have a genetic basis. Nurturists interpret differences in behavior and social organization among human groups as cultural responses to different environments, as differences in learning experiences.

Nonanthropologists writing for the public have often used anthropological data inappropriately in support of naturist arguments. An early example was Robert Ardrey's widely read *African Genesis* (1961). That book claimed that humans still carry the bloodthirsty instincts of our meat-eating ancestors who took over the African savannas a million years ago by hunting down and killing off an earlier, gentler vegetarian hominid. Ardrey, a playwright, cited gang warfare of the sort portrayed in *West Side Story* as evidence of our aggressive legacy. In this view, killer genes doom humans to fight forever. There is no hope of stopping war, since it's biologically determined.

Naturists have argued that many aspects of human social behavior arise from animal instincts. Fighting, status seeking, hierarchy, greed, nationalism, inequality, and aggression are some of the social traits that have been assigned genetic causes. The usual naturist strategy is to mention only the animals and cultures that support their theory. Naturists use only the positive cases, the ones that confirm their ideas. They ignore negative cases, data from other cultures showing that the behavior the naturists claim to be universal isn't universal at all.

For example, Ardrey (1966) also argued that humans exhibit **territoriality**—we are genetically programmed to fight to defend our exclusive use of a tract of land. He maintained that war occurs because of genes we share with animals. However, most social scientists and historians believe that the causes of war are economic, political, and social. In characteristic naturist fashion, Ardrey picks his animals arbitrarily. He cites gibbons as proof of primate territoriality, but he ignores the less territorial chimps, gorillas, and orangs.

The naturists never address a key logical point: If instincts are shared by all animals, all primates, or all humans, they must be displayed everywhere. We know, however, that behavior and social life vary with environmental conditions. Territoriality, ranking, status seeking, and greed are not universal among either primates or humans. Humans have a capacity, not a compulsion, to be aggressive. Humans and other primates can be mild and docile when resources are abundant and very aggressive when supplies are scarce. Even in a particular troop, aggression can increase or decrease as the environment changes.

The psychologist Sigmund Freud shared the naturist belief in universal human aggression, as do many of his followers. To explain why this drive is not always expressed in behavior, Freudians suggest that it may be diverted or displaced into activities, such as sports, that don't harm society. This theory implies that cultures with the most aggressive sports tend to be the least warlike, because their sports so effectively express their innate aggression. However, a cross-cultural study by an anthropologist (Sipes 1973) found just the opposite. Aggressive sports don't replace war; they *correlate* with it. Warfare, raiding, and combat sports were almost always found together. If a culture had one, it tended to have them all. If it lacked warfare, it also tended to lack aggressive sports. We can conclude that if a society stresses aggression in some areas, that emphasis tends to permeate the culture. There *is* hope for the future. War is part of human culture rather than human nature.

traits that are not so obviously foreshadowed by the apes.

Sharing, Cooperation, and Division of Labor

Early humans lived in small social groups called bands, with economies based on hunting and gathering. Some band-organized societies have survived into the modern world, and ethnographers have studied them. From those studies we can say that in such groups the strongest and most aggressive members do not dominate, as they do in a troop of terrestrial monkeys. Sharing and curbing of aggression are as basic to technologically simple humans as dominance and threats are to baboons.

Monkeys fend for themselves in the quest for food. However, among human foragers, men generally hunt and women gather. People bring resources back to the camp and share them. The most successful hunters are expected to be generous. Everyone shares the meat from a large animal. Older people who did not engage in the food quest receive food from younger adults. Nourished and protected by younger band members, elders live past reproductive age. They receive special respect for their age and knowledge. The amount of information stored in a human band is far greater than that in any other primate society. Sharing, cooperation, and language are intrinsic to information storage.

Among all primates except *Homo*, most food comes from individual foraging, usually for vegetation. The rarity of meat eating and the concentration on vegetation are fundamental differences between apes and humans. Through millions of years of adaptation to an omnivorous diet, hominids have come to rely on hunting, meat eating, food sharing, and cooperative behavior. These are universal features in human adaptive strategies.

Mating, Exogamy, and Kinship

Another difference between humans and other primates concerns mating. Among baboons and chimpanzees, sexual intercourse occurs when females ''go into heat'' or enter **estrus**, a period of sexual receptivity. Estrus is signaled by swelling and coloration of the vaginal skin. Receptive females form temporary bonds with males. Among

humans, sexual activity occurs throughout the year. Related to this more constant sexuality, all human societies have some form of marriage. Marriage gives mating a reliable basis and grants each spouse special, though not always exclusive, sexual rights in the other.

Marriage creates another major contrast between human and nonhumans: exogamy and kinship systems. Most cultures have rules of exogamy requiring marriage outside one's kin or local group. Coupled with the recognition of kinship, exogamy confers adaptive advantages. It creates ties between the spouses' groups of origin. Their children have relatives, and therefore allies, in two kin groups rather than just one.

The key point here is that ties of affection and mutual support between members of different local groups are absent among primates other than *Homo*. There is a tendency among primates to disperse at adolescence. Both male and female gibbons leave home when they become sexually mature. Once they find mates and establish their own territories, ties with their native groups cease. Long-term studies of terrestrial monkeys have suggested that males leave the troop at puberty, eventually finding places elsewhere. The troop's core members are females. They sometimes form **uterine** groups made up of mothers, sisters, daughters, and sons that have not yet emigrated. This dispersal of males reduces the incidence of incestuous matings. Females mate with males born elsewhere, which join the troop at adolescence. Although kin ties are maintained between female monkeys, no close lifelong links are preserved through males. Among chimps and gorillas, females tend to migrate seeking mates in other groups (Wrangham 1987).

Humans choose mates from outside the native group (the family), and at least one spouse moves. However, *humans maintain lifelong ties with sons and daughters*. The systems of kinship and marriage that preserve these links provide a major contrast between humans and other primates.

SOCIOBIOLOGY AND INCLUSIVE FITNESS

According to evolutionary theory, when the environment changes, natural selection starts to modify the *population's* pool of genetic material.

Natural selection has another key feature: the differential reproductive success of *individuals* within the population. **Sociobiology**, the study of the evolutionary basis of social behavior, assumes that individuals compete to maximize their genetic contribution to future generations—their *fitness*. Primate illustrations include cases in which male monkeys kill infants after entering a new troop in order to clear a place for their own progeny (Hausfater and Hrdy 1984).

Besides competition, one's genetic contribution to future generations can be maximized by cooperation, sharing, and other apparently unselfish behavior. This is because of **inclusive fitness** (the sociobiological theory that individuals strive to maximize their fitness), which is based on the fact that close relatives share genes. Individuals may be willing to sacrifice for their relatives and thus limit their own direct reproduction. By doing so, however, they may increase their personal genetic contribution to the future. If self-sacrifice perpetuates more of their genes than does direct reproduction, it makes sense in sociobiological terms. The following cases show how inclusive fitness theory can help us understand aspects of primate behavior and social organization.

Sex, Aggression, and Parenting

By focusing on primate mating patterns and parental investment strategies, researchers are enlarging our understanding of social organization, behavior, and evolution. We are discovering clues about the origins and functions of such human social institutions as friendship, courtship, and child care. Evolution through natural selection can operate on primate social behavior, because behavioral strategies help some individuals reproduce more effectively than others. Modern evolutionary biologists assume that organisms attempt to maximize their inclusive fitness.

Maternal care always makes sense in terms of inclusive fitness because females can be sure that their offspring are their own. However, it's harder for males to be sure about paternity. Inclusive fitness theory predicts that males will invest most in offspring when they are surest the offspring are theirs. Gibbons, for example, have strict male-female pair bonding, which makes it likely that the offspring are those of both members of the pair.

Here we would expect males to offer care and protection to their young, and they do. When a male can't be sure about paternity, it may be more rational—in terms of maximizing fitness—to invest in a sister's child than a mate's because that niece or nephew definitely shares some of that male's genes.

For years anthropologists have speculated that human pair bonding and, eventually, monogamy originated for economic reasons. All foraging populations divide labor by gender (women usually gather and men hunt). Because of this, some anthropologists have assumed that hominids started pairing to ensure that women got meat and men had access to gathered products. Pair bonding also increases the chance that the husband is the father of the wife's children. This justifies greater paternal investment.

Barbara Smuts's detailed study (1985) of long-lasting male-female "friendship" bonds among Kenyan baboons suggests that human pair bonding might have developed much earlier. Among baboons, male-female friendships are useful for females, infants, and males. Females and infants need the protection provided by adult males' much larger size. Infants run to their mother's male friends when threatened.

One way for a male to win a place in a new troop is to find a friendly female as a sponsor. Friendship often leads to mating and thus helps maximize the male's fitness, because his friend's future infants are likely to be his own. However, males also bolster friendships by protecting infants born before their arrival. Baboon friendships have benefits and costs. Rivals sometimes attack another male's female friend. When threatened, males sometimes pick up a nearby infant to keep an antagonist at bay—the baboon equivalent of "Don't shoot, I've got the kid!"

Another primate study has also shed light on human mating and parenting patterns. Charles Janson (1986) studied two closely related but contrasting species of monkeys—brown- and white-fronted capuchin monkeys—in the forests of Amazonian Peru. The brown monkeys are bigger and live in smaller groups dominated by one male. They inhabit smaller trees and lower branches and eat tougher fruits. The dominant male has preferential access to food and to females. He gets the females not through competition with other males

White-fronted capuchin monkeys range from the forests of Amazonian Peru to Costa Rica, shown here. White-fronted capuchin males compete for females, but all males get to mate. Thus male cooperation to defend the troop makes sense from the inclusive fitness perspective, because all the troop's infants have a chance to be the offspring of any one of its males.

but because females seek him out and refuse to mate with anyone else. He is very aggressive with other males but tolerant and protective toward infants, which are likely to be his own. Only that dominant male defends the troop against threats from eagles or other monkeys. Subdominant males run away. According to inclusive fitness theory, they don't help out because they have a minimal genetic stake in the outcome.

White-fronted monkey males are much less aggressive with members of their own troops than are dominant brown-fronted males. However, they aren't as attentive to infants. Dominance is less marked among these monkeys. White males cooperate to defend the troop against eagles—or to displace brown monkeys when they wish to feed in the same tree. White males compete for females, but all males get to mate. Here, male cooperation to benefit the entire troop makes sense from the perspective of inclusive fitness: All the troop's infants may be any individual male's offspring.

These primate studies suggest that pair bonds and other stable social links between hominid males and females might have preceded the hunter-gatherer division of labor. Human pair bonding might have originated for social, protective, and reproductive reasons rather than economic ones.

SUMMARY

Humans, apes, monkeys, and prosimians belong to the primate order. This order is subdivided into suborders, infraorders, superfamilies, families, subfamilies, genera, species, and subspecies. Organisms included within the same subdivision, or taxon, should share more recent common ancestry and more homologies with each other than with organisms in other taxa.

Difficulties in distinguishing homologies, which reflect common ancestry, from analogies, which reflect convergent evolution, have influenced primate taxonomy. For example, gorillas and chimpanzees are often placed in the family Pongidae with orangs, to which they are distantly related, rather than in Hominidae with humans, their closer phylogenetic relatives.

Primates share several trends that are most developed among the anthropoids. These involve grasping, vision, touch, brain complexity, litter size, and social organization. Differences between humans and other primates have often been stressed, but their many similarities have been ignored. Recent research shows that similarities are extensive and that many differences are quantitative rather than qualitative. A unique concentration and combination of ingredients makes humans distinct.

Some of our most important adaptive traits are foreshadowed in other primates, particularly the African apes. For example, chimpanzees make tools for several purposes. Furthermore, it is now apparent that learning ability, the basis of culture, is also an adaptive advantage of many other primates.

Although wild primates have only call systems, chimpanzees and gorillas can understand and manipulate nonverbal symbols based on language. Primates emit calls only in the presence of particular environmental stimuli. Calls cannot be combined when different stimuli are present simultaneously. At some point in hominid evolution our ancestors became capable of displaced speech. Other contrasts between language and call systems include productivity and cultural transmission. Over time, our ancestral call systems developed into true language. Call systems grew too complicated for genetic transmission and began to rely on learning.

Primates other than humans sometimes hunt cooperatively. Chimps, which are more omnivorous than once was thought, occasionally hunt and share meat. Hunting and the killing of chimp by chimp, like sexual antagonism among orangutans, reflect pressure on strategic resources, especially human encroachment on their natural habitat. Chimps, baboons, and orangs, like humans, are flexible animals that increase or reduce their aggression as environmental conditions warrant. None of these animals is a slave of its genes. Primate social organization varies with environment.

Although most contrasts are of degree rather than kind, important differences between humans and other primates remain. Aggression and dominance are characteristic of terrestrial monkeys, whereas sharing and cooperation are equally significant among primitive human populations. Connected with sharing is the traditional division of subsistence labor by age and gender.

Other primates avoid incest through dispersal at adolescence. However, only humans use explicit, linguistically expressed incest taboos to promote exogamy as a means of linking themselves to other social groups. Only humans have systems of kinship and marriage that permit us to maintain lifelong ties with relatives in different local groups.

From the perspective of sociobiology, individuals within a population strive to maximize their genetic contribution to future generations. Evolution through natural selection may operate on primate social behavior, since behavioral strategies help some individuals reproduce more effectively than others. Maternal care makes sense from an inclusive fitness perspective because females can be sure that their offspring are their own. Because it's harder for males to be sure about paternity, inclusive fitness theory predicts that they will invest most in offspring when they are surest that the offspring are theirs. The idea of inclusive fitness, based on the fact that individuals share their DNA with relatives, is also used to explain individual self-sacrifice and altruism as well as human pair bonding.

GLOSSARY

Ameslan: American Sign Language, a medium of communication for apes and deaf and mute humans.

analogies: Similarities produced by selective forces operating in similar environments.

Anthropoidea: One of two suborders of primates; includes monkeys, apes, and humans.

arboreal: Pertaining to life in the trees.

call systems: Systems of communication among nonhuman primates, composed of a limited number of sounds that vary in intensity and duration. Tied to environmental stimuli.

convergent evolution: Development of similar traits or behavior patterns as a result of adaptation to similar environments and selective forces.

cultural transmission: A basic feature of language; transmission through learning.

displacement: A basic feature of language; the ability to speak of things and events that are not present.

estrus: Period of sexual receptivity in some female primates; signaled by swelling and coloration of the vaginal skin.

extrasomatic: Nonbodily; pertaining to culture, including language, tools, and other cultural means of adaptation.

gibbons: The smallest apes, natives of Asia; arboreal and territorial.

Hominidae: Zoological superfamily that includes fossil and living humans; according to some taxonomists, also includes the African apes.

Hominoidea: Zoological superfamily that includes fossil and contemporary apes and humans.

homologies: Similarities present among related species or populations because of inheritance from a common ancestor.

inclusive fitness: In the sociobiological view, individuals strive to maximize their fitness, which includes not just their own genes but those they share with close relatives.

opposable thumb: One that can touch all the other digits of the same hand; basic to tool manufacture.

phylogeny: Genetic relatedness based on common ancestry.

precision grip: Grasping an object between index finger and opposable thumb; basic to tool manufacture.

primatology: The study of fossil and living apes, monkeys, and prosimians, including their behavior and social life.

productivity: A basic feature of language; the ability to use the rules of one's language to create new expressions comprehensible to other native speakers.

prosimians: The primate suborder that includes lemurs, loris, and tarsiers.

sexual dimorphism: Marked differences in male and female anatomy and temperament besides the contrasts in breasts and genitals.

sociobiology: The study of the evolutionary basis of social behavior.

speciation: The formation of a new species through reproductive isolation.

species: Group of organisms capable of interbreeding and producing viable and fertile offspring whose own offspring are viable and fertile.

stereoscopic vision: Ability to see in depth.

taxonomy: The assignment of organisms to categories (*taxa*; singular, *taxon*) according to phylogenetic relationship and structural resemblance.

terrestrial: Pertaining to life on the ground rather than in trees, air, or water.

territoriality: A group's behavior in defending its right to exclusive use of a tract of land.

uterine: Related through female kinship ties.

STUDY QUESTIONS

1. What is the basis of zoological taxonomy?
2. What is the importance of behavioral plasticity (flexibility) in primate adaptation?
3. How do tools distinguish between humans and other animals?
4. What are the features of primate call systems?
5. What attributes are basic to language? Does language use by apes show these characteristics?
6. Explain this statement: "Apes aren't people, but they aren't just animals either."
7. How might the use of Ameslan by apes affect interpretations of human evolution?
8. What is the most important reason for the different adaptations of early hominids and monkeys to terrestrial life in the savanna?
9. What environmental conditions might trigger predatory behavior among chimpanzees?
10. What causes sexual antagonism among orangs?
11. What behavioral differences distinguish humans from other primates?
12. Why is it significant that among primates, only hominids maintain ties of affection and mutual support between different local groups?
13. How does inclusive fitness theory help us understand differences between female and male parental investment strategies?
14. How might baboon "friendship" patterns shed light on the origin of marriage?

SUGGESTED ADDITIONAL READING

BARASH, D. P.
1977 *Sociobiology and Behavior*. Amsterdam: Elsevier. Basics of sociobiology.

FEDIGAN, L. M.
1982 *Primate Paradigms: Sex Roles and Social Bonds*. Montreal: Eden Press. Focuses on sex roles in primate social organization.

GOODALL, J.
1986 *The Chimpanzees of Gombe: Patterns of Behavior*. Cambridge, MA: Belknap Press of Harvard University Press. Results of decades of research on primate behavior in Tanzania.
1988 *In the Shadow of Man*. rev. ed. Boston: Houghton Mifflin. Popular account of the author's life among the chimps.

GRAY, J. P.
1985 *Primate Sociobiology*. New Haven, CT: HRAF Press. A comparative study of parental investment and inclusive fitness in primate society.

HAMBURG, D. A., AND E. R. McCOWN, EDS.
1979 *The Great Apes*. Menlo Park, CA: Benjamin Cummings. Collection of twenty-two papers based on field studies of chimps, gorillas,

and orangutans. Excellent data and detailed bibliography.

HILL, J. H.
1978 Apes and Language. *Annual Review of Anthropology* 7: 89–112. Thorough review of Ameslan and other language use by chimps and gorillas.

HINDE, R. A., ED.
1983 *Primate Social Relationships: An Integrated Approach.* Sunderland, MA: Sinaeur Associates. Theoretical implications of aspects of social life among various primates.

MITTERMEIER, R. A., AND M. J. POLTKIN, EDS.
1982 *Primates and the Tropical Forest.* Washington, DC: World Wildlife Fund. Well-illustrated introduction to many primate species.

MONTAGU, A.
1975 *The Nature of Human Aggression.* New York: Oxford University Press. Well-known anthropologist refutes instinctive human aggression.

MOWAT, F.
1987 *Woman in the Mists: The Story of Dian Fossey and the Mountain Gorillas of Africa.* New York: Warner Books. Account of the well-known primatologist whose story was told in the film *Gorillas in the Mist.*

SEBEOK, T. A., AND J. UMIKER-SEBEOK, EDS.
1980 *Speaking of Apes: A Critical Anthology of Two-Way Communication with Man.* New York: Plenum. Articles disputing the linguistic abilities of Ameslan-using primates.

SMALL, M., ED.
1984 *Female Primates: Studies by Women Primatologists.* New York: Alan R. Liss. Differences in female strategies in various primate groups.

SMUTS, B. B.
1985 *Sex and Friendship in Baboons.* New York: Aldine. Pair bonding, mutual support, and parental investment in baboon social organization, with implications for early human evolution.

CULTURAL EVOLUTION AND ADAPTIVE STRATEGIES

Some 12,000 to 10,000 years ago, ancient Middle Easterners started to intervene in the reproduction of plants and animals. These people were pioneers in **food production**—plant cultivation and animal domestication. They added new, domesticated foods (wheat and barley, sheep and goats) to their diet. For hundreds of thousands of years before this, humans, like other primates, had relied on wild foods, nature's bounty. Humans had always supported themselves by **foraging**—hunting and gathering.

This chapter examines the implications of food production and compares this economy with the old one based on foraging. First, however, a brief review of previous human evolution will be helpful. Between 4 million and 2 million years ago strong-toothed *australopithecine* hominids lived off the tough, gritty vegetation of the African savanna. Some of the australopithecines evolved into our own genus, *Homo*, around 2 million years ago. Greater reliance on hunting, made possible by anatomical and cultural changes, was a primary cause of this evolution.

All modern humans belong to *Homo sapiens*, the species that first colonized Australia, the Pacific islands, and North and South America (the New World). The previous species, *Homo erectus*—whose earliest fossil remains, in East Africa, date back 1.6 million years—spread into tropical and subtropical Asia, eventually to reach temperate Europe. *Homo erectus* had more than a million years to perfect the foraging mode of existence.

Fossils assigned to *Homo sapiens* date back 300,000 years. The early subspecies *Homo sapiens neanderthalensis*, the Neandertals, had fully upright locomotion, large brains, and sophisticated tools. The modern subspecies *Homo sapiens*, which includes all contemporary humans, goes back some 40,000 years. Scientists still dispute the exact relationship between the Neandertals and modern humans. However, it is likely that some subpopulations of Neandertals were among our ancestors.

Homo sapiens, including the "Cro-Magnons" who lived in France around 30,000 years ago, continued to rely on foraging. This remained the sole human economic strategy until food production emerged in the Middle East. A parallel and comparable emergence took place in **Mesoamerica** (Mexico, Guatemala, Belize) somewhat later. In both areas people added domesticates to wild foods. Wheat and barley were the main Middle Eastern crops. Corn (maize), cassava (manioc), and potatoes were the staples of the New World.

Food production led to major changes in human life, as the pace of cultural evolution increased enormously. This chapter provides a framework for applying evolutionary principles to cultural change. Like other primates, humans adapt through biological traits and learned behavior pat-

Peruvian women work in a high-altitude field near Lake Titicaca. The "Irish" potato, originally domesticated in the Andes and still important in Peruvian subsistence—was one of the caloric staples of the pre-Columbian New World.

terns, which help them cope with problems posed by specific environments. Once a viable and stable relationship with the environment is established, that relationship tends to persist until something—internal or external—causes the environment to change.

In the context of environmental change, humans experiment with new coping mechanisms. The possession of both cultural and biological means of adaptation doesn't free us from nature, nor does culture guarantee that humans can or will adapt to new circumstances. Reliance on culture merely allows *Homo sapiens* to cope with change more flexibly than other species do. Still, if the environmental change is too severe or the adaptive potential of the group too limited or inflexible, extinction rather than evolution will result.

EVOLUTION

Anthropologists examine both general and specific dimensions of human evolution. **General evolution** concerns major changes, biological and cultural, in the genus *Homo* as a whole. It involves long-term trends—major changes across a sweep of time. Ethnologists and archeologists ascertain these trends by considering human populations from many times and places. **Specific evolution,** by contrast, involves particular populations. It describes their long-term adaptation and changes within particular environments—a valley in Mexico, a plain in Iran, the Nile delta, or Australia, for example.

General Evolution

Trends in the evolution of the stone tools used by our foraging ancestors illustrate general evolution. Thus, during hominid evolution:

1. Reliance on tools has increased.
2. Tools have become more numerous.
3. Tools have become diversified and functionally differentiated; they are designed for more specialized tasks.

Here are some other general evolutionary observations. During hominid evolution, reliance on culture has increased. The number of people and the range of human activities have expanded.

Methods by which humans control energy have become more complex, if not always more efficient. Changes in human control over energy have created new adaptive possibilities. Thus fire, an energy source tamed by *Homo erectus*, permitted adaptation to new environments. Cooking, for example, allowed hominids to eat more types of foods.

Plants, through photosynthesis, capture solar energy and transform it into carbohydrates. Some animals eat plants, and higher up the food chain, some eat other animals. When people gather plants or hunt animals, they exploit some of this stored solar energy to keep themselves alive. Then, when humans shift from foraging to food production, growing crops and managing animal reproduction, they concentrate and control other forms of nonhuman energy. There are many ways of controlling energy sources: harnessing an ox to a plow, using the wind to sail boats, using rivers to run industrial plants, and employing natural gas or solar radiation for heat.

The Main Trends of General Evolution

Enlarging our frame of reference from humans to the history of life itself, certain general evolutionary trends are also apparent. They are the following:

1. Parts and subparts have increased.
2. Parts and subparts have become functionally specialized.
3. More effective coordinating mechanisms—means of regulation and integration—have evolved.
4. Population size and adaptability (range of environments occupied) have expanded.

First, parts and subparts have increased. Multicelled organisms evolved from early plants and animals that had only one cell. Social evolution shows a similar trend toward an increase in parts. Early hominids lived in small **bands** (groups of fewer than 100 people that often split up seasonally). Like monkey troops, bands belonged to no larger group. Each band was structurally like any other, just as one amoeba resembles another. By the time of *Homo erectus,* however, larger social units (macrobands) formed seasonally as their

Anthropologist Nadine Peacock studies Efe "pygmies" in Zaire's Ituri forest. The Efe have a foraging economy and live in small mobile groups called bands. The number of human groups, the size of each, and their reliance on others has steadily increased during human evolution.

parts (microbands) came together to hunt. The number of human groups, the size of each, and their reliance on others have increased steadily during human evolution.

Functional specialization is a second general evolutionary trend. In one-celled organisms, a single structure has many functions or jobs. More advanced organisms have several systems, each with a special function. Our bodies, for example, have reproductive, circulatory, and excretory systems, among others. In cultural evolution the trend toward specialization shows up in the appearance of separate economic, political, and religious spheres in more complex societies. Simple cultures are unspecialized, whereas complex societies have such special-purpose systems and subsystems as military, judiciary, and administrative.

The third trend involves regulation, coordination, and integration. We can compare the integrative social role of a central government with that of the nervous system, which coordinates bodily parts and systems.

The fourth trend is toward increasing population size and **adaptability**—greater tolerance of environmental diversity. Over billions of years life forms have proliferated and diversified. More sophisticated adaptive means have enabled life to spread (radiate) into a wider range of environments. This process of population increase and adaptation to varied environments is called **adap-**

tive radiation, as exemplified by hominid evolution. Human reproductive success shows up in steady population growth, particularly during the past 10,000 years. *Homo's* widening environmental and geographic range illustrates this increasing adaptability.

Village life came before food production in certain areas where natural resources were abundant and concentrated. However, the domestication of plants and animals permitted widespread **sedentary** life (a nonmobile existence in permanent settlements). Food production supported larger populations and allowed *Homo* to expand its range. The evolution of social complexity accelerated with food production.

These general evolutionary trends permit a rough comparison of cultures. "Simple," "primitive," or "less complex" societies score low on the trends, whereas "complex" societies score higher. Ethnography and archeology applied to hundreds of cultures shows that the trends tend to be less developed among foragers than among food producers. Thus, foraging groups, including all human societies before food production, tend to be less complex.

Leslie White and the Evolution of Culture

Leslie White was a major and controversial figure in mid-twentieth-century American anthropology.

MENTAL HEALTH, SPECIALIZATION, AND CULTURAL EVOLUTION

In September 1984, from interviews with thousands of adults in three American cities, the National Institute of Mental Health (NIMH) arrived at the astounding estimate that 19 percent of the American population—43 million people—are mentally ill (Albee 1985). The estimate of our mentally ill has risen from 10 percent in the 1950s, through 15 percent in the 1970s, to the 1984 estimate of almost 20 percent. To help these people, American society has trained thousands of psychiatrists, clinical psychologists, and counseling psychologists. There are also millions of social workers, marriage counselors, psychiatric nurses, guidance counselors, special education instructors, and other "helping professionals" with less exalted degrees.

How should we interpret this rise in mental illness? Psychiatrists offer basically two kinds of explanation. One is genetic-biochemical. In this view, mental conditions are caused by genetic and biological factors and may be treated chemically. The second model attributes mental illness to environment, particularly poor socioeconomic conditions.

But there is a third explanation, derived from an anthropological, cross-cultural, and cultural evolutionary perspective. General evolution involves an increase in functionally specialized parts and subparts. Trends observed over thousands of years of cultural evolution and in field studies in hundreds of societies confirm the growth of specialization and diversity in the contemporary United States. The evolutionary, comparative viewpoint suggests that the main reason American society has so many people labeled mentally ill has more to do with our extreme occupational specialization than with individual psychopathology. Much of the increase in our mentally ill population may be due not to behavioral changes in the diagnosed but to an increase in diagnosticians. Let's assume that 25 percent of mental disorders have a biological basis and respond to drugs. Another 25 percent may have a socioeconomic basis and may respond to corrective programs and therapy. I believe that the other half may very well be labels that have little to do with concrete behavioral manifestations of real mental problems.

Doubts about a claim that one of every five Americans is mentally ill inevitably surface in an anthropologist who has worked in countries where the "helping" establishment is less developed and prestigious. Obvious mental disorders occur in non-Western societies, but no anthropologist has ever discovered a culture in which 20 percent of the people are mentally ill. If, as seems likely, socioeconomic stresses are a major cause of mental illness, underdeveloped countries should have more mental problems than does the richest nation in history. Of course, the mental health establishment would probably contend that a wave of mental problems does exist, undetected, throughout the Third World. However, since the typical North American helping professional sees everything from the perspective of a single culture, he or she can't be sure.

Mental illness is culturally defined and treated. Therapists from different cultures diagnose mental illness differently. Furthermore, even in North America, definitions of mental illness have changed. The *Diagnostic and Statistical Manual of Mental Disorders* published by the American Psychiatric Association has consistently expanded the types and subtypes (parts and subparts) of mental illness (Albee 1985). The figure rose from 60 in 1952 to 145 in 1968. It stands at 230 in the latest edition (1987). Mental disorders arbitrarily appear and disappear. Often this occurs not because of a behavioral change in the population but because the psychological community has changed its mind about what is and isn't mentally aberrant. Homosexuality, for example, came off the official disorder list in 1973. Tobacco dependence and an array of developmental disorders and sexual dysfunctions were added. To this anthropologist, it seems that when crime, juvenile delinquency, and cigarette smoking become mental illnesses (rather than sociocultural phenomena), something is suspect about the system of classification.

American health problems may be increasing. Nevertheless, the evolutionary viewpoint suggests that an important cause of the apparent increase is growth in the number, percentage, and prominence of specialists. This denies neither the reality of mental illness nor the need for professional helpers. It merely raises doubts about whether actual mental disorders are increasing. Or is it only their identification, scope, and treatment?

Concerned with general evolution, White (1959) looked at major developments in culture from early foragers through the fall of Rome. He described the transition from primitive society, which relied almost exclusively on human energy, to the complex societies that emerged with food production. White applied his grand-movement view of evolution to historical developments from foraging through food production to civilization (nation-states and empires), as revealed by archeology.

He applied the same general evolutionary perspective to contemporary cultures. Thus he viewed the foragers and simple cultivators who survive today as kinds of "living fossils," similar in their economies, social structures, and political institutions to ancient foragers and the earliest cultivators, respectively. Applying this perspective, ethnography has been used to complement archeology: living societies whose economies mirror those of extinct groups are used to infer similarities in other correlated cultural features.

Technological determinism dominated White's theories. He asserted that culture advanced through improvements in technology, particularly those which permitted greater energy capture. Improved tools and new economic practices produced social changes. For example, agriculture led to many social, political, and legal changes, including notions of property and distinctions in wealth, class, and power. White compared past and present cultures, using such terms as *primitive* or *simple* versus *complex* or *civilized* to describe them. However, he did not mean these labels to imply moral progress; on the contrary, he believed that simpler social systems are better social environments for humans than are civilizations.

Unilinear Evolution

Many social scientists of the late nineteenth century believed in a process of **unilinear evolution.** In this view, all cultures have evolved in the same order through a set sequence of stages. Any society at a "higher" (more complex) stage must have passed through all the "lower" ones. We know now that the evolution of culture is not unilinear. Societies may develop the same traits in different order. Cultures may even "devolve" (move to a less complex condition).

Specific, Multilinear, and Convergent Evolution

A study of specific evolution focuses on long-term adaptive changes (adaptive processes—see below) in a particular environment. It examines the evolution of only one group rather than that of all of humanity. However, by comparing specific evolutionary sequences, we can detect generalized causes of human evolution. Julian Steward, the best-known such comparativist, introduced the term *multilinear evolution* for the cultural phenomena he studied (Steward 1955). *Multi-* means "many." **Multilinear evolution** refers to the fact that cultures have followed many different lines of evolution. Any one of these lines or sequences considered individually is a case of specific evolution.

Steward chose a middle ground between general and specific studies of the evolution of culture. He concentrated on cases in which unrelated populations had followed *convergent* evolutionary paths. Given long-term adaptation by different cultures to similar environments, the same institutions tend to develop, in the same order. Steward, an influential advocate of the position that scientific laws govern human behavior and culture change, sought to explain convergent cultural evolution. He contributed to anthropological theory by showing that parallel cultural changes have occurred repeatedly and independently in different places.

Steward also contributed to cultural **typology** (the grouping of cultures into types). One type he defined was the **irrigation state.** According to Steward, the evolution of civilization in five arid areas (Mesopotamia, Egypt, Peru, China, and Mesoamerica), as reconstructed archeologically, exemplified a single **developmental type** (a category based on convergent evolution and environmental similarity). There had been different developmental types in nonarid areas (e.g., tropical rain forests).

By comparing specific evolutionary sequences as Steward did, we may discover trends in cultural development. Analogous selective forces in similar environments have produced *convergent,* or *parallel,* cultural evolution in different areas. Thus, certain environmental conditions and stimuli may produce the same cultural adaptive response in separate populations.

STRATEGIES OF ADAPTATION

John Bennett (1969) divided the concept of cultural adaptation into two parts. First, **adaptive strategies** are patterns formed by the many separate adjustments individuals make to obtain and use resources and to solve immediate problems in a particular society. Second, **adaptive processes** are long-term (*specific* evolutionary) changes resulting from the repeated use of such strategies in a particular locale. People are usually conscious of their adaptive strategies but often do not discern adaptive processes, which are detected by observers and analysts such as the archeologist and the historically oriented ethnologist.

Yehudi Cohen (1974) used *adaptive strategy* to describe a group's system of economic production. He argued that the most important reason for similarities between two unrelated cultures is their possession of a similar adaptive strategy. Similar economic causes, in other words, produce similar cultural effects. For example, there are striking similarities among most cultures that have a *foraging* strategy. Cohen developed a useful typology of cultures based on correlations between economies and social features. His typology includes six adaptive strategies: foraging, horticulture, agriculture, pastoralism, mercantilism (trade), and industrialism. I examine the last two strategies in Chapter 9. I focus on the first four here.

FORAGING

Until 12,000 years ago all humans were foragers. However, environmental specifics created contrasts between foraging populations. Some were big game hunters; others hunted and collected a wider range of animals and plants. Nevertheless, foraging economies shared one essential feature: People relied on nature for food and other necessities.

Food production began 12,000 to 10,000 years ago in the Middle East. Cultivation, based on different crops, emerged 3,000 to 4,000 years later in the Western Hemisphere, in Mexico. In both hemispheres the new economy spread rapidly. Most foragers eventually turned to food production.

However, foraging held on in a few places. There are still two broad areas of foraging in Africa. One is the Kalahari Desert of southern Africa. This is the home of the **San** ("Bushmen"). The San include the **!Kung**. (The exclamation point stands for a distinctive sound made in their language, a click.) Richard Lee (Lee 1984; Lee and DeVore 1977) and other anthropologists have spent years studying !Kung foragers. I shall draw on their findings throughout this book. The other main African foraging area is the equatorial forest of central and eastern Africa, home of the Mbuti and other "pygmies."

Foraging populations also survive in remote forested areas of Madagascar, Southeast Asia, Malaysia, and on isolated islands off the Indian coast. Some of the best-known contemporary foragers are the aborigines of Australia, who lived on their island continent for more than 30,000 years without developing food production.

There are also foragers in the Western Hemisphere. The Eskimos, or Inuit, of Alaska and Canada are well-known hunters. The native populations of California, Oregon, Washington, and British Columbia were all foragers, as were those of inland subarctic Canada and the Great Lakes. Coastal foragers lived near the southern tip of South America. On the grassy plains of Argentina, southern Brazil, Uruguay, and Paraguay there were other hunters and gatherers.

Throughout the world, foragers survived mainly in environments that posed major obstacles to food production. (Some took refuge in such areas after the rise of food production, the state, and the world system.) The difficulties of cultivating at the North Pole are obvious. However, environmental impediments to other adaptive strategies aren't the only reason foragers survived. Their niches have one thing in common—their marginality. Their environments have not been of immediate interest to those with other adaptive strategies.

Even today foragers survive in areas where food production and industrialism have not yet spread. However, the number of foraging groups continues to decline. (I consider issues of the cultural survival of foragers and other groups in Chapters 9 and 18.) Finally, I should note that foraging has held on in a few areas that can be cultivated, even after contact with cultivators. These foragers did not become food producers because they were supporting themselves adequately by hunting and gathering.

Correlates of Foraging

Typologies, such as Cohen's adaptive strategies, are useful because they suggest **correlations**—that is, associations or covariation between two or more variables. (Correlated variables are factors that are linked and interrelated, such as height and weight, such that when one increases or decreases, the other tends to change, too.) Ethnographic studies in hundreds of cultures have revealed many correlations between the economy and social life.

Associated (correlated) with each adaptive strategy is a bundle of particular cultural features. For example, foragers tend to live in band-organized societies. Their basic social unit, the band, is a small group of fewer than a hundred people, all related by kinship or marriage. Band size varies between cultures and often from one season to the next in a given culture. In some foraging societies, band size stays about the same year-round. In others, the band splits up for part of the year. Families leave to gather resources that are better exploited by just a few people. Later, they regroup for cooperative work and ceremonies. Several examples of seasonal splits and recongregation are known from archeology and ethnography.

One important characteristic of band life is mobility. Of interest here are the San Bushmen of the Kalahari in southern Africa and the Mbuti "pygmies" of Zaire. A San or Mbuti shifts band membership many times in a lifetime. One may be born, for example, in a band where one's mother has kin. Later, one's family may move to a band where the father has relatives. Because bands are exogamous, one's parents come from two different bands and one's grandparents may come from four. People may affiliate with any band to which they have kinship or marriage links. A San couple may live in either the husband's or the wife's band. Later they may decide to move to the band of the other spouse for a while.

One may also affiliate with a band through **fictive kinship**—personal relationships modeled on kinship, such as that between godparents and godchildren. San have a limited number of personal names. People with the same name have a special relationship; they treat each other like siblings. San expect the same hospitality in bands where they have **namesakes** as they do in a band in which a real sibling lives. Namesakes share a strong identity. They call everyone in a namesake's band by the kin terms the namesake uses. Those people reply as if they were addressing a real relative. Thus kinship, marriage, and fictive kinship permit the San to join many bands, and people do change bands often. Band membership therefore changes tremendously from year to year.

All human societies have a division of labor on the basis of gender. Among foragers, men typically hunt and women collect, but the nature of the work varies among cultures. Sometimes women's work provides most of the diet. Sometimes male hunting and fishing predominate. Excellent quantitative data on production and consumption gathered by Richard Lee among the !Kung San helped correct widespread misconceptions about foragers (Lee 1968/1974). First, Lee showed that gathering—not hunting—was the mainstay of their diet. Second, he found that foragers' work, rather than being a constant struggle against starvation, was much less time-consuming than, and can support at least as many dependents as, the average American's job.

Lee also gathered quantitative data on consumption. Rather than being marginal, the !Kung diet turned out to be as nutritious as that enjoyed by middle-class Americans. !Kung food output was found to exceed their minimum daily requirements (1,965 calories and 60 grams of protein per person per day, given their size and level of activity) by 165 calories and 33 grams of protein. The !Kung, working only two or three days per week on the average, could even have increased production a bit. They could have obtained more calories and protein without danger of degrading their environment. They did not do so simply because there was no need to work harder.

All foragers make social distinctions based on age. Often old people receive great respect as guardians of myths, legends, stories, and traditions. Younger people value the elders' special knowledge of ritual and practical matters. Most foraging societies are *egalitarian*. This means that contrasts in status are minor and are based on age and gender.

When considering issues of "human nature," we should not forget that the egalitarian band has been the basic form of human social life for most of our history. Food production has existed less than 1 percent of the time *Homo* has spent on

In slash-and-burn cultivation horticulturalists clear land by cutting down (slashing) and burning forest or bush. The ashes remain to fertilize the soil.

earth. However, it has produced huge social differences. We now consider the main economic features of food-producing strategies.

CULTIVATION

The three adaptive strategies based on food production in nonindustrial societies are horticulture, agriculture, and pastoralism. In non-Western cultures, as in our own, people carry out many economic tasks. Each adaptive strategy refers to the *main* economic activity. Pastoralists (herders), for example, consume milk, butter, blood, and meat from their animals as mainstays of their diet. However, they also add grain to the diet by doing some cultivating or by trading with neighbors. Food producers may also hunt or gather to supplement a diet based on domesticated species.

Horticulture

Horticulture and agriculture are two types of cultivation found in nonindustrial societies. Both differ from the **farming** systems of industrial nations such as the United States. Farming uses large land areas, machinery, and petrochemicals. Horticulture makes intensive use of *none* of the factors of production: permanently owned land, labor, capital, and machinery. Horticulturalists use simple tools such as hoes and digging sticks to grow their crops. Their fields are not permanent property and lie fallow for varying lengths of time.

Horticulture is also known as **slash-and-burn** cultivation. Each year horticulturalists clear land by cutting down (slashing) and burning forest or bush or by setting fire to the grass covering the plot. The ashes remain to fertilize the soil. Crops are then sown, tended, and harvested. Use of the plot is not continuous. Often it is cultivated for only a year. This depends, however, on soil fertility and weeds, which compete with cultivated plants for nutrients.

When horticulturalists abandon a plot because of soil exhaustion or a thick weed cover, they clear another piece of land, and the original plot reverts to forest. After several years of fallowing (the duration varies in different societies), the cultivator returns to farm the original plot again. Because the relationship between people and land is not permanent, horticulture is also called *shifting cultivation*. Shifting cultivation does not mean that whole villages must move when plots are abandoned. Horticulture can support large permanent villages. Among the Kuikuru of the South American tropical forest, for example, one village of 150 people remained in the same place for ninety years (Carneiro 1956). Kuikuru houses are large and well made. Because the work involved in building them is great, the Kuikuru would rather walk farther to their fields than construct a new village. They shift their plots rather than their settlements. On the other hand, horticulturalists in the *montaña* (Andean foothills) of Peru live in small villages of about thirty people (Carneiro 1961/1968). Their houses are small and simple. After a few years in one place, these people build new villages near virgin land. Because their houses are so simple, the prefer rebuilding to walking even a half mile to their fields.

Agriculture

Agriculture is cultivation that requires more labor than horticulture and uses land intensively and continuously. The labor demands associated with agriculture reflect its use of domesticated animals, irrigation, and terracing.

Domesticated Animals

Agriculturalists use animals as means of production, for transport, as cultivating machines, and for their manure. The Betsileo of central Madagascar (Kottak 1980) sow rice in nursery beds. When the seedlings get big enough, they are transplanted into flooded rice fields. Before transplanting, the Betsileo till and flood their fields. Cattle are brought to trample the prepared fields just before transplanting. Young men yell at and beat the cattle, striving to drive them into a frenzy so that they

will trample the fields properly. Trampling breaks up clumps of earth and mixes irrigation water with soil to form a smooth mud into which women transplant seedlings. Like many other agriculturalists, the Betsileo collect manure from their animals, using it to fertilize their plots, thus increasing the yield.

Irrigation

While horticulturalists must await the rainy season, agriculturalists can schedule their planting in advance, because they control water. The Betsileo irrigate their fields with canals from rivers, streams, springs, and ponds. Irrigation makes it possible to cultivate a plot year after year. Irrigation enriches the soil because the irrigated field is a unique ecosystem with several species of plants and animals, many of them minute organisms, whose wastes fertilize the land.

An irrigated field is a capital investment that increases in value. It takes time for a field to start yielding; it reaches full productivity only after several years of cultivation. The Betsileo, like other irrigators, have farmed the same fields for generations. In some agricultural areas, including the Middle East, however, salts carried in the irrigation water can make fields unusable after fifty or sixty years.

In some areas of Irian Jaya, Indonesia (which is on the island of New Guinea), labor-intensive cultivation in valleys involves the construction of long drainage ditches. Here, members of the Dani tribe use their bare hands and feet to maintain such a canal.

Terracing

Terracing is another agricultural technique that the Betsileo have mastered. Central Madagascar has small valleys separated by steep hillsides. Because the population is dense, people need to farm the hills. However, if they simply planted on the steep hillsides, fertile soil and crops would be washed away during the rainy season. To prevent this, the Betsileo, like the rice-farming Ifugao of the Philippines, cut into the hillside and build stage after stage of terraced fields rising above the valley floor. Springs located above the terraces supply their irrigation water. The labor necessary to build and maintain a system of terraces is great. Terrace walls crumble each year and must be partially rebuilt. The canals that bring water down through the terraces also demand attention.

The Cultivation Continuum

Because nonindustrial economies can have features of both horticulture and agriculture, it is useful to discuss cultivators as being arranged along a **cultivation continuum.** Horticultural systems stand at one end—the "low-labor, shifting-plot" end. Agriculturalists are at the other—"labor-intensive, permanent-plot"—end.

We speak of a continuum because there are today intermediate economies, combining horticultural and agricultural techniques, such as those which developed historically in early archeological sequences leading from horticulture to agriculture in the Middle East and Mexico. Nonintensive horticulturalists farm a plot just once before fallowing it. However, the South American Kuikuru grow two or three crops of **manioc,** or cassava—an edible tuber—before abandoning their plots. Cultivation is even more intense in certain densely populated areas of Papua–New Guinea, where plots are planted for two or three years, allowed to rest for three to five, and then recultivated. Plots are abandoned for longer fallowing after several of these cycles. This pattern is called **sectorial fallowing** (Wolf 1966). Besides Papua–New Guinea, such systems occur in areas as far apart as West Africa and highland Mexico. Sectorial fallowing is associated with denser populations than is simple horticulture. The simpler system is the norm in tropical forests, where weed invasion and delicate soils prevent more intensive cultivation.

The key difference between horticulture and agriculture is that horticulture always uses a fallowing period whereas agriculture does not. The earliest cultivators in the Middle East and Mexico were rainfall-dependent horticulturalists. Until recently, horticulture was the main form of cultivation in several areas, including parts of Africa, Southeast Asia, Indonesia, the Philippines, the Pacific islands, Mexico, Central America, and the South American tropical forest.

Increasing labor intensity and permanent land use have several demographic, social, and political consequences. These consequences illustrate general evolutionary trends, as discussed earlier. Because of their permanent fields, agriculturalists are sedentary. People live in larger and more permanent communities located closer to other settlements. Growth in population size, density, and stability increases contact between groups. There is more need to regulate interpersonal relations and conflicts of interest. Economies that support more people require more coordination in the use of land, labor, and other resources.

Intensive agriculture poses many regulatory problems, and central governments have often arisen to solve them. Agriculturalists are much more likely than are horticulturalists to live in societies organized as **states** or **nation-states**—complex sociopolitical systems that administer a territory and populace with substantial contrasts in occupation, wealth, prestige, and power.

Intensive Agriculture

Intensive agriculture requires human labor to build and maintain irrigation systems and terraces. People must feed, water, and care for their animals. Given sufficient labor input and management, agricultural land can yield one or two crops annually for years or even generations. An agricultural field does not necessarily produce a higher single-year yield than does a horticultural plot. The first crop grown by horticulturalists on long-idle land may be larger than that from an agricultural plot of the same size. Furthermore, because agriculturalists work harder than horticulturalists do, agriculture's yield relative to labor is also lower. Agriculture's main advantage is that the *long-term yield* per area is far greater and more dependable. Because a single field sustains its own-

Agriculture requires more labor than horticulture does and uses land intensively and continuously. Labor demands associated with agriculture reflect its use of domesticated animals, irrigation, and terracing. The Ifugao of the Philippines are famous for their terraced rice fields.

ers year after year, there is no need to maintain a reserve of uncultivated land as horticulturalists do. This is why agricultural societies are more densely populated than are horticultural ones.

The range of environments open to human use widens as people increase their control over nature. Agricultural populations exist in many areas that are too arid for nonirrigators or too hilly for nonterracers. Many ancient civilizations in arid lands arose on an agricultural base. The demographic, social, and political consequences of plant cultivation are most extensive among agriculturalists, illustrating the general evolutionary trends discussed earlier. Most agriculturalists live in nation-states. In such societies, cultivators play their role as one part of a differentiated, function-

ally specialized, and tightly integrated sociopolitical system.

PASTORALISM

Pastoralists live in North Africa, the Middle East, Europe, Asia, and sub-Saharan Africa. These herders are people whose activities focus on such domesticated animals as cattle, sheep, goats, camels, and yak. East African pastoralists, like many others, live in **symbiosis** with their herds. (Symbiosis is an obligatory interaction between groups—here humans and animals—that is beneficial to each.) Herders protect their animals and ensure their reproduction in return for food and other necessities, such as leather. Herds provide dairy products and meat. East Africans also dine on cooked cattle blood. Animals are slaughtered at ceremonies which occur throughout the year, and so beef is available on a fairly constant basis.

People put their livestock to many different uses. Natives of North America's Great Plains, for example, didn't eat, but only rode, their horses. (Europeans *re*introduced horses to the Western Hemisphere; the native American horse had become extinct thousands of years earlier.) For Plains Indians horses served as "tools of the trade," means of production used to hunt bison, the target of their economies. So the Indians were not true pastoralists but *hunters* who used horses—as many agriculturalists use animals—as means of production.

Unlike the use of animals merely as productive machines, pastoralists typically make direct use of their herds for food. They consume their meat, blood, and milk, from which they make yogurt and butter. Although some pastoralists rely on their herds more completely than do others, it is impossible to base subsistence solely on animals. Most pastoralists therefore supplement their diet by hunting, gathering, fishing, cultivating, or trading.

To get crops, pastoralists either trade with cultivators or do some cultivating or gathering themselves. Since their beginning, herding and cultivation have often been interdependent. Nineteenth-century anthropologists, lacking today's knowledge, speculated about whether cultivation or animal domestication came first. We now know that pastoralism and cultivation emerged and spread together in the Old World as interrelated parts of a pattern of increasing human intervention in nature.

Unlike foraging and cultivation, which were practiced globally before the Industrial Revolution, pastoralism was almost totally confined to the Old World. Before European conquest, the only pastoralists in the Americas lived in the Peruvian Andes. They used their llamas and alpacas for food and in agriculture and transport. Much more recently, the Navajo of the southwestern United States developed a pastoral economy based on sheep, which were brought to North America by Europeans. The populous Navajo are now the major pastoral population in the New World.

Two patterns of movement occur with pastoralism: nomadism and transhumance. Both are based on the fact that herds must move to take advantage of pasture available in particular places in different seasons. In pastoral **nomadism,** the entire group—women, men, and children—moves with the animals throughout the year. With **transhumance,** only part of the group follows the herds while the rest remain in home villages. During their annual trek, nomads trade for crops and other products with more sedentary people. Transhumants don't have to trade for crops. Because only part of the population accompanies the herds, transhumants can maintain year-round villages and grow their own crops. Another name for groups that divide their subsistence between agriculture and pastoralism is agro-pastoralists. **Agro-pastoralism** is a common form of economic adaptation in the Himalayas (being found among such peoples as the Tamang, Sherpa, and Gurungs) and in the Andes.

The Jie of Uganda, a transhumant population of some 18,000 people (Gulliver 1955), have a territory about 105 kilometers (65 miles) long by 40 kilometers (25 miles) wide. Because the western area has year-round water, the Jie have their villages there and grow crops using horticultural techniques. When the rainy season begins, grass appears in eastern pastures, and the men take the herds there. Later they move west of the villages, where pasture remains after the east is dry. Having exhausted the western pastures, they return to the villages to spend the rest of the year in the best-watered area of all. While younger men are accompanying the herds, women, older men, and children stay home.

The Alps also have people who live by transhumance. The annual movement to spring and summer pastures at higher elevations is familiar to anyone who has read the children's book *Heidi*. Transhumance and nomadism once again illustrate a continuum: the proportion of the population accompanying the herds, the time spent in any one place, and the amount of labor devoted to other activities are all matters of "more or less" rather than absolute contrasts.

Some pastoralists rely on their herds more completely than others. Most pastoralists also hunt, gather, fish, cultivate, or trade. This Spanish shepherd lives in a region with a mixed economy, alongside peasants and townsfolk.

SUMMARY

General evolution refers to long-term trends in hominid evolution, including the consequences of food production. Specific evolution refers to particular human populations adapting to changing environments. Julian Steward compared cases of specific evolution to discover cross-cultural regularities, instances of convergent cultural evolution. Leslie White described the general evolution of culture. He believed that technological changes, particularly new ways of harnessing nonhuman energy, caused social and political evolution.

Yehudi Cohen's six adaptive strategies are foraging (hunting and gathering), horticulture, agriculture, pastoralism, mercantilism (trade), and industrialism. Foraging was the only human strategy until food production (cultivation and animal domestication) appeared 12,000 to 10,000 years ago. Food production eventually replaced foraging in most areas. Foragers survive in certain marginal zones.

Among most foragers, the band is the basic social unit. Often band members split up seasonally into microbands or families. Kinship, marriage, and other arrangements link band members. Foragers assign tasks by gender and age. Men usually hunt, and women gather. Old people guard traditions.

Cultivation is often combined with other adaptive strategies, for example, pastoralism and foraging. Horticulture and agriculture stand at different ends of a continuum based on labor intensity and continuity of land use. Horticulture does not use land or labor intensively. Horticulturalists cultivate a plot one or two years and then abandon it. Further along the continuum, horticulture becomes more intensive, but there is always a fallowing period. Horticulturalists can shift plots while living in permanent villages. The first cultivating economies were horticultural. Horticulture still occurs in many areas of both hemispheres.

Agriculturalists farm the same plot of land continuously and use labor intensively. They use one or more of the following practices: irrigation, terracing, domesticated animals as means of production, and manuring. Because of permanent land use, agricultural populations are denser than are those associated with other adaptive strategies. Agriculturalists often have complex regulatory systems, including state organization.

The mixed nature of the pastoral strategy is obvious. Nomadic pastoralists trade with cultivators. Transhumants grow their own crops. Part of the transhumant population cultivates while another part takes the herds to pasture. Except for some Peruvians and the Navajo, who are recent herders, the New World lacks native pastoralists.

GLOSSARY

adaptability: Tolerance of environmental diversity.

adaptive processes: Long-term (*specific* evolutionary) changes resulting from repeated use of adaptive strategies (in Bennett's sense) in a particular locale.

adaptive radiation: Process of population increase and adaptation to varied environments.

adaptive strategies: Patterns formed by the many separate adjustments individuals make to obtain and use resources and solve immediate problems; in Cohen's sixfold typology of cultures, foraging, horticulture, agriculture, pastoralism, mercantilism (trade), and industrialism.

agriculture: Nonindustrial system of plant cultivation characterized by continuous and intensive use of land and labor.

agro-pastoralism: Subsistence economy based on both agriculture and (transhumant) pastoralism; the most common form of economic adaptation in the Himalayas.

band: Basic unit of social organization among foragers. A band includes fewer than 100 people; it often splits up seasonally.

correlation: An association between two or more variables such that when one changes (varies), the other(s) also change(s) (covaries); for example, temperature and sweating.

cultivation continuum: A continuum based on the comparative study of nonindustrial cultivating societies in which labor intensity increases and fallowing decreases.

developmental type: Category based on convergent evolution and environmental similarity; includes societies in ecologically similar areas that evolved in an analogous fashion.

farming: Cultivation in industrial nations; relies on large land areas, machinery, and petrochemicals.

fictive kinship: Personal relationships modeled on kinship, such as that between godparents and godchildren.

food production: Plant cultivation and animal domestication.

foraging: Hunting and gathering.

general evolution: Study of major changes, biological and cultural, in *Homo*; abstracted from a variety of times, places, and populations.

horticulture: Nonindustrial system of plant cultivation in which plots lie fallow for varying lengths of time.

irrigation state: Nonindustrial state, e.g., ancient Mesopotamia, Egypt, Peru, China, and Mesoamerica, based on irrigation in an arid area; one of Julian Steward's developmental types.

!Kung: Group of San (Bushmen) foragers of southern Africa; the exclamation point indicates a click sound in the San language.

manioc: Cassava, a tuber abundant in South American tropical forests. Along with maize and white potatoes, it is one of the three major caloric staples of the aboriginal New World.

Mesoamerica: Middle America—Mexico, Guatemala, and Belize.

multilinear evolution: Study of the evolution of human society "along its many lines" through examination of specific evolutionary sequences; associated with Julian Steward.

namesakes: People who share the same name; a form of fictive kinship among the San, who have a limited number of personal names.

nation-state: A complex sociopolitical system administering a territory and populace with substantial contrasts in occupation, wealth, prestige, and power.

nomadism: Movement throughout the year by the whole pastoral group (men, women, and children) with their animals. More generally, such constant movement in pursuit of strategic resources.

pastoralists: People who use a food-producing strategy of adaptation based on care of herds of domesticated animals.

San: Foragers of southern Africa, also known as Bushmen; speakers of San languages.

sectorial fallowing: Intensive horticulture; plots are cultivated for two to three years, then fallowed for three to five, with a longer rest after several of these shorter cycles.

sedentary: Remaining in one place; a sedentary village is one in which people remain together year-round and for several years.

slash and burn: Form of horticulture in which the forest cover of a plot is cut down and burned before planting to allow the ashes to fertilize the soil.

specific evolution: Studies of changes in relationships between specific populations and their environments.

state: See *nation-state*.

symbiosis: An obligatory interaction between groups that is beneficial to each.

transhumance: One of two variants of pastoralism; part of the population moves seasonally with the herds while the other part remains in home villages.

typology: A system of classification of cultures into types.

unilinear evolution: The view that all cultures have evolved in the same order through a set sequence of stages.

STUDY QUESTIONS

1. How do general and specific evolution differ?
2. What is the relationship between specific, convergent, and multilinear evolution?
3. What are the four main general evolutionary trends?
4. What was Leslie White's view of cultural evolution?
5. What are Cohen's four nonindustrial strategies of adaptation? What are the main characteristics of each?
6. How do social ties facilitate individual mobility between bands?
7. What are the main differences between horticulture, agriculture, and farming?
8. What are the advantages and disadvantages of irrigation?
9. What is the difference between nomadism and transhumance?

SUGGESTED ADDITIONAL READING

BOSERUP, E.
1965 *The Conditions of Agricultural Growth*. Chicago: Aldine. Influential book linking population increase, agricultural intensity, and level of sociopolitical development.

BOYD, R., AND P. J. RICHERSON
1985 *Culture and the Evolutionary Process*. Chicago: University of Chicago Press. Social evolution within the larger context of human evolution and recent evolutionary theory.

COHEN, Y., ED.
1974 *Man in Adaptation: The Cultural Present*. 2nd ed. Chicago: Aldine. Sets forth Cohen's typology of strategies of adaptation and uses it

to organize interesting essays on cultural anthropology.

HUGHES, J. D.

1983   *American Indian Ecology.* El Paso, TX: Texas Western Press. Traditional adaptations in Native North America.

JOHNSON, A. W., AND T. EARLE

1987   *The Evolution of Human Societies: From Foraging Group to Agrarian State.* Stanford, CA: Stanford University Press. Most recent synthesis of findings on human cultural evolution.

LEE, R. B., AND I. DEVORE, EDS.

1977   *Kalahari Hunter-Gatherers: Studies of the !Kung*

San and Their Neighbors. Cambridge, MA: Harvard University Press. Long-term interdisciplinary study of well-known foragers.

SAHLINS, M. D., AND E. R. SERVICE

1960   *Evolution and Culture.* Ann Arbor: University of Michigan Press. Application of evolutionary principles to cultural anthropological data a century after Darwin.

WHITE, L. A.

1965   *The Evolution of Culture: The Development of Civilization to the Fall of Rome.* New York: McGraw-Hill. Classic sketch of human cultural evolution and diversity.

C H A P T E R 7

BANDS AND TRIBES

several years ago anthropologist Elman Service (1962) listed four types, or levels, of social and political organization: band, tribe, chiefdom, and state. *Bands,* as we have seen, are small kin-based groups that typify foragers. **Tribes,** which are associated with nonintensive food production (horticulture and pastoralism), have villages and descent groups but lack a government (centralized rule) and social classes (socioeconomic stratification). In a tribe, there is no reliable means of enforcing political decisions. The **chiefdom,** a form of sociopolitical organization that is intermediate between the tribe and the state, is kin-based, but it has differential access to resources and a permanent political structure. The **state** is a form of sociopolitical organization based on central government and socioeconomic stratification.

Many anthropologists have criticized Service's typology as being too simple. However, it does offer a handy set of labels for highlighting cross-cultural similarities and differences in social and political organization. Accordingly, most anthropologists use the classification occasionally. Service's four types reflect the general evolutionary trends discussed in Chapter 6. To restate those trends, as we move from band to tribe to chiefdom to state:

1. Parts and subparts increase.
2. Parts and subparts become more functionally specialized.
3. More effective coordinating mechanisms (means of regulation and integration) appear.
4. Population size increases, along with the range or scale of the sociopolitical system (from local to regional to national).

Parts and subparts proliferate as villages and descent groups are added to families and kin-based bands. Functional specialization increases as political, economic, and religious figures and institutions crystallize out of a less complex social organization. Regulatory systems expand from local (band or village) to regional to national (the state) levels as the population grows and political control strengthens.

POLITICS

Anthropologists and political scientists share an interest in political organization, but the anthropological approach is global and comparative. Anthropological data reveal substantial variations in power, authority, and legal systems in different cultures. (*Power* is the ability to exercise one's will over others; *authority* is the socially approved use of power.) In bands and tribes, the political order, or **polity,** is not a separate entity but is submerged in the total social order. It is difficult to characterize an act or event as political rather than merely social.

Recognizing that political organization is sometimes just an aspect of social organization, Morton Fried offered this definition:

> Political organization comprises those portions of social organization that specifically relate to the individuals or groups that manage the affairs of *public policy* or seek to control the appointment or activities of those individuals or groups (Fried 1967, pp. 20–21, emphasis added).

This definition certainly fits contemporary North America. Under "individuals or groups that manage the affairs of public policy" come federal, state (provincial), and local (municipal) governments. Those who "seek to control . . . appointment or activities" include such familiar interest groups as political parties, unions, corporations, consumers, activists, action committees, and religious groups.

Fried's definition is much less applicable to bands and tribes, where it is often difficult to detect any "public policy." For this reason, I prefer to speak of *socio*political organization in discussing cross-cultural similarities and differences in the **regulation** or management of interrelationships among groups and their representatives. Regulation assures that variables stay within their normal ranges, corrects deviations from the norm, and thus maintains the system's integrity. This includes such things as the settling of conflicts between individuals and groups and methods of decision making within the group. It draws our attention to questions about who performs these tasks (are there formal leaders?) and how they are managed.

TYPES AND TRENDS

Ethnographic and archeological studies in hundreds of places have revealed many correlations between economy and social and political organization. Band, tribe, chiefdom, and state are classified in a system of **sociopolitical typology.** These types are correlated with the adaptive strategies (**economic typology**) discussed in Chapter 6. Thus, foragers (an economic type) tend to have band organization (a sociopolitical type). Similarly, many horticulturalists and pastoralists live in tribal societies (or, more simply, tribes). The economies of chiefdoms tend to be based on intensive horticulture or agriculture. Nonindustrial states have an agricultural base.

Food producers tend to have larger, denser populations and more complex economies than do foragers. These features create new regulatory problems, which give rise to more complex relationships and linkages. Many sociopolitical trends reflect the increased regulatory demands associated with food production. Archeologists have studied these trends through time, and cultural anthropologists have observed them among contemporary groups.

This chapter and Chapter 8 examine societies that differ in their adaptive strategies and levels of sociopolitical complexity. A common set of questions will be considered for different types of societies. What kinds of social groups do they have? How do people affiliate with those groups? How do the groups link up with larger ones? How do the groups represent themselves to each other? How are their internal and external relations regulated? This chapter focuses on bands and tribes. Chapter 8 deals with chiefdoms and states.

FORAGING BANDS

The groups that are significant in a given society tend to reflect that society's sociopolitical type and adaptive strategy. For example, in most foraging societies only two kinds of groups are significant: the nuclear family and the band. Unlike sedentary villages (which appear in tribal societies), bands are impermanent. They form seasonally as component nuclear families assemble. The particular combination of families in a band may vary from year to year.

In such settings the main social building blocks (linking principles) are the personal relationships of individuals. For example, marriage and kinship create ties between members of different bands. Because one's parents and grandparents come from different bands, a person has relatives in several of these groups. Trade and visiting also link local groups, as does fictive kinship, such as the !Kung namesake system described in Chapter 6. Similarly, Eskimo men traditionally had trade partners, whom they treated almost like brothers, in different bands. The natives of Australia had an institution known as the section system that had similar linking functions.

In a foraging band there is very little differential authority and no differential power, although particular talents lead to special respect. For example, someone can sing or dance well, is an especially good storyteller, or can go into a trance and communicate with spirits. Band leaders are leaders in name only. They are first among equals. Sometimes they give advice or make decisions, but they have no means of enforcing their decisions.

Although foragers lack formal **law** in the sense of a legal code that includes trial and enforcement, they do have methods of social control and dispute settlement. The absence of law does not mean total anarchy. The aboriginal Eskimos (Hoebel 1954, 1968), or Inuit, as they are called in Canada, provide a good example of methods of settling disputes in stateless societies. In the **ethnographic present** (the time at which a group was first studied by an ethnographer), a sparsely settled population of some 20,000 Eskimos spanned 9,500 kilometers (6,000 miles) of the Arctic region. The most significant Eskimo social groups were the nuclear family and the band. Personal relationships linked the families and bands. Some bands had headmen. There were also shamans (part-time religious spe-

As is true of most foragers, the most significant social groups among the Eskimos (or Inuit, as they are called in Canada) were the nuclear family and the band. This historic photo shows a family group of eleven Eskimo men, women, and children in Port Clarence, Alaska.

cialists). However, these positions conferred little power on those who occupied them.

In contrast to most foraging societies, in which gathering—usually a female task—is more important, hunting and fishing by men were the primary Eskimo subsistence activities. The diverse and abundant plant foods available in warmer areas were absent in the Arctic. Traveling on land and sea in a bitter environment, Eskimo men faced more dangers than women did. The traditional male role took its toll in lives. Adult women would have outnumbered men substantially without occasional female **infanticide** (killing of a baby), which Eskimo culture permitted.

Despite this crude (and to us unthinkable) means of population regulation, there were still more adult women than men. This permitted some men to have two or three wives. The ability to support more than one wife conferred a certain amount of prestige, but it also encouraged envy. (*Prestige* is esteem, respect, or approval for culturally valued acts or qualities.) If a man seemed to be taking additional wives just to enhance his reputation, a rival was likely to steal one of them. Most disputes were between men and originated over women, caused by wife stealing or adultery.

If a man discovered that his wife had been having sexual relations without his permission, he considered himself wronged.

Although public opinion would not let the husband ignore the matter, he had several options. He could try to kill the wife stealer. However, if he succeeded, one of his rival's kinsmen would surely try to kill him in retaliation. One dispute could escalate into several deaths as relatives avenged a succession of murders. No government existed to intervene and stop such a **blood feud** (a feud between families). However, one could also challenge a rival to a song battle. In a public setting, contestants made up insulting songs about each other. At the end of the match, the audience declared one of them the winner. However, if a man whose wife had been stolen won, there was no guarantee she would return. Often she would decide to stay with her abductor.

Several acts of killing that are crimes in contemporary North America were not considered criminal by the Eskimos. Infanticide has already been mentioned. Furthermore, people who felt that because of age or infirmity they were no longer useful might kill themselves or ask others to kill them. Old people or invalids who wished to die would ask a close relative, such as a son, to end their lives. It was necessary to ask a close relative in order to ensure that the kin of the deceased did not take revenge on the killer.

Thefts are common in state-organized societies, which have marked property differentials. However, thefts were not a problem for the Eskimos—or for most foragers. Each Eskimo had access to the resources needed to sustain life. Every man could hunt, fish, and make the tools necessary for subsistence. Every woman could obtain the implements and materials needed to make clothing, prepare food, and do domestic work. Eskimos could even hunt and fish in territories of other local groups. There was no notion of private ownership of territory or animals.

To describe certain property notions of people who live in societies without state organization, Elman Service (1966) coined the term **personalty** (note the spelling). Personalty refers to items other than strategic resources that are indelibly associated with a specific person. These items include things such as arrows, a tobacco pouch, clothing, and personal ornaments. The term points to the personal relationship between such items and their owner. Personalty is so tied to specific people that theft is inconceivable (think of your toothbrush). The "grave goods" that are often found in archeological sites dating to the period before food production probably represent personalty. These items were not passed on to heirs. Their association with the deceased was too definite.

One of the most basic Eskimo beliefs was that "all natural resources are free or common goods" (Hoebel 1968). Band-organized societies usually lack differential access to strategic resources. The only private property is personalty. If people want something from someone else, they ask for it, and it is usually given.

TRIBAL CULTIVATORS

Tribes usually have a horticultural or pastoral economy and are organized by village life and/or descent-group membership. Socioeconomic stratification (i.e., a class structure) and centralized rule are absent. Many tribes have small-scale warfare, often in the form of intervillage raiding. Tribes have more effective regulatory mechanisms than

do foragers, but tribalists have no secure means of enforcing political decisions. The main regulatory officials are village heads, "big men," descent-group leaders, village councils, and leaders of pan-tribal associations. All these figures and groups have limited authority.

Like foragers, horticulturalists tend to be egalitarian, although some have marked gender stratification—an unequal distribution of resources, power, prestige, and personal freedom between men and women. Horticultural villages are usually small, with low population density and open access to strategic resources. Age, gender, and personal traits determine how much respect people receive and how much support they get from others. Egalitarianism diminishes, however, as village size and population density increase. Horticultural villages usually have headmen—rarely, if ever, headwomen.

Descent-Group Organization

Kin-based bands are basic social units among foragers. An analogous group among food producers is the **descent group.** A descent group is a permanent social unit whose members claim common ancestry. The group endures even though its membership changes as members are born and die, move in and move out. Often, descent-group membership is determined at birth and is lifelong.

Descent groups frequently are exogamous (members must seek their mates from other descent groups). Two common rules serve to admit certain people as descent-group members while excluding others. With a rule of **matrilineal descent,** people join the mother's group automatically at birth and stay members throughout life. Matrilineal descent groups therefore include only the children of the group's women. With **patrilineal descent,** people automatically have lifetime membership in the father's group. The children of all the men join the group, but the children of the women are excluded. Matrilineal and patrilineal descent are types of **unilineal descent.** This means that the descent rule uses *one line* only, either the female or the male (Figures 7.1 and 7.2). Patrilineal descent is much more common than is matrilineal descent. In a sample of 564 societies (Murdock 1957), about three times as many were found to be patrilineal (247 to 84).

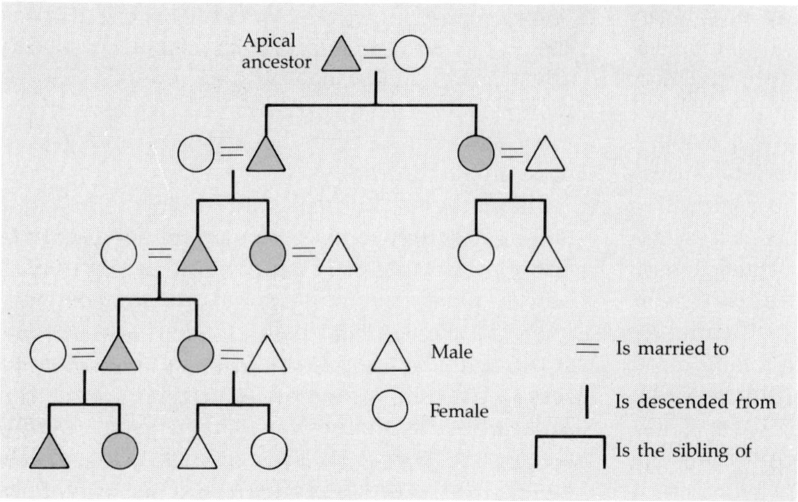

Figure 7.1 *A patrilineage five generations deep. Lineages are based on demonstrated descent from an apical ancestor. With patrilineal descent children of men (blue) are included as descent-group members. Children of women are excluded; they belong to their father's patrilineage. Also notice lineage exogamy.*

Descent groups may be **lineages** or **clans.** Common to both is the belief that members descend from the same **apical ancestor.** This person stands at the apex, or top, of the common genealogy. How do lineages and clans differ? A lineage uses **demonstrated descent.** Members can recite the names of their forebears in each generation from the apical ancestor through the present. (This doesn't mean that their recitations are accurate, only that lineage members think they are.) Clans

Figure 7.2 *A matrilineage five generations deep. Matrilineages are based on demonstrated descent from a female ancestor. Only the children of women (red) belong to the matrilineage. The children of men are excluded; they belong to their mother's matrilineage.*

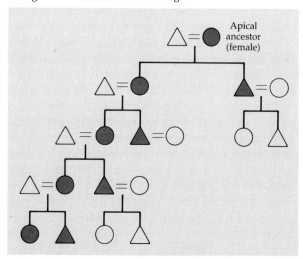

use **stipulated descent.** Clan members merely say they descend from the apical ancestor. They don't try to trace the actual genealogical links between themselves and that ancestor.

Some societies have both lineages and clans. In this case, clans have more members and cover a larger geographical area than lineages do. Sometimes a clan's apical ancestor is not a human at all but an animal or plant (called a **totem**). Whether human or not, the ancestor symbolizes the social unity and identity of the members, distinguishing them from other groups.

A tribal society normally contains several descent groups. Any one of them may be confined to a single village, but they usually span more than one village. Any branch of a descent group that lives in one place is a **local descent group.** Two or more local branches of different descent groups may live in the same village. Descent groups in the same village or different villages establish alliances through frequent intermarriage.

The Village Headman

The Yanomami (Chagnon 1983) are Native Americans who live in southern Venezuela and adjacent Brazil. Their tribal society has about 15,000 people living in 125 dispersed villages, each with a population between 40 and 250. The Yanomami are horticulturalists who also hunt and gather. Their staple crops are bananas and plantains (a banana-like crop). There are more significant social groups among the Yanomami than exist in a foraging society. The Yanomami have nuclear families, villages, and descent groups. Their descent groups are patrilineal and exogamous. They span more than one village. However, local branches of two different descent groups may live in the same village and intermarry.

As in many village-based tribal societies, the only leadership position among the Yanomami is that of **village head** (always a man). His authority, like that of the foraging band leader, is severely limited. If a headman wants something done, he must lead by example and persuasion. The headman lacks the right to issue orders. He can only persuade, harangue, and try to influence public opinion. For example, if he wants people to clean up the central plaza in preparation for a feast, he must start sweeping it himself, hoping that his covillagers will take the hint and relieve him.

When conflict erupts, the headman may be called on as a mediator who listens to both sides. He will give an opinion and advice. If a disputant is unsatisfied, the headman can do nothing. He has no power to back his decisions and no way to impose punishments. Like the band leader, he is first among equals.

A Yanomami village headman must also lead in generosity. Because he must be more generous than any other villager, he cultivates more land. His garden provides much of the food consumed when his village holds a feast for another village. The headman represents the village in its dealings with outsiders. Sometimes he visits other villages to invite people to a feast.

The way a person acts as headman depends on his personal traits and the number of supporters he can muster. One village headman, Kaobawa, intervened in a dispute between a husband and wife and kept him from killing her (Chagnon 1983). He also guaranteed safety to a delegation from a village with which a covillager of his wanted to start a war. Kaobawa was a particularly effective headman. He had demonstrated his fierceness in battle (in a population labeled "the fierce people" by one of its principal ethnographers, Napoleon Chagnon [1983]). Kaobawa diplomatically used his influence to avoid offending other villagers. No one had a better personality for the headmanship. Nor (because Kaobawa had many brothers) did anyone have more supporters.

Among the Yanomami, when a group is dissatisfied with a village headman, its members can leave and found a new village; this is done from time to time.

Village Raiding

Yanomami society, with its many villages and descent groups, is more complex than a band-organized society. The Yanomami also face more regulatory problems. A headman can sometimes prevent a specific violent act, but there is no government to maintain order. In fact, intervillage raiding in which men are killed and women are captured has been a feature of some areas of Yanomami territory, particularly those studied by Chagnon (1983).

Traditional Yanomami intratribal warfare is similar to, but more extreme than, raiding in other tribal societies. Chagnon describes male supremacy as a central theme in Yanomami culture. Gender stratification is so extreme that we may speak of a *male supremacist complex,* in which males are valued more than females and women are deprived of prestige, power, and personal freedom. The Yanomami prefer sons to daughters, especially as firstborn children. If the firstborn is a girl, she may be killed, but boys are allowed to live. Females also die in warfare, and there are more male than female Yanomami (449 to 391 in seven villages that Chagnon studied). Furthermore, although there are too few women to provide even one wife for each man, 25 percent of the men are polygynous—they have multiple mates. The scarcity of women is one reason men go on fighting. They want to capture additional women, as wives. Figure 7.3 summarizes the way in which the pattern of Yanomami warfare perpetuates itself.

There is very lively debate among anthropologists about the nature and causes of intervillage raiding among the Yanomami (Albert 1989; Chagnon 1988; Ferguson 1989a,b,c; Heider 1988; Lizot 1985; Ramos 1987). However, we must also point out that the Yanomami are not isolated from the external world but live in two nation-states—Venezuela and Brazil. External warfare waged by Brazilian ranchers and miners has increasingly threatened these Indians (*Cultural Survival Quarterly* 1989). On the average, one Yanomami dies each day as a result of this external warfare (including

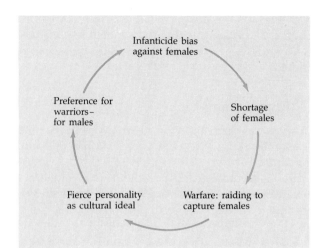

Figure 7.3 *Continued selection for warfare among the Yanomami.*

biological warfare—introduced diseases to which the Yanomami lack resistance). This new warfare poses a much more serious threat to Yanomami survival than does the traditional pattern.

Tribal Warfare

In a cross-cultural study of tribal warfare, Divale and Harris (1976) used the **Human Relations Area Files (HRAF),** a voluminous archive housed in New Haven, Connecticut, but available on microfiche in most college and university libraries. The HRAF is assembled from ethnographic reports and historical accounts of more than 300 cultures. Harris and Divale define *warfare* as

> all organized forms of intergroup homicide involving combat teams of two or more persons, including feuding and raiding (1976, p. 521).

Divale and Harris located 112 societies with good information about warfare. In 49 percent of them, warfare was going on at the time of the report. In 30 percent, it had stopped between five and twenty-five years earlier. In the remaining 21 percent, warfare had ceased more than twenty-five years before the report.

Divale and Harris argue that warfare is a common way of regulating population size among tribal cultivators. This is not mainly because of deaths in battle. Warfare also reduces population size *indirectly* by leading in a complex way to female infanticide. To understand how, consider

Figure 7.3. According to Divale and Harris, tribal warfare perpetuates a cultural preference for warriors, and thus for boys over girls, which promotes female infanticide. Wherever preindustrial warfare exists, they contend, cultures that raise aggressive warriors have an advantage over those that don't.

In nonindustrial societies men always do the fighting because, on the average, they are taller and heavier than are the women of their group. Size confers an advantage in combat with hand-held, muscle-powered weapons. Any nonindustrial population that assigned defense to women would probably be beaten by societies with male warriors. Note that the military significance of physical size and strength declines in industrial societies. A few North American women with rifles or even handguns could easily best a party of tribal raiders.

When warfare is frequent, and once fighting has been assigned to men, the male supremacist complex pervades the culture. Men control access to resources and labor. Descent rules, residence customs, and marital privileges emphasize and maintain male solidarity. Sexual favors go to successful warriors, who have multiple wives. This polygyny intensifies any shortage of females that may already exist and stimulates additional fighting—to capture women. As a result—as Figure 7.3 diagrams—the preference for warriors and the practice of female infanticide continue. (Female infanticide is not always direct. There is also preferential treatment of boys and neglect of girls, leading to girls' deaths.)

In the study by Divale and Harris, in societies where warfare was still going on, the ratio of males to females in the junior age group (fourteen years and under) was 127:100. In those in which warfare had stopped, junior sex ratios approached that of our own society (106:100).

Divale and Harris consider the spread of warfare to be one consequence of the emergence and expansion of plant cultivation. Food production increased the rate of population growth. To understand why, we must consider the relationship between diet and fertility. Foragers have diets that are high in protein and low in fats and carbohydrates. Cultivators have a diet that is just the opposite. Diet affects the ratio of body fat to total weight. Foragers have less fat per unit of body weight than do food producers. The physical re-

In aboriginal times, no state intervened to curb intervillage warfare among the tribal Asmat of West Irian, Indonesia, shown here with their war canoes.

sults of diet affect fertility in two ways. First, high-fat diets promote earlier puberty and lengthen the childbearing period. Second, high-fat diets make women more likely to get pregnant, even when they are nursing.

Foragers, with their low body fat, can delay conception by nursing their babies for years. **Lactation** (milk production) keeps body fat down and disrupts normal ovulation, so sexual intercourse is less likely to result in a new pregnancy. However, because prolonged lactation is only partially effective as contraception, infanticide also occurs among foragers.

The high-fat and high-carbohydrate diet of cultivators reduces the effectiveness of lactation as contraception. In cultivating societies, nursing women often get pregnant. To regulate population growth, other practices are inevitable. For example, there may be a **postpartum taboo:** women must avoid sexual intercourse for a culturally determined period after giving birth.

Abortion, although practiced in some cultures—for example, among certain tropical forest groups in South America—often kills the pregnant woman. Divale and Harris contend that without effective contraception and abortion, the most widespread cultural means of regulating population among tribal cultivators is female infanticide, which intensifies with warfare and the male supremacist complex. Females are valued less than males are, and this makes it psychologically easier for members of such groups (often the mothers) to kill female babies. Reliable contraception, based on recent inventions, permits more humane population limitation.

Village Councils

Whatever the reasons for increased population density and the presence of larger villages in an area, these demographic changes pose new regulatory problems. As the number of people living together increases, the potential for interpersonal conflict grows. Nigeria has villages of more than 1,000 people in areas where population densities exceed 200 people per square mile (about 75 people per square kilometer). In Amazonia, native horticulture has supported villages with 1,400 people (Carneiro 1961/1968). When village population exceeds 1,000, there may be a dozen descent groups in a village instead of just one or two.

In large villages, not only are there many interpersonal relationships requiring regulation, but there are intergroup relations as well. In societies with a well-developed descent-group structure, a person's allegiance is mainly to the descent group and only secondarily to the village and tribe. People must take the side of their group in any dispute with another descent group residing in the same village.

MURDER, LIFE, AND PERSONHOOD

Americans have different opinions about when life begins and when one person can take it from another. So do different cultures. Although American law defines infanticide as murder, it has been widespread in non-Western cultures. One of the keenest moral dilemmas that some anthropologists face in the field is how to deal with infanticide. Understandably, ethnographers have trouble standing by while their hosts carry out a custom that to us is considered murder. Fortunately, I have never seen overt infanticide, nor did the villagers I studied in Brazil and Madagascar practice it. However, other anthropologists have seen babies put to death, usually because the culture being studied considered it immoral or unethical to let certain kinds of infants survive. Many cultures, for example, required that one or both twins be killed. They viewed twin births as inhuman; only animals should have multiple births.

In cultures with infanticide, *parents* (usually the mother) must sometimes kill their own progeny. Powerful moral and religious rules and standards compel such an intrinsically difficult act. Natives believe that the survival of unusual children or those born under exceptional, dubious, or culturally inappropriate circumstances poses a threat to the entire group. Letting both twins live, for instance, might damage the survival chances of either twin because of scarce resources, including mother's milk. (A side effect of killing *both* twins is to remove genes that lead to twinning from the population.)

Among the Tapirapé Indians of Brazil, couples could raise two children of one sex, three in all. Tapirapé culture banned parents from raising more, because additional mouths would siphon resources needed by other families. The Tapirapé considered it selfish and immoral to try to keep a surplus baby. The death of the infant, who was not defined as human, was considered morally necessary for other members of the group to survive.

Among the world's cultures, infanticide may be overt or covert. When there is another small child or many children in the family, if a baby is not killed at birth, it is often neglected until it dies. This is covert infanticide. If the baby survives, the mother may change her strategy and begin to invest more in its care, particularly if it shows culturally valued characteristics (Scheper-Hughes 1987).

Most cultures that practice overt infanticide justify it by excluding newborn babies from their definition of human life. They do not consider baby killing to be murder. When does humanity begin? In the United States, the question was answered judicially in 1973. In its *Roe v. Wade* decision, the U.S. Supreme Court divided the genesis of human life into three parts. During the first trimester of pregnancy, a woman may seek abortion on demand. In the second trimester, abortions may be obtained in specified circumstances. During the third trimester, abortions are normally prohibited because the fetus may be able to survive independently. That judicial decision suggested that human life begins with the third trimester.

The ancestors of the Betsileo of Madagascar, whom I studied in 1966–1967, practiced occasional infanticide. Their culture did not define it as murder, because in the Betsileo view it takes several years for a child to become fully human. Parental and social investment gradually increases as the child survives and matures.

Even today, although infanticide has ended, the Betsileo do not define a baby as fully human. When a baby is born, an astrologer calculates its lifetime horoscope. Formerly, when the horoscope was unlucky or seemed to threaten the parents or the group, the infant could be subjected to a death ordeal. It was placed at the entrance to the cattle corral, where it was likely to be trampled by livestock returning in the evening. If it survived, it was assumed to have positive qualities that offset its apparent negative destiny.

Although infanticide has ended, the process by which a Betsileo child grows into a human being (the acquisition of personhood) is still gradual. During the first two years of its life, people call the baby such derogatory names as "little dog," "slave," and "pile of feces." By devaluing the child in this way, the Betsileo think they are increasing its chances for survival. They are trying to divert ancestral spirits who might want to seize the child for the spirit world. The American anthropologist, whom a different culture has trained to say, "Oh, how cute," must repress the urge to compliment a baby and produce an insult instead. If a Betsileo baby dies during its first two years, it is buried in the rice fields. Until adolescence, it can be buried in the children's tomb. Only in adolescence does it acquire full personhood and the right to a place in the ancestral tomb, which has tremendous cultural significance in Betsileo culture.

If disorder is not to reign in such larger-scale cultivating societies, political leaders must arbitrate disputes. Large villages have more effective heads than the Yanomami have. The specific activities and manner of selection of the head (usually a man) vary, but the task of regulator is demanding. Heads may direct military actions or hunting expeditions. They may reallocate land if, because of different rates of population increase, some descent groups have grown too big for their estates while others are still too small to make full use of their own.

In smaller-scale societies a person's position depends on age, gender, and personality traits. When societies have descent groups, however, another basis for status develops—descent-group leadership. In villages with multiple descent groups, each descent group has a head. All the heads together may form a council of advisers or elders to work with the village head. In cooperation, they make up the local power structure. The council backs the village head's authority and ensures that decisions are carried out by the descent groups the members represent.

The village head must obtain council support for decisions applying to the entire village. Sometimes, however, it is difficult to reach agreement, since decisions that are good for the community at large may harm the interests of a particular descent group. Decisions usually are not enforced through physical means. If the head of one descent group refuses to cooperate, persuasion and public opinion are used. If people refuse to follow the advice of their elders, they may be asked to leave the village. However, in tribes, as in bands, community opinion and persuasion are usually sufficient.

Despite their enlarged powers, the descent-group leaders and the village head must still be generous. Their wealth and life styles are not noticeably superior to those of their fellow villagers. They are only part-time political specialists. They are also subsistence farmers. If they control more land and larger and more productive households, they must give more feasts and support more dependents.

The manner of choosing the village head varies from one tribal society to another. Sometimes the headship rotates among descent groups. In other cultures the office is confined to one descent group, perhaps the largest, but the incumbent re-

lies on the support and approval of representatives of the others. Finally, the choice of the village head may be associated with religion. Heads may be chosen because of supernatural powers. Their abilities may be a result of training, or people may believe they are inherited or come from divine revelation.

The "Big Man"

In many areas of the South Pacific, particularly the Melanesian Islands and Papua–New Guinea, native cultures have a kind of political leader that we call the **big man.** The big man (almost always a male) is an elaborate version of the village head, but there is one very significant difference. The

The "big man" is an important regulator of regional events. He persuades people to organize feasts, which distribute pork and wealth. Shown here is such a regional event, drawing on several villages, in Papua–New Guinea. Big men owe their status to their individual personalities rather than to inherited wealth or position.

village head's leadership is within one village; the big man has supporters in several villages. He is therefore a more effective (but still limited) regulator of *regional* political organization. Here we see the trend toward expansion in the scale of sociopolitical regulation—from village to region.

The Kapauku Papuans live in Irian Jaya, Indonesia (which is on the island of New Guinea). Anthropologist Leopold Pospisil (1963) studied the Kapauku (45,000 people), who grow crops (with the sweet potato as their staple) and raise pigs. Their economy is too complex to be described as simple horticulture. Beyond the household, the only political figure among the Kapauku is the big man, known as a *tonowi*. A *tonowi* achieves his status through hard work, amassing wealth in the form of pigs and other native riches. Characteristics that can distinguish a big man from his fellows include wealth, generosity, eloquence, physical fitness, bravery, and supernatural powers. Notice that big men are what they are because they have certain personalities, not because they have inherited their wealth or position.

Any man who is determined enough can become a big man, because people create their own wealth through hard work and good judgment. Wealth depends on successful pig breeding and trading. As a man's pig herd and prestige grow, he attracts supporters. He sponsors ceremonial pig feasts in which pigs are slaughtered and their meat is distributed to guests.

The big man has some advantages that the Yanomami village headman lacks. His wealth exceeds that of his fellows. His primary supporters, in recognition of past favors and anticipation of future rewards, recognize him as a leader and accept his decisions as binding. He is an important regulator of regional events in Kapauku life. He helps determine the dates for feasts and markets. He persuades people to sponsor feasts, which distribute pork and wealth. He regulates intervillage contacts by sponsoring dance expeditions. He initiates economic projects that require the cooperation of a regional community.

The Kapauku big man again exemplifies a generalization about leadership in tribal societies: If people achieve wealth and widespread respect and support, they must be generous. The big man works hard not to hoard wealth but to be able to *give away* the fruits of his labor, to convert wealth

into prestige and gratitude. If a big man is stingy, he loses his supporters, and his reputation plummets. The Kapauku take even more extreme measures against big men who hoard. Selfish and greedy rich men may be murdered by their fellows.

Political figures such as the big man emerge as regulators both of demographic growth and of economic complexity. Kapauku cultivation uses varied techniques for specific kinds of land. Labor-intensive cultivation in valleys involves mutual aid in turning the soil before planting. The digging of long drainage ditches is even more complex. Kapauku plant cultivation supports a larger and denser population than does the simpler horticulture of the Yanomami. Kapauku society could not survive in its present form without collective cultivation and political regulation of the more complex economic tasks.

Segmentary Lineage Organization

The big man is a *temporary* regional regulator. Big men can mobilize supporters in several villages to pool produce and labor on specific occasions. Another temporary form of regional political organization in tribal society is **segmentary lineage organization (SLO).** This means that the descent-group structure (usually patrilineal) has several levels—nested segments—that are like dolls nesting inside other dolls or boxes placed within boxes (Figure 7.4). The largest segments are maximal lineages, segments of which are known as major lineages. Major lineages are divided up into minor lineages. Minor lineages in turn are segmented into minimal lineages, whose common ancestor lived fairly recently—no more than four generations ago. The larger segments have spread throughout a region, but members of the minimal lineage occupy the same village. New minimal lineages develop when people move away and establish new settlements. Over time, minimal lineages grow into minor ones, minor into major ones, and major into maximal ones.

Segmentary lineage organization exists in broad outline in many cultures, such as the traditional societies of North Africa and the Middle East, including prestate Arabs and biblical Jews. However, the classic examples of SLO are two African groups, the Tiv of Nigeria and the Nuer of the

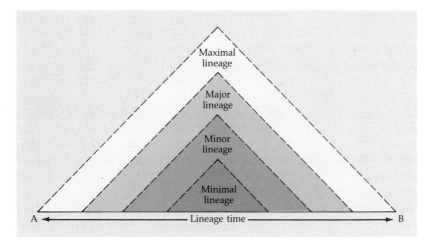

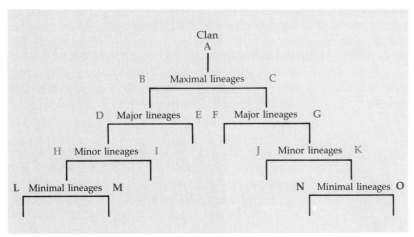

Figure 7.4 *Two views of segmentary lineage organization. (Reprinted by permission from E. E. Evans-Pritchard,* The Nuer: A Description of the Modes of Livelihood and Political Institutions of a Nilotic People *[Oxford: Clarendon Press, 1940].)*

(top) *Minimal lineages nest within minor lineages, which nest within major lineages, which nest within maximal lineages, which may in turn belong to a clan, as in bottom figure. Common ancestry is most recent in the minimal lineage.*

(bottom) *Clan A is segmented into* maximal lineages *B and C. These have* divided into major lineages *D, E, F, and G. At the next level down,* minor lineages *H, I, J, and K are segments of major lineages D and G. L, M, N, and O are* minimal lineages *which are segments of H and K. For simplification, the minor lineages of E and F and the minimal lineages of I and J aren't shown.*

Sudan (Sahlins 1961). Segmentary lineage structure organizes more than 1 million Tiv, who believe that they all share the same remote ancestor, a man named Tiv who settled in their homeland many generations ago. They trace the line of descent leading from Tiv to the present, listing his male descendants in each generation.

Although the Nuer cannot demonstrate patrilineal descent that far back, they believe that they have a common ancestry separate from that of their neighbors. One of several **Nilotic** populations (populations that inhabit the Upper Nile region of eastern Africa), the Nuer (Evans-Pritchard 1940), numbering some 200,000, live in the Sudan. Cattle pastoralism is fundamental to their mixed economy, which also includes horticulture. The Nuer have many institutions that are typical of tribal societies, including patrilineal descent groups arranged into a segmentary structure.

Their political organization is based on descent rules and genealogical reckoning.

Brothers are very close in segmentary societies, especially when the father is alive. He manages their joint property and stops them from quarreling too much. He also arranges their marriages. When he dies, the brothers usually keep on living in the same village, but one may take his share of the herds and start a settlement of his own. However, his brothers are still his closest allies. He will live as close as he can to them. Even if the brothers all stay in the same village, some of the grandchildren will move away in search of new pastures. However, each will try to remain as close to the home village as possible, settling nearest his brothers and nearer to his first cousins than to more distant relatives.

With SLO, the basic principle of solidarity is that the closer the descent-group relationship, the greater the mutual support. The more distant the shared ancestor, the greater the potential for hostility. This extends right up the genealogy; maximal lineages are more likely to fight each other than are major lineages.

Segmentary lineage organization seems to have been advantageous for the Tiv and the Nuer, allowing them to expand at their neighbors' expense. This sociopolitical organization confers a feeling of tribal identity. It provides an orderly way to mobilize temporarily against other societies. When the need arises, the Nuer or the Tiv can easily present a common front against outsiders—people who claim different genealogical and ethnic identity (Sahlins 1961).

Segmentary descent also regulates disputes and their resolution. If a fight breaks out between men who share a living patrilineal ancestor, he intervenes to settle it. As head of the minimal descent

A leopard-skin man, mediator among the Nuer—tribal cattle herders and horticulturalists of the Sudan. The Nuer mediator has recourse only to supernatural sanctions when arbitrating descent-group feuds in this segmentary society.

group that includes the disputants, he backs his authority with the threat of banishment. However, when there is no common living ancestor, a blood feud may develop.

Nuer disputes do not arise over land, which a person acquires as a member of a lineage. As a member of a minimal descent group, one has a right to its estate. A frequent cause of quarrels is adultery, and if a person injures or kills someone, a feud may develop. Conflicts also arise over divorce.

There is an alternative to a blood feud. The disputants may consult the leopard-skin man, so called because he customarily wears a leopard skin over his shoulders. Leopard-skin men conduct rituals, but their most important role is to mediate disputes. For instance, elders may ask a leopard-skin man to persuade a murder victim's kin to accept a certain number of cattle in recompense. While the mediator attempts to arrange a peaceful settlement, the murderer may take refuge in the leopard-skin man's village, which offers sanctuary until the mediator resolves the dispute or withdraws.

The leopard-skin man relies on persuasion and avoids blaming either side. He cannot enforce his decisions, but in theory he can use the threat of supernatural punishment. If one of the disputing groups is adamant, he may, in disgust, threaten to curse it. If, after seeking mediation, the disputants refuse to agree, the leopard-skin man may withdraw.

Negotiations involve the disputants, their elders, and other close kin. There is full and free discussion before a settlement is reached. The disputants may gradually come to accept the collective opinion of the mediator and the elders. However, although the peace-making abilities of the leopard-skin man are greater than anything found among the Yanomami and Eskimos, blood feuds still exist among the stateless Nuer.

With SLO, no one has a constant group of allies. One's allies change from one dispute to the next, depending on genealogical distance. Still, common descent does permit a temporary common front, as minimal lineages unite to form minor ones. Minor lineages form majors, and major lineages come together in a maximal lineage that, in the presence of an outside threat, unites all Nuer or Tiv society through its claim of common patrilineal descent.

Some unigender groups (all male or all female) are confined to a single village. This is true of the Turkoman women's quarters in Central Asia shown here. Other unigender groups span several local groups. Only the latter, the pantribal groups, are important in regional political organization.

Arabs claim to demonstrate their segmentary descent patrilineally from the biblical Ishmael. There is an Arab adage, "I and my brother against my cousin [father's brother's son]. I, my brother, and my cousin against all other Arabs. I, my brother, my cousin, and all other Arabs against all the world" (Murphy and Kasdan 1959, p. 20). Jews believe themselves to be descended from Isaac, half-brother of Ishmael. The Jews and Arabs share a common ancestor, Abraham, the father of both Ishmael and Isaac.

Pantribal Sodalities, Associations, and Age Grades

We have seen that events initiated by big men temporarily unite people from different villages. Segmentary lineage organization permits short-term mobilization of an entire society against an outside threat. There are many other kinds of sociopolitical linkages between local groups in a region. Clans, for example, often span several villages.

Kinship and descent provide important social linkages in tribal societies. Principles other than kinship also may link local groups. In a modern nation, a labor union, national sorority or fraternity, political party, or religious denomination may provide such a non-kin-based link. In tribes, nonkin groups called associations or **sodalities** may serve the same linking function. Often sodal-

ities are based on common age or gender, with all-male sodalities more common than all-female ones.

Pantribal sodalities (those which extend across the whole tribe, spanning several villages) tend to be found in areas where two or more different cultures come into regular contact. They are especially likely to develop when there is warfare *between tribes* (as opposed to raiding between villages of the same tribe, as practiced by the Yanomami). Sodalities help organize the warfare that men wage against neighboring cultures. Since sodalities draw their members from different villages of the same tribe, they can mobilize men in many local groups for attack or retaliation against another tribe. Like SLO, pantribal sodalities have military value because they facilitate temporary regional mobilization. In particular, pantribal sodalities are common among pastoralists. One culture's sodality may organize raids to steal cattle or horses from another.

In the cross-cultural study of nonkin groups, we must distinguish between those which are confined to a single village and those which span several local groups. Only the *pantribal* groups are important in general military mobilization and regional political organization. *Localized* men's houses and clubs, limited to particular villages, are found in many horticultural societies in tropical South America, Melanesia, and Papua–New

Plains Indians were originally foragers who hunted bison (buffalo) on foot. Later they adopted a mixed economy based on hunting, gathering, and horticulture but then changed to a much more specialized economy based on hunting bison on horseback (eventually with rifles).

Guinea. These groups may organize village activities and even intervillage raiding, but their political role is like that of village councils, and their leaders are similar to village heads. The following discussion, which continues our examination of the growth in scale of regional sociopolitical organization, concerns pantribal groups.

The best examples of pantribal sodalities come from the Central Plains of North America and from tropical Africa. During the eighteenth and nineteenth centuries, native populations of the Great Plains of the United States and Canada experienced a rapid growth of pantribal sodalities. This development reflected an economic change that followed the spread of horses, which had been brought to the New World by the Spanish, to the states between the Rocky Mountains and the Mississippi River. Many Plains Indian societies changed their adaptive strategies because of the horse. At first they had been foragers who hunted bison (buffalo) on foot. Later they adopted a mixed economy based on hunting, gathering, and horticulture. Finally they changed to a much more specialized economy based on horseback hunting of bison (eventually with rifles).

As the Plains tribes were undergoing these changes, other Indians also adopted horseback hunting and moved into the Plains. Attempting to occupy the same ecological niche, groups came into conflict. A pattern of warfare developed in which the members of one tribe raided another, usually for horses. The new economy demanded that people follow the movement of the bison herds. During the winter, when the bison dispersed, a tribe fragmented into small bands and families. In the summer, as huge herds assembled on the Plains, members of the tribe reunited. They camped together for social, political, and religious activities, but mainly for communal bison hunting.

Only two activities in the new adaptive strategy demanded strong leadership: organizing and carrying out raids on enemy camps (to capture horses) and managing the summer bison hunt. All the Plains cultures developed pantribal sodalities, and leadership roles within them, to police the summer hunt. Leaders coordinated hunting efforts, making sure that people did not, say, cause a stampede with an early shot or an ill-advised action. Leaders imposed severe penalties, including seizure of a culprit's wealth, for disobedience.

Some of the Plains sodalities were **age sets** of increasing rank. Each set included all the men—from that tribe's component bands—born during a certain time span. Each set had its distinctive dance, songs, possessions, and privileges. Members of each set had to pool their wealth to buy admission to the next higher level as they moved up the age hierarchy. Most Plains societies had pantribal warrior associations whose rituals celebrated militarism. As noted previously, the leaders of these associations organized bison hunting and raiding. They also arbitrated disputes during the summer, when large numbers of people came together.

Many of the tribes that adopted this Plains strategy of adaptation had once been foragers for whom hunting and gathering had been individual or small-group affairs. They had never come together previously as a single social unit. *Age and gender were available as social principles that could quickly and efficiently forge unrelated people into pantribal groups.* Other means of creating and intensifying tribal spirit also developed, for example, the fervent Sun Dance religion, which spread rapidly among the Plains groups as a summertime ceremony. Common participation in the Sun Dance ceremonies became a powerful forger of new tribal ethnic identities.

Raiding of one tribe by another, this time for cattle rather than horses, was also common in eastern and southeastern Africa, where pantribal sodalities, including age sets, also developed. Among the pastoral Masai of Kenya, men born during the same four-year period were circumcised together and belonged to the same named group, an age set, throughout their lives. The sets moved through grades, the most important of which was the warrior grade. Members of the set who wished to enter the warrior grade were at first discouraged by its current occupants, who even-

tually vacated the warrior grade and married. Members of a set felt a strong allegiance to one another and eventually had sexual rights to each other's wives. Masai women lacked comparable set organization, but they also passed through culturally recognized age grades: initiate, married woman, and postmenopausal woman.

To understand the difference between an *age set* and an *age grade,* think of a college class, the Class of '96, for example, and its progress through the university. The age set would be the group of people constituting the Class of '96, while the first ("freshman"), sophomore, junior, and senior years would represent the age grades.

Not all cultures with age grades also have age sets. When there are no sets, men can enter or leave a particular grade individually or collectively, often by going through a predetermined ritual. The grades most commonly recognized in Africa are these:

1. Recently initiated youths
2. Warriors
3. One or more grades of mature men who play important roles in pantribal government
4. Elders, who may have special ritual responsibilities

In certain parts of West Africa and Central Africa, the pantribal sodalities are **secret societies,**

Among the pastoral Masai of Kenya, men born during the same four-year period were circumcised together and belonged to the same named group, an age set, throughout their lives. The sets moved through grades, of which the most important was the warrior grade. Two Masai age sets are shown here.

Political organization is well-developed among the Qashqai, who share their nomadic route and strategic resources with several other tribes. Here Qashqai nomads cross a river in Iran's Fars province.

made up exclusively of men or women. Like our college fraternities and sororities, these associations have secret initiation ceremonies. Among the Mende of Sierra Leone, men's and women's secret societies are very influential. The men's group, the Poro, trains boys in social conduct, ethics, and religion and supervises political and economic activities. Leadership roles in the Poro often overshadow village headship and play an important part in social control, dispute management, and tribal political regulation. Like descent, then, age, gender, and ritual can link members of different local groups into a single social collectivity in tribal society and thus create a sense of ethnic identity, of belonging to the same cultural tradition.

PASTORALISTS

Tremendous demographic and sociopolitical diversity is associated with pastoralism. A comparison of pastoralists shows that as regulatory problems increase, political hierarchies become more complex. Political organization becomes less personal, more formal, and less kinship-oriented. The pastoral strategy of adaptation does not dictate any particular political organization. A range of authority structures manage regulatory problems associated with specific environments. Some pastoralists (such as the Nuer and other East African

herders) live in tribal societies. Others have powerful chiefs and live in nation-states. This reflects pastoralists' need to interact with other populations—a need that is less characteristic of the other adaptive strategies.

The scope of political authority among pastoralists expands considerably as regulatory problems increase in densely populated regions. Consider two Iranian pastoral nomadic tribes—the Basseri and the Qashqai (Salzman 1974). In the ethnographic present, these groups followed a nomadic route more than 480 kilometers (300 miles) long. Starting each year from a plateau near the coast, they took their animals to grazing land 5,400 meters (17,000 feet) above sea level. These tribes shared this route with one another and with several other ethnic groups.

Use of the same pasture land at different times was carefully scheduled. Ethnic-group movements were tightly coordinated. Expressing this schedule is *il-rah*, a concept common to all Iranian nomads. A group's *il-rah* is its customary path in time and space. It is the schedule, different for each group, of when specific areas can be used in the annual trek.

Each tribe had its own leader, known as the *khan* or *il-khan*. The Basseri *khan*, because he dealt with a smaller population, faced fewer problems in coordinating its movements than did the leaders of the Qashqai. Correspondingly, his rights, privileges, duties, and authority were weaker. Nevertheless, his authority exceeded that of any political figure we have discussed so far. However, the *khan*'s authority still came from his personal traits rather than from his office. That is, the Basseri followed a particular *khan* not because of a political position he happened to fill but because of their personal allegiance and loyalty to him as a man. The *khan* relied on the support of the heads of the descent groups into which Basseri society was divided, following a rough segmentary lineage model.

In Qashqai society, however, allegiance shifts from the person to the office. The Qashqai had multiple levels of authority and more powerful *khans*. Managing 400,000 people required a complex hierarchy. Heading it was the *il-khan*, helped by a deputy, under whom were the heads of constituent tribes, under each of whom were descent-group heads.

A case illustrates just how developed the Qashqai authority structure was. A hailstorm prevented some nomads from joining the annual migration at the appointed time. Although everyone recognized that they were not responsible for their delay, the *il-khan* assigned them less favorable grazing land, for that year only, in place of their usual pasture. The tardy herders and other Qashqai considered the judgment fair and didn't question it. Thus Qashqai authorities regulated the annual migration. They also adjudicated disputes between people, tribes, and descent groups.

These Iranian cases illustrate the fact that pastoralism is often just one among many specialized economic activities within complex nation-states and regional systems. As part of a larger whole, pastoral tribes are constantly pitted against other ethnic groups. In these nations, the state becomes a final authority, a higher-level regulator that attempts to limit conflict between ethnic groups. State organization arose not just to manage agricultural economies but also to regulate the activities of ethnic groups within expanding social and economic systems. We turn in Chapter 8 to chiefdoms and states.

SUMMARY

Anthropologists may use a sociopolitical typology of bands, tribes, chiefdoms, and states along with an economic typology based on adaptive strategy. Through these classification schemes we can compare the scale and effectiveness of social linkages and political regulation and of variations in power, authority, and legal systems cross-culturally. There are important cross-cultural contrasts in the kinds of groups that are significant, determinants of leadership, reasons for disputes, and means for resolving them.

Illustrating trends in the evolution of sociopolitical complexity, parts and subparts proliferate as villages and descent groups are added to families and bands. Functional specialization increases as political, economic, and religious figures and institutions crystallize out of less complex social organization. Regulatory systems expand from local (band or village) to regional to national (the state) levels as the population grows and political control strengthens.

Foragers usually have egalitarian societies, with bands and families as characteristic groups. Personal networks link individuals, families, and bands. There is little differential power. Band leaders are first among equals and have no means of enforcing decisions. Disputes rarely arise over strategic resources, because the resources are available to everyone. Among the Eskimos, used in this chapter to exemplify sociopolitical regulation among foragers, disputes traditionally originated in adultery or wife stealing. Aggrieved individuals might kill offenders, but this could trigger a blood feud. Although no government existed to halt blood feuds, there were certain customary means of resolving disputes.

The descent group is a basic kin group in tribal societies. Unlike families, descent groups have perpetuity—they last for generations. There are several types of descent groups. Lineages are based on demonstrated descent; clans, on stipulated descent. Patrilineal and matrilineal descent are unilineal descent rules.

Political authority increases as population size and density and the scale of regulatory problems grow. Egalitarianism diminishes as village size increases. With more people, there are more interpersonal relationships to regulate. Increasingly complex economies pose further regulatory problems.

Horticultural villages generally have heads with limited authority. The heads lead by example and persuasion and have no sure means of enforcing their decisions. The Yanomami are tribal horticulturalists. Their sociopolitical organization has more varied groups than does the foraging society. There are villages and patrilineal descent groups. Authority is more developed than it is among foragers. However, village heads, the main Yanomami political figures, have no sure power. The Yanomami also illustrate a pattern of warfare that is widespread among tribal cultivators. Warfare produces a male supremacist complex, which leads to female infanticide.

Other tribal societies have councils of elders or descent-group heads who deliberate and make decisions about village affairs. Their authority varies with the scale of regulatory problems. Big men are temporary regional regulators. Their influence extends beyond the village; they mobilize the labor of supporters in several villages. Big men have prestige, commanding the loyalty of many, but they must be generous. Sponsorship of feasts leaves them with little wealth but with a reputation for generosity, which must be maintained if the big man is to retain his influence.

Another form of temporary regional sociopolitical organization is segmentary lineage organization (SLO). The Nuer, tribal pastoralists of the Upper Nile, have SLO, as do the horticultural Tiv of Nigeria. The closest allies of the Tiv and the Nuer are their patrilineal relatives. The term *segmentary* describes the organization of descent groups into segments at different genealogical levels. Nuer belong to minimal lineages, which are residential units. Groups of these lineages constitute minor lineages. Groups of minor lineages make up major lineages. Groups of major lineages make up maximal lineages, and groups of maximal lineages make up clans. Although Nuer clans do not trace descent from the same ancestor, they believe that they share a common ethnic origin separate from that of their neighbors.

Among populations with segmentary descent organization, alliance is relative, depending on genealogical distance. Social solidarity is proportional to the closeness of patrilineal ancestry and geographical proximity. The Nuer have disputes over murder, injuries, and adultery. People support the disputant with whom they share the closest ancestor. Despite mediators, there is no sure way of halting feuds. Disputes can mobilize the entire segmentary lineage—that is, the entire society—against outsiders.

Age and gender are obvious social variables that, like SLO, can be used in regional political integration. The Plains cultures of native North America developed pantribal sodalities during the eighteenth and nineteenth centuries as they changed from generalized foraging and horticulture to horseback hunting of bison. Men's associations organized raiding parties and communal hunting and maintained order in the summer camp.

Religion can also bolster ethnic identity among local groups who assemble for the same ceremonies. This was true in the Sun Dance religion of the Plains and in the initiation ceremonies of African age sets, grades, and secret societies. Pantribal sodalities, often emphasizing the warrior grade, develop in areas where people from different cultures come into contact, particularly when there is intertribal raiding for domesticated animals.

Differential authority relationships among pastoralists reflect population size and density, interethnic relationships, and pressure on resources. Regulatory problems increase and political organization is well-developed among the Basseri and especially the Qashqai of Iran. Each group shares its nomadic route and its strategic resources with several others.

GLOSSARY

age set: Group uniting all men or women (usually men) born during a certain time span; this group controls property and often has political and military functions.

apical ancestor: In a descent group, the individual who stands at the apex, or top, of the common genealogy.

big man: Figure often found among tribal horticulturalists and pastoralists. The big man occupies no office but creates his reputation through entrepreneurship and generosity to others. Neither his wealth nor his position passes to his heirs.

blood feud: Feud between families, usually in a non-state society.

chiefdom: Form of sociopolitical organization intermediate between the tribe and the state; kin-based with differential access to resources and a permanent political structure.

clan: Unilineal descent group based on stipulated descent.

demonstrated descent: Basis of the lineage; descent-group members cite the names of their forebears in each generation from the apical ancestor through the present.

descent group: A permanent social unit whose members claim common ancestry; fundamental to tribal society.

economic typology: Classification of societies based on their adaptive strategies, e.g., foraging, horticulture, pastoralism, agriculture.

ethnographic present: Time at which a group was first studied by an ethnographer.

head, village: A local leader in a tribal society who has limited authority, leads by example and persuasion, and must be generous.

Human Relations Area Files (HRAF): Voluminous archive assembled from ethnographic reports and historical accounts of more than 300 cultures.

infanticide: Killing a baby; a form of population control in some societies.

lactation: Milk production.

law: A legal code, including trial and enforcement; characteristic of state-organized societies.

lineage: Unilineal descent group based on demonstrated descent.

local descent group: All the members of a particular descent group who live in the same place, such as the same village.

matrilineal descent: Unilineal descent rule in which people join the mother's group automatically at birth and stay members throughout life.

Nilotic populations: Populations, including the Nuer, that inhabit the Upper Nile region of eastern Africa.

pantribal sodality: A non-kin-based group that exists throughout a tribe, spanning several villages.

patrilineal descent: Unilineal descent rule in which people join the father's group automatically at birth and stay members throughout life.

personalty: Items other than strategic resources that are indelibly associated with a particular person; contrasts with property.

polity: The political order.

postpartum taboo: Prohibition of sexual relations for a culturally determined period after childbirth.

regulation: Management of variables within a system of related and interacting variables. Regulation assures that variables stay within their normal ranges, corrects deviations from the norm, and thus maintains the system's integrity.

secret societies: Sodalities, usually all-male or all-female, with secret initiation ceremonies.

segmentary lineage organization (SLO): Political organization based on descent, usually patrilineal, with multiple descent segments that form at different genealogical levels and function in different contexts.

sociopolitical typology: Classification scheme based on the scale and complexity of social organization and the effectiveness of political regulation; includes band, tribe, chiefdom, and state.

sodality: See *pantribal sodality*.

state: Sociopolitical organization based on central government and socioeconomic stratification—a division of society into classes.

stipulated descent: Basis of the clan; members merely say they descend from their apical ancestor; they don't trace the actual genealogical links between themselves and that ancestor.

totem: An animal or plant apical ancestor of a clan.

tribe: Form of sociopolitical organization usually based on horticulture or pastoralism. Socioeconomic stratification and centralized rule are absent in tribes, and there is no means of enforcing political decisions.

typology, economic: See *economic typology*.

typology, sociopolitical: See *sociopolitical typology*.

unilineal descent: Matrilineal or patrilineal descent.

STUDY QUESTIONS

1. What is the rationale for using the term *sociopolitical organization* rather than *political organization*?
2. How is the sociopolitical typology discussed in this chapter related to the previously discussed economic typology based on adaptive strategy?
3. How would you characterize the usual sociopolitical organization of foragers?
4. How does comparative sociopolitical organization illustrate the four general evolutionary trends?
5. What are the main types of descent groups, and how do they differ?
6. What is the significance of Yanomami warfare?
7. How do the political roles of headman and big man differ?
8. What is segmentary lineage organization (SLO), and how does it work politically? How is it similar to a big man system?
9. What are sodalities, and how do they work politically? How are they similar to SLO?
10. What conclusions can be drawn from this chapter about the relationship between population density and political hierarchy?
11. List the local, regional, temporary, and permanent forms of sociopolitical organization discussed in this chapter.

SUGGESTED ADDITIONAL READING

CHAGNON, N.
1983 *Yanomamo: The Fierce People,* 3rd ed. New York: Holt, Rinehart & Winston. Account of the Yanomami, including their warfare.

HARRIS, M.
1989 *Our Kind: Who We Are, Where We Came From, Where We Are Going.* New York: Harper & Row. Popular anthropology; origins of humans, culture, and major sociopolitical institutions.

LIZOT, J.
1985 *Tales of the Yanomami: Daily Life in the Venezuelan Forest.* New York: Cambridge University Press. Account of the Yanomami by a French anthropologist who has spent about two decades in the field with them.

NEWMAN, C.
1983 *Law and Economic Organization: A Comparative Study of Pre-Industrial Societies.* New York: Cambridge University Press. Based on data from sixty societies; synthesizes the economic underpinnings of variation in legal systems.

ROBERTS, S.
1979 *Order and Dispute: An Introduction to Legal Anthropology.* New York: Penguin Books. Social control in Africa and New Guinea.

CHAPTER 8

CHIEFDOMS AND NONINDUSTRIAL STATES

aving looked at bands and tribes, we turn to more complex forms of sociopolitical organization—chiefdoms and states. The first states (or *civilizations*, a near synonym) emerged in the Old World about 5,500 years ago. The first chiefdoms developed perhaps a thousand years earlier, but few survive today. The chiefdom was a transitional form of sociopolitical organization that emerged during the evolution of tribes into states. State formation began in Mesopotamia (currently Iran and Iraq) and then occurred in Egypt, the Indus Valley of Pakistan and India, and northern China. A few thousand years later states also arose in two parts of the Western Hemisphere—Mesoamerica (Mexico, Guatemala, Belize) and the central Andes (Peru and Bolivia). Early states are known as **archaic,** or nonindustrial, states, in contrast to modern industrial nation-states. Robert Carneiro defines the state as

an autonomous political unit encompassing many communities within its territory, having a centralized government with the power to collect taxes, draft men for work or war, and decree and enforce laws (Carneiro 1970, p. 733).

The chiefdom and the state, like many categories used by social scientists, are **ideal types.** That is, they are labels that make social contrasts seem more extreme than they really are. In reality there is a continuum from tribe to chiefdom to state (Table 8.1). Some societies have many attributes of chiefdoms but retain tribal features. Some advanced chiefdoms have many attributes of archaic states and thus are difficult to assign to either cate-

gory. We see this when our sample of societies in time and space is large enough. Recognizing this "continuous change" (Johnson and Earle 1987), some anthropologists speak of "complex chiefdoms" (Earle 1987).

POLITICAL AND ECONOMIC SYSTEMS IN CHIEFDOMS

As we shall see later in this chapter (for Peru and Buganda), archaic state formation has often gone through a chiefdom phase. However, state formation remained incomplete and only chiefdoms emerged in several areas, including the circum-Caribbean (e.g., Caribbean islands, Panama, Colombia), lowland Amazonia, what is now the southeastern United States, and Polynesia. Chiefdoms created the megalithic cultures of Europe, such as the one that built Stonehenge. Indeed, between the emergence and spread of food production and the expansion of the Roman empire, much of Europe was organized at the chiefdom level, to which it reverted after the fall of Rome. The foundations of historic Europe (and thus of the modern world system) emerged as some of those chiefdoms developed into states during the Dark Ages (Johnson and Earle 1987).

Much of our ethnographic knowledge about chiefdoms comes from Polynesia, where they were common at the time of European exploration. In chiefdoms, social relations are regulated solely by kinship, marriage, descent, age, generation, and gender—just as they are in bands and tribes. This

Table 8.1 *Correlates of sociopolitical types*

Sociopolitical Type	Adaptive Strategy	Ranking/Stratification	Kin/Nonkin Basis	Political Structure
Band	Foraging	Egalitarian/gender	Kinship/marriage	Rudimentary
Tribe	Horticulture/pastoralism	Prestige/gender	Kinship/marriage/descent	Temporary Regional
Chiefdom	Intensive cultivation	Differential access/ranked	Kinship/descent/seniority	Permanent Regional
State				
Archaic	Agriculture	Differential access/ stratification	Territorial/government	Permanent Regional
Industrial	Industrialism	Class system	Territorial/government	Permanent Regional

is a fundamental difference between chiefdoms and states. States bring nonrelatives together and oblige them all to pledge allegiance to a government.

Unlike bands and tribes, chiefdoms are characterized by *permanent political regulation* of the territory they administer, which includes thousands of people living in many villages and/or hamlets. Regulation is carried out by the chief and his or her assistants, who occupy political offices. An **office** is a permanent position which must be refilled when it is vacated by death or retirement. Because offices are systematically refilled, the structure of a chiefdom endures across the generations, ensuring permanent political regulation.

In the Polynesian chiefdoms, the chiefs were full-time political specialists in charge of regulating production, distribution, and consumption. Polynesian chiefs relied on religion to buttress their authority. They regulated production by commanding or prohibiting (using religious taboos) the cultivation of certain lands and crops. Chiefs also regulated distribution and consumption. At certain seasons—often on a ritualized occasion such as a first-fruit ceremony—people would offer part of their harvest to the chief through his or her representatives. Products moved up the hierarchy, eventually reaching the chief. Conversely, illustrating obligatory sharing with kin, chiefs sponsored feasts at which they gave back much of what they had received.

Such a flow of resources to and then from a central office is known as *chiefly redistribution*. Redistribution offers economic advantages. If different areas specialized in particular crops, goods, or services, chiefly redistribution made those products available to the whole society. Chiefly redistribution also played a role in risk management. It stimulated production beyond the immediate subsistence level and provided a central storehouse for goods that might become scarce at times of famine. Chiefdoms and archaic states had similar economies, often based on intensive cultivation, and both administered systems of regional trade or exchange. (Earle [1987] reviews the economic foundations of chiefdoms.) The more limited scale of political and economic regulation associated with chiefdoms tended to be short-lived, developing rapidly into a central government, one of the defining features of the state.

Chiefdoms were common in Polynesia at the time of European exploration. Some "complex" chiefdoms, such as ancient Hawaii, had many attributes of archaic states. Monument building begins in chiefdoms, where "ceremonies of place" are associated with the creation of a "sacred landscape" through temples and sculptures, such as the Hawaiian statues shown here.

SOCIAL STATUS IN CHIEFDOMS

Social status in chiefdoms was based on seniority of descent. Because rank, power, prestige, and resources came through kinship and descent, Polynesian chiefs kept extremely long genealogies. Some chiefs (without writing) managed to trace their ancestry back fifty generations. All the people in the chiefdom were thought to be related to each other. Presumably, all were descended from a group of founding ancestors.

The chief (usually a man) had to demonstrate seniority in descent. Degrees of seniority were calculated so intricately on some islands that there

Social status in chiefdoms is based on seniority of descent. In the modern world system, seniority may still confer prestige, but the differences in wealth and power between chiefs and their juniors are often minor. Shown here is a contemporary chief (center) in the Marquesas Islands, Polynesia.

were as many ranks as people. For example, the third son would rank below the second, who in turn would rank below the first. The children of an eldest brother, however, would all rank above the children of the next brother, whose children would in turn outrank those of younger brothers. However, even the lowest-ranking person in a chiefdom was still the chief's relative. In such a kin-based context, everyone, even a chief, had to share with his or her relatives.

Because everyone had a slightly different status, it was difficult to draw a line between elites and common people. Although other chiefdoms calculated seniority differently and had shorter genealogies than did those in Polynesia, the concern for genealogy and seniority and the absence of sharp gaps between elites and commoners are features of all chiefdoms.

STATUS SYSTEMS IN CHIEFDOMS AND STATES

The status systems of chiefdoms and states are similar in that both are based on **differential access** to resources. This means that some men and women had privileged access to power, prestige, and wealth. They controlled strategic resources such as land, water, and other means of production. Earle characterizes chiefs as "an incipient aristocracy with advantages in wealth and lifestyle"

(1987, p. 290). Nevertheless, differential access in chiefdoms was still very much tied to kinship. The people with privileged access were generally chiefs and their nearest relatives and assistants.

Compared with chiefdoms, archaic states drew a much firmer line between elites and masses, distinguishing at least between nobles and commoners. Kinship ties did not extend from the nobles to the commoners because of *stratum endogamy*—marriage within one's own group. Commoners married commoners; elites married elites. Such a division of society into socioeconomic strata contrasts strongly with the status systems of bands and tribes, which are based on prestige, not resources. The prestige differentials that do exist in bands reflect special qualities, talents, and abilities. Good hunters get respect from their fellows as long as they are generous. So does a skilled curer, dancer, storyteller—or anyone else with a talent or skill that others appreciate.

In tribes, some prestige goes to descent-group leaders, to village heads, and especially to the big man, a regional figure who commands the loyalty and labor of others. However, all these figures must be generous. If they accumulate more resources—i.e., property or food—than others in the village, they must share them with the others. Since strategic resources are available to everyone, social classes based on the possession of unequal amounts of resources can never exist.

In many tribes, particularly those with patri-

lineal descent, men have much greater prestige and power than women do. The gender contrast in rights diminishes in chiefdoms, where prestige and access to resources are based on seniority of descent, so that some women are senior to some men. Unlike big men, chiefs are exempt from ordinary work and have rights and privileges that are unavailable to the masses. However, like big men, they still return much of the wealth they take in.

The status system in chiefdoms, although based on differential access, differed from the status system in states because the privileged few were always relatives and assistants of the chief. However, this type of status system didn't last very long. Chiefs would start acting like kings and try to erode the kinship basis of the chiefdom. In Madagascar they would do this by demoting their more distant relatives to commoner status and banning marriage between nobles and commoners (Kottak 1980). Such moves, *if accepted by the society,* created separate social strata—*unrelated* groups that differ in their access to wealth, prestige, and power. (A **stratum** is one of two or more groups that contrast in regard to social status and access to strategic resources. Each stratum includes people of both sexes and all ages.) The creation of separate social strata is called **stratification,** and its emergence signified the transition from chiefdom to state. *The presence and acceptance of stratification is one of the key distinguishing features of a state.*

The influential sociologist Max Weber (1922) defined three related dimensions of social stratification: (1) Economic status, or **wealth,** encompasses all a person's material assets, including income, land, and other types of property (Schaefer 1989). (2) **Power,** the ability to exercise one's will over others—to do what one wants—is the basis of political status. (3) **Prestige**—the basis of social status—refers to esteem, respect, or approval for acts, deeds, or qualities considered exemplary. Prestige, or "cultural capital" (Bourdieu 1984), provides people with a sense of worth and respect, which they may often convert into economic advantage (Table 8.2).

Table 8.2 *Max Weber's three dimensions of stratification*

wealth	→	economic status
power	→	political status
prestige	→	social status

These Weberian dimensions of stratification are present to varying degrees in chiefdoms. However, chiefdoms lack the sharp division into classes that characterizes states. Wealth, power, and prestige in chiefdoms are all tied to kinship factors.

Historically, the emergence of differential access, the chiefdom, stratification, and the state was a gradual process. In some societies, evolution was slowed by temporary collapses of developing political machinery, as happened in Europe after the Roman collapse. Because of this, anthropologists must sometimes decide arbitrarily whether a particular society with political regulation and differential access should be called a chiefdom or a state.

In archaic states—for the first time in human evolution—there were contrasts in wealth, power, and prestige between entire groups (social strata) of men and women. Each stratum included people of both sexes and all ages. The **superordinate** (the higher or elite) stratum had privileged access to wealth, power, and other valued resources. Access to resources by members of the **subordinate** (lower or underprivileged) stratum was limited by the privileged group.

Socioeconomic stratification continues as a defining feature of all states, archaic or industrial. The elites control a significant part of the means of production, e.g., land, herds, water, capital, farms, or factories. Those born at the bottom of the hierarchy have reduced chances of social mobility. Because of elite ownership rights, ordinary people lack free access to resources. Only in states do the elites get to keep their differential wealth. Unlike big men and chiefs, they don't have to give it back to the people whose labor has built and increased it.

STATUS AND ROLE

Before discussing the state, we pause to note that **status** has two meanings in social science. One (as in Weber's discussion of social status) is close to the definition of *prestige* and refers to social ranking. Thus, someone (such as a chief) may have more (or higher) social status than someone else does. The other meaning is neutral. Here a status is simply a position in a social structure—any position that determines where someone fits within society (Light, Keller, and Calhoun 1989). Such social statuses include mother, father, professor, student, factory worker, Democrat, shoe salesperson, labor leader, and—in our own society—thousands of others (Figure 8.1).

People always occupy multiple statuses (e.g., Hispanic, Catholic, infant, sister). Among the statuses we occupy, particular ones dominate in particular settings, such as son or daughter at home and student in the classroom. Moving through life, we leave some statuses behind (e.g., high school senior) and enter others (e.g., first-year college student). When we vacate one status or die, we leave those positions, and others fill them. The occupant changes while the status endures as part of the social structure.

Some statuses are **ascribed:** people have little or no choice about occupying them. Gender is normally an ascribed status, although some cultures permit gender changes. Age is another ascribed status; people have no choice about getting older. In unilineal societies, descent-group membership is ascribed. People automatically belong to the father's descent group in a patrilineal society and to the mother's in a matrilineal one. In chiefdoms and states, many contrasts in wealth, prestige, and power are ascribed. In chiefdoms they are ascribed

Figure 8.1 *Social statuses. The person in this figure— "ego," or "I,"—occupies many social statuses. The green circles indicate ascribed status; the orange circles represent achieved statuses.*

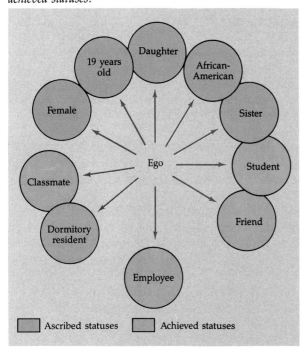

by genealogy and seniority. In states some people are born into rich or noble families while others are born into poverty. In archaic states the paramount ruling status known as king or queen was usually ascribed, as was the status of chief in chiefdoms.

Achieved statuses, in contrast, aren't automatic but come through traits, talents, actions, efforts, activities, and accomplishments. Achieved statuses in bands include healer, dancer, and storyteller. In tribes, people may become leaders through work, generosity, charisma, and particular skills. Achieved statuses in tribes include polygynist, warrior, magician, trading partner, and trance specialist, among hundreds of others. *The number of social statuses increases with (and is a measure of) social complexity.* More complex societies offer more choices; the number of achieved statuses in particular increases. In the modern world we choose to marry or not and have children or not, so that even our statuses as spouse or parent are achieved. People in traditional societies have less choice about marriage and fertility.

The distinction between ascribed status and achieved status isn't always clear-cut. For example, although we choose our colleges (from those to which we apply and are accepted) and our jobs (from those we seek out and are offered), family background influences our success. Despite the North American value of individual achievement (including the possibility of rising from "rags to riches"), it is easier for offspring of the middle and upper classes to succeed than it is for people born in poverty.

Each status has an associated **role**—a set of expected (culturally "proper") behaviors, attitudes, rights, and obligations. Through enculturation, we come to expect certain behavior to characterize certain statuses. Cultures develop images of how a "good" or "proper" boss, teacher, mother, or coach acts. For example, "fatherly" behavior might be defined as affectionate, nurturing, and supportive. In some societies, the status of son-in-law entails strict avoidance of the mother-in-law—to the point of leaping off the road if she approaches. In other cultures, the son-in-law role is to treat the mother-in-law like his own mother (or, in still other cultures, like his wife). Cultures may define a girl's younger brother as a pal, a pest, or some-

Elizabeth II, Queen (left), and Margaret Thatcher, former Prime Minister (right), of Great Britain. Elizabeth gained office through ascription—a formal rule of succession—whereas Thatcher achieved her status by her election as a member of Parliament and as head of Britain's Conservative party. While Elizabeth will remain ruler until her death or abdication, prime ministers come and go, depending on which party has a majority in Parliament. However, both women belong to the elite—the rich, famous, privileged, and powerful—and both occupy offices that survive even though their occupants change.

one who is socially distant and to be avoided.

Anthropologist Ralph Linton (1936) drew a distinction between status and role by saying that people *occupy* a status but *play* a role. A status is a position in the social structure, but a role involves thought and action. People differ in how well they play the roles that go with the various statuses they occupy. There are disruptive students, sinful ministers, and lousy bosses. A man may be a skilled craftsman but an inattentive father.

STATES

Although multiple statuses and roles exist in all societies, they are more numerous, complex, and specialized in states than they are in bands, tribes, and chiefdoms. Illustrating general evolutionary trends, certain statuses, systems, and subsystems

with specialized functions are found in all states. They include the following:

1. *Population control:* fixing of boundaries, establishment of citizenship categories, and the taking of a census
2. *Judiciary:* laws, legal procedure, and judges
3. *Enforcement:* permanent military and police forces
4. *Fiscal:* taxation

In archaic states, these subsystems were integrated by a ruling system or government composed of civil, military, and religious officials (Fried 1960).

Population Control

To know whom they govern, all states conduct censuses. States demarcate boundaries that sepa-

RIDDLES OF ANCIENT CIVILIZATIONS

Anthropologist Marvin Harris (1978) uses a theoretical approach called *cultural materialism* to answer questions raised by the rise and fall of archaic states. Cultural materialism begins with the assumption that cultures are influenced by material conditions: physical resources, plants and animals, relationships (such as trade and war) with other groups, and systems of production and reproduction. According to Harris, history's prime movers have been continually repeated economic cycles. Population pressure promotes intensification of production; eventually this depletes the environment; renewed population pressure then leads to new systems of production.

For example, Harris has cast a materialist eye on the Maya of Mexico's Yucatán peninsula and adjacent Guatemala. For years archeologists have wondered how, between A.D. 300 and 900, the Maya supported state organization with an economy seemingly based only on nonintensive slash-and-burn cultivation. How did they feed dense urban populations? How did they build and maintain impressive ceremonial centers? For some scholars, the mysterious Maya seem to contradict the tendency for archaic states to have dense populations and a sedentary agricultural economy.

However, Harris showed that the Mayas' economy was more productive than was once thought. For instance, high-yield breadnut trees could have provided 80 percent of the calories in their diet. Aerial photographs taken during the rainy season revealed a previously undetected pattern of canals. This suggests that the Maya, like most ancient state builders, did some irrigated farming.

Nonetheless, the Maya material base really was poorer than that of other states. It is not surprising, then, that Maya civilization collapsed around A.D. 900 and that nothing comparable reappeared in the depleted area, where slash-and-burn cultivation now supports a sparse population. In contrast to the Mexican highlands, where successive cycles of agricultural intensification supported the rise, fall, and reappearance of state organization (Teotihuacan, Toltecs, and Aztecs), the Maya state rose just once and fell forever.

Harris's views have been criticized as mechanical and simple-minded, but they are almost always intriguing. One of the most controversial is his interpretation of Aztec religion (Harner 1977). When the emperor Montezuma II showed Cortés and his men around Tenochtitlan, the Aztec capital, the Spaniards were struck not just by the city's bustling population and imposing architecture but by bloodstains on the pyramids. Atop those imposing structures, priests regularly cut out the hearts of prisoners of war to slake the blood cravings of the Aztec gods.

Why were these gods so bloodthirsty, and why did the Aztecs sacrifice so many people? It isn't enough, says Harris, to explain Aztec sacrifice in terms of religious motives. We need to know why Aztec religion differed from other state religions and to explain a key difference: Aztec victims weren't just sacrificed—they were cannibalized.

Many Old World state religions sacrificed animals to the gods and distributed their meat to humans, but all those societies tabooed cannibalism. In Aztec sacrifice, "all edible parts were used in a manner strictly comparable to the consumption of the flesh of domesticated animals" (Harris 1978 p. 164). The ultimate fate of many victims was to be stewed with tomatoes and chili peppers in Tenochtitlan's residential compounds.

According to Harris, ancient Mexico's distinctive material conditions provide the solution to the puzzle. Ecological conditions in the Valley of Mexico made it possible to support population growth by intensifying agriculture. However, in contrast to all Old World civilizations—and to Peru's Incas, who feasted on sacrificial llamas and guinea pigs rather than people—ancient Mexico lacked domesticated animals that could be used to increase the food supply. Old World societies and the Incas had sheep, goats, cattle, camels, or llama; the Aztecs had only dogs and turkeys.

It was no accident that the Aztecs, faced with these material conditions, presided over the only major ancient state that didn't ban cannibalism. Harris believes that the Aztecs developed a taste for human flesh because their diet was meat-poor. Dense populations, especially urban ones, are subject to food crises. Disastrous famines occasionally plagued the Aztecs, and their legends recall times when ancestors had to eat snakes, vermin (Coe 1962), and algae skimmed from the lake. Aztec sacrifice thus had both a religious purpose and a material result—distribution of animal protein to the urban population. According to Harris, lack of domesticated animals and the dietary needs of a dense population were the conditions responsible for Aztec sacrifice and cannibalism. For an opposing view, see the review of Harris's book by Sahlins (1978).

Unequal rights in state-organized societies persist in today's world. Under South Africa's apartheid system, blacks, whites, and Asians have had their own separate (and unequal) neighborhoods, schools, laws, and punishments. There has been both social and legal resistance to the weakening of apartheid.

rate them from other societies. Customs agents, immigration officers, navies, and coast guards patrol frontiers, regulating passage from one state to another. Even nonindustrial states have boundary-maintenance forces. In Buganda, an archaic state on the shores of Lake Victoria in Uganda, the king rewarded military officers with estates in outlying provinces. They became his guardians against foreign intrusion.

States also control population through administrative subdivision: provinces, districts, "states," counties, subcounties, and parishes. Lower-level officials manage the populations and territories of the subdivisions.

In nonstates, people work and relax with their relatives, in-laws, fictive kin, and age mates—people with whom they have a personal relationship. Such a personal social life existed throughout most of human history, but food production spelled its eventual end. After millions of years of human evolution, it took a mere 4,000 years for the population increase and regulatory problems spawned by food production to lead from tribe to chiefdom to archaic state. With state organization, kinship's pervasive role diminished. Descent groups may continue as kin groups within archaic states, but their importance in political organization declines, and their exclusive control over their members ends.

States—archaic and modern—foster geographic mobility and resettlement, severing long-standing ties between people, land, and kin. Population dis-

placements have increased in the modern world. War, famine, and job seeking across national boundaries churn up migratory currents. People in states come to identify themselves by new statuses, both ascribed and achieved, including ethnic background, place of birth or residence, occupation, party, religion, and team or club affiliation, rather than as members of a descent group or extended family.

States also manage their populations by granting different rights and obligations to (making status distinctions between) citizens and noncitizens. Distinctions among citizens are also common. Many archaic states granted different rights to nobles, commoners, and slaves. Unequal rights within state-organized societies persist in today's world, very obviously in South Africa. In recent American history, before the Emancipation Proclamation, there were different laws for slaves and free people. In European colonies, separate courts judged cases involving only natives and those which involved Europeans. In contemporary America, a military code of justice and court system continue to coexist alongside the civil judiciary.

Judiciary

States have *laws* based on precedent and legislative proclamations. Without writing, laws may be preserved in oral tradition, with justices, elders, and other specialists responsible for remembering them. Oral traditions as repositories of legal wisdom have continued in some nations with writing, such as Great Britain. Laws regulate relations between individuals and groups.

Crimes are violations of the legal code, with specified types of punishment. However, a given act, such as killing someone, may be legally defined in different ways (e.g., as manslaughter, justifiable homicide, or first-degree murder). Furthermore, even in contemporary North America, where justice is supposed to be "blind" to social distinctions, the poor are prosecuted more often and more severely than are the rich.

To handle disputes and crimes, all states have courts and judges. Precolonial African states had subcounty, county, and district courts, plus a high court formed by the king or queen and his or her advisers. Most states allow appeals to higher courts, although people are encouraged to solve problems locally.

A striking contrast between states and nonstates is intervention in family affairs. In states, aspects of parenting and marriage enter the domain of public law. Governments step in to halt blood feuds and regulate previously private disputes. States attempt to curb *internal* conflict, but they aren't always successful. About 85 percent of the world's armed conflicts since 1945 have begun within states—in efforts to overthrow a ruling regime or as disputes over tribal, religious, and ethnic minority issues. Only 15 percent have been fights across national borders (Barnaby 1985).

People in modern nations no longer fight for spouses and cattle but for political, economic, religious, and ideological reasons. Nations battle over philosophies of government—to subdue "the infidel," to "halt the spread of communism," or to undermine "capitalist imperialism." Rebellion, resistance, repression, terrorism, and warfare continue. Indeed, recent states have perpetrated some of history's bloodiest deeds.

Enforcement

All states have agents to enforce judicial decisions. Confinement requires jailers, and a death penalty calls for executioners. Agents of the state collect fines and confiscate property. These officials wield power that is much more effective than the curse of the Nuer leopard-skin man.

A major concern of government is to defend hierarchy, property, and the power of the law. The government suppresses internal disorder (with police) and guards the nation against external threats (with the military). As a relatively new form of sociopolitical organization, states have competed successfully with less complex societies throughout the world. Military organization helps states subdue neighboring nonstates, but this is not the only reason for the spread of state organization. Although states impose hardships, they also offer advantages. Most obviously, they provide protection from outsiders and preserve internal order. They curb the feuding that plagues tribes such as the Yanomami and the Nuer. By promoting internal peace, states enhance production. Their economies support massive, dense populations, which supply armies and colonists to promote expansion.

Fiscal

A financial or **fiscal** subsystem is needed in states to support rulers, nobles, officials, judges, military personnel, and thousands of other specialists. As in the chiefdom, the state intervenes in production, distribution, and consumption. The state may decree that a certain area will produce certain things or forbid certain activities in particular places. Although, like chiefdoms, states also have redistribution (through taxation), generosity and sharing are played down. A smaller proportion of what comes in flows back to the people.

In nonstates, people customarily share with relatives, but residents of states face added obligations to bureaucrats and officials. Citizens must turn over a substantial portion of what they produce to the state. Of the resources that the state collects, it reallocates part for the general good and uses another part (often larger) for the elite.

The state does not bring more freedom or leisure to the common people, who usually work harder than do the people in nonstates. They may be called on to build monumental public works. Some of these projects, such as dams and irrigation systems, may be economically necessary. However, people also build temples, palaces, and tombs for the elites.

Monument building began in chiefdoms, where "ceremonies of place" were associated with the creation of a "sacred landscape" through construc-

The state does not mean more leisure time for the common people, who may be called on to build monuments for the elite, as in this illustration of slave labor in ancient Egypt.

tions such as (stone) henges of Europe, the mounds of the southeastern United States, and the temples of Hawaii (Earle 1987). Like chiefs, state officials may use religion to buttress their authority. Archeology shows that temples abounded in early states. Even in mature states, rulers may link themselves to godhood through divine right or claim to be deities or their earthly representatives. Rulers convoke peons or slaves to build magnificent castles or tombs, cementing the ruler's place in history or status in the afterlife. Monumental architecture survives as an enduring reminder of the exalted prestige of priests and kings.

Markets and trade are usually under at least some state control, with officials overseeing distribution and exchange, standardizing weights and measures, and collecting taxes on goods passing into or through the state. States also set standards for artisans, manufacturers, and members of other professions.

Taxes support government and the ruling class, which is clearly separated from the common people in regard to activities, privileges, rights, and obligations. Elites take no part in subsistence activities. Taxes also support the many specialists—administrators, tax collectors, judges, lawmakers, generals, scholars, and priests. As the state matures, the segment of the population freed from direct concern with subsistence grows.

The elites of archaic states revel in the consumption of **sumptuary goods**—jewelry, exotic food and drink, and stylish clothing reserved for, or affordable only by, the rich. Peasants' diets suffer as they struggle to meet government demands. Commoners perish in territorial wars that have little relevance to their own needs.

THE ORIGIN OF THE STATE

Why were people willing to give up so many of the freedoms, pleasures, and personal bonds that their ancestors had enjoyed throughout human history? The answer is that people didn't choose but were *forced* to accept state organization. Because state formation may take centuries, people experiencing the process at any time rarely perceive the significance of the long-term changes. Later generations find themselves dependent on government institutions that took generations to develop.

The state develops to handle regulatory problems encountered as the population grows and/or the economy increases in scale and diversity. Anthropologists and historians have identified the causes of state formation and have reconstructed the rise of several states. Many factors always contribute to state formation, with the effects of one magnifying those of the others. Although some contributing factors appear again and again, no single one is always present. In other words, state formation has generalized rather than universal causes.

Hydraulic Systems

One suggested cause of state formation is the need to regulate **hydraulic** (water-based) agricultural economies (Wittfogel 1957). States have emerged in certain arid areas to manage systems of irrigation, drainage, and flood control. Nevertheless, hydraulic agriculture is neither a sufficient nor a necessary condition for the rise of the state. That is, many societies with irrigation never developed state structure, and many states developed without hydraulic systems.

However, hydraulic agriculture does have certain implications for state formation. Water control increases production in arid lands. Irrigated agriculture fuels population growth because of its labor demands and its ability to feed more people. This in turn leads to enlargement of the system. The expanding hydraulic system supports larger and denser concentrations of people. Interpersonal problems increase, and conflicts over access to water and irrigated land become more frequent. Political systems may arise to regulate interpersonal relations and the means of production.

Larger hydraulic works can sustain towns and cities and become essential to their subsistence. Given such urban dependence, regulators protect the economy by mobilizing crews to maintain and repair the hydraulic system. These life-and-death functions enhance the authority of state officials. Thus, growth in hydraulic systems is often, but not always, associated with state formation.

Ecological Diversity

Some anthropologists have suggested that states tend to arise in areas of ecological diversity in order to regulate the production and exchange of products between zones. What about this theory? Although ecological diversity and interzonal regulation do strengthen state organization, such diversity is neither necessary nor sufficient to cause state formation. Diversity is a matter of scale, and state formation has occurred in places without much environmental diversity—the Nile Valley, for example. Furthermore, in many areas with environmental diversity, no indigenous states developed. Finally, diversity is as much a result as a cause of state formation. As states grow, they create diversity, promoting regional and local spe-

cialization in the production, manufacture, and supply of goods and services.

Long-Distance Trade Routes

Another theory is that states develop at strategic locations in regional trade networks. These sites include points of supply or exchange, such as crossroads of caravan routes, and places (e.g., mountain passes and river narrows) situated so as to threaten or halt trade between centers. Like ecological diversity, features of regional trade can certainly contribute to state formation. Here again, however, the cause is generalized but neither necessary nor sufficient. Although long-distance trade has been important in the evolution of many states and does eventually develop in all states, it can follow rather than precede state formation. Furthermore, long-distance trade also occurs in tribal societies, such as those of Papua–New Guinea, where no states developed.

Population Growth, Warfare, and Environmental Circumscription

Anthropologist Robert Carneiro (1970) proposed a theory that incorporates three factors working together instead of a single cause of state formation. (We call a theory involving multiple factors or variables a **multivariate** theory.) Wherever and whenever *environmental circumscription* (or *resource concentration*), *increasing population*, and *warfare* exist, says Carneiro, state formation will begin. Environmental circumscription may be physical or social. Physically circumscribed environments include small islands and, in arid areas, river plains, oases, and valleys with streams. Social circumscription exists when neighboring societies block expansion, emigration, or access to resources. When strategic resources are concentrated in limited areas—even when no obstacles to migration exist—the effects are similar to those of circumscription.

Coastal Peru, one of the world's most arid areas, illustrates the interaction of environmental circumscription, warfare, and population increase. Early cultivation was limited to valleys with springs. Each valley was circumscribed by the Andes mountains to the east, the Pacific Ocean to the west, and desert to the north and south. The transition from foraging to food production triggered population increase in these valleys (Figure 8.2). In each valley, villages got bigger. Colonists split off from the old villages and founded new ones. Rivalries and raiding developed between villages in the same valley. As villages proliferated and the valley population grew, a scarcity of land developed.

Population pressure and land shortages were developing in all the valleys. Because the valleys were circumscribed, when one village conquered another, the losers had to submit to the winners—they had nowhere else to go. Conquered villagers could keep their land only if they agreed to pay tribute to their conquerors. To do this, they had to intensify production, using new techniques to produce more food. By working harder, they managed to pay tribute while meeting their subsistence needs. Villagers brought new areas under cultivation by means of irrigation and terracing.

Those early Peruvians didn't work harder because they chose to. They were *forced* to pay tribute, accept political domination, and intensify production by factors beyond their control. Once established, all these trends accelerated. Population grew, warfare intensified, and villages were eventually united in chiefdoms. The first states developed when one chiefdom in a valley conquered the others (Carneiro 1987). Eventually, different valleys began to fight, and the winners brought the losers into growing empires. States expanded from the coast to the highlands. By the sixteenth century, from their capital, Cuzco, in the high Andes, the Incas ruled one of the major empires of the tropics.

Carneiro's theory is very useful, but again, the association between population density and state organization is generalized rather than universal. States do tend to have large and dense populations (Stevenson 1968). However, population increase and warfare within a circumscribed environment were insufficient to trigger state formation in highland Papua–New Guinea. Certain valleys there are socially or physically circumscribed and have population densities similar to those of many states. Warfare was also present, but no states emerged. Again we are dealing with an important theory that explains many but not all cases of state formation.

States arose in different areas for many reasons.

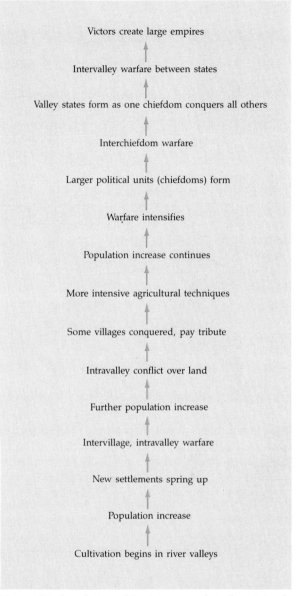

Figure 8.2 *Carneiro's multivariate approach to the origin of the state as applied to coastal Peru. In this very arid area, food production developed in narrow river valleys where water for cultivation was available (resource concentration). With cultivation, the population increased. Population pressure on land led to warfare, and some villages conquered others. Physical circumscription (an arid area) meant that the losers had no way to escape. The process accelerated as the population grew and as warfare and cultivation intensified. Chiefdoms, states, and empires eventually developed.*

By the sixteenth century, the Incas ruled one of the major empires of the tropics from their capital, Cuzco, in the high Andes. Shown here is the Sacsahuayman Inca fortress at Cuzco—a powerful defensive structure built without cement.

In each case, interacting causes (often comparable ones) magnified each other's effects. To explain any instance of state formation, we must search for the specific changes in access to resources and in regulation that fostered stratification and state machinery.

CONVERGENCE IN STATE FORMATION

One of the first anthropologists to demonstrate **convergence** (parallel development without contact or mutual influence) in state formation was Julian Steward (1949). He did this by comparing five areas: Mesopotamia, Egypt, northern China, Peru, and Mexico. These were all arid places where irrigation, flood control, and other hydraulic techniques became significant. What impressed Steward was not so much that the final product—the state—was the same but that in all five areas social, religious, and military patterns and institutions had developed similarly and in the same order. Although these developments occurred 3,000 to 4,000 years later in the New World, in both hemispheres foraging was succeeded by food production, which set off a series of changes that led eventually to the formation of states.

The process began with communities based on food production, which supported growing population density. At first, irrigation systems (necessary for food production in these arid areas) were simple. They were managed by individual cultivators, kin groups, and communities. Eventually, however, some people were allowed to withdraw from subsistence to become chiefs and managers. Differences in wealth, prestige, and power appeared as chiefdoms emerged. Craft specialists made varied goods, including sumptuary goods for the elite, marking a contrast in life style between chiefs, their nearest relatives and assistants, and the common people.

As chiefdoms evolved into early states, religion continued to bolster managerial authority. Temples and pyramids were built in new ceremonial centers. Priests emerged who combined ritual, political, and economic functions. They coordinated manufacturing, exchange, and irrigation. As states grew, militarism increased. Powerful states arose as others were conquered or collapsed. Towns multiplied, and major cities appeared. Agricultural techniques became more intensive to sustain a growing population, and a larger group engaged in nonsubsistence activities. Hydraulic systems were enlarged.

Although political authority was still buttressed by religion, stronger rule with a more secular basis developed, along with growing militarism. Conflicts grew more frequent as states collided. States conquered others and became empires. Local, regional, and long-distance trade expanded with improved means of transportation. The scale of architecture continued to increase, and art and manufactured items—many destined for consumption by elites—were produced. Eventually, manufacturing became more standardized, oriented toward mass production and consumption.

Stratification also grew more complex. As an illustration of stratification in a mature archaic state, consider the Aztecs of sixteenth-century Mexico, as described in Spanish documents. Heading the Aztec state was the monarch; the last one, conquered by the Spanish, was named Montezuma. He was surrounded by an elaborate court—the palace elite. Immediately below him were princes and nobles.

Next came the commoners, internally divided into groups based on occupation and urban versus rural residence. City dwellers ranked highest among the commoners. They included warriors, merchants, and artisans such as goldsmiths, stone workers, and feather workers. The lowest of the commoners were peasants, agriculturists who lived in villages.

Below the Aztec commoners were three oppressed groups: serfs attached to estates, slaves who had been criminals or debtors, and slaves who had been prisoners of war (Sanders and Price 1968). Soldiers, merchants, and artisans paid tribute to the state in the form of military service, taxes, and manufactures, respectively. Those below them paid in produce and public labor. Aztec serfs and slaves, of course, bore heavier burdens.

ETHNOHISTORY

Archeologists have documented many cases of early state formation. Cultural anthropologists have also studied state formation through historical, ethnohistorical, and ethnographic data. For example, this has been done in Africa, where there were diverse precolonial sociopolitical types and environmental adaptations. Some of the most complex and tightly organized preindustrial states, including Buganda in the Great Lakes area of East Africa, developed in the African tropics.

Ethnohistory encompasses oral and written accounts of a culture's past by insiders and outsiders. Written historical records about precolonial

Africa are rich compared with those of the precolonial New World. Centuries of accounts by Arab, European, and Chinese merchants, travelers, explorers, and missionaries are available. Also, even when there are no written records, African states preserved detailed oral traditions, one of whose main concerns was tracing genealogies.

However, there are certain risks in using oral traditions (a culture's accounts of its own past) to reconstruct history. In any society, present realities affect memories. History is often fictionalized in various ways and for various reasons. Nevertheless, oral traditions often contain useful historical data. Reconstructions and hypotheses based on oral traditions often can be tested later by archeologists. And cross-cultural regularities known from better-documented sequences can be used to judge the probability of oral traditions. Such an approach has been used in reconstructing the evolution of the state in Buganda (Kottak 1972).

STATE FORMATION IN BUGANDA

The former kingdom of Buganda, northwest of Lake Victoria, is now a province of the nation of Uganda. When the English travelers John Speke and Richard Francis Burton, searching for the source of the Nile, visited Buganda in 1862, it was the most populous and powerful state in this area (Figure 8.3). Because rainfall was heavy and was evenly distributed throughout the year, the Ganda (people of Buganda) were able to grow many varieties of bananas and the closely related **plantains.** These crops are perennial and highly productive and have many advantages as subsistence crops.

Unlike grains, they are not harvested all at once but are picked during the year as needed. Once planted, banana and plantain trees can yield for up to forty years. Like irrigated cereals, such as wheat and barley in the ancient Middle East, Buganda's plantains and bananas were concentrated and reliable sources of calories. They could support a dense sedentary population.

In sharp contrast to irrigated agriculture, however, labor investment in bananas was very low. The low labor requirements of subsistence farming meant that women could maintain the subsistence economy while men's labor was put to work for

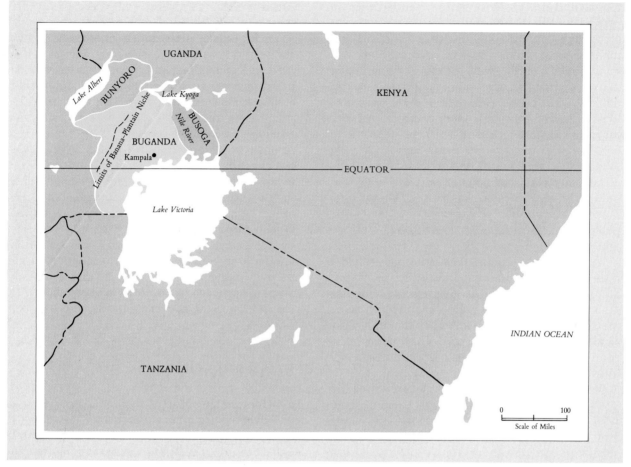

Figure 8.3 *Map of precolonial Buganda. Borders fluctuated but increased through militarism as Buganda extended its influence north, east, and west.*

higher-level authorities. Men were withdrawn from cultivation to take part in public works, the army, and manufacturing.

Nutrition required that bananas and plantains be supplemented with other foods, particularly protein sources. This promoted a varied economy and interregional trade, which influenced state formation. The Ganda hunted, fished, and kept sheep, goats, cattle, poultry, and buffalo. Near Lake Victoria, fish were an important part of the diet. (Regulation of the inland trade of fish and other lake products was one way in which the government controlled areas distant from the capital.)

All states promote economic specialization, so that some people withdraw from subsistence and work as artisans and administrators, among other specialized jobs. Buganda had an even more obvious specialization based on gender. It is very un-

usual in states with cultivation-based economies for men to be freed totally from subsistence activities. The low labor requirements of plantains and bananas permitted this in Buganda.

Men were able to be full-time soldiers. They could specialize in crafts or trade. They could build canoes for the navy. They could work on the roads, bridges, and public works that extended the transportation network and facilitated Buganda's military advance at its neighbors' expense.

By the nineteenth century, Buganda had a four-level administrative and **settlement hierarchy** (a ranked series of communities differing in size, function, and type of building). Such a four-level hierarchy has been used (Wright and Johnson 1975) to characterize state (versus chiefdom) organization.

1. The lowest level (and smallest settlement) was

the peasant village, actually a string of households along a ridge.

2. Villages were administered by subchiefs, whose settlements were somewhat larger.
3. Chiefs lived in still larger villages, some with over 1,000 people, where their estates supported a large retinue consisting of several wives, musicians, artisans, bodyguards, and other dependents.
4. The highest level was the capital, which had a population in 1862 estimated at 77,000—perhaps the largest city in interior Africa then.

How did Buganda develop, and what can this process tell us about state formation in general? As in other cases of state formation, Buganda's rise can ultimately be traced to the emergence of food production. Plant cultivation, accompanied by iron tools, spread rapidly in eastern Africa during the first centuries A.D. The emergence of plantain and banana cultivation near the lakes was part of this change in subsistence economy. Reliance on plantains and bananas did not replace foraging. It merely added a secure source of calories to hunting, fishing, and gathering, which continued alongside cultivation. The early tribal Ganda, with their iron tools, plantains, and bananas, were free to expand until they were blocked by neighboring groups or reached the natural limits of the banana and plantain niche. In other words, they could expand until they encountered factors that led to their social or physical circumscription, to recall Carneiro's theory of state formation.

The population increased and spread; new villages were built farther from Lake Victoria. To maintain a diversified diet that included fish, inland people relied on trade with lakeshore communities. A basis for the ranking of descent groups arose through their differential population growth—some got to be larger and more widespread than did others. Given warfare, which was present in Buganda by the year 1600, the larger descent groups had more members in more places and thus more widespread support. Buganda had reached the chiefdom level.

The largest descent groups gained power. They managed the regional economy that was developing. They administered the sociopolitical system that was evolving from chiefdom into state. By the nineteenth century, when Buganda was at its height, the regulation of ecological diversity and

interregional trade had become a major concern of state officials.

Buganda's subsistence base and lakeshore location gave it a crucial advantage in warfare. Plantain-banana subsistence favored Buganda's domination of its region, as did its position near water transport and lakeshore trade. Remember that Buganda's men could be mobilized into an army without endangering the food supply, which female labor guaranteed. Eventually the army became a powerful offensive force, extending Buganda's boundaries by encroaching on its neighbors. The expanding trade network and military apparatus required roads and bridges, which were built and maintained under the supervision of state of-

Figure 8.4 *The process of state formation in Buganda. Several variables interacted throughout the sequence. Permanent cultivation based on plantains and bananas enabled men to be diverted to military operations. This favored Buganda's military success, conquest of its neighbors, and further expansion. Expansion and conquest continued to add new areas, contributing to ecological diversity and interregional trade.*

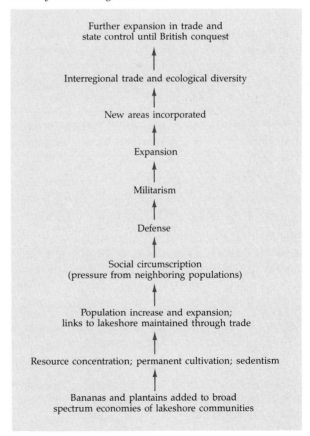

ficials. The land and water transportation system facilitated the movement of people, troops, and goods. A fleet of large canoes formed the navy, which conquered other lakeshore populations and permitted Buganda to control Lake Victoria's mammoth trade. Buganda's men had no choice but to fight or participate in public works projects.

The main factors that contributed to state formation in Buganda can now be summarized. Plantain and banana cultivation were added to an economy based on lakeshore foraging. Eventually, banana-plantain cultivation spread to the natural limits of its ecological niche as the human population grew. Trade, warfare, and differential descent-group growth contributed to the emergence of contrasts in wealth and power. Eventually, stratification and state organization developed. Because bananas and plantains offered long-term reliable yields for little labor, men could withdraw from subsistence and pursue military service, trade, and manufacture. As in other cases of state formation, several factors contributed to the process in Buganda. Population increase, warfare, environmental circumscription, ecological diversity, trade, and permanent cultivation (but not irrigation) were all important (Figure 8.4).

SUMMARY

The first states emerged in the Old World, in Mesopotamia, about 5,500 years ago. The first chiefdoms developed a thousand years earlier, but few survive today. States also arose in two parts of the Western Hemisphere—Mesoamerica and the central Andes. The state is an autonomous political unit encompassing many communities; its central government has the power to collect taxes, draft people for work or war, and decree and enforce laws. The state is defined as a form of sociopolitical organization based on central government and socioeconomic stratification—a division of society into classes. Early states are known as archaic, or nonindustrial, states, in contrast to modern industrial nation-states.

The chiefdom is a form of sociopolitical organization intermediate and transitional between tribes and states. Like states and unlike tribes, chiefdoms are characterized by permanent regional regulation and differential access to strategic resources, but chiefdoms lack stratification. Unlike states but like bands and tribes, chiefdoms are organized by kinship, descent, and marriage.

State formation remained incomplete, and only chiefdoms emerged in several areas, including the circum-Caribbean, lowland Amazonia, the southeastern United States, and Polynesia. Between the rise of food production and the Roman empire, much of Europe was organized at the chiefdom level, to which it reverted after Rome's collapse. Much of our ethnographic knowledge of chiefdoms comes from Polynesia, where they were common at the time of European exploration. Although other chiefdoms calculated seniority differently and had shorter genealogies, the concern for genealogy and seniority and the absence of sharp gaps between elites and commoners are features of all chiefdoms. Chiefdoms feature redistribution, a flow of resources to and then from a central office.

The sociologist Max Weber defined three related dimensions of social stratification: wealth, power, and prestige. In archaic states—for the first time in human evolution—contrasts in wealth, power, and prestige between entire groups (social strata) of men and women came into being. A socioeconomic stratum includes people of both sexes and all ages. The superordinate—higher or elite—stratum enjoys privileged access to wealth, power, and other valued resources. The lower stratum is subordinate. Its members' access to resources is limited by the privileged group.

Status has two meanings. One is close to the definition of prestige and refers to social ranking. The other is neutral: a status is simply a position in a social structure. Some statuses are ascribed; others are achieved. The number of social statuses increases with (and is a measure of) social complexity. Each status has an associated role—a set of expected (culturally "proper") behaviors, attitudes, rights, and obligations. A status is a position in the social structure, but a role involves thought and action. People occupy a status but play a role.

Illustrating general evolutionary trends, certain systems and subsystems with specialized functions are found in all states. They include population control, judiciary, enforcement, and fiscal. In archaic states, these subsystems were integrated by a ruling system or government composed of civil, military, and religious officials. To know whom they govern, all states conduct censuses and demarcate boundaries. States have laws based on precedent and legislative proclamations. To handle disputes and crimes, all states have courts and judges. Governments intervene to preserve internal peace, halt blood feuds, and regulate previously private disputes. All states have agents to enforce judicial decisions.

The major concern of government is to defend hierarchy, property, and the power of the law. The government suppresses internal disorder (with the police) and defends the nation against external threats (with the military). As a relatively new form of sociopolitical organization, states have competed successfully with less complex societies throughout the world.

A financial or fiscal subsystem is necessary to support rulers, nobles, officials, judges, military personnel, and other specialists. The state does not bring more freedom or leisure to the common people, who usually work harder than people do in nonstates.

People did not choose but were forced to accept state organization. Complex political organization develops to handle regulatory problems as the population grows and the economy increases in scale and diversity. Anthropologists and historians have reconstructed evolutionary sequences leading to formation of the state in several areas. Many factors always contribute to this process, with the effects of one magnifying those of the others. Although some contributing factors appear again and again, no single one is always present. The most important contributing factors are hydraulic (water-based) agricultural economies, ecological diversity, long-distance trade, population growth, warfare, and envi-

ronmental circumscription. Coastal Peru, one of the world's most arid areas, illustrates the interaction of environmental circumscription, warfare, and population increase.

Archeologists have documented many cases of early state formation. Cultural anthropologists have also studied state formation through historical, ethnohistorical, and ethnographic data. Such an approach has been used in reconstructing the evolution of the state in Buganda.

In Buganda, plantain-banana cultivation supported population growth; permitted the release of male labor for military service, trade, and other special functions; and thus paved the way for state formation. Trade, warfare, and differential descent-group growth led to contrasts in wealth and power. Both Buganda and coastal Peru illustrate the effects of warfare, population increase, environmental circumscription, and resource concentration. In all cases of state formation, there are several contributing factors. Population increase, warfare, environmental circumscription, ecological diversity, trade, and permanent cultivation are some of the most important ones.

GLOSSARY

achieved status: Position that people occupy through their own efforts, activities, and accomplishments, for example, big man.

archaic state: Nonindustrial state.

ascribed status: Position occupied without choice by an individual, for example, gender and age.

convergence: Parallel development without contact or mutual influence.

differential access: Unequal access to resources; basic attribute of chiefdoms and states. Superordinates have favored access to such resources, while the access of subordinates is limited by superordinates.

ethnohistory: Oral and written accounts of a culture's past by insiders and outsiders.

fiscal: Pertaining to finances and taxation.

hydraulic systems: Systems of water management, including irrigation, drainage, and flood control. Often associated with agricultural societies in arid and river environments.

ideal types: Labels that make contrasts seem more extreme than they really are (e.g., big and little). Instead of discrete categories, there is actually a continuum from one type to the next.

multivariate: Involving multiple factors or variables.

office: Permanent political position.

plantain: Bananalike staple of the Yanomami and Ganda.

power: The ability to exercise one's will over others—to do what one wants; the basis of political status.

prestige: Esteem, respect, or approval for acts, deeds, or qualities considered exemplary.

role: A set of expected (culturally "proper") behaviors, attitudes, rights, and obligations attached to a particular status.

settlement hierarchy: A ranked series of communities differing in size, function, and type of building.

status: A position within a social structure; alternatively, differential social ranking.

stratification: Characteristic of a system with socioeconomic strata; see *stratum*.

stratum: One of two or more groups that contrast in regard to social status and access to strategic resources. Each stratum includes people of both sexes and all ages.

subordinate: The lower, or underprivileged, group in a stratified system.

sumptuary goods: Items whose consumption is limited to the elite.

superordinate: The upper, or privileged, group in a stratified system.

wealth: All a person's material assets, including income, land, and other types of property; the basis of economic status.

STUDY QUESTIONS

1. What are the similarities and differences between chiefdoms and tribes?
2. What are the similarities and differences between chiefdoms and states?
3. What is redistribution, and what are its economic advantages? How does it differ from taxation?
4. What is the difference between the two meanings of *status*? Give examples of each.
5. What is the difference between ascribed status and achieved status? Give three examples of each.
6. What is the difference between status and role? Give examples of each.
7. What are the four special-purpose subsystems found in all states? How do they illustrate the four general evolutionary principles?
8. What is the relationship between state organization, conflicts, and warfare?
9. What are the advantages and disadvantages of the state from the citizen's perspective? Why have people been willing to sacrifice personal freedom to live in states?
10. How have anthropologists attempted to explain state formation? Which do you think is the best explanation, and why?
11. What is ethnohistory, and why do anthropologists study it?
12. What were the common variables in state formation in Peru and Buganda? What were the main differences?

SUGGESTED ADDITIONAL READING

COHEN, R., AND E. R. SERVICE, EDS.
1978 *Origins of the State: The Anthropology of Political Evolution.* Philadelphia: Institute for the Study of Human Issues. Several articles on state formation in many areas.

DRENNAN, R. D., AND C. A. URIBE, EDS.
1987 *Chiefdoms in the Americas.* Landon, MD: University Press of America. Chiefdoms in the precolonial Western Hemisphere.

EARLE, T.
1987 Chiefdoms in Archaeological and Ethnohistorical Perspective. *Annual Review of Anthropology* 16: 279–308. Comprehensive review of early and recent chiefdoms worldwide; includes economy, stratification, and ideology.

FLANNERY, K. V.
1972 The Cultural Evolution of Civilizations. *Annual Review of Ecology and Systematics* 3: 399–426. Survey of theories of state origins.

FOX, J. W.
1987 *Maya Postclassic State Formation.* Cambridge: Cambridge University Press. The role of the "segmentary state" among the Mayas.

FRIEDMAN, J., AND M. J. ROWLANDS, EDS.
1978 *The Evolution of Social Systems.* Pittsburgh, PA: University of Pittsburgh Press. Twenty studies of social change, including the rise of the state.

JOHNSON, A. W., AND T. EARLE, EDS.
1987 *The Evolution of Human Society: From Forager Group to Agrarian State.* Stanford, CA: Stanford University Press. Most recent comprehensive look at sociocultural evolution.

JONES, G., AND R. KRAUTZ
1981 *The Transition to Statehood in the New World.* Cambridge: Cambridge University Press. Processes of state formation, including chiefdoms, in the Americas.

KIRSCH, P. V.
1984 *The Evolution of the Polynesian Chiefdoms.* Cambridge: Cambridge University Press. Diversity and sociopolitical complexity in native Oceania.

KOTTAK, C. P.
1980 *The Past in the Present: History, Ecology, and Cultural Variation in Highland Madagascar.* Ann Arbor: University of Michigan Press. Examines the process of state formation using ethnohistorical and ethnographic data and relates this historical process to contemporary cultural variation.

PFFEIFER, J.
1977 *The Emergence of Society.* New York: McGraw-Hill. A journalist with considerable anthropological expertise surveys the implications of food production and the rise of complex societies throughout the world.

SERVICE, E. R.
1975 *Origins of the State and Civilization: The Process of Cultural Evolution.* New York: W. W. Norton. State formation accessed through several case studies.

STEPONAITIS, V.
1986 Prehistoric Archaeology in the Southeastern United States. *Annual Review of Anthropology* 15: 363–404. Overview of the archeology of an area of chiefdoms.

CHAPTER 9

THE WORLD SYSTEM, INDUSTRIALISM, AND STRATIFICATION

THE EMERGENCE OF THE WORLD SYSTEM

INDUSTRIALIZATION
Causes of the Industrial Revolution

STRATIFICATION
Marx and Weber on Stratification
Open and Closed Class Systems

Box: The American Periphery

**INDUSTRIAL AND NONINDUSTRIAL
SOCIETIES IN THE WORLD SYSTEM TODAY**

Box: Spirit Possession in Malaysian Factories

The Effects of Industrialization on the
World System

143

Although field work in small communities is anthropology's hallmark, isolated groups are impossible to find today. Truly isolated cultures probably have never existed. For thousands of years, human groups have been in contact with one another. Local societies have always participated in a larger system, which today has global dimensions. We call it the modern world system, by which we mean a world in which nations are economically and politically interdependent.

City, nation, and world increasingly invade local communities. Today, if anthropologists want to study a fairly isolated society, they must journey to the highlands of Papua–New Guinea or the tropical forests of South America. Even in those places they will probably encounter missionaries or prospectors. In contemporary Australia sheep owned by people who speak English graze where totemic ceremonies once were held. Farther in the outback some descendants of those totemites work in a movie crew making *Crocodile Dundee IV*. A Hilton hotel stands in the capital of faraway Madagascar, and a paved highway now has an exit for Arembepe, the Brazilian fishing village I have been studying since 1962. My son and I have a bet about when the first McDonald's will open there. When and how did the modern world system begin?

THE EMERGENCE OF THE WORLD SYSTEM

As Europeans took to ships, developing a trans-oceanic trade-oriented economy, people throughout the world entered Europe's sphere of influence. The origins of the European Age of Discovery, which was well under way by 1400, can be traced back to the Crusades, which began in 1096. The Crusades were Christian military expeditions undertaken between the eleventh and fourteenth centuries to recapture the Holy Land (particularly the city of Jerusalem) from the Moslems. Rising European powers (particularly Italian city-states) used the Crusades to establish and extend trade routes.

Marco Polo journeyed to China between 1271 and 1295, and in 1352 the Arab geographer Muhammad ibn-Batuta explored the Sahara desert. In the fifteenth century Europe established regular contact with Asia, Africa, and eventually the Americas. During the early years of exploration Europeans visited Asia and Africa as transient sailors, traders, missionaries, and officials sent to govern small outposts. Contact with Asia led to a trade relationship in which Europeans imported highly refined cottons and porcelains from India and China.

The pace of social change is accelerating within the modern world system, based on international capitalism. This Malaysian woman pumps gasoline produced from Middle Eastern petroleum by a multinational organization (Shell) based in the Netherlands.

Trade was also established with the New World (the Caribbean and the Americas). Christopher Columbus's first voyage from Spain to the Bahamas and the Caribbean in 1492 was soon followed by additional voyages. These journeys opened the way for a major exchange of people, resources, diseases, and ideas (Crosby 1972) as the Old and New Worlds were forever linked. Led by Spain and Portugal, Europeans extracted silver and gold, conquered the natives (taking some as slaves), and colonized their lands.

Previously in Europe as throughout the world, rural people had produced mainly for their own needs, growing their own food and making clothing, furniture, and tools from local products. Production beyond immediate needs was undertaken to pay taxes and purchase trade items such as salt and iron. In the preindustrial cities of Europe craftspeople worked in their own shops, using simple tools to make hardware, cloth, jewelry, silverware, guns, cannon, and ammunition. As late as 1650 the English diet, like those in 75 percent of the world today, centered on locally grown starches (Mintz 1985). However, in the 200 years that followed, the English, who had formerly subsisted mainly on foods produced within their national boundaries, became extraordinary consumers of imported goods. One of the earliest and most popular of those goods was sugar (Mintz 1985).

By 1650 England's nobility and wealthy classes were habitual sugar eaters. After 1650 sugar began to change from a luxury and rarity into a necessity, as tobacco had done a century earlier. By 1750 even the poorest English farm woman took sugar in her tea. The English consumed sugar in the form of rum and with coffee, chocolate, and especially tea.

Sugar was originally domesticated in Papua–New Guinea and was first processed in India. Reaching Europe via the Middle East and the eastern Mediterranean, it was carried to the New World by Columbus (Mintz 1985). The climate of Brazil and the Caribbean proved ideal for growing sugarcane, and Europeans built plantations there to supply the growing demand for sugar. This led to the development in the seventeenth century of a plantation economy based on a single cash crop—a system known as **monocrop production**.

The demand for sugar and the emergence of a sugar supply geared to an international market spurred the development of one of the most inhumane—and profitable—trade systems in the preindustrial world—the slave trade. Two triangles of trade involving sugar and slaves arose in the seventeenth century and matured in the eighteenth. In the first triangle, English manufactured goods were sold to Africa, African slaves were sold to the Americas, and American tropical commodities (especially sugar) were sold to England and its neighbors. (**Commodities** are articles of trade, products with commercial value.) In the second triangle, New England rum was shipped to Africa, slaves were sent from Africa to the Caribbean, and molasses (from sugar) was shipped to New England to make rum. In the eighteenth century an increased English demand for raw cotton led to the rapid settlement of what is now the southeastern United States and the emergence of monocrop production there. This was another instance of a plantation economy based on slave labor.

In the Americas the labor power of African slaves created wealth, which returned mostly to Europe. Products grown by slaves were consumed in Europe. The Caribbean and Brazil supplied European nations with spices, beverages (coffee and chocolate), dyes, sugar, and rum (Mintz 1985). The United States supplied cotton and additional rum.

Like sugar, cotton was a key trade item that spurred the development of the world system and industrialization. Cotton cloth, which initially was imported from India, became increasingly fashionable in England after 1690. Cotton's popularity grew steadily during the eighteenth century. The English cotton industry began to thrive when Parliament banned the importation of Indian cotton. Some of the cotton spun in England found its way back to the Americas to clothe slaves on English plantations in the Caribbean (Mintz 1985).

The increasing dominance of international trade led to the **capitalist world economy** (Wallerstein 1982)—a single world system committed to production for sale or exchange, with the object of maximizing profits rather than supplying domestic needs. The defining attribute of capitalism is *economic orientation to the world market for profit*.

The world system and the relations between the countries within that system are shaped by the world economy. World-system theory can be traced to the French social historian Fernand Braudel. In his three-volume work *Civilization and Capitalism, 15th–18th Century* (1981, 1982, 1984), Braudel argues that society consists of parts assembled into an interrelated system. Societies are subsystems of bigger systems, with the world system as the largest.

The key claim of world-system theory is that an identifiable social system extends beyond individual states and nations. That system is formed by a set of economic and political relations that has characterized much of the globe since the sixteenth century, when the Old World established regular contact with the New World.

According to Wallerstein (1982), the nations within the world system occupy three different positions: core, periphery, and semiperiphery. The position a nation occupies is based on the degree of political and economic specialization within that nation. There is a geographic center or **core**, the dominant position in the world system, which consists of the strongest and most powerful nations, with advanced systems of production. In core nations, "the complexity of economic activities and the level of capital accumulation is the greatest" (Thompson 1983, p. 12). Core countries specialize in producing the most "advanced" goods, using the most sophisticated technologies and mechanized means of production. The core produces capital-intensive high-technology goods and exports some of them to the periphery and semiperiphery.

Semiperiphery and **periphery** nations, which roughly correspond to what is usually called the Third World, have less power, wealth, and influence. The semiperiphery is intermediate between the core and the periphery. Contemporary nations of the semiperiphery are industrialized. Like core nations, they export both industrial goods and commodities, but they lack the power and economic dominance of core nations. Thus Brazil, a semiperiphery nation, exports automobiles to Nigeria and auto engines, orange juice extract, and coffee to the United States.

Economic activities in the periphery are less mechanized and use human labor more intensively than do those in the semiperiphery. The periphery produces raw materials and agricultural commodities for export to the core and the semiperiphery. However, in the modern world, industrialization is invading even peripheral nations. Although the weakest structural position in the world system, the periphery is an essential part of the world economy. Peripheral nations exist to serve the interests of the core (see the box "Spirit Possession in Malaysian Factories" in this chapter). The relationship between the core and the periphery is fundamentally exploitative. Trade and other forms of economic relations between core and periphery benefit capitalists in the core at the expense of the periphery (Shannon 1989).

Usually, at a given time, one state dominates the core, but dominance shifts over time. The northern Italian city-states dominated world trade in the fourteenth century. Holland dominated in the seventeenth, England after 1750, and the United States after 1900. In 1560 (Figure 9.1) the core of the world system was in western Europe (England, France, the Netherlands, Portugal, and Spain). The northern Italian city-states, which had once been more powerful, had joined the semiperiphery. Northeastern Europe and particularly Latin America formed the periphery. Many societies (particularly in Oceania and in the interior of Africa and Asia) were still beyond the periphery. They had not yet joined the world capitalist economy and were still self-sufficient, producing and consuming their own goods. Today there are virtually no societies beyond the periphery, although the Soviet bloc ("Second World") nations, traditionally excluded from the world capitalist economy, are now moving rapidly toward the semiperiphery.

INDUSTRIALIZATION

By the eighteenth century the stage had been set for the **Industrial Revolution**—the historical transformation (in Europe, after 1750) of "traditional" into "modern" societies through industrialization of the economy. Industrialization required capital

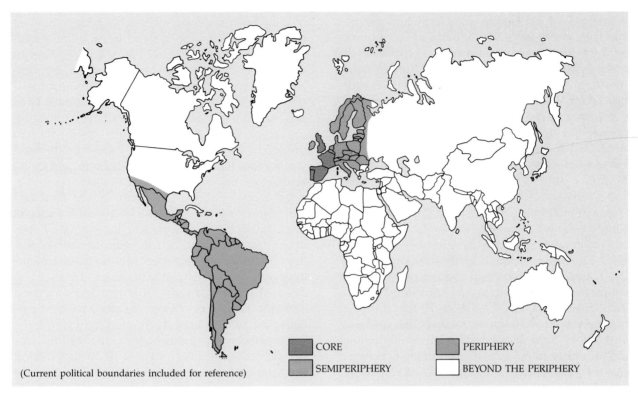

CORE

SEMIPERIPHERY

PERIPHERY

BEYOND THE PERIPHERY

(Current political boundaries included for reference)

Figure 9.1 *The world system in 1560. (Reprinted by permission of Westview Press from* An Introduction to the World-System Perspective *by Thomas Richard Shannon. Copyright Westview Press 1989, Boulder, Colorado.)*

for investment. The established system of transoceanic trade and commerce, which was controlled by a small group of merchants and mercantile companies, supplied this capital from the enormous profits it generated. Wealthy people sought investment opportunities and eventually found them in machines and engines to drive machines. Industrialization increased production in both farming and manufacturing, as capital and scientific innovation fueled invention.

European industrialization developed from (and eventually replaced) the **domestic system** (or home handicraft system) of manufacture. In this system, an organizer-entrepreneur supplied raw materials to workers in their homes and collected finished products from them. The entrepreneur, whose sphere of operations might span several villages, owned the materials, paid for the work, and arranged the marketing.

Causes of the Industrial Revolution

The Industrial Revolution began in the cotton products, iron, and pottery trades, whose growing markets were very attractive to capitalists with money to risk. The manufacture of cotton, iron, and earthenware could be broken down into simple routine motions that machines could perform. Factories could produce cheap staple goods.

Industrialization began in industries that produced *goods that were widely used already*. This illustrates **Romer's rule**—a generalization about evolutionary processes, biological or cultural, originally proposed by the paleontologist Alfred S. Romer (1960). The key is that an innovation that evolves to maintain an existing system can play a major role in changing that system. Romer used the rule to explain the evolution of land-dwelling vertebrates from fish. The ancestors of land vertebrates were animals that lived in pools of water that dried up seasonally. Fins gradually evolved into legs, not to permit vertebrates to live full-time on the land but to enable them to get back to the water when particular pools dried up. In other words, an innovation (legs) that proved essential to land life originated to maintain life in the water.

We can apply Romer's rule to many major changes in human adaptive strategies. One example is the transition to food production in the Middle East. The "first farmers" did not start cultivating in order to become cultivators but to maintain the basis of their traditional foraging economy. Population increase forced colonists into a marginal zone that lacked the bountiful wild fields of wheat and barley of their nearby homeland. They began sowing seeds (cultivating) in the marginal zone in order to create fields like the ones in which they once had gathered. As often happens in cultural evolution, the actions of those ancient Middle Easterners had unintended consequences. The process they set in motion led to full-fledged food production, as farmers eventually developed new varieties of wheat and barley that outyielded the wild forms.

Similarly, the Industrial Revolution led to a dramatic increase in production. Manufacturing moved from home and workshop to factory, where machinery replaced handwork. Agrarian societies evolved into urban industrial ones. Industrialization fueled urban growth and created a new kind of city, with factories crowded together in places where coal and labor were cheap.

Revolution is not the right term to describe either food production or industrialism, because both were long-term processes that began in order to maintain rather than to change. Romer's lesson is that evolution (biological or cultural) tends to occur in small increments. Gradually changing systems make adaptations to maintain themselves as they change. The rule also applies to conscious economic changes: people usually want to *change just enough to maintain what they have*. Motives to modify behavior arise within a particular culture and reflect the small concerns and demands of daily life, such as improved crop yields and increased profit (assuming that the profit motive has been established in that culture).

Romer's rule helps us understand why the Industrial Revolution began in England rather than France. The French were able to maintain the form

of their manufacturing system (even as they were changing their *political* system through the French Revolution and Napoleon). With a late eighteenth-century population at least twice that of Great Britain, France could simply expand its domestic system of production by drawing in new homes. Thus the French could increase production without innovating—they could enlarge the existing system rather than adopt a new one. However, to meet mounting demand for staples—at home and in the colonies—England had to industrialize.

Anthropologist Marvin Harris (1978) contends that history's prime movers are economic cycles of intensification, depletion, and innovation. Population pressure promotes intensification of production, but this eventually depletes the environment. Renewed pressure (resulting from depleted resources) spurs innovative solutions in production systems. This process seems to apply (at least partially) to the Industrial Revolution in England.

Accompanying English industrialization was agrarian intensification stimulated by population pressure and demand for food. The English population was increasing faster than the food supply was. In response, the eighteenth-century enclosure movement created more efficient farming, as more easily cultivated compact private holdings replaced common pastures and fields. Experiments with root crop rotation and shifts between pastureland and farmland also enhanced productivity. Inventions bolstered both farming and industry. Fewer farmers were able to feed a growing manufacturing work force.

Britain's population doubled during the eighteenth century (particularly after 1750) and did so again between 1800 and 1850. This demographic explosion fueled consumption, but British entrepreneurs couldn't meet increased demand with traditional production methods. This spurred experimentation, innovation, and rapid technological change. English industrialization also rested on the accumulation of capital from land and overseas trade. This capital had been growing through saving, and banking stimulated the industrial market economy. By 1800 factory-based mechanization was rapidly replacing Britain's domestic system.

According to Sidney Mintz (1985), Caribbean sugar plantations played a key role in the emergence of industrialism. Mintz makes the unorthodox suggestion that industrialism was invented in the Third World rather than in Europe. Specifically, he traces industrialization back to the Caribbean sugar plantations of the seventeenth century. Those enterprises shared many features with, and thus might have served as models for, the industrial factories that developed a century later. The plantations, where cane was grown and chemically transformed into sugar, were a synthesis of field and factory unlike anything known in Europe during the seventeenth century. Sugar plantations were like factories because they had specialization by job and skill level. They maintained a division of labor by age, gender, and condition (slave, free, or indentured worker). As in factories, workers were organized into crews, shifts, and gangs, and punctuality and discipline were stressed in the coordinated operations.

As we saw in the discussion of theories of state formation (Chapter 8), multivariate approaches are more convincing than single-factor explanations of major socioeconomic changes. Just as several factors contributed to state formation, several also propelled industrialization. English industrialization could draw on national advantages in natural resources. Great Britain was rich in coal and iron ore and had navigable waterways and easily negotiated coasts. It was a seafaring island nation located at the crossroads of international trade. These features gave Britain a favored position for importing raw materials and exporting manufactured goods.

The national manufacturing tradition was also important. In contrast to France, which specialized in luxury goods and items requiring detailed handwork, England's manufacturing economy emphasized staples that could be made using routine processes. French manufactures (within the domestic system) doubled between 1788 and 1812. Eventually, however, a limited supply of raw materials (partially due to English control of the seas) slowed France's further economic expansion under Napoleon.

Another factor in England's industrial ascendancy was the fact that much of its eighteenth-century colonial empire was occupied by English settler families who looked to the mother country as they tried to replicate European civilization in the New World. These colonies bought large quantities of English staples. By contrast, in the French New World colonies there were fewer French set-

The Caribbean sugar plantations of the seventeenth century shared many features with, and may have served as models for, industrial factories, which developed a century later. On sugar plantations as in factories, workers were organized into crews, shifts, and gangs, and punctuality and discipline were stressed in the coordinated operations. Here a contemporary team of workers in Puerto Rico loads cane for transport to the factory for processing.

tlers. Neither Caribbean slaves, who worked on the sugar plantations, nor French Canadian and Indian trappers, who provided furs, formed a particularly lucrative market for French manufactures.

Social and political factors also stimulated English industrialization. In England (in contrast to Germany and Italy) early political and economic unification aided the emergence of industrialization. Other European countries had internal tariffs, but there was free trade throughout England. While France maintained customs taxes between its provinces, England lacked such internal restrictions. England also managed to escape the invading armies that plagued continental Europe during the eighteenth century.

It has also been argued that particular cultural values and religion contributed to industrialization. Thus, many members of the emerging English middle class were Protestant nonconformists. Their beliefs and values encouraged industry, thrift, the dissemination of new knowledge, inventiveness, and willingness to accept change (Weber 1904/1949).

STRATIFICATION

The worldwide effects of the Industrial Revolution continue today, extending our familiar general evolutionary trends: proliferation, specialization, integration, and expansion. Thus parts and subparts have proliferated with the emergence of new social categories and occupations. Functional differentiation and specialization have increased. For example, each European nation promoted differentiation within its trade zone and functional specialization in its colonies in order to supply particular commodities. Transoceanic trade, which grew with industrialization, encouraged economic specialization on a global level. Integration and system scale increased as new areas entered the world capitalist economy and colonialism engulfed the globe. The growth rate of world population also increased. The Industrial Revolution produced another quantum leap in the rate of cultural evolutionary change, which had previously accelerated with food production and again with state formation.

How does social stratification in the industrial world system compare with that in archaic states, as examined in Chapter 8? The hereditary rulers and elites of archaic states and ancient empires, like the feudal nobility that ruled Europe before 1500, viewed the state as their property (conferred by gods, tradition, or war) to control and do with as they pleased (Shannon 1989). The most basic distinction in archaic states was between those who controlled the state machinery and those who did not. In the world system of the industrial era, particularly after industrialization, the main differentiating factor became ownership of the means of production.

Marx and Weber on Stratification

Karl Marx and Max Weber focused on the stratification systems associated with industrialization.

The socioeconomic effects of industrialization were mixed. English national income tripled between 1700 and 1815 and increased thirty times more by 1939. Standards of comfort rose, but prosperity was uneven. At first, factory workers got wages higher than those available in the domestic system. Later, owners started recruiting labor in places where living standards were low and labor (including that of women and children) was cheap.

Social ills increased with the growth of factory towns and industrial cities, with conditions like those Charles Dickens described in *Hard Times*. Filth and smoke polluted nineteenth-century cities. Housing was crowded and unsanitary, with insufficient water and sewage disposal facilities and rising disease and death rates. This was the world of Ebenezer Scrooge, Bob Cratchit, Tiny Tim—and Karl Marx.

From his observations in England and his analysis of nineteenth-century industrial capitalism, Marx (Marx and Engels 1848/1976) saw socioeconomic stratification as a sharp and simple division between two opposed classes: the bourgeoisie (capitalists) and the proletariat (propertyless workers). The bourgeoisie traced its origins to overseas ventures and the world capitalist economy, which had transformed the social structure of northwestern Europe, creating a wealthy commercial class.

Industrialization shifted production from farms and cottages to mills and factories, where mechanical power was available and where workers could be assembled to operate heavy machinery. The **bourgeoisie** were the owners of the factories, mines, large farms, and other means of production. The **working class**, or proletariat, was made up of people who had to sell their labor to survive. With the decline of subsistence production and with the rise of urban migration and the possibility of unemployment, the bourgeoisie came to stand between workers and the means of production.

Industrialization hastened the process of **proletarianization**—the separation of workers from the means of production. The bourgeoisie also came to dominate the means of communication, the schools, and other key institutions. Marx viewed the nation-state as an instrument of oppression and religion as a method of diverting and controlling the masses.

Faulting Marx for an overly simple and exclusively economic view of stratification, Weber

Social ills increased with the growth of factory towns and industrial cities. This drawing depicts nineteenth-century air pollution in England's "Black Country" (Wolverhampton)—a coal and iron producing district covered with manufacturing towns, mines, blasting furnaces, and forges.

(1922) defined the three related dimensions of social stratification examined in Chapter 8: wealth (economic status), power (political status), and prestige (social status). Having one of the three doesn't entail having the others. Band societies have slight contrasts in prestige and power but none in wealth; lottery winners gain wealth but usually not prestige. Although, as Weber showed, wealth, power, and prestige are distinct components of social ranking, they do tend to be correlated.

Class consciousness (recognition of collective interests and personal identification with one's economic group) was a vital part of Marx's view of class. He saw bourgeoisie and proletariat as socioeconomic divisions with radically opposed interests. Marx viewed classes as powerful collective forces that could mobilize human energies to influence the course of history. Finding strength through common experience, workers would develop organizations to protect their interests and increase their share of industrial profits.

And so they did. During the nineteenth century trade unions and socialist parties emerged to express a rising anticapitalist mass spirit. The concerns of the English labor movement were to remove young children from factories and limit the hours during which women and children could work. The profile of stratification in industrial core nations gradually became clear: capitalists controlled production, but labor was organizing to improve wages and working conditions. By 1900 many governments had factory legislation and social-welfare programs. Mass living standards in core nations rose as population grew.

The modern capitalist world system maintains the distinction between those who own the means of production and those who don't. The class division into capitalists and propertyless workers is now worldwide. Nevertheless, modern stratification systems aren't simple and dichotomous. They include (particularly in core and semiperiphery nations) a growing middle class of skilled and professional workers. Gerhard Lenski (1966) argues that social equality tends to increase in advanced industrial societies as the masses acquire and use political power and get economic benefits. In his scheme, the shift of political power to the masses reflects the growth of the middle class, which reduces the polarization between owning and working classes. The proliferation of intermediate occupations creates opportunities for social mobility, and the stratification system grows more complex (Giddens 1973).

There are also distinctions among propertyless workers. Hopkins and Wallerstein (1982) distinguish between (1) lifetime or full proletarians and (2) part-time proletarians or semiproletarians. The former get their full lifetime support from work for capitalists; the latter supplement wage work with independent commodity production (for example, part-time farming).

Weber believed that social solidarity based on ethnicity, religion, race, nationality, and other attributes could take priority over class (social identity based on economic status). In addition to class contrasts, the modern world system is cross-cut by status groups, such as ethnic and religious groups and nations (Shannon 1989). Class conflicts tend to occur within nations, and nationalism has prevented global class solidarity, particularly of proletarians.

Although the capitalist class dominates politically in most modern nations, the leaders of core nations have found it to be in their interest to allow proletarians to organize and make demands of the state and the capitalist class. Growing wealth has made it easier for core nations to become less authoritarian and to grant higher wages (Hopkins and Wallerstein 1987). However, the improvement in core workers' living standards wouldn't have occurred without the world system, in which the added surplus that comes from the periphery allows core capitalists to maintain their profits while satisfying the demands of core workers. In the periphery, where investment typically goes to enterprises designed to meet the needs of core nations, wages and living standards are much lower. A system of intense labor exploitation is maintained at low levels of compensation. We see, then, that the current *world stratification system* features a substantial contrast between both capitalists and workers in core nations and workers on the periphery.

In times of economic stagnation in the core, class conflict intensifies as workers and capitalists compete to increase their share of declining national wealth. The conflict ends only with some income redistribution to workers and the middle class. Once workers have more to spend, market demand increases, triggering renewed economic expansion. Workers in core nations benefit from economic expansion, but increased demand fuels the process of proletarianization in the periphery (Shannon 1989).

With the expansion of the world capitalist economy, people on the periphery have been removed from the land by large landowners and multinational agribusiness interests. One result is increased poverty, including food shortages. Displaced people can't earn enough to buy the food they can no longer grow. The effects of the world economy can also create peripheral regions within core nations, such as areas of the rural South in the United States (see the box "The American Periphery" in this chapter).

Bangladesh illustrates some of the causes of Third World poverty and food shortages. Climate, soils, and water availability in Bangladesh are favorable for productive agriculture. Indeed, before the arrival of the British in the eighteenth century, Bangladesh (then called Bengal) had a prosperous local cotton industry. There was some stratification, but peasants had enough land to provide an adequate diet. Land was neither privately owned nor part of the market economy. Under colonialism, the British forced the Bengalis to grow cash crops (indigo and jute) for export and converted land into an individually owned commodity that could be bought and sold.

Increased stratification was a result of colonialism and tighter linkage with the world capitalist economy. The peasantry gradually lost its land. A study done in 1977 (Bodley 1985) showed that a small group of wealthy people owned most of the land. Sixty percent of rural households owned less than 10 percent of the land, and one-third of the households owned no land at all. Poverty was expressed in food shortages. Landless peasants ate 22 percent less grain than small landholders did, but they had to burn 40 percent more calories because of increased work loads. Many landless people worked as sharecroppers, with landowners claiming at least half the crop. The local elite used its power to manipulate wages and prices. The peasants were underpaid for their crops and overcharged for the commodities they needed. Local landowners (capitalists of the periphery) also monopolized international development aid and even emergency food aid.

Open and Closed Class Systems

Inequalities, which are built into the structure of state organization, tend to persist across the generations. The extent to which they do or don't is a measure of the openness of the stratification system, the ease of social mobility it permits. Within the world capitalist economy, stratification has taken many forms, including caste, slavery, and class systems.

Caste systems are closed, hereditary systems of stratification that are often dictated by religion. Hierarchical social status is ascribed at birth, so that people are locked into their parents' social position. Caste lines are clearly defined, and legal and religious sanctions are applied against those who seek to cross them. The world's best-known caste system, associated with Hinduism in traditional India, Pakistan, and Sri Lanka, is described more fully in Chapter 13. Another castelike system, **apartheid,** exists today in South Africa. In that legally maintained hierarchy, blacks, whites, and Asians have their own separate (and unequal) neighborhoods, schools, laws, and punishments.

In **slavery** people are treated as property. In the Atlantic slave trade millions of human beings were treated as commodities. The plantation systems of the Caribbean, the southeastern United States, and Brazil were based on forced slave labor. Slaves were like proletarians in that they lacked control over the means of production, but proletarians have some control over where they work, how much they work, for whom they work, and what they do with their wages. Slaves, in contrast, have nothing to sell—not even their own labor (Mintz 1985). Slavery is the most extreme and coercive form of legalized inequality.

Vertical mobility is an upward or downward change in a person's social status. A truly **open class system** would facilitate mobility, with individual achievement and personal merit determining social rank. Hierarchical social statuses would be achieved on the basis of people's efforts. As-

Plantation systems in the New World were based on forced slave labor. Proletarians, such as these "white slaves of England" also lacked control over the means of production, but they did have some control over where and for whom they worked.

cribed statuses (family background, ethnicity, gender, religion) would be less important. Open class systems would have blurred class lines and a wide range of status positions.

Compared with archaic states and contemporary peripheral and semiperipheral nations, core industrial nations tend to have more open class systems. Under industrialism, wealth is based to some extent on **income**—earnings from wages and salaries. Economists contrast such a *return on labor* with interest, dividends, and rent, which are *returns on property* or capital.

THE AMERICAN PERIPHERY

In a comparative study of two counties at opposite ends of Tennessee, Thomas Collins (1989) reviews the effects of industrialization on poverty and unemployment. Hill County, with an Appalachian white population, is on the Cumberland Plateau in eastern Tennessee. Delta County, predominantly African-American, is sixty miles from Memphis in western Tennessee's lower Mississippi region. Both counties once had economies based on agriculture and timber, but jobs in those sectors declined sharply with the advent of mechanization. Both counties have unemployment rates more than twice that of Tennessee as a whole. More than a third of the people in each county live below the poverty level. Such poverty pockets represent a slice of the world periphery within modern America. Given very restricted job opportunities, the best-educated local youths have migrated to northern cities for three generations.

To increase jobs, local officials and business leaders have tried to attract industries from outside. Their efforts exemplify a more general rural southern strategy, which began during the 1950s, of courting industry by advertising "a good business climate"—which means low rents, cheap utilities, and a non-union labor pool. However, few firms are attracted to an impoverished and poorly educated work force. All the industries that have come to such areas have very limited market power and a narrow profit margin. Such firms survive by offering low wages and minimal benefits, with frequent layoffs. These industries tend to emphasize traditional female skills such as sewing and mostly attract women.

The garment industry, which is highly mobile, is Hill County's main employer. The knowledge that a garment plant can be moved to another site very rapidly tends to reduce employee demands. Management can be as arbitrary and authoritarian as it wishes. The un-employment rate and low educational level ensure that many women will accept sewing jobs for a bit more than the minimum wage.

In neither county has new industry brought many jobs for men, who have a higher unemployment rate than do women (as do blacks, compared with whites). Collins found that many men in Hill County had never been permanently employed; they had just done temporary jobs, always for cash.

The effects of industrialization in Delta County have been similar. That county's recruitment efforts have also drawn only marginal industries. The largest is a bicycle seat and toy manufacturer, which employs 60 percent women. Three other large plants, which make clothing and auto seat covers, employ 95 percent women. Egg production was once significant in Delta County but folded when the market for eggs fell in response to rising national concern over the effects of cholesterol.

Even in advanced industrial nations, stratification is more marked in wealth than it is in income. Thus in 1985 the bottom fifth of American households got 4.6 percent of total national income, compared with 43.5 percent for the top fifth. However, if we consider wealth rather than income, the contrast is much more extreme: One percent of American families hold one-third of the nation's wealth (Light, Keller, and Calhoun 1989).

INDUSTRIAL AND NONINDUSTRIAL SOCIETIES IN THE WORLD SYSTEM TODAY

World-system theory stresses the existence of a global culture. It emphasizes historical contacts and linkages between local people and international forces. The major forces influencing cultural interaction during the past 500 years have been commercial expansion and industrial capitalism (Wolf 1982; Wallerstein 1982). As state formation had done previously, industrialization accelerated local participation in larger networks. According to Bodley (1985), perpetual expansion (whether in population or consumption) is the distinguishing feature of industrial economic systems. Unlike bands and tribes, which are small, self-sufficient, subsistence-based systems, industrial economies are large, highly specialized systems in which local areas don't consume the products they produce and in which market exchanges occur with profit as the primary motive (Bodley 1985).

There is a *world* economy because the first loyalty of capitalism is to itself rather than to any community, region, or nation. Because capitalists do not freely subordinate their profit-seeking goals to

In both counties the men, ignored by industrialization, maintain an informal economy. They sell and trade used goods through personal networks. They take casual jobs, such as operating farm equipment on a daily or seasonal basis. Collins found that maintaining an automobile was the most important and prestigious contribution these men made to their families. Neither county has public transportation; Hill County even lacks school buses. Families need cars to get women to work and kids to school. Men who keep an old car running longest get special respect.

Reduced opportunities for men to do well at work—to which American culture attributes great importance—lead to a feeling of lowered self-worth, which is expressed in physical violence. The rate of domestic violence in Hill County exceeds the state average. Spousal abuse arises from men's demands to control women's paychecks. (Men regard the cash they earn themselves as their own, to spend on male activities.)

One important difference between the two counties involves unionization. In Delta County, organizers have waged campaigns for unionization. There is just one unionized plant in Delta County now, but recent campaigns in two other factories failed in close votes. Attitudes toward workers' rights in Tennessee correlate with race. Rural southern whites usually don't vote for unions when they have a chance to do so, whereas African-Americans are more likely to challenge management about pay and work rules. Local blacks view their work situation in terms of black against white rather than from a position of working-class solidarity. They are attracted to unions because they see only whites in managerial positions and resent differential advancement of white factory workers. One manager told Collins that "once the work force of a plant becomes more than one-third black, you can expect to have union representation within a year" (Collins 1989, p. 10). Responding to the probability of unionization, canny core capitalists

from Japan don't build plants in the primarily African-American counties of the lower Mississippi. The state's Japanese factories cluster in eastern and central Tennessee.

Poverty pockets of the rural South (and other regions) represent a slice of the world periphery within modern America. Through mechanization, industrialization, and other changes promoted by larger systems, local people have been deprived of land and jobs. After years of industrial development, a third of the people of Hill and Delta counties remain below the poverty level. Emigration of educated and talented locals continues as opportunities shrink. Collins concludes that rural poverty won't be reduced by attracting additional peripheral industries because these firms lack the market power to improve wages and benefits. Different development schemes are needed for these counties and the rural South generally.

national interests, most countries have erected protective barriers designed to protect their own products from foreign competition. In world-system theory, **mercantilism** refers to the system of tariffs, trade laws, and other barriers designed to protect national products and industries from (often cheaper) foreign competition.

The twentieth-century world economy and the nations within it have witnessed cycles of expansion, overproduction, falling demand, and depression. Industrial capitalism depends on distant markets, which can expand rapidly and contract unpredictably. Colonization, international competition, and the diffusion of fads and fashions have fueled industrial expansion. However, massive unemployment may follow when distant wars or fads run their course.

During the nineteenth century, industrialization

spread beyond England. Belgium became the first nation in continental Europe to industrialize—in the 1820s—on the strength of its iron and coal resources. France followed in the 1830s, as did Prussia in the 1840s. By the middle of the nineteenth century the United States had joined the roster of industrializing nations.

American industrialization was confined to the Northeast before becoming widespread after the Civil War. Eli Whitney's 1793 invention of the cotton gin, which vastly increased the flow of fiber to textile mills, kindled the New England textile industry. A later stimulus to the American industrial economy was Cyrus McCormick's reaper (1831), a major mechanical invention for harvesting. Labor-saving devices such as these freed American laborers to enter factories, which also drew heavily on immigrant labor (Fraser 1980).

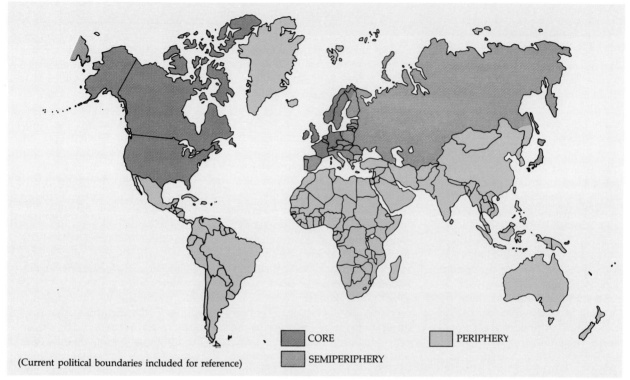

(Current political boundaries included for reference)   CORE   PERIPHERY   SEMIPERIPHERY

Figure 9.2 *The world system in 1900. (Reprinted by permission of Westview Press from* An Introduction to the World-System Perspective *by Thomas Richard Shannon. Copyright Westview Press 1989, Boulder, Colorado.)*

After 1870 European business began a concerted search for more secure markets in Asia, Africa, and other less-developed areas. This process, which led to European imperialism in Africa, Asia, and Oceania, was aided by improved transportation, which brought huge new areas within easy reach. Europeans also colonized vast areas of previously unsettled or sparsely settled lands in the interior of North and South America and Australia. The new colonies purchased masses of goods from the industrial centers and shipped back wheat, cotton, wool, mutton, beef, and leather. Thus began the second phase of colonialism (the first had been in the New World after Columbus) as European nations competed for colonies between 1875 and 1914, a process that helped cause World War I.

By 1900 the United States had become a core nation within the world system (Figure 9.2). It had overtaken Great Britain in iron, coal, and cotton production. With its older plants and equipment, Britain faced increased international competition.

Electric generators replaced steam engines and the internal combustion engine (an 1890s invention) led to the automobile. England began to lag behind Germany (in chemicals) and the United States (in electric and automobile industries), eventually (by 1980) to fall to the semiperiphery.

Industrialization spread to many other nations in a process that continues today (Table 9.1). In a few decades (1868–1900) Japan changed from a medieval handicraft country to an industrial one, joining the semiperiphery by 1900 and moving to the core between 1945 and 1970. Italy and the Netherlands industrialized by 1914. Russian industrialization had begun somewhat earlier. However, World War I and the 1917 Bolshevik Revolution halted industrialization, which resumed in the 1930s—no longer as a response to market forces but as planned economic development by the Soviet state. The basis of Soviet industrialization was state investment in plants, machinery, and heavy industrial goods—with restricted con-

Table 9.1 *Ascent and decline of nations within the world system*

Periphery to Semiperiphery	Semiperiphery to Core	Core to Semiperiphery
United States (1800–1860)	United States (1860–1900)	Spain (1620–1700)
Japan (1868–1900)	Japan (1945–1970)	
Taiwan (1949–1980)	Germany (1870–1900)	
S. Korea (1953–1980)		

SOURCE: Reprinted by permission of Westview Press from *An Introduction to the World-System Perspective* by Thomas Richard Shannon. Copyright Westview Press 1989, Boulder, Colorado.

sumerism. In the 1950s China also embarked on planned industrial development, seeking to accomplish in a decade what had taken Britain a century.

Twentieth-century industrialization has added hundreds of new industries and millions of new jobs. Its early hallmarks were mass production and the assembly line. Jobs in offices and stores also increased, and more young women began to do wage work. Production increased, often beyond immediate demand, and this spurred strategies such as advertising to sell everything that industry could churn out. Mass production gave rise to a culture of overconsumption, which valued acquisitiveness and conspicuous consumption.

Bodley defines overconsumption as "consumption in a given area that exceeds the rates at which natural resources are produced by natural processes, to such an extent that the long-run stability of the culture involved is threatened" (1985,

p. 39). Industrialization entailed a shift from reliance on renewable resources to the use of fossil fuels. Fossil fuel energy, stored over millions of years, is being rapidly depleted to support a previously unknown and probably unsustainable level of consumption (Bodley 1985). Table 9.2 com-

Table 9.2 *Energy consumption in various contexts*

Type of Society	Daily Kilocalories per Person
Bands and tribes	4,000–12,000
Preindustrial states	26,000 (maximum)
Early industrial states	70,000
Americans in 1970	230,000
Americans in 1990	275,000

SOURCE: From John H. Bodley, *Anthropology and Contemporary Human Problems*, 1985. Reprinted by permission of Mayfield Publishing.

Twentieth century industrialization created hundreds of new industries and millions of new jobs. Its hallmarks were mass production and the assembly line, such as the one shown in this Highland Park, Michigan, Ford plant in 1914.

SPIRIT POSSESSION IN MALAYSIAN FACTORIES

Successive waves of integration into the world system have washed Malaysia, a former British colony. The Malays have witnessed sea trade, conquest, the influx of British and Chinese capital, and immigration from China and India. For centuries Malaysia has been part of the world system, but the immediate effects of industrialization are recent. The Malaysian government has promoted export-oriented industry to bring rural Malays into the capitalist system. This has been done in response to rural discontent over poverty and landlessness as some 10,000 families per year are pushed off the land. Since 1970 transnational companies have been installing labor-intensive manufacturing operations in rural Malaysia. Between 1970 and 1980 agriculture's contribution to the national labor force fell from 53 to 41 percent as manufacturing jobs proliferated.

The industrialization of Malaysia is part of a global strategy. To escape mounting labor costs in the core, corporations headquartered in Japan, Western Europe, and the United States have been moving labor-intensive factories to the periphery. Malaysia now has hundreds of Japanese and American subsidiaries, which mainly produce garments, foodstuffs, and electronics components. In electronics plants in rural Malaysia, thousands of young women from peasant families now assemble microchips and microcomponents for transistors and capacitors. Aihwa Ong (1987) did a study of electronics assembly workers in an area where 85 percent of the workers were young unmarried females from nearby villages.

Ong found that factory discipline and social relations contrast strongly with traditional community life. Previously, agricultural cycles and daily Islamic prayers, rather than production quotas and work shifts, had framed the rural economy and social life. Villagers had planned and done their own work, without bosses. In factories, however, village women had to cope with a rigid work routine and unyielding supervision by men.

Factory relations of production featured a hierarchy, pay scale, and division of labor based on ethnicity and gender. Japanese men filled top management, while Chinese men were the engineers and production supervisors. Malay men also worked as supervisors of the factory work force, which consisted of nonunion female semiskilled workers from poor Malay peasant families.

The Japanese firms in rural Malaysia were paternalistic. Managers assured village parents that they would care for their daughters as though they were their own. Unlike the American firms, the Japanese subsidiaries worked hard at maintaining good relations with rural elders. Management gave money for village events, visited workers' home communities, and invited

pares energy consumption in various types of cultures. Americans are the world's foremost consumers of non·.ewable resources. Since becoming a core nation in 1900, the United States has tripled its per capita energy use while increasing its total energy consumption thirtyfold.

The Effects of Industrialization on the World System

How has industrialization affected the Third World—Latin America, Africa, the Pacific, and the less-developed parts of Asia? One effect is the destruction of indigenous economies, ecologies, and populations. Two centuries ago, as industrialization was developing, 50 million people still lived beyond the periphery in politically independent bands, tribes, and chiefdoms. Occupying vast areas, those nonstate societies, although not totally isolated, were only marginally affected by nation-states and the world capitalist economy. Bands, tribes, and chiefdoms controlled half the globe and 20 percent of its population in 1800 (Bodley, ed. 1988). Industrialization then tipped the balance in favor of states. The war of conquest between states and tribes, under way for 6,000 years, continues in just a few remote places today. In the rest of the world, states now govern.

Industrialization is "a global process that has destroyed or transformed all previous cultural adaptations and has given humanity the power not only to bring about its own extinction as a species, but also to speed the extinction of many other species and to alter biological and geological processes as well" (Bodley 1985, p. 4). The negative effects of an expanding industrial world system include genocide, ethnocide, and ecocide. **Genocide** is the physical destruction of ethnic groups by murder,

parents to the plant for receptions. In return, village elders accorded high status to the Japanese managers. The elders colluded with the managers to urge young women to accept and stay with factory work.

The discipline, diligence, and obedience that factories value is learned in local schools, where uniforms help prepare girls for the factory dress code. Peasant women wear loose, flowing tunics, sarongs, and sandals, but factory workers must don tight overalls and heavy rubber gloves, in which they feel constrained and controlled.

Assembling electronics components requires precise, concentrated labor. Demanding, exhausting, depleting, and dehumanizing, labor in these factories illustrates the separation of intellectual and manual activity that Marx considered the defining feature of industrial work. One woman said about her bosses, "They exhaust us very much, as if they do not think that we too are human beings" (Ong 1987, p. 202).

Nor does factory work bring women a substantial financial reward, given low wages, job uncertainty, and family claims on wages. Young women typically work just a few years. Production quotas, three daily shifts, overtime, and constant surveillance take their toll in mental and physical exhaustion.

One response to factory discipline and relations of production is spirit possession, which Ong interprets as an unconscious protest against labor discipline and male control of the industrial setting. Sometimes possession takes the form of mass hysteria. Spirits have simultaneously invaded as many as 120 factory workers. Weretigers (the Malay equivalent of the werewolf) arrive to avenge the construction of a factory on aboriginal burial grounds. Disturbed earth and grave spirits swarm on the shop floor. First the women see the spirits; then their bodies are invaded. The women become violent and scream abuses. Vengeful weretigers send

maidens into sobbing, laughing, and shrieking fits. To deal with possession, factories employ local medicine men, who sacrifice chickens and goats to fend off the spirits. This solution works only some of the time; possession still goes on. Factory women continue to act as vehicles to express the anger of avenging ghosts and their own frustrations.

Ong argues that spirit possession expresses anguish caused by and resistance to capitalist relations of production. However, she also notes that by engaging in this form of ritual rebellion, factory women avoid a direct confrontation with the source of their distress. Ong concludes that spirit possession, while expressing repressed resentment, doesn't do much to modify factory conditions. (Unionization would probably do more.) Spirit possession may even help maintain the current conditions of inequality and dehumanization by operating as a safety valve for accumulated tensions.

warfare, and introduced diseases. When ethnic groups survive but lose or severely modify their ancestral cultures, we speak of **ethnocide**. The term for the destruction of local ecosystems is **ecocide**.

As industrial states have conquered, annexed, and "developed" nonstates, there has been genocide on a grand scale. Bodley (1988) estimates that an average of 250,000 indigenous people perished annually between 1800 and 1950. Foreign diseases (to which natives had no resistance), warfare, slavery, land grabbing, and other forms of dispossession and impoverishment contributed to this genocide.

In the South Pacific, the population of the Solomon Islands, which had numbered at least 500 before contact, fell to 100 soon after 1900 as forty-six villages were reduced to three. Depopulation plagued Melanesia to such an extent that colonial

authorities worried about maintaining the native labor force (Bodley, ed. 1988). By 1800 the world capitalist economy had penetrated Alaska, where, during the nineteenth century, the fur trade, the commercial use of marine animals and salmon, and the gold rush combined to undermine the traditional resource base. Indigenous bands, tribes, and chiefdoms from Alaska down the North Pacific Coast suffered impoverishment, disease, and depopulation. (Chapter 10 considers some of the economic and cultural effects of this process there.)

After initial contact and conquest, many native groups, having been incorporated as ethnic minorities within nation-states, recouped their population. Many indigenous peoples survive and maintain their ethnic identity despite having lost their ancestral cultures to varying degrees (partial ethnocide).

In the wake of industrialism—seemingly a cultural evolutionary advance—comes ecological disaster. Indigenous cultures have been devastated along with their environments as local resources have become fodder for global industrial growth. Shown here is deforestation on tribal lands—once covered by properly managed rainforests—in Rondonia, Brazil.

During the nineteenth century, with the abolition of slavery in the Caribbean and the Americas, many of the plantation economies that had been based on slavery became monocrop economies using free but poorly paid labor. After World War II many Asian, African, and Oceanian colonies gained political independence. Often, however, their economic dependence on the industrial world continued. Peripheral and semiperipheral nations continue to specialize in cash crops, raw materials, and unskilled and semiskilled labor.

The American economy has recently shifted from heavy-goods manufacture toward a high-tech economy based on information processing and the provision of specialized services. The term *post-industrial* has been coined to describe this economic transformation. However, this term seems inappropriate, because industrialization certainly continues today in a world economy in which the United States is a full participant. Manufacturing is declining in the United States but not internationally. Continuing to place capital above national loyalty, American (and Western European and Japanese) businesses pursue their search for markets, profits, and cheap labor abroad. Thus industrialization continues, and the world system goes on evolving.

The notion of a constant human struggle to tame nature—missing in bands and tribes but a hall-mark of industrialism—promotes increasing exploitation of the earth's finite store of natural resources. Industrialism, seemingly a cultural evolutionary advance, may eventually prove disastrous because of the ecological destruction left in its wake. Indigenous cultures have been devastated along with their environments as resources within their territories have become necessary components of industrial growth.

Today's world contains some 200 million people who are members of conquered tribes or of still autonomous tribal nations, of which, however, only a handful survive. Compare this with 75 million people living in perhaps 150,000 independent bands and tribes 10,000 years ago at the dawn of food production (Bodley 1988). Many descendants of tribespeople live on as culturally distinct colonized peoples, many of whom aspire to autonomy. As the original inhabitants of their territories, they are called **indigenous peoples.** They become *peasants* when their dependency and integration within states are complete and they remain on the land. When they move to urban areas, they are often called **ethnic minorities.** Bodley (1988) argues that indigenous peoples have consistently resisted integration within nation-states because such integration—usually into the impoverished classes—is likely to lead to a decline in their quality of life.

Many contemporary nations are repeating—at an accelerated rate—the process of resource depletion that occurred in Europe and the United States during the Industrial Revolution. Fortunately, however, today's world has some environmental watchdogs that were absent during the first centuries of the Industrial Revolution. Given national and international cooperation and sanctions, the modern world may benefit from the lessons of the past.

Although the more isolated societies that represent anthropology's traditional concern are disappearing, the subject matter open to anthropology is actually expanding. This book examines the many ways in which people modify their customs

and behavior in adapting to environmental change. Alterations in the wider environments of human groups—that is, in their relationship with foreigners—represent changes to which people must adapt. Furthermore, although the pressure to change may come from the outside, people are not always the helpless prey of social processes beyond their control. They should be seen as potential or actual participants, rather than mere victims, in a process of change generated by larger forces. Not only are today's international safeguards more effective than were those of 1800, there is often local mobilization against threats from larger-scale systems.

SUMMARY

Local societies increasingly participate in wider systems—regional, national, and global. Columbus's voyages opened the way for a major and continuing exchange between the Old and New Worlds. The first plantation economies based on a single cash crop (most notably sugar) appeared in the seventeenth century. The plantations of Brazil and the Caribbean spurred the development of two triangles of trade involving sugar and slaves. In the eighteenth century a monocrop economy based on slave labor also emerged in the cotton plantations of the southeastern United States. Cotton was another key trade item that spurred the development of the world system and industrialization.

The capitalist world economy is based on production for sale, with the goal of maximizing profits. The capitalist world economy has political and economic specialization based on three positions. Core, semiperiphery, and periphery have existed within the world system since the sixteenth century, although the particular countries filling these niches have changed.

The Industrial Revolution—the historical transformation of "traditional" into "modern" societies through industrialization of the economy—began around 1760. Transoceanic trade and commerce supplied capital for industrial investment.

Industrialization developed from the domestic system of manufacture, and increased production in farming and manufacturing. Industrialization began in industries that produced goods that were widely used already. This illustrates Romer's rule: an innovation that evolves to maintain an existing system can play a major role in changing that system. The Industrial Revolution started in England rather than France because French industry could grow through expansion of the domestic

system. England, with fewer people, had to industrialize. A demographic explosion fueled consumption and demand.

The Caribbean sugar plantation played a key role in the emergence of industrialism. Sugar plantations of the seventeenth century might have served as models for the industrial factories that developed a century later. Just as several factors contributed to state formation, several also propelled industrialization, including natural resources, social and political factors, and the nature of demand.

The worldwide effects of industrialism continue today, extending the general evolutionary trends of proliferation, specialization, integration, and expansion. The most basic distinction in archaic states was between those who controlled the state machinery and those who did not. In the world system, particularly after industrialization, the main differentiating factor became ownership of the means of production. Marx saw socioeconomic stratification as a sharp and simple division between the bourgeoisie (capitalists) and the proletariat (propertyless workers). Industrialization hastened the separation of workers from the means of production. Class consciousness was a vital part of Marx's view of class. Weber, on the other hand, believed that social solidarity based on ethnicity, religion, race, or nationality could take priority over class.

The modern capitalist world system maintains the distinction between those who own the means of production and those who don't, but the division is now worldwide. Modern stratification systems also include a middle class of skilled and professional workers.

In addition to class contrasts, the modern world system is cross-cut by status groups, of which nations are the most important. Class conflicts tend to occur within nations, and nationalism has prevented global class solidarity. The added surplus from the periphery allows core capitalists to maintain their profits while satisfying the demands of core workers. World stratification features a substantial contrast between capitalists and workers in core nations and workers on the periphery. With the expansion of world capitalism, Third World peoples have been removed from the land by large landowners and multinational agribusiness interests. One result is increased poverty, as the case of Bangladesh illustrates.

The extent to which inequalities persist across the generations is a measure of the openness of the stratification system, the ease of social mobility it permits. Within the world capitalist economy, stratification has taken many forms, including caste, slavery, and class systems. Caste systems are closed, hereditary systems of stratification, often dictated by religion. In slavery, the most extreme and coercive form of legalized inequality, people are treated as property. Core industrial nations tend to have the most open class systems.

The major forces influencing cultural interaction during the past 500 years have been commercial expansion and industrial capitalism. Perpetual expansion is a distinguishing feature of industrial economic systems. The first loyalty of capitalism is to itself rather than to any community, region, or nation. Mercantilism refers to the system of tariffs, trade laws, and other barriers designed to protect national products and industries from foreign competition.

During the first half of the nineteenth century, industrialization spread to Belgium, France, Germany, and the United States. After 1870 businesses began a concerted search for more secure markets. This process led to European imperialism in Africa, Asia, and Oceania. Europeans also colonized vast areas of previously unsettled or sparsely settled lands in the interior of North and South America and Australia. This was the second phase of colonialism. The first had occurred in the New World after Columbus.

By 1900 the United States had become a core nation within the world system. Industrialization spread to many other countries, including Japan, Italy, the Netherlands, Russia, and China, in a process that continues today. Mass production gave rise to a culture of overconsumption, which valued acquisitiveness and conspicuous consumption. Industrialization shifted reliance from renewable resources to fossil fuels.

One effect of industrialization is the destruction of indigenous economies, ecologies, and populations. Two centuries ago, 50 million people still lived in politically independent bands, tribes, and chiefdoms, which controlled half the globe and 20 percent of its population. Industrialization tipped the balance in favor of states. The negative effects of the industrial world system include genocide, ethnocide, and ecocide. The specialization and peripheralization promoted by world capitalism and colonialism are basic to much of the poverty in the world today. Many former colonies remain economic satellites.

The American economy has recently shifted from manufacture toward information processing and services. The term *postindustrial,* sometimes used to describe this change, is inappropriate because industrialization continues today in a world economy in which the United States is a full participant.

The more isolated societies that represent anthropology's traditional concern are disappearing, but the subject matter open to anthropology is expanding. Alterations in the wider environments of human groups—that is, in their relationships with foreigners—represent changes to which people must adapt.

GLOSSARY

apartheid: Castelike system in South Africa; blacks, whites, and Asians have separate (and unequal) neighborhoods, schools, laws, and punishments.

bourgeoisie: One of Marx's opposed classes; owners of the means of production (factories, mines, large farms, and other sources of subsistence).

capitalist world economy: The single world system, which emerged in the sixteenth century, committed to production for sale, with the object of maximizing profits rather than supplying domestic needs.

caste system: Closed, hereditary system of stratification, often dictated by religion; hierarchical social status is ascribed at birth, so that people are locked into their parents' social position.

class consciousness: Recognition of collective interests and personal identification with one's economic group (particularly the proletariat); basic to Marx's view of class.

commodities: Articles of trade, products with commercial value.

core: Dominant structural position in the world system; consists of the strongest and most powerful states with advanced systems of production.

domestic system (of manufacture): Also known as home handicraft production; preindustrial manufacturing system in which organizer-entrepreneurs supplied raw materials to people who worked at home and collected finished products from them.

ecocide: Destruction of local ecosystems.

ethnic minorities: Indigenous peoples who have moved to urban areas.

ethnocide: Process in which ethnic groups survive but lose or severely modify their ancestral cultures.

genocide: Physical destruction of ethnic groups by murder, warfare, and introduced diseases.

income: Earnings from wages and salaries.

indigenous peoples: The original inhabitants of particular territories; often descendants of tribespeople who live on as culturally distinct colonized peoples, many of whom aspire to autonomy.

Industrial Revolution: The historical transformation (in Europe, after 1750) of "traditional" into "modern" societies through industrialization of the economy.

mercantilism: System of tariffs, trade laws, and other barriers designed to protect national products and industries from (often cheaper) foreign competition.

monocrop production: System of production, often on plantations, based on the cultivation of a single cash crop.

open class system: Stratification system that facilitates social mobility, with individual achievement and personal merit determining social rank.

periphery: Weakest structural position in the world system.

proletarianization: Separation of workers from the means of production through industrialism.

Romer's rule: Evolutionary rule stating that an innovation that evolves to maintain an existing system can play a major role in changing that system.

semiperiphery: Structural position in the world system intermediate between core and periphery.

slavery: The most extreme and coercive form of legalized inequality; people are treated as property.

vertical mobility: Upward or downward change in a person's social status.

working class: Or proletariat; those who must sell their labor to survive; the antithesis of the bourgeoisie in Marx's class analysis.

STUDY QUESTIONS

1. What is the world-system perspective, and why is it important in anthropology?
2. What were the two triangles of trade involving sugar and slaves?
3. How did the Caribbean sugar plantation play a key role in the emergence of world capitalism and industrialism?
4. What was the Age of Discovery, and how did it contribute to the Industrial Revolution?
5. What is the capitalist world economy? When did it originate, and what are its features?
6. What is the defining feature of capitalism? Why does capitalism require a world economy?
7. What are core, semiperiphery, and periphery? What is their relationship to world capitalism?
8. How do the worldwide effects of industrialism illustrate the general evolutionary trends of proliferation, specialization, integration, and expansion?
9. What was the Industrial Revolution, and how did it differ from previous life in villages, towns, and cities?
10. Why might the Industrial "Revolution" be better viewed in an evolutionary context?
11. What is Romer's rule, and how does it apply to food production and the Industrial Revolution?
12. Why did the Industrial Revolution begin in the cotton, iron, and pottery trades?
13. Why did the Industrial Revolution begin in England rather than France?
14. How did population growth and the accumulation of capital contribute to the Industrial Revolution?
15. How did proletarianization change human work?
16. How did the views of Marx and Weber on stratification differ?
17. What are the differences between open and closed class systems?
18. How is the world stratification system related to structural positions within the world capitalist economy?
19. What have been the major forces influencing cultural interaction during the past 500 years?
20. What was the second phase of colonialism, and what caused it?
21. How does industrialization destroy indigenous economies, ecologies, and populations?
22. What is mercantilism, and what is its relationship to capitalism?
23. What is *postindustrialism,* and why is this a problematic term?

SUGGESTED ADDITIONAL READING

BRAUDEL, F.

1973   *Capitalism and Material Life: 1400–1800.* London: Weidenfeld and Nicolson. The role of the masses in the history of capitalism.

1977   *Afterthoughts on Material Civilization and Capitalism.* Baltimore: Johns Hopkins University Press. Reflections on the history of industrial capitalism.

1982   *Civilization and Capitalism 15th–18th Century. Volume II: The Wheels of Commerce.* New York: Harper & Row. On the history of capitalism and the role of trade from precapitalist mercantilism to the present.

1984   *Civilization and Capitalism 15th–18th Century. Volume III: The Perspective of the World.* New York: Harper & Row. On the emergence of the world capitalist economy; case histories of European countries and various areas of the rest of the world.

CROSBY, A. W., JR.

1972   *The Columbian Exchange: Biological and Cultural Consequences of 1492.* Westport, CT: Greenwood Press. Describes how Columbus's voyages opened the way for a major exchange of people, resources, and ideas as the Old and New Worlds were forever joined together.

MINTZ, S.

1985   *Sweetness and Power: The Place of Sugar in Modern History.* New York: Viking Penguin. The place of sugar in the formation of the modern world system.

ROSEBERRY, W.

1988   Political Economy. *Annual Review of Anthropology* 17: 161–185. Review of recent works on industrialization, political economy, local and regional social history, and world-system studies.

WALLERSTEIN, I.

1974   *The Modern World-System: Capitalist Agriculture and the Origins of the European World-Economy in the Sixteenth Century.* New York: Academic Press. The origins of the capitalist world economy; a classic work.

1980   *The Modern World-System II: Mercantilism and the Consolidation of the European World-Economy, 1600–1750.* New York: Academic Press. Further development of the world system and the underpinnings of industrialization.

WOLF, E. R.

1982   *Europe and the People without History.* Berkeley: University of California Press. An anthropologist examines the effects of European expansion on tribal peoples and sets forth a world-system approach to anthropology.

C H A P T E R 1 0

ECONOMIC SYSTEMS

Economic anthropology looks at economics in a comparative perspective. A population's **economy** is its system of production, distribution, and consumption of resources. *Economics* is the study of such systems. **Comparative economics** examines these systems in different societies. It is in this last area that anthropologists have made a great contribution. Economists concentrate on modern nations, usually on capitalist systems but sometimes on the more managed economies of the Soviet Union and other socialist states. It has remained for anthropologists to broaden economics by gathering data on nonindustrial economies.

Economic anthropologists are concerned with two questions:

1. How are production, distribution, and consumption organized in different societies? This question focuses on *systems* of human behavior and their organization.
2. What motivates people in different cultures to produce, distribute or exchange, and consume? Here the focus is not on systems of behavior but on the *individuals* who participate in those systems.

Anthropologists view both economic systems and motivations in a cross-cultural perspective. Motivation is a concern of psychologists, but it has also been, implicitly or explicitly, a concern of economists and anthropologists. American economists assume that producers and distributors make decisions rationally using the *profit motive,* as do consumers when they shop around for the best value. However, anthropologists know that the motives of people in one culture are not necessarily the same as those of people in another. We compare the motivations, beliefs, and values that influence personality formation and cause individuals to behave differently in different cultures.

ECONOMIZING AND MAXIMIZATION

Although anthropologists know that the profit motive is not universal, the assumption that individuals try to maximize profits is basic to the capitalist world economy and to Western economic theory. In fact, the subject matter of economics is often

defined as **economizing,** or the rational allocation of scarce means (or resources) to alternative ends (or uses). What does that mean? Classical economic theory assumes that our wants are infinite and that our resources are limited. Since means are always scarce, people have to make choices. They must decide how they will use their scarce resources—their time, labor, money, and capital. Western economists assume that when confronted with alternatives, people tend to choose the one that maximizes profit. This is assumed to be the most rational (reasonable) choice.

The idea that individuals maximize profits was a basic assumption of the classical economists of the nineteenth century and one that is held by many contemporary economists. However, certain economists now recognize that individuals in Western cultures, as in others, may be motivated by many other goals. Depending on the society and the situation, people may try to maximize profit, wealth, prestige, pleasure, comfort, or social harmony. Individuals may want to realize their personal or family ambitions or those of another group to which they belong.

Alternative Ends

To what uses do people in various societies put their scarce resources? Throughout the world, people devote some of their time and energy to building up a **subsistence fund** (Wolf 1966). In other words, they have to work to eat, to replace the calories they use in their daily activity. People must also invest in a **replacement fund.** They must maintain their technology and other items essential to production. If a hoe or plow breaks, they must repair or replace it. They must also obtain and replace items that are essential not to production but to everyday life, such as clothing and shelter.

People everywhere also have to invest in a **social fund.** They have to help their friends, relatives, inlaws, and, especially in states, unrelated neighbors. It is useful to distinguish between a social fund and a **ceremonial fund.** The latter term refers to expenditures on ceremonies or rituals. To prepare a festival honoring one's ancestors, for example, requires time and the outlay of wealth.

Citizens of states must also allocate scarce resources to a **rent fund.** We think of rent as payment for the use of property. However, *rent fund* has a wider meaning. It refers to resources that people must render to an individual or agency that is superior politically or economically. Tenant farmers and sharecroppers, for example, either pay rent or give some of their produce to their landlords, as peasants did under feudalism.

Peasants are small-scale agriculturalists who live in states with rent fund obligations. They produce to feed themselves and to sell. All peasants have two things in common:

1. They live in state-organized societies.
2. They produce food without the elaborate technology—chemical fertilizers, tractors, airplanes to spray crops, and so on—of modern American farming or agribusiness.

In addition to paying rent to landlords, peasants must satisfy government obligations, paying taxes in the form of money, produce, or labor. The rent fund is not simply an *additional* obligation for peasants. Often it becomes their foremost and unavoidable duty. Sometimes, to meet the obligation to pay rent, their own diets suffer. The demands of social superiors may divert resources from subsistence, replacement, social, and ceremonial funds.

Social and ceremonial funds assume new functions in states. Many states use ceremonies as occasions to collect fees. In the Merina kingdom of Madagascar, circumcision, which once had been just a ritual and social event, became a device for collecting taxes and carrying out a census. In pre-state times circumcision had been a small-scale ritual uniting the boy, other members of his household, and his close relatives on his mother's and father's sides. It affirmed kinship between the boy, usually a member of his father's group, and his maternal relatives. As the Merina state developed, however, the king made circumcision a concern of the state. Every seventh year, boys were circumcised. Their sponsors, similar to godparents, had to pay a set fee (a single coin) to state officials. The coins collected were tallied to get a census of the boys born during the cycle.

Motivations vary from society to society, and people often lack freedom of choice in allocating their resources. Because of obligations to pay rent, peasants may allocate their scarce means toward

ends that are not their own but those of state officials. Thus, even in societies where there is a profit motive, people are often prevented from rationally maximizing self-interest by factors beyond their control.

PRODUCTION

Organization in Nonindustrial Populations

Strategies of adaptation, as discussed in Chapter 6, are based on the system (mode) of production that predominates in a particular society. Production varies somewhat within any adaptive strategy, depending on the environment. Thus the social organization of the foraging mode of production—for example, individual hunters or teams—depends on whether the game is a solitary or a herd animal. Gathering is usually more individualistic than hunting. People may fish alone or in crews.

Although some kind of division of economic labor related to age and gender is a cultural universal, the specific tasks assigned to each sex and to people of different ages vary. Some horticulturalists assign a major productive role to women; others make men's work primary. Similarly, among pastoralists men generally tend large animals, but in some cultures women do the milking. Jobs accomplished through teamwork in some cultivating societies are done by smaller groups or individuals working over a longer period of time in others.

Among the Betsileo of Madagascar there are two stages of teamwork in rice cultivation: transplanting and harvesting. Team size varies with the size of the field. Both transplanting and harvesting feature a traditional division of labor by age and gender which is well known to all Betsileo and is repeated across the generations. The first job in transplanting is the trampling of a flooded field by young men driving cattle in order to mix earth and water. Once the tramplers leave the field, older men arrive. With their spades they break up the clumps that the cattle missed. Meanwhile, the owner and other adults uproot rice seedlings and bring them to the field. Women plant the seedlings.

At harvest time, four or five months later, young men cut the rice off the stalks. Young women carry it to a clearing above the field. Older women ar-

The cultivation of rice, one of the world's most important food crops, often features a division of task by age and gender. Women often transplant; men often thresh. These young women are transplanting rice seedlings in Sulawesi, Indonesia, and these men are threshing rice, to separate the grains from the stem, in Bangladesh.

range and stack it. The oldest men and women then stand on the stack, stomping and compacting it. Three days later, young men thresh the rice, beating the stalks against a rock to remove the grain. Older men then attack the stalks with sticks to make sure all the grains have fallen off.

Most of the other tasks in Betsileo rice cultivation are done by owners and their immediate families. Men maintain and repair the irrigation and drainage systems and the earth walls that separate one plot from the next. Men also till with spade or plow. All members of the household help weed the rice field.

In any culture, the organization of production may change over time. The Betsileo no longer use teams to maintain the irrigation network. Each man cleans the sections of the canals that irrigate and drain his own field. Irrigation ditches start at stone dams built across the shallow parts of rivers. Canals that run for miles irrigate the fields of as many as thirty people. These systems were originally constructed and repaired by work parties or-

SCARCITY AND THE BETSILEO

From October 1966 through December 1967 my wife and I lived among the Betsileo people of Madagascar, studying their economy and social life (Kottak 1980). Soon after our arrival we met two well-educated schoolteachers who were interested in our research. The woman's father was a congressman who became a cabinet minister during our stay. Our schoolteacher friends told us that their family came from a historically important and typical Betsileo village called Ivato, which they invited us to visit with them.

We had traveled to many other villages, where we were often displeased with our reception. As we drove up, children would run away screaming. Women would hurry inside. Men would retreat to doorways, where they lurked bashfully. Eventually someone would summon the courage to ask what we wanted. This behavior expressed the Betsileos' great fear of the *mpakafo*. Believed to cut out and devour his victim's heart and liver, the *mpakafo* is the Malagasy vampire. These cannibals are said to have fair skin and to be very tall. Because I have light skin and stand six feet four inches tall, I was a natural suspect. The fact that such creatures were not known to travel with their wives helped convince the Betsileo that I wasn't really a *mpakafo*.

When we visited Ivato, we found that its people were different. They were friendly and hospitable. Our very first day there we did a brief census and found out who lived in which households. We learned people's names and relationships to our schoolteacher friends and to each other. We met an excellent informant who knew all about the local history. In a few afternoons I learned much more than I had in the other villages in several sessions.

Ivatans were willing to talk because I had powerful sponsors, village natives who had made it in the outside world, people the Ivatans knew would protect them. The schoolteachers vouched for us, but even more significant was the cabinet minister, who was like a grandfather and benefactor to everyone in town. The Ivatans had no reason to fear me because their most influential native son had asked them to answer my questions.

Once we moved to Ivato, the elders established a pattern of visiting us every evening. They came to talk, attracted by the inquisitive foreigners but also by the wine, cigarettes, and food we offered. I asked questions about their customs and beliefs. I eventually developed interview schedules about various subjects, including rice production. I mimeographed these forms to use in Ivato and in two other villages I was studying less intensively. Never have I interviewed as easily as I did in Ivato. So enthusiastic were the Ivatans about my questions that even people from neighboring villages came to join the study. Since these people know nothing about social scientists' techniques, I couldn't discourage them by saying that they weren't in my sample. Instead, I agreed to visit each village, where I filled out the interview schedule in just one house. Then I told the other villagers that the household head had done such a good job of teaching me about their village I wouldn't need to ask questions in the other households.

As our stay drew to an end, the elders of Ivato began to lament, saying, "We'll miss you. When you leave, there won't be any more cigarettes, any more wine, or any more questions." They wondered what it would be like for us back in the United States. Ivatans had heard of American plans to send a man to the moon. Did I think it would succeed? They knew that I had an automobile and that I regularly purchased things, including the wine, cigarettes, and food I shared with them. I could afford to buy products they would never have. They commented, "When you go back to your country, you'll need a lot of money for things like cars, clothes, and food. We don't need to buy those things. We make almost everything we use. We don't need as much money as you, because we produce for ourselves."

The Betsileo are not unusual among people whom anthropologists have studied. Strange as it may seem to an American consumer, who may believe that he or she can never have enough money, some rice farmers actually believe that *they have all they need*. The lesson from the Betsileo is that scarcity, which economists view as universal, is variable. Although shortages do arise in nonindustrial societies, the concept of scarcity (insufficient means) is much less developed in stable subsistence-oriented societies than in societies characterized by industrialism, particularly as consumerism increases.

ganized by political officials. Now, however, they are individually maintained without teamwork and political regulation.

Means of Production

In nonindustrial societies there is a more intimate relationship between the worker and the **means of production** than there is in industrial nations. Means, or factors, of production include land, labor, technology, and capital.

Territory

Among foragers, ties between people and land are less permanent than they are among food producers. Although many bands have territories, the boundaries are not usually marked, and there is no way they can be enforced. The hunter's stake in an animal that is being stalked or has been hit with a poisoned arrow is more important than where the animal finally dies. A person acquires the right to use a band's territory by being born in the band or by joining it through a tie of kinship, marriage, or fictive kinship. In Botswana in southern Africa, !Kung San women, whose work provides over half the food, habitually use specific tracts of berry-bearing trees. However, when a woman changes bands, she immediately acquires a new gathering area.

Among food producers, rights to the means of production also come through kinship and marriage. Descent groups are common among nonindustrial food producers, and those who descend from the founder share the group's territory and resources. If the adaptive strategy is horticulture, the estate includes garden and fallow land for shifting cultivation. As members of a descent group, pastoralists have access to animals to start their own herds, to grazing land, to garden land, and to other means of production.

In states, the means of production are unequally distributed. Stratification implies the existence of rent. Among the Betsileo, however, even after two centuries of life in nation-states, descent still plays a role in allocating land, although that role has weakened considerably. Today land is held in common by people with the same grandfather. The Betsileo have the legal right to end the condominium (joint holding) at any time and register their share of the rice field as private property, which may be sold. However, the Betsileo dis-

courage the sale of rice fields to outsiders. If people wish to sell a field and still have good relations with their kin, they must sell it to a fellow descent-group member.

Labor, Technology, Technical Knowledge, and Specialization

Like land, labor is a means of production. In nonindustrial societies, access to both land and labor comes through social links such as kinship, marriage, and descent. Mutual aid in production is merely one aspect of ongoing social relationships that are expressed on many other occasions.

Nonindustrial societies contrast with industrial nations in regard to another means of production—technology. In bands and tribes manufacturing is often linked to age and gender. Women may weave and men may make pottery or vice versa. Most people of a particular age and gender share the technical knowledge associated with that age and gender. If married women customarily make baskets, most married women know how to make baskets. Neither technology nor technical knowledge is as specialized as it is in states.

However, some tribal societies do promote specialization. Among the Yanomami of Venezuela and Brazil, for instance, certain villages manufacture clay pots and others make hammocks. They don't specialize, as one might suppose, because certain raw materials happen to be available near particular villages. Clay suitable for pots is widely available. Everyone knows how to make pots, but not everybody does so. Craft specialization reflects the social and political environment rather than the natural environment. Such specialization promotes trade, which is the first step in creating an alliance with enemy villages (Chagnon 1983). Specialization contributes to keeping the peace, although it has not prevented intervillage warfare.

Among the Trobriand Islanders of the South Pacific, Malinowski (1922/1961) found that only two out of several villages manufactured certain ceremonial items that were important in a regional exchange network called the kula ring. As among the Yanomami, this specialization was unrelated to the location of raw materials. We don't know why this specialization began, but we do know that it persisted within the kula ring, which allied several communities and islands in a common trade network.

Manufacturing is often linked to age and gender. Men may make pottery and women, baskets (like these Malaysians)— or vice versa. In traditional societies most people of a particular age and gender share the technical knowledge associated with that age and gender. Thus, if married women customarily make baskets, most married women know how to make baskets.

Alienation and Impersonality in Industrial Economies

What are the most significant contrasts between industrial and nonindustrial economies? When factory workers produce for sale and for the employer's profit rather than for their own use, they may be alienated from the items they make. Such alienation means they do not feel strong pride in or personal identification with their products. In nonindustrial societies people see their work through from start to finish and have a sense of accomplishment in the product.

In nonindustrial societies the economic relation-

In nonindustrial communities people usually see their work through from start to finish and have a sense of accomplishment. By contrast, assembly-line workers may be alienated from production—feeling no strong pride in or personal identification with their products. Compare this Dai woman weaving a fishing net in China's Yunnan province with these Japanese line workers sorting out substandard oranges.

ship between coworkers is just one aspect of a more general social relationship. They aren't just coworkers but kin, in-laws, or cocelebrants in a ritual. In industrial nations, people don't usually work with relatives and neighbors. If coworkers are friends, the personal relationship usually develops during their common employment rather than being based on a previous association.

Thus, industrial workers have impersonal relationships with their products, coworkers, and employers. People sell their labor for cash. They don't give it to members of their personal networks as readily or as often as they do in tribes. In bands, tribes, and chiefdoms people work for their relatives toward family or community goals. The goals of the factory owner, by contrast, usually differ from those of workers and consumers.

In industrial nations the economic domain stands apart from ordinary social life. In nonindustrial societies, however, the relations of production, distribution, and consumption are *social relations with economic aspects*. The economy is not a separate entity but is *embedded* in the society.

DISTRIBUTION, EXCHANGE

Besides studying production cross-culturally, economic anthropologists investigate exchange or distribution systems. The economist Karl Polanyi (1957) stimulated the comparative study of exchange, and several anthropologists followed his lead. To study exchange cross-culturally, Polanyi defined three principles orienting exchanges: the **market principle, redistribution,** and **reciprocity.** These principles can all be present in the same society, but in that case they govern different kinds of transactions. In any society, one of them usually dominates. The principle of exchange that dominates is the one that allocates the means of production. Roughly speaking, the market principle dominates in states, particularly industrial states. Redistribution is the main exchange principle of chiefdoms, and reciprocity dominates in band and tribal societies.

The Market Principle

In nonsocialist industrial nations, as in the world capitalist economy, the market principle domi-

nates. Thus, in the United States it governs the distribution of the means of production—land, labor, natural resources, technology, and capital. "Market exchange refers to the organizational process of purchase and sale at money price" (Dalton 1967). With market exchange, items are bought and sold with an eye to maximizing profit, and value is determined by the **law of supply and demand** (things cost more the scarcer they are and the more people want them).

Bargaining is characteristic of market-principle exchanges. The buyer and seller strive to maximize—to get their "money's worth." Bargaining doesn't require that the buyer and seller meet. Consumers bargain whenever they shop around or use advertisements in their decision making.

Redistribution

Redistribution is the dominant exchange principle in chiefdoms and some nonindustrial states and in states with managed economies. Redistribution operates when goods, services, or their equivalent move from the local level to a center. In states, the center is often a capital or a regional collection point. In chiefdoms, it may be a storehouse near the chief's residence. Products move through a hierarchy of officials for storage at the center. Along the way officials and their dependents consume some of them, but the exchange principle here is *re*distribution. The flow of goods eventually reverses direction—out from the center, down through the hierarchy, and back to the common people.

Reciprocity

Reciprocity is exchange between social equals, who are normally related by kinship, marriage, or another close personal tie. Because it occurs between social equals, it is dominant in egalitarian societies—among foragers, cultivators, and pastoralists living in bands and tribes. There are three degrees of reciprocity: generalized, balanced, and negative (Sahlins 1968, 1972; Service 1966). These may be imagined as areas on a continuum determined by these questions:

1. How closely related are the parties to the exchange?
2. How quickly are gifts reciprocated?

Sharing the fruits of production, which is the keystone of egalitarian societies, has also been a goal of modern socialist nations, such as China. These workers in Yunnan province strive for an equal distribution of meat.

Generalized reciprocity, the purest form of reciprocity, is characteristic of exchanges between closely related people. In **balanced reciprocity,** social distance increases, as does the need to reciprocate. In **negative reciprocity,** social distance is greatest and reciprocation is most urgent.

With generalized reciprocity, someone gives to another person and expects nothing concrete or immediate in return. Such exchanges (including parental gift giving in contemporary North America) are not primarily economic transactions but expressions of personal relationships. Most parents don't keep accounts of every penny they spend on their children. They merely hope that the children will respect their culture's customs involving love, honor, loyalty, and other obligations to parents.

Among foragers, generalized reciprocity tends to govern exchanges. People routinely share with other band members. A study of the !Kung San found that 40 percent of the population contributed little to the food supply (Lee 1974). Children, teenagers, and people over sixty depended on other people for their food. Despite the high proportion of dependents, the average worker hunted or gathered less than half as much (twelve to nineteen hours a week) as the average American works. Nonetheless, there was always food because different people worked on different days.

So strong is the ethic of reciprocal sharing that most foragers lack an expression for "thank you."

To offer thanks would be impolite, because it would imply that a particular act of sharing, which is the keystone of egalitarian society, was unusual. Among the Semai, foragers of central Malaysia (Dentan 1979), to express gratitude would suggest surprise at the hunter's generosity or success (Harris 1974).

Balanced reciprocity applies to exchanges between people who are more distantly related than are members of the same band or household. In a tribal society, for example, a man presents a gift to someone in another village. The recipient may be a cousin, a trading partner, or a brother's fictive kinsman. The giver expects something in return. This may not come immediately, but the social relationship will be strained if there is no reciprocation.

Foragers and members of tribes also have negative reciprocity, which applies to people on the fringes of their social systems. To people who live in a world of close personal relations, exchanges with outsiders are full of ambiguity and distrust. Exchange is one way of establishing friendly relations with outsiders, but when trade begins, the relationship is still tentative. The initial exchange is as close to being purely economic as anything that ever happens in tribal society. People want something back immediately, and just as in market economies, they try to get the best possible immediate return for their investment.

One example of negative reciprocity is silent

trade or barter between the "pygmy" foragers of the African equatorial forest and neighboring horticultural villagers. There is no personal contact during the exchange. A "pygmy" hunter leaves game, honey, or another forest product at a customary site. Villagers collect it and leave crops in exchange. Thus the parties can bargain silently. If one feels that the return is insufficient, he or she simply leaves it at the trading site. If the other party wants to continue trade, it will be increased.

As people exchange with more and more distantly related individuals, they move along the continuum from generalized toward negative reciprocity. However, because the differences are of degree rather than kind, exchange relationships may shift as personal relationships change. A good example, which also illustrates the role of exchange in establishing alliances, comes from the Yanomami. Two hostile villages may initiate an alliance by beginning reciprocal exchange. The first step is an exchange of products in which each of the villages specializes. The next step is the exchange of food and hospitality, with each village inviting the other to a feast.

Exchanges have now moved from negative reciprocity, in which hostility, fear, distrust, immediate return, and equivalence are characteristic, toward balanced reciprocity, in which gifts may be returned later. Mutual feasting doesn't guarantee that an alliance between villages will last, but it is a closer relationship than is one based on intervillage trade of arrows, pots, and hammocks.

The final stage in establishing an alliance between two Yanomami villages is intermarriage. Many Yanomami marriages result from an arrangement called sister exchange. If two men have unmarried sisters, each man marries the other's sister. The notion of equivalence operates here: a sister is given "in exchange for" a wife. Once the marriages take place, the brother-in-law relationship becomes one of generalized reciprocity, because a close personal relationship has been established.

However, Yanomami villages can fall out of alliance the way modern North Americans fall out of love. Villages may split and stop exchanging spouses. They go on feasting for a while and still trade. Finally, one village may invite the other to a "treacherous feast" in which the hosts attack and try to kill their guests. With the alliance ended, there is

no longer even negative reciprocity. Instead, there is open hostility and feuding (Chagnon 1983).

Coexistence of Modes of Exchange

In contemporary North America, the market principle governs the means of production and most exchanges, for example, those involving consumer goods. We also have redistribution, but it is not highly developed. Much of our tax money goes to support the government, but some of it comes back as social services, education, Medicare, and road building. We also have reciprocal exchanges. Generalized reciprocity characterizes the relationship between parents and children. However, even here the dominant market mentality surfaces in comments about the high cost of raising children and in the stereotypical statement of the disappointed parent: "We gave you everything money could buy."

Exchanges of gifts, cards, and invitations exemplify reciprocity, usually balanced. Everyone has heard remarks like "They invited us to their daughter's wedding, so when ours gets married, we'll have to invite them" and "They've been here for dinner three times and haven't invited us yet. I don't think we should ask them back until they do." Such precise balancing of reciprocity would be out of place in a foraging band, where resources are communal (common to all) and daily sharing based on generalized reciprocity is an essential ingredient of social life and survival.

It often takes time for Western ethnographers to get used to generalized reciprocity in the societies they study. For example, among the Betsileo (Kottak 1980) and Merina (Bloch 1971) of Madagascar, men routinely march up to covillagers and demand chewing tobacco. Kinsmen are expected to share with one another. This test of kin loyalty, which none dares refuse, helps maintain village solidarity.

Once anthropologists are accepted within the community, they often find *their* possessions disappearing at an alarming rate. People are using up the ethnographer's resources just as they do with those of their own relatives. Anthropologists gradually learn that our culture's "stealing" is another's kin-based sharing. The ethnographer is simply being treated as part of community life. Of course, he or she must also devise a way of preserving necessary items for the remainder of the field stay.

MONEY AND SPHERES OF EXCHANGE

Money is of such overwhelming importance to us that it is difficult to conceive of its absence. However, it is not a cultural universal. Money has several different functions (Bohannan 1963). First, it may be a *means of exchange*. In contemporary North America it is the most common means of exchange. We don't give food to a bank teller and expect our accounts to be credited or give a cashier a dozen roses in exchange for a steak. We give money in exchange for food.

Second, money may function as a *standard of value*. Indeed, it is the main standard we use to evaluate what something is worth. A washing machine is worth $400, not 225 chickens or 4 pigs. Third, money functions as a *means of payment*. We pay money to the government, often not in exchange for anything but simply to fulfill an obligation, such as paying a parking ticket.

Because the currencies of modern nations serve all three functions, each is a **general-purpose money**. Any currency that doesn't serve all three functions is a **special-purpose money** (Bohannan 1963). In some societies a cow is a means of exchange but not a standard of value. To understand the difference between general-purpose and special-purpose money, we need to discuss multicentric exchange systems.

Many tribal societies have **multicentric exchange systems**, or systems which are organized into different categories or spheres. Bohannan (1955) found that the Tiv of Nigeria had such a system. They assigned relative value to exchanges and divided them into three spheres: subsistence, prestige, and marriage partners. The Tiv thought that items within a given sphere should be exchanged only for each other. The subsistence sphere included food, small livestock, and tools. The prestige sphere encompassed slaves, cattle, large bolts of white cloth, and metal bars. The third sphere included only one "item"—women.

Although the number of spheres and the items they contain vary from society to society, multicentric economies are common in tribes and chiefdoms. How do they work? Exchanges for items in the same sphere are called **conveyances**, which are considered normal and appropriate. Tiv examples include yams for pots (subsistence conveyances) and cloth or brass rods for slaves (prestige conveyances). Like Yanomami men, who exchange sisters as marriage partners, Tiv men were found to control the marriage system. Tiv society had a system of wardship in which men tried to obtain female wards in order to arrange marriages for them. In return, the men received wives.

Viewing conveyances as proper, the Tiv avoided exchanging higher-sphere for lower-sphere items. Occasionally, however, exchanges between different spheres, called **conversions**, did take place, for example, a brass rod for food. The people who managed to convert subsistence into prestige items were pleased, whereas those who had to do the contrary were shamed.

We can return now to the matter of money. Despite their multicentric economy, the Tiv had a general-purpose money consisting of metal bars. However, this general-purpose money worked in just one sphere—the prestige sphere. Contemporary nations, participating in an international economy, have eliminated spheres of exchange. General-purpose currencies regulate the entire modern exchange system.

POTLATCHING

Spheres of exchange are widespread because they are cultural adaptive mechanisms that help populations adapt to their environments. In societies without banks, the higher spheres serve some of the same functions that banks do in modern nations. In times of plenty, people convert subsistence surpluses into higher categories. In times of need, they reconvert the surpluses back into subsistence goods. In multicentric economies, as in our own, people save for a rainy day. However, the context of their saving is personal, and the situations in which deposits and withdrawals take place are social and ceremonial. Consider the following case.

One of the most famous cultural practices studied by ethnographers is the **potlatch**, which was widely practiced by tribes of the North Pacific Coast of North America, including the Salish and

Piling up blankets to burn in a Kwakiutl potlatch on Vancouver island in British Columbia. As European trade goods poured in, some Kwakiutl hosts became so wealthy that they destroyed most of their property. They even burned down their houses in impressive displays of the conversion of wealth into prestige.

Kwakiutl of Washington and British Columbia. The potlatch, which some tribes still practice (sometimes as a memorial to the dead) (Kan 1986), was a festive event. Assisted by members of their communities, sponsors gave away food, blankets, pieces of copper, and other items. In return for this, they got prestige. To give a potlatch enhanced one's reputation. Prestige increased with the lavishness of the potlatch, the value of the goods given away in it.

Within the spreading world capitalist economy of the nineteenth century, the potlatching tribes, particularly the Kwakiutl, began to trade with Europeans (fur for blankets, for example), and their wealth increased as a result. Simultaneously, a huge proportion of the population died from previously unknown diseases brought by the Europeans. The increased wealth from trade flowed into a drastically reduced population. With many of the traditional sponsors dead, the Kwakiutl extended the right to give a potlatch to the entire population, and this stimulated intense competition for prestige. Given trade, increased wealth, and a decreased population, the Kwakiutl also started converting wealth into prestige by *destroying* wealth items such as blankets and pieces of copper (Vayda 1961/1968).

Both the Salish and the Kwakiutl had multicentric economies with a subsistence sphere and a wealth sphere. The third sphere, the highest one, contained a nonmaterial item—prestige. Included in the subsistence sphere were several foods. The potlatching tribes were hunters and gatherers, but compared with other foragers, they were more like food producers. They lived in sedentary tribes and chiefdoms rather than in bands. In contrast to most foragers, their environments were not marginal. They had access to a wide variety of land and sea resources. Their most important foods were salmon, herring, candlefish, berries, mountain goats, seals, and porpoises (Piddocke 1969).

There were some differences in the diets of the Salish and the Kwakiutl, and their wealth spheres also differed. Among the Salish, blankets, shell ornaments, hide shirts, and fine baskets were wealth items. The Kwakiutl wealth sphere included slaves, canoes, skins, blankets, and pieces of copper. Nevertheless, people in both societies could convert wealth into prestige by giving away (or destroying, among the Kwakiutl) wealth items at potlatches.

Scholars once regarded Kwakiutl potlatching as economically wasteful behavior, the result of an irrational drive for social status and prestige. They stressed the destructiveness of the Kwakiutl to support their contention that in some societies people strive irrationally to maximize prestige— even by destroying valuable resources.

However, a more recent interpretation views potlatching not as wasteful but as a useful cultural adaptive mechanism. This view not only helps us understand potlatching, it also has comparative value because it helps us understand similar feasts and multicentric economies throughout the world. This is the new interpretation: *Customs such as the potlatch are adaptations to alternating periods of local abundance and shortage.*

How did this work? The overall natural environment of the North Pacific Coast is favorable, but resources fluctuate from year to year and place to place. Salmon and herring aren't equally abundant every year in a given locality. One village can have a good year while another is experiencing a bad one. Later their fortunes reverse. In this context, the multicentric economies of the Kwakiutl and Salish had adaptive value, and the potlatch was not an irrational competitive display.

A village enjoying an especially good year had a surplus of subsistence items, which it could exchange for wealth, and wealth could be converted into prestige. Potlatches distributed food and wealth to other communities that needed it. In return, the sponsors and their villages got prestige. The decision to potlatch was determined by the health of the local economy. If there had been a subsistence surplus, and thus a buildup of wealth over several good years, the village could afford a potlatch to convert food and wealth into prestige.

The adaptive value of intercommunity feasting becomes clear when we consider what happened when a formerly prosperous village had a bad year. Its people started accepting invitations to potlatches in villages that were doing better. The tables were turned as the temporarily rich became temporarily poor and vice versa. The newly needy accepted food and wealth items. They were willing to receive rather than bestow gifts and thus to relinquish some of their stored-up prestige. Later, if the village's fortunes continued to decline, its people could exchange wealth items for food, for example, slaves for herring or canoes for cherries (Vayda 1961/1968). They hoped that their luck would eventually improve so that the process of converting up could resume.

Note that potlatching also impeded the development of socioeconomic stratification. Wealth relinquished or destroyed was converted into a nonmaterial item—prestige. Under capitalism we reinvest our profits (rather than burning our cash) with the hope of making an additional profit. However, the potlatching tribes were content to destroy their surpluses rather than use them to widen the social distance between themselves and fellow tribe members.

Multicentric economies and regional systems of intervillage feasting can therefore have adaptive value. Similar to our banks, their wealth and prestige spheres are places where people can store surpluses. Multicentric economies also provide for communities in need. As fortunes fluctuate, food is converted into wealth and prestige, wealth is converted into prestige, prestige is converted back

into wealth and food, and wealth is converted back into food.

The potlatch linked local groups along the North Pacific Coast into a regional alliance and exchange network. Potlatching and multicentric exchange had adaptive functions, regardless of the motivations of the individual participants. The anthropologists who stressed rivalry for prestige were not wrong. They were merely emphasizing motivations at the expense of an analysis of economic and ecological systems.

The use of feasts to enhance individual and community reputations and to redistribute wealth is not peculiar to the Kwakiutl and the Salish. Competitive but adaptive feasting is widely characteristic of tribal economies. Among foragers in marginal areas, resources are too meager to support feasting on such a level. Further along the evolutionary continuum, chiefdoms and states have more effective means of distributing resources among local groups.

SIPHONING

Tribal feasting thus redistributes scarce resources between communities and *levels* differences in wealth. However, in states, ceremonial obligations often siphon wealth from poor people to rich people. This *magnifies* contrasts in wealth and helps maintain inequality, stratification, and poverty.

Latin American peasant communities provide an ethnographic illustration of how this happens. Anthropologist Eric Wolf (1955) has distinguished between two types of communities in Latin America: the **closed, corporate peasant community** and the **open, noncorporate peasant community**. Indian communities located in the highlands are closed and corporate. Non-Indian (mestizo) communities in the lowlands are open and noncorporate. Closed, corporate communities are found in the highlands of Mexico, Guatemala, Ecuador, Peru, Bolivia, and Colombia.

As we noted in discussing the potlatching tribes of North America, Old World diseases, which spread through the world system, also ravaged native populations further south—throughout the New World. However, the effects of depopulation were more severe in the Latin American lowlands than in the densely populated highlands, which had chiefdoms and states before the arrival of the *conquistadors*. In the Latin American highlands, in nations with closed, corporate peasant communities, much of the national population is still Indian.

The precolonial lowlands, by contrast, had horticultural and foraging economies and tribes rather than chiefdoms and states. Population densities were much lower. Here foreign diseases, slave raids, and warfare proved more devastating and completely destroyed some groups. In the lowlands today, Native Americans are fewest and their cultural contribution is least marked. Here the open, noncorporate community is the characteristic rural settlement.

The term **mestizo** ("mixed") describes lowland communities in Latin America. The populations of these communities are mixtures of Europeans, Indians, and Africans who speak the national language. In such plantation nations as Brazil, large numbers of slaves were imported from Africa during the seventeenth, eighteenth, and nineteenth centuries. These people left their physical and cultural mark on lowland Latin America just as they did in the Caribbean and the United States. Brazilian peasants show an array of physical types and cultural features because of the intermingling of Europeans, Africans, and Indians.

The Highland Peasant Community

The peasant community of highland Latin America is *corporate*. Like a modern corporation, it has an estate (property), usually consisting of land. All members have access to this estate. Such communities are usually located in marginal areas of the highlands, places that Europeans could not use for plantation crops. Production for subsistence rather than cash is characteristic of these communities.

Highland communities are also *closed*. That is, a person's status as a community member is determined at birth and cannot easily be shifted. Further isolating the community is the custom of endogamy: most marriages take place between natives of the community.

Living in communities that are closed socially and corporate economically, highlanders have a feeling of internal solidarity and distinctiveness from neighboring towns. People in nearby communities sometimes speak different dialects or even different languages. Communities are also set apart by different clothing styles. Finally, although the Indians are all Roman Catholics and thus participate in a world religious system, each community has its own patron saint, who is honored in an annual celebration—a festival, or *fiesta*.

The Lowland Peasant Community

Lowland and highland communities differ in several ways. Lowlanders do not farm a joint estate held in trust from generation to generation. People individually own or manage the land they farm. Nor is the lowland community closed. Membership is not ascribed at birth, and people move. Finally, there is no cultural preference for endogamy. People marry both insiders and outsiders. The lowland community, not being corporate, has few of the features of solidarity and distinctiveness that are characteristic of the highlands. For example, Arembepe, an open community in Brazil, has a patron saint, as do neighboring communities. Every February a festival is held in his honor. However, the traditional lowland festival is less ostentatious than is the highland fiesta, and its consequences are different. The patron saint is not a powerful symbol for lowland identification and pride. Many of the people who live in Arembepe, for example, cannot even name the saints of nearby villages.

Unlike highlanders, who have subsistence economies, lowlanders produce for cash. They sell crops in markets and to marketers who visit the community; between half and two-thirds of what they produce is exchanged for cash. However, this does not mean that lowlanders eat better than' highlanders do. It merely means that they can buy more and that they depend more on the outside world. Arembepeiros sold nutritious fish to purchase manioc flour and sugar, which are high in calories but much lower in protein. Lowland peasants also use cash for clothing, household items, and other externally manufactured products.

Lowlanders speak the national language—Portuguese in Brazil, Spanish in the rest of Latin America. This allows them to partake more in national life than highlanders do. They follow national events and vote in state and national elections. Lowlanders celebrate national holidays. They are increasingly drawn into national culture through exposure to the mass media. In Brazil, lotteries, soccer, and commercial television are national pastimes.

Although lowlanders feel more attached to the nation than highlanders do, it would be wrong to suppose that highland Indians are isolated from their nations and from the world capitalist economy. It would be equally erroneous to assume that life in lowland communities is better, happier, or more fulfilling. Many lowlanders are just as poor as highlanders, eat just as badly, and are equally illiterate. Their health conditions are as poor, and their life expectancies are equally short. Furthermore, obstacles to improving living conditions are often as severe in the lowlands and the highlands.

Poverty in Highland Latin America: The Cargo System

In a tribal setting, competitive feasting redistributes resources between communities. In a state setting (for example, modern Peru), highland Indian feasting not only levels wealth contrasts among Indians, it also *siphons* wealth from Indians to wealthier mestizos. This helps maintain Indian poverty. Highland feasting proceeds within a political and religious hierarchy characteristic of each community—the **cargo system.** (This derives from the Spanish word *cargo,* meaning "charge" or "burden." It should not be confused with the cargo cults discussed in Chapter 18.)

In highland communities men move up through the local prestige hierarchy by undertaking progressively heavier cargos. Young men begin this process by doing errands for older men. As they get older, they occupy political offices as the equivalents of sheriffs, city council members, and mayors. Religious burdens are associated with each office. Highland communities celebrate several saints' days, culminating in a large festival honoring the patron saint of the community. As men advance within the political hierarchy, they must contribute more of their time and wealth to religious celebrations. In return, they receive prestige.

Large quantities of time and wealth are invested in organizing fiestas. The wealthiest Indians are always chosen to hold the highest offices and to assume the major cargos. Many expenses devolve on the fiesta organizers, who pay for food, liquor, church services, candles, costumes, musicians,

fireworks, bulls, and bullfighters. Since the organizers must serve on the village council, they are away from their fields much of the year. They lose both time and money (Harris 1964).

On the surface, cargo-system feasting resembles the potlatch. However, its effects are quite different. Highland communities exist within stratified, multiethnic nations in which Indians are members of the lowest stratum. These countries also have mestizos. The main difference between Indians and mestizos is not genetic but cultural. Mestizos don't participate directly in the cargo system, but they profit from it.

The cargo system helps maintain inequalities between Indians and mestizos. To understand this, recall the economy of the highland community. Indians grow crops for subsistence rather than cash. They sell and buy little. However, fiestas require *cash expenditures for goods produced outside.* This forces Indians into market relationships. Mestizo storekeepers, who supply items consumed during the fiesta, profit.

Mestizos benefit from the system in another way. Nations with highlands generally also include lowland zones with cash-crop plantation economies. Highland Indians are a source of cheap labor for these plantations. But how, given the solidarity of the closed, corporate peasant community, do plantation owners entice Indians to join the world capitalist economy? How do capitalists get Indians to leave home to work for wages?

The cargo system provides the answer. Labor recruiters from the lowlands regularly travel through the highlands to find Indians who have assumed heavy cargos. Because cargo obligations usually leave Indians with prestige but destitute, *cargueros* are often willing to sign work contracts or take loans from recruiters. The Indians get cash to repay these loans only by selling their labor on the national market. Their cargo participation complete, they go off to work a few years on a mestizo-owned lowland plantation at rock-bottom wages. In these ways, the cargo system funnels cheap Indian labor into the capitalist world economy.

Understandably, highland Indians are often reluctant to assume cargos. In an ethnographic study in Guatemala, Ruth Bunzel (1952) described Indians so reluctant to fill elective posts that they literally had to be dragged into office. Often community members force others to assume cargos. Indians who have served their terms are unwilling to excuse others from the same obligations. Church and government officials also encourage compliance.

We see that contemporary nations, such as Peru, have institutions that are similar in form to those of tribes. However, in tribal societies such customs help maintain an *unstratified* society by acting as **leveling mechanisms.** They even out, or level, temporary fluctuations in wealth and resources be-tween communities. In states, however, comparable customs can act to preserve a *stratified* society by siphoning wealth and labor from Indians to upper-status mestizos. Ceremonial burdens have this effect in many stratified nations throughout the world. Indeed, religious obligations have become one of the main ways of drawing subsistence-oriented people into the world cash economy.

SUMMARY

Economic anthropologists study systems of production, distribution, and consumption cross-culturally. Economics has been defined as the science of allocating scarce means to alternative ends. Western economists assume that the notion of scarcity is universal—which it isn't—and that in making choices, people strive to maximize personal profit. However, in nonindustrial societies, as in our own, people maximize values other than individual profit. Furthermore, people often lack free choice in allocating their resources.

In bands and tribes, people invest in subsistence, replacement, social, and ceremonial funds. States add a rent fund: People must share their output with government officials and other social superiors. In states, the obligation to pay rent often becomes primary, and family subsistence may suffer.

Strategies of adaptation are actually systems of production. In nonindustrial societies, production is personal. The relations of production are aspects of continuous social relationships. One acquires rights to resources through membership in bands, descent groups, villages, and other social units, not impersonally through purchase and sale. Labor is also recruited through personal ties. Work is merely one aspect of social relationships that are expressed in a variety of social and ceremonial contexts.

Manufacturing specialization can exist in tribal societies, promoting trade and alliance between groups. In nonindustrial societies there is usually a personal relationship between producer and commodity, in contrast to the alienation of labor, product, and management in industrial economies.

Besides production, economic anthropologists study and compare exchange systems. The three principles of exchange are the market principle, redistribution, and reciprocity. The market principle, based on supply and demand and the profit motive, is dominant in states. Its characteristics are impersonal purchase and sale and bargaining. Redistribution is the characteristic exchange mode in chiefdoms, some nonindustrial states, and managed economies. Goods are collected at a central place, and some of them are eventually given back, or redistributed, to the people.

Reciprocity governs exchanges between social equals. It is the characteristic mode of exchange in bands and tribes. There are different degrees of reciprocity. With generalized reciprocity, there is no immediate expectation of return. With balanced reciprocity, which is characteristic of exchanges between more distantly related people, donors expect their gifts to be returned, although not immediately. Exchanges on the fringes of the social system are governed by negative reciprocity. As with the market principle, there is concern about immediate return, as well as bargaining. Reciprocity, redistribution, and the market principle may coexist in a society, but the primary exchange mode is the one that allocates the means of production.

A general-purpose money is a standard of value, a means of exchange, and a means of payment. Special-purpose monies are currencies that don't serve all these functions. Multicentric exchange systems, which are common in tribal societies, are organized into ranked spheres of exchange (subsistence, wealth, and prestige). Multicentric economies have adaptive relevance: conversions of subsistence goods to wealth or prestige are ways of saving in tribal societies. Conversions to such nonmaterial items as prestige also impede the emergence of socioeconomic stratification.

Latin America has two types of peasant communities: the closed, corporate (generally Indian) peasant community of the highlands and the open, noncorporate (generally mestizo) peasant community of the lowlands. Both have some customs similar in form to those of tribal societies. However, comparing similar forms—for example, ceremonial feasting—in states and nonstates, we find that their functions may be very different. The cargo systems of highland Latin America force Indians into market relations, siphon Indian wealth, and maintain poverty. This contrasts with the adaptive, intercommunity redistribution of resources associated with tribal feasting, such as potlatching.

GLOSSARY

balanced reciprocity: See *generalized reciprocity.*

cargo system: A series of obligations associated with the political and religious hierarchies of highland Latin American Indian communities.

ceremonial fund: Resources invested in ceremonial or ritual expenses or activity.

closed, corporate peasant community: Generally Indian, located in the highlands of Latin America; corporate in sharing an estate and closed by birth and through endogamy.

comparative economics: The study of economic systems in different societies.

conversion: Exchange between different spheres of a multicentric economy.

conveyance: Exchange within the same sphere of a multicentric economy.

economizing: The rational allocation of scarce means (or resources) to alternative ends (or uses); often considered the subject matter of economics.

economy: A population's system of production, distribution, and consumption of resources.

generalized reciprocity: Principle that characterizes exchanges between closely related individuals: As social distance increases, reciprocity becomes *balanced* and finally *negative.*

general-purpose money: Currency that functions as a means of exchange, a standard of value, and a means of payment.

Kwakiutl: A potlatching society on the North Pacific Coast of North America.

leveling mechanism: Sociocultural custom that acts to even out or reduce differences in wealth and resources.

market principle: Profit-oriented principle of exchange that dominates in states, particularly industrial states. Goods and services are bought and sold, and values are determined by supply and demand.

means (or factors) of production: Land, labor, technology, and capital—major productive resources.

mestizo: Mixed. In Latin America, having a combination of European, African, and Native American ancestors. Mestizos speak the national language.

multicentric exchange system: Economy organized into different categories or spheres.

negative reciprocity: See *generalized reciprocity.*

open, noncorporate peasant community: Located in the lowlands of Latin America; admixture of Indians, Europeans, and Africans. Noncorporate; members do not farm a joint estate. Not closed; flexible in admitting new members.

peasant: Small-scale agriculturalist living in a state with rent fund obligations.

potlatch: Competitive feast among Indians on the North Pacific Coast of North America.

reciprocity: One of the three principles of exchange. Governs exchange between social equals; major exchange mode in band and tribal societies.

redistribution: Major exchange mode of chiefdoms, many archaic states, and some states with managed economies.

rent fund: Scarce resources that a social inferior is required to render to an individual or agency that is superior politically or economically.

replacement fund: Scarce resources invested in technology and other items essential to production.

social fund: Scarce resources invested to assist friends, relatives, in-laws, and neighbors.

special-purpose money: Currency that serves only one or two of the three functions associated with general-purpose money.

subsistence fund: Scarce resources invested to provide food in order to replace the calories expended in daily activity.

supply and demand, law of: Economic rule that things cost more the scarcer they are and the more people want them.

STUDY QUESTIONS

1. What do economists mean by *economizing?*
2. What are the main differences between the economies of bands and tribes and peasant economies?
3. What are some of the main contrasts between industrial and nonindustrial economies?
4. What are the main differences between reciprocity, redistribution, and the market principle?
5. What examples can you give from your own culture to illustrate each of these three types of exchange?
6. What are the main differences between the three degrees of reciprocity?
7. How are multicentric exchange systems adaptive?
8. What were the adaptive functions of the potlatch?

9. What are the main differences between peasant communities in the highlands and those in the lowlands of Latin America?

10. What are the main differences in the context, functions, and effects of ceremonial feasting in tribal versus peasant settings?

SUGGESTED ADDITIONAL READING

CLAMMER, J., ED.
1976 *The New Economic Anthropology*. New York: St. Martin's Press. Essays link economic anthropology to problems affecting Third World nations and to Marxist analysis.

GOODY, J.
1977 *Production and Reproduction: A Comparative Study of the Domestic Domain*. New York: Cambridge University Press. Relationships between agriculture, property transmission, and domestic relations in Africa, Asia, and Europe.

HARRIS, M.
1974 *Cows, Pigs, Wars, and Witches: The Riddles of Culture*. New York: Random House. Good discussion of different exchange systems and general evolution.

LeCLAIR, E. E., AND H. K. SCHNEIDER, EDS.
1968 (orig. 1961). *Economic Anthropology: Readings in Theory and Analysis*. New York: Holt, Rinehart & Winston. Defines the "substantive" approach in economic anthropology and advocates the study of exchange systems in different societies.

LEE, R. B., AND I. DEVORE, EDS.
1977 *Kalahari Hunter-Gatherers: Studies of the !Kung San and Their Neighbors*. Cambridge, MA: Harvard University Press. Long-term interdisciplinary study of well-known foragers.

MAUSS, M.
1954 (orig. 1925). *The Gift: Forms and Functions of Exchange in Archaic Societies*. New York: Free Press. Uses comparative data to emphasize the positive values of giving. Has influenced generations of anthropologists, especially French.

PLATTNER, S., ED.
1989 *Economic Anthropology*. Stanford, CA: Stanford University Press. Most recent comprehensive text in economic anthropology, including original articles by twelve authors on bands, tribes, states, peasants, and industrial economies.

WOLF, E. R.
1966 *Peasants*. Englewood Cliffs, NJ: Prentice-Hall. Fascinating theoretical and comparative introduction to peasants.

GENDER

Because anthropologists consider human biology, psychology, society, and culture, they are in a unique position to comment on nature (biological predispositions) and nurture (environment) as determinants of human behavior. Human attitudes, values, and behavior are limited not only by our genetic predispositions—which are difficult to identify—but also by our experiences during enculturation. Our attributes as adults are determined both by our genes and by our environment during growth and development.

Debate about the effects of nature and nurture proceeds today in scientific and public arenas. **Naturists** assume that some—they differ about how much—human behavior and social organization is biologically determined. **Nurturists,** or **environmentalists,** do not deny that in theory some universal aspects of human behavior may have a genetic base. However, they find most attempts to link behavior to genes unconvincing. The basic environmentalist assumption is that human evolutionary success rests on flexibility, or the ability to adapt in various ways. Because human adaptation relies so strongly on cultural learning, we can change our behavior more readily than members of other species can.

The nature-nurture debate emerges in the discussion of human sex-gender roles and sexuality. Men and women differ genetically. Women have two X chromosomes, and men have an X and a Y. The father determines a baby's sex, because only he has the Y chromosome to transmit. The mother always provides an X chromosome.

The chromosomal difference is expressed in hormonal and physiological contrasts. Humans are sexually dimorphic. Men and women differ not just in primary (genitalia and reproductive organs) and secondary (breasts, voice, hair distribution) sexual characteristics but in average weight, height, and strength.

Just how far, however, do these genetically and physiologically determined differences go? What effect do they have on the way men and women act and are treated in different cultures? On the environmentalist side, anthropologists have discovered substantial variability in the roles of men and women in different cultures. The anthropological position on sex-gender roles and biology may be stated as follows:

The biological nature of men and women [should be seen] not as a narrow enclosure limiting the human organism, but rather as a broad base upon which a variety of structures can be built (Friedl 1975, p. 6).

Although in most cultures men tend to be somewhat more aggressive than women, many of the behavioral and attitudinal differences between the sexes emerge from culture rather than biology. *Sex* differences are biological, but *gender* encompasses all the traits that a culture assigns to and inculcates in males and females. Gender, in other words, refers to the cultural construction of male and female characteristics. A person's sense of self includes a sense of gender, cultural identity, and social class (Rosaldo 1980b).

Given "rich and various constructions of gender" within the anthropological realm of cultural diversity, Susan Bourque and Kay Warren (1987) note that the same images of masculinity and feminity do not always apply. Margaret Mead did an early ethnographic study of variation in gender roles. Her book *Sex and Temperament in Three Primitive Societies* (1935/1950) was based on field work in three societies in Papua–New Guinea: Arapesh, Mundugumor, and Tchambuli. The extent of personality variation in men and women in these three societies on the same island amazed Mead. She found that Arapesh men and women acted as Americans have traditionally expected women to act—in a mild, parental, responsible way. Mundugumor men and women, in contrast, acted as she believed we expect men to act—fiercely and aggressively. Tchambuli men were "catty," wore curls, and went shopping, but Tchambuli women were energetic and managerial and placed less emphasis on personal adornment than did the men. (Drawing on their recent case study of the Tchambuli, Errington and Gewertz [1987], while recognizing gender malleability, have disputed the specifics of Mead's account.)

There is a growing field of feminist scholarship within anthropology (Nash and Safa 1986; Rosaldo 1980b), and in recent years ethnographers have been gathering systematic ethnographic data about gender in many cultural settings (Mukhopadhyay and Higgins 1988). We can see that gender roles vary with environment, economy, adaptive strategy, and level of social complexity. Before we examine the cross-cultural data, some definitions are in order.

Gender roles are the tasks and activities that a culture assigns to the sexes. Related to gender roles are **gender stereotypes,** which are oversimplified but strongly held ideas about the characteristics of males and females. **Gender stratification** describes an unequal distribution of rewards (socially valued resources, power, prestige, and personal freedom) between men and women, reflecting their different positions in a social hierarchy (Light, Keller, and Calhoun 1989). According to Ann Stoler (1977), the "economic determinants of female status" include freedom or autonomy (in disposing of one's labor and its fruits) and social power (control over the lives, labor, and produce of others).

In stateless societies, gender stratification is often much more obvious in regard to prestige than it is in regard to wealth. In her study of the Ilongots of northern Luzon in the Philippines, Michelle Rosaldo (1980a) described gender differences related to the positive cultural value placed on adventure, travel, and knowledge of the external world. More often than women, Ilongot men, as headhunters, visited distant places. They acquired knowledge of the external world, amassed experiences there, and returned to express their knowledge, adventures, and feelings in public oratory. They received acclaim as a result. Ilongot women had inferior prestige because they lacked external experiences on which to base knowledge and dramatic expression. On the basis of Rosaldo's study and findings in other stateless societies, Ong (1989) argues that we must distinguish between gender categories (pronounced or muted), prestige systems, and actual power in a given society. High male prestige may not entail economic or political power held by men over their families.

GENDER ISSUES AMONG FORAGERS

Several studies have linked aspects of gender stratification to economic roles. Cross-culturally, women's cultural value rises when they contribute about as *much* to subsistence as men do (Sanday 1974). Among nonindustrial food producers, women's prestige tends to diminish when they contribute either *much more* or *much less* than men do.

Among foragers, however, female status falls *only* when women contribute substantially less, as among the Eskimo, Inuit, and other northern hunters and fishers. Among foragers in tropical and semitropical areas, gathering contributes more to the diet than do hunting and fishing. Gathering is generally women's work; men usually hunt and fish. When gathering is prominent, gender status tends to be more equal than it is when hunting and fishing are dominant subsistence activities.

Gender status is also more equal when the domestic and public spheres are not sharply separated, with a corresponding devaluation of women's work and worth. Sharp differentiation between the home and the external world is called the **domestic-public dichotomy** or the *private-public contrast*. The external world can include politics, trade, warfare, or work. Cross-culturally, as traditionally in the United States, women's rights and duties tend to be closer to home than men's are. Another reason foragers have more equal gender status is that the domestic-public dichotomy is less developed among them than it is among food producers.

A division of labor linked to gender has been found in all cultures. However, the particular tasks assigned to men and women don't always reflect differences in strength and endurance. Gathering just two or three days per week, !Kung San women travel about 2,500 kilometers (1,500 miles) in a year. For half that distance, they carry children plus up to fifteen kilograms (thirty-three pounds) of food (Friedl 1975).

Food producers often assign the arduous tasks of carrying water and firewood and pounding grain to women. In 1967 Soviet women filled 47 percent of factory positions, including many unmechanized jobs, which required the hardest physical labor. Most Soviet sanitation workers, physicians, and nurses are women (Martin and Voorhies 1975). Many jobs that men do in some societies are done by women in others, and vice versa.

Certain roles are more sex-linked than others. Men are the usual hunters and warriors. Given such weapons as spears, knives, and bows, men make better fighters because they are bigger and stronger on the average than are women in the same population (Divale and Harris 1976). The male hunter-fighter role also reflects a tendency toward greater male mobility.

In foraging societies women are either pregnant or lactating during most of their childbearing period. Late in pregnancy and after childbirth, carrying the baby limits a woman's movements, even her gathering. Given the effects of pregnancy and lactation on mobility, it is rarely feasible for women to be the primary hunters (Friedl 1975). Warfare, which also requires mobility, is not found in most foraging societies, nor is interregional trade well developed. Warfare and trade are two public arenas that contribute to status inequality of males and females among food producers.

The !Kung San illustrate the extent to which the activities and spheres of influence of men and women may overlap among foragers (Draper 1975). Traditional !Kung gender roles were interdependent. During gathering, women discovered information about game animals, which they passed on to the men. Men and women spent about the same amount of time away from camp, but neither worked more than three days a week. Between one-third and one-half of the band stayed home while the others worked.

The !Kung saw nothing wrong in doing the work of the other gender. Men often gathered food and collected water. A general sharing ethos dictated that men distribute meat and women share the fruits of gathering. Boys and girls of all ages played together. Fathers took an active role in raising children. Resources were adequate, and competition and aggression were discouraged. Exchangeability and interdependence of roles are adaptive in small groups.

Patricia Draper's field work among the !Kung is especially useful in showing the relationships between economy, gender roles, and stratification because she studied both foragers and a group of former foragers who had become sedentary. Just a few thousand !Kung continue their culture's traditional foraging pattern. Most are now sedentary, living near food producers or ranchers.

Draper studied sedentary !Kung at Mahopa, a village where they herded, grew crops, worked for wages, and did a small amount of gathering. Their gender roles were becoming more rigidly defined. A domestic-public dichotomy was developing as men traveled farther than women did. With less gathering, women were confined more to the home. Boys could gain mobility through herding, but girls' movements were more limited. The equal and communal world of the bush was yielding to the social features of sedentary life. A differential ranking of men according to their herds, houses, and sons began to replace sharing. Males came to be seen as the most valuable producers.

If there is some degree of male dominance in every contemporary society, it may be because of changes such as those which have drawn the !Kung into wage work, market sales, and thus the world capitalist economy. A historical interplay between local, national, and international forces influences systems of gender stratification (Ong 1989). In traditional foraging cultures, however, egalitarianism extends to the relations between the sexes. The social spheres, activities, rights, and obligations of men and women overlap. Foragers' kinship systems tend to be bilateral (calculated equally through males and females) rather than favoring either the mother's side or the father's side. Foragers may live with either the husband's or the wife's kin and often shift between one group and the other.

One last observation about foragers: It is among them that the public and private spheres are least separate, hierarchy is least marked, aggression and competition are most discouraged, and the rights, activities, and spheres of influence of men and women overlap the most. Our ancestors lived entirely by foraging until 10,000 years ago. If there is any "natural" form of human society, it is best (although imperfectly) represented by foragers. Despite the popular stereotype of the club-wielding caveman dragging his mate by the hair, relative gender equality is a much more likely ancestral pattern.

GENDER ISSUES AMONG HORTICULTURALISTS

Gender roles and stratification among cultivators vary widely, depending on specific features of the economy and social structure. Demonstrating this, Martin and Voorhies (1975) studied a sample of 515 horticultural societies, representing all parts of the world. They looked at several variables, including descent and postmarital residence, the percentage of the diet derived from cultivation, and the productivity of men and women.

Women have high status in matrilineal, uxorilocal societies because descent-group membership, succession to political positions, allocation of land, and overall social identity come through female links. Among these Minangkabau of Negeri Sembilan (Malaysia), matriliny gave women sole inheritance of ancestral rice fields and promoted clusters of female kin.

Women were found to be the main producers. In 50 percent of the horticultural societies women did most of the cultivating. In 33 percent contributions to cultivation by men and women were equal, and in only 17 percent did men do most of the work. Women tended to do a bit more cultivating in matrilineal compared with patrilineal societies. They dominated horticulture in 64 percent of the matrilineal societies versus 50 percent of the patrilineal ones. However, even more important for women's overall status than their contribution to subsistence is their control over what is produced (Sanday 1974). This is usually linked to factors such as kinship and the extent to which men are away from the community.

Matriliny, Uxorilocality, and High Female Status

Cross-cultural variation in gender status is related to rules of descent and postmarital residence (Martin and Voorhies 1975; Friedl 1975). Among horticulturalists with matrilineal descent and **uxorilocality** (customary residence after marriage with the wife's kin), female status is usually high. Matriliny and uxorilocality disperse rather than consolidate related males. Their effects are very different from those of patriliny and **virilocality** (customary residence after marriage with the husband's relatives).

Women have high status in matrilineal, uxori-local societies because descent-group membership, succession to political positions, allocation of land, and overall social identity come through female links. Among the Minangkabau in Malaysia (Peletz 1988), matriliny gave women sole inheritance of ancestral rice fields and promoted clusters of female kin. Minangkabau women had considerable influence beyond the household (Swift 1963). In such matrilineal contexts, women are the basis of the entire social structure. Although public authority may be (or appear to be) assigned to men, much of the power and decision making may belong to senior women.

Anthropologists have never discovered a **matriarchy,** a society ruled by women. However, some matrilineal societies, including the **Iroquois** (Brown 1975), a confederation of tribes in aboriginal New York, show that women's political and ritual influence can rival that of the men.

We saw that among foragers gender status is more equal when there is not a sharp separation between male and female activities and between the public and domestic spheres. However, gender equality can also be enhanced by roles that remove men from the local community. We now refine our generalizations: Female status falls only when the male and female spheres are sharply differentiated *within* the local community. Iroquois women played a major subsistence role, while men left home for long periods. As is usual in matrilineal societies, *internal* warfare was uncommon among the Iroquois, whose men waged war only on distant groups. However, this could keep them away for years.

Iroquois men hunted and fished, but women controlled the local economy. Women did some fishing and occasional hunting, but their major productive role was in horticulture. Women owned the land, which they inherited from matrilineal kinswomen. Women controlled the production and distribution of food.

Iroquois women lived with their husbands and children in the family compartments of a communal longhouse. Women born in a longhouse remained there for life. Senior women, or **matrons,** decided which men could join the longhouse as husbands, and they could evict incompatible men. Women therefore controlled alliances between descent groups, an important political job in tribal society.

Iroquois women thus managed production and distribution. Social identity, succession to office and titles, and property all came through the female line, and women were prominent in ritual and politics. Related tribes made up a confederacy, the League of the Iroquois, with chiefs and councils.

A council of male chiefs managed military operations, but chiefly succession was matrilineal. The matrons of each longhouse nominated a man as their representative. If the council rejected their first nominee, the women proposed others until one was accepted. Matrons constantly monitored the chiefs and could impeach them. Women could veto war declarations, withhold provisions for war, and initiate peace efforts. In religion, too, women shared power. Half the tribe's religious practitioners were women, and the matrons helped select the others.

Matrifocality and High Female Status

Surveying the **matrifocal** (mother-centered, often with no resident husband-father) organization of certain societies in Indonesia, West Africa, and the Caribbean, anthropologist Nancy Tanner (1974) also found that male travel, when combined with a major female role in subsistence, promotes high female status. Matrifocal societies are not necessarily matrilineal. A few are even patrilineal.

For example, Tanner (1974) found matrifocality

among the Igbo of eastern Nigeria, who are patrilineal, virilocal, and polygynous (men have multiple wives). Each wife had her own house, where she lived with her children. Women planted crops next to their houses and traded surpluses. Women's associations ran the local markets, while men did the long-distance trading.

In a case study of the Igbo, Ifi Amadiume (1987) noted that either sex could fill male gender roles. Before Christian influence, successful Igbo women and men used wealth to take titles and acquire wives. Wives freed husbands (male and female) from domestic work and helped them accumulate wealth. Female husbands were not considered masculine but preserved their femininity. Igbo women asserted themselves in women's groups, including those of lineage daughters, lineage wives, and a communitywide women's council led by titled women. The high status and influence of Igbo women rested on the separation of males from local subsistence and on a marketing system that allowed women to leave home and gain prominence in distribution and—through these accomplishments—in politics.

The Patrilineal-Virilocal Complex and Low Female Status

The Igbo are unusual among patrilineal-virilocal societies, in which female status is usually lower. Martin and Voorhies (1975) link the decline of matriliny and the spread of the **patrilineal-virilocal complex** (consisting of patrilineality, virilocality, warfare, male supremacy, female infanticide, and polygyny) to pressure on resources. Cross-cultural research by Divale and Harris (1976) has supported this finding. Both studies suggest that patrilineal-virilocal societies share several contexts and characteristics.

Faced with scarce resources, patrilineal-virilocal cultivators often adopt the interrelated cultural responses of intervillage warfare (as contrasted with long-distance, intertribal warfare) and polygyny. Intervillage warfare devalues women and favors the localization of related men—and thus virilocality and patriliny. Polygyny can also be a social response to scarcity and the need to increase food production. Women are the main subsistence workers, and polygyny increases household production by bringing women together.

Among patrilineal-virilocal cultivators, men and

women live in the same village but have sharply different activities and interests. The domestic-public dichotomy is apparent. Men use their public roles in distribution, including intervillage trade, to symbolize and reinforce their oppression of women. In patrilineal-virilocal societies world-wide, men dominate the allocation of prestige.

In parts of highland Papua–New Guinea the patrilineal-virilocal complex has extreme social repercussions. Women raise pigs, but men trade the pigs and control their use in ritual. Men grow and distribute prestige crops and arrange strategic marriages. They prepare food for feasts, as do the patrilineal, virilocal, male-supremacist Yanomami. Women do domestic cooking, grow and process subsistence crops, and tend pigs before the pigs are slaughtered and cooked. Women are isolated from the public domain.

In the most densely populated areas of the Papua–New Guinea highlands, there is severe sexual antagonism that is associated with strong pressure on resources (Lindenbaum 1972). Men fear that sexual contact with women will weaken them. Indeed, men see everything female as dangerous and polluting. Men segregate themselves in men's houses and hide their precious ritual objects from women. They fear all female contacts, including sex. They delay marriage, and some never marry.

In contrast, sparsely populated areas of Papua–New Guinea, such as recently settled areas, lack taboos on male-female contacts. The image of woman as polluter fades, heterosexual intercourse is valued, men and women live together, and reproductive rates are high.

Etoro Homosexuality

One of the most extreme examples of male-female sexual antagonism in Papua–New Guinea comes from the **Etoro** (Kelly 1976), a group of 400 people who subsist by hunting and horticulture in the Trans-Fly region. The Etoro also reveal the power of culture in molding human sexuality. The following account applies only to Etoro males and their beliefs. Etoro cultural norms prevented the male anthropologist who studied them from gathering information about female attitudes. Etoro opinions about sexuality are linked to beliefs about the cycle of birth, physical growth, maturity, senescence, and death.

The Etoro believe that semen is necessary to give

In some parts of Papua–New Guinea, the patrilineal-virilocal complex has extreme social repercussions. Regarding females as dangerous and polluting, men may segregate themselves in men's houses (such as this one, located near the Sepik River), where they hide their precious ritual objects from women.

life force to a fetus, which is said to be placed within a woman by an ancestral spirit. Because men are believed to have a limited supply of semen, sexuality saps male vitality. The birth of children, nurtured by semen, symbolizes a necessary (and unpleasant) sacrifice that will lead to the husband's eventual death. Heterosexual intercourse, which is needed only for reproduction, is discouraged. Women who want too much sex are viewed as witches, hazardous to their husbands' health. Etoro culture permits heterosexual intercourse only about 100 days a year. The rest of the time it is tabooed. Seasonal birth clustering shows that the taboo is respected.

So objectionable is heterosexuality that it is removed from community life. It can occur neither in sleeping quarters nor in the fields. Coitus can happen only in the woods, where it is risky, be-

HIDDEN WOMEN, PUBLIC MEN—PUBLIC WOMEN, HIDDEN MEN

For the past few years, one of Brazil's top sex symbols has been Roberta Close, whom I first saw in a furniture commercial. Roberta, whose looks reminded me of the young Natalie Wood, ended her pitch with an admonition to prospective furniture buyers to accept no substitute for the advertised product. "Things," she warned, "are not always what they seem."

Nor was Roberta. This petite and incredibly feminine creature was actually a man. Nevertheless, despite the fact that he—or she (speaking as Brazilians do)—is a man posing as a woman, Roberta has won a secure place in Brazilian mass culture. Her photos decorate magazines. She has been a panelist on a TV variety show and has starred in a stage play in Rio with an actor known for his super-macho image. Roberta even inspired a well-known, apparently heterosexual pop singer to make a "video" honoring her. In it she pranced around Rio's Ipanema Beach in a bikini, showing off her ample hips and buttocks.

The video depicted widespread male appreciation of Roberta's beauty. As confirmation, one heterosexual man told me that he had recently been on the same plane as Roberta and had been struck by her looks. Another man said he wanted to have sex with her. These comments, it seemed to me, illustrated striking cultural contrasts about gender and sexuality. In Brazil, a Latin American country noted for its *machismo,* heterosexual men do not feel that attraction toward a transvestite blemishes their masculine identities.

Roberta Close exists in relation to a gender-identity scale that jumps from extreme femininity to extreme masculinity, with little in between. Masculinity is stereotyped as active and public, femininity as passive and domestic. The male-female contrast in rights and behavior is much stronger in Brazil than it is in North America. Brazilians confront a more rigidly defined masculine role than North Americans do.

The active-passive dichotomy

Things aren't always what they seem. Roberta Close, a known transvestite (a transsexual as of 1989) who for years has been one of Brazil's top sex symbols, is genetically male.

also provides a stereotypical model for male homosexuality: One man is supposed to be the active, masculine (inserting) partner, whereas the other is the passive, effeminate one. The latter man is derided as a *bicha* (intestinal worm), but little stigma attaches to the inserter. However,

cause poisonous snakes, the Etoro say, are attracted by the sounds and smells of sex.

Although coitus is discouraged, homosexual acts are viewed as essential. Etoro believe that boys cannot produce semen on their own. To grow into men and eventually give life force to their children, boys must acquire semen orally from older men. From the age of ten until adulthood, boys are inseminated by older men. No taboos are attached to this. Homosexual activity can go on in the sleeping area or garden. Every three years a group of boys around the age of twenty are formally initiated into manhood. They go to a secluded mountain lodge, where they are visited and inseminated by several older men.

Etoro homosexuality is governed by a code of propriety. Although homosexual relationships between older and younger males are culturally essential, those between boys of the same age are discouraged. A boy who gets semen from other youths is believed to be sapping their life force and preventing their proper development. When an adolescent boy develops very rapidly, this suggests that he is ingesting semen from other boys. Like a sex-hungry wife, he is shunned as a witch.

Etoro homosexuality rests not on hormones or genes but on cultural traditions. The Etoro represent one extreme of a male-female avoidance pattern that is widespread in Papua–New Guinea and in patrilineal-virilocal societies.

for Brazilian men who are unhappy with active masculinity or passive effeminacy there is one other choice—active femininity. For Roberta Close and others like her, the cultural demand of ultramasculinity has yielded to a performance of ultrafemininity. These men-women form a third gender in relation to Brazil's more polarized male-female identity scale.

Transvestites such as Roberta are particularly prominent in Rio's annual Carnival, when an ambience of inversion rules the city. In the culturally accurate words of the American popular novelist Gregory McDonald, who sets one of his books in Brazil at Carnival time:

> Everything goes topsy-turvy . . . . Men become women; women become men; grown-ups become children; rich people pretend they're poor; poor people, rich; sober people become drunkards; thieves become generous. Very topsy-turvy. (McDonald 1984, p. 154)

Most notable in this costumed inversion (DaMatta 1981), men dress as women. Carnival reveals and expresses normally hidden tensions and conflicts as social life is turned upside down. Reality is illuminated through a dramatic presentation of its opposite.

This is the final key to Roberta's cultural meaning. She emerged in a setting in which male-female inversion is part of the year's most popular festival. Transvestites are the pièces de résistance at Rio's Carnival balls, where they dress as scantily as the real women do. They wear postage-stamp bikinis, sometimes with no tops. Photos of real women and transformed ones vie for space in the magazines. It is often impossible to tell the born women from the hidden men. Roberta Close is a permanent incarnation of Carnival—a year-round reminder of the spirit of Carnivals past, present, and yet to come.

Roberta emerges from a Latin culture whose gender roles contrast strongly with those of the United States. From small village to massive city, Brazilian males are public and Brazilian females are private creatures. Streets, beaches, and bars belong to the men. Although bikinis adorn Rio's beaches on weekends and holidays, there are many more men than women there on weekdays. The men revel in their ostentatiously sexual displays. As they sun themselves and play soccer and volleyball, they regularly stroke their genitals to keep them firm. They are living publicly, assertively, and sexually in a world of men.

Brazilian men must work hard at this public image, constantly acting out their culture's definition of masculine behavior. Public life is a play whose strong roles go to men. Roberta Close, of course, is a public figure. Given that Brazilian culture defines the public world as male, we can perhaps better understand now why the nation's number one sex symbol is a man who excels at performing in public as a woman.

GENDER ISSUES AMONG PASTORALISTS

Because it rarely occurs as a "pure" adaptive strategy, pastoralism has diverse social correlates, including gender roles and stratification. Most pastoralists also cultivate, using either horticultural or agricultural techniques. They are classified as pastoralists, however, if dairy products and meat provide more than 50 percent of their diet. Among pastoralists who practice intensive cultivation (such as the Balkan case discussed below) or who are descended from agricultural parent communities, women's status reflects the domestic-public dichtomy characteristic of intensive cultivators (see the next section). The patrilineal-virilocal complex also characterizes pastoralists. Both of these factors contribute to low female status within this strategy of adaptation.

Transhumants residing in the Balkan peninsula of Greece, Yugoslavia, Albania, and Bulgaria provide an extreme illustration of this gender stratification. Balkan men follow a transhumant pattern between summer and winter pastures, and they practice plow agriculture. Herding and plowing are male activities, although women do some cultivating in addition to their domestic work and crafts. Women also carry firewood and water. The domestic-public dichotomy and the patrilineal-virilocal complex are fully expressed in "patricentric" Balkan social organization (Denich 1974). Men control all property. Women inherit neither land nor livestock.

Balkan pastoralists belong to patrilineal-virilocal tribes and descent groups. The father is the patriarch in a joint household that includes his wife, his married sons, their wives and children, and his own unmarried children. Joint households split up after the patriarch's death. The sons become patriarchs in their own right.

Gender stratification involving low female prestige and subordination is extreme. When identifying their children, men mention only sons. Male ancestors, but never female ones, are remembered—for as many as twenty generations. Men arrange all marriages. Brothers' wives must come from different villages. Therefore, when they marry, women must enter a totally alien social world where they have no relatives.

Men have total authority and power. A woman must defer to her husband and his kinsmen. Women may be beaten and, if adulterous, killed. Their sexual activity is rigidly controlled. Exclusion of women from a major role in production has helped maintain patricentric organization in the Balkans.

GENDER ISSUES AMONG AGRICULTURALISTS

We have seen that horticulturalists faced with pressure on resources may develop the patrilineal-virilocal complex and intensify production. Agriculture continues trends toward intensification and a fall in female status. As horticulture evolved into agriculture, men were forced to work more in the fields in order to increase production. Women were no longer the primary cultivators. New agricultural techniques, particularly plowing, were assigned to men because of their greater average size and strength (Martin and Voorhies 1975). Except when irrigation was used, plowing eliminated the need for constant weeding, an activity usually done by women.

Cross-cultural data illustrate these changes in productive roles. Women were the main workers in 50 percent of the horticultural societies surveyed but in only 15 percent of the agricultural groups. Male labor dominated 81 percent of the agricultural societies but only 17 percent of the horticultural ones (Martin and Voorhies 1975) (see Table 11.1).

With agriculture, women were cut off from production for the first time in cultural evolution. Belief systems started contrasting the inferior **domestic** (within or pertaining to the home) role of women with men's valuable **extradomestic** (within or pertaining to the public domain) productive labor. Related changes in kinship and postmarital residence patterns also hurt women. Descent groups and polygyny declined with agriculture, and the nuclear family became more common. Living with her husband and children, a woman was isolated from her kinswomen and cowives. Female sexuality is carefully supervised in agricultural economies; this gives men easier access to divorce and extramarital sex, reflecting a "double standard."

However, woman's status in agricultural economies is not inevitably bleak. Low female status is associated with plow agriculture rather than with intensive cultivation per se. Studies of peasant gender roles and stratification in France and Spain (Harding 1975; Reiter 1975), which have plow agriculture, show that people think of the house as the female sphere and the fields as the male sphere. However, such a dichotomy is not inevitable, as my own research among Betsileo agriculturalists in Madagascar shows.

Betsileo women play a prominent role in agriculture, contributing a third of the hours invested in rice production. They have their customary tasks in the division of labor, but their work is more seasonal than men's is.

Table 11.1 *Male and female contributions to production in cultivating societies*

	Horticulture (percentage of 104 societies)	Agriculture (percentage of 93 societies)
Women are primary cultivators	50	15
Men are primary cultivators	17	81
Equal contributions to cultivation	33	3

SOURCE: Martin and Voorhies 1975, p. 283.

No one has much to do during the ceremonial season, between mid-June and mid-September. Men work in the rice fields almost daily the rest of the year. Women's cooperative work occurs during transplanting (mid-September through November) and harvesting (mid-March through early May). Along with other members of the household, women do daily weeding in December and January. After the harvest, all family members work together winnowing the rice and transporting it to the granary.

If we consider the strenuous daily task of husking rice by pounding (a part of food preparation rather than production per se), women actually contribute slightly more than 50 percent of the labor devoted to producing and preparing rice before cooking.

Not just women's prominent economic role but traditional social organization enhances female status among the Betsileo. Although postmarital residence is mainly virilocal, descent rules permit married women to keep membership in and a strong allegiance to their own descent groups. Kinship is broadly and bilaterally (on both sides—as in contemporary North America) calculated. The Betsileo exemplify Aihwa Ong's (1989) generalization that bilateral (and matrilineal) kinship systems, combined with subsistence economies in which the sexes have complementary roles in food production and distribution, are characterized by reduced gender stratification. Such societies are common among South Asian peasants (Ong 1989).

The Betsileo woman assumes obligations to her husband and his kin, but they are also obligated to her and her relatives. Often accompanied by their husbands and children, women pay regular visits to their home villages. The husband and his relatives help the wife's kin in agriculture and attend ceremonials hosted by them. When a woman dies, she is normally buried in her husband's ancestral tomb. However, a delegation from her own village always comes to request that she be buried at home. Women often marry into villages where some of their kinswomen have previously married; thus, even after marriage a woman lives near some of her own relatives.

Betsileo men do not have exclusive control over the means of production. Women can inherit rice fields, but most women, on marrying, relinquish their shares to their brothers. Sometimes a woman

Bilateral kinship systems, combined with subsistence economies in which the sexes have complementary roles in food production and distribution, have reduced gender stratification. Such features are common among Asian rice cultivators, such as the Ifugao of the Philippines (shown here).

and her husband cultivate her field, eventually passing it on to their children.

Traditionally, Betsileo men participate more in politics, but women also hold political office. Women sell their produce and products in markets, invest in cattle, sponsor ceremonials, and are mentioned during offerings to ancestors. Arranging marriages, an important extradomestic activity, is more women's concern than men's. Sometimes Betsileo women seek their own kinswomen as wives for their sons, reinforcing their own prominence in village life and continuing kin-based female solidarity in the village.

The Betsileo illustrate the idea that intensive cultivation does not necessarily entail a degraded status for women. We can see that gender roles and stratification reflect not just the type of adaptive strategy but also specific environmental variables and cultural attributes. Betsileo women continue to play a significant role in their society's major economic activity, rice production.

Plowing has become prominent in Betsileo agriculture only recently, but irrigation makes weeding, in which women participate, continue to be necessary. If new tools and techniques eventually reduce women's roles in transplanting, harvesting, and weeding, female status may fall. In the meantime, several features of the economy and social organization continue to draw the Betsileo away from the stereotype of the degraded woman in agricultural and virilocal societies.

We have seen that virilocality and polygyny are usually associated with low female status. However, some cultures with these institutions, including the Betsileo and the matrifocal Igbo of eastern Nigeria, permit women to improve their lot. The Igbo and Betsileo are not alone in allowing women a role in trade. Many patrilineal, polygynous so-

In many parts of West Africa, including Ibadan, Nigeria (shown here), women are active in commerce. Polygyny may even help the aspiring woman trader, who can leave her children with co-wives while she pursues a business career.

cieties in West Africa also allow women to have careers in commerce. Polygyny may even help an aspiring woman trader, who can leave her children with her cowives while she pursues a business career. She repays them with cash and other forms of assistance.

In tribal societies, the patrilineal-virilocal complex can isolate and devalue women. In chiefdoms and states, new possibilities are opened for some women. With general social stratification, some men, women, and children have privileged access to resources while other strata have more limited opportunities. In such contexts elite women manipulate wealth and power as effectively as do men—as they did among the Betsileo. They can become queens, chiefs, and headwomen. They can direct rituals, convoke and sponsor regional ceremonials, trade, exchange, and arrange marriages.

Tribal society, under some conditions, discriminates against women. In stratified society, not only does discrimination against women continue but some women join some men in discriminating against other men, women, and children.

GENDER ISSUES AND INDUSTRIALISM

The domestic-public dichotomy, which is developed most fully among patrilineal-virilocal food producers and plow agriculturalists, has also affected the status of women in industrial societies, including the United States and Canada. However, gender roles have been changing rapidly in North America (Margolis 1984; Martin and Voorhies 1975).

We can trace the belief that a woman's place is in the home, particularly for biological reasons, to growth in American industrialization late in the nineteenth century. Earlier, pioneer women in the Midwest and West had been perceived as fully productive work partners in farming and home industry. Western frontier women were among the first American women to gain the right to vote.

As industrialism began, attitudes about women's work varied with class and region. In early industrial Europe, men, women, and children flocked to factories as wage laborers. American slaves of both sexes did grueling work in cotton fields. With abolition, southern African-American women continued working as field hands and domestics. Poor white women labored in the South's early cotton mills. In the 1890s more than 1 million American women held menial, repetitive, and unskilled factory positions.

Early in the twentieth century an influx of European immigrants who were willing to accept wages lower than those of American-born men helped push women out of the factories. As machine tools and mass production also reduced the need for female labor, the notion that women are biologically unfit for factory work began to gain ground (Martin and Voorhies 1975).

Twentieth-century American attitudes about women and actual female participation in extradomestic labor have varied in response to economic needs (Margolis 1984). Wartime shortages of men have promoted the idea that extradomestic labor is woman's patriotic duty. During the world wars the notion that women are biologically unfit for hard physical labor faded. Inflation and the culture of consumption have also spurred female employment. When prices and demand rise, multiple paychecks help maintain family living standards.

The steady increase in female paid employment since World War II also reflects the baby boom and industrial expansion. American culture has traditionally defined clerical work, teaching, and nursing as female occupations. With rapid postwar population growth and business expansion, the demand for women to fill such jobs grew steadily. Employers also discovered that they could increase profits by paying women lower wages than they would have to pay returning veterans.

Anthropologist Maxine Margolis (1984) has argued that changes in the economy lead to changes in attitudes toward women. Woman's role in the home is stressed during periods of high unemployment, although if inflation occurs simultaneously, female employment may still be accepted. Between 1970 and 1989 the proportion of women in the American work force increased from 38 percent to 45 percent, and more than 56 million American women now work at paid jobs (Cowan 1989). Figures on the ever-increasing cash employment of American mothers are given in Table 11.2.

The average American man made $26,660 in 1988 versus $17,610 for the average woman (66 percent of the male rate, up from 62 percent in 1982 and 65 percent in 1987) (Barringer 1989). Table

Wartime shortages of men have promoted the idea that extradomestic labor is woman's patriotic duty. During the world wars the notion that women were biologically unfit for hard physical labor faded. Shown here is World War II's famous Rosie the Riveter.

11.3 details employment in the United States in 1987 by gender and job type. Notice that the income gap between women and men was least pronounced—but still obvious—in professional jobs,

Table 11.2 *Cash employment of American mothers, 1950–1985*

Year	Percentage of Mothers with Children under 18
1950	19
1960	28
1970	40
1980	52
1985	60

SOURCE: Bureau of the Census.

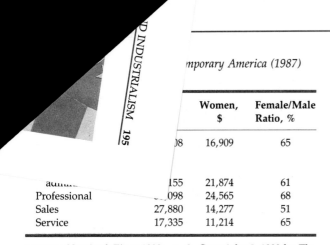

...mporary America (1987)

	Women, $	Female/Male Ratio, %
	...08	16,909	65
...adm...	...155	21,874	61
Professional	...098	24,565	68
Sales	27,880	14,277	51
Service	17,335	11,214	65

SOURCE: *New York Times* 1988a, p. 9. Copyright © 1988 by The New York Times Company. Reprinted by permission.

where women averaged 68 percent of the male income. The gap was widest in sales, where women averaged half the male salary.

According to political scientist Andrew Hacker (1984), American women are replacing men in certain occupations for three reasons. First, because of increasing automation, physical strength is less necessary for many jobs. Second, American women tend to be better educated than American men are. Employers prefer to hire more literate people, particularly when—and here is Hacker's third reason—women are willing to work for lower wages.

In particular, many American men between fifty-five and sixty are encouraged to retire earlier, and less expensive women workers are replacing them. (Later, many of the men will accept lower-paying part-time jobs.) There is also a group of younger men, including many ethnic minorities, who are too poorly educated to find any work openings in an economy that increasingly stresses services and information over farm and factory.

Table 11.4, which shows the percentage of female workers in certain occupations in 1950 and 1985, seems to support Hacker's contention that women are replacing men in certain professions, particularly in fields that require an advanced education. However, even as more women enter engineering, medicine, law, and college teaching, certain positions with less prestige and income (e.g., clerical workers) still have a higher proportion of women (Bourque and Warren 1987).

Economist George Gilder, author of *The Spirit of Enterprise* (1984), argues that American women are not actually taking jobs away from men. Rather,

because the economy is expanding, there are more men *and* more women working. Between 1970 and 1985, the American economy added 27 million jobs, while European economies were adding none (Rowan 1985). No matter which view one takes (that women are displacing men or that an expanding economy is providing new jobs for everyone), one thing is clear: Americans are working more than ever before. It is not that today's jobs are particularly demanding in terms of physical labor. Machines have ended much of the "tote that barge, lift that bale" drudgery that plagued our ancestors. With machines to do the heavy work, the smaller average body size and lesser strength of women are no longer impediments to blue-collar employment.

The main reason we don't see more modern-day Rosies working alongside male riveters is that the U.S. work force itself is abandoning heavy-goods manufacture. In the 1950s two-thirds of American jobs were blue-collar, compared with 16 percent today. The location of those jobs has shifted within the world capitalist economy. Third World countries with cheaper labor produce steel, automobiles, and other heavy goods less expensively than the United States can, but the United States excels at services. The American mass education system

Table 11.4 *Employment of women in selected occupations, 1950 and 1985*

Occupation	WOMEN AS PERCENT OF ALL WORKERS IN THE OCCUPATION	
	1950	1985
Professional workers	40	49
Engineers	1	7
Lawyers and judges	4	18
Physicians	7	17
Dentists	N/A	7
Registered nurses	98	95
College teachers	23	35
Other teachers	75	73
Managers	14	36
Sales workers	35	48
Clerical workers	62	80
Artisans	3	8
Operatives	34	40
Transport operatives	1	8
Service workers	57	61

N/A—Not available.
SOURCE: Schaefer 1989, p. 283.

has many inadequacies, but it does train millions of people for service and information-oriented jobs, from sales clerks to computer operators.

The Feminization of Poverty

Alongside the economic gains of many American women, particularly professionals, stands an opposite extreme: the feminization of poverty. This refers to the increasing proportion of America's poor who are women. More than half of U.S. households with sub-poverty-level incomes (3.6 million of 6.9 million families) have female heads. The feminization of poverty accounts for virtually the entire increase (53 percent) in poverty in the United States since 1970 (Barringer 1989).

Feminine poverty has been a trend in the United States since World War II, but it has accelerated recently. In 1959 female-headed households accounted for 26 percent of the American poor. That figure had doubled by 1986. About half the female poor are "in transition," facing an economic crisis caused by the departure, disability, or death of a husband. The other half are more permanently dependent on the welfare system or on friends or relatives living nearby (Schaefer 1989). The feminization of poverty and its consequences in regard to living standards and health are pervasive even among wage earners. Many American women, especially African-American women, work part time for low wages and meager benefits. Fifteen percent of the American population, some 37 million people, had no health insurance in 1988 (*New York Times* 1988b).

The fate of America's less fortunate children, whose poverty has increased by 25 percent since 1970, is linked to the feminization of poverty. Almost 40 percent of poor people in the United States today are children under age eighteen. Twenty percent of American children now live with one parent, usually the mother. Among single mothers with children under eighteen, the 1984 poverty rate was 43 percent for whites, 67 percent for Hispanics, and 68 percent for African-Americans (Schaefer 1989).

The Index of Social Health for Children and Youth is calculated from national statistics on infant mortality, child abuse, children in poverty, teenage suicide, teenage drug abuse, and the high school dropout rate. With 100 a perfect and ideal score, the index declined from 68 in 1970 to 37 in 1987 (the most favorable score was 72 in 1973) (Goleman 1989).

WHAT DETERMINES VARIATION IN GENDER ISSUES?

We have seen that gender roles and stratification vary widely across cultures and through history. Among the causes of this variation are the needs of particular economies and, more generally, adaptive strategy, level of sociopolitical complexity, and degree of participation in the capitalist world economy. The degradation of women, female subordination, and sharp differentiation between the public and private spheres are not cultural universals. Among many foragers and matrilineal cultivators, there is little gender stratification.

Competition for resources leads to warfare and the intensification of production. These conditions favor patriliny and virilocality. To the extent that women lose their productive roles in agricultural and pastoral societies, the domestic-public dichotomy is accentuated and female degradation becomes extreme.

With industrialism, attitudes about gender vary in the context of female extradomestic employment. The variability of gender in time and space suggests that it will continue to change. Gender is flexible and reflects culture, society, politics, and economics more than biological imperatives.

SUMMARY

In recent years anthropologists have been gathering systematic ethnographic data about gender in many cultural settings. Gender roles and gender stratification vary with environment, economy, adaptive strategy, level of social complexity, and degree of participation in the capitalist world economy. Gender roles are the tasks and activities that a culture assigns to each sex. Related to gender roles are gender stereotypes—oversimplified but strongly held ideas about the characteristics of males and females. Gender stratification describes an unequal distribution of rewards (socially valued resources, power, prestige, and personal freedom) between men and women, reflecting their different positions in a social hierarchy. In stateless societies, gender stratification is often much more obvious in regard to prestige than it is in regard to wealth or power.

Where gathering is prominent, gender status is more symmetrical than is the case when hunting or fishing dominates the foraging economy. Gender status is more equal when the domestic and public spheres are not sharply separated. Foragers lack two public arenas that contribute to higher male status among food producers: warfare and organized interregional trade. Among foragers, hierarchy is least marked, aggression and competition are most discouraged, and the rights, activities, and spheres of influence of men and women overlap the most.

Female status falls as cultivation intensifies. Women's status is also linked to descent and postmarital residence. Matrilineal-uxorilocal systems occur in societies where population pressure on strategic resources is minimal and warfare is infrequent. Women's status is high in such societies, because descent-group membership, political succession, land allocation, and overall social identity come through female links. Although there are no matriarchies, women in many societies wield power and make decisions. If women play a major subsistence role while men leave home for long periods, sexual equality is favored. Women's status falls when male and female spheres are sharply differentiated *within* the local community.

Scarcity of resources favors the development of patriliny and virilocality. The localization of related males is adaptive for military solidarity. Intervillage warfare and polygyny are cultural responses to resource scarcity. Women remain the main subsistence workers. Polygyny brings several female workers under the control of one household. It may thus intensify production and generate surpluses, which male heads of households can then invest for prestige and alliance formation. Men use their public roles in extradomestic distribution to symbolize and reinforce their oppression of women.

Pastoralism, since it rarely occurs as a "pure" adaptation, has diverse gender roles, but the status of female pastoralists is generally low. Agriculture intensifies production and reliance on crops. With plow agriculture, women's status keeps falling as men assume responsibility for subsistence.

With the advent of plow agriculture, women were removed from production for the first time in cultural evolution. The distinction between women's domestic work and men's extradomestic "productive" labor reinforced the contrast between men as public and valuable and women as domestic and inferior. The Betsileo illustrate, however, that intensive cultivation per se does not entail a degraded status for women.

Americans' attitudes toward gender vary with class and region. The attitude that woman's place is in the home was nourished during certain periods of industrialism. When the need for female labor declines, the idea that women are unfit for many jobs increases. Forces such as war, inflation, the baby boom, and employment patterns help account for female cash employment and Americans' attitudes toward it. Alongside the economic gains of many American women, particularly, professionals, stands an opposite extreme: the feminization of poverty. The feminization of poverty, which refers to the increasing proportion of America's poor who are women, accounts for virtually the entire increase in poverty in the United States since 1970. The degradation of women, female subordination, and sharp differences between the public and private spheres do not appear to be cultural universals.

GLOSSARY

domestic: Within or pertaining to the home.

domestic-public dichotomy: Contrast between women's role in the home and men's role in public life, with a corresponding social devaluation of women's work and worth.

environmentalists: See *nurturists*.

Etoro: Papua–New Guinea culture in which males are culturally trained to prefer homosexuality.

extradomestic: Outside the home; within or pertaining to the public domain.

gender roles: The tasks and activities that a culture assigns to each sex.

gender stereotypes: Oversimplified but strongly held ideas about the characteristics of males and females.

gender stratification: Unequal distribution of rewards (socially valued resources, power, prestige, and personal freedom) between men and women, reflecting their different positions in a social hierarchy.

Iroquois: Confederation of tribes in aboriginal New York State; matrilineal with communal longhouses and a prominent political, religious, and economic role for women.

matriarchy: A society ruled by women; unknown to ethnography.

matrifocal: Mother-centered; often refers to a household with no resident husband-father.

matrons: Senior women, as among the Iroquois.

naturists: Those who argue that human behavior and social organization are biologically determined.

nurturists: Those who link behavior and social organization to environmental factors. Naturists focus on variation rather than universals and stress learning and the role of culture in human adaptation.

patrilineal-virilocal complex: An interrelated constellation of patrilineality, virilocality, warfare, male supremacy, female infanticide, and polygyny; particularly characteristic of tribes.

uxorilocality: Customary residence with the wife's relatives after marriage.

virilocality: Customary residence with the husband's relatives after marriage.

STUDY QUESTIONS

1. What is the dominant position in anthropology regarding the argument that the destinies of men and women are linked with their respective anatomies and genetic makeups?
2. What is the difference between gender roles, gender stereotypes, and gender stratification?
3. How do gender roles in traditional !Kung society compare with those in U.S. society?
4. How does female status differ in societies that are matrilineal and uxorilocal compared with those which are patrilineal and virilocal?
5. How are Etoro sexual practices related to patterns of male-female relations in Papau–New Guinea and in patrilineal-virilocal cultures generally?
6. How does female status differ in agricultural versus horticultural societies?
7. How did gender roles change as the United States became industrialized?
8. What determines variation in gender roles, and what does this variation suggest for societies of the future?

SUGGESTED ADDITIONAL READING

BOSERUP, E
   1970   *Women's Role in Economic Development.* London: Allen & Unwin. An examination of woman's changing role as cultivation intensifies, including plow agriculture and the domestic-public dichotomy.
BOURQUE, S.C., AND K. B. WARREN
   1981   *Women of the Andes: Patriarchy and Social Change in Two Peruvian Villages.* Ann Arbor: University of Michigan Press. Comparison of two communities with respect to traditional and modern gender hierarchies, capitalization, and directions of development.
DAHLBERG, F., ED.
   1981   *Women the Gatherer.* New Haven, CT: Yale University Press. Female roles and activities among prehistoric and contemporary foragers.
ETIENNE, M., AND E. LEACOCK, EDS.
   1980   *Women and Colonization: Anthropological Perspectives.* New York: Praeger and J. F. Bergin. Women and the growth of the world system.

MARGOLIS, M.
   1984   *Mothers and Such: American Views of Women and How They Changed.* Berkeley: University of California Press. The evolution of the female role, women's work, and attitudes about female nature and activities in the United States since its settlement.
MORGEN, S., ED.
   1989   *Gender and Anthropology: Critical Reviews for Research and Teaching.* Washington, DC: American Anthropological Association. Most up-to-date review of scholarship on gender in many areas of the world and in a biosocial perspective.
MUKHOPADHYAY, C., AND P. HIGGINS
   1988   Anthropological Studies of Women's Status Revisited: 1977–1987. *Annual Review of Anthropology* 17: 461–495. Most recent extensive review of the cross-cultural literature on the subject.

NASH, J., AND P. FERNANDEZ-KELLY, EDS.

1983 *Women, Men and the International Division of Labor*. Albany: State University of New York Press. Essays on global accumulation; the labor process; production, reproduction, and the household economy; and labor flow and capital expansion, with case studies from electronics and trade.

NASH, J., AND H. SAFA, EDS.

1986 *Women and Change in Latin America*. South Hadley, MA: Bergin and Garvey. Recent articles by anthropologists on gender, political economy, and social change in Latin America.

REITER, R., ED.

1975 *Toward an Anthropology of Women*. New York: Monthly Review Press. Classic anthology, with a particular focus on peasant societies.

ROSALDO, M. Z.

1980 *Knowledge and Passion: Notions of Self and Social Life*. Stanford, CA: Stanford University Press. Role of travel, experience, knowledge, and emotion in the gender hierarchy of a stateless society in the Philippines.

ROSALDO, M. Z., AND L. LAMPHERE, EDS.

1974 *Woman, Culture, and Society*. Stanford, CA: Stanford University Press. Another classic anthology, covering many areas of the world.

SILVERBLATT, I.

1988 Women in States. *Annual Review of Anthropology* 17: 427–460. Issues of gender stratification and politics in ancient and modern states.

WOLF, M.

1985 *Revolution Postponed: Women in Contemporary China*. Stanford, CA: Stanford University Press. One of the few studies of women based on anthropological field research in China; discusses urban and rural women, marriage, and China's controversial birth control policy.

CHAPTER 12

KINSHIP AND DESCENT

The kinds of societies that anthropologists have traditionally studied have stimulated a strong interest in systems of kinship and marriage. Kinship—as vitally important in daily life in nonindustrial societies as work outside the home is in our own—has become an essential part of anthropology because of its importance to the people we study. We are ready to take a closer look at the systems of kinship and descent that have organized human life for much of our history. We consider actual kin groups, along with the more personal matter of how people think about kinship and classify their relatives.

KINSHIP GROUPS AND KINSHIP CALCULATION

Anthropologists study the kinship *groups* that are significant in a society as well as **kinship calculation**—the system by which people in a society reckon kin relationships. Ethnographers quickly recognize social divisions (groups) within any society they study. During field work, they learn about significant groups by observing their activities and composition. People often live in the same village or neighborhood or work, pray, or celebrate together because they are related in some way. To understand the social structure, an ethnographer must investigate such kin ties. For example, the most significant local groups may consist of descendants of the same grandfather. These people may live in neighboring houses, farm adjoining fields, and help each other in everyday tasks. Other groups, perhaps based on other kin links, get together less often.

To study kinship calculation an ethnographer must first determine the word or words for different types of "relatives" used in a particular language and then ask questions such as, "Who are your relatives?" Kinship, like gender, is culturally constructed. This means that some biological kin are considered to be relatives whereas others are not. Through questioning, the ethnographer discovers the specific genealogical relationships between "relatives" and the person who has named them—the **ego**. By posing the same questions to several informants, the ethnographer learns about the extent and direction of kinship calculation in that society. The ethnographer also begins to un-

derstand the relationship between kinship calculation and kinship groups—how people use kinship to create and maintain personal ties and to join social groups. In several of the kinship charts that follow, the black square labeled "ego" (Latin for *I*) identifies the person whose kinship calculation is being examined.

Biological Kin Types and Kinship Calculation

At this point we may distinguish between **kin terms** (the words used for different relatives in a particular language) and **biological kin types.** We designate biological kin types with the letters and symbols shown in Figure 12.1. *Biological kin type refers to an actual genealogical relationship (e.g., father's brother) as opposed to a kin term (e.g., uncle).*

Figure 12.1. *Kinship symbols and biological kin type notation.*

△	Male
○	Female
□	Individual regardless of sex
=	Is married to
≠	Is divorced from
|	Is descended from
⌐	Is the sibling of
●	Female ego whose kin are being shown
▲	Male ego whose kin are being shown
⊘ △	Individual is deceased
F	Father
M	Mother
S	Son
D	Daughter
B	Brother
Z	Sister
C	Child (of either sex)
H	Husband
W	Wife

Kin terms reflect the social construction of kinship in a given culture. A kin term may (and usually does) lump together several genealogical relationships. In English, for instance, we use *father* primarily for one kin type—the genealogical father. However, *father* can be extended to an adoptive father or stepfather—and even to a priest. *Grandfather* includes mother's father and father's father. The term *cousin* lumps several kin types. Even the more specific *first cousin* includes mother's brother's son (MBS), mother's brother's daughter (MBD), mother's sister's son (MZS), mother's sister's daughter (MZD), father's brother's son (FBS), father's brother's daughter (FBD), father's sister's son (FZS), and father's sister's daughter (FZD). *First cousin* thus lumps together at least eight biological kin types.

Uncle encompasses mother's and father's brothers, and *aunt* includes mother's and father's sisters. We also use *uncle* and *aunt* for the spouses of our "blood" aunts and uncles. We use the same term for mother's brother and father's brother because we perceive them as being the same sort of relative. Calling them *uncles*, we distinguish between them and another kin type, F, whom we call *Father, Dad,* or *Pop.* In many societies, however, it is common to call a father and a father's brother by the same term. Later we'll see why.

In the United States and Canada, the *nuclear family* (a kin group composed of parents and children residing together) continues to be the most important group based on kinship. This is true despite an increased incidence of divorce and remarriage. The nuclear family's prevalence (and its relative isolation from other kin groups) in modern nations reflects an industrial economy, sale of labor for cash, and geographical mobility. (The nuclear family is also the most important kin group in many foraging societies for reasons that will be discussed later.)

It's reasonable for Americans to distinguish between relatives who belong to their nuclear families and those who don't. We are more likely to grow up with our parents than with our aunts or uncles. We tend to see our parents more often than we see our uncles and aunts, who may live in different towns and cities. We often inherit from our parents, but our cousins have first claim to inherit from our aunts and uncles. If our marriage is stable, we see our children daily as long as they re-

main at home. They are our heirs. We feel closer to them than to our nieces and nephews.

American kinship calculation and kin terminology reflect these social features. Thus the term *uncle* distinguishes between the kin types MB and FB on the one hand and the kin type F on the other. However, this term also lumps kin types together. We use the same term for MB and FB, two different kin types. We do this because American kinship calculation is **bilateral**—traced equally through males and females, e.g., father and mother. Both kinds of uncle are brothers of one of our parents. We think of both as roughly the same kind of relative.

"No," you may object, "I'm closer to my mother's brother than to my father's brother." That may be. However, in a representative sample of American students, we would find a split, with some favoring one side and some favoring the other. We'd actually expect a bit of **matrilateral skewing**—a preference for relatives on the mother's side. This occurs because—for many reasons—when contemporary children are raised by just one parent, it's more likely to be the mother than the father. Thus, in the United States in 1988, 21 percent of all children lived in fatherless homes versus 3 percent residing in motherless homes and 73 percent living with both parents (Johnson 1989).

Bilateral kinship means that people tend to perceive kin links through males and females as being similar or equivalent. This bilaterality is expressed in interaction with, living with or near, and rights to inherit from relatives. We don't usually inherit from uncles, but if we do, there's about as much chance that we'll inherit from the father's brother as from the mother's brother. We don't usually live with either aunt, but if we do, the chances are about the same that it will be the father's sister as the mother's sister.

KIN GROUPS

The nuclear family is one kind of kin group that is widespread in human societies. Other kin groups include extended families and descent groups—lineages and clans. *Descent groups,* which are composed of people claiming common ancestry, are basic units in the social organization of nonindustrial food producers.

There are important differences between nuclear families and descent groups. A descent group is *permanent*; a nuclear family lasts only as long as the parents and children remain together. Descent-group membership often is ascribed at birth (by a rule of patrilineal or matrilineal descent, as discussed in Chapter 7) and lifelong. In contrast, most people belong to at least two nuclear families at different times in their lives. They are born into a nuclear family consisting of their parents and siblings. When they reach adulthood, they may marry and establish a nuclear family that includes the spouse and eventually the children. Since most societies permit divorce, some people establish more than one family through marriage.

Anthropologists distinguish between the **family of orientation** (the nuclear family in which one is born and grows up) and the **family of procreation** (formed when one marries and has children). From the individual's point of view, the critical relationships are with parents and siblings in the family of orientation and with spouse and children in the family of procreation.

Defining Marriage

Marriage (discussed more fully in Chapter 13) is often the basis of a new nuclear family. No definition of marriage is broad enough to apply easily to all societies. A commonly quoted definition comes from *Notes and Queries in Anthropology:*

> Marriage is a union between a man and a woman such that the children born to the woman are recognized as legitimate offspring of both partners (Royal Anthropological Institute 1951, p. 111).

This definition may describe marriage in contemporary North America, but it isn't universally valid for several reasons. For example, in many societies marriages unite more than two spouses. Here we speak of *plural marriages,* as when a woman weds a group of brothers—an arrangement called *fraternal polyandry* that is characteristic of certain Himalayan cultures. Furthermore, in certain societies (usually patrilineal), a woman may marry another woman. This can happen in West Africa when a successful market woman (perhaps already married to a man) wants a wife of her own to take care of her home and children while she works outside (Amadiume 1987).

In the African Sudan a Nuer woman can marry a woman if her father has only daughters but no male heirs, who are necessary if his patrilineage is to survive. He may ask his daughter to stand as a son in order to take a bride. This is a symbolic and social relationship rather than a sexual one. Indeed, the woman who serves as a man may already be living in another village as a man's wife!

The Nuer woman doesn't live with her "wife," who has sex with a man or men until she becomes pregnant. What's important here is *social* rather than *biological paternity;* we see again how kinship is socially constructed. The bride's children are considered the legitimate offspring of her "husband," who is biologically a woman but socially a man, and the descent line continues.

The British anthropologist Edmund Leach (1955) despaired of ever arriving at a universal definition of marriage. Instead, he suggested that depending on the society, several different kinds of rights are allocated by institutions classified as marriage. These rights vary from one culture to another, and no single one is widespread enough to provide a basis for defining marriage.

According to Leach, marriage can do the following:

1. Establish the legal father of a woman's children and the legal mother of a man's
2. Give the husband a monopoly in the wife's sexuality and the wife a monopoly in the husband's
3. Give either or both spouses rights to the labor of the other
4. Give either or both spouses rights over the other's property
5. Establish a joint fund of property—a partnership—for the benefit of the children
6. Establish a socially significant "relationship of affinity" between spouses and their relatives

This list highlights particular aspects of marriage in different cultural contexts. However, I believe that we need some definition—even a loose one—to identify an institution found in some form in all human societies. I suggest the following:

Marriage is a socially approved relationship between a socially recognized male (the husband) and a socially recognized female (the wife) such that the children born to the wife are accepted as the offspring of both husband and wife. The husband may be the actual **genitor** (biological father) of the children or only the **pater** (socially recognized father).

THE NUCLEAR FAMILY

Because marriage is a cultural universal, necessary for the formation of a nuclear family, some anthropologists argue that the nuclear family itself is universal. G. P. Murdock (1949), for example, viewed the nuclear family as universal because, he argued, its component relationships (wife-husband and parent-child) fulfill four essential social functions: sexual, reproductive, economic, and educational. Unlike Murdock, most contemporary anthropologists recognize that nuclear family organization is widespread but not universal. In certain societies, the nuclear family is rare or nonexistent. In other cultures, the nuclear family has no special role in social life. Other social units—most notably descent groups and extended families—can assume most or all of the functions otherwise associated with the nuclear family. In other words, there are many alternatives to nuclear family organization.

Sex

Murdock argued that because the nuclear family includes the husband-wife relationship, it fulfills a sexual function. More accurately, it is marriage that has a sexual function—granting social approval to regular mating. (Many societies also permit premarital and extramarital sex.) Although marriage is a cultural universal, it doesn't always lead to the same kind of family organization.

Reproduction

Murdock viewed the nuclear family as necessary for a society's reproduction, but again, reproduction is better seen as a function of marriage, which legitimizes children and thus provides them with social rights. However, we may note certain exceptions.

In most societies, most adult men and women marry and become parents. However, in certain Caribbean island societies, many women head households with no permanently resident husband-father. We call these *matrifocal* families or

households because the mother (*mater*) is the household head.

The Trans-Fly region of Papua-New Guinea is the homeland of several homosexual tribes. Here, although men must marry, they prefer homosexual acts to heterosexual coitus with their wives. One of the Trans-Fly groups, the Etoro, are so disapproving of heterosexual intercourse that they prohibit it for more than 200 days annually (Kelly 1976). Men of the neighboring Marind-anim tribe (van Baal 1966) also prefer homosexuality, and their birth rate is so low that in order to reproduce the population, villages must raid their neighbors. Many children who grow up to be Marind-anim have been captured in raids on other tribes rather than born into Marind-anim society.

Another exception to reproduction through marriage and the nuclear family is provided by the Nayars, who live on the Malabar Coast of southern India. Their kinship system is matrilineal (descent is traced only through females). Nayar marriages are mere formalities. Adolescent females go through a marriage ceremony with a man, after which the girl returns home, usually without having had sex with her husband. The man returns to his own household. Thereafter, Nayar women have many sexual partners. Children become members of the mother's household and kin group; they are not considered to be relatives of

The matrilineal Nayars of southern India's Malabar Coast (shown here with ethnographer Kathleen Gough) lacked ordinary marriage and the nuclear family. Nayar marriages were mere formalities. Children belonged to their mother's kin group and household—with no co-resident father.

the biological father. Indeed, many Nayar children don't even know who their father is. However, for children to be legitimate, a man, usually neither the actual genitor nor the mother's original "husband," must go through a ritual acknowledging paternity. Nayar society therefore reproduces itself biologically without the nuclear family.

Family Economics

The supposed universality of the nuclear family has also been attributed to an economic function related to the fact that all cultures have some kind of division of labor by gender. The nuclear family's economic function is especially important in societies where it is a self-contained unit of production and consumption. However, the division of labor is often much more complex. Among the agricultural Betsileo of Madagascar, for example, traditional tasks are allocated by gender, age, and gen-

In many cultures grandparents, uncles, aunts, and other nonnuclear kin play important roles in childrearing. Grandmothers take an active role in child care in Czechoslovakia.

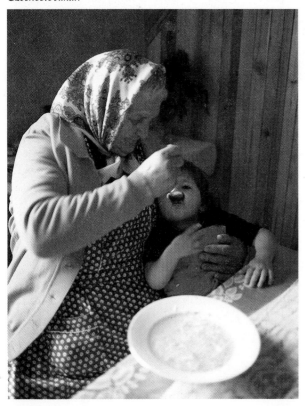

eration. Grandfathers have certain jobs, and adolescent boys and girls have others. In such agricultural settings the nuclear family does not encompass in microcosm all the significant economic roles, as it may among foragers. Food-producing societies usually have larger kinship groups that bridge at least three generations.

Education

Education isn't the same thing as enculturation—the universal process by which children internalize their culture by learning how they are supposed to act. *Education* refers to the acquisition of more formal knowledge and normally occurs in a place called a school. Education exposes certain—not all—people in a society to a body of formal knowledge or lore. Studying education cross-culturally, we see that it is usually found in state-organized societies. Furthermore, education is a strategic resource to which there is differential access based on stratification. All nations have educational systems, but access to the full range of educational possibilities is always unequal.

There are exceptions to the correlation between education and state-organized societies. Certain populations in West Africa, and even the Tiwi, foragers of northern Australia (Hart and Pilling 1960), traditionally had "bush" schools in the hinterland. Even here, however, there was differential access based on gender. Only Tiwi boys received formal instruction in tribal lore. By finishing bush school, Tiwi boys became men in a rite of passage from one social status to another.

It is clear that education is not normally a function of the nuclear family, as Murdock contended, but a function of a state or church institution. The nuclear family isn't even the exclusive enculturative agent. In modern societies it isn't just parents and siblings who transmit culture but friends, schoolmates, age peers, teachers, and neighbors.

The nuclear family's enculturative role is most prominent in societies that isolate the married couple and the nuclear family from other kin. In many cultures, however, grandparents, uncles, aunts, and other nonnuclear kin play important roles in child rearing. Among the Betsileo of Madagascar, for example, grandparents often spend more time with a child and have more to say about its upbringing than do its parents.

In summary, in cultures in which the nuclear family is the most important kin group, its sexual, reproductive, economic, and enculturative functions stand out. However, enculturation is never confined to the nuclear family, and in most societies economic activities are carried out by larger groups. In fact, in only two types of society does the nuclear family tend to be the most important kinship group: industrial nations and foraging societies. Why should such different economies have similar family organization?

Industrialism, Stratification, and Family Organization

For many Americans and Canadians, the nuclear family is the only well-defined kin group. Because family isolation arises from geographic mobility, which is associated with industrialism, a nuclear family focus is characteristic of many modern nations. Born into a family of orientation, Americans leave home for work or college, and the break with parents is under way. Eventually most Americans marry and start a family of procreation. Because less than 3 percent of the American population now farms, most people aren't tied to the land. Selling our labor on the market, we often move to places where jobs are available.

Many married couples live hundreds of miles from their parents. Their jobs have determined where they live. Such a postmarital residence pattern is called **neolocality**: married couples are expected to establish a new place of residence—a "home of their own." Among middle-class Americans, neolocal residence is both a cultural preference and a statistical norm. Most middle-class Americans eventually establish households and nuclear families of their own.

Within stratified nations, value systems vary to some extent from class to class, and so does kinship. There are significant differences between middle-class, poorer, and richer Americans. For example, in the lower class the incidence of **expanded family households** (those which include nonnuclear relatives) is greater than it is in the middle class. When an expanded family household includes three or more generations, it is an **extended family**. Another type of expanded family is the **collateral household**, which includes siblings and their spouses and children.

An extended family household (like this one in Yuba City, California) includes three or more generations.

The higher proportion of expanded family households in certain American ethnic groups and classes has been explained as an adaptation to poverty (Stack 1975). Unable to survive economically as nuclear family units, relatives band together in an expanded household and pool their resources.

Poverty causes kinship values and attitudes to diverge from middle-class norms. Thus, when Americans raised in poverty achieve financial success, they often feel obligated to provide considerable financial help to less fortunate relatives. Upper-class households, living in bigger homes supported by greater wealth, may also diverge from the nuclear family norm. Upper-class households can afford to lodge and feed extended family kin, guests, and servants.

North American neolocality is therefore linked to both the geographical mobility and the distri-

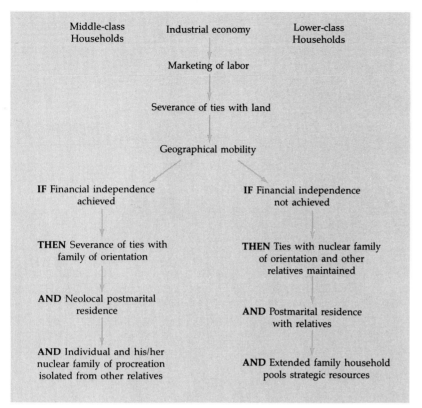

Middle-class Households

Industrial economy

Lower-class Households

Marketing of labor

Severance of ties with land

Geographical mobility

IF Financial independence achieved

IF Financial independence not achieved

THEN Severance of ties with family of orientation

THEN Ties with nuclear family of orientation and other relatives maintained

AND Neolocal postmarital residence

AND Postmarital residence with relatives

AND Individual and his/her nuclear family of procreation isolated from other relatives

AND Extended family household pools strategic resources

Figure 12.2 *The relationship between industrial economy, social class, and kinship-group organization.*

bution of wealth associated with industrialism. Neolocal residence tends to isolate the nuclear family, making it the best defined kinship group. Figure 12.2 categorizes the relationship between these factors and household composition by class. The arrows show the direction of causality.

Recent Changes in American Kinship Patterns

Although the nuclear family remains a cultural ideal for many Americans, Table 12.1 shows that nuclear families accounted for just 28 percent of American households in 1986. *Nonnuclear family arrangements now outnumber the "traditional" American household by more than three to one.* There are several reasons for changing household composition. Americans leave home to work, often in a different community. Women are increasingly joining men in the work force. This often removes them from the family of orientation while making it economically feasible to delay marriage. Furthermore, job demands compete with romantic attachments. Ac-

cording to the U.S. Census Bureau, the average age at first marriage for American women rose from 20.2 years in 1955 to 23.6 years in 1988. The comparable figures for men were 22.6 and 25.9 (*Ann Arbor News* 1989).

The U.S. divorce rate rose steeply during the 1970s and early 1980s, so that more than one-third

Table 12.1 *Classification of American households, 1980 and 1986*

	PERCENTAGE OF ALL HOUSEHOLDS	
Type of Household	**1980**	**1986**
Nuclear family	33	28
Married couple	30	30
One adult	22	25[†]
One parent and child(ren)	7	8
Other*	8	9[†]

*Includes unmarried couples, roommates, and extended families, adult siblings, etc.
[†]Estimated based on trends.
SOURCE: Bureau of the Census.

of marriages now end in divorce. In 1960 there were 35 divorced Americans for every 1,000 married people living with a spouse; by 1988 there were 133 (*Ann Arbor News* 1989). Single-parent families are increasing at a rapid rate. In 1970, 85 percent of American children lived with both parents, versus 73 percent in 1988 (Johnson 1989). The percentage of American children living in fatherless households rose from 11 percent in 1970 to 21 percent in 1988. The percentage living in motherless households increased from 1 percent in 1970 to 3 percent in 1988 (Table 12.2).

The cost of maintaining a middle-class life style forces men, women, and teenagers to work outside the home. Job demands compete with child care, which has become an expensive proposition in itself—it now costs more than $100,000 to raise an American child to age eighteen. In response, nuclear families have shrunk, and more couples now raise one child than two children. "Beaver Cleaver" families, consisting of children, a working father, and a homemaker mother, now constitute less than 10 percent of all households.

The numbers in Table 12.1 suggest that life is growing increasingly lonely for many Americans. The disappearance of extended families and descent groups reflects the mobility of industrialism. However, even nuclear families are breaking up. In the United States the single population aged eighteen and over rose from 38 million in 1970 (28 percent of all adults) to 66 million in 1988 (37 percent of all adults) (*Ann Arbor News* 1989). To be sure, contemporary Americans maintain social lives through work, friendship, sports, clubs, religion, and organized social activities. However, the isolation from kin that these figures suggest is unprecedented in human evolution. Because primates are intensely social animals, many observers of contemporary society see the decline of kinship

The Cleavers, a traditional American family of the 1950s and 1960s, consisting of breadwinner Ward, homemaker June, and sons Wally and "Beav." Outmoded in prime time, where single, divorced, and professional mothers now abound, the Cleavers live on in black-and-white daytime syndication, where they still figure in the enculturation of American children.

as unfortunate and wonder how these trends are harming our mental health.

Our changing household organization has been reflected in the mass media. During the 1950s and early 1960s such television sitcoms as *Ozzie and Harriet* and *Leave It to Beaver* portrayed "traditional" nuclear families. The incidence of **blended families** (kin units formed when parents remarry and bring their children into a new household) is rising, as represented in programs such as *The Brady Bunch*. Three-quarters of divorced Americans remarry (*Ann Arbor News* 1989). Television programs and other media presentations now routinely feature coresident "roommates," unmarried couples, "singles," unrelated retirees, hired male housekeepers, working mothers, and even "two dads." Changes in life styles are reflected by the media, which in turn help promote further modifications in our values concerning kinship, marriage, and living arrangements (Kottak 1990).

Table 12.2 *Percentage of American children residing with one or both parents, 1970 and 1988*

	1970	1988
Both parents present	85	73
No resident father	11	21
No resident mother	1	3
Other	3	3

SOURCE: Johnson 1989.

The Brady Bunch, *a blended family, created not through divorce, as happens so frequently in the media and in "real life" today, but through the deaths of former spouses.*

The entire range of kin attachments is narrower for Americans, particularly those in the middle class, than it is for nonindustrial peoples. Al-

though we recognize ties to grandparents, uncles, aunts, and cousins, we have less contact with, and depend less on, those relatives than people in other cultures do. We see this when we answer a few questions: Do we know exactly how we are related to all our cousins? How much do we know about our ancestors, such as their full names and where they lived? How many of the people with whom we associate regularly are our relatives?

Differences in the answers to these questions by people from industrial and those from nonindustrial societies confirm the declining importance of kinship in contemporary nations. Most of the people whom middle-class Americans see every day are either nonrelatives or members of the nuclear family. On the other hand, Stack's (1975) study of welfare-dependent families in a ghetto area of a midwestern city shows that sharing with nonnuclear relatives is an important strategy that the urban poor use to adapt to poverty. In this sense, lower-class kinship patterns in America are more like those of nonindustrial societies than are those of the middle class, as you will see below.

One of the most striking contrasts between the United States and Brazil, the two most populous nations of the Western Hemisphere, is in the meaning and role of the family. Contemporary American adults usually define their families as consisting of their husbands or wives and their children. However, when Brazilians talk about

Although "Beaver Cleaver" families may be less common among African-Americans than among white Americans, blacks maintain very strong ties with their kin. African-American children tend to see their extended kin more often than their white middle-class compatriots do. Shown here, an African-American family reunion.

IS THERE ANYTHING WRONG WITH THE BLACK FAMILY?

A social issue that receives frequent media attention is "the problem of the black family"—the problematic status of which, from the anthropologist's perspective, originates in the American cultural preference for marriage and the nuclear family. The apparent problem is that half the African-American babies born in the United States today are born to unmarried mothers. Furthermore, more than half (52 percent) of African-American households with children are classified as single-parent families.

We must first recognize the role of the state in creating "the problem of the black family." Welfare policies that deny Aid to Families with Dependent Children to households with able-bodied male residents have helped create the pattern of unwed mothers and female-headed households.

Just how serious are these problems, and what does the view of such families as constituting a problem tell us about American culture? For Americans, the ideal family consists of a married couple and their children. American culture favors this kind of family and is biased against others. Even anthropologists sometimes fall into the trap, teaching a course entitled "Marriage and the Family" rather than the more neutral "Kinship and Social Organization."

A cross-cultural perspective makes it obvious (although American culture tends to deny it) that families can exist without a marital tie. Unmarried Brazilians, for example, easily perceive the ethnocentrism in the American viewpoint. Adult Brazilians certainly believe they have families (parents, siblings, aunts, nephews, cousins, etc.) even though they may lack a husband or wife.

Even in the United States, there can be families without marriage. Although many Americans don't realize it, strong kin relationships exist among African-Americans, as anthropologist Carol Stack (1975) showed in a classic field study of black family structure and kin relations in urban America. Stack demonstrated that although "Beaver Cleaver" families are less common among poverty-level blacks than among middle-class whites, blacks still maintain very strong ties with their kin. Even if fathers live elsewhere, children often know and visit their fathers and paternal kin. Furthermore, children see their extended kin—grandparents, uncles, aunts, great-aunts and uncles, and cousins—more often than their white middle-class counterparts do.

Confirming Stack's findings are comprehensive statistical surveys done by the Institute of Social Research of the University of Michigan. This research has shown that families and churches are very important sources of emotional support and sustenance for African-Americans. Twenty percent of the black households surveyed were extended families. Sixty percent of the respondents saw, phoned, or wrote to relatives outside their own households at least once a week. Ninety-two percent had attended a church regularly since age eighteen (*Ann Arbor Observer* 1985). Indeed, compared with blacks, many American whites are more cut off from their kin, living alone or in nuclear family houses in suburban neighborhoods. Significantly, every one of the unmarried black teenage mothers shown in a *Today* show report of October 1984 was living not as an isolated young woman but with her own mother.

The most severe problems facing African-Americans today do not arise from black family structure but from the increasing social and economic polarization of American society. More than three times more African-American than white children are born poor. On the average, black children spend more than five years of their lives in poverty, versus less than one year for white children (*Ann Arbor News* 1985). Contemporary urban African-Americans must also cope with other forms of social oppression, including drugs and disease. Welfare laws that make coresidence of adult men and women an economically irrational decision make coping even more difficult and fuel the "problem of the black family."

their families, they mean their parents, siblings, aunts, uncles, grandparents, and cousins. Later they add their children, but rarely the husband or wife, who has his or her own family. The children are shared by the two families. Because middle-class Americans lack an extended family support system, marriage assumes more importance. The husband-wife relationship is supposed to take precedence over either spouse's relationship with his or her own parents. This places a significant strain on North American marriages.

The cultural contrast runs even deeper. Family relationships themselves are more important in Brazil than they are in the United States. Living in a less mobile society, Brazilians stay in closer contact with their relatives, including members of the extended family. Residents of Rio de Janeiro and São Paulo, two of South America's largest cities, are reluctant to leave those urban centers to live away from family and friends. Brazilians find it hard to imagine, and unpleasant to live in, social worlds without relatives. Contrast this with a characteristic American theme—learning to live with strangers. We live with strangers more and more, even at home. According to U.S. census data, only 71 percent of American households were composed of family members in 1988, compared with 80 percent in 1980 and 89 percent in 1950 (Barringer 1989).

The Nuclear Family among Foragers

Populations with foraging economies are far removed from industrial societies in terms of social complexity. Here again, however, the nuclear family is often the most significant kin group, although in no foraging culture is the nuclear family the only group based on kinship. The two basic social units of foraging societies are the nuclear family and the band.

Unlike middle-class couples in industrial nations, foragers don't usually reside neolocally. Instead, they join a band in which either the husband or the wife has relatives. However, couples and families may move from one band to another several times. Although nuclear families are ultimately as impermanent among foragers as they are in any other society, they are usually more stable than bands are.

Many foraging societies lacked year-round band organization. The Native American Shoshone of the Great Basin in Utah and Nevada provide an example. The resources available to the Shoshone were so meager that for most of the year families traveled alone through the countryside hunting and gathering. In certain seasons families assembled to hunt cooperatively as a band; after a few months together they dispersed.

Industrial and foraging economies do have something in common. In neither type are people tied permanently to the land. The mobility and the emphasis on small, economically self-sufficient family units select for the nuclear family as a basic kin group in both types of societies.

TRIBAL SOCIAL ORGANIZATION

Lineages and Clans

We have seen that the nuclear family is important among foragers and in industrial nations. The analogous group among nonindustrial food producers is the descent group (described in Chapter 7, where we distinguished between clans and lineages). In many societies, lineages are **corporate groups**. Like businesses in modern nations, corporate descent groups manage an *estate*, a pool of property and resources. Such an estate may include fields, an irrigation system, house sites, and herds. American culture teaches that people should acquire management positions through individual achievement rather than through kinship ties. We tend to disapprove of employees who hold their positions not because of special competence but because they happen to be the boss's son, daughter, or spouse. In contrast, rights in nonindustrial corporations, such as lineages and their estates, usually come through kinship and descent.

Another characteristic shared by industrial corporations and corporate descent groups is *perpetuity*. Descent groups, unlike nuclear families, are permanent and enduring units, with new members added in every generation. Members have access to the lineage estate. Unlike the nuclear family, the descent group lives on even though specific members die.

Unilineal Descent Groups and Unilocal Residence

Most cultures have a prevailing opinion about where couples should live after they marry. Neolocality, which is the rule for most middle-class Americans, is not very common outside modern North America, Western Europe, and the European-derived cultures of Latin America. Much more common is *virilocality* (*vir* in Latin means "husband"): married couples live with the husband's relatives. Often virilocality is associated with patrilineal descent. This makes sense. If the children of males are to become descent-group members, with rights in the father's estate, it's a good idea to raise them on that estate. This can be done if a wife moves to her husband's village rather than vice versa.

A less common postmarital residence rule that often is associated with matrilineal descent is *uxorilocality* (*uxor* in Latin means "wife"): married couples live with the wife's relatives. Together, virilocality and uxorilocality are known as **unilocal** rules of postmarital residence.

Flexibility in Descent-Group Organization

Some descent rules admit certain people as members while excluding others. A unilineal rule uses one line only, either the female or the male. Besides the unilineal rules, there is another descent rule called nonunilineal or **ambilineal** descent. As in any descent group, membership comes through descent from a common ancestor. However, ambilineal groups differ from unilineal groups in that they do not *automatically* exclude either the children of sons or those of daughters. With unilineal descent, membership is automatic—with no choice permitted. People are born members of the father's group in a patrilineal society or of the mother's group in a matrilineal society. They stay members of that group for the rest of their lives.

Before 1950, descent groups were generally described simply as patrilineal or matrilineal. If the society tended toward patrilineality, the anthropologist classified it as patrilineal rather than ambilineal. The treatment of ambilineal descent as a separate category was a formal recognition that many descent systems are flexible—some more so than others.

Descent, Ecology, and Evolution

We are ready now for some generalizations about relationships between kin groups, descent, ecology, and cultural evolution. There is a definite relationship between ecological factors and principles of social organization, including kinship and descent. Thus, because foragers live off nature rather than controlling it, families move about during the year and throughout their lives. Industrialism also fosters nuclear family organization (and even more severe kinship disintegration), because ties with the land are cut and the economy rewards geographical mobility.

Descent-group organization is especially characteristic of populations whose economies are based on a stable relationship between people and estates. By admitting some people and excluding others, a descent rule regulates access to resources. Descent is a flexible cultural means of adaptation. If there are too many people for a given estate to support, descent rules get stricter. If, by contrast, the population exploiting the estate starts to decline, descent rules become more flexible (Kottak 1971). Principles such as descent that serve over time to maintain stable relationships between human populations and their resource base are known as *homeostats* because they maintain equilibrium, or **homeostasis**.

We would expect descent rules to be most rigid when there is great pressure on resources, for example, in densely populated agricultural societies. However, if the population has not approached *carrying capacity* (the maximum number of people that the environment *could* support given the society's needs and its techniques of satisfying them), descent rules should be weaker. We would therefore expect descent rules to be least severely enforced in sparsely populated pastoral and horticultural societies. In these societies, the relationship between the human population and specific plots of land is less permanent than it is among agriculturalists.

However, the functions of descent and descent-group organization extend well beyond the context of population pressure on resources. In the discussion of segmentary lineage organization (Chapter 7) we saw that people may use common descent to create a regional political organization in order to unite and expand against other tribes.

KINSHIP TERMINOLOGY

People define kin relationships differently in different cultures, using different patterns of kinship terminology to refer to relatives. In any culture, kinship terminology is a classification system, a taxonomy or typology. However, it is not a system developed by anthropologists. Rather, it is a **native taxonomy**, developed over generations by the people who live in a particular society. A native classification system is based on how people perceive similarities and differences in the things being classified.

However, anthropologists have discovered that there are a limited number of ways in which people classify their kin. People who speak very different languages may use exactly the same system of kinship terminology. This section examines the four main ways of classifying kin on the parental generation: lineal, bifurcate merging, generational, and bifurcate collateral. We also consider the social correlates of these classification systems.

Several factors influence the way people interact with, perceive, and classify relatives. For example, do certain kinds of relatives customarily live together or apart? How far apart? What benefits do they derive from each other, and what are their obligations? Are they members of the same descent group or of different descent groups? With these questions in mind, let's examine systems of kinship terminology.

Kinship Terminology on the Parental Generation

Figure 12.3 applies to kin types on the generation above ego, the first ascending generation. The letters at the top identify six biological kin types. Numbers and colors indicate the manner of classification. Where the same number and color is shown below two biological kin types, the kin types are called by the same term.

Lineal Terminology

Our system of kinship classification is called the *lineal system* (Figure 12.4). The number 3 and the color green, which appear below the kin types FB and MB in Figures 12.3 and 12.4, stand for the term *uncle*, which we apply both to FB and to MB. **Lineal kinship terminology** is found in societies such as the United States and Canada, in which the nuclear family is the most important group based on kinship.

Lineal kinship terminology distinguishes lineal relatives from collateral relatives. A **lineal relative** is an ancestor or descendant, anyone on the direct

Figure 12.3 *Types of kinship classification on the first ascending generation.*

	MB	MZ	M	F	FB	FZ
Lineal	3	4	1	2	3	4
Bifurcate merging	3	1	1	2	2	4
Generational	2	1	1	2	2	1
Bifurcate collateral	3	6	1	2	5	4

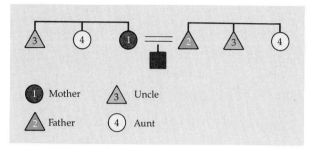

Figure 12.4 *Lineal kinship terminology.*

line of descent that leads to and from ego (Figure 12.5). Thus, lineal relatives are one's parents, grandparents, great-grandparents, and other direct forebears. Lineal relatives also include children, grandchildren, and great-grandchildren.

Collateral relatives are all other biological kin types. They include siblings, nieces and nephews, aunts and uncles, and cousins (Figure 12.5). **Affinals** are relatives by marriage, whether of lineals (e.g., son's wife) or collaterals (sister's husband).

Bifurcate Merging Kinship Terminology

Bifurcate merging kinship terminology is the most common way of classifying kin types (Figure 12.6). People use this system in societies with unilineal descent rules and unilocal postmarital residence. When the society is both unilocal and unilineal, the logic of bifurcate merging terminology is fairly clear. In a patrilineal society, for example, father and father's brother belong to the same descent group, gender, and generation. Since patrilineal societies usually have virilocal residence, the father and his brother live in the same local group. Because they share so many attributes that are socially relevant, ego regards them as social equivalents and calls them by the same kinship term—2. However, the mother's brother belongs to a different descent group, lives elsewhere, and has a different kin term—3.

What about mother and mother's sister in a patrilineal society? They belong to the same descent group, the same gender, and the same generation. Often they marry men from the same village and go to live there. These social similarities help explain the use of the same term—1—for both.

Similar observations apply to matrilineal societies. Consider a society with two matrilineal clans,

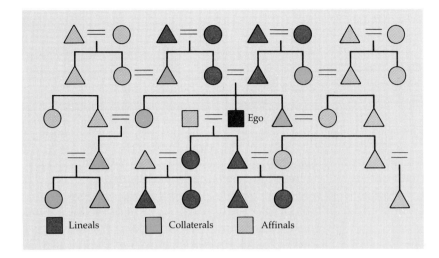

Figure 12.5 *The distinction between lineals, collaterals, and affinals as perceived by ego.*

the Ravens and the Wolves. Ego is a member of his mother's clan, the Raven clan. Ego's father is a member of the Wolf clan. His mother and her sister are female Ravens of the same generation. If there is uxorilocal residence, as there often is in matrilineal societies, they will live in the same village. Because they are so similar socially, ego calls them by the same kin term—1.

The father's sister, however, belongs to a different group, the Wolves, lives elsewhere, and has a different kin term—4. Ego's father and father's brother are male Wolves of the same generation. If they marry women of the same clan and live in the same village, this creates additional social similarities that reinforce this usage.

Generational Kinship Terminology

Like bifurcate merging kinship terminology, **generational kinship terminology** uses the same term

for parents and their siblings, but the lumping is more complete (Figure 12.7). With generational terminology, there are only two terms for the parental generation. We may translate them as "father" and "mother," but more accurate translations would be "male member of the parental generation" and "female member of the parental generation."

Generational kinship terminology does not distinguish between the mother's and father's sides. It uses just one term for father, father's brother, and mother's brother. In matrilineal and patrilineal societies, these three kin types do not belong to the same descent group. Generational kinship terminology also uses a single term for mother, mother's sister, and father's sister. In a unilineal society, these three would never be members of the same group.

Nevertheless, generational terminology suggests closeness between ego and his or her aunts

Figure 12.6 *Bifurcate merging kinship terminology.*

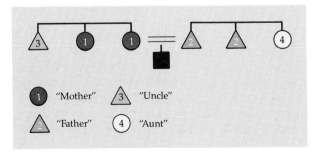

Figure 12.7 *Generational kinship terminology.*

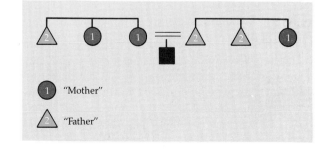

and uncles—much more closeness than exists between Americans and these kin types. We would therefore expect to find generational terminology in cultures in which kinship is much more important than it is in our own but in which there is no rigid distinction between the father's side and the mother's side.

It is no surprise, then, that generational kin terminology is typical of societies with ambilineal descent. In such contexts, descent-group membership is not automatic. People may choose the group they join, change their descent-group membership, or belong to two or more descent groups simultaneously. Generational terminology fits these conditions. The use of intimate kin terms allows people to maintain close personal relationships with all their relatives on the parental generation. People exhibit similar behavior toward aunts, uncles, and parents. Someday they will have to choose a descent group to join. Furthermore, in ambilineal societies, postmarital residence is usually **ambilocal**. This means that the married couple can live with either the husband's or the wife's group.

Significantly, generational terminology also characterizes certain foraging bands, including Kalahari groups and several native cultures of North America. Use of the same kinship terminology reflects certain similarities between foraging bands and ambilineal descent groups. In both societies, people have a choice about their kin-group affiliation. Foragers always live with kin, but they often shift band affiliation and so may be members of several different bands during their lifetimes. Just as in food-producing societies with ambilineal descent, generational kinship terminology among foragers helps maintain close personal relationships with several parental-generation relatives whom ego may eventually use as a point of entry into different groups.

Bifurcate Collateral Kinship Terminology

Of all the kinship classification systems, **bifurcate collateral terminology** is the most specific. It has separate terms for each of the six kin types on the parental generation (Figure 12.8). Bifurcate collateral terminology isn't as common as the other types. Most of the societies that use it are in North

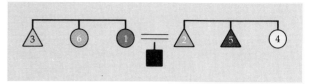

Figure 12.8 *Bifurcate collateral kinship terminology.*

Africa and the Middle East, and many of them are offshoots of the same ancestral group. They are also geographically close and have experienced many of the same historical events.

How can we explain bifurcate collateral terminology? Perhaps it arose accidentally in one society in this region and then diffused to others. Or perhaps bifurcate collateral terminology emerged in an ancient Middle Eastern society and now exists among descendant societies because of their common cultural heritage. Either explanation would be an example of a **historical explanation**. Similar customs often exist in different societies because those cultures have shared a period of common history or common sources of information.

Notice that the explanation being proposed for bifurcate collateral terminology is unlike the **functional explanations** that were offered for the other systems of kinship terminology. Functional explanations attempt to relate particular customs to other aspects of behavior in a society. Certain features of a culture are so closely related that when one of them changes, the others inevitably change too. For lineal, bifurcate merging, and generational terminologies, the social correlates (as discussed above) are very clear. However, because we lack a satisfactory functional explanation for bifurcate collateral terminology, a historical explanation was proposed instead. This discussion has a more general aim: it helps illustrate the kinds of explanations that anthropologists have proposed or considered for many other aspects of culture.

Relevance of Kinship Terminology

Anthropologists have to pay attention to kinship terminology because kinship is vitally important in bands, tribes, and chiefdoms. We saw in earlier chapters that kinship and descent play basic roles in regulating both interpersonal relations and political organization in such cultures. Kinship terms provide useful information about social patterns.

If two relatives are designated by the same term, we can assume that they are perceived as sharing socially significant attributes.

Nevertheless, cross-cultural studies have found that kinship *terminology* is one of the slowest-changing aspects of social organization. Land ownership, inheritance patterns, residence rules, and descent rules all change more easily and quickly than terminology does. As a result, many societies have kinship terminology that doesn't fit their other social patterns. If we find generational terminology in a society with virilocal residence and patrilineal descent, for example, we may conclude that kinship terminology has lagged behind changes in residence and descent. We expect that the kinship terminology will eventually become bifurcate merging.

SUMMARY

In non-Western, nonindustrial cultures, kinship is very important. In fact, kinship, descent, and marriage form the basis of social life and political organization. We must distinguish between kinship groups, whose composition and activities can be observed, and kinship calculation—the manner in which people identify and designate their relatives.

One widespread but nonuniversal kin group is the nuclear family, which consists of a married couple and their children. There are many functional alternatives to the nuclear family. These are social forms that assume functions that devolve on the nuclear family in other societies.

The nuclear family is a variable form of social organization that is most important in foraging and industrial societies. Food producers have kinship-based ties to estates, and other kinds of kinship and descent groups often overshadow the nuclear family.

In contemporary North America, the nuclear family is the characteristic kinship group for the middle class. Other kin groups assume somewhat greater importance in different social strata. Expanded households and sharing with extended family kin occur more frequently among disadvantaged minorities. The greater significance of expanded kinship in the lower class is an adaptation to poverty. It entails pooling of strategic resources by people with limited access to wealth and power. Today, however, even in the American middle class, nuclear family households are declining as single-person households and other domestic arrangements increase.

The descent group is the basic kin group among nonindustrial food producers. Unlike nuclear families, descent groups have perpetuity—they last for several generations. Descent-group members share and manage a common estate. Because of this, anthropologists have compared corporate descent groups to modern business. Descent rules may be unilineal or ambilineal. Unilineal (patrilineal and matrilineal) descent is associated with unilocal (respectively, virilocal and uxorilocal) postmarital residence rules.

Like many cultural features, descent rules help people adapt to their environments. Usually, these rules don't govern people's lives rigidly. The rules are often flexible. Ecological conditions help determine the types of kin groups that exist in a society and the extent to which people observe or depart from the rules.

Kinship terms, in contrast to biological kin types, are parts of native taxonomies. These are culturally specific ways of dividing up the world of kin relations on the basis of perceived differences and similarities. Although perceptions and classifications vary from culture to culture, comparative research has revealed a limited number of systems of kinship terminology. Because there are correlations between kinship terminology and other social practices, we can, with fair accuracy, predict kinship terminology from other aspects of culture.

Four basic classification systems, three of which are widely distributed throughout the world, categorize kin types on the parental generation. Many foraging and industrial societies have lineal terminology, which is correlated with nuclear family organization. Cultures with unilocal residence and unilineal descent tend to have bifurcate merging terminology. Generational terminology correlates with ambilineal descent and ambilocal residence. The more restricted bifurcate collateral terminology is concentrated among societies of the Middle East and North Africa. Its social functions and correlates are unclear. Kinship terminology changes more slowly than do patterns of inheritance, postmarital residence, and descent-group organization. Therefore, the correlation between kin terms and social structure is often incomplete.

GLOSSARY

affinals: Relatives by marriage, whether of lineals (e.g., son's wife) or collaterals (e.g., sister's husband).

ambilineal: Principle of descent that does not automatically exclude the children of either sons or daughters.

ambilocal: Postmarital residence pattern in which the couple may reside with either the husband's or the wife's group.

bifurcate collateral kinship terminology: Kinship terminology employing separate terms for M, F, MB, MZ, FB, and FZ.

bifurcate merging kinship terminology: Kinship terminology in which M and MZ are called by the same term, F and FB are called by the same term, and MB and FZ are called by different terms.

bilateral kinship calculation: A system in which kinship ties are calculated equally through both sexes: mother and father, sister and brother, daughter and son, and so on.

biological kin types: Actual genealogical relationships, designated by letters and symbols (e.g., FB), as opposed to the kin terms (e.g., *uncle*) used in a particular society.

blended family: Kin unit formed when parents remarry and bring their children into a new household.

collateral household: Type of expanded family household including siblings and their spouses and children.

collateral relative: A biological relative who is not a lineal.

corporate groups: Groups that exist in perpetuity and manage a common estate; include descent groups and modern corporations.

ego: Latin for *I*. In kinship charts, the point from which one views an egocentric genealogy.

expanded family household: Coresident group that can include siblings and their spouses and children (a *collateral* household) or three generations of kin and their spouses (an *extended family* household).

extended family: Expanded household including three or more generations.

family of orientation: Nuclear family in which one is born and grows up.

family of procreation: Nuclear family established when one marries and has children.

functional explanation: Explanation that establishes a correlation or interrelationship between social customs. When customs are functionally interrelated, if one changes, the others also change.

generational kinship terminology: Kinship terminology with only two terms for the parental generation, one designating M, MZ, and FZ and the other designating F, FB, and MB.

genitor: Biological father of a child.

historical explanation: Demonstration that a social institution or practice exists among different populations because they share a period of common history or have been exposed to common sources of information; includes diffusion.

homeostasis: Equilibrium, or a stable relationship, between a population and its resource base.

kin terms: The words used for different relatives in a particular language, as opposed to actual genealogical relationships (*biological kin types*).

kinship calculation: The system by which people in a particular society reckon kin relationships.

lineal kinship terminology: Parental generation kin terminology with four terms: one for M, one for F, one for FB and MB, and one for MZ and FZ.

lineal relative: Any of ego's ancestors or descendants (e.g., parents, grandparents, children, grandchildren) on the direct line of descent that leads to and from ego.

marriage: Socially approved relationship between a socially recognized male (the husband) and a socially recognized female (the wife) such that the children born to the wife are accepted as the offspring of both husband and wife.

matrilateral skewing: A preference for relatives on the mother's side.

native taxonomy: Classification system invented and used by natives rather than anthropologists.

neolocality: Postmarital residence pattern in which a couple establishes a new place of residence rather than living with or near either set of parents.

pater: Socially recognized father of a child; not necessarily the genitor.

unilocal: Either virilocal or uxorilocal postmarital residence; requires that a married couple reside with the relatives of either the husband (*vir*) or the wife (*uxor*), depending on the society.

STUDY QUESTIONS

1. Why has kinship been so important in ethnographic studies?
2. What is the nuclear family, and why is it significant?
3. What is the difference between the family of orientation and the family of procreation?
4. What kinds of rights may marriage transmit?
5. What is the relationship between the nuclear family and marriage?
6. What four "essential" social functions have been attributed to the nuclear family, and what is the argument against this view?
7. What is the difference between education and enculturation?
8. How does Nayar society reproduce itself biologically without the nuclear family?
9. What three factors are linked with neolocal postmarital residence and household composition?
10. Nuclear families account for what percentage of American households? What are the other household types?
11. How is the content of television programs related to changes in household organization in twentieth-century North America?
12. What is the key causal factor underlying the nuclear family's role in both foraging and industrial societies?
13. How is descent related to ecological adaptation?
14. What is lineal kinship terminology, and how is it related to American culture?
15. What types of explanations do anthropologists use for systems of kinship terminology?

SUGGESTED ADDITIONAL READING

AMADIUME, I.
    1987 *Male Daughters, Female Husbands.* Atlantic Highlands, NJ: Zed. How women fill male roles, including husband, among the Igbo of Nigeria.

BUCHLER, I. R., AND H. A. SELBY
    1968 *Kinship and Social Organization: An Introduction to Theory and Method.* New York: Macmillan. Introduction to comparative social organization; includes several chapters on interpretations of kinship classification systems.

COLLIER, J. F., AND S. J. YANAGISAKO, EDS.
    1987 *Gender and Kinship: Essays toward a Unified Analysis.* Stanford, CA: Stanford University Press. Recent consideration of kinship in the context of gender issues.

GRABURN, N., ED.
    1971 *Readings in Kinship and Social Structure.* New York: Harper & Row. Several important articles on kinship terminology.

MORGEN, S., ED.
    1989 *Gender and Anthropology: Critical Reviews for Research and Teaching.* Washington, DC: American Anthropological Association. Reviews aspects of gender, kinship, marriage, and household organization in many areas and in a biosocial perspective.

NETTING, R. M. C., E. R. WILK, AND E. J. ARNOULD, EDS.
    1984 *Households: Comparative and Historical Studies of the Domestic Group.* Berkeley: University of California Press. Excellent collection of articles on household research.

RADCLIFFE-BROWN, A. R.
    1950 Introduction to *African Systems of Kinship and Marriage,* ed. A.R. Radcliffe-Brown and D. Forde, pp. 1–85. London: Oxford University Press. Classic introduction to kinship and classification systems.

SAHLINS, M. D.
    1968 *Tribesmen.* Englewood Cliffs, NJ: Prentice-Hall. Kinship, descent, and marriage in tribal societies.

SERVICE, E. R.
    1971 *Primitive Social Organization: An Evolutionary Perspective,* 2nd ed. New York: Random House. Includes a theoretical discussion, from a general evolutionary point of view, of kinship terms in bands, tribes, and chiefdoms.

MARRIAGE

I n stateless societies a person's social world includes two main categories—friends and strangers. Strangers are potential or actual enemies. Marriage is one of the primary ways of converting strangers into friends, of creating and maintaining personal and political alliances. The incest taboo forces people to practice **exogamy,** to seek their mates outside their own groups. Exogamy has adaptive value because it links people into a wider social network that nurtures, helps, and protects them in times of need.

THE INCEST TABOO AND EXOGAMY

Incest refers to sexual relations with a close relative. All cultures have taboos against it. However, although the taboo is a cultural universal, cultures define incest differently. As an illustration, consider some implications of the distinction between two kinds of first cousins, cross cousins and parallel cousins.

The children of two brothers or two sisters are **parallel cousins.** The children of a brother and a sister are **cross cousins.** Your mother's sister's children and your father's brother's children are your parallel cousins. Your father's sister's children and your mother's brother's children are your cross cousins.

The American kin term *cousin* doesn't distinguish between cross and parallel cousins, but in many societies, especially those with unilineal descent, the distinction is essential. As an example, consider a community with only two descent groups. This exemplifies what is known as **moiety** organization—from the French *moitié,* which means "half." Descent bifurcates the community so that everyone belongs to one half or the other. Some societies have patrilineal moieties; others have matrilineal moieties.

In Figures 13.1 and 13.2, notice that cross cousins are always members of the opposite moiety and parallel cousins always belong to your (ego's) own moiety. With patrilineal descent (Figure 13.1), people take the father's descent-group affiliation; in a matrilineal society (Figure 13.2), they take the mother's. You can see from these diagrams that your mother's sister's children (MZC) and your father's brother's children (FBC) belong to your group. Your cross cousins—that is, FZC and MBC—belong to the other moiety.

Parallel cousins therefore belong to the same generation and the same descent group, and they are like brothers and sisters. They are called by the same kin terms as brother and sister are. Defined as close relatives, parallel cousins are tabooed as sex or marriage partners. They fall within the incest taboo, but cross cousins don't.

In societies with unilineal moieties, cross cousins belong to the opposite group. Sex with cross cousins isn't incestuous, because they aren't considered relatives. In fact, in many unilineal societies people must marry either a cross cousin or someone from the same descent group as a cross cousin. A unilineal descent rule ensures that the cross cousin's descent group is never one's own. With moiety exogamy, spouses must belong to different moieties.

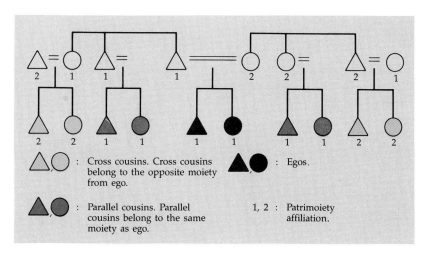

Cross cousins. Cross cousins belong to the opposite moiety from ego.

Parallel cousins. Parallel cousins belong to the same moiety as ego.

: Egos.

1, 2 : Patrimoiety affiliation.

Figure 13.1 *Parallel and cross cousins and patrilineal moiety organization.*

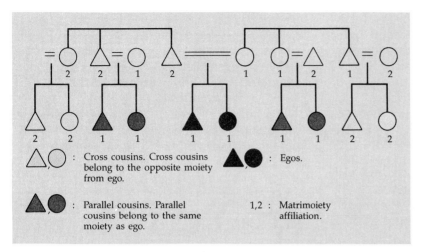

Figure 13.2 *Matrilineal moiety organization.*

Among the Yanomami of Venezuela and Brazil (Chagnon 1974, 1983), men anticipate eventual marriage to a cross cousin by calling her "wife." They call their male cross cousins "brother-in-law." Yanomami women call their male cross cousins "husband" and their female cross cousins "sister-in-law." Among the Yanomami, as in many societies with unilineal descent, sex with cross cousins is proper but sex with parallel cousins is considered incestuous.

A custom that is much rarer than cross-cousin marriage also illustrates that people define their kin, and thus incest, differently in different societies. When unilineal descent is very strongly developed, the parent who does not belong to one's own descent group isn't considered a relative.

First-cousin marriage, though permitted or even required in many tribal societies, is illegal in many parts of the United States, although marriage of more distant cousins, such as Eleanor and Franklin Roosevelt, is not.

Thus, with strict patrilineality, the mother is not a relative but a kind of in-law who has married a member of ego's group—ego's father. With strict matrilineality, the father isn't a relative, because he belongs to a different descent group.

The Lakher of Southeast Asia are strictly patrilineal (Leach 1961). Using the male ego in Figure 13.3, let's suppose that ego's father and mother get divorced. Each remarries and has a daughter by a second marriage. A Lakher always belongs to his or her father's group, all the members of which (one's **agnates,** or patrikin) are considered too closely related to marry because they are members of the same patrilineal descent group. Therefore, ego can't marry his father's daughter by the second marriage, just as in contemporary North America it's illegal for half-siblings to marry.

However, in contrast to our society, where all half-siblings are tabooed, the Lakher permit ego to marry his mother's daughter by a different father. She is not ego's relative, because she belongs to her own father's descent group rather than ego's. The Lakher illustrate very well that definitions of relatives, and therefore of incest, vary from culture to culture.

Figure 13.3 *Patrilineal descent-group identity and incest among the Lakher.*

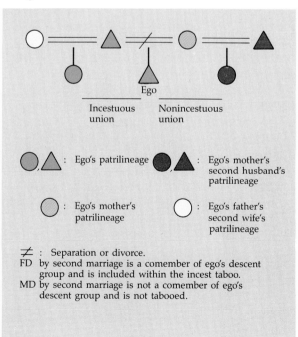

We can extend these observations to strict matrilineal societies. If a man's parents divorce and his father remarries, ego may marry his paternal half-sister. By contrast, if his mother remarries and has a daughter, the daughter is considered ego's sister, and sex between them is taboo. Cultures therefore have different definitions of relationships that are biologically or genetically equivalent.

EXPLANATIONS FOR THE INCEST TABOO

Instinctive Horror

There is no simple or universally accepted explanation for the fact that all cultures ban incest. Do primate studies offer any clues? Research with primates does show that adolescent males (among monkeys) or females (among apes) often move away from the group in which they were born. This emigration helps reduce the frequency of incestuous unions. The human avoidance of mating with close relatives may therefore express a generalized primate tendency.

One argument (Westermarck 1894; Hobhouse 1915; Lowie 1920/1961) is that the incest taboo is universal because incest horror is instinctive— *Homo sapiens* has a genetically programmed disgust toward incest. Because of this feeling, early humans banned it. However, cultural universality doesn't necessarily entail an instinctual basis. Fire making, for example, is a cultural universal, but it certainly is not an ability transmitted by the genes. Furthermore, if people really did have an instinctive horror of mating with blood relatives, a formal incest taboo would be unnecessary. No one would ever do it. However, as social workers, judges, psychiatrists, and psychologists know, incest isn't rare but happens all the time.

A final objection to the instinctive horror theory is that it can't explain why in some societies people can marry their cross cousins but not their parallel cousins. Nor does it tell us why the Lakher can marry their maternal, but not their paternal, half-siblings. No known instinct can distinguish between parallel and cross cousins.

The specific kin types included within the incest taboo—and the taboo itself—have a cultural rather than a biological basis. Even among nonhuman primates there is no evidence for an instinct against incest. Adolescent dispersal does not prevent—but merely limits the frequency of—incestuous unions. Among humans, cultural traditions determine the specific relatives with whom sex is considered incestuous. They also deal with people who violate prohibited relationships in different ways. Banishment, imprisonment, death, and threats of supernatural retaliation are some of the punishments imposed.

Biological Degeneration

Another theory is that the taboo emerged because early *Homo* noticed that abnormal offspring were born from incestuous unions (Morgan 1877/1963). To prevent this, our ancestors banned incest. The human stock produced after the taboo originated was so successful that it spread everywhere.

What is the evidence for this theory? Laboratory experiments with animals that reproduce faster than humans do (such as mice and fruit flies) have been used to investigate the effects of inbreeding: A decline in survival and fertility does accompany brother-sister mating across several generations. However, despite the potentially harmful biological results of systematic inbreeding, human marriage patterns are based on specific cultural beliefs rather than universal concerns about biological de-

generation several generations in the future. Neither instinctive horror nor fear of biological degeneration explains the very widespread custom of marrying cross cousins. Nor can fears about degeneration explain why breeding with parallel cousins but not cross cousins is so often tabooed.

Marry Out or Die Out

One of the best explanations for the incest taboo is that it arose in order to ensure exogamy, to force people to marry outside their kin groups (Tylor 1889; White 1959; Lévi-Strauss 1949/1969). In this view, the taboo originated early in human evolution because it was adaptively advantageous. Marrying someone from one's own group, with whom one is already on peaceful terms, would be counterproductive. There is more to gain by extending peaceful relations to a wider network of groups.

This view emphasizes the role of marriage in creating and maintaining alliances. By forcing members to marry out, a group increases its allies. Marriage within the group, by contrast, would isolate that group and might ultimately lead to its extinction. Exogamy and the incest taboo that propels it help explain human adaptive success. Besides the sociopolitical function, exogamy also ensures genetic mixture between groups and thus maintains a successful human species.

In nonindustrial societies, marriage and exogamy play key roles in forming alliances between groups. One marries not just an individual but an entire kin group. Here a groom's sister mimics her brother's role as husband, dressing as a man and embracing "their" bride.

Cultural Continuity and Family Roles

Bronislaw Malinowski (1927) explained the incest taboo with reference to enculturation and the family. Malinowski believed in the generalized importance of nuclear family relationships. He saw the family as the setting in which the knowledge and feelings on which culture is based are transmitted. Cultural continuity across the generations requires feelings of family dependence and respect.

Malinowski's interest in family sentiments and attachments reflected his reading of early twentieth-century psychologists, especially Sigmund Freud. Malinowski rejected the Freudian theory that children have strong sexual feelings before puberty. Instead, he argued that young children have different kinds of affectionate feelings. He believed that nonsexual affection between parents and prepubescent children is important. Malinowski thought that only at puberty do sexual urges develop. He argued that children entering puberty would naturally attempt to gratify their emerging sexual urges with the people who are already emotionally closest to them. They would therefore seek members of their nuclear family as sexual partners. To phrase it with a pun, "familiarity breeds attempt."

Malinowski argued that the incest taboo arose to displace and direct outward this universal temptation toward incestuous unions. If sexual urges were satisfied within the family, conflict would arise and halt the group's normal functioning. Fundamental social bonds—the child's relationships with its parents—would be destroyed, and cultural transmission could not continue. Thus, the incest taboo became a cultural universal to keep all this from happening.

Much of Malinowski's argument seems reasonable. As a child grows up, he or she learns that father, mother, brother, and sister have different and distinct roles (behavioral expectations and obligations) within the family. A boy's attempt to emulate his father by having sex with his mother could destroy the role structure on which the family is based. However, Malinowski's interpretation is not so satisfactory when it comes to the taboo against sex between siblings.

A more complete and satisfactory explanation for the taboo combines several views. Thus, exogamy and its alliances do have adaptive value and biologically desirable results. Close relatives do provide enculturative models for role differentiation by age and gender. Incestuous gratification of sexual urges *would* threaten relationships among close relatives and create conflict. The universal combination of incest taboo plus exogamy therefore does all the following:

1. It establishes alliances and extends peaceful relations beyond the group.
2. It promotes genetic mixture.
3. It preserves family roles, guarding against socially destructive conflict.

ENDOGAMY

Exogamy pushes social organization outward, establishing and preserving alliances among groups. In contrast, rules of **endogamy** dictate mating or marriage within a group to which one belongs. Endogamic rules are less common but are still familiar to anthropologists. Indeed, most cultures *are* endogamous units, although they usually do not need a formal rule requiring people to marry someone from their own society. Members of the endogamic groups would never consider doing anything else.

Some societies have both exogamic and endogamic rules. However, these rules cannot apply to the same social unit. In stratified societies, for example, people are often expected to marry someone from the same social class. However, the classes, or strata, themselves may be divided into descent groups or other subdivisions, each of which may be an exogamous unit. Exogamy links groups together and merges their resources. However, endogamy keeps groups apart and prevents their resources from blending. Endogamic rules in stratified societies help maintain social, economic, and political distinctions in order to preserve differential access to culturally valued resources.

Caste

An extreme example of endogamy is India's caste system. Castes are stratified groups in which membership is ascribed at birth and is lifelong. Castes are usually endogamous groups, and the caste system has rules that automatically and unambiguously classify a person at birth. People

This street sweeper in New Delhi is a member of India's untouchable caste. Occupational specialization and notions about ritual impurity have been features of the Indian caste system.

have no choice about their caste affiliation. The main difference between castes and unilineal descent groups, which also automatically and unambiguously recruit members at birth, is that castes are stratified and endogamous.

Indian castes are grouped into five major categories, or *varna*. Each is ranked relative to the other four, and these categories extend throughout India. Each *varna* includes a large number of castes (*jati*), each of which includes people within a region who may intermarry. All the *jati* in a single *varna* in a given region are ranked, just as the *varna* themselves are ranked.

Occupational specialization often sets off one caste from another. A community may include castes of agricultural workers, merchants, artisans, priests, and sweepers. The untouchable *varna*, found throughout India, includes castes whose ancestry, ritual status, and occupations are considered so impure that higher-caste people consider even casual contact with untouchables to be defiling.

The belief that intercaste sexual unions lead to ritual impurity for the higher-caste partner is important in maintaining endogamy. A man who has sex with a lower-caste woman can restore his purity with a bath and a prayer. However, a woman who has intercourse with a man of a lower caste has no such recourse. Her defilement cannot be undone. Because the women have the babies, these differences protect the purity of the caste line, ensuring the pure ancestry of high-caste children. Although Indian castes are endogamous groups, many of them are internally subdivided into exogamous lineages. This means that Indians must marry a member of another descent group from the same caste.

A long history, an ideology that includes notions of ritual purity and contamination, and intricate occupational and economic distinctions buttress the Indian caste system. However, the principle of caste, without all these particular cultural features, is widely encountered in stratified societies. For example, the two ethnic groups called black and white, which are known as "races" in the contemporary United States, have traditionally been castelike groups.

A dual stratified hierarchy exists in the United States. American society includes lower, middle, and upper classes and their subdivisions. To a certain extent, class status in the United States is achieved. American culture values the self-made man or woman, the rugged individualist, and rags-to-riches stories. We preach individual achievement as a way of moving up in society.

The second dimension of the American stratification system is the black-white contrast. Many states once prohibited marriages between blacks and whites. However, the rule that did the most to create and perpetuate this castelike system was that of *hypodescent*, which states that the child of a black-white union is always black. This arbitrary rule disregards both the actual physical appearance of the child and the equal shares of its genetic composition that come from each parent. Hypodescent automatically assigns the children of intercaste unions to membership in the socioeconomically disadvantaged group—to the black "race" in the United States.

Royal Incest

Royal incest is similar to caste endogamy. The best-known examples come from Inca Peru, ancient Egypt, and traditional Hawaii. Those cultures allowed royal brother-sister marriages. Privileged endogamy, a violation of the incest taboo that applied to commoners in those cultures, was a means of differentiating between rulers and subjects.

Manifest and Latent Functions

To understand why royalty did not observe the incest taboo, it is useful to distinguish between the manifest and latent functions of behavior. The **manifest function** of a custom refers to the reasons natives give for it. Its **latent function** is an effect the custom has on the society that the native people don't mention or may not even recognize.

Royal incest illustrates this distinction. Hawaiians and other Polynesians believed in an impersonal force called *mana*. Mana could exist in things or people, in the latter case marking them off from other people and making them divine. The Hawaiians believed that no one had as much mana as the ruler. Mana depended on genealogy. The person whose own mana was exceeded only by the king's was his sibling. The most appropriate wife for a king was his own full sister. Notice that brother-sister marriage also meant that royal heirs would be as mana-ful, or divine, as possible. The manifest function of royal incest in ancient Hawaii involved that culture's beliefs about mana and divinity.

Royal incest also had latent functions—political repercussions. The ruler and his spouse had the same parents. Since mana was believed to be inherited, they were almost equally divine. When the king and his sister married, their children indisputably had the most mana in the land. No one could question their right to rule. However, if the king had taken a wife with less mana than his sister, his sister's children with someone else might eventually cause problems. Both sets of children could assert their divinity and right to rule. Royal sibling marriage therefore limited conflicts about succession because it reduced the number of people with claims to rule. Other kingdoms have solved this problem differently. Some succession rules, for instance, specify that only the oldest child (usually the son) of the reigning monarch can succeed; this custom is called **primogeniture.** Commonly, rulers have banished or killed claimants who rival the chosen heir.

Royal incest also had a latent economic function. If the king and his sister had rights to inherit the ancestral estate, their marriage to each other, again by limiting the number of heirs, kept it intact. Power often rests on wealth, and royal incest tended to ensure that royal wealth remained concentrated in the same line.

Patrilateral Parallel-Cousin Marriage

Functionally similar to royal incest is **patrilateral parallel-cousin marriage** (marriage of the children of brothers) among Islamic, or Moslem, societies of the Middle East and North Africa, particularly the Arabs. Arabs trace their descent patrilineally from Abraham's son Ishmael in the Bible. The Arabs' genealogy enhances their feelings of ethnic identity, because they all belong to a huge patrilineage.

Arabs say that a man likes to marry his father's brother's daughter in order to keep property in the family. This manifest function originated as patrilineal Arabs adapted to the imposition of Islamic inheritance laws. In contrast to patrilineality, in which only males inherit, Islam stipulates that daughters must share in their parents' estates. Patrilateral parallel-cousin marriage helps prevent fragmentation of estates that brothers have inherited from their parents.

EXOGAMY

We move now from endogamy, which isolates groups, back to exogamy, which forges them into social and political networks. In many tribal societies, rules of exogamy are rigid and very specific. For example, some cultures with strongly developed unilineal descent organization not only prohibit descent-group endogamy but also specify where people should seek their spouses.

Generalized Exchange

Directing his attention toward such societies, the renowned French anthropologist Claude Lévi-Strauss (1949/1969) analyzed the exogamic rules that give rise to what he calls *generalized exchange systems*. In societies with generalized exchange, there is an established marital relationship between descent groups. The men of B always marry women from A, and the women of B always marry men from C. Generalized exchange is associated with patrilineal descent and virilocal residence. Men stay put, and women marry out.

Virilocal residence always ensures that patrilineally related men stay together; uxorilocal residence does the same for women in a matrilineal society. Combined with virilocality, generalized exchange means that a patrilineage's men live together and that its women marry into the same village. This rule thus grants both men and women lifelong residence with members of their own descent groups. This can provide important psychological support for women who might otherwise have to leave their kinsmen and kinswomen behind and live with strangers in a husband's village. To be sure, women do live in the husband's village. However, that village is filled with women from their own descent group, including their sisters, paternal aunts, and brother's daughters.

MARRIAGE IN TRIBAL SOCIETIES

Outside of industrial societies, marriage is often more a relationship between groups than one between individuals. We think of marriage as an individual matter. Although the bride and groom usually seek their parents' approval, the final choice (to live together, to marry, to divorce) lies with the couple. The idea of romantic love symbolizes this individual relationship.

In nonindustrial societies, marriage is a group concern. People don't just take a spouse; they assume obligations to a group of in-laws. When residence is virilocal, for example, a woman must leave the community where she was born. Unless there is generalized exchange, she must leave most of her relatives behind. She faces the prospect of spending the rest of her life in her husband's village, with his relatives. She may even have to transfer her major allegiance from her own group to her husband's. If there are disputes between her group and her husband's, she may have to side with him.

Bridewealth

In societies with descent groups, people enter marriage not alone but with the help of the descent group. Descent-group members often have to contribute to **bridewealth,** a customary gift before, at, or after marriage from the husband and his kin to the wife and her kin. Another word for bridewealth is **brideprice,** but this term is inaccurate, because people with the custom don't usually regard the exchange as a sale. They don't think of

Marriage usually entails a shift in residence for wife, husband, or both. Shown here, a traditional procession associated with Confucian weddings in rural South Korea.

Gift-giving customs, including dowry and brideprice, are associated with marriage throughout the world. Here guests bring presents in baskets to a wedding in Wenjiang, China.

marriage as a commercial relationship between a man and an object that can be bought and sold.

Bridewealth compensates the bride's group for the loss of her companionship and labor. More important, it makes the children born to the woman full members of her husband's descent group. For this reason, the institution is also called **progeny price.** Rather than the woman herself, it is her children who are permanently transferred to the husband's group. Whatever we call it, such a transfer of wealth at marriage is common in patrilineal tribes. In matrilineal societies, children are members of the mother's group, and there is no reason to pay a progeny price. **Dowry** is a marital exchange in which the wife's group provides substantial gifts to the husband's family. Dowry, best known from India, correlates with low female status. Women are perceived as burdens. When husbands and their families take a wife, they expect to be compensated for the added responsibility.

Bridewealth exists in many more cultures than dowry does, but the nature and quantity of transferred items differ. In many African societies, cattle constitute bridewealth, but the number of cattle given varies from society to society. *As the value of bridewealth increases, marriages become more stable.* Bridewealth is insurance against divorce.

Imagine a patrilineal society in which a marriage requires the transfer of about twenty-five cattle from the groom's descent group to the bride's. Mi-

chael, a member of descent group A, marries Sarah from group B. His relatives help him assemble the bridewealth. He gets the most help from his close agnates—his older brother, father, father's brother, and closest patrilineal cousins. His maternal grandfather or uncle also contributes on behalf of Michael's mother's group as a token of a continuing alliance established a generation earlier, when Michael's father and mother married.

Michael's marriage is the concern of his entire corporate lineage, especially his father or, if his father is dead, his older brother or father's brother. Some of the cattle are from the herds of Michael's descent group. Others have come in as bridewealth for the women of Michael's group, for example, his sister Jennifer and his paternal aunts.

The distribution of the cattle once they reach Sarah's group mirrors the manner in which they were assembled. Sarah's father, or her oldest brother if the father is dead, receives her bridewealth. He keeps most of the cattle to use as bridewealth for his sons' marriages. However, a share also goes to everyone who will be expected to help when Sarah's brothers marry.

When Sarah's brother David gets married, many of the cattle go to a third group—C, which is David's wife's group. Thereafter, they may serve as bridewealth to still other groups. Men constantly use their sisters' bridewealth cattle to acquire their own wives. In a decade, the cattle given when Michael married Sarah will have been exchanged widely.

In tribal societies, marriage entails an agreement between descent groups. Cultural traditions define specific roles for husband and wife. Everyone understands that neither Sarah nor Michael should stray too far from the behavior expected of a married couple in that society. Sarah owes certain things to Michael's group and can expect certain things from him and his relatives, and vice versa.

Still, several problems may arise. Sarah may find that Michael is a poor husband. She may have trouble getting along with him or his relatives, with whom she resides virilocally. If she convinces her relatives that her complaints are justified and if the bridewealth is easy to repay, her group may return the cattle, and a divorce will take place.

However, marriages in such societies aren't usually so brittle. A woman's relatives generally try to persuade her to work things out with her husband. This is especially true if the bridewealth was substantial and has been distributed among many of Sarah's relatives or if most of it has been used to obtain a wife for her brother. We may generalize: the more difficult it is to reassemble the bridewealth, the more stable is marriage and the rarer is divorce.

If Sarah and Michael try to make their marriage succeed but fail to do so, both groups may conclude that the marriage can't last. Here it becomes especially obvious that tribal marriages are relationships between groups as well as between individuals. If Sarah has a younger sister or niece (her older brother's daughter, for example), the concerned parties may agree to Sarah's replacement by a kinswoman.

There is another possibility. When a woman divorces a man, he may sometimes claim her brother's wife. After all, Sarah's father might have used Michael's cattle to obtain a wife for his son (Sarah's brother) David. Thus, through his bridewealth cattle, Michael has a claim on David's wife. This practice existed among the Ba-Thonga of southeastern Africa.

However, incompatibility isn't the main problem that threatens marriage in societies with bridewealth. Infertility is a more important concern. If Sarah has no children, she and her group have not fulfilled their part of the marriage agreement. If the relationship is to endure, Sarah's group must furnish another woman, perhaps her younger sister, who can have children.

So important is fertility among the Betsileo of Madagascar that it is often only after a woman is pregnant that the marriage takes place and bridewealth is given. During a period of trial marriage, the woman lives in her husband's village. She may demonstrate her fertility by getting pregnant. She also learns whether she is compatible with her prospective husband and his relatives. If she gets pregnant and the couple doesn't want to marry, the child can join its mother's descent group, with full rights.

In societies with descent groups and bridewealth, every marriage entails an agreement between groups. An infertile woman's group must return the progeny price or provide a substitute child bearer. The original wife may choose to stay in her husband's village. Perhaps she will someday have a child. If she does stay on, her husband will have established a plural marriage.

Most nonindustrial food-producing societies, unlike most foraging societies and industrial nations, allow **plural marriages,** or **polygamy.** There are two varieties, one common and the other very rare. The more common variant is **polygyny,** in which a man has more than one wife. The rare variant is **polyandry,** in which a woman has more than one husband. If the infertile wife remains married to her husband after he has taken a substitute wife provided by her descent group, this is polygyny. I will discuss reasons for polygyny other than infertility shortly.

Durable Alliances

It is possible to exemplify the group-alliance nature of marriage in tribal societies by examining still another common practice—continuation of marital alliances when one spouse dies.

Sororate

What happens if Sarah dies young? Michael's group will ask Sarah's group for a substitute, often her sister. This custom is known as the **sororate** (Figure 13.4). If Sarah has no sister or if all her sisters are already married, another woman from her group may be available. Michael marries her, there is no need to return the bridewealth, and the alliance continues. The sororate exists in both matrilineal and patrilineal societies. In a matrilineal society with uxorilocal postmarital residence, a widower may remain with his wife's group by marrying her sister or another female member of her matrilineage (Figure 13.4).

Levirate and Other Arrangements

What happens if the husband dies? In many societies, the widow may marry his brother. This custom is known as the **levirate** (Figure 13.4). Like the sororate, it is a continuation marriage that maintains the alliance between descent groups, in this case by replacing the husband with another member of his group. The implications of the levirate vary with age.

Returning to Michael, Sarah, and company, what happens if Michael dies after Sarah has had children? When they married, it was understood that his group would care for Sarah. She fulfilled her part of the agreement by producing the children necessary to perpetuate Michael's descent group. When Michael dies, the levirate assigns one of his brothers to Sarah. If that brother already has a wife, he will now be polygynous. Michael's brother must care for Sarah and treat her as his wife. Depending on their ages, their marriage may or may not involve sex. A recent study found that

Figure 13.4 *Sororate and levirate.*

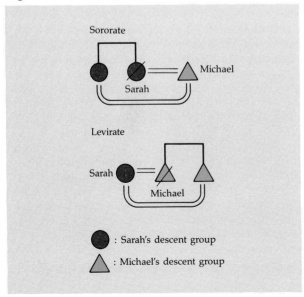

Sororate

Sarah

Michael

Levirate

Sarah

Michael

● : Sarah's descent group

▲ : Michael's descent group

in African societies the levirate, though widely permitted, rarely involves coresidence of the widow and her new husband. Furthermore, widows don't automatically marry the husband's brother just because they are allowed to. Often they prefer to make other arrangements (Potash 1986).

PLURAL MARRIAGES

In contemporary North America, where divorce is fairly easy and common, polygamy (marriage to more than one spouse at the same time) is against the law. Marriage in industrial nations joins individuals, and relationships between individuals can be severed more easily than can those between groups. As divorce grows more common, North Americans practice **serial monogamy:** individuals have more than one spouse but never, legally, more than one at the same time. As stated earlier, the two forms of polygamy are polygyny and polyandry. Polyandry is practiced in only a few cultures, notably among Polynesia's Marquesas Islanders and among certain groups in Tibet, Nepal, and India. Polygyny is much more common.

Polygyny

We must distinguish between the social approval of plural marriage and its actual frequency in a particular society. Many cultures approve of a man's having more than one wife. However, even when polygyny is encouraged, most people are monogamous, and polygyny characterizes only a fraction of the marriages. Why?

One reason is equal sex ratios. In the United States, about 105 males are born for every 100 females. In adulthood the ratio of men to women equalizes, and eventually it reverses. The average North American woman outlives the average man. In many nonindustrial societies as well, a male-biased sex ratio among children also reverses in adulthood. This occurs because many cultures allocate dangerous tasks to men. They have to climb, hunt, make war, fish, sail, and travel, sometimes into alien territory. The Eskimos, who traditionally assigned dangerous jobs to men, practiced female infanticide. The practice of killing girl babies ensured that there were approximately equal numbers of adult Eskimo men and women.

BRADY BUNCH NIRVANA

The freshmen I teach at the University of Michigan belong to the first generation raised after the almost total diffusion of television into the American home. Most young Americans have never known a world without TV. The tube is as familiar as Mom or Dad. Indeed, considering how common divorce has become, TV sets outlast the father in many homes. One habit I began about ten years ago, taking advantage of my students' familiarity with television, is to demonstrate changes in American kinship and marriage patterns by contrasting the programs of the fifties with more recent ones. Four decades ago, the usual TV family was a nuclear family made up of father (who often knew best), homemaker mother, and children. Examples include *Father Knows Best, Ozzie and Harriet,* and *Leave It to Beaver.* These programs were appropriate for the 1950s market, but they are out of sync with today's social and economic realities. Only 16 million American women worked outside the home in 1950, compared with three times that number today. Today just 7 percent of American households fit the former ideal: breadwinner father, homemaker mother, and two children.

Virtually all my students have seen reruns of the more recent family series *The Brady Bunch.* The social organization of *The Brady Bunch* provides an instructive contrast with 1950s programs, because it illustrates what we call blended family organization. A new (blended) family forms when a widow with three daughters marries a widower with three sons. Blended families have been increasing in American society because of more frequent divorce and remarriage. During *The Brady Bunch*'s heyday, divorce remained controversial and could not give rise to a TV family. However, the first spouse's death may also lead to a blended family, as in *The Brady Bunch.*

The Brady husband-father is a successful architect. Even today, the average TV family tends to be more professional, successful, and rich than the average real-life family. The Bradys were wealthy enough to employ a housekeeper, Alice. Mirroring American culture when the program was produced, the wife's career was part-time and subsidiary. Women lucky enough to find wealthy husbands did not compete with other women—even professional housekeepers—in the work force. (It is noteworthy that when *The Bradys* was revived as a weekly series in 1990, Mrs. Brady had a full-time job.)

Students enjoy learning about anthropological techniques through culturally familiar examples. Each time I begin my kinship lecture, a few people in the class immediately recognize (from reruns) the nuclear families of the 1950s. However, as soon as I begin diagramming the Brady characters (without saying what I'm doing), students start shouting out their names: "Jan," "Bobby," "Greg," "Cindy," "Marsha," "Peter," "Mike," "Carol," "Alice." The response mounts. As the cast of characters nears completion, almost everyone has joined in. Whenever I give my kinship lecture, Anthropology 101 is guaranteed to resemble a revival meeting, as hundreds of TV-enculturated American natives shout out in unison names made almost as familiar as their parents' through exposure to television reruns.

Furthermore, as the natives participate in this chant, based on common knowledge acquired by growing up in the post-1950s United States, there is an enthusiasm, a warm glow, that my course will not recapture until the next semester's rerun of my *Brady Bunch* lecture. My students seem to find *nirvana* (a feeling of religious ecstasy) through their collective remembrance of the Bradys and in the rituallike incantation of their names.

Some segments of our society stigmatize television as "trivial," yet the average American family owns 2.2 television sets, 1.8 of them color (*USA Today* 1985). Given this massive penetration of the modern home, television's effects on our socialization and enculturation can hardly be trivial. Indeed, the common information and knowledge we acquire by watching the same TV programs is indisputably culture in the anthropological sense. Culture is collective, shared, meaningful. It is transmitted by conscious and unconscious learning experiences acquired by humans not through their genes but as a result of growing up in a particular society. Of the hundreds of culture bearers who have passed through the Anthropology 101 classroom over the past decade, many have been unable to recall the full names of their parents' first cousins. Some have forgotten their grandmother's maiden name. But most have absolutely no trouble identifying names and relationships in a family that exists only in television land.

Societies without birth control often use infanticide to limit population growth. The horticultural Tapirapé of Brazil controlled their population by killing the fourth baby born in each family (Wagley 1977). A couple could have two girls and a boy or two boys and a girl. If the third child was of the same sex as the previous two, it was killed. The fourth child was always killed. This custom allowed the Tapirapé to maintain a stable population size.

There are demographic reasons why polygyny is more common than polyandry. Without female infanticide, if customary male tasks are more dangerous, more females survive into adulthood. Polygyny is the cultural response. The custom of men marrying later than women also promotes polygyny. Among Nigeria's Kanuri people (Cohen 1967), men get married between the ages of eighteen and thirty; women, between twelve and fourteen. The age difference between spouses means that there are more widows than widowers. Most of the widows remarry, some in polygynous unions. Among the Kanuri and in other polygynous societies, widows make up a large number of the women involved in plural marriages (Hart and Pilling 1960).

In many societies, including the Kanuri, the number of wives is a measure of a man's prestige and social position. The Kanuri live in expanded family households headed by men. The man's wives and unmarried children also live there. Because residence is virilocal, married sons and their

wives and children (Figure 13.5) are also household members.

The household is the main productive unit. The more wives, the more workers. Increased productivity means more wealth. This wealth in turn attracts additional wives. Wealth and wives bring greater prestige to the household and head. In many societies, the first wife requests a second wife to help with household chores. The second wife's status is lower than that of the first; they are senior and junior wives. The senior wife sometimes chooses the junior one from among her close kinswomen.

Among the Betsileo of Madagascar, the different wives always lived in different villages. A man's first and senior wife, called "Big Wife," lived in the village where he cultivated his best rice field and spent most of his time. However, the Betsileo inherit from several different ancestors and cultivate different areas. High-status men with several rice fields had households near each field. They spent most of their time with the senior wife but visited the others occasionally throughout the year.

Plural wives can also play important political roles in nonindustrial states. The king of the Merina, a society with more than 1 million people in the highlands of Madagascar, had palaces for each of his twelve wives in different provinces. He stayed with them when he traveled through the kingdom. They were his local agents, overseeing and reporting on provincial matters. The king of

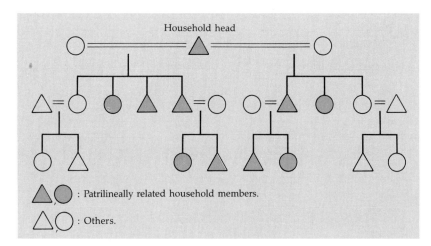

Figure 13.5 *A polygynous expanded Kanuri household.*

In many societies polygyny is a measure of a man's prestige and social position. Shown here, a Masai chief, his two wives, and their children (in Kenya).

Buganda, the major precolonial state of Uganda, took hundreds of wives, representing all the clans in his nation. Everyone in the kingdom became the king's in-law, and all the clans had a chance to provide the next ruler. This was a way of giving the common people a stake in the government.

These examples show that there is no single explanation for polygyny. Its context and function vary from society to society and even within the same society. Some men are polygynous because they have inherited a widow from a brother. Others have plural wives because they seek prestige or want to increase household productivity. Still others use marriage as a political tool or a means of economic advancement. Men and women with political and economic ambitions cultivate marital alliances that serve their aims. In many societies, including the Betsileo of Madagascar and the Igbo of Nigeria, women arrange the marriages.

Polyandry

Polyandry is very rare and is practiced under very specific conditions. Most of the world's polyandrous peoples live in South Asia—Tibet, Nepal, India, and Sri Lanka. India's polyandrous groups inhabit the lower ranges of the Himalayas, in northern India. They are known as Paharis, which means "people of the mountains." Gerald Berreman (1962, 1975) did a comparative study of two

Pahari groups, one in the foothills of the western Himalayas and the other in the central foothills.

The western and central Paharis are historically and genetically related and speak dialects of the same language. Polyandry exists among the western, but not the central, Paharis. Because there are so many other cultural and social similarities between the western and central Paharis, including caste stratification and patrilineal clans, Berreman wondered why one group practiced polyandry and the other didn't.

Pahari marriage customs turned out to correlate with demographic contrasts. Sex ratios were different in the two areas. In the polyandrous west, there was a shortage of females (789 per 1,000 males). Although female infanticide was not documented in the area, neglect of girls (*covert* female infanticide) helped explain the shortage of women (Levine 1988). Western Pahari polyandry was always **fraternal**: husbands were brothers. The oldest brother arranged the marriage, which made all the brothers legal husbands of the wife. Subsequently, they could marry additional women. All these women were joint wives and sexual partners of the brothers. Children born to any wife called all the brothers "father."

Nevertheless, there was considerable variation in the actual marriage arrangements in western Pahari households (Berreman 1975). In one village only 9 percent of the households were polyan-

Polyandry in northwest Nepal. The seated young women is Terribal, age 15. She holds her youngest husband, age 5. To her left is another husband, age 12. Standing directly behind her is her third husband, age 9. The two older standing men are brothers who are married to the same woman, standing to the right. These are Terribal's "fathers" and mother.

drous, 25 percent were polygynous, and 34 percent were monogamous. Variation in marriage type and household composition reflected household wealth, the age of the brothers, and divorce. Household composition went through a developmental cycle. For example, one group of three brothers took their first wife in 1910. In 1915 they added a second wife. This changed simple fraternal polyandry into a polyandrous-polygynous household. A few years later they added a third wife, and later they added a fourth. By a decade later, one of the brothers had died and two of the wives had divorced and remarried elsewhere. By 1955 the household had become monogamous, as only one husband and one wife survived.

This flexible marriage system was adaptive because it allowed the western Paharis to spread people and labor out over the land. The number of working adults in a western Pahari household was proportional to the amount of farmland it owned. Because women did as much agricultural work as men, given the same amount of land, two brothers might require and support three or four wives whereas three or four brothers might have only one or two. Plural marriages were uncommon in landless households, whose resources and labor needs were lowest. Landless people were more monogamous (43 percent) than were landowners (26 percent).

Among the nonpolyandrous central Paharis, by

contrast, there were more women than men. Most (85 percent) marriages were monogamous. Only 15 percent were plural—polygynous. Despite the absence of formal polyandry here, it was customary for brothers to contribute to each other's bridewealth, and they could have sex with each other's wives. The major difference was that central Pahari children recognized only one father. However, because brothers had common sexual rights, socially recognized fathers were not necessarily the true genitors.

Polyandry in other parts of South Asia seems to be a cultural adaptation to mobility associated with customary male travel for trade, commerce, and military operations. Polyandry ensures that there is always a man at home. Fraternal polyandry is also an effective strategy when resources are scarce. Like poverty-level Americans, brothers with limited resources (in land) pool their resources in expanded (polyandrous) households. They take just one wife. Polyandry restricts the number of wives and heirs. Less competition among heirs means that land can be transmitted with minimal fragmentation.

The reasons for polyandry among the Marquesan Islanders of Polynesia were different. Marquesan polyandry was not fraternal. During the nineteenth century, intertribal raiding, warfare with European explorers, smallpox, and famine produced a substantial population decline (Otterbein

1963/1968). More women than men died. By 1900, the ratio was six males to five females. Polyandry, in a variety of forms, was the response.

The Marquesans developed four types of marriage. One was monogamy. Another was simple polyandry. A third type was the polygynous-polyandrous household. Here a woman and her husband moved in with a new husband (always a richer man) and his wife. All spouses had sexual rights to those of the opposite sex. In the final type—the composite household—unmarried men attached themselves to one of the other three types. These bachelors did not marry but were permissible sexual partners for the women in the household.

The Marquesan example is rare and highly unusual. Like marriage in South Asia, however, it illustrates that monogamy, polyandry, and polygyny can all coexist in the same culture as part of a flexible set of marriage rules with value for cultural adaptation.

SUMMARY

All societies have incest taboos. However, different cultures taboo different biological kin types. Among the explanations that have been offered for the taboo's universality are the following: (1) it codifies instinctive human horror of incest, (2) it results from concern about the biological degeneration that can follow from incestuous unions, (3) it has a selective advantage because it promotes exogamy and intergroup alliances, and (4) it is necessary to maintain family role structure and cultural continuity. The third and fourth explanations are the most useful. The taboo promotes exogamy, therefore increasing networks of friends and allies. Furthermore, sex between close relatives, especially parents and children, would create conflict that could impair sociocultural cohesion and continuity.

The main adaptive advantage of exogamy is the extension of social and political ties outward. This is confirmed by a consideration of endogamy—marriage within the group. Endogamic rules are common in stratified societies. One example is India, where castes are the endogamous units. However, castes are subdivided into exogamous descent groups. The same culture can therefore have both endogamic and exogamic rules. The U.S. "racial" system is structurally similar to the Indian caste system, although it lacks many of the specific cultural features.

Certain ancient kingdoms encouraged royal incest while condemning incest by commoners. The manifest functions of royal incest in ancient Hawaii were linked to the idea of mana. However, royal incest also served latent functions in the political and economic domains—limiting succession struggles and keeping royal wealth intact. Preferential marriage of brothers' children among Arabs is another example of endogamy.

Many tribal societies not only prohibit people from marrying within their own group but also rigidly dictate their choice of spouses. Generalized exchange exemplifies such marriage systems. Generalized exchange links exogamous descent groups in an established system of marital relationships. Women from group B always marry men from group C, men from group B always take wives from group A, and so on.

In societies with descent groups, marriages are relationships between groups as well as between spouses. With the custom of bridewealth, the groom and his relatives transmit wealth to the bride and her relatives. As the bridewealth's value increases, the divorce rate declines.

Bridewealth customs show that marriages among nonindustrial food producers create and maintain group alliances. So do the sororate, by which a man marries the sister of his deceased wife, and the levirate, by which a woman marries the brother of her deceased husband. Replacement marriages in cases of spousal incompatibility also confirm the importance of group alliances.

Many cultures permit plural marriages. The two kinds of polygamy are polygyny and polyandry. The former involves multiple wives; the latter, multiple husbands. Polygyny and polyandry are found in varied social and cultural contexts and occur for many reasons. Polygyny is much more common than is polyandry. There are demographic, economic, and ecological reasons for plural marriage systems.

GLOSSARY

agnates: Members of the same patrilineal descent group.

brideprice: See *progeny price.*

bridewealth: See *progeny price.*

cross cousins: Children of a brother and a sister.

dowry: A marital exchange in which the wife's group provides substantial gifts to the husband's family.

endogamy: Marriage between people of the same social group.

exogamy: Rule requiring people to marry outside their own group.

fraternal polyandry: Marriage of a group of brothers to the same woman or women.

incest: Sexual relations with a close relative.

latent function: A custom's underlying function, often unperceived by natives.

levirate: Custom by which a widow marries the brother of her deceased husband.

manifest function: The reasons that natives offer for a custom.

moiety: One of two descent groups in a given population; usually moieties intermarry.

parallel cousins: Children of two brothers or two sisters.

patrilateral parallel-cousin marriage: Marriage of the children of brothers.

plural marriage: See *polygamy.*

polyandry: Variety of plural marriage in which a woman has more than one husband.

polygamy: Any marriage with more than two spouses.

polygyny: Variety of plural marriage in which a man has more than one wife.

primogeniture: Inheritance rule that makes the oldest child (usually the oldest son) the only heir.

progeny price: A gift from the husband and his kin to the wife and her kin before, at, or after marriage; legitimizes children born to the woman as members of the husband's descent group.

serial monogamy: Marriage of a given individual to several spouses, but not at the same time.

sororate: Custom by which a widower marries the sister of the deceased wife.

STUDY QUESTIONS

1. What explanations have been offered for the universality of the incest taboo? Which do you prefer, and why?
2. What are the respective functions of endogamy and exogamy within the Indian caste system?
3. What aspect of contemporary American stratification most resembles the Indian caste system?
4. What were the manifest and latent functions of privileged royal incest?
5. What is generalized exchange, and what is its advantage for women?
6. What is bridewealth? What else is it called, and why?
7. What is the difference between sororate and levirate? What do they have in common?
8. What is the difference between polygyny and polyandry?
9. What are some of the reasons for polygyny?
10. What are some of the reasons for polyandry?
11. What general conclusions do you draw from the two chapters on kinship and marriage?

SUGGESTED ADDITIONAL READING

BOHANNAN, P., AND J. MIDDLETON, EDS.
　1968　*Marriage, Family, and Residence.* Garden City, NY: Natural History Press. Articles about marriage, incest, exogamy, and family and household organization.

COLLIER, J.F., ED.
　1988　*Marriage and Inequality in Classless Societies.* Stanford, CA: Stanford University Press. Marriage and issues of gender stratification in bands and tribes.

COMAROFF, J., ED.
　1980　*The Meaning of Marriage Payments.* New York: Academic Press. Economic, symbolic, and social organizational components of marital gifts in varied cultures.

FOX, R.
　1985　*Kinship and Marriage.* New York: Viking Penguin. Well-written survey of kinship and marriage systems and theories about them.

GOODY, J., AND S.T. TAMBIAH
　1973　*Bridewealth and Dowry.* Cambridge: Cambridge University Press. Marital exchanges in comparative perspective.

HENDRY, J.

  1981   *Marriage in Changing Japan*. London: Croom Helm. A thorough look at the institution of marriage in post– versus pre–World War II Japan.

LEACH, E.

  1985   *Social Anthropology*. New York: Oxford University Press. A well-known British anthropologist who studied the kinship and marriage systems of many peoples wrote this nontechnical survey of social anthropology and the anthropologists who have contributed to it.

LEVINE, N.

  1988   *The Dynamics of Polyandry: Kinship, Domesticity, and Population in the Tibetan Border*. Chicago: University of Chicago Press. Case study of fraternal polyandry and household organization in northwestern Nepal.

POTASH, B., ED.

  1986   *Widows in African Societies: Choices and Constraints*. Stanford, CA: Stanford University Press. Ten case studies giving widows' perspectives on African marriage systems.

RELIGION

Anthropologist Anthony F. C. Wallace has defined **religion** as "belief and ritual concerned with supernatural beings, powers, and forces" (1966, p. 5). In studying religion cross-culturally, anthropologists pay attention to religious acts, actions, events, processes, settings, practitioners, specialists, and organizations. We also consider such verbal manifestations of religious beliefs as prayers, chants, invocations, myths, fables, tales, texts, and statements about ethics, standards, and morality.

The supernatural is the extraordinary realm outside (but believed to touch on) the observable world. It is nonempirical, unverifiable, mysterious, and inexplicable in ordinary terms. Supernatural beings—gods and goddesses, ghosts, and souls—are not of the material world. Nor are supernatural forces, some of which are wielded by beings. Other sacred forces are impersonal—they simply exist. In many societies, however, people believe that they can benefit from, become imbued with, or manipulate supernatural forces.

Religion, as defined here, exists in all human societies. It is a cultural universal. However, we'll see that it isn't always easy to distinguish the supernatural from the natural and that different cultures conceptualize supernatural entities very differently.

ORIGINS, FUNCTIONS, AND EXPRESSIONS OF RELIGION

When did religion begin? Neandertal burials provide the earliest archeological suggestion of religion. The fact that Neandertals buried their dead and put objects in graves has convinced many anthropologists that they conceived of an afterlife. However, we have no way of knowing the specifics of Neandertal religion or determining whether religion predates them. Any statement about when, where, why, and how religion arose or any description of its original nature is pure speculation. Nevertheless, although such speculations are inconclusive, many of them have revealed important functions and effects of religious behavior. Several theories will be examined now.

Animism

The Englishman Sir Edward Burnett Tylor (1871/1958) was a founder of the anthropology of religion. Religion was born, Tylor thought, as people tried to comprehend conditions and events they could not explain by reference to daily experience. Tylor believed that our ancestors—and contemporary nonindustrial peoples—were particularly intrigued with death, dreaming, and trance. In dreams and trances people experience a form of suspended animation. On waking, they recall images from the dream world.

Tylor argued that attempts to explain dreams and trances led primitives to believe that two entities inhabit the body, one active during the day and the other—a double or soul—active during sleep and trance states. Although they never meet, they are vital to each other. When the double permanently leaves the body, the person dies. Death is departure of the soul. From the Latin for soul, *anima*, Tylor named this belief **animism.**

Tylor proposed that religion had evolved through stages, beginning with animism. Polytheism and then monotheism developed later. Because religion originated to explain things people didn't understand, Tylor thought it would decline as science offered better explanations. To an extent, he was right. We now have scientific explanations for many things that religion once elucidated. Nevertheless, because religion persists, it must do something more than explain the mysterious. It must, and does, have other functions.

Animatism, Mana, and Taboo

There was a competing view to Tylor's theory of animism as the first religion. The alternative was that early humans saw the supernatural as a domain of impersonal power, or force, which people could control under certain conditions. Such a conception of the supernatural, called **animatism,** is particularly prominent in Melanesia, the area of the South Pacific that includes Papua–New Guinea and adjacent islands. Melanesians (like the ancient Hawaiians discussed in Chapter 13) believed in **mana,** a sacred impersonal force existing in the universe. Mana can reside in people, animals, plants, and objects.

Melanesian mana was similar to our notion of luck. Melanesians attributed success to mana, which people could acquire or manipulate in different ways, such as through magic. Objects with mana could change someone's luck. For example, a charm belonging to a successful hunter might transmit the hunter's mana to the next person who held it. A woman might put a rock in her garden, see her yields improve dramatically, and attribute the change to the sacred force contained in the rock.

Beliefs in manalike forces are widespread, although the specifics of the religious doctrines vary. The contrast between mana in Melanesia and Polynesia, for example, reflects the difference between Melanesian tribes and Polynesian chiefdoms and states (such as ancient Hawaii). In Melanesia, one could acquire mana by chance, or by working hard to get it. In Polynesia, however, mana was not potentially available to everyone but was attached to particular political offices. Rulers and nobles had more mana than ordinary people did.

So charged with mana were the highest chiefs that contact with them was dangerous to commoners. The mana of high chiefs flowed out of their bodies everywhere they went. It could infect the ground, making it dangerous for others to walk in the chief's footsteps. It could permeate the containers and utensils chiefs used in eating. Contact between chief and commoners was dangerous because mana could have an effect like an electric shock. Because high chiefs had so much mana, their bodies and possessions were **taboo** (subject to supernatural sanctions). Contact between a high chief and commoners was forbidden. Because ordinary people couldn't bear as much sacred current as royalty could, when commoners were accidentally exposed, purification rites were necessary.

One function of religious beliefs is to explain. The belief in souls explains what happens in sleep, trance, and death. Melanesian mana explains success that people can't understand in ordinary, natural terms. People fail at hunting, warfare, or gardening not because they are lazy, stupid, or inept but because success comes—or doesn't come—from the supernatural world. Animism, animatism, and mana all fit into the definition of religion given at the beginning of this chapter. Most of the religions that anthropologists have studied include both personal spirits and impersonal forces. The supernatural beliefs of contemporary North America include beings (gods, saints, souls, demons) and forces (lucky charms, talismans, and sacred objects).

Beliefs in mana—supernatural force or power, which people may manipulate for their own ends—are widespread. Mana can reside in people, animals, plants, and objects, such as the skull held here by a member of the head-hunting Iban tribe of Malaysia.

Magic and Religion

Magic refers to supernatural techniques designed to accomplish specific aims. These techniques include spells, formulas, and incantations used with deities or with impersonal powers and forces. Magicians use *imitative magic* to produce a desired effect by imitating it. If magicians wish to injure or kill someone, they may imitate that effect on an image of the victim. Sticking pins in "voodoo dolls" is an example. With *contagious magic*, whatever is done to an object is believed to affect a person who once had contact with it. Sometimes practitioners of contagious magic use body products from prospective victims—their nails or hair, for example. The spell performed on the body product is believed to reach the person eventually and work the desired result.

We find magic in cultures with diverse religious beliefs. It can be associated with animism, animatism, polytheism, and even monotheism. Magic and religion can be found not just in the same society but even in the same rites. Magic is neither simpler nor more primitive than animism and animatism.

Anxiety, Control, Solace

Religion and magic don't just explain things and help people accomplish goals. They also enter the context of feelings. In other words, they do not have just explanatory (cognitive) functions but have emotional ones as well. For example, supernatural beliefs and practices can help reduce anxiety. Magical techniques can dispel doubts that arise when outcomes are beyond rational human control. Similarly, religion helps people face death and endure life crises.

Although all societies have techniques to deal with everyday matters, there are certain aspects of people's lives over which they have no control. When people are confronted with these aspects, according to Malinowski, they turn to magic.

> [H]owever much knowledge and science help man in allowing him to obtain what he wants, they are unable completely to control chance, to eliminate accidents, to foresee the unexpected turn of natural events, or to make human handiwork reliable and adequate to all practical requirements (1931/1978, p. 39).

Malinowski found that the Trobriand Islanders used magic when sailing, a hazardous activity. He proposed that because people can't control matters such as wind, weather, and the fish supply, they turn to magic. This happens whenever people come to an unbridgeable gap in their knowledge or powers of practical control yet have to continue in a pursuit (Malinowski 1931/1978).

Religion, by contrast, "is born out of . . . the real tragedies of human life, out of the conflict between human plans and realities" (Malinowski 1931/1978, p. 45). Religion offers emotional comfort, particularly when people face a crisis. Malinowski saw primitive religion as concerned mainly with such

crises of life as conception, birth, puberty, marriage, and death.

The Social Functions of Ritual Acts

Magic and religion can reduce anxiety and allay fears. Ironically, rituals and beliefs can also *create* anxiety and a sense of insecurity and danger (Radcliffe-Brown 1962/1965). Anxiety may arise *because* a rite exists. Indeed, participation in a rite may build up a common stress whose reduction, through successful completion of the rite, enhances the social solidarity of participants.

Rites of Passage

The traditional vision quests of Native Americans, particularly the Plains Indians, illustrate **rites of passage** (culturally defined activities associated with the transition from one place or stage of life to another), which are found throughout the world. To move from boyhood to manhood, a youth temporarily separated himself from his community. After a period of isolation in the wilderness, often featuring fasting and drug consumption, the young man would see a vision, which would become his personal guardian spirit. He would then return to his community as an adult.

The rites of passage of contemporary cultures include confirmations, baptisms, bar and bat mitzvahs, and fraternity hazing. Passage rites involve changes in social status, such as from boyhood to manhood and from nonmember to sorority sister. More generally, a rite of passage may mark any change in place, condition, social position, or age.

All rites of passage have three phases: separation, margin, and aggregation. In the first phase, people withdraw from the group and begin moving from one place or status to another. In the third phase, they reenter society, having completed the rite. The *margin* phase is the most interesting. It is the period between states, the limbo during which people have left one place or state but haven't yet entered or joined the next. We call this the liminal phase of the passage rite (Turner 1974).

Liminality always has certain characteristics. Liminal people occupy ambiguous social positions. They exist apart from ordinary distinctions and expectations, living in a time out of time. They are cut off from normal social contacts. A variety of contrasts may ritually demarcate liminality from regular social life. For example, among the Ndembu of Zambia, a newly chosen chief traditionally had to undergo a passage rite before taking office. During the liminal period, his past and future positions in society were ignored, even reversed. He was subjected to a variety of insults, orders, and humiliations.

Unlike the vision quest and the Ndembu initiation, which are individual experiences, passage rites are often collective. A group—boys being circumcised, fraternity or sorority initiates, men at military boot camps, football players in summer training camps, women becoming nuns—pass through the rites together. Table 14.1 summarizes the contrasts or oppositions between liminality and normal social life.

Most notable is a social aspect of *collective liminality* called **communitas** (Turner 1978), an intense community spirit, a feeling of great social solidar-

Rites of passage, found throughout the world, mark changes in place, condition, social position, and age. This girl from Monrovia, Liberia, illustrates liminality, the middle phase of a passage rite. A variety of symbolic contrasts with the ordinary—such as her bodily puberty painting—may ritually demarcate liminality from regular social life.

Table 14.1 *Oppositions between liminality and normal social life.*

Liminality	Normal Social Structure
transition	state
homogeneity	heterogeneity
communitas	structure
equality	inequality
anonymity	names
absence of property	property
absence of status	status
nakedness or uniform dress	dress distinctions
sexual continence or excess	sexuality
minimization of sex distinctions	maximization of sex distinctions
absence of rank	rank
humility	pride
disregard of personal appearance	care for personal appearance
unselfishness	selfishness
total obedience	obedience only to superior rank
sacredness	secularity
sacred instruction	technical knowledge
silence	speech
simplicity	complexity
acceptance of pain and suffering	avoidance of pain and suffering

SOURCE: Adapted from Victor W. Turner, *The Ritual Process.* Copyright © 1969 by Victor W. Turner. By permission of Aldine de Gruyter, New York.

ity, equality, and togetherness. People experiencing liminality together form a community of equals. The social distinctions that have existed before or will exist afterward are temporarily forgotten. Liminal people experience the same treatment and conditions and must act alike. Liminality may be marked ritually and symbolically by *reversals* of ordinary behavior. For example, sexual taboos may be intensified or, conversely, sexual excess may be encouraged.

Liminality is part of every passage rite. Furthermore, in certain societies, it can become a permanent feature of particular groups. This happens most notably in complex societies—state-organized societies. Religious sects or brotherhoods often use liminal characteristics to set themselves off from others. Humility, poverty, equality, obedience, sexual abstinence, and silence may be

Passage rites are often collective. A group—such as these initiates in Togo and Marine recruits in South Carolina—pass through the rites together. Such liminal people experience the same treatment and conditions and must act alike. They share communitas, an intense community spirit, a feeling of great social solidarity or togetherness.

conditions of membership in a sect. Liminal features may also signal the sacredness of persons, settings, and events by setting them off as extraordinary—outside normal social space and regular time.

Totems: Symbols of Society

Thus rituals may serve the social function of creating temporary or permanent solidarity between people—forming a social community. We see this also in religious practices known as totemism. Totemism was particularly important in the religions of the Native Australians. *Totems* could be animals, plants, or geographical features. In each tribe, groups of people had particular totems. Members of each totemic group believed themselves to be descendants of their totem. They customarily neither killed nor ate it, but this taboo was lifted once a year, when people assembled for ceremonies dedicated to the totem. These annual rites were believed to be necessary for the totem's survival and reproduction.

Totemism is a religion that uses nature as a model for society. The totems are usually animals and plants, which are part of nature. People relate to nature through their totemic association with natural species. Because each group has a different totem, social differences mirror natural contrasts. Diversity in the natural order becomes a model for specialization in the social order. However, although totemic plants and animals occupy different niches in nature, on another level they are united because they all are part of nature. The unity of the human social order is enhanced by symbolic association with and imitation of the natural order (Durkheim 1912/1961; Radcliffe-Brown 1962/1975; Levi-Strauss 1963).

One role of religious rites and beliefs is to affirm, and thus maintain, the social solidarity of a religion's adherents. ("A family that prays together stays together.") Totems are sacred emblems symbolizing common social identity. In totemic rites, people gather together to honor their totem. In so doing, they use ritual to maintain the social oneness that the totem symbolizes.

The Nature of Ritual

Several features distinguish **rituals** from other kinds of behavior (Rappaport 1974). Rituals are formal—stylized, repetitive, and stereotyped. People perform them in special (sacred) places and at set times. Rituals include **liturgical orders**—set sequences of words and actions invented prior to the current performance of the ritual in which they occur.

These features link rituals to plays, but there are important differences. Plays have audiences rather than participants. Actors merely *portray* something, but ritual performers—who make up congregations—are *in earnest*. Rituals convey information about the participants and their cultural traditions. Repeated year after year, generation after generation, rituals translate enduring messages, values, and sentiments into observable actions.

Rituals are *social* acts. Inevitably, some participants are more committed than others are to the beliefs that lie behind the rites. However, just by taking part in a joint public act, the performers signal that they accept a common social and moral order, one that transcends their status as individuals.

ANALYSIS OF MYTH

Cross-cultural research has documented a rich variety of ideas about the supernatural, including animism, mana, taboo, and totemism. We have seen that participation in a ritual is a powerful creator of social solidarity. Regardless of their particular thoughts and varied degrees of commitment, the participants temporarily submerge their individuality in a community. Like descent, marriage, gender, and the other social forces we have examined, religion can be a powerful molder of social solidarity.

Nevertheless, the anthropological study of religion is not limited to religion's social effects or its expression in rites and ceremonies. Anthropology also studies religious and quasi-religious stories about supernatural entities—the myths and tales of long ago or far away that are retold across the generations in every society.

Myths often include people's own account of their creation, of the beginning of their world and the extraordinary events that affected their ancestors. They may also tell of the continuing exploits and activities of deities or spirits either in an alternative world or as they come into occasional contact with mortals. Myths, legends, and folk tales express cultural beliefs and values. They offer hope, excitement, and escape. They also teach lessons that society wants taught.

Structural Analysis

One way of studying myth cross-culturally is structural analysis, or **structuralism,** developed by Claude Lévi-Strauss, a prolific French anthropologist. Lévi-Straussian structuralism (1967) aims not at *explaining* relations, themes, and connections among aspects of culture but at *discovering* them. It differs sharply in its goals and results from the methods of gathering, interpreting, and explaining data normally used in the sciences. Because structuralism is as akin to the humanities as it is to science, structuralist methods have been used in analyzing literature and art as well as in anthropology. Myths and folk tales are the oral literature of nonliterate societies. Lévi-Strauss used structuralism to analyze the cultural creations of such societies, including their myths.

Structuralism rests on Lévi-Strauss's belief that human minds have certain universal characteristics which originate in common features of the *Homo sapiens* brain. These common mental structures lead people everywhere to think similarly regardless of their society or cultural background. Among these universal mental characteristics are the need to classify: to impose order on aspects of nature, on people's relation to nature, and on relations between people.

According to Lévi-Strauss, a universal aspect of classification is opposition, or contrast. Although many phenomena are continuous rather than discrete, the mind, because of its need to impose order, treats them as being more different than they are. Things that are quantitatively rather than qualitatively different are made to seem absolutely dissimilar. Scientific classification is the Western academic outgrowth of the universal need to impose order. One of the most common means of classifying is by using **binary opposition.** Good and evil, white and black, old and young, high and low are oppositions that, according to Lévi-Strauss, reflect the universal human need to convert differences of degree into differences of kind.

Lévi-Strauss has applied his assumptions about classification and binary opposition to myths and folk tales. He has shown that these narratives have simple building blocks—elementary structures or "mythemes." Examining the myths of different cultures, Lévi-Strauss shows that one tale can be converted into another through a series of simple operations, for example, by doing the following:

1. Converting the positive element of a myth into its negative
2. Reversing the order of the elements
3. Replacing a male hero with a female hero
4. Preserving or repeating certain key elements

Through such operations, two apparently dissimilar myths can be shown to be variations on a common structure, that is, to be transformations of each other. One example is Lévi-Strauss's analysis of "Cinderella" (1967), a widespread tale whose elements vary between neighboring cultures. Through reversals, oppositions, and negations, as the tale is told, retold, diffused, and incorporated within the traditions of successive societies, "Cinderella" becomes "Ash Boy," after a series of simple contrasts related to the change in hero's gender.

Structuralism has been widely applied to the myths of nonindustrial cultures, but we can also use it to analyze narratives in our own society. Interested students may wish to read the Appendix, which includes several examples—including *Star Wars* and *The Wizard of Oz*—drawn from contemporary American popular culture.

Fairy Tales

In his book *The Uses of Enchantment: The Meaning and Importance of Fairy Tales* (1975) psychologist Bruno Bettelheim draws a useful distinction between two kinds of tale: the tragic myth and the hopeful folk tale. Tragic myths include many Old Testament accounts (that of Job, for example) and Greco-Roman myths that confront humans with powerful, capricious, and awesome supernatural entities. Such tales, which are characteristic of state-organized societies, focus on the huge gap between ordinary mortals and the supernatural. In contrast, the folk or fairy tales found in many cultures use fantasy to offer hope and to suggest the possibility of growth and self-realization. Bettelheim argues that this message is particularly important for children. The characters in the myths and tales of bands and tribes are not powerful supernatural beings but plants, animals, humans, and nature spirits who use intelligence, physical prowess, or cunning to accomplish their ends. State societies retain hopeful tales along with the tragedies.

Bettelheim urges parents to read or tell folk or fairy tales to their children. He chides American parents and librarians for pushing children to read "realistic" and "prosocial" stories, which often are dull, complex, and psychologically empty. Folk or fairy tales, in contrast, allow children to identify with heroes who win out in the end. These stories offer confidence that no matter how bad things seem now, they will eventually improve. They

HALLOWEEN: AN AMERICAN RITUAL OF REBELLION

Brazil is famous for *Carnaval,* a pre-Lenten festival celebrated the four days before Ash Wednesday. Carnival occurs, but has a limited distribution, in the United States. Here we know it as the Mardi Gras for which New Orleans is famous. Mardi Gras (Fat Tuesday) is part of a Latin tradition that New Orleans, because of its French background, shares with Brazil. France and Italy also have carnival. Nowhere, however, do people invest as much in carnival—in money, costumes, time, and labor—as they do in Rio de Janeiro. There, on the Saturday and Sunday before Mardi Gras, a dozen samba schools, each with thousands of members, take to the streets to compete in costumes, rhythmic dancing, chanting, singing, and overall presentation.

The United States lacks any national celebration that is exactly equivalent to carnival, but we do have Halloween, which is similar in some respects. Even if Americans don't dance in the street on Halloween, children do go out ringing bells and demanding "trick or treat." As they do things they don't do on ordinary nights, they also disguise themselves in costumes, as Brazilians do at carnival.

The common thread in the two events is that they are times of culturally permitted *inversion*—carnival much more strongly and obviously than Halloween (see the box in Chapter 11). In the United States Halloween is the only nationally celebrated occasion that dramatically inverts the normal relationship between children and adults. Halloween is a night of disguises and reversals. Normally, children are at home or in school, taking part in supervised activities. Kids are domesticated and diurnal—active during the day. Halloween permits them to become—once a year—nocturnal invaders of public space. Furthermore, *they can be bad.* Halloween's symbolism is potent. Children love to cloak themselves in evil as they enjoy special privileges of naughtiness. Darth Vader and Freddy Krueger are much more popular Halloween figures than are Luke Skywalker and the Smurfs.

Properly enculturated American kids aren't normally let loose on the streets at night. They aren't usually permitted to ask their neighbors for doles. They don't generally walk around the neighborhood dressed as witches, goblins, or vampires. Traditionally, the expectation that children be good little boys and girls has been overlooked on Halloween. "Trick or treat" recalls the days when children who didn't get treats would pull tricks such as soaping windows, turning over flower boxes, and setting off firecrackers on a grouch's porch.

Halloween is like the "rituals of rebellion" that anthropologists have described in African societies, times when normal power relations are inverted, when the powerless turn on the powerful, expressing resentments they suppress during the rest of the year. Halloween lets kids meddle with the dark side of the force. Children can command adults to do their bidding and punish the adults if they don't. Halloween behavior inverts the scoldings and spankings that adults inflict on kids. For adults, Halloween is a minor occasion, not even a holiday. For children, however, it's a favorite time, a special night. Kids know what rituals of rebellion are all about.

Halloween is therefore a festival that inverts two oppositions important in American life: the adult-child power balance and expectations about good and evil. Halloween's origin can be traced back 2,000 years to Samhain, the Day of the Dead, the most significant holiday in the Celtic religion (Santino 1983). Given its historical development through pagan rites, church suppression, and beliefs about witches and demons, Halloween continues to turn the distinction between good and bad on its head. Innocent children dress as witches and demons and act out their fantasies of rebellion and destruction. Once during the year, real adult witches are interviewed on talk shows, where they have a chance to describe their beliefs as solemnly as orthodox religious figures do. Puritan morality and the need for proper public behavior are important themes in American society. The rules are in abeyance on Halloween, and normal things are inverted. This is why Halloween, like *Carnaval* in Brazil, persists as a ritual of reversal and rebellion, particularly as an escape valve for the frustrations and resentments that build during enculturation.

give reassurance that although small and insignificant now, the child will eventually grow up and achieve independence from parents and siblings.

Similar to the way Lévi-Strauss focuses on binary oppositions, Bettelheim analyzes how fairy tales permit children to deal with their ambivalent feelings (love and hate) about their parents and siblings. Bettelheim tells of a girl who, when scolded and yelled at by her mother, developed the fantasy that a Martian was temporarily inhabiting her mother's body as an explanation for her change in mood. Fairy tales often split the good and bad aspects of the parent into separate figures of good and evil. Thus, in "Cinderella," the mother is split in two, an evil stepmother and a fairy go(o)dmother. Cinderella's two evil stepsisters disguise hostile and rivalrous feelings toward real siblings. A tale such as "Cinderella" permits the child to deal guiltlessly with hostile feelings toward parents and siblings, since positive feelings are preserved in the idealized good figure.

Bettelheim contends that it doesn't matter much whether the hero is male or female, because children of both sexes can usually find psychological satisfaction of some sort in a fairy tale. However, male heroes usually slay dragons, giants, or monsters (representing the father) and free princesses from captivity, whereas female characters accomplish something, such as spinning straw into gold or capturing a witch's broomstick, and then return home or establish a home of their own.

Secular Rituals

We must recognize certain problems in the cross-cultural study of religion and in the definition of religion given earlier. The first problem: If we define religion with reference to supernatural beings, powers, and forces, how do we classify rituallike behavior that occurs in secular contexts? Some anthropologists believe that there are both sacred and secular rituals. Secular rituals include formal, invariant, stereotyped, earnest, repetitive behavior that takes place in nonreligious settings.

A second problem: If the distinction between the ordinary and the supernatural is not consistently made in certain societies, how can we tell what is religion and what is not? The Betsileo of Madagascar, for example, view witches and dead ancestors as real people who play roles in ordinary life.

Nevertheless, their powers are not empirically demonstrable.

A third problem: The kind of behavior considered appropriate for religious occasions varies tremendously from culture to culture. One society may consider drunken frenzy the surest sign of faith, whereas another may inculcate quiet reverence. Who is to say which is "more religious"?

RELIGION AND CULTURAL EVOLUTION

Religion is a cultural universal because it has so many causes, effects, and meanings for the people who take part in it. We have looked at the cognitive, emotional, psychological, and social dimensions of religion. Now we examine its evolutionary, ecological, and economic context. Religious forms do not vary randomly from society to society. Religion is part of culture, and cultural differences show up systematically in religion. Specifically, anthropologists have found correlations between religion and cultural type. State religions are unlike those of tribes, just as foragers' religions differ from those of food producers. We focus now on the religious expressions of different types of society, and we see how such forms of religious expression have causes and effects right here on earth.

STATE RELIGIONS

Many nonindustrial states have had a state religion managed by specialized religious officials. In ancient Mesopotamia, literate priests preserved sacred lore and texts along with utilitarian information about agricultural production, exchanges, and other economic transactions. While priests manage the state religion, folk beliefs and rites may persist in the countryside. Folk religion often coexists with monotheistic or polytheistic state religions.

State religion has often been used to maintain social order and stratification. Misfortune, conquest, and slavery can be borne more easily if the oppressed believe that an afterlife holds better things. Tragic myths portraying awesome deities warn people not to question the authority of the gods or of the rulers and religious leaders who represent them on earth.

Some state-organized societies never developed a state religion. The Merina of Madagascar, for example, created a state that ruled over 2 million people. Early in the nineteenth century, Protestant missionaries from England brought their religion (and writing skills) to the Merina elite, who readily accepted Christianity and championed its spread. So ripe was Merina society for state religion that most people became Christians.

Today 75 percent of the people of Madagascar are nominal Christians—a missionary success story in sub-Saharan Africa. However, as in other nonindustrial states, elements of prestate religions, such as ancestor worship and indigenous ceremonials, have survived in Madagascar alongside Christianity. Readiness for a state religion similarly helped Islam's rapid spread in West African states.

DEITIES

Leslie White (1959) pointed out differences between the religions of foragers and those of food producers. Foragers have *zoomorphic gods*—animals and plants (as in totemism)—or worship natural phenomena such as the sun, moon, and stars. Actually, foragers tend to *identify with* rather than worship spiritual beings. Rituals enact events associated with mythical people and animals as participants assume their identities.

As people gain more control over the environment through food production, new kinds of gods appear—*anthropomorphic,* or humanlike, ones. Just as food producers manage the reproduction of plants and animals, their deities control such natural phenomena as thunder, lightning, and soil fertility.

State religions have more powerful gods (and officials) than do tribes. Many indigenous states of Africa, Polynesia, Mexico, Peru, China, India, and the Middle East had powerful deities and priests, with rituals requiring worship and sacrifice. In some states, kings were considered divine and rulers assumed priestly duties. A hierarchy of gods might control various aspects of nature. Religious doctrine and organization have mirrored the political and administrative structures of chiefdoms and states.

Throughout history, nation-states have used religion to promote and justify political policy. Religious fervor inspired Christians on crusades against the infidel and led Moslems to undertake *jihads,* holy wars against non-Islamic peoples. Fueling Iran's Islamic revolution was opposition to the "Great Satan," the ayatollahs' term for the United States. Guy Swanson's carefully documented study *The Birth of the Gods* (1960), based on cross-cultural research, shows that high gods, believed to be omnipresent (present everywhere), all-knowing, and all-powerful, are present in complex societies, absent in primitive groups.

RELIGIOUS PRACTITIONERS AND TYPES

In developing an evolutionary typology of world religions, Wallace (1966) defined religion as consisting of all a society's **cult institutions**—rituals and associated beliefs. Considering several cultures, Wallace proposed that there are four types of religion: shamanic, communal, Olympian, and monotheistic (Figure 14.1).

The simplest type is shamanic religion. Unlike priests, **shamans** aren't full-time religious officials but part-time religious figures who mediate between ordinary people and supernatural beings and forces. Nevertheless, along with hunter and gatherer, shaman completes the trio of "the world's oldest professions." All cultures have medico-magico-religious specialists. *Shaman* is the general term encompassing curers ("witch doctors"), mediums, spiritualists, astrologers, palm readers, and other diviners. Expectably, Wallace found shamanic religions to be most characteristic of foragers, particularly those living in the northern latitudes, such as the Eskimos and the native peoples of Siberia.

Although they are only part-time specialists, shamans often set themselves off symbolically from ordinary people by assuming a different sex or gender role. (In more complex societies, priests, nuns, and vestal virgins do something similar by taking vows of celibacy and chastity. The ambiguous sexuality of religious figures continues to fascinate Americans, as media accounts of televangelists in the late 1980s confirmed.)

Transvestism provides one way of being sexually ambiguous. Among the Chukchee of Siberia (Bogoras 1904), where coastal populations fished and interior groups hunted reindeer, male sha-

Type of religion (Wallace)	Religious practitioners; conception of supernatural	General evolutionary continuum
Monotheistic	priesthood; supreme being	State
Olympian	priesthood; hierarchical pantheon with powerful high gods	Chiefdom
Communal	occasional, community-sponsored rituals; several major deities with some control over nature	Food-producing tribe
Shamanic	part-time practitioners	Foraging band

Figure 14.1 *Wallace's typology of religious types and general evolution. Associations with areas of the general evolutionary continuum are only approximate. Communal religions, for example, are found among Australian foragers as well as tribal food producers, where such religions are most typical.*

In this historic photo, an Alaskan shaman, wearing a spirit mask and wielding a spirit knife, attempts to cure a sick man. Shamans often adopt special patterns of dress and behavior. Hunter, gatherer, and shaman are the world's oldest professions. Shamanic religions are typically found among foragers.

mans copied the dress, speech, hair arrangements, and general life styles of women. These shamans took other men as husbands and sex partners and received respect for their supernatural and curative expertise. Female shamans could join a fourth gender, copying men and taking wives.

Among the Crow Indians of the North American Plains, certain ritual duties were reserved for **ber-daches,** men who rejected the usual male role of bison hunter, raider, and warrior and joined a third gender (Lowie 1935). *Berdaches* dressed, spoke, and styled their hair like women and pursued such traditionally female activities as cooking and sewing. The fact that certain key rituals could be done only by *berdaches* confirmed their regular and normal place in Crow social life.

Each of Wallace's four types of religion retains the cult institutions of each simpler type while developing distinctive ones of its own. **Communal religions** have, in addition to shamanic cults, cults in which people organize community rituals, such as harvest ceremonies and rites of passage. Although communal religions lack *full-time* religious specialists, they believe in several deities (**polytheism**) who control aspects of nature. Although some foragers, including Australian totemites, have communal religions, these religions are more typical of food producers.

For the first time in cultural evolution, **Olympian religions,** which develop with state organization, add full-time religious specialists—professional priesthoods. Like the state itself, the priesthood is hierarchically and bureaucratically organized. The term *Olympian* comes from Mount Olympus, home of the classical Greek gods. Olympian religions are polytheistic. They include powerful anthropomorphic gods with specialized functions, for example, gods of love, war, the sea, and death. Olympian **pantheons** (collections of supernatural beings) were prominent in the religions of many nonindustrial states, including the Aztecs and Incas of the Americas, several African and Asian kingdoms, and classical Greece and Rome.

Wallace's fourth type—**monotheism**—also has priesthoods and notions of divine power, but it views the supernatural differently. In monotheism, all supernatural phenomena are manifestations of or are under the control of a single eternal, omniscient, omnipotent, and omnipresent supreme being. Such religions occur in states and empires and survive in modern organized religions. Hinduism, Buddhism, Islam, Judaism, and Christianity are all examples. Table 14.2 compares the numbers of contemporary adherents of monotheistic religions.

These men cleanse themselves in the Ganges River, considered sacred by Hinduism, a monotheistic, world-rejecting religion associated with state organization.

World-Rejecting Religions

A distinctive type of religion (usually monotheistic), the **world-rejecting religion** (Bellah 1978), arose in ancient states along with literacy and a specialized priesthood. For the first time religion rejected the natural world and focused on a different realm of reality. The supernatural world was no longer viewed as superior simply because it was more powerful. The divine became a domain of exalted *morality* to which humans could only aspire. Salvation through fusion with the supernatural was the main goal.

In *modern* monotheistic religions, such as Protestantism, the hierarchical structure of previous monotheistic religions has collapsed. Salvation is directly available to individuals, who, regardless of social status, have unmediated access to the supernatural. The role of the priest declines. Protestantism and other forms of Christianity are world-rejecting religions. In contrast to the primitive fusion of nature and religion, they sharply separate the world of here and now from the sacred realm. Notions of the afterlife and of the salvation that it offers dominate their ideologies.

RELIGION, STABILITY, AND CHANGE

Revitalization Movements

Religion helps maintain social order, but it can also be an instrument of change, sometimes even of revolution. As a response to conquest or foreign domination, religious leaders often undertake to alter or revitalize a society. In the recent "Islamic Revolution," Iranian ayatollahs marshaled religious fervor to create national solidarity and radical change. We call such movements *nativistic movements* (Linton 1943) or **revitalization movements** (Wallace 1956).

Christianity originated as a revitalization movement. Jesus was one of several prophets who preached new religious doctrines while the Middle East was under Roman rule. It was a time of social unrest, when a foreign power ruled the land. Jesus inspired a new, enduring, and major religion. His contemporaries were not so successful.

The Handsome Lake religion arose around 1800 among the Iroquois of New York State (Wallace 1970b). Handsome Lake, the founder of this revi-

Table 14.2 *Adherents of all religions by seven continental areas.*

	Africa	Asia	Europe	Latin America	Northern America	Oceania	U.S.S.R.	World	%	Countries
Christians	293,547,000	236,700,000	410,310,000	410,240,000	234,600,000	21,700,000	104,800,000	1,711,897,000	32.9	251
Roman Catholics	110,264,000	111,028,000	260,450,000	381,800,000	95,200,000	7,660,000	5,300,000	971,702,000	18.7	242
Protestants	77,327,000	73,563,000	73,330,000	15,500,000	94,600,000	7,600,000	9,300,000	351,220,000	6.7	230
Orthodox	26,262,000	3,300,000	35,860,000	1,660,000	5,900,000	540,000	90,100,700	163,622,700	3.1	98
Anglicans	24,108,000	645,000	32,690,000	1,230,000	7,200,000	5,336,000	300	71,209,300	1.4	148
Other Christians	55,586,000	48,164,000	7,980,000	10,050,000	31,700,000	564,000	99,000	154,143,000	3.0	110
Muslims	263,132,000	608,500,000	12,360,000	1,200,000	5,220,000	99,500	34,100,000	924,611,500	17.8	172
Nonreligious	1,700,000	690,000,000	52,158,000	16,000,000	21,700,000	3,100,000	84,855,500	869,513,500	16.7	220
Hindus	1,450,000	685,000,000	594,000	750,000	1,100,000	310,000	1,100	689,205,100	13.2	88
Buddhists	14,000	310,000,000	222,000	495,000	400,000	17,000	290,000	311,438,000	6.0	86
Atheists	250,000	150,000,000	18,460,000	2,900,000	1,200,000	530,000	58,500,000	231,840,000	4.5	130
Chinese folk religionists	10,000	170,000,000	50,000	60,000	101,000	15,000	200	170,236,200	3.3	56
New-Religionists	15,000	125,000,000	35,000	460,000	1,300,000	9,000	500	126,819,500	2.4	25
Tribal religionists	66,240,000	23,500,000	200	950,000	50,000	70,000	0	90,810,200	1.7	98
Sikhs	23,000	17,350,000	217,000	7,000	230,000	8,000	100	17,735,100	0.3	20
Jews	300,000	4,310,000	1,447,000	1,010,000	7,100,000	90,000	3,100,000	17,357,000	0.3	125
Shamanists	900	10,500,000	400	200	500	200	200,000	10,702,200	0.2	10
Confucians	800	5,800,000	1,000	800	18,000	300	500	5,821,400	0.1	3
Baha'is	1,310,000	2,510,000	85,000	750,000	340,000	71,000	6,000	5,072,000	0.1	205
Jains	45,000	3,520,000	10,000	3,000	2,500	1,000	0	3,581,500	0.1	10
Shintoists	300	3,200,000	400	1,000	3,000	500	100	3,205,300	0.1	3
Other religionists	279,000	5,719,000	736,000	4,237,000	405,000	87,500	7,000	11,570,500	0.2	170
Total Population	**628,317,000**	**3,051,609,000**	**496,686,000**	**439,064,000**	**273,770,000**	**26,109,000**	**285,861,000**	**5,201,416,000**	**100.0**	**251**

SOURCE: Reprinted with permission from the 1990 *Britannica Book of the Year*, copyright 1990, Encyclopaedia Britannica, Inc., Chicago, Illinois.

252

talization movement, was a chief of one of the Iroquois tribes. The Iroquois had suffered because of their support of the British against the American colonials. After the colonial victory and a wave of immigration to their homeland, the Iroquois were dispersed on small reservations. Unable to pursue traditional horticulture and hunting in their homeland, the Iroquois became heavy drinkers and quarreled among themselves.

Handsome Lake was an alcoholic who started having visions from heavenly messengers. The spirits warned him that unless the Iroquois changed their ways, they would be destroyed. His visions offered a plan for coping with the new order. Witchcraft, quarreling, and drinking would end. The Iroquois would copy European farming techniques, which, unlike traditional Iroquois horticulture, stressed male rather than female work. Handsome Lake preached that the Iroquois should also abandon their communal longhouses and matrilineal descent groups for more permanent marriages and individual family households. The teachings of Handsome Lake produced a new church and religion, one that still has members in New York and Ontario. This revitalization movement helped the Iroquois survive in a drastically modified environment. They eventually gained a reputation among their non-Indian neighbors as sober family farmers.

RELIGIOUS TABOOS AND CULTURAL ECOLOGY

We have considered religious beliefs, practices, and personnel in different types of society. We have seen that state religions differ markedly from those of egalitarian societies. We now turn to the cultural ecology of religion. How does behavior motivated by beliefs in supernatural beings, powers, and forces help people survive in their material environments? In this section we will see how beliefs and rituals function as part of a group's cultural adaptation to its environment.

The Adaptive Significance of Sacred Cattle in India

The people of India worship zebu cattle, which are protected by the Hindu doctrine of *ahimsa,* a prin-

ciple of nonviolence that forbids the killing of animals generally. Western economic development experts occasionally (and erroneously) cite the Hindu cattle taboo to illustrate the idea that religious beliefs can stand in the way of rational economic decisions. Hindus seem to be ignoring a valuable resource (beef) because of their cultural or religious traditions. The economic developers also comment that Indians don't know how to raise proper cattle. They point to the scraggly zebus that wander about town and country. Western techniques of animal husbandry grow bigger cattle that produce more beef and milk. Western planners lament that Hindus are set in their ways. Bound by culture and tradition, they refuse to develop rationally.

However, these assumptions are both ethnocentric and wrong. Sacred cattle actually play an important adaptive role in an Indian ecosystem that has evolved over thousands of years (Harris 1974, 1978). Peasants' use of cattle to pull plows and carts is part of the technology of Indian agriculture. Indian peasants have no need for large, hungry cattle of the sort that economic developers, beef marketers, and Texas cattle ranchers prefer. Scrawny animals pull plows and carts well enough but don't eat their owners out of house and home. How could peasants with limited land and marginal diets feed supersteers without taking food away from themselves?

Indians use cattle manure to fertilize their fields. Not all the manure is collected, because peasants don't spend much time watching their cattle, which wander and graze at will during certain seasons. In the rainy season, some of the manure that cattle deposit on the hillsides washes down to the fields. In this way, cattle also fertilize the fields indirectly. Furthermore, in a country where fossil fuels are scarce, dry cattle dung, which burns slowly and evenly, is a basic cooking fuel.

Far from being useless, as the development experts contend, sacred cattle are essential to Indian cultural adaptation. Biologically adapted to poor pasture land and a marginal environment, the scraggly zebu provides fertilizer and fuel, is indispensable in farming, and is affordable for peasants. The Hindu doctrine of *ahimsa* puts the full power of organized religion behind the command not to destroy a valuable resource even in times of extreme need.

Yams for the Ancestors

Consider another case of supposedly irrational, culture-bound behavior in which religion also has an adaptive function. This time, however, anthropologists perceived that function only after a long period of study. Customarily, the yam-growing Trobriand Islanders offer pounds of surplus yams to their ancestors. They store the yams in a sacred house, where they eventually rot, because dead ancestors have poor appetites.

Ethnocentrically again, Westerners might be tempted to see this custom as irrational. Trobrianders appear to grow more yams than they can possibly eat because they are slaves to their religious beliefs. However, there is another interpretation. Yam overproduction is part of the Trobrianders' long-term environmental adaptation. Normally, Trobriand horticulture produces good harvests, leaving a surplus of yams for the ancestors. However, islands are vulnerable to droughts and typhoons, and every decade or so a drought destroys much of the Tobriand yam crop. Of course, when they plant, Trobrianders never know just how large a crop they will get. If conditions are normal, there will be a surplus for the ancestors. In drought years, however, while able to make only a token offering to the ancestors, Trobrianders at least have enough yams to meet their own subsistence needs.

Their custom of overproduction is adaptive because in the long run it provides a margin of safety. If Trobrianders didn't grow surplus yams for religious purposes, they'd run the risk of insufficient harvests in lean years. This custom therefore illustrates long-term cultural adaptation to unpredictable and unusual conditions. Although droughts happen only occasionally, if Trobrianders stopped the custom, they might starve when the limiting event took place.

CEREMONIES, FEASTS, AND CULTURAL ECOLOGY

In previous chapters we saw that feasts hosted by big men and chiefs bring people together from several places and thus forge communities and political alliances. We saw that potlatching on the Pa-

cific Coast of North America evened out variations in local production by distributing resources throughout the region. Potlatching also prevented economic differentiation, because wealth was either destroyed or given away (and thus converted into prestige) rather than being hoarded or reinvested to create additional differential wealth.

Intercommunity potlatching also ensures production that exceeds the minimum needed in normal years. This provides a cushion if harvests are smaller than normal. In lean years suffering villages can scale down their local ceremonies, invite fewer outsiders, and accept more invitations to feast elsewhere. They can consume more of their own harvest and give away less, just as Trobriand yam growers make smaller offerings to their ancestors when food is scarce.

In many tribes, intercommunity feasting is a leveling, redistributive mechanism, helping to even out imbalances in access to strategic resources. Although intercommunity feasting is often done for religious purposes, particularly to fulfill obligations to dead ancestors, this religious behavior has real-world effects that are more obvious to anthropologists than to natives, as the following two cases illustrate.

Betsileo Ceremonial

The first example comes from my own field work among the Betsileo, who grow rice and use cattle as draft animals. The Betsileo live in dispersed hamlets and villages. Hamlets begin as small settlements with two or three households. Over time many grow into villages. All the settlements have ancestral tombs, which are very important in Betsileo culture. It costs much more to build a tomb than to build a house. It's right to spend more on the tomb, say the Betsileo, because one spends eternity in it. A house is only a temporary home.

Betsileo may be buried in the same tomb as any one of their eight great-grandparents. When a woman has children, she also earns burial rights in her husband's tomb. Most men belong to their father's descent group, live in his village, and will be buried in his tomb. Nevertheless, Betsileo attend ceremonies at all their ancestral tombs, in all of which they have burial rights.

After the annual rice harvest in April and May comes the ceremonial season, when agricultural work is least taxing. Ceremonies honor the ancestors as the Betsileo open the tombs. Sometimes they simply rewrap corpses and bones in new shrouds. Sometimes, in more elaborate ceremonies, they take the bodies and bones outside, dance with them, wrap them in new cloth, and return them to the tomb. Whenever a tomb is built, bodies and bones are moved in from an older family tomb.

During their ceremonies, the Betsileo kill cattle. They offer a small part of the beef to the ancestors; living people eat the rest. After offering meat to the ancestors, people remove it from the altar and eat it as well. The custom of cattle sacrifice developed at a time when there were no markets and the Betsileo lived in small hamlets. At that time, ceremonial distribution was the Betsileo's only source of beef. It was not feasible to slaughter and eat an entire animal in a small hamlet, because there were too few people to consume it. Nor could the Betsileo buy meat in markets. They got beef by attending ceremonials in villages where they had kinship, descent, and marriage links.

Betsileo also kill cattle for funerals. Again, some beef is dedicated to the ancestors but eaten by the living. People attend the funerals of neighbors, kin, in-laws, and fictive kin. Because funerals occur throughout the year, the Betsileo eat beef and thus obtain animal protein regularly. However, although people can die at any time, Betsileo deaths cluster in certain seasons—especially November to February, the rainy season. This is a period of food shortages, when much of the rice harvested the previous April has been eaten. Many funerals, occasions on which beef and rice are distributed, occur at precisely the time of year (the preharvest season of food scarcity) when people are hungriest. In Betsileo cultural adaptation, funerals distribute food beyond the local group and to the poorest people, helping them survive the lean season.

Today, settlements are larger and the Betsileo have markets. Ceremonies persist, but there are fewer big postharvest feasts than there once were. Naturally, any discussion of the adaptive functions of Betsileo religion raises the question whether the Betsileo created the ceremonies because they recognized their potential adaptive usefulness. The answer is no, but the question is instructive.

The Betsileo maintain these rituals because they honor, commemorate, or appease ancestors, relatives, fictive kin, in-laws, and neighbors. The tomb ceremonies serve many of the social and psychological functions of religion we have discussed. However, although Betsileo receive invitations to several ceremonies each year, they don't attend them all. What determines the individual's decision to attend? If a distant relative or acquaintance dies when people are eating well, they may decide not to go or to send someone junior in their place. However, if an equally distant relative dies during the season of scarcity, many Betsileo, especially poorer people, opt for a day or two of feasting. Some of my Betsileo friends, usually those with small rice fields, became funeral hoppers during the lean season. They used a series of personal connections to attend every available funeral and ceremony. Betsileo ceremonies do not simply maintain social solidarity. They also play a role in cultural adaptation by regulating access to strategic resources, including the nutrients that people need to resist disease and infection and to survive (Kottak 1980).

Ritual Regulation of Environmental Relations

Roy Rappaport (1984) documented another example of the adaptive functions of ritual among the Tsembaga Maring of the Papua–New Guinea highlands. This time it is the ceremonial slaughter of pigs that has adaptive significance. Pig sacrifice functions within two levels of ecosystems. The first is the local ecosystem, consisting of the Tsembaga, their territory, and its plants and animals. The second is a wider, or regional, ecosystem that consists of the Tsembaga and other Maring groups, along with the territory and plants and animals of a wider geographical region.

Until the Australian government brought them under control in 1962, the Maring engaged in intratribal warfare. Local groups such as the Tsembaga fought their neighbors. Usually, the fighting ended in a truce. Occasionally, however, one group prevailed and the other vacated its ancestral territory. When the fighting stopped, the group or groups remaining in ancestral territory carried out a ritual known as planting the rumbim plant. They sacrificed all their adult pigs, feasted, and gave pork to all their allies to repay them for their aid.

The pig feast also thanked the ancestors for their role in the victory.

Nevertheless, obligations to ancestors and allies didn't end with this sacrifice. As they planted the rumbim, the Tsembaga vowed that they would hold a **kaiko**, a larger pig festival, when the pig herd grew back to its original size. This might take as long as twenty years.

When the big festival did come, the Tsembaga had to kill pigs throughout the entire *kaiko* year, which ended when the rumbim was uprooted. This symbolic gesture announced the full repayment of ancestors and allies. The group was also signaling its readiness to fight again.

Fighting was taboo as long as the rumbim stayed planted, a custom which limited the frequency of hostilities among the Maring. The taboo brought occasional peace to a society that lacked state organization. It functioned within the regional political organization by regulating relationships between different local groups.

Besides the occasional slaughter of the entire herd, the Maring also sacrificed individual pigs when people were ill or injured. Afflicted people and their close kin and neighbors ate this pork. Illness and injury bring stress and increase an individual's protein needs. This custom provided pork, which helped the sick person recover, while also providing protein to other members of the local group, whose diets might have been suffering as well. Demands of this sort affected the growth of the pig herd. The herds of healthier populations grew faster.

Maring pigs normally ate substandard yams and sweet potatoes. Pigs roamed the village and its territory during the day and were rounded up at night. As the herd grew, however, Maring women had to start giving the pigs food intended for people. They also had to plant extra gardens. At this point, the Maring, especially Maring women, were working harder, laboring for their surplus pigs.

Besides the additional work, the pig herd created other problems as pigs started invading gardens. Garden owners sometimes shot pigs that uprooted their crops. This usually provoked retaliation by the pig owner, who might shoot the garden owner or the garden owner's spouse or pig. Disputes became frequent, and women complained to their husbands that they had more pigs than they could handle. It was time for the *kaiko*. Women's complaints pushed the men to plan the festival. Throughout the year of the *kaiko*, groups of allies visited. They danced, talked, traded things, and arranged marriages. They stuffed themselves with pork and took leftovers home. When all the adult pigs had been sacrificed, the rumbim was uprooted. The men could again wage war.

After uprooting its rumbim, a group could occupy any territory vacated by its opponents during the last fighting period. Because the enemies had dispersed, joining relatives in other local groups, they had been unable to plant rumbim. It was a rule of Maring culture that if one group could uproot its rumbim before its opponents could plant theirs, the first group could occupy the second group's territory (Rappaport 1984). The ancestors of the routed group, like its living members, were believed to have left the territory.

In these ways, the ritual cycle gradually redistributed people over Maring territory. Significantly, the time between warfare's end, rumbim planting, and the *kaiko* was twelve to twenty years. This was exactly the time it normally took gardens, in the cycle of Maring shifting horticulture, to recover their productivity. The twelve- to twenty-year taboo against occupying enemy territory allowed precisely the time needed for the losers' fields to regain their fertility. The timing of the Maring ritual cycle was adapted to the optimal functioning of the productive system.

SUMMARY

Religion, a cultural universal, consists of belief and behavior concerned with supernatural beings, powers, and forces. Cross-cultural studies have revealed many functions of religion. Tylor focused on religion's explanatory role, suggesting that animism—the belief in souls—is religion's most primitive form. He argued that religion evolved from animism through polytheism to monotheism. As science provided better explanations, Tylor thought that religion would eventually disappear. However, a different view of the supernatural also occurs in primitive societies. This is animatism, which sees the supernatural as a domain of raw, impersonal power or force (called mana in Polynesia and Melanesia). People can manipulate and control mana under certain conditions.

When ordinary technical and rational means of doing things fail, people may turn to magic, using it when they lack control over outcomes. Religion offers comfort and psychological security at times of crisis. However, rites can also create anxiety. Rituals are formal, invariant, stylized, earnest acts that require people to subordinate their particular beliefs to a social collectivity. Rites of passage have three stages: separation, liminality or margin, and aggregation. Passage rites can mark any change in social status, age, place, or social condition. Collective rites are often cemented by communitas, a feeling of intense solidarity.

The study of religion also leads anthropologists to the cross-cultural analysis of myths and folk tales. These forms of creative expression reveal native theories about the creation of the world and supernatural entities. Myths express cultural values, offer hope, and teach enculturative lessons. The myths of state-organized societies include cautionary tragedies as well as hopeful tales typical of bands and tribes. Lévi-Strauss, the inventor of the structural analysis of myth, has argued that people universally classify aspects of nature and culture by means of binary opposition. Such opposition makes phenomena that are continuous seem more distinct. Structural analysis aims not to explain but to discover otherwise hidden connections among aspects of culture. This approach links anthropology to the humanities.

Religion varies with cultural evolutionary status. The religions of state-organized societies often have high gods—all-knowing, all-powerful deities—and state religion supports secular authority. Religion has evolved through several types, each of which has characteristic ceremonies and practitioners. Shamans are part-time, priests full-time, religious specialists. From simplest to most recently evolved, the types of religion are shamanic, communal, Olympian, and monotheistic. World-rejecting religions, which appeared more recently, are well represented among the organized religions of contemporary North America. Unlike the religions of bands, tribes, and chiefdoms, they view the supernatural realm as morally superior to the real world.

Religion helps maintain the social and ecological order, but it can also promote change. Revitalization movements incorporate old and new beliefs and have helped people adapt to changing environments.

Besides their psychological and social functions, religious beliefs and practices play a role in the adaptation of human populations to their environments. The Hindu doctrine of *ahimsa*, which prohibits harm to living things, makes cattle sacred and beef a tabooed food. The taboo's force stops peasants from killing their draft cattle even in times of extreme need. This preserves a vital resource for Indian agriculture. Western economic planners should investigate the adaptive significance of a religious prohibition before condemning it as economically irrational.

Intercommunity feasting also falls within a cultural ecological framework. Betsileo tomb ceremonies redistribute food and other scarce resources. The ceremonial slaughter of pigs among the Maring of New Guinea shows that ritual prohibitions help regulate relationships in local and regional ecosystems.

GLOSSARY

ahimsa: Hindu doctrine that prohibits harming life, and thus cattle slaughter.

animatism: Concept of the supernatural as an impersonal power.

animism: Belief in souls or doubles.

berdaches: Among the Crow Indians, members of a third gender, for whom certain ritual duties were reserved.

binary opposition: Pairs of opposites, such as good-evil and old-young, produced by converting differences of degree into qualitative distinctions; important in structuralism.

communal religions: In Wallace's typology, these religions have, in addition to shamanic cults, communal cults in which people organize community rituals such as harvest ceremonies and rites of passage.

communitas: Intense community spirit, a feeling of great social solidarity, equality, and togetherness; characteristic of people experiencing liminality together.

cult institutions: A society's rituals and associated beliefs; basis of Wallace's evolutionary typology of world religions.

kaiko: Pig festival among the Maring of Papua–New Guinea.

liminality: The critically important marginal or in-between phase of a rite of passage.

liturgical order: A set sequence of words and actions invented prior to the current performance of the ritual in which it occurs.

magic: Use of supernatural techniques to accomplish specific aims.

mana: Sacred impersonal force in Melanesian and Polynesian religions.

monotheism: Worship of an eternal, omniscient, omnipotent, and omnipresent supreme being.

Olympian religions: In Wallace's typology, develop with state organization; have full-time religious specialists—professional priesthoods.

pantheon: A collection of supernatural beings in a particular religion.

polytheism: Belief in several deities who control aspects of nature.

religion: Belief and ritual concerned with supernatural beings, powers, and forces.

revitalization movements: Movements that occur in times of change, in which religious leaders emerge and undertake to alter or revitalize a society.

rites of passage: Culturally defined activities associated with the transition from one place or stage of life to another.

ritual: Behavior that is formal, stylized, repetitive, and stereotyped, performed earnestly as a social act; rituals are held at set times and places and have liturgical orders.

shaman: A part-time religious practitioner who mediates between ordinary people and supernatural beings and forces.

structuralism: Structural analysis; technique developed by Lévi-Strauss not to explain sociocultural similarities and differences but to uncover themes, relations, and other cross-cultural connections.

taboo: Prohibition backed by supernatural sanctions.

world-rejecting religions: Religions that sharply separate the material world from the sacred; include notions of an afterlife and salvation.

STUDY QUESTIONS

1. How do anthropologists define religion, and what are the problems with this definition?
2. What are the cognitive (explanatory), psychological (emotional), and social functions of religion?
3. What are rituals, and how do they differ from other acts?
4. What is a rite of passage, and what are its phases?
5. Can you give examples of rites of passage from your own experience or from American culture in general?
6. What is structural analysis, and how do its aims differ from those of science?
7. Can you suggest an aspect of your culture that might be appropriate for a structural analysis? Sketch such an analysis.
8. How do state religions differ from those of nonstate societies?
9. What are shamans? How are they similar to and different from priests?
10. How do world-rejecting religions differ from those found in bands and tribes?
11. How do revitalization movements function as an instrument of social change?
12. What ethnographic example could illustrate how religious beliefs and practices have material consequences or ecological functions?

SUGGESTED ADDITIONAL READING

BETTELHEIM, B.
   1975 *The Uses of Enchantment: The Meaning and Importance of Fairy Tales.* New York: Vintage. Neo-Freudian perspective on fairy tales and myths.
FRIED, M. N., AND M. H. FRIED
   1980 *Transitions: Four Rituals in Eight Cultures.* New York: W. W. Norton. Rituals surrounding birth, adolescence, marriage, and death compared cross-culturally.

HARGROVE, E. C.
   1986 *Religion and Environmental Crisis.* Athens: University of Georgia Press. Religion and ecological issues.
LESSA, W. A., AND E. Z. VOGT, EDS.
   1978 *Reader in Comparative Religion: An Anthropological Approach,* 4th ed. New York: Harper & Row. Excellent collection of major articles on the origins, functions, and expressions of religion in comparative perspective.

MAIR, L.

1969 *Witchcraft.* New York: McGraw-Hill. Analysis of the social contexts and functions of witchcraft and witchcraft accusations; relies heavily on African data.

MOORE, S. F., AND B. G. MYERHOFF, EDS.

1978 *Secular Ritual.* Atlantic Highlands, NJ: Humanities Press. Political rallies, carnivals, athletic contests, theater, and national celebrations in several cultures.

MORRIS, B.

1987 *Anthropological Studies of Religion: An Introductory Text.* New York: Cambridge University Press. Up-to-date text on religion crossculturally.

RAPPAPORT, R. A.

1979 *Ecology, Meaning, and Religion.* Richmond, CA: North Atlantic Books. Various essays on religion in cultural and ecological perspective.

TURNER, V. W.

1974 *The Ritual Process.* Harmondsworth, United Kingdom: Penguin. Liminality among the Ndembu discussed in a comparative perspective.

WALLACE, A. F. C.

1966 *Religion: An Anthropological View.* New York: Random House. Excellent survey of anthropological approaches to religion.

C H A P T E R 1 5

PERSONALITY AND WORLDVIEW

Culture is both public and individual, both in the world and in people's heads" (Quinn and Strauss, 1989, p. 1). Anthropologists are interested not only in public and collective behavior but also in how *individuals* think, feel, and act. The individual and culture are linked because human social life is a process in which individuals internalize the meanings of *public* (i.e., cultural) messages. Then, alone and in groups, people influence culture by converting their private understandings into new public objects and actions (D'Andrade 1984). We may study this process by focusing on shared, public aspects of culture or by focusing on individuals. Anthropology and psychology intersect in **psychological anthropology,** the ethnographic and cross-cultural study of differences and similarities in human psychology. Focusing on the individual, psychological anthropology exists because a complete account of cultural process requires both perspectives—private and public.

THE INDIVIDUAL AND CULTURE

One area of psychological anthropology is **cognitive anthropology**—the ethnographic and cross-cultural study of cognition—which includes learning, ways of knowing, and the organization of knowledge, perceptions, and meaning. Cognitive anthropology examines private understanding by analyzing aspects of individual behavior, including speech. (This links it to some areas of linguistic anthropology, including the study of meaning, as discussed in Chapter 16.)

Drawing on recent discoveries in cognitive science, Naomi Quinn and Claudia Strauss (1989) have developed an approach that explicitly links the individual and culture. They start with the assumption that every culture is both (1) a network of shared understandings and (2) a changing product involving negotiation by its individual members. Quinn and Strauss draw on **schema theory,** which is prominent in modern cognitive science (Casson 1983). According to this theory, the mind builds schemata (the plural of *schema*) to filter new experience and reconstruct past experience, shaping memories to conform to current expectations. Linked to schema theory is **connectionism**—the idea that things that consistently occur together in

an individual's experience become strongly associated in that person's mind. A schema develops when a set of linked experiences forms a network of strong mental associations.

Schemata produce simplified versions of experience, so that we remember the typical, or modal, event rather than the unusual one. Remembering typical events, we fill in missing information according to expectations created by strong associations. To describe how a child internalizes associations—develops and uses schemata—Quinn and Strauss use the example of a middle-class American girl born just after World War II. During childhood the girl builds up a chain of associations in which mother goes with "food, kitchen, home, indoors, everyday routine. Father goes with basement, garage, office, outdoors, special occasions" (Quinn and Strauss 1989, pp. 6–7). These associations are strengthened because the girl's experience constantly reinforces them. The tendency to remember the typical rather than the unusual can lead individuals to forget or misremember (mistakenly reconstruct in memory) times when the father cooked or the mother worked in the garage.

Diversity among the world's cultures reflects the fact that babies have malleable neural networks, permitting varied learning paths during enculturation. However, as individuals grow, their schemata harden. They make new experience fit the established pattern more than they change with new experience. One reason why schemata are shared by people in the same culture is the tendency to rely on modal mental images. Although my experience has differed somewhat from yours, if we both have experienced the same pattern, our schemata retain it. As we enact our shared schemata in our public behavior, the typical pattern is reinforced further in our separate minds.

Schemata strongly influence our behavior because they have conscious and unconscious elements of all kinds—cognitive, emotional, and motivational. Cognition and emotions develop together as part of schema formation. Thus if a child learns that mother goes with food, he or she also builds associations of feelings around motherhood and food.

Schemata explain not only the shared aspect of culture but also its openness to diverse individual interpretations and outlooks and the possibility of cultural change. To illustrate this, Quinn and

Strauss (1989) add a second middle-class American girl to their example. Both girls may have learned that mother goes with kitchen and father goes with office, but beyond that there may be great differences. One may associate her father's arrival home with anticipation; the other, with dread. Individual feelings and experiences give rise to differences in schemata among people who grow up in the same culture.

Society has both unifying and divisive forces. Unique schemata arise from distinct individual experiences, while shared schemata are built up from common experience. In modern nations some schemata are shared by millions because of people's exposure to the mass media. Other schemata are shared by smaller groups—ethnic and regional subcultures, people who accidentally share similar experiences, and experts with the same formal training (such as anthropologists). Schemata are like the *levels of culture* discussed in Chapter 3 in that both are associated with a continuum of shared experience and learning. However, schema theory focuses on the cognitive attributes of the *individuals* who share understandings.

Schema theory leaves room for individual creativity, disagreement, resistance, and change. People aren't doomed to re-create all the patterns they observed in childhood. New social options can provide fresh models for adult behavior. New experiences can create new associations, and associations may be altered by conscious intervention. In such ways behavior (and culture) can change. Our children's schemata and behavior will be both like and unlike our own.

PERSONALITY

Psychological anthropology is sometimes described as the study of "culture and personality." According to one definition, **personality**

> is a more or less enduring organization of forces within the individual associated with a complex of fairly consistent attitudes, values, and modes of perception which account in part for the individual's consistency of behavior (Barnouw 1985, p. 10).

The consistency of an individual's personality reveals itself in varied settings—work, rest, play, creative activities, and interaction with others.

Thus, we can think of personality as an individual's characteristic ways of thinking and acting.

People have different personalities because, except for identical twins, everyone is genetically unique. Furthermore, from conception on, no two people encounter exactly the same environment. The experiences of childhood and later life combine with genetic predispositions to form the psychological attributes of the adult. However, as we saw in the discussion of schema theory, personality attributes can change as adults encounter new problems, situations, and experiences or through conscious intervention.

Psychologists are correct in assuming that despite cultural diversity, humans share certain universal mental traits. These similarities aren't necessarily genetic but may arise from universal or nearly universal experiences—birth itself; stages of physiological development; interaction with parents, siblings, and others; and experiences with light and dark, heat and cold, and wet and dry objects.

Anthropologists only occasionally comment on—usually to question—the existence of psychological universals. Instead, the study of culture and personality pursues anthropology's characteristic interest in diversity by examining psychological data cross-culturally. Psychological anthropologists draw on techniques developed by psychologists to examine personality variation within a society and between societies. Research methods include observing behavior in varied settings, conversing about wide-ranging topics, administering psychological tests, analyzing dreams, and collecting life histories. Because child rearing is crucial in personality formation, anthropologists have investigated this process in many societies. As a result, we can generalize about factors that produce certain personalities.

In modern nations, regional, ethnic, and socioeconomic variation influences child-rearing patterns, individual opportunities, and thus personality formation. In studying relationships between personality and culture, anthropologists must examine (1) personality traits common to all or most members of a society and (2) those associated only with social subdivisions. We also consider personality variation that is *not* typical of either society at large or its subgroups, which we call *deviant* behavior.

Margaret Mead's controversial book Coming of Age in Samoa *(1928/1961), based on a nine-month study, compared Samoan and American adolescence. Samoan personality and culture have changed since Mead did her fieldwork. These young women are celebrating Flag Day in Pago Pago, American Samoa.*

EARLY CULTURE AND PERSONALITY RESEARCH

Margaret Mead: Child Training and Gender Roles

Margaret Mead (profiled in Chapter 1) did comparative studies of culture and personality in the Pacific islands, focusing on childhood and adolescence. Her early book *Coming of Age in Samoa* (1928/1961), based on a nine-month study of Samoan girls, compared Samoan and American adolescence. Mead's hypothesis was that the psychological changes associated with puberty are not biologically based but culturally determined. She described Samoan adolescence as a relatively easy period, lacking the sexual frustrations and stresses characteristic of American adolescence.

Later researchers in other Samoan villages reached different conclusions. A study by Derek Freeman (1983) offers a particularly harsh judgment of Mead's ethnography. Rather than the carefree sexual experimentation Mead described, Freeman found a strict virginity complex. Instead of casual and friendly relations between the sexes, Freeman found male-female hostility. His Samoan boys competed in macho contests that involved sneaking up on girls and raping them with their fingers.

How do other anthropologists evaluate Freeman's findings and his criticisms of Mead? We know that in any culture, customs vary from village to village and decade to decade. Mead and Freeman worked at different times (fifteen years apart) and in different villages. Freeman's Samoans may well have differed from the people Mead observed in 1930. Furthermore, anthropologists have particular interests, skills, and biases which affect their interpretations. Ethnographers (even those from the same culture) have different schemata, which influence the way they do field work and the conclusions they reach.

Besides their own biases, ethnographers should be aware of variation within any culture they are studying. They must avoid the tendency to imply that a particular village represents an entire culture. Freeman's attack on Mead is merely the most publicized in a series of disagreements between anthropologists who offer contrasting interpretations of a given culture. Ethnographers need to be more sensitive to variation within a culture as well as to ways in which their particular interests may influence their field work.

Culture and personality research has been criticized more than most other aspects of ethnography. Long before Freeman's attack, anthropologists (e.g., Harris 1968) had faulted Mead's work for being too impressionistic. Mead relied heavily on her own impressions about the emotions of Samoan girls. Although she did report deviant cases, Mead focused on the *typical* adolescent experience. However, because she presented little statistical

VARIETIES OF HUMAN SEXUALITY

Margaret Mead showed that sexual behavior varies from culture to culture. A later, more systematic cross-cultural study (Ford and Beach 1951) found wide variation in attitudes about masturbation, bestiality (sex with animals), and homosexuality. Even in a single culture, such as the United States, attitudes about sex differ with socioeconomic status, region, and rural versus urban residence. However, even in the 1950s, before the "age of sexual permissiveness" (the late 1960s and 1970s) began, research showed that almost all American men (92 percent) and more than half of American women (54 percent) admitted to masturbation. Between 40 and 50 percent of American farm boys had sex with animals. In the famous Kinsey report (Kinsey, Pomeroy, and Martin 1948), 37 percent of the men surveyed admitted having had at least one homosexual experience leading to orgasm. In a later study of 1,200 unmarried

women, 26 percent reported homosexual activities.

Attitudes toward homosexuality, masturbation, and bestiality in other cultures differ strikingly, as I find when I contrast the cultures I know best—the United States, urban and rural Brazil, and Madagascar. During my first stay in Arembepe, Brazil, when I was nineteen years old and unmarried, young men told me details of their occasional experiences with prostitutes in the city. In Arembepe, a rural community, sex with animals was common. Targets of the male sex drive included cattle, horses, sheep, goats, and turkeys, with no particular regard for gender. Small boys began with chickens. Arembepe's women were also more open about their sex lives than their North American counterparts were.

Arembepeiros talked about sex so willingly that I wasn't prepared for the silence and avoidance of sexual subjects that I encountered in Mad-

agascar. My wife's and my discreet attempts to get the Betsileo to tell us at least the basics of their culture's sexual practices led nowhere. I did discover from city folk that, as in many non-Western cultures, traditional ceremonies were times of ritual license, when normal taboos lapsed and Betsileo men and women engaged in what Christian missionaries described as "wanton" sexuality. Only during my last week in Madagascar did a young man in the village of Ivato, where I had spent a year, take me aside and offer to write down the words for genitals and sexual intercourse. He still could not say these tabooed words, but he wanted me to know them so that my knowledge of Betsileo culture would be complete.

I have never worked in a culture with institutionalized homosexuality of the sort that exists among several tribes in Papua–New Guinea, such as the Kaluli (Schieffelin 1976). The Kaluli believe that semen has a

data, the ratio of normal to deviant could not be established. In defending her research, Mead stated that "the student of the more intangible and psychological aspects of human behavior is forced to illuminate rather than demonstrate a thesis" (1928/1961, p. 260). More recent approaches to culture and personality research that are less impressionistic than Mead's are discussed below.

Ruth Benedict: Cultures as Individuals

Like Mead's work, Ruth Benedict's widely read book *Patterns of Culture* (1934/1959) influenced research on culture and personality. Using published sources rather than personal field experiences, Benedict contrasted the cultural orientations of the Kwakiutl of the Northwest Coast of North America and the Zuni of the Amer-

ican Southwest. The Kwakiutl, whose potlatch system was described in Chapter 10, are unusual foragers. They inhabit a rich environment and have tribal or chiefdom rather than band organization. The Zuni, tribal agriculturalists, are a Pueblo group in the American Southwest.

Benedict proposed that particular cultures are integrated by one or two dominant psychological themes and that entire cultures—here the Zuni and the Kwakiutl—can be labeled by means of their psychological attributes. Thus, she called the Kwakiutl *Dionysian* and the Zuni *Apollonian*, from the Greek gods of wine and light, respectively. Benedict portrayed the Dionysian Kwakiutl as striving to escape limitations, achieve excess, and break into another order of experience. Given these goals, they valued drugs and alcohol, fasting, self-torture, and frenzy. In contrast, Bene-

magical quality that promotes knowledge and growth. Before traveling into alien territory, boys must eat a mixture of ginger, salt, and semen to enhance their ability to learn a foreign language. At age eleven or twelve, a Kaluli boy forms a homosexual relationship with an older man chosen by his father. (This man cannot be a relative, because that would violate their incest taboo.) The older man has anal intercourse with the boy. The Kaluli cite the boy's peach-fuzz beard, which appears thereafter, as evidence that semen promotes growth. Young Kaluli men also have homosexual intercourse at hunting lodges, where they spend an extended period learning the lore of the forest and the hunt from older bachelors.

Homosexual activities were absent, rare, or secret in only 37 percent of seventy-six societies for which data were available (Ford and Beach 1951). In the others, various forms of homosexuality were considered normal and acceptable. Sometimes sexual relations between people of the same sex involved transvestism on the part of one of the partners. However, this was not true of homosexuality among the Sudanese Azande, who valued the warrior role (Evans-Pritchard 1970). Prospective warriors—boys aged twelve to twenty—left their families and shared quarters with adult fighting men, who paid bridewealth for, and had sex with, them. During this apprenticeship, the boys performed the domestic duties of women. Upon reaching warrior status, young men took their own boy brides. Later, retiring from the warrior role, Azande men married women. Flexible in their sexual expression, Azande men had no difficulty shifting to heterosexual coitus.

There appears to be greater cross-cultural acceptance of homosexuality than of bestiality or masturbation. Most societies in the Ford and Beach (1951) study discouraged masturbation, and only five allowed human-animal sex. However, these figures measure only the social approval of sexual practices, not their actual frequency. As in our own society, socially disapproved sex acts are more widespread than people admit.

We see nevertheless that flexibility in human sexual expression is an aspect of our primate heritage. Both masturbation and homosexual behavior exist among chimpanzees and other primates. Primate sexual potential is molded both by the environment and by reproductive necessity. Heterosexuality is natural and practiced in all human societies—which, after all, must reproduce themselves—but alternatives are also widespread (Davis and Whitten 1987). The sexual component of personality—just how humans express their "natural" sexual urges—is a matter that culture and environment determine and limit.

In her famous book Patterns of Culture, *Ruth Benedict portrayed the Puebloan Zuni (shown here) as noncompetitive, gentle, and peace-loving. According to her stereotypical account, they valued a middle-of-the-road existence and distrusted excess.*

dict's Apollonian Zuni were noncompetitive, gentle, and peace-loving. She found no Dionysian traits (strife, factionalism, painful ceremonies, disruptive psychological states) among the Zuni. They valued a middle-of-the-road existence and distrusted excess.

Benedict's approach was **configurationalism.** In this view, cultures are integrated wholes, each uniquely different from all others. She thought that cross-cultural comparison of particular features is less feasible than demonstrating each culture's distinctive patterning. However, later scholars have faulted Benedict for having overly stereotypical views of cultures—for ignoring cooperative features of Kwakiutl life and strife, suicide, and alcoholism among the Zuni. Unfortunately, Benedict's risky use of individual psychological labels to characterize whole cultures influenced later descriptions of national character.

National Character

Studies of **national character** were popular in the United States from World War II until the early 1950s. These studies were flawed because they used a few informants to generalize about the psychological features of entire nations. Several anthropologists tried to help the American war effort by describing Japanese culture and personality structure (Benedict 1946; Gorer 1943). Because the war precluded field work in Japan, American anthropologists had to do "studies of culture at a distance." They interviewed Japanese people in the United States, watched Japanese films, and read books, magazines, and histories. Because their aim was to describe *common* behavior patterns and personality traits, these anthropologists often ignored variation. They assumed that each individual represented groupwide patterns, at least partially. However, these national character researchers never used samples that properly encapsulated the range of variation in a complex nation.

Sigmund Freud's psychoanalytic influence was apparent in national character studies. The most famous example was the purported relationship between Japanese toilet training, said to be severe and early, and a "compulsive" Japanese personality preoccupied with ritual, order, and cleanliness (Benedict 1946; Gorer 1943; LaBarre 1945). Some anthropologists even argued that the compulsion engendered by strict toilet training made the Japanese particularly aggressive in warfare. However, later research showed that modal Japanese were actually *less* preoccupied with toilet training than Americans were.

Many early descriptions of personality and national character contained ethnocentric and personal impressions. Without careful field work, objectivity and cultural relativism faded. (From the perspective of cultural relativism, the moral standards of one culture shouldn't be used to evaluate another.) It's difficult to believe that anthropologist Ralph Linton, a contributor to culture and personality research, wrote in a professional report about tribes of Madagascar that

> the Betsimisaraka are stupid and lazy, and insolent unless kept in check. . . . The Tsimahety are moderately straightforward and courageous, and are courteous to whites, but indifferent. . . . The Sakalava are by far the bravest of the . . . tribes, and are also fairly intelligent (1927, pp. 296–297).

As difficult as it is to maintain scholarly objectivity during an ethnographic survey, it is much more difficult to provide a balanced description of an enemy nation. This reveals major flaws—impressionism and ethnocentrism—in national character studies, which are rarely done today.

CROSS-CULTURAL STUDIES

In the late 1930s, in a series of seminars at Columbia University, the psychoanalyst Abram Kardiner (1939) developed the idea of **basic personality structure** (personality traits acquired by adapting to a culture). Several anthropologists gave accounts of societies they had studied, which Kardiner interpreted psychoanalytically. Kardiner's theoretical framework is more useful than those of other early culture and personality researchers. He believed that a basic personality structure typifies people in a society. Basic personality exists in the context of cultural institutions—patterned ways of doing things in that society.

Cultural institutions fall into two categories: primary and secondary. *Primary institutions* include kinship, child care, sexuality, and subsistence. In adapting to primary institutions, the individual develops his or her personality. Because the primary patterns are similar throughout the society, many personality traits are shared. These shared traits make up the society's basic personality structure. *Secondary institutions* arise as individuals deal with the primary ones. Images of the gods, for example, may be modeled on a primary institution—children's relationship to their parents. Secondary institutions encompass religion, rituals, and folk tales.

Kardiner's theoretical framework also linked personality changes to changes in basic institutions. In this view, an alteration in a primary institution, such as subsistence, changes basic personality structure and secondary institutions. Kardiner compared the Tanala and Betsileo of Madagascar—closely related cultures that differed in types of subsistence economy. The Tanala were horticulturalists; the Betsileo, intensive cultivators of irrigated rice. Kardiner argued that certain Betsileo secondary institutions, such as an emphasis on magic and spirit possession, came from anxieties that the demands of irrigated agriculture produced in their basic personality structure. Kardiner also recognized that the diversity of personality types in a culture increases with that culture's social and political complexity. He identified some of the anxieties associated with social stratification, private property, warfare, and state organization.

Since the 1950s, culture and personality studies have tended to follow a comparative strategy like Kardiner's, using data from several societies rather than one or two. There have been noteworthy attempts to improve data quality, to permit accurate cross-cultural generalization about personality formation. For example, one project (Whiting, ed. 1963) dispatched six teams for a coordinated investigation of child rearing in northern India, Mexico, Okinawa, the Philippines, New England, and East Africa. The teams used a common field guide and research techniques. Focusing on 50 to 100 families in each culture, the teams studied interactions between mothers and young children. They interviewed and observed behavior, paying particular attention to nurturing, self-reliance, responsibility, achievement orientation, dominance, obedience, aggression, and sociability. The teams rated the societies on the basis of psychological tones of child rearing. For example, mothers in some societies were rated more affectionate than were those in others. Child-rearing patterns were

then linked to certain culture traits, such as the presence or absence of warfare.

Also in the 1960s, Walter Goldschmidt (1965) organized a project to investigate cultural, psychological, and ecological variation among four groups in East Africa: the Hehe, Kamba, Pokot, and Sebei. All four had mixed economies. In each group, some communities cultivated, others herded, and some did both. Project researcher Robert Edgerton (1965) gathered psychological information in eight communities, one pastoral and one agricultural for each group. He drew a sample of at least thirty adults of each gender for each community and interviewed a total of 505 people.

To assess personality differences between the groups, Edgerton (1965) analyzed responses to questions, inkblot plates, and color slides. What kinds of conclusions did he reach? He found the Kamba to have extreme male dominance, fear of poverty, and restrained emotions. The Hehe were aggressive, formal, mistrusting, and secretive. Different personality traits marked the Pokot and the Sebei.

Some psychological similarities correlated with language. The Pokot and Sebei spoke languages of the Kalenjin group, and the Hehe and Kamba spoke Bantu languages. The Kalenjin speakers valued both sons and daughters; the Bantu speakers, just sons. The Bantus worried about sorcery and witchcraft and valued land over cattle. The Bantu groups respected wealthy people; the Kalenjins, prophets.

Economic contrasts also were found to influence personality. The cultivators consulted sorcerers and made group decisions, whereas the pastoralists were more individualistic. The farmers valued hard work; the herders didn't. The cultivators were more hostile and suspicious, indirect, abstract, and anxious and less able to control their emotions and impulses. The herders, by contrast, were more direct, open, and realistic.

Unlike earlier, more impressionistic culture and personality studies, this one used statistical data, collected in accordance with objective standards. This made it possible to evaluate the respective contributions of culture, history, and economy to personality formation. If personality traits correlate with economic systems in East Africa, do similar associations exist on a worldwide scale? Several anthropologists have answered yes.

When the image of limited good operates, peasants try to hide differences in wealth. Their dress, homes, and diet remain ordinary. George Foster found the image of limited good to be most obvious among Latin American and European peasants, such as the couple shown here near Avila, Spain.

WORLDVIEW

Peasants and Limited Good

George Foster (1965), for example, found that a distinctive cognitive orientation, ideology, or **worldview** characterizes "classic" peasant economies—nonindustrial farming communities within nation-states. (A *worldview* is a culture's characteristic way of perceiving, interpreting, and explaining the world.) Foster cited several ethnographic cases to illustrate this peasant worldview, which he called the **image of limited good.** In this ideology everything is perceived as finite: land, wealth, health, love, friendship, honor, respect, status, power, influence, safety, and security. Viewing everything as scarce, peasants believe that individuals can excel only by taking more than their fair share from a common pool, therefore depriving others.

Fatalism, quarreling, individualism, and an emphasis on luck rather than achievement, hard work, or thrift are associated with the image of limited good. In Foster's view, peasants rarely cooperate for social welfare—only to satisfy specific obligations. They exhaust their wealth on rituals rather than reinvesting it to create new wealth.

If someone does manage to increase his or her wealth, there are several possible responses. Peasants accept differential wealth that comes from outside the village and clearly hasn't required dipping into the finite local pool. Thus peasants may prosper from external wage work or favors from external patrons. Profit also may come from sheer luck (winning a lottery, finding a treasure). In all these cases the community supply of good remains intact.

If, however, wealth comes from local activity, forces of public opinion act as leveling mechanisms. Prosperous people may be forced to sponsor ceremonies, which reduce differential wealth, leaving only prestige, which isn't dangerous. Prosperous peasants may also become targets of gossip, envy, ostracism, and physical violence. Given such community responses, peasants try to hide good fortune. Their dress, homes, and diet remain ordinary. Furthermore, people who have had bad luck and sink below the community norm are also distrusted, for they are thought to be envious of everyone else.

Foster found the image of limited good to be most obvious among Latin American and European peasants. African peasants were less individualistic; their competition and rivalry occurred between descent groups rather than between individuals or families. The image of limited good develops when peasant societies emphasize nuclear family organization but not when corporate descent groups are important. Foster also pointed out that the image of limited good is a response to the subordinate position of peasants within a larger society. Often, good really is limited by land-ownership patterns, poor health care, and inadequate government services. Foster suggested—and there is considerable evidence to support him—that when access to wealth, power, and influence is more open, the image of limited good declines.

The (Sub)Culture of Poverty

Anthropologist Oscar Lewis (1959) described another constellation of values, the "subculture of poverty," which he often shortened to "culture of poverty." Economically, the **culture of poverty** is marked by low incomes, unemployment, unskilled occupations, little saving, and frequent pawning. Its social attributes include crowded living quarters, lack of privacy, alcoholism, physical violence, early sex, informal and unstable marriages, and mother-centered households. Psychologically, Lewis argued, the culture of poverty has a distinctive set of values and feelings. These include marginality, insecurity, fatalism, desperation, aggression, gregariousness, sensuality, adventurousness, spontaneity, impulsiveness, absence of planning, and distrust of government.

Lewis argued that these values and customs marginalize people, limiting their chances for success and social mobility. He was explicit about the conditions that give rise to the culture of poverty: a cash economy, unemployment, low wages, and a certain set of values in the dominant class—stressing wealth and property accumulation and regarding poverty as resulting from personal inferiority. According to Lewis, poverty doesn't always produce the culture of poverty. For example, when poor people become class-conscious or active in labor unions, they may escape the culture of poverty—although they may still be poor.

Before he began to study the culture of poverty in Mexico City and San Juan, Puerto Rico, Lewis had done field work in India, where he found poverty but no subculture of poverty. Although Hindu villages were poorer than the slums of Mexico City and San Juan, the caste system gave people a sense of social identity and solidarity that was missing in Latin America. Lewis argued that the culture of poverty developed in the absence of such a feeling of belonging and in the context of bilateral kinship systems. In areas with corporate descent groups, such as India and Africa, the subculture would not develop, even though poverty might be great. Lewis saw something positive in descent-group organization—the feeling that a corporate body continues to exist while individuals come and go. This feeling offers a sense of past and future even to the desperately poor.

Although the culture of poverty first emerged in Europe, with capitalism, industrialization, and urban migration, Lewis found the best contemporary examples in Latin America. It was less marked in the United States, where the welfare system had eliminated many of its causes. Critics have suggested that the poor really don't have a separate subculture (Valentine 1968; Stack 1975); they are merely unable to live up to dominant norms because of their economic disadvantages. Others have suggested that the poor hold two sets of values simultaneously, one shared with the larger society and the other a response to poverty (Parker

Oscar Lewis argued that the culture of poverty developed when the poor lacked a sense of social solidarity. Its values, he contended, limited their chances for success and social mobility. Among the conditions leading to the culture of poverty were a cash economy, unemployment, and low wages. Shown here, an urban slum in Mexico.

and Kleiner 1970). The second value set helps the poor adjust psychologically and thus preserves their mental health. Lewis and his critics agreed that if poverty were totally eradicated, the culture of poverty, with its distinctive values and feelings of marginality, would disappear as well.

The Protestant Ethic and Capitalism

Consider now the emergence of a worldview and personality structure—the **Protestant ethic**—valuing hard work, thrift, wealth, and capital accumulation. In *The Protestant Ethic and the Spirit of Capitalism* (1920/1958), sociologist Max Weber argued that capitalism demanded an entrepreneurial personality type, which he linked to the values preached by early Protestant leaders. Weber observed that European Protestants tended to be more successful financially than Catholics were, and he attributed this contrast to values stressed by their religion. Weber characterized Catholics as more concerned with immediate happiness and security, Protestants as more ascetic and future-oriented.

Capitalism required that the traditional attitudes of Catholic peasants be replaced by values more compatible with an industrial economy fueled by capital accumulation. Protestantism offered a worldview that valued hard work, an ascetic life, and profit seeking. Early Protestants believed that success on earth is a sign of divine favor. According to some Protestant credos, individuals can gain favor through good works. Other sects stressed predestination, the doctrine that only a few mortals are selected for eternal life and that people cannot change their fates. However, material success, achieved through hard work, can signal that an individual is one of the elect. Here, hard work was valued because success helped convince individuals of their salvation.

The English Puritan variety of Protestantism stressed physical and mental labor; it discouraged leisure and the enjoyment of life. Waste of time was the deadliest sin because work was a duty demanded by God. The Puritans valued the simplicity of the middle-class home and condemned ostentation as worldly enjoyment. Profits, the fruits of successful labor, could be given to the church or reinvested. However, they could not be hoarded, because excess wealth might lead to temptation. People could increase their profit-making activity as long as they kept in mind the common good and didn't engage in harmful, illegal, greedy, or dishonest activity.

According to Weber, the change in the European worldview that accompanied the Protestant Reformation led to modern industrial capitalism. However, residues of the traditional Catholic peasant mentality slowed the pace of change. Early Protestants who produced more than they needed for subsistence—who tried to make a profit—stirred up the mistrust, hatred, and moral indignation of others. Successful innovators were people of strong character who could persevere despite resistance and command the confidence of customers and workers.

Weber also argued that rational business organization entailed removing production from the household, its setting in peasant societies. Protestant doctrines made such a split possible by emphasizing individualism: individuals rather than families would be saved or not. The family was a secondary matter for Weber's Protestants.

Controversy surrounds Weber's ideas, mainly because he neglected economic forces, historical events, and political structures—all of which are known causes of capitalism's emergence and spread (see Chapter 9). Today, people of many religions and worldviews are successful capitalists. Furthermore, the old Protestant emphasis on honesty and hard work often has little relationship to modern economic maneuvers. Still, there is no denying that the individualistic focus of Protestantism was compatible with the severance of ties to land and kin that the Industrial Revolution demanded. Might a similar worldview exist in nonindustrial areas as an example of convergent evolution? In the case that follows, I argue that it does.

Personality and Cognition among Fishermen

Individualistic personality types, like nuclear families, tend to be found at opposite ends of the general evolutionary continuum—among foragers and industrialists. One cross-cultural study (Barry, Bacon, and Child 1959) found that foragers, like Weber's Protestant capitalists, tended to emphasize achievement, competition, self-reliance, and independence. Arembepe, a fishing community in

Brazil, illustrates this orientation toward achievement among foragers. (Remember that foraging encompasses fishing as well as hunting and gathering.)

When I began to study Arembepe (Kottak 1983) in the mid-1960s, the basis of the village economy was Atlantic Ocean fishing. However, Arembepe was not an isolated foraging community; it was tied to the Brazilian nation economically, politically, and socially. Arembepeiros sold their fish to marketers from outside, often to the detriment of their own subsistence needs.

Although Arembepeiros lacked a peasantlike, land-based economy, their behavior and ideology and their economic and political ties to the nation-state were similar to those of peasants. Since Arembepeiros were like peasants in some important ways, one might expect them to have some of the features of the image of limited good, and they did. However, since most men fished—a form of foraging—they might also be expected to be independent and achievement-oriented.

Arembepe's main social unit was the household, generally inhabited by a nuclear family. Local social organization was individualistic and atomistic, though not to the extent that Foster (1965) leads us to expect in a peasant community. Arembepe was a fairly homogeneous community socially and economically. Everyone belonged to the national lower class, with only minor differences in wealth and status. Ambitious young men had a relatively equal chance to climb the local ladder of achievement.

Success came through fishing. Sailboats normally fished with crews of four or five men, one of whom was the captain, who usually was also the owner of the boat. Arembepe's fishermen formed four groups: (1) successful young captains, (2) older captains, who had once belonged to the first group, (3) the least successful captains, who fished irregularly, primarily because of alcoholism, and (4) ordinary fishermen.

These groups had different opinions about what determines success in fishing. Ordinary fishermen said that captains needed good *eyesight* to see distant landmarks that marked profitable fishing spots. They mentioned their own poor eyesight as a reason why they weren't captains. They also said that *luck* helped some people catch more fish than others did. Older, formerly successful captains

Successful sea fishing requires hard work, discipline, vigor, and risk-taking—traits also associated with Max Weber's "Protestant ethic." Shown here, a lobster fisherman from New Brunswick, Canada.

blamed their declining catches on their failing eyesight, which prevented them from fishing as effectively as in the past. The third group of captains attributed differential success only to luck, refusing to admit that some captains were better than others.

The most successful captains (the first group) explained success differently, linking it to personality traits recalling Weber's Protestant ethic. They cited their hard and constant work and sobriety, rarely mentioning luck or eyesight. My analysis of success in fishing supports this explanation. The traits and behavior of successful captains differed from those of less successful fishermen. Because they were in their twenties and thirties, they had good health, which permitted them to fish regularly. They attracted hard-working crew members because they were dependable and could remain at sea longer. Like Weber's Protestant entrepreneurs, successful captains took calculated risks. They sometimes traveled to farther fishing zones during the season of storms and rough seas. They experimented more, seeking out new fishing areas. Often their risks paid off in the form of larger catches.

Although they weren't teetotalers, they drank only on festive occasions, and they preferred beer to the rum that ordinary fishermen and less successful captains drank. Young captains missed no fishing because of drunkenness. They commanded better crew allegiance and attracted more energetic crew members. They were respected within the community and became officers of the fishermen's society. Other villagers were aware of their success and eager to join their crews. Like Protestant entrepreneurs, successful captains reinvested their profits to produce additional wealth. They bought livestock, planted coconut trees, and invested in new technology to increase fishing productivity.

Unlike peasants, Arembepeiros did not depend on the land, an easily limitable resource. Their subsistence came from the sea, a more open frontier where it's harder to assign and maintain property rights. Hard work at sea does pay off. Furthermore, the high rate of inflation that plagued Brazil also promoted reinvestment. With continual devaluation, hoarding would have been disastrous.

Arembepeiros didn't restrict their kinship ties as severely as Weber's Protestant capitalists did. Because fishing required hard work and vigor, even the most successful fishermen knew that their productivity would eventually decline. They planned for their declining years by building up sources of income on the land. However, because there was no social security system, successful people knew they might eventually depend on their kin for help. Anticipating this, good fishermen shared some of their wealth with relatives.

Arembepeiros didn't think of good as limited. No doubt this reflected the combination of an open local economy and ties to the external world. However, social mechanisms similar to those Foster (1965) described for peasant societies did operate to ensure that individuals acted appropriately. Consider the case of Laurentino, Arembepe-born son of an immigrant. Like his father, Laurentino never fished but ran a store. His store prospered, he bought four boats, and he inherited his father's store. Arembepeiros attributed Laurentino's business success to a pact they believed he had made with the devil.

Between 1962 and 1965 I observed the social gap between Laurentino and other Arembepeiros widen steadily. Villagers warned me about devil worship in his house and about a demon he had caged in his store. They distrusted Laurentino because unlike other local storekeepers, he refused to extend credit. Laurentino cultivated social distance, perhaps in an effort to free himself from the community obligations that all other Arembepeiros had to face. He found it amusing that other villagers thought of him as a witch or devil worshiper. Flouting Catholic doctrine and local practice, he bought birth control pills for his wife and demanded that she take them. When she did get pregnant, he let it be known that his child wouldn't be baptized.

Laurentino eventually suffered because of his unconventional behavior. Villagers started avoiding his stores. More important, he could no longer find men to serve as captains of his boats. Eventually, all four boats rotted and he chopped them up for firewood. Not only did he become the most isolated man in Arembepe, his efforts to increase his wealth were blocked by public opinion. The lesson is that one can prosper in Arembepe only within limits set by community opinion.

Arembepe illustrates that many different cognitive orientations and ideological themes can coexist in a fairly homogeneous community. The explanations for success that people offer, like other aspects of their worldview, reflect their reference groups. Yet certain ideologies, for example, that of sharing with less fortunate villagers, can override differences in outlook among subgroups. This analysis of one village suggests that despite the value of cross-cultural studies of relationships between personality and culture, we also need to study particular cases intensively in order to understand the subtle influences of culture on cognition and personality. Internal variation within a community or society may turn out to be as interesting as variation between cultures.

SUMMARY

Anthropologists are interested in public and collective behavior and in how individuals, think, feel, and act. The individual and culture are linked in a process by which individuals internalize the meanings of public messages. Anthropology and psychology intersect in psychological anthropology. With its focus on the individual, psychological anthropology exists because a complete account of cultural processes requires both perspectives—private and public.

One area of psychological anthropology is cognitive anthropology—the ethnographic and cross-cultural study of cognition (the organization of knowledge, perceptions, and meaning). A culture is both a network of shared understandings and a changing product involving negotiation by its individual members.

According to schema theory, the mind builds schemata to filter new experience and reconstruct past experience. Schemata construct simplified versions of experience; we remember the typical (modal) rather than the unusual. Cognition and emotions develop together as part of people's schemata. As individuals grow, their schemata harden. In a given culture, if people experience the same typical pattern, their schemata retain it. However, individual feelings and experiences give rise to differences in schemata among people who grow up in the same culture. Like the idea of levels of culture, schema theory recognizes a continuum of shared experience and learning.

Culture and personality studies examine the personality types that characterize different cultures. Early students of culture and personality, such as Margaret Mead, were criticized for relying too heavily on personal impressions in gathering field data. Assuming that individuals in a culture would share personality traits, certain anthropologists tried to define basic personality structures and national character. National character studies, which were popular during World War II, were criticized on several grounds, including their impressionistic basis and overemphasis on childhood determinism.

Kardiner proposed that a culture's basic personality structure results from individual adaptation to primary institutions, including family organization and type of economy. The basic personality structure then influences secondary institutions, including religion and ideology. More recent, less impressionistic culture and personality generalizations have emerged from problem-oriented field work that uses more objective techniques to get data on personality formation.

Several studies have suggested or documented correlations between economic systems and personality type or worldview. Foster found an "image of limited good" to be part of the cognitive orientation of "classic" peasant societies. Lewis identified a gregarious, spontaneous, fatalistic, marginalizing subculture of poverty associated with real poverty, capitalism, and bilateral kinship. Weber attributed the emergence of industrial capitalism to asceticism, emphasis on hard and constant work, and profit seeking, all of which he associated with Protestantism.

The case of Arembepe, a Brazilian fishing community, shows that cognition varies with a person's reference group even in a fairly homogeneous village. Nevertheless, all Arembepeiros have a general ideology of sharing. Both ethnographic and comparative studies promise to increase our understanding of psychological and cognitive variation between cultures and social groups.

GLOSSARY

basic personality structure: According to Abram Kardiner, personality traits shared by members of a society; acquired in adapting to a culture's primary institutions.

cognitive anthropology: Area of psychological anthropology; the ethnographic and cross-cultural study of cognition, including learning, ways of knowing, and the organization of knowledge, perceptions, and meaning.

configurationalism: View associated with Ruth Benedict. Cultures are integrated wholes, each uniquely different from all others.

connectionism: Linked to schema theory; the idea that things that consistently occur together in an individual's experience become strongly associated in that person's mind.

culture of poverty: Coined by Oscar Lewis; has economic, social, and psychological characteristics—gregariousness, spontaneity, fatalism, marginality; associated with real poverty, capitalism, and bilateral kinship.

image of limited good: Peasant worldview in which all desired things are considered finite; belief that when one person takes too much, everyone else is deprived.

national character: Personality traits shared by the inhabitants of a nation.

personality: An individual's characteristic ways of thinking and acting and the underlying structure that produces this consistency.

Protestant ethic: Worldview associated with early ascetic Protestantism; values hard and constant work as a sign of salvation; concept developed by Max Weber.

psychological anthropology: Ethnographic and cross-cultural study of differences and similarities in human psychology.

schema theory: Theory that the mind builds schemata (the plural of schema) to filter new experience and reconstruct past experience, shaping memories to conform to current expectations.

worldview: A culture's characteristic way of perceiving, interpreting, and explaining the world.

STUDY QUESTIONS

1. What is psychological anthropology, and why is it necessary?
2. What is cognitive anthropology, and what is its value?
3. What is schema theory, and how does it deal with similarities and differences within cultures?
4. How does schema theory deal with cultural change?
5. What does Derek Freeman's criticism of Margaret Mead teach us about ethnography and psychological anthropology?
6. What were the contributions and shortcomings of the studies of culture and personality by Mead, Benedict, and Kardiner?
7. What were the aims and limitations of national character studies?
8. What kinds of correlations between ecology-economy and personality have been discovered?
9. What is Foster's concept of the image of limited good, and how does it help us understand peasant behavior?
10. What is the culture of poverty, and under what conditions does it emerge and persist?
11. How did Weber relate the Protestant ethic to the development of capitalism?
12. Why and how is the case analysis of Arembepe fishermen relevant to the discussion (in the section on Mead and Freeman) of the need to pay attention to variation in a culture?

SUGGESTED ADDITIONAL READING

BARNOUW, V.
1985 *Culture and Personality,* 4th ed. Homewood, IL: Dorsey Press. One of the most readable and complete introductions to the field.

BOCK, P. K.
1980 *Continuities in Psychological Anthropology.* San Francisco: W. H. Freeman. Overview of psychological anthropology.

BOURGUIGNON, E.
1979 *Psychological Anthropology: An Introduction to Human Nature and Cultural Differences.* New York: Holt, Rinehart & Winston. Textbook with a focus on child development and socialization.

BRADY, I., ED.
1983 Special Section: Speaking in the Name of the Real: Freeman and Mead on Samoa. *American Anthropologist* 85: 908–947. Several anthropologists evaluate Freeman's charges, Mead's work, and the implications of the controversy for psychological anthropology and ethnography.

DAVIS, D. L., AND R. G. WHITTEN
1987 The Cross-Cultural Study of Human Sexuality. *Annual Review of Anthropology* 16: 69–98. Review of recent research.

FREEMAN, D.
1983 *Margaret Mead and Samoa: The Making and Unmaking of an Anthropological Myth.* Cambridge, MA: Harvard University Press. Controversial work criticizing the renowned anthropologist.

HOLLAND, D., AND N. QUINN, EDS.
1987 *Cultural Models in Language and Thought.* Cambridge: Cambridge University Press. Cognition through linguistic examples.

LEVINE, R. A.
1982 *Culture, Behavior, and Personality: An Introduction to the Comparative Study of Psychosocial Adaptation,* 2nd ed. Chicago: Aldine. Original, sophisticated text of psychological anthropology by an anthropologist-psychoanalyst.

MEAD, M.
1961 (orig. 1928). *Coming of Age in Samoa.* New York: New American Library. Popular report of Mead's first field work, a study of female adolescents in a Polynesian society.

SCHWEDER, R. A., AND R. A. LEVINE, EDS.
1984 *Culture Theory: Essays on Mind, Self, and Emotion.* Cambridge: Cambridge University Press. Papers on social and emotional development during childhood.

SPINDLER, G. D., ED.
1978 *The Making of Psychological Anthropology.* Berkeley: University of California Press. Various anthropologists describe their personal experiences in contributing to culture and personality research.

CHAPTER 16

LANGUAGE

In linguistic anthropology, we again encounter anthropology's characteristic interest in comparison, variation, and change. Anthropologists study language in its social and cultural context. Some make inferences about universal features of language, linking them to uniformities in the human brain. Others reconstruct ancient languages by comparing their contemporary descendants and in so doing make discoveries about history. Still others study linguistic differences to discover varied worldviews and patterns of thought in a multitude of cultures. Sociolinguists examine dialects and styles in a single language to show how speech reflects social differences (Labov 1972a, b). Linguistic anthropologists also explore the role of language in colonization, capitalist expansion, state formation, class relations, and political and economic dependence.

THE STRUCTURE OF LANGUAGE

Until the late 1950s linguists thought that the study of a language should proceed through a sequence of separate stages of analysis. The first stage was **phonology,** the study of sounds used in speech. Phonological analysis would determine which speech sounds (**phones**) were present and significant in that language. Speech sounds can be recorded using the International Phonetic Alphabet, a series of symbols devised to describe dozens of sounds that occur in different languages. The next analytic stage was **morphology,** the study of the forms in which sounds combine to form **morphemes**—words and their meaningful constituents. Thus, the word *cats* would be analyzed as containing two morphemes—*cat*, the name for a kind of animal, and *-s*, a morpheme indicating plurality. The language's **lexicon** was a dictionary containing all its morphemes and their meanings. The next step was to study **syntax,** the arrangement and order of words in phrases and sentences. This stage-by-stage analysis sometimes created the erroneous impression that phonology, morphology, lexicon, and syntax were unconnected. All this was revolutionized by an approach known as *transformational-generative grammar*, to which we shall return after a brief consideration of phonology.

Phonemes and Phones

No single language includes all the sounds designated by the symbols in the International Phonetic Alphabet. Nor is the number of **phonemes**—significant sound contrasts in a given language—infinite. Phonemes lack meaning in themselves, but they are the smallest sound contrasts that distinguish meaning. We discover them by comparing **minimal pairs,** words that resemble each other in all but one sound. An example is the minimal pair *pit/bit*. These two words are distinguished by a single sound contrast between /p/ and /b/ (we enclose phonemes in slashes). Thus /p/ and /b/ are phonemes in English. Another example is the different vowel sound of *bit* and *beat* (Figure 16.1). This contrast serves to distinguish these two words in English.

Standard (American) English (SE), the "region-

Figure 16.1 *Vowel phonemes in Standard American English shown according to height of tongue and tongue position at front, center, or back of mouth. Phonetic symbols are identified by English words that include them; note that most are minimal pairs. (Adaptation of excerpt and Figure 2-1 from* Aspects of Language, *Third Edition, by Dwight Bolinger and Donald Sears, copyright © 1981 by Harcourt Brace Jovanovich, Inc., reprinted by permission of the publisher.)*

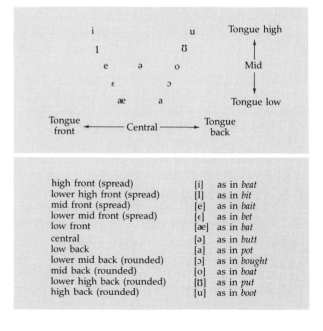

high front (spread)	[i]	as in *beat*
lower high front (spread)	[I]	as in *bit*
mid front (spread)	[e]	as in *bait*
lower mid front (spread)	[ɛ]	as in *bet*
low front	[æ]	as in *bat*
central	[ə]	as in *butt*
low back	[a]	as in *pot*
lower mid back (rounded)	[ɔ]	as in *bought*
mid back (rounded)	[o]	as in *boat*
lower high back (rounded)	[ʊ]	as in *put*
high back (rounded)	[u]	as in *boot*

free'' dialect of TV network newscasters, has about thirty-five phonemes—at least eleven vowels and twenty-four consonants. The number of phonemes varies markedly from language to language—from fifteen to sixty, averaging between thirty and forty. There is no correlation between the number of phonemes and the cultural complexity of a language's speakers. English, spoken in some of the most technologically complex countries, has just an average number of phonemes.

The number of phonemes also varies between dialects of a given language. In American English, for example, vowel phonemes vary noticeably from dialect to dialect. Readers should pronounce the words in Figure 16.1, paying attention to (or asking someone else) whether they distinguish each of the vowel sounds. Most Americans don't pronounce them all.

Phonetics is the study of speech sounds in general, what people actually say in various languages. **Phonemics** studies the significant sound contrasts (phonemes) of a *particular* language. In English, /b/ and /v/ are phonemes, occurring in minimal pairs such as *bat* and *vat.* In Spanish, however, the contrast between [b] and [v] doesn't distinguish meaning, and they are therefore not phonemes. Spanish speakers normally use the [b] sound to pronounce words spelled with either *b* or *v.*

In any language a given phoneme extends over a phonetic range. Thus in English the phonetic distinction between the [pʰ] in *pin* and the [p] in *spin* is not phonemic. Most English speakers don't even notice that there is a phonetic difference. [pʰ] is aspirated, so that a puff of air follows the [p]. The [p] in *spin* is not. (To see the difference, light a match and watch the flame as you pronounce the two words.) However, the contrast between [pʰ] and [p] is phonemic in some languages. That is, there are words whose meaning is distinguished only by the contrast between an aspirated and an unaspirated [p].

Native speakers vary in their pronunciation of certain phonemes. This variation is important in the evolution of language. With no shifts in pronunciation, there can be no linguistic change. The section on sociolinguistics below considers phonetic variation and its relationship to social divisions and the evolution of language.

TRANSFORMATIONAL-GENERATIVE GRAMMAR

Noam Chomsky's influential book *Syntactic Structures* (1957) advocated a new method of linguistic analysis—**transformational-generative grammar.** In Chomsky's view, a language is more than the surface phenomena just discussed (sounds, words, and word order). Beneath the surface features discovered through stage-by-stage analysis of particular languages, all languages share a limited set of organizing principles.

Chomsky views language as a uniquely human possession, qualitatively different from the communication systems of other animals, including primate call systems. Every normal child who grows up in a society develops language easily and automatically. Chomsky thinks that this occurs because the human brain contains a genetically transmitted blueprint, or basic linguistic plan, for building language. He calls this plan a **universal grammar.** When children learn a language, they don't start from scratch, because they already know the outline. As they learn their native language, children experiment with different parts of the blueprint. In so doing, they discover that their language uses some sections but not others. They gradually reject principles used in other languages and accept only the ones in their own.

The fact that children everywhere begin to speak at about the same age buttresses Chomsky's theory. Furthermore, people master features of language at similar rates. There are universals in language acquisition, for example, such as improper generalizations (*foot, foots; hit, hitted*), which are eventually corrected. This illustrates the process by which children experiment with linguistic rules, accepting and refining some while rejecting others.

As we learn to speak, we master a specific **grammar,** a *particular* set of abstract rules—the ones our language has taken from the universal set. These rules let us convert what we want to say into what we do say. People who hear us and speak our language understand our meaning. Our knowledge of the rules enables us to use language creatively, to *generate* an infinite number of sentences according to a finite number of rules. We can produce sentences that no one has ever uttered be-

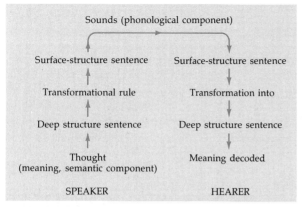

Sounds (phonological component)

Surface-structure sentence	Surface-structure sentence
↑	↓
Transformational rule	Transformation into
↑	↓
Deep structure sentence	Deep structure sentence
↑	↓
Thought (meaning, semantic component)	Meaning decoded
SPEAKER	HEARER

Figure 16.2 *How a message passes from speaker to hearer according to Chomsky's model. The speaker translates meaning (the semantic component) into sound (the phonological component) through grammar (deep structure, a transformation rule, and a surface-structure sentence). The hearer decodes in reverse order to find meaning.*

fore, and we can understand other people's original statements.

Chomsky distinguishes between a native speaker's linguistic **competence** (what the speaker must—and does—know about his or her language in order to speak and understand) and **performance** (what the person actually says in social situations). Competence develops during childhood and becomes an unconscious structure. The linguist's job is to discover this structure by looking at deep structures, surface structures, and the transformational rules that link them.

When a speaker wishes to express a thought, a sentence is formed at what Chomsky calls the level of **deep structure** (the mental level) in the speaker's mind. That sentence rises to **surface structure** (the actual speech event)—expressed in sound— and passes from speaker to hearer. When a *sentence* (roughly defined as a complete thought) is spoken, the hearer figures out its meaning by translating it back into his or her own deep structure (Figure 16.2).

On the surface—the object of traditional linguistics—languages seem more different than they really are. Similarities are more obvious at the level of deep structure. Chomsky proposed that by studying the deep structures of many languages, linguists might eventually discover the grammati-

cal building blocks on which all languages are founded.

LANGUAGE, THOUGHT, AND CULTURE

According to Chomsky, the human brain has a limited set of rules for organizing language. The fact that people can learn foreign languages and that words and ideas can be translated from one language into another tends to support Chomsky's position that all humans have similar linguistic abilities and thought processes.

The Sapir-Whorf Hypothesis

Other linguists and anthropologists have a different view of the relationship between language and thought. Rather than seeking universal linguistic structures as clues to universal mental processes, they believe that different languages produce different ways of thinking. This position is sometimes known as the **Sapir-Whorf hypothesis** after Edward Sapir (1931) and Benjamin Lee Whorf (1956), its prominent early advocates. They argued that particular languages lead their speakers to think about things in different ways. For example, the third-person singular pronouns of English (*he, she; him, her; his, hers*) distinguish gender, whereas those of the Palaung, a small tribe in Burma, do not (Burling 1970). Gender exists in English, although a fully developed noun-gender and adjective-agreement system, as in French and other Romance languages (*la belle fille, le beau fils*), does not. The Sapir-Whorf hypothesis therefore suggests that English speakers can't help paying more attention to differences between males and females than do the Palaung and less than do French or Spanish speakers.

English divides time into past, present, and future. Hopi, a language of the Pueblo region of the Native American Southwest, does not. However, Hopi distinguishes between events that exist or have existed (what we use past and present to discuss) and those which don't or don't yet (our future events, along with imaginary and hypothetical events). Whorf argued that this difference gives English and Hopi speakers different perceptions of time and reality. Language thus causes differences in thought.

Focal Vocabulary

A lexicon (or vocabulary) is a language's dictionary, its set of names for things, events, and ideas. Lexicon influences perception. Thus, Eskimos have several distinct words for different types of snow that in English are all called *snow*. Most English speakers never notice the differences between these types of snow and might have trouble seeing them even if someone pointed them out. Eskimos recognize and think about differences in snow that English speakers don't see because our language provides us with just one word.

Similarly, the Nuer of the Sudan have an elaborate vocabulary to describe cattle. Eskimos have several words for snow and Nuer have dozens for cattle because of their particular histories, economies, and environments (Eastman 1975; Brown 1958). When the need arises, English speakers can also elaborate their snow and cattle vocabularies. For example, skiers name varieties of snow with words that are missing from the lexicons of Florida retirees. Similarly, the cattle vocabulary of Texas ranchers is much more extensive than that of a salesperson in a New York City department store. Such specialized sets of terms and distinctions that are particularly important to certain groups (those with particular *foci* of experience or activity) are known as **focal vocabulary.**

Vocabulary and lexical distinctions belong to the area of language that changes most readily. New words and distinctions, when needed, appear and spread. For example, who would have "faxed" anything a decade ago? Often-used words tend to be or become simple (*monolexemes*) rather than compound expressions (*rain* versus *tropical storm*) (Brown 1958). Names for items get simpler as they become common and important. A television has become a *TV*, an automobile a *car*, and a videocassette recorder a *VCR*.

Language, culture, and thought are interrelated. However, it would be more accurate to say that changes in culture produce changes in language and thought than the reverse. Consider differences between female and male Americans in regard to the color terms they use (Lakoff 1975). Dis-

In the American Southwest, a Hopi woman prepares corn meal. The tense system of the Hopi language differs from that of English. According to the Sapir-Whorf hypothesis, this leads Hopi speakers to think about the world differently than English speakers do.

tinctions implied by such terms as *salmon, rust, peach, beige, teal, mauve, cranberry,* and *dusky orange* aren't in the vocabularies of most American men. However, many of them weren't even in American women's lexicons fifty years ago. These lexical changes reflect changes in American economy, society, and culture. Color terms and distinctions have increased with the growth of the fashion and cosmetic industries. A similar gender-based contrast in Americans' lexicons shows up in football, basketball, and hockey vocabularies. Sports fans, more often males than females, use more terms in reference to and make more elaborate distinctions between the games they watch. Thus cultural contrasts and changes affect lexical distinctions (for instance, *peach* versus *salmon*) within semantic domains (for instance, color terminology). **Semantics** refers to a language's meaning system.

Meaning

Speakers of particular languages use sets of terms to organize, or categorize, their experiences and perceptions. Linguistic terms and contrasts encode (embody) differences in meaning that people perceive. **Ethnoscience,** or **ethnosemantics,** studies such native classification systems in various languages. Well-studied ethnosemantic *domains* (sets of related things, perceptions, or concepts named in a language) include kinship terminology and color terminology. When we study such domains, we are examining how those people perceive and distinguish between particular kin relationships or colors. Other ethnosemantic domains include ethnomedicine—the terminology for causes, symptoms, and cures of disease (Frake 1961); ethnobotany—native classification of plant life (Conklin 1954; Berlin, Breedlove, and Raven 1974); and ethnoastronomy (Goodenough 1953).

The ways in which people divide up the world—the contrasts they perceive as meaningful or significant—reflect their experiences. Anthropologists have discovered that certain lexical domains and vocabulary items evolve in a determined order. For example, after studying color terminology in more than 100 languages, Berlin and Kay (1969) discovered ten basic color terms: *white, black, red, yellow, blue, green, brown, pink, orange,* and *purple* (they evolved in more or less that order). The number of terms varied with cultural complexity. Representing one extreme were Papua–New Guinea cultivators and Australian hunters and gatherers, who used only two basic terms, which translate as *black* and *white* or *dark* or *light.* At the other end of the continuum were European and Asian languages with all the color terms. Color terminology was most developed in areas with a history of using dyes and artificial coloring.

SOCIOLINGUISTICS

No language is a homogeneous system in which everyone speaks just like everyone else. Linguistic *performance* is the concern of sociolinguists. The field of **sociolinguistics** investigates relationships between social and linguistic variation, or language in its social context. How do different speakers use a given language? How do linguistic features correlate with social stratification, including class, ethnic, and gender differences? How is language used to express, reinforce, or resist power?

Sociolinguists don't deny that people who speak the same language share common deep structures and rules which permit mutually intelligible communication. However, sociolinguists focus on features that vary systematically with social position and situation. To study variation, sociolinguists must do field work in order to define, observe, and measure variable aspects of language. The use of these aspects by different speakers must be quantified. To show that linguistic features correlate with social, economic, and political differences, the social attributes of speakers must also be measured and related to speech (Labov 1972*a*).

Variation within a language at a given time is change in progress. According to the principle of *linguistic uniformitarianism,* the same forces that have produced large-scale linguistic changes over the centuries are still at work in linguistic events taking place today (Labov 1972*b*). Linguistic change doesn't occur in a vacuum but in society. Only when new ways of speaking are associated with social factors can they be imitated, spread, and play a role in linguistic change.

Linguistic Diversity in Nation-States

As an illustration of the linguistic variation encountered in all nation-states, consider the contemporary United States. Ethnic diversity is revealed by the fact that millions of Americans learn first languages other than English. Spanish is the most common. Most of these people eventually become bilinguals, adding English as a second language. In many multilingual (including colonized) nations, people use two languages on different occasions—one in the home, for example, and the other on the job or in public.

Whether bilingual or not, we all vary our speech in different contexts; we engage in **style shifts.** In certain parts of Europe, people regularly switch dialects. This phenomenon, known as **diglossia,** applies to "high" and "low" variants of the same language, for example, in German and Flemish (spoken in Belgium). People employ the "high"

Ethnic and linguistic diversity characterizes many nations, especially in big cities, as is illustrated by this multilingual advertising on New York's Lower East Side.

In stratified societies, people constantly shift linguistic styles. Linguistic performance varies in formal and informal contexts. The Portuguese woman on the left uses an animated, informal style with her neighbor in Lisbon's Alfama.

variant at universities and in writing, professions, and the mass media. They use the "low" variant for ordinary conversation with family members and friends.

Just as social situations influence our speech, so do geographical, cultural, and socioeconomic differences. Many dialects coexist in the United States with Standard (American) English (SE). SE itself is a dialect that differs, say, from "BBC English," which is the preferred dialect in Great Britain. According to the principle of **linguistic relativity,** all dialects are equally effective as systems of communication, which is language's main job. Our tendency to think of particular dialects as better or worse than others is a social rather than a linguistic judgment. We rank certain speech patterns because we recognize that they are used by groups that we also rank. People who say *dese, dem,* and *dere* instead of *these, them,* and *there* communicate perfectly well with anyone who recognizes that the *d* sound systematically replaces the *th* sound in their speech. However, this form of speech has become an indicator of low social rank. We call it, like the use of *ain't,* "uneducated speech." The use of *dem, dese,* and *dere* is one of many phonological differences that Americans recognize and look down on.

Gender Speech Contrasts

Women's speech tends to be more similar to the standard dialect than men's is. Consider the data in Table 16.1, gathered in Detroit. In all social classes, but particularly in the working class, men were more apt to use double negatives (e.g., "I don't want none"). Women are more careful about

Depending on where we live, Americans have certain stereotypes about how people in other regions talk. Some stereotypes, spread by the mass media, are more generalized than others. Most Americans think they can imitate a "southern accent." We also have nationwide stereotypes about speech in New York City (the pronunciation of *coffee,* for example) and Boston ("I pahked the kah in Hahvahd Yahd").

Many Americans also believe that midwesterners don't have accents. This belief stems from the fact that midwestern dialects don't have many stigmatized linguistic variants—speech patterns that people in other regions recognize and look down on, such as *r*lessness and *dem, dese,* and *dere* (instead of *them, these,* and *there*).

Actually, regional patterns influence the way all Americans speak. Midwesterners do have detectable accents. College students from out of state easily recognize that their in-state classmates speak differently. In-state students, however, have difficulty hearing their own speech peculiarities, because they are accustomed to them and view them as normal.

In Detroit-area high schools, sociolinguist Penelope Eckert, as described in her book *Jocks and Burnouts* (1990), studied variation in speech correlated with high school social categories. Eckert's study has revealed links between speech and social status—the high school manifestation of a larger and underlying American social class system. Social variation showed up most clearly in the division of the high school population into two main categories— "jocks" and "burnouts."

Along with teachers, administrators, and parents (particularly "jock parents"), jocks helped maintain the school's formal and traditional social structure. They participated more in athletics, student government, and organized school-based activities. In contrast, burnouts (a social label derived from their tendency to smoke cigarettes) had their main social networks in their neighborhoods. They took school social structure less seriously.

A comparable split exists in many public high schools, although the specific names of the two categories vary from place to place. Jocks have also been called "preppies" or "tweeds," and burnouts have been called "freaks," "greasers," "hoods," and "rednecks." This social division correlates with linguistic differences. Many adult speech habits are set when people are teens, as adolescents copy the speech of people they like and admire. Because jocks and burnouts move in different social systems, they come to talk differently. Eckert is still analyzing the specific differences.

The first step in a sociolinguistic study is to find out which speech forms vary. In New York City, the pronunciation of *r* varies systematically with social class and thus can be used in studies of sociolinguistic variation. However, this feature doesn't vary much among midwesterners, most of whom are adamant *r* pronouncers. However, vowel pronunciation does vary considerably among midwesterners and can be used in a sociolinguistic study.

Far from having no accents, midwesterners, even in the same high school, exhibit sociolinguistic variation. Furthermore, dialect differences in Michigan are immediately obvious to people, like myself, who come from other parts of the country. One of the best examples of variable vowel pronunciation is the /e/ phoneme, which occurs in words like *ten, rent, French, section, lecture, effect, best,* and *test.* In southeastern Michigan there are four different ways of pronouncing this phoneme. Speakers of Black English and immigrants from Appalachia often pronounce *ten* as *tin,* just as southerners habitually do. Some Michiganians say *ten,* the correct pronunciation in Standard English. However, two other pronunciations are more common. Instead of *ten,* many Michiganians say *tan,* or *tun* (as though they were using the word *ton,* a unit of weight).

My students often astound me with their pronunciation. One day I met one of my Michigan-raised teaching assistants in the hall. She was deliriously happy. When I asked why, she replied, "I've just had the best suction."

"What?" I said.

"I've just had a wonderful suction," she repeated.

"What?" I still wasn't understanding.

She finally spoke more precisely. "I've just had the best saction." She considered this a clearer pronunciation of the word *section.*

Another TA complimented me, "You luctured to great effuct today." After an exam a student lamented that she hadn't been able to do her "bust on the tust." Once I lectured about uniformity in fast-food restaurant chains. One of my students had just vacationed in Hawaii, where, she told me, hamburger prices were higher than they were on the mainland. It was, she said, because of the runt. Who, I wondered, was this runt? The very puny owner of Honolulu's McDonald's franchise? Perhaps he advertised on television "Come have a hamburger with the runt." Eventually I figured out that she was talking about the high cost of *rent* on those densely packed islands.

Table 16.1 *Multiple negation ("I don't want none")*
according to gender and class (in percentages).

	Upper Middle Class	Lower Middle Class	Upper Working Class	Lower Working Class
Male	6.3	32.4	40.0	90.1
Female	0.0	1.4	35.6	58.9

SOURCE: From *Sociolinguistics: An Introduction to Language and Society* by Peter Trudgill (London: Pelican Books, 1974, revised edition 1983), p. 85, copyright © Peter Trudgill, 1974, 1983. Reproduced by permission of Penguin Books Ltd.

"uneducated speech." This trend shows up in both the United States and England. Men may adopt working-class speech because they associate it with masculinity. Perhaps women pay more attention to the mass media, where standard dialects are employed. Also, women may compensate for the socioeconomic barriers they have faced by copying the linguistic norms of upper-status groups.

According to Robin Lakoff (1975), the use of certain types of words and expressions has reflected women's lesser power in American society. For example, *Oh dear, Oh fudge,* and *Goodness!* are less forceful than *Hell* and *Damn.* Men's customary use of "forceful" words reflects their traditional public power and presence. Furthermore, men can't normally use certain "women's words" (*adorable, charming, sweet, cute, lovely, divine*) without raising doubts about their masculinity.

Stratification and Symbolic Domination

We use and evaluate speech—and language changes—in the context of *extralinguistic* forces—social, political, and economic. Mainstream Americans evaluate the speech of low-status groups negatively, calling it "uneducated." This is not because these ways of speaking are bad in themselves but because they have come to symbolize low status. Consider variation in the pronunciation of *r*. In some parts of the United States *r* is regularly pronounced, and in other (*r*less) areas it is not. Originally, American *r*less speech was modeled on the fashionable speech of England. Because of its prestige, *r*lessness was adopted in many areas and continues as the norm around Boston and in the South.

New Yorkers sought prestige by dropping their *r*'s in the nineteenth century, after having pronounced them in the eighteenth. However, contemporary New Yorkers are going back to the eighteenth-century pattern of pronouncing *r*'s. What matters, and what governs linguistic change, is not the reverberation of a good strong midwestern *r* but *social* evaluation, whether *r*'s happen to be "in" or "out."

Studies of *r* pronunciation in New York City have clarified the mechanisms of phonological change. William Labov (1972b) focused on whether *r* was pronounced after vowels in such words as *car, floor, card,* and *fourth.* To get data on how this linguistic variation correlated with social class, he used a series of rapid encounters with employees in three New York City department stores, each of whose prices and locations attracted a different socioeconomic group. Saks Fifth Avenue (68 encounters) catered to the upper middle class, Macy's (125) attracted middle-class shoppers, and S. Klein's (71) had predominantly lower-middle-class and working-class customers. The class origins of store personnel tended to reflect those of their clients.

Having already determined that a certain department was on the fourth floor, Labov approached ground-floor salespeople and asked where that department was. After the salesperson had answered, "Fourth floor," Labov repeated his "Where?" in order to get a second response. The second reply was more formal and emphatic, the salesperson presumably thinking that Labov hadn't heard or understood the first answer. For each salesperson, therefore, Labov had two samples of /r/ pronunciation in two words.

Labov calculated the percentages of workers who pronounced /r/ at least once during the interview. These were 62 percent at Saks, 51 percent at Macy's, but only 20 percent at S. Klein's. He also found that personnel on upper floors, where he asked "What floor is this?" (and where more expensive items were sold), pronounced *r* more often than ground-floor salespeople did.

In Labov's study, *r* pronunciation was clearly associated with prestige. Certainly the job interviewers who had hired the salespeople never counted *r*'s before offering employment. However, they did use speech evaluations to make judgments about how effective certain people would be in selling particular kinds of merchandise. In other words, they practiced sociolinguistic discrimination, using linguistic features in deciding who got certain jobs.

In stratified societies, our speech habits help determine our access to employment and other material resources. Because of this, "proper language" itself becomes a strategic resource—and a path to wealth, prestige, and power (Gal 1989). Illustrating this, many ethnographers have described the importance of verbal skill and oratory in local-level politics (Bloch, ed. 1975). Remember, too, that a "great communicator" dominated American society in the 1980s as a two-term President.

The French anthropologist Pierre Bourdieu views linguistic practices as *symbolic capital* which properly trained people may convert into economic and social capital. The value of a dialect—its standing in a "linguistic market"—depends on the extent to which it provides access to desired positions in the labor market. In turn, this reflects its legitimation by formal institutions—the educational establishment, state, church, and prestige media. In stratified societies, where there is always differential control of prestige speech, even people who don't use the prestige dialect accept its authority and correctness, its "symbolic domination" (Bourdieu 1982, 1984). Thus, linguistic forms, which lack power in themselves, take on the power of the groups and relationships they symbolize. The education system, however (defending its own worth), denies this, misrepresenting prestige speech as being inherently better. The linguistic insecurity of lower-class and minority speakers is a result of this symbolic domination.

Black English Vernacular (BEV)

Many linguists have analyzed variation based on ethnic background. In particular, Labov and several associates, both white and black, have conducted detailed studies of what they call **Black English Vernacular (BEV). (Vernacular** means ordinary, casual speech.) BEV is the

> relatively uniform dialect spoken by the majority of black youth in most parts of the United States today, especially in the inner city areas of New York, Boston,

Detroit, Philadelphia, Washington, Cleveland, . . . and other urban centers. It is also spoken in most rural areas and used in the casual, intimate speech of many adults (Labov 1972a, p. xiii).

Researchers have collected data from adolescent and adult BEV speakers in New York City and other cities.

Contrary to popular belief, BEV, which is usually called simply Black English, is not an ungrammatical hodge-podge but a complex linguistic system with its own rules. It developed as a variant of southern speech, with a phonology and a syntax similar to those of southern dialects. Nearly every feature distinguishing BEV from SE (Standard English) also characterizes the speech of some southern whites, although less often than is the case among speakers of BEV.

Among the phonological differences between BEV and SE, BEV speakers are less likely to pronounce *r*. Although many SE speakers fail to pronounce *r* before other consonants (ca*r*d) or at the end of words (ca*r*), most do pronounce *r* before a vowel, either at the end of a word (fou*r* o'clock) or within a word (Ca*r*ol). BEV speakers are much more likely to omit the *r* before a vowel or between vowels. The result is that speakers of the two dialects have different **homonyms** (words that sound the same but have different meanings). If they don't pronounce *r* between vowels, BEV speakers have the following homonyms: *Carol/Cal; Paris/ pass.*

Because of phonological contrasts between BEV and SE, BEV-speaking students systematically pronounce certain words differently than SE-speaking students do. The homonyms of BEV-speaking students differ from those of SE-speaking teachers. To evaluate reading accuracy, the teacher must take care to determine whether students are recognizing the different meanings of such homonyms as *passed, past,* and *pass.* Teachers need to make sure that students grasp what they are reading, which is more important than whether they are pronouncing words "correctly" according to the SE norm.

Phonological contrasts between BEV and SE speakers often have grammatical consequences. One of these is **copula deletion,** the absence of SE forms of the verb *to be.* For example, any of the following may contrast BEV and SE:

BEV	SE
you tired	you are tired
he tired	he is tired
we tired	we are tired
they tired	they are tired

In its deletion of the present tense of *to be,* BEV is similar to many languages, including Russian, Hungarian, and Hebrew, but it contrasts with SE. BEV copula deletion is a grammatical result of BEV's phonological rules. Notice that BEV omits the copula only where SE has contractions. SE contracts "you are tired" to "you're tired." Through contraction, SE produces "he's," "we're," and "they're." The phonological rules of BEV dictate that *r*'s and word-final *s*'s be dropped. However, BEV speakers do pronounce *m.* The BEV first-person singular is "I'm tired," just as in SE. When BEV omits the copula, it is merely carrying contraction one step further. This is an automatic result of BEV's phonological rules.

Also, phonological rules may lead BEV speakers to omit *-ed* as a past-tense marker and *-s* as a marker of plurality. These, however, are differences in surface structure rather than deep structure. BEV speakers *do* understand the difference between past and present verbs and singular and plural nouns. Confirming this are irregular verbs (for instance, *tell, told*) and irregular plurals (for instance, *child, children*), in which BEV works the same as SE.

BEV, like SE, is a complex, rule-governed dialect. SE is not superior to BEV as a linguistic system, but it does happen to be the dialect used in the mass media, in writing, and in most public and professional contexts. In areas of Germany where there is diglossia, speakers of Plattdeusch (Low German) learn the High German dialect to communicate appropriately in the national context. Similarly, upwardly mobile BEV-speaking students need to learn SE.

In a recent study, Labov (Williams 1985) discovered that despite the use of SE on radio and television, American dialect variance is growing not just between blacks and whites but between whites in different cities. Labov and coauthor Wendell Harris note that language is not learned from remote experience (such as the mass media) but from an individual's personal social network, particularly from peers. Speech responds to primary influences, people who make a difference in your life, such as supervisors, coworkers, and classmates. Urban ghetto existence tends to isolate blacks from whites. Many black children have never talked to white children before entering school.

Although BEV is diverging from SE, the dialects are still close. This means that teachers need to know something about the phonology and grammar of both dialects if they are to teach successfully. Schoolteachers should be able to show BEV-speaking students exactly how SE differs in phonology and syntax.

Many Americans who spoke other regional and

Like SE, BEV is a rule-governed dialect of American English. Most of the contrasts between BEV and other dialects involve surface structure. Language is not learned from remote experience (such as the mass media), but from an individual's personal social network, particularly from peers.

Breughel's Tower of Babel. The Bible traces the origin of different languages to God's punishment of humans who dared approach heaven by building the tower of Babel: all at once, the tower builders started speaking mutually incomprehensible languages. Opposing this creationist explanation is linguistic uniformitarianism, which states that new languages evolve out of old ones as minor linguistic variations, of the sort observable in any language today, gradually accumulate. This gradual process is illustrated by differences and similarities between Middle and modern English.

ethnic dialects as children have eventually learned to shift their linguistic styles outside the home. Since BEV is a bit more different from SE than other American English dialects are, mastery of the prestige dialect requires more effort. If learning and teaching SE are to be goals of blacks and whites within our educational system, school personnel need linguistic knowledge and sensitivity. Otherwise, as Labov notes, "We're in danger of forming a permanent underclass" (of ghetto blacks). Dialect divergence has the effect of "locking" blacks out of "important networks that lead to jobs, housing, and basic rights and privileges" (Williams 1985, p. 10).

HISTORICAL LINGUISTICS

Sociolinguists study contemporary variation in speech—language change in progress. **Historical linguistics** deals with longer-term change. Historical linguists can reconstruct many features of past languages by studying contemporary **daughter languages.** These are languages that descend from the same parent language and that have been changing separately for hundreds or even thousands of years. We call the original language from which they diverge the **protolanguage** (Figure 16.3). French and Spanish, for example, are daughter languages of Latin, their common protolanguage. Historical linguists also classify contemporary languages according to their degrees of relationship.

Language changes over time. It evolves—varies, spreads, divides into **subgroups** (languages within a taxonomy of related languages that are most closely related). Dialects of a single parent language become distinct daughter languages, especially if they are isolated from one another. Some of them split, and new "granddaughter" languages develop. If people remain in the ancestral homeland, their speech patterns also change. The evolving speech in the ancestral homeland should be considered a daughter language like the others. Language may also unify as groups that once spoke different languages occupy a new homeland, develop a national identity, or come under a common system of political domination (Bourdieu 1982; Gal 1989; Weber 1976).

A close relationship between languages doesn't necessarily mean that their speakers are closely related biologically or culturally, because people can

Figure 16.3 *Main languages and subgroups of the Indo-European language stock. All these daughter languages have developed out of the protolanguage (Proto-Indo-European) spoken in northern Europe about 5,000 years ago. Note subgrouping: English, a member of the Germanic branch, is more closely related to German and Dutch than it is to Italic (or Romance) languages such as French and Spanish. However, English shares many linguistic features with French through borrowing and diffusion. (Figure 8.6 from* An Introduction to Language, *Fourth Edition, by Victoria Fromkin and Robert Rodman, copyright © 1988 by Holt, Rinehart & Winston, Inc., reprinted by permission of the publisher.)*

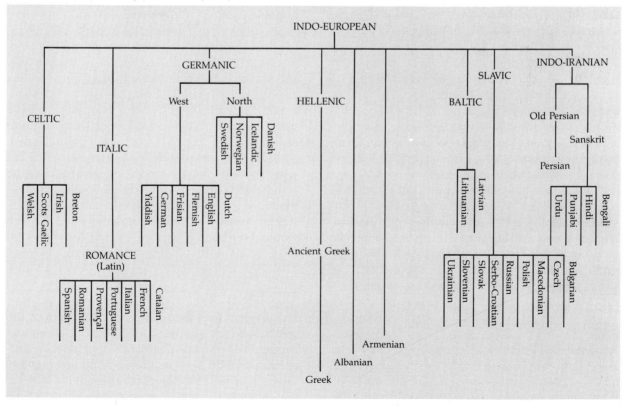

Immigrants to the United States have spoken many different languages on arrival, but their descendants now speak fluent English. People with very different cultures may speak a single language. Similarly, people who are culturally similar may speak different languages.

learn new languages. In the equatorial forests of Africa, "pygmy" hunters have discarded their ancestral languages and now speak those of the cultivators who have migrated to the area. Immigrants to the United States spoke many different languages on arrival, but their descendants now speak fluent English. People with very different customs may speak a single language. However, people who are culturally similar over a large area, such as Central African hunters and gatherers, may speak different languages.

How does linguistic evolution differ from biological evolution? Biological species originate in reproductive isolation, and gene sharing or borrowing is not possible after speciation. In language and in culture, however, complete isolation never occurs. Diffusion, borrowing, conquest, and consolidation go on all the time. In the world system, linguistic and cultural items keep passing from group to group. Linguistic change is influenced by contact between languages and cultures.

Historical Linguistics and Other Anthropological Concerns

Knowledge of linguistic relationships is often valuable to anthropologists interested in history, particularly events during the past 5,000 years. Cultural features may (or may not) correlate with the distribution of language families. Groups that speak related languages may (or may not) be more culturally similar to each other than they are to groups whose speech derives from different linguistic ancestors. Of course, cultural similarities aren't limited to speakers of related languages. Even groups whose members speak unrelated languages have contact through trade, intermarriage, and warfare. Ideas and inventions diffuse widely among human groups. Many items of vocabulary in contemporary English come from French. Even without written documentation of France's influence after the Norman Conquest of England in 1066, linguistic evidence in contemporary English would reveal a long period of important firsthand contact with France. Similarly, linguistic evidence may confirm cultural contact and borrowing when written history is lacking. By considering which words have been borrowed, we can also make inferences about the nature of the contact.

Language and Adaptation

Language is a major adaptive advantage that differentiates *Homo sapiens* from other species and has been partially responsible for the evolutionary success of humans. Just as there are no documented differences in brain complexity or intelligence between contemporary human populations, no one has ever shown the superiority of any language or dialect to any other. The doctrine of linguistic relativity states that all known languages and dialects are effective means of communication. This contradicts popular stereotypes. Many French people believe that theirs is the only appropriate language for civilized conversation. Many British and Americans assert the superiority of their language for commercial negotiations.

These claims, however, reflect cultural rather than linguistic facts. They originate in world politics and economy rather than in inherent linguistic properties. In creating a nation-state, and thereafter a world empire, the French spread their culture through their language. They asserted to the provinces they attached and the people they conquered that they were engaged in a civilizing mission. They came to equate the French language with civilization itself.

The contemporary use and distribution of a language reflect factors other than features of the language itself. One language spoken in China has more native speakers than English does not because it is a better language but because the population that speaks it has multiplied as a result of nonlinguistic factors. English is the native language of British people, North Americans, Australians, New Zealanders, and many South Africans because of English colonization and conquest. The success of this colonization and conquest had nothing to do with language. Weapons, ships, commerce, and sociopolitical organization played decisive roles.

Between 2,000 and 3,000 years ago a West African (proto-Bantu) population lived in a small area of what is now Nigeria and Cameroon. Today the linguistic descendants of the proto-Bantu cover most of Central Africa and southern Africa. Speakers of **Bantu** did not expand because their languages were superior means of communication. Rather, they grew, prospered, and spread because they developed a highly competitive cultural adaptation based on iron tools and weapons and very productive food crops.

We have seen that no language or dialect can confer, because of its purely linguistic qualities, a differential advantage on its speakers. Only the social evaluation of its speakers and, by extension, of the language itself can do this. Languages are flexible and—at least at the surface level—constantly changing systems. They easily admit and adopt new items and new terms. Speakers modify old forms, borrow foreign words, and create entirely new expressions.

Through surface changes, languages adjust to rapid cultural changes. However, the central core of a language—its deep structure—may remain virtually intact while its speakers' lives are revolutionized. In many respects the daily lives of rural Europeans before the Industrial Revolution were more similar to those of precolonial West Africans than to those of their contemporary European descendants. Yet linguistic change in English or in French has proceeded very slowly compared with the rate of economic, political, and social change.

SUMMARY

Linguistic anthropologists share anthropology's general interest in uniformity and diversity in time and space. Linguistic anthropology examines meaning systems, relationships between language and culture, linguistic universals, sociolinguistics, and linguistic change.

No language includes all the sounds (phones) that the human vocal apparatus can make. Phonology—the study of speech sounds—focuses on sound contrasts (phonemes) that distinguish meaning in a given language. In sociolinguistics, variation among speakers of the same language correlates with social contrasts and exemplifies linguistic change in progress.

In his transformational-generative approach, Chomsky argues for an innate blueprint for building language in the human brain. All people share this genetically determined capacity for language, though not for any particular language. Each language's grammar is a particular set of rules taken from the universal set. Once we master our language's rules, we can generate an infinite number of statements. Surface structures, the object of traditional linguistic study, make languages seem more different than they are. The similarities lie deeper, at the level of deep structure.

There are culturally distinctive as well as universal relationships between language and mental processes. The lexicons and grammars of particular languages can lead speakers to perceive and think in particular ways. Studies of domains such as kinship, color terminologies, and pronouns show that speakers of different languages categorize their experiences differently. However, language does not tightly restrict thought, because cultural changes can produce changes in thought and in language, particularly in surface structure.

Sociolinguistics investigates relationships between social and linguistic variation. It focuses on performance (the actual use of language) rather than competence (rules shared by all speakers of a given language). Sociolinguists do field work with several informants and quantify their observations. Only when features of speech acquire social meaning are they imitated. If they are valued, they spread.

People vary their speech on different occasions, shifting styles, dialects, and languages, particularly in the modern world system. As linguistic systems, all languages and dialects are equally complex, rule-governed, and effective for communication. However, speech is used, is evaluated, and changes in the context of political, economic, and social forces. The linguistic traits of a low-status group are negatively evaluated (often even by members of that group) not because of their *linguistic* features but because they are associated with and symbolize low *social* status. One dialect, supported by the dominant institutions of the state, exercises symbolic domination over the others.

Black English Vernacular, a dialect of contemporary English, shares, despite certain surface differences, most of its deep structural rules with Standard English and other American English dialects. Both SE and BEV are complex, rule-governed systems. Neither dialect communicates more effectively than the other.

Historical linguistics is useful for anthropologists interested in historical relationships between populations. Cultural similarities and differences often correlate with linguistic ones. Linguistic clues can suggest past contacts between cultures. Related languages—members of the same language family—descend from an original protolanguage. Relationships between languages don't necessarily mean that there are biological ties between their speakers, because people can learn new languages.

Linguistic relativity views each language as a communication system that is as adequate as any other for the exchange of information.

GLOSSARY

Bantu: Group of related languages spoken over a large area of Central Africa and eastern and southern Africa.

Black English Vernacular (BEV): Like Standard English, a rule-governed dialect of contemporary English; spoken by many inner-city African-Americans.

competence: What native speakers must (and do) know about their language in order to speak and understand it.

copula deletion: Absence of the verb *to be.*

daughter languages: Languages developing out of the same parent language; for example, French and Spanish are daughter languages of Latin.

deep structure: In transformational grammar, the mental level; a sentence is formed in the speaker's mind and then interpreted by the hearer.

diglossia: The existence of "high" (formal) and "low" (familial) dialects of a single language, such as German.

ethnoscience: See *ethnosemantics.*

ethnosemantics: The study of lexical (vocabulary) contrasts and classifications in various languages.

focal vocabulary: A set of words and distinctions that are particularly important to certain groups (those with particular foci of experience or activity), such as types of snow to Eskimos or skiers.

grammar: The formal organizing principles that link sound and meaning in a language; the set of abstract rules that makes up a language.

historical linguistics: Subdivision of linguistics that studies languages over time.

homonyms: Words that sound the same but have different meanings, such as *bear* and *bare.*

lexicon: Vocabulary; a dictionary containing all the morphemes in a language and their meaning.

linguistic relativity: Notion that all languages and dialects are equally effective as systems of communication.

minimal pairs: Words that resemble each other in all but one sound; used to discover phonemes.

morpheme: Minimal linguistic form (usually a word) with meaning.

morphology: The study of form; used in linguistics (the study of morphemes and word construction) and for form in general—for example, biomorphology relates to physical form.

performance: What people actually say; the use of speech in social situations.

phone: Any speech sound.

phoneme: Significant sound contrast in a language that serves to distinguish meaning, as in minimal pairs.

phonemics: The study of the sound contrasts (phonemes) of a particular language.

phonetics: The study of speech sounds in general; what people actually say in various languages.

phonology: The study of sounds used in speech.

protolanguage: Language ancestral to several daughter languages.

Sapir-Whorf hypothesis: Theory that different languages produce different ways of thinking.

semantics: A language's meaning system.

sociolinguistics: Study of relationships between social and linguistic variation; study of language (performance) in its social context.

style shifts: Variations in speech in different contexts.

subgroups: Languages within a taxonomy of related languages that are most closely related.

surface structure: In transformational grammar, the message that passes from speaker to hearer; an actual speech event.

syntax: The arrangement and order of words in phrases and sentences.

transformational-generative grammar: Approach associated with Noam Chomsky; views language as set of abstract rules with deep and surface structures.

universal grammar: According to Chomsky, a genetically transmitted blueprint for language, a basic linguistic plan in the human brain.

vernacular: Ordinary, casual speech.

STUDY QUESTIONS

1. Why is linguistic anthropology a subdiscipline of anthropology? What does it share with the other subdisciplines? How does it link up with cultural anthropology?
2. What is Chomsky's transformational-generative grammar, and how does it relate to the issue of "human nature"?
3. What is the Sapir-Whorf hypothesis, and how does it relate to cultural diversity?
4. What is sociolinguistics, and how does it relate to the distinction between competence and performance?
5. Several examples of interrelationships between social and linguistic variation have been given. Can you cite comparable sociolinguistic examples from your own experience?
6. How do men and women differ in their use of language?
7. What is historical linguistics, and what are the issues it studies?
8. What is linguistic relativity, and how does it relate to symbolic domination by prestige dialects?

SUGGESTED ADDITIONAL READING

APPEL, R., AND P. MUYSKEN
    1987 *Language Contact and Bilingualism.* London: Edward Arnold. Issues of linguistic contact.
BURKE, P., AND R. PORTER
    1987 *The Social History of Language.* Cambridge: Cambridge University Press. Language in society through history.
BURLING, R.
    1970 *Man's Many Voices: Language in Its Cultural Context.* New York: Holt, Rinehart & Winston. Readable introduction to sociolinguistics and language and culture.
COOK-GUMPERZ, J.
    1986 *The Social Construction of Literacy.* Cambridge: Cambridge University Press. Literacy in its social and cultural context.

CRANE, L. B., E. YEAGER, AND R. L. WHITMAN
    1981 *An Introduction to Linguistics.* Boston: Little, Brown. A thorough introductory text covering the field of linguistics.
DI LEONARDO, M., ED.
    1990 *Toward a New Anthropology of Gender.* Berkeley: University of California Press. Discusses case studies of gender and language.
EDWARDS, J.
    1985 *Language, Society, and Identity.* London: Basil Blackwell. Self and speech in society.
FERGUSON, C. A., AND S. B. HEATH, EDS.
    1981 *Language in the U.S.A.* New York: Cambridge University Press. Bilingualism, professional jargon, languages of Native Americans, Spanish, and varieties of American English.

GUMPERZ, J. J.
  1982 *Language and Social Identity.* Cambridge: Cambridge University Press. Well-known sociolinguist discusses language and social identification.
HELLER, M.
  1988 *Codeswitching: Anthropological and Sociolinguistic Perspectives.* Berlin: Mouton de Gruyter. Style shifting and diglossia.
HEWITT, R.
  1986 *White Talk, Black Talk.* Cambridge: Cambridge University Press. Recent research on Black English Vernacular and its relationship to Standard English and white dialects.
HYMES, D., ED.
  1964 *Language in Culture and Society: A Reader in Linguistics and Anthropology.* New York: Harper & Row. Excellent reader, strong in ethnoscience and other linguistic developments of the early 1960s.
KRAMARAE, R., M. SHULZ, AND M. O'BARR, EDS.
  1984 *Language and Power.* Beverly Hills, CA: Sage. Issues of language, politics, and symbolic domination.
LAKOFF, R.
  1975 *Language and Woman's Place.* New York: Harper & Row. Nontechnical discussion of how women use and are treated in Standard American English.

MUHLHAUSLER, P.
  1986 *Pidgin and Creole Linguistics.* London: Basil Blackwell. New languages of travel, trade, and colonialism.
SANKOFF, G.
  1980 *The Social Life of Language.* Philadelphia: University of Pennsylvania Press. Important sociolinguistic study.
STEEDMAN, C., C. URWIN, AND V. WALKERDINE, EDS.
  1985 *Language, Gender, and Childhood.* London: Routledge and Kegan Paul. The learning of gender differentiation through language.
THOMASON, S. G., AND T. KAUFMAN
  1988 *Language Contact, Creolization, and Genetic Linguistics.* Berkeley: University of California Press. Language in the world system.
TRUDGILL, P.
  1983 *Sociolinguistics: An Introduction to Language and Society,* rev. ed. Harmondsworth, United Kingdom: Penguin. Readable short introduction to the role and use of language in society.
WOOLARD, K. A.
  1989 *Double Talk: Bilingualism and the Politics of Ethnicity in Catalonia.* Stanford, CA: Stanford University Press. Field study of diglossia.

CHAPTER 17

APPLIED ANTHROPOLOGY

Anthropology helps reduce ethnocentrism by instilling an appreciation of cultural diversity. This broadening, educational role affects the knowledge, values, and attitudes of most people who are exposed to anthropology. Now we must ask: What contribution can anthropology make in identifying and solving human problems stirred up by contemporary currents of economic, social, and cultural change?

APPLIED ANTHROPOLOGY

Anthropologists have held three different positions about applying anthropology—using it to identify and solve social problems. People who hold the **ivory tower view** contend that anthropologists should avoid practical matters and concentrate on research, publication, and teaching. Those who favor the **schizoid view** think that anthropologists should help carry out, but not make or criticize, policy. In this view, personal "value judgments" should be kept strictly separate from scientific investigation. The third view is **advocacy.** Its proponents assert that precisely because anthropologists *are* experts on human problems and social change and because they study, understand, and respect cultural values, they should make policy affecting people.

I join many other anthropologists in favoring advocacy. I share the belief that no one is better qualified to propose and evaluate guidelines for society than are those who study anthropology. To be effective advocates, anthropologists must present their views clearly, thoughtfully, and forcefully (Gough 1968/1973) to policy makers and the public. Many anthropologists do serve as social commentators, problem solvers, and policy makers, advisers, and evaluators. We express our policy views through professional associations, in books and journals, and through participation in social and political movements.

Some advocates work in social-change organizations. Others investigate social issues as independent researchers. More and more anthropologists work in organizations that promote, manage, and assess programs that influence human life. The scope of applied anthropology includes change and development abroad and social problems and policies in North America.

One definition of **applied anthropology** is "the use of anthropological findings, concepts, and methods to accomplish a desired end" (Clifton 1970, p. viii). Modern applied anthropology (Kimball 1978) differs from an earlier version that mainly served the goals of colonial regimes. Before turning to the new, we should consider some dangers of the old.

Anthropology and Colonialism

Bronislaw Malinowski (1929) proposed that "practical anthropology" (his term for colonial applied anthropology) should focus on the westernization of African societies. The diffusion of European culture into tribal societies was of special interest to Malinowski. He argued that anthropologists can avoid politics by concentrating on facts and processes. However, he was actually expressing his own political views, because he questioned neither the legitimacy of colonialism nor the anthropologist's role in helping it work. He saw nothing wrong with aiding colonial regimes by studying land tenure and land use to determine how much land natives should keep and how much Europeans should get. Malinowski's comments exemplify a historical association between anthropology, particularly in Europe, and colonialism (Maquet 1964).

The Third World Talks Back

In the postcolonial world, anthropologists from industrial core nations have paid attention to criticisms leveled against them by Third World colleagues. For example, the Mexican anthropologist Guillermo Batalla (1966) has decried certain "conservative and essentially ethnocentric assumptions" of applied anthropology in Latin America. He laments the heavy psychological emphasis of many studies. These studies, he says, focus too much on attitudes and beliefs about health and nutrition rather than on the basic material causes of poor health and malnutrition. Another problem he mentions is misuse of cultural relativism by certain anthropologists. He faults these researchers for refusing to interfere in existing social situations because they consider it inappropriate to judge and guide.

Batalla also criticizes the *multiple causation theory,* which assumes that any social event has countless small and diverse causes. Such a theory does not

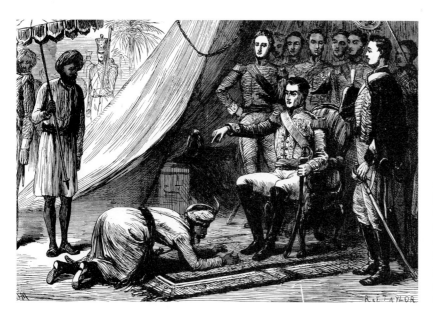

In the postcolonial world, anthropologists from industrial nations have paid attention to criticisms leveled against them by Third World colleagues. Modern applied anthropology differs from an earlier version that mainly served the goals of colonial regimes. This scene depicts nineteenth-century British colonial rule in Nepal.

perceive major social and economic inequities as targets for attack. Batalla also faults anthropologists who see communities as isolated units, because (as our world-system approach recognizes) local-level changes are always accepted or opposed in a larger context. He argues that applied anthropologists should pay more attention to regional, national, and international contexts. Finally, Batalla criticizes anthropologists for thinking that diffusion, usually of skills from the United States, is the most significant process involved in change.

Batalla doesn't argue that *all* applied anthropology suffers from these faults. However, his points are generally valid, and many Third World social scientists agree with him. Those scholars have also criticized American anthropology for the links that exist between some anthropologists and government agencies that don't promote the best interests of the people.

Applied anthropologists should recognize these pitfalls and be wary of programs that would use them merely as technicians (Eddy and Partridge 1978). Anthropologists should do more than supply information to officials who have preconceived assumptions about social problems and policies (Berreman 1969/1973a). Today's applied anthropologists have two codes of professional conduct. One is the code of the Society for Applied Anthropology. The other is the more general code of the American Anthropological Association (AAA).

ETHICS AND ANTHROPOLOGY

In 1971 the AAA adopted a code of ethics entitled "AAA: Principles of Professional Responsibility." This code reveals strong differences between contemporary anthropologists and those who hold the schizoid view. The preamble suggests that anthropologists should avoid research that can potentially damage either the people studied or the scholarly community. The code covers six areas of professional responsibility.

1. Responsibility to Those Studied. Anthropologists' main responsibility is to the people they study. Anthropologists should do all they can to protect their informants' welfare and to honor their dignity and privacy. If interests conflict, these people come first. Their rights and interests must be protected. Specifically, anthropologists should let informants know the aims and anticipated consequences of their research. They should ensure that informants preserve their anonymity in data collection. Informants should not be exploited for personal gain. Anthropologists must anticipate and take steps to avoid potentially damaging effects of the publication of their results. Reflecting the AAA's disapproval of secret research, reports should be available to the general public.

2. Responsibility to the Public. As scholars who devote their lives to understanding human diversity, anthropologists should speak out publicly about what they know and believe as a result of their professional expertise. They should contribute to an adequate definition of social reality, upon which public opinion and policy can be based. Anthropologists should also be aware of the limitations of their expertise.

3. Responsibility to the Discipline. Anthropologists are responsible for the reputations of their discipline and their colleagues. They should maintain their integrity in the field so that their behavior will not jeopardize future research by others.

4. Responsibility to Students. Anthropologists should be fair, candid, nonexploitative, and committed to the welfare and academic progress of their students. They should make students aware of ethical problems in research.

5. Responsibility to Sponsors. Anthropologists should be honest about their qualifications, capabilities, and aims. They should not agree to working conditions or terms of employment that violate professional ethics. They should retain the right to make their own decisions on ethical issues during research.

6. Responsibility to One's Own and to Host Governments. Anthropologists should demand assurance that agreements with governments do not require them to compromise their professional responsibilities and ethics in order to pursue their research.

This statement of principles of professional responsibility was designed to offer guidelines. However, the code also provides for censure of unprofessional conduct. When the actions of one anthropologist jeopardize others or appear unethical, colleagues may examine those actions and take measures that lie within the mandate of the AAA. A committee on ethics is now a permanent part of the AAA.

ACADEMIC AND APPLIED ANTHROPOLOGY

There was a time—the 1940s—when most anthropologists focused on practical problems. Many anthropologists worked for governments during World War II. American anthropologists studied Japanese and German "culture at a distance" and

aided the Pacific war effort. Applied anthropology did not disappear during the 1950s and 1960s, but academic anthropology did most of the growing after World War II. The baby boom, which began in 1945 and peaked in 1957, fueled expansion of the American educational system and thus of academic jobs. New junior, community, and four-year colleges opened. Anthropology became a standard part of the college curriculum. During the 1950s and 1960s most American anthropologists were college professors, although some still worked in agencies and museums.

This era of academic anthropology continued through the early 1970s. Especially during the Vietnam War, undergraduates flocked to anthropology classes to learn about the cultures of the Third World. Students were particularly interested in Southeast Asia, whose traditional lifeways were threatened by war. Many anthropologists protested the superpowers' blatant disregard for the values, customs, social systems, and lives of Third World peoples.

A shift in the interests of college students and in the jobs available to anthropologists occurred during the 1970s with the end of the Vietnam War and the baby boom. Students started turning away from a broad liberal education and toward a curriculum that seemed more practical. Computer science, engineering, business, accounting, economics, and even psychology seemed more likely to lead to a job than did anthropology, philosophy, history, and literature.

Anthropology itself followed this shift toward the practical. Anthropologists sought jobs in international organizations, government, business, hospitals, and schools. The shift toward application, though only partial, benefited the profession. It forced anthropologists to consider the wider social value and implications of their research.

Massive changes in human life are going on today, and many anthropologists feel obliged not simply to study but also to try to solve contemporary problems. Contemporary applied anthropologists work in diverse settings. Some hold academic positions but also consult for firms and organizations. Some do independent research on the social context and effects of planned and unplanned changes. Still others work full-time as nonacademic anthropologists. Recognizing their increasing importance, the AAA now publishes a directory of practicing anthropologists that paral-

During the Vietnam War, many anthropologists protested the superpowers' blatant disregard for the values, customs, social systems, and lives of Third World peoples. Several anthropologists, including the author (nearer of two men with glasses and chin-in-hand, on lower level), attended this all-night Columbia University "teach-in" against the War in 1965.

lels the long-published *AAA Guide* [to Departments of Anthropology].

Ethnography in Applied Anthropology

The applied anthropologist's most valuable research tool is the ethnographic method. Ethnographers study societies firsthand, living with and learning from ordinary people. Ethnographers are participant-observers, taking part in the events they study in order to understand native thought and behavior. Ethnographic techniques guide applied anthropologists in both foreign and domestic settings.

Other "expert" participants in social-change programs may be content to converse with officials, read reports, and copy statistics. However, the applied anthropologist's likely early request is some variant of "take me to your villagers." Anthropologists know that local people must play an active role in the changes that affect them and that "the people" have information that "experts" lack.

Theory and Practice

Besides the ethnographic approach, a few other features of anthropology deserve reemphasis here. Anthropological theory—the body of findings and generalizations of the subdisciplines—also guides applied anthropology. Anthropology's holistic perspective—its interest in biology, society, culture, and language—permits the evaluation of many issues that affect people.

Anthropology's **systemic perspective** recognizes that changes do not occur in a vacuum. A project or program always has multiple consequences, some unforeseen. For example, dozens of economic development projects intended to increase productivity through irrigation have worsened health conditions by creating waterways where disease microorganisms thrive. In an American example of unintended consequences, a program aimed at enhancing teachers' appreciation of cultural differences led to ethnic stereotyping (Kleinfeld 1975). Specifically, Native American students did not welcome teachers' frequent comments about their Indian heritage. The students felt set apart from their classmates and saw this attention to their ethnicity as patronizing and demeaning.

Theory aids practice, and application fuels theory. As we compare projects, our understanding of cause and effect increases. We add new generalizations about culture change to those discovered in traditional and ancient cultures.

Applied Anthropology and the Subdisciplines

Applied anthropologists come from all four subdisciplines. Biological anthropologists work in public health, nutrition, genetic counseling, substance abuse, epidemiology, aging, and mental illness. They apply their knowledge of human anatomy and physiology to the improvement of automobile safety standards and to the design of airplanes and spacecraft. In forensic work, biological anthropologists help police identify skeletal remains. Similarly, forensic archeologists reconstruct crimes by analyzing physical evidence.

An important role for applied archeologists has been created by legislation requiring surveys of prehistoric and historic sites threatened by dams, highways, and other projects supported by federal funds. To save as much as possible of the past when actual sites cannot be preserved is the work of **salvage archeology.** Applied cultural anthropologists sometimes work alongside the applied

Because linguistic differences may affect children's schoolwork and teachers' evaluations, applied linguistic anthropology can aid education. Knowledge of linguistic differences is important in an increasingly multi-cultural society whose populace grows up speaking many languages and dialects. Shown here, French instruction in Canada, a bilingual nation (English and French).

archeologists, assessing the human problems generated by the change and determining how they can be reduced.

Cultural anthropologists work with social workers, business people, media researchers, advertising professionals, factory workers, gerontologists, nurses, physicians, mental-health professionals, school personnel, and economic development experts. Linguistic anthropology, particularly sociolinguistics, aids education. Knowledge of linguistic differences is important in an increasingly multicultural society whose populace grows up speaking many languages and dialects. Because linguistic differences may affect children's schoolwork and teachers' evaluations, many schools of education now require courses in sociolinguistics.

ANTHROPOLOGY AND EDUCATION

Ethnography brings a novel perspective to education, with practical applications (Eddy 1978). **Anthropology and education** refers to anthropological research in classrooms, homes, and neighborhoods. Some of the most interesting research has been done in classrooms, where anthropologists observe interactions between teachers, students, parents, and visitors. Jules Henry's classic account of the American elementary school classroom (1955) shows how students learn to conform to and compete with and criticize their peers. Anthropologists also follow students from classrooms into their homes and neighborhoods, viewing children as total cultural creatures whose enculturation and attitudes toward education belong to a larger context that includes family and peers.

Sociolinguists and cultural anthropologists work side by side in education research, for example, in a study of Puerto Rican seventh graders in the urban Midwest (Hill-Burnett 1978). In classrooms, neighborhoods, and homes, anthropologists uncovered some misconceptions by teachers. For example, the teachers had mistakenly assumed that Puerto Rican parents valued education less than did non-Hispanics. However, in-depth interviews revealed that the Puerto Rican parents valued it more.

Researchers also discovered that certain practices were preventing Hispanics from being adequately educated. For example, the teachers' union and the Board of Education had agreed to teach "English as a foreign language." However, they had not provided bilingual teachers to work with Spanish-speaking students. The school started assigning all students (including non-Hispanics) with low reading scores and behavior problems to the "English as a foreign language" classroom.

This educational disaster brought together a teacher who spoke no Spanish, children who barely spoke English, and a group of English-speaking students with reading and behavior problems. The Spanish speakers were falling farther behind not just in reading but in all subjects. They could at least have kept up in the other subjects if a Spanish speaker had been teaching them science, social studies, and math until they were ready for English-language instruction in those areas.

The researchers also discovered that Anglo-Americans and Hispanics reacted differently to humor and teasing. Many Hispanic youths believed that teachers' kidding comments went too far. They heard the remarks as insults and slurs rather than jokes. The Hispanics who adapted most successfully were those who had learned the general American norm about kidding, so that teachers' attempts at humor didn't damage their self-esteem.

A dramatic illustration of the relevance of sociolinguistics to education comes from Ann Arbor, Michigan. In 1979 the parents of several black students at the predominantly white Dr. Martin Luther King Jr. Elementary School sued the Board of Education. They claimed that their children faced linguistic discrimination in the classroom.

The children, who lived in a neighborhood housing project, spoke Black English Vernacular (BEV, see Chapter 16) at home. At school, most had encountered problems with their classwork. Some had been labeled "learning-impaired" and placed in remedial reading courses. (Consider the embarrassment that children suffer and the effect on self-image of such labeling.)

The African-American parents and their attorney contended that the children had no intrinsic learning disabilities but simply did not understand everything their teachers said. Nor did their teachers always understand them. The lawyer argued that because BEV and Standard English (SE) are so

similar, teachers often misinterpreted a child's correct pronunciation (in BEV) of an SE word as a reading error.

The children's attorney recruited several sociolinguists to testify on their behalf. The school board, by contrast, could not find a single qualified linguist to support its contention that there was no linguistic discrimination.

The judge ruled in favor of the children and ordered the following solution: Teachers at the King School had to attend a full-year course designed to improve their knowledge of nonstandard dialects, particularly BEV. The judge did *not* advocate that the teachers learn to speak BEV or that the children do their assignments in BEV. The school's goal remained to teach the children to use SE, the standard dialect, correctly. Before this could be accomplished, however, teachers and students alike had to learn how to recognize the differences between these similar dialects. At the end of the year most of the teachers interviewed in the local newspaper said the course had helped them.

In a diverse, multicultural populace, teachers should be sensitive to and knowledgeable about linguistic and cultural differences. Children need to be protected so that their ethnic or linguistic background is not used against them. That is what happens when a social variation is regarded as a learning disability.

URBAN ANTHROPOLOGY

As social complexity, industrialization, and urbanization spread globally, anthropologists increasingly study these processes and the social problems they create. *Urban anthropology*, which has theoretical (basic research) and applied dimensions, is the cross-cultural and ethnographic study of global urbanization and life in cities. The United States has also become a popular arena for urban anthropological research on topics such as ethnicity, poverty, class, and subcultural variations (Mullings, ed. 1987).

Recognizing that a city (even a preindustrial one) is a social context that is very different from a tribal or peasant village, an early student of Third World urbanization, the anthropologist Robert Redfield, focused on contrasts between rural and urban life. He contrasted rural communities, whose social relations are on a face-to-face basis, with cities, where impersonality characterizes many aspects of life. Redfield (1941) proposed that urbanization be studied along a rural-urban continuum. He described differences in values and social relations in four sites that spanned such a continuum. In Mexico's Yucatán peninsula, Redfield compared an isolated Maya-speaking Indian community, a rural peasant village, a small provincial city, and a large capital. Several studies in Africa (Little 1971) and Asia were influenced by Redfield's view that cities are centers through which cultural innovations spread to rural and tribal areas.

In any nation, urban and rural represent different social systems. However, cultural diffusion occurs as people, products, and messages move from one to the other. Migrants bring rural practices and beliefs to town and take urban patterns back home. The experiences and social forms of the rural area affect adaptation to city life. For example, principles of tribal organization, including descent, provide migrants to African cities with coping mechanisms that Latin American peasants lack. City folk also develop new institutions to meet specific urban needs (Mitchell 1966).

African urban groups include ethnic associations, occupational groups, social clubs, religious groups, and burial societies. Through membership in these groups, urban Africans have networks of personal support. Ethnic or "tribal" associations, which build a bridge between one social system and another (rural and urban), are common both in West and East Africa (Little 1965; Banton 1957).

City dwellers from the Luo tribe in Kampala, Uganda (Parkin 1969), for example, are organized in accordance with migrants' traditional clan ties and rural areas of origin. Luo associations provide economic and moral support, including transportation of destitute people back to the country. Nigerian associations also use a tribal-descent model to organize city dwellers, with extended families and lineages grouped into clans. The urban clans belong to district associations, which combine to make up the entire urban ethnic association. Although most members of such Nigerian urban associations are laborers, some are doctors, lawyers, and other professionals.

The ideology of such associations is that of a gigantic kin group. Members call one another "brother" and "sister." As in an extended family, rich members help their poor relatives. When members fight among themselves, the association acts as judge. A member's improper behavior can lead to expulsion—an unhappy fate for a migrant in an ethnically heterogeneous city.

ETHNIC GROUPS, POVERTY, AND CRIME

These associations reduce the stress of urban life on migrants. Researchers in American cities have studied similar kin-modeled, ethnic, and voluntary associations—which even play a role in organizing crime. Francis Ianni (1977) has studied criminal organizations among African-Americans and Hispanics. He views organized crime as a long-established feature of American economic life—a response to poverty and differential power. Ianni sees criminal organizations as representing one end of an economic continuum, with legitimate businesses at the other end.

Most African-Americans and Hispanics, even those who face severe poverty, don't become criminals. Historically, however, some poor ethnics have used crime as a route to financial and psychological security. Crime appears when legitimate economic opportunities are limited by unemployment which is caused by state organization and industrialization. In nonstate societies everyone who wants to work can do so. Only states have joblessness.

Crime is also a creation of state organization. By definition, a crime is an illegal act, and only states have legal codes. According to Ianni, poverty and powerlessness rather than ethnic background cause crime. After all, in American history successive ethnic groups with very different cultural backgrounds (but facing similar conditions of poverty) have used crime to better themselves economically.

Ianni found that several types of personal relationships introduce African-American and Hispanic criminals to each other and to crime. Links between adult criminals often grow out of childhood friendships or membership in a gang. Commonly, however, boys begin their careers in crime as apprentices to older men. Established criminals, who become role models, recruit boys for criminal ventures. Links established in prison also lead to

Cementing urban gangs, such as this one in Los Angeles, is social solidarity—an espirit de corps. Here gang members demonstrate special hand and finger signs that contribute to their in-group solidarity.

later criminal association. Women occasionally join criminal organizations through male friends or husbands.

Once people are committed to crime, their common activity holds the networks together. Networks link partners, employers and employees, and buyers and sellers of goods and services. Social solidarity—an *esprit de corps*—cements criminal networks. The stronger this spirit is, the more successful the ventures in crime tend to be.

One kind of criminal association is the entrepreneurial organization, which Ianni compares to a legitimate business. Consisting of a head and the head's agents in illegality, it has a code of rules designed to protect itself and its activities. The rules stress secrecy (don't tell the police or nonmembers), honesty (don't cheat on members), and competence.

Ianni discusses the ethnic succession of crime in American cities. Segments of Italian, Cuban, Puerto Rican, African-American, and other ethnic groups have all used crime to escape poverty and powerlessness. However, the criminal networks of each group have differed. Kinship is one of the most obvious differences. Kinship has played a stronger role in organizing Italian-American and Cuban-American criminals than it has in organizing African-American and Puerto Rican criminals.

MEDICAL ANTHROPOLOGY

Both biological and cultural anthropologists work in **medical anthropology,** which focuses on dis-

ease, health problems, health-care systems, and theories about illness in different cultures and ethnic groups. Disease problems vary among cultures. Such epidemic diseases as cholera, typhoid, and bubonic plague are associated with dense populations and thus with agriculture and urbanization. Malaria spread as a result of forest clearing and population increase associated with plant cultivation. Certain diseases tend to accompany economic development. **Schistosomiasis,** or **bilharziasis** (liver flukes), is spread by snails that inhabit ponds, lakes, and waterways, often ones created by irrigation projects.

The incidence of particular diseases varies between cultures, and different cultures interpret and treat illness differently. All societies have "disease-theory systems" to identify, classify, and explain illness. According to George Foster and Barbara Anderson (1978), there are three basic theories of causation: personalistic, naturalistic, and emotionalistic. **Personalistic disease theories** blame illness on sorcerers, witches, ghosts, or ancestral spirits. **Naturalistic disease theories** (including scientific medicine) explain illness in impersonal systemic terms. This includes microorganisms and (in some traditional medical systems) unbalanced body fluids. Many Latin cultures classify food, drink, and environmental conditions as "hot" or "cold." People believe their health suffers when they eat or drink hot or cold substances under inappropriate conditions. Thus, one should not drink something cold after a hot bath or eat a pineapple (a "cold" fruit) when one is menstruating (a "hot" condition).

Emotionalistic disease theories assume that intense emotional experiences cause illness. For example, Latin American women are believed to be susceptible to *susto,* an illness caused by fright. Its symptoms (lethargy, vagueness, distraction) are similar to those of "soul loss," a diagnosis of similar symptoms made by people in Madagascar. Modern psychoanalysis also focuses on the role of the emotions in physical and psychological well-being.

All societies have **health-care systems**—beliefs, customs, and specialists concerned with ensuring health and preventing and curing illness. A society's disease-causation theory is important in regard to treatment. When illness has a personalistic cause, shamans and other magicoreligious specialists may be good curers. They draw on varied techniques (occult and practical), which constitute their specialized knowledge and expertise. A shaman may cure soul loss by enticing the lost spirit back to the body. In societies without the possibility of Caesarian section, shamans may aid difficult childbirths by calling on spirits to travel up the vagina and guide the baby out (Lévi-Strauss 1967). A shaman may cure a persistent cough by counteracting a curse or removing an evil substance introduced by a sorcerer.

All cultures have health-care professionals. If there is a "world's oldest profession" besides hunter and gatherer, it is **curer,** or shaman. The curer's role has some universal features (Foster and Anderson 1978). Thus curers become specialists through a culturally appropriate process of selection (parental prodding, inheritance, visions, dream instructions) and training (apprentice shamanship, medical school). Eventually, the curer is certified by established practitioners and acquires a professional image. Patients, who believe in the curer's special powers, consult and compensate him or her.

Non-Western systems (traditional medicine) have certain lessons for Western medicine. Traditional practitioners may be more successful in treating mental illness than psychotherapists are. This may be due to non-Western systems which explain mental illness in terms of causes that are easier to identify and cure. It may be simpler to rid a body of a spirit possessor than to undo all the psychological damage that a Freudian might attribute to an unresolved Oedipus complex.

Another reason why non-Western therapy succeeds is that the mentally ill are diagnosed and treated in small, cohesive groups with the full support of their kin. Curing may be an intense community ritual in which the shaman heals by temporarily taking on and then rejecting the patient's illness (Lévi-Strauss 1967).

In the impersonal mental institutions of contemporary North America, no preexisting social ties link patients to each other or to doctors and nurses. Mental illness is seen as the patient's lone, individual burden. The social context of treatment is one of isolation and alienation rather than intense participation by a social group in a ritual.

We should not lose sight, ethnocentrically, of the difference between **scientific medicine** and Western medicine per se (Lieban 1977). Despite advances in pathology, microbiology, biochemistry, surgery, diagnostic technology, and applications, many Western medical procedures have no clear justification in logic or fact. Overprescription of tranquilizers and drugs, unnecessary surgery, and the impersonality and inequality of the physician-patient relationship are dubious features of our medical system.

However, there is no doubt that *scientific* medicine surpasses tribal treatment in many ways. Although medicines such as quinine, coca, opium, ephedrine, and rauwolfia were discovered in nonindustrial societies, traditional medicines are not as effective against bacteria as antibiotics are. Preventive health care has advanced significantly during the twentieth century. Today's surgical procedures are much better than those of traditional societies.

Still, industrialization has spawned its own special health problems. Modern stressors include noise, air and water pollution, poor nutrition habits, dangerous industrial machinery, impersonal work organization, social isolation, homelessness, and substance abuse. With the conquest of most infectious diseases, health problems in industrial nations, other than AIDS, are due more to economic, social, political, and cultural factors than to pathogens (Lieban 1977). In the United States, for example, poverty is linked to many illnesses, including arthritis, heart conditions, back problems, and hearing and vision impairment.

Medical anthropology, which is based on biological, social, and cross-cultural research, has the-

Western medicine and scientific medicine are not the same thing. Many Western medical procedures have no clear justification, but scientific medicine surpasses tribal health-care systems in several ways. Clinics such as this one bring antibiotics, minor surgery, and preventive medicine to the Masai of Kenya.

oretical and applied dimensions. Health programs must pay attention to native theories about the cause and treatment of illness. Once scientific medicine arrives, people tend to continue using traditional procedures while also accepting the new. Shamans may treat certain conditions (such as spirit possession), whereas M.D.s may deal with others. If both scientific and traditional specialists are consulted and the patient is cured, the native curer may get as much credit as or more credit than the physician.

A more personal, social treatment of illness that emulates the non-Western curer-patient-community relationship could benefit Western systems. Western medicine tends to draw an overly rigid line between biological and psychological causation. Non-Western theories usually make no such distinction, accurately recognizing that impaired health often has intertwined physical, emotional, and social causes. The mind-body opposition is part of Western folk taxonomy, not of science.

Rather than seeking causes, non-Western practitioners often treat symptoms, and their aim is an immediate cure. Traditional curers have a high rate of success with health problems that our medical establishment classifies as psychosomatic (Foster and Anderson 1978) and dismisses as not needing treatment—despite the feelings of the patient. Non-Western systems tell us that patients should be treated as whole beings, to be treated with

whatever combination of procedures may prove beneficial.

SOCIAL WORK, BUSINESS, AND MEDIA ANTHROPOLOGY

A program of study linking anthropology and social work began at the University of Michigan in Ann Arbor in 1981. After obtaining master's degrees in both fields, students use anthropological techniques in their doctoral research, which might, for example, be an ethnographic investigation of a community-health center in an urban ethnic neighborhood. The main difference between this kind of research and traditional doctoral research in anthropology is that anthropology–social work dissertations use research to make recommendations about social policy.

Carol Taylor (1978) discusses the value of an "anthropologist-in-residence" in a complex organization such as a hospital. A free-ranging ethnographer can be a valuably perceptive oddball when information and decisions usually move through a rigid hierarchy. If allowed to converse freely with all levels of personnel, from orderly to chief surgeon, the anthropologist may acquire a unique perspective on organizational conditions and problems.

For many years anthropologists have used eth-

Solidarity-enhancers used by businesses include common meals, distinctive costumes or work uniforms, and joint participation in special company events and "rituals." In Japan, this sake distillery uses calisthenics to promote physical fitness and social solidarity among its employees.

nography to study businesses (Arensberg 1978), working directly with workers, managers, planners, and executives (Serrie, ed. 1986). For example, ethnographic research in an auto factory views workers, managers, and executives as different social categories participating in a common social system. Each group has characteristic attitudes, values, and behavior patterns that are transmitted through **microenculturation,** the process by which people learn particular roles in a limited social system. The free-ranging nature of ethnography takes the anthropologist from worker to executive. Each of these people is both an individual with a personal viewpoint and a cultural creature whose perspective is, to some extent, shared with other members of a group. Applied anthropologists have acted as "cultural brokers," translating managers' goals or workers' concerns to the other group.

Not just ethnography but the cross-cultural perspective is of interest to business, especially when other nations have higher productivity than we do (Ferraro 1990). The reasons for differential productivity are cultural, social, and economic. To find them, anthropologists must focus on key features in the organization of production. For example, Japanese auto workers earn less but have more secure jobs than do their American counterparts. The salary differential between worker and executive is greater in the United States. There is less of an economic basis for an adversary relationship between workers and management in Japan.

Furthermore, Japanese businesses use varied techniques to increase productivity (McGraw, ed. 1986). Profit sharing enhances company loyalty, but more subtle social and symbolic techniques also strengthen the social fiber. Solidarity enhancers vary from culture to culture but may include common meals, agreeable working conditions, distinctive costumes or work uniforms, and joint participation in special company events and "rituals."

Because cultural anthropologists have always studied values, attitudes, and opinions, anthropology links up with media research and advertising (Eiselein and Topper 1976; Kottak 1990). The media play a powerful integrative role in contemporary culture. The popularity, themes, and content of television, films, and literature reflect underlying culture. It is obvious to many anthropologists that advertising employs techniques borrowed from religion to sell products (Arens and Montague 1981; Kottak 1982). Similarly, contemporary religion—particularly televangelism—uses techniques borrowed from advertising to propagate religion. Anthropology's holistic perspective recognizes that the media both reflect and influence the beliefs, attitudes, opinions, and behavior of the natives at whom they are aimed.

CAREERS IN ANTHROPOLOGY

Many college students find anthropology interesting and consider majoring in it. However, their

Twenty percent of McDonald's fast-food sales are outside the United States. One area in which McDonald's is expanding successfully is Brazil, where 30 million to 40 million middle-class people, most living in densely packed cities, provide a concentrated market for a fast-food chain. In 1980 I visited Brazil after a seven-year absence. One manifestation of Brazil's growing participation in the world economy was the appearance of two McDonald's restaurants in Rio.

There wasn't much difference between Brazilian and American McDonald's. The restaurants looked alike. The menu was more or less the same, as was the taste of the quarter-pounders. I picked up an artifact, a white paper bag with yellow lettering, exactly like the take-out bags used in American McDonald's. An advertising device, it carried several messages about how Brazilians could bring McDonald's into their lives. However, it seemed to me that McDonald's Brazilian ad campaign was missing some important points about how fast-food should be marketed in a culture that values large, leisurely lunches.

The bag proclaimed, "You're going to enjoy the [McDonald's] difference," and listed several "favorite places where you can enjoy McDonald's products." This list confirmed that the marketing people were trying to adapt to Brazilian middle-class culture, but they were making some mistakes. "When you go out in the car with the kids" transferred the uniquely developed North American cultural combination of highways, affordable cars, and suburban living to the very different context of urban Brazil. A similar suggestion was "traveling to the country place." Even Brazilians who own country places can't find

McDonald's, still confined to the cities, on the road. The ad creator had apparently never attempted to drive up to a fast-food restaurant in a neighborhood with no parking spaces.

Several other suggestions pointed customers toward the beach, where *cariocas* (Rio natives) do spend much of their leisure time. One could eat McDonald's products "after a dip in the ocean," "at a picnic at the beach," or "watching the surfers." These suggestions ignored the Brazilian custom of consuming cold things, such as beer, soft drinks, ice cream, and ham and cheese sandwiches, at the beach. It's hard enough to keep sand off a Popsicle. Brazilians do not consider a hot, greasy hamburger proper beach food.

Also culturally dubious was the suggestion to eat McDonald's hamburgers "lunching at the office." Brazilians prefer their main meal at midday, often eating at a leisurely pace with business associates. Many firms serve ample lunches to their employees. Other workers take advantage of a two-hour lunch break to go home to eat with the spouse and children. Nor did it make much sense to suggest that children should eat hamburgers for lunch, since most kids attend school for half-day sessions and have lunch at home. Two other suggestions— "waiting for the bus" and "in the beauty parlor"—did describe popular aspects of daily life in a Brazilian city. However, these settings have not proved especially inviting to hamburgers or fish filets.

The homes of Brazilians who can afford McDonald's products have cooks and maids to do many of the things that fast-food restaurants do in the United States. The suggestion that McDonald's products be eaten

"while watching your favorite television program" is culturally appropriate, because Brazilians watch TV a lot. However, Brazil's consuming classes can ask the cook to make a snack when hunger strikes. Indeed, much televiewing occurs during the light dinner served when the husband gets home from the office.

Most appropriate to the Brazilian life style was the suggestion to enjoy McDonald's "on the cook's day off." Throughout Brazil, Sunday is that day. The Sunday pattern for middle-class families is a trip to the beach, liters of beer, a full midday meal around 3 P.M., and a light evening snack. McDonald's has found its niche in the Sunday evening meal, when families flock to the fast-food restaurant, and it is to this market that its advertising is now appropriately geared.

McDonald's is expanding rapidly in Brazilian cities, and in Brazil as in North America, teenage appetites are fueling the fast-food explosion. As McDonald's outlets appeared in urban neighborhoods, Brazilian teenagers used them for after-school snacks, while families had evening meals there. As an anthropologist could have predicted, the fast-food industry has not revolutionized Brazilian food and meal customs. Rather, McDonald's is succeeding because *it has adapted to preexisting Brazilian cultural patterns*.

The main contrast with North America is that the Brazilian evening meal is lighter. McDonald's now caters to the evening meal rather than to lunch. Once McDonald's realized that more money could be made by fitting in with, rather than trying to Americanize, Brazilian meal habits, it started aiming its advertising at that goal.

parents or friends sometimes discourage them by asking, "What kind of job are you going to get with an anthropology major?" The purpose of this section is to answer that question. You may want to show it to your parents and other skeptics if you decide to take additional anthropology courses or to major in the field.

The first step in answering "What do you do with an anthropology major?" is to consider the more general question "What do you do with any college major?" The answer is "Not much, without a good bit of effort, thought, and planning." A survey of recent graduates of the literary college of the University of Michigan showed that few had jobs that were clearly linked to their majors. Medicine, law, and many other professions require advanced degrees. Although many colleges offer bachelor's degrees in engineering, business, accounting, and social work, master's degrees are sometimes needed to get the best jobs in those fields.

A broad college education, and even a major in anthropology, can be an excellent basis for success in many fields. A recent survey of women executives showed that most had not majored in business but in the social sciences or humanities. Only after graduating did they study business, obtaining a master's degree in business administration. These executives felt that the breadth of their college educations had contributed to their business careers. Anthropology majors go on to medical, law, and business schools and find success in many professions that often have little explicit connection to anthropology.

A few years ago I helped give a workshop on "Working Abroad" at a meeting of the American Anthropological Association. The organizer and participants discussed their experiences using anthropology in their work outside the United States. All reported a common experience: none had ever been offered a job as an anthropologist per se. They all had convinced their eventual employers—most of whom knew little or nothing about anthropology—that they had particular skills that made them good choices for the work they sought. The employers didn't care where the skills came from as long as the applicants had them.

Anthropology's breadth provides knowledge and an outlook on the world that are useful in many kinds of work. For example, an anthropol-

ogy major combined with a master's degree in business is excellent preparation for work in international business and economic development. However, job seekers must convince employers that they have a special and valuable "skillset."

Getting an interesting job takes work. Prepare by reading job descriptions. Figure out the distinctive skillset your training gives you and then convince your future boss that you're the best-qualified applicant. Never say, "Hire me because I was an anthropology major." Instead, illustrate your qualifications. Be specific, in terms of the job description, about what you may know that the other applicants don't.

Many employers attended college many years ago, before anthropology courses were as common as they are now. Most people you will have to persuade to hire you have never heard of applied anthropology, although if told what it does, they might see its relevance to their own work with people. Ignorance of anthropology's content and scope is common among people over forty. Thus, your own enthusiasm and ability to "sell yourself" will be necessary if you are to get an interesting job.

This is also true for almost any field in which you may major. Despite tales of ten jobs for each applicant in certain fields, students tend to flock to areas in current demand. However, it doesn't take very long for faddish fields to get overcrowded. Not only do jobs get scarce, but if you choose a narrowly specialized field merely because it is popular now, you may be left with a specialty you never liked much anyway. It may also be too narrow to use as an entry point for a variety of careers or advanced degree programs.

From their work in kin-based societies, anthropologists know that personal connections are important to success. Even in the United States and Canada, personal relationships still count. A personal connection to someone in an organization is usually more helpful than an impersonal interview with an unknown personnel director.

Breadth is anthropology's hallmark. Anthropologists study people biologically, culturally, socially, and linguistically, in time and space, in developed and underdeveloped nations, in simple and complex settings. Most colleges have anthropology courses that compare cultures and others that focus on particular world areas, such as Latin

America, Asia, and Native North America. The knowledge of foreign areas acquired in such courses can be useful in many jobs. Anthropology's comparative outlook, its longstanding Third World focus, and its appreciation of diverse life styles combine to provide an excellent foundation for overseas employment.

Even for work in modern North America, the focus on culture is valuable. Every day we hear about cultural differences, about social problems whose solutions require a multicultural viewpoint—an ability to recognize and reconcile ethnic differences. Government, schools, and private firms constantly deal with people from different social classes, ethnic groups, and tribal backgrounds. Physicians, attorneys, social workers, police officers, judges, teachers, and students can all do a better job if they understand social differences in a part of the world that is one of the most ethnically diverse in history.

The cross-cultural perspective is one reason why some North American businesses have become interested in anthropology. Business practices in other cultures can suggest techniques that improve efficiency here. A trend in many business schools is to recognize that organizations include **microcultures**—several restricted social circles and traditions of particular social groups within a complex organization. (In a plant these might involve assembly-line workers, union representatives, professionals, middle managers, engineers, and top management.) Microcultures have different viewpoints, goals, and perceptions. Along with organizational psychologists, anthropologists have worked to increase communication between levels and microcultures. Often there is a need to reduce social distinctions and enhance company loyalty in order to increase worker productivity and profits. An ethnographic focus on behavior in the daily social setting can help locate problems that plague American businesses, which tend to be overly hierarchical.

Attention to the social dimension of business can only gain importance as more and more executives recognize that proper human relations are as important as economic forecasts are in maximizing productivity. Contemporary applied anthropologists design plans for deploying employees better and increasing job satisfaction. This is part of "the new humanism," which is of growing importance as a management strategy. A noted proponent of this approach, James O'Toole, a management professor in southern California and editor of *New Management* magazine, has a Ph.D. in anthropology from Oxford.

Anthropologists also work to help natives threatened by external systems. As highways and power-supply systems cross tribal boundaries, the "modern" world comes into conflict with historic land claims and traditions. An anthropological study is often considered necessary before permission is granted to extend a public system across native lands.

Because dams, reservoirs, and other public works may threaten archeological sites, fields such as salvage archeology and cultural resource management have developed. Government agencies, engineering firms, and construction companies now have jobs for people with an anthropological background because of federal legislation to protect historic and prehistoric sites.

Knowledge about the traditions and beliefs of subgroups within a nation is important in planning and carrying out programs that affect those subgroups. Attention to social background and cultural categories helps ensure the welfare of affected ethnic groups, communities, and neighborhoods. Experience in planned social change—whether community organization in North America or economic development overseas—shows that a proper social study should be done before a project begins. When local people want the change and it fits their life style and traditions, it will be more successful, beneficial, and cost-effective. There will be not only a more humane but a more economical solution to a real social problem.

Some agencies working overseas place particular value on anthropological training. Others seek employees with certain skills without caring much about specific academic backgrounds. Among the government agencies that hire anthropologists are **USAID** (the United States Agency for International Development) and **USDA** (the United States Department of Agriculture). These organizations hire anthropologists both full-time and as short-term consultants.

Several consulting firms with "social experts" are located near Washington, D.C. Although these firms have regular staffs, they also use outside experts for particular projects. For instance, I was once offered a part-time consultancy requiring fluency in French and Portuguese and research experience among rice cultivators and fishermen. My work among fishermen in Brazil and rice farmers in Madagascar made me one of a limited number of people qualified to do the social planning for a group of development projects in two African nations. The **World Bank** (the International Bank for Reconstruction and Development, or **IBRD**), along with USAID, USDA, and other such organizations, often hires anthropologists for this type of work abroad.

Private voluntary organizations working overseas offer other opportunities. These **PVO**s include Care, Save the Children, Catholic Relief Services, Foster Parents Plan International, and Oxfam (a hunger relief organization operating out of Boston and Oxford). Some of these groups employ anthropologists full-time. Anthropologists, including anthropology majors seeking overseas employment, should consult the book *Who Owns Whom in North America* (1984), which lists organizations with international divisions.

Anthropologists apply their expertise in surprisingly diverse areas. They negotiate business deals, suggest organizational changes, and testify as expert witnesses. Anthropologists have also worked for pharmaceutical firms interested in potential conflicts between traditional and Western medicine and in culturally appropriate marketing of their products in new settings.

These are some of the opportunities potentially available to college graduates with a background in the broadest of the disciplines (Bernard and Sibley 1975; American Anthropological Association 1982). Some jobs, of course, require a doctorate. Others, however, are possibilities for someone who has taken several anthropology or foreign-area courses and can "sell" himself or herself as the best-prepared candidate for a particular job. No matter what the major, the best jobs come through preparation, perseverance, and creativity.

People with anthropology backgrounds are doing well in many fields. Furthermore, even if the job has little or nothing to do with anthropology in a formal or obvious sense, anthropology is always useful when we work with fellow human beings. For most of us, this means every day of our lives.

SUMMARY

Anthropologists have different opinions about the relationship between scientific research and its application. In the ivory tower view, anthropologists should teach, do independent research, and publish but avoid applications and political issues. In the schizoid view, anthropologists may work for agencies; however, their role is not to set but to carry out policies or to investigate reasons for the acceptance or rejection of changes. Advocates believe that anthropologists, as experts on social life and cultural diversity, should seek to influence policy and should participate only in projects they approve.

In the applied anthropology of earlier periods, anthropologists supported colonialism by working on projects aimed at economic and cultural change. Colonial anthropologists faced, and modern applied anthropologists may still face, problems posed by their inability to set or influence policy and the difficulty of criticizing programs in which they have participated. Anthropology's professional organizations have addressed these problems with codes of ethics and ethics committees.

The American Anthropological Association (AAA) has issued a statement of professional conduct that lays out the responsibilities of anthropologists to informants, universities, colleagues, students, sponsors, and governments. The AAA has also committed itself to taking action against breaches of professional ethics.

Modern applied anthropology keeps ethical problems and guidelines in mind. Its practitioners attempt to help the people anthropologists have traditionally studied as formerly isolated communities are increasingly confronted with worldwide currents of economic and social change. Applied anthropology draws its practitioners from biological, archeological, linguistic, and cultural anthropology.

Ethnography has become one of applied anthropology's most valuable research tools, along with the comparative, cross-cultural perspective. Holism allows applied anthropologists to perceive the biological, social, cultural, and linguistic dimensions of policy issues. A systemic perspective helps anthropologists recognize that all changes have multiple consequences, some unintended.

Applied anthropology has many domains. Anthropology and education researchers work in classrooms, homes, neighborhoods, and other settings relevant to education. Some of their research leads to policy recommendations. Courses in cultural anthropology and sociolinguistics are making teachers more aware of how linguistic and ethnic differences should be handled in the classroom.

As complex societies expand, anthropologists increasingly study such societies and the issues involved in their expansion. Urban anthropology includes the study of life in cities and the process of urbanization that affects people throughout the world. The United States has become a popular arena for urban anthropological research on topics such as ethnicity, poverty, class, and subcultural variation.

Rural social relations are personal and face to face, but impersonality characterizes many aspects of life in cities. Although urban and rural are different social systems, there is cultural diffusion from one to the other. Rural and tribal social forms affect adjustment to the city. For example, principles of tribal organization, including descent, provide migrants to African cities with adaptive mechanisms. Urban associations have also been important in organizing crime among segments of certain ethnic groups in the United States. Crime has been linked to poverty and powerlessness rather than to the subcultural norms of ethnic groups.

Medical anthropology unites biological and cultural anthropologists in the cross-cultural study of health problems and conditions, disease, disease theories, and health-care systems. Characteristic diseases reflect diet, population density, economy, and social complexity. The three main native theories of illness are personalistic, naturalistic, and emotionalistic. Personalistic causes refer to such agents as witches and sorcerers. In this context, shamans can be effective curers.

Western medicine is not the same as scientific medicine. The latter has made many advances, particularly in bacterial diseases and surgery. However, non-Western treatment of psychosomatic illness is often more effective, because it occurs in a personal, community-support context with no rigid distinction drawn between mind and body.

Ethnography has also proved useful in studying businesses, factories, and hospitals. Free-ranging anthropologists translate messages and viewpoints between microcultures and hierarchical levels in complex organizations. Research on work organization in other countries can enlighten North American businesses. Anthropologists also study the mass media, showing their reflection of cultural themes and their role in enculturating and in promoting social change.

A broad college education, including anthropology and foreign-area courses, offers excellent preparation for many fields. Anthropology's comparative outlook, longstanding Third World focus, and cultural relativism provide an excellent basis for overseas employment. Among the agencies that hire anthropologists are USAID, USDA, independent consulting firms, the World Bank, and such private voluntary organizations as Care, Save the Children, Catholic Relief Services, Foster Parents Plan International, and Oxfam.

Even for work in North America, a focus on culture is valuable. Anthropological training is useful in dealing with issues that reflect cultural contrasts and problems whose solutions require an ability to recognize and reconcile social or ethnic differences. The cross-cultural perspective and the focus on daily social life of anthropologists help locate problems that plague American businesses, which tend to be too hierarchical. Anthropologists have worked for and with natives threatened by external systems. Anthropology majors attend medical, law, and business schools and succeed in many fields, some of which have little explicit connection with anthropology.

Experience with social-change programs, whether community organization in North America or economic development abroad, offers a common lesson. If local people want the change and it fits their life style and traditions, the change will be more successful, beneficial, and cost-effective.

GLOSSARY

advocacy: View that because anthropologists are experts on human problems and social change, they should make and influence policies affecting people.

anthropology and education: Anthropological research in classrooms, homes, and neighborhoods, viewing students as total cultural creatures whose enculturation and attitudes toward education belong to a larger context that includes family, peers, and society.

applied anthropology: Use of anthropological findings, concepts, data, and methods to identify and solve social problems.

bilharziasis: See *schistosomiasis*.

curer: Specialized role acquired through a culturally appropriate process of selection, training, certification, and acquisition of a professional image; the curer is consulted by patients, who believe in his or her special powers, and receives some form of special consideration; a cultural universal.

emotionalistic disease theories: Theories that assume that illness is caused by intense emotional experiences.

health-care systems: Beliefs, customs, and specialists concerned with ensuring health and preventing and curing illness; a cultural universal.

IBRD: See *World Bank*.

ivory tower view: View that anthropologists should avoid practical matters and concentrate on research, publication, and teaching.

medical anthropology: Unites biological and cultural anthropologists in the study of disease, health problems, health-care systems, and theories about illness in different cultures and ethnic groups.

microculture: Restricted traditions of particular social groups within a complex organization. See *microenculturation.*

microenculturation: The process by which people learn particular roles in a limited social system; creates microcultures.

naturalistic disease theories: Includes scientific medicine; theories that explain illness in impersonal systemic terms.

personalistic disease theories: Theories that attribute illness to sorcerers, witches, ghosts, or ancestral spirits.

PVOs: Private voluntary organizations, such as Care, Save the Children, Catholic Relief Services, Foster Parents Plan International, and Oxfam.

salvage archeology: Branch of applied archeology aimed at preserving sites threatened by dams, highways, and other projects.

schistosomiasis: Disease caused by liver flukes transmitted by snails inhabiting ponds, lakes, and waterways, often created by irrigation projects.

schizoid view: View that anthropologists can collect facts for development agencies but should neither make nor criticize policy because personal value judgments should be kept strictly separate from scientific investigation.

scientific medicine: As distinguished from Western medicine, a health-care system based on scientific knowledge and procedures, encompassing such fields as pathology, microbiology, biochemistry, surgery, diagnostic technology, and applications.

systemic perspective: View that changes have multiple consequences, some unforeseen.

USAID: The United States Agency for International Development.

USDA: The United States Department of Agriculture.

World Bank: Also called the International Bank for Reconstruction and Development (IBRD); a major international lending organization that funds development projects.

STUDY QUESTIONS

1. What are the three viewpoints on anthropology's role in practical affairs?
2. Which of these viewpoints do you prefer, and why?
3. What is applied anthropology?
4. What was the relationship between the old applied anthropology and colonialism? What's different about modern applied anthropology?
5. What are Batalla's criticisms of applied anthropology?
6. How do anthropologists deal with the matter of professional ethics?
7. What is the ethnographic method? What is its relevance for modern society, contemporary problems, and applied anthropology?
8. Why have many anthropologists turned from academic to applied work?
9. What is educational anthropology, and what are its applications?
10. What is urban anthropology, and what are its applications?
11. What causes crime? Why is crime a creation of the state?
12. What is medical anthropology, and what are its applications?
13. How can anthropology be relevant to business?
14. How can anthropology be relevant to the study of the media?
15. What is the relevance of anthropological training to employment opportunities abroad?
16. How has federal legislation concerning historic and prehistoric sites affected anthropologists?
17. What governmental, international, and private organizations concern themselves with socioeconomic change abroad?

SUGGESTED ADDITIONAL READING

APPELL, G. N.
  1978 *Ethical Dilemmas in Anthropological Inquiry: A Case Book.* Waltham, MA: Crossroads Press. Ninety-one cases illustrating ten broad categories of ethical problems that may confront anthropologists.
ARENS, W., AND S. P. MONTAGUE, EDS.
  1981 *The American Dimension: Cultural Myths and*

Social Realities, 2nd ed. Sherman Oaks, CA: Alfred. Anthropologists analyze movies, television, commercials, fast food, and graffiti.

DOUGLAS, M., AND A. WILDAVSKY
1982 *Risk and Culture: An Essay on the Selection of Technological and Environmental Dangers.* Berkeley: University of California Press. Controversial analysis and comparison of ideologies concerning pollution in tribal and industrial societies.

EDDY, E. M., AND W. L. PARTRIDGE, EDS.
1978 *Applied Anthropology in America.* New York: Columbia University Press. Historical review of applications of anthropological knowledge in the United States.

FOSTER, G. M., AND B. G. ANDERSON
1978 *Medical Anthropology.* New York: Wiley. Very good, thorough introduction to this field.

GOLDSCHMIDT, W., ED.
1979 *The Uses of Anthropology.* Washington, DC: American Anthropological Association. Diverse applications of anthropology are described in several articles.

HILL, C. E., ED.
1986 *Current Health Policy Issues and Alternatives: An Applied Social Science Perspective.* Southern Anthropological Society Proceedings. Athens: University of Georgia Press. Ten articles, including anthropological case studies of health-care policy in the United States and abroad.

HUMAN ORGANIZATION
The quarterly journal of the Society for Applied Anthropology. An excellent source for articles on applied anthropology and development.

MCGRAW, T. K., ED.
1986 *America versus Japan.* Boston: Harvard Business School Press. A collection of articles dealing with Japanese and American business interactions.

MULLINGS, L., ED.
1987 *Cities of the United States: Studies in Urban Anthropology.* New York: Columbia University Press. Includes several case studies and argues for more applied and advocacy research in American cities.

SERRIE, H., ED.
1986 *Anthropology and International Business.* Studies in Third World Societies, No. 28. Williamsburg, VA: Department of Anthropology, College of William and Mary.

Introduction to business anthropology—national and international.

SPINDLER, G., ED.
1982 *Doing the Ethnography of Schooling: Educational Anthropology in Action.* New York: Holt, Rinehart & Winston. Recent efforts by anthropologists to throw light on the sources of inequality and other problems found in schools.

VAN WILLINGEN, J.
1986 *Applied Anthropology: An Introduction.* South Hadley, MA: Bergin and Garvey. Excellent review of the growth of applied anthropology and its links to general anthropology.
1987 *Becoming a Practicing Anthropologist: A Guide to Careers and Training Programs in Applied Anthropology.* NAPA Bulletin 3. Washington, DC: American Anthropological Association/ National Association for the Practice of Anthropology. Useful brief guide for students contemplating a career in applied anthropology.

WAX, M. L., AND J. CASSELL, EDS.
1979 *Federal Regulations: Ethical Issues and Social Research.* Boulder, CO: Westview Press. Papers from a symposium of the American Association for the Advancement of Science on ethical considerations, privacy, and anthropological research, particularly in the United States.

WEAVER, T., GEN. ED.
1973 *To See Ourselves: Anthropology and Modern Social Issues.* Glenview, IL: Scott, Foresman. Timely anthology of articles on the social responsibility of the anthropologist, anthropology and the Third World, race and racism, poverty and culture, education, violence, environment, intervention, and anthropology in the contemporary United States.

WOLCOTT, H. F.
1977 *Teachers versus Technocrats: An Educational Innovation in Anthropological Perspective.* Eugene: Center for Educational Policy and Management, University of Oregon. Well-done ethnographic study of the work of a group of educational developers.

WULFF, R. M., AND S. J. FISKE, EDS.
1987 *Anthropological Praxis: Translating Knowledge into Action.* Boulder, CO: Westview Press. Recent cases illustrating the use of anthropology in solving human problems in various areas.

CHAPTER 18

SOCIAL CHANGE AND DEVELOPMENT

In previous chapters we have considered many aspects of social change, including the political and economic effects of colonialism and the world system. The bands and tribes that survive today live in nation-states. Most indigenous peoples have been drawn at least partially into the world capitalist economy, which is based on private ownership of resources and huge contrasts in wealth. Contact with "civilized" outsiders has led to economic dependency and loss of political autonomy. Governments rarely tolerate politically sovereign tribes within their national boundaries (Bodley 1988).

Since the 1920s anthropologists have been investigating changes arising from contact between industrial and nonindustrial societies. Studies of "social change" and "acculturation" are abundant. British and American ethnographers, respectively, have used these terms to describe the same process.

ACCULTURATION

Acculturation has been defined as including

> those phenomena which result when groups of individuals come into continuous firsthand contact, with subsequent changes in the original cultural patterns of either or both groups. (Redfield, Linton, and Herskovits 1936, p. 149)

This definition is broad enough to refer to any case in which people from different cultures meet and change their customs as a result. One precolonial example would be the mutual influences of Mbuti "pygmy" culture and that of horticultural villagers in the forests of Zaire.

History includes thousands of cases of acculturation as different groups have come into contact. Acculturation differs from *diffusion,* or cultural borrowing, which can occur without firsthand contact. For example, most Americans who eat hot dogs ("frankfurters") have never been to Frankfurt, nor have most American Honda owners or sushi eaters ever visited Japan.

Although *acculturation* can apply to many cases of cultural contact and change, the term most often describes the influence of Western expansion on native cultures. Thus natives who wear store-bought clothes, learn Indo-European languages, and otherwise adopt Western customs are called acculturated.

Syncretisms are cultural blends or mixtures that emerge from acculturation, particularly under colonialism. One example is the blend of African, Native American, and Roman Catholic saints and deities in Caribbean vodun, or "voodoo," cults. This blend is also present in *candomblé,* an "Afro-Brazilian" cult.

Acculturation, including syncretisms, is a broad area of study. Because its focus is interethnic re-

Exemplifying cultural syncretism is the blend of African, Native American, and Roman Catholic saints and deities in Caribbean vodun or "voodoo" cults and in candomblé, *an "Afro-Brazilian" cult (shown here).*

HOW TV LIBERATED SONIA

My most recent research project was a study of the social impact of television in Brazil, which has the world's most watched commercial network (TV Globo). Its most popular programs are *telenovelas,* locally made serials that are similar to American soap operas. The Globo network transmits three *telenovelas* each night (except Sunday) to some 60 million to 80 million viewers throughout the nation.

It's hard for modern Americans to perceive the full range of TV's social impact, because we so rarely encounter anyone who hasn't been raised in the daily presence of television. Here ethnographic research in another culture can contribute significantly to our understanding.

In using portraits of other cultural patterns to reflect self-critically on our own ways, anthropology disrupts common sense and makes us reexamine our taken-for-granted assumptions. (Marcus and Fisher 1986, p. 1)

Most Americans will never have a chance to observe, through a before-and-after comparison of individual cases, the dramatic role that television can play in (1) stimulating curiosity and a thirst for knowledge and (2) increasing skills in social navigation and communication with outsiders. To illustrate these effects, I introduce Sonia, a woman who lives in Arembepe, Brazil.

In July 1984, when I was testing a questionnaire for my TV research project, I interviewed my next-door neighbor, Sonia, who at that time was a media-deprived person in her midtwenties. Sonia was barely literate and had spent a lifetime without TV. She did have a radio, with which she listened mostly to music. Sonia had moved to Arembepe with her husband, a caretaker for a summer home, in 1981. They came from a remote village that was much more isolated from urban life than is Arembepe.

Although an Arembepe resident

for three years, Sonia lived in substantial isolation from the local social system. She dared visit just one of her neighbors and even let her husband do most of the shopping. Sonia found interactions with strangers, including most Arembepeiros, threatening. She and her husband didn't let their three young sons play in the street even during the day, because they were afraid of problems with the neighbors.

Sonia had trouble talking to strangers. As I interviewed her, I found myself feeling guiltier and guiltier for "inflicting" my questions. Sonia responded reluctantly, tears occasionally streaking her face. She said she had no friends and lamented that she missed her mother, the most important person in her life—more important than her husband and her sons, she said.

Sonia longed for a home of her own. She would build one (and feed her family better) if she won the lottery. Sonia knew almost nothing

lations, it is relevant to many of the changes taking place in the modern world. Local people are increasingly being drawn into larger systems—and changing as a result. Sources of exposure to external institutions and currents of social change include the mass media, migration, and improved transportation.

Cargo Cults

There is often a "shock phase" (Bodley 1988) when routine contact is established between indigenous cultures and representatives of a national society or the world system. This may lead to the tribe's cultural collapse (*ethnocide*) or physical extinction (*genocide*). There may be civil repression backed by military force. Unregulated traders and settlers may exploit the native people. The shock phase

may include increased mortality, disruption of subsistence activities, kin-group dispersion, breakdown of social support systems, emergence of new religious movements, or armed tribal resistance (Bodley 1988).

Religion can be a powerful force in social change. Many religious movements have arisen in response to the spread of colonialism, European domination, and the world capitalist economy. Often such movements emerge from acculturation, particularly when natives come into sustained contact with citizens of industrial societies but are denied their wealth, technology, and living standards. Some of these movements attempt to explain European domination and wealth and achieve similar success magically by mimicking European behavior and manipulating symbols of the desired life style.

about Rio or São Paulo and found it hard to imagine life in those places. My impression was that Sonia was a terrible informant, unaccustomed to and uninterested in talking with strangers. The interview was like pulling teeth, an unpleasant experience for me and a terrifying one for her.

No doubt some of Sonia's behavior reflected her individual personality, gender, and class position. A member of the lower working class, she had little personal contact with elites, particularly men. Her life experience provided no clue as to why someone like me would want to talk to her for more than a minute—particularly to elicit her opinions. Whenever I encountered her that year, Sonia displayed the obsequious, eye-averting, voice-lowering, limp-handed demeanor that is often adopted by poor rural Bahians—especially women—when they deal with perceived social superiors. For Sonia that meant almost everyone she met.

Nevertheless, there is also reason to conclude that some of Sonia's fearful and obsequious behavior reflected a lack of media exposure. In July 1985, a year after the disastrous interview, I returned to Arembepe to do formal interviewing. In the meantime Sonia's family had acquired a black-and-white TV set, which they watched constantly.

I soon noticed a change in Sonia's demeanor. She was no longer quite the shy, quiet person she had been in 1984. She now visited her neighbors, conversed with my wife, usually looked me in the eye when we talked, sang as she worked, and even made a few jokes. She proved to be an average respondent when I formally interviewed her again.

These changes were obvious to my wife and me. However, for Sonia and the people who saw her every day, she had changed gradually, unspectacularly, and without any obvious relationship to television. Although Sonia could say that she was "happier" in 1985 and

that she felt more at home in Arembepe, she couldn't conclude that "television had changed her life." But it had.

From my research in Brazil I have no doubt that the changes in demeanor and social behavior that took place in Sonia are effects of televiewing. Television familiarizes provincial people with urban-national norms. It makes them less reluctant and less uncertain in dealing with strangers, including representatives of higher social classes. Many Americans make the erroneous "commonsense" assumption that television isolates people. Cross-cultural evidence says otherwise. Far from cutting Sonia off from society, television increased her social skills and connectedness.

Source: Adapted from *Prime-Time Society: An Anthropological Analysis of Television and Culture* by Conrad Phillip Kottak. © 1990 by Wadsworth, Inc. Used by permission of the publisher.

Some of the best-known examples of these movements are the **cargo cults** of Melanesia. They take their name from their focus on cargo—European goods of the sort natives have seen unloaded from the cargo holds of ships and airplanes. Cargo cults often develop around charismatic prophets. **Charisma** (Weber 1947) is a quality that sets certain people apart from others. Charismatic figures have unusual qualities and talents that often are perceived as superhuman or supernatural powers.

In an early cargo cult, members believed that the spirits of the dead would arrive in a ship. They would bring manufactured goods for the natives and would kill all the whites. More recent cults replaced ships with airplanes (Worsley 1959/1985). Many cults have used elements of European culture as sacred objects. The rationale is that Europeans use these objects, have wealth, and there-

fore must know the "secret of cargo." By mimicking how Europeans use or treat objects, natives hope also to come upon the secret knowledge needed to gain cargo.

For example, having observed Europeans' reverent treatment of flags and flagpoles, the members of one cult began to worship flagpoles. They believed the flagpoles were sacred towers capable of transmitting messages between the living and the dead. Other natives constructed airstrips to entice planes bearing canned goods, portable radios, clothing, wristwatches, and motorcycles. Near the airstrips they built effigies of towers and airplanes and tin-can radios. They talked into the cans in a magical attempt to establish radio contact with the gods.

Some cargo cult prophets proclaimed that success would come through a reversal of European

Many religious movements, including the Melanesian (New Hebrides) cargo cult shown here, have arisen in response to the spread of colonialism, European domination, and the world capitalist economy. Cult members may try to attract wealth (cargo) by mimicking European behavior and manipulating symbols of the desired life-style.

domination and native subjugation. The day was near, they preached, when natives, aided by God, Jesus, or native ancestors, would turn the tables. Native skins would turn white, and those of Europeans would turn brown; Europeans would die or be killed.

Cargo cults are syncretic, blending Christian doctrine with aboriginal beliefs. Melanesian myths told of ancestors shedding their skins and changing into powerful beings and of dead people returning to life. Christian missionaries, who had been in Melanesia since the late nineteenth century, also spoke of resurrection. Cult members believed that masters would become slaves and slaves would become masters; the white would turn brown, and the brown would turn white. They had heeded well the Christian promise that the meek will inherit the earth.

Cargo cults adapted native social structure and ideology to the acculturative environment created by contact with Europeans (Belshaw 1972; Harris 1974; Lawrence and Worsley 1970). Native beliefs fused with Christian millennarian doctrines in cult ideology. The cults' preoccupation with cargo is also related to traditional Melanesian big-man systems (Chapter 7). Previously we saw that a Melanesian big man had to be generous. People worked for the big man, helping him amass wealth, but eventually the big man had to give a huge feast in which all that wealth would be given away. Big men who weren't generous were subject to social censure, including murder.

Because of their experience with big-man systems, Melanesians believed that all wealthy people eventually had to give their wealth away. For decades they had attended Christian missions and worked on plantations. All the while they expected Europeans to return the fruits of their labor as their own big men did. When the Europeans refused to distribute the wealth or even to let natives know the secret of its production and distribution, cargo cults developed.

Like arrogant big men, Europeans would be leveled, by death if necessary. However, natives lacked the physical means of doing what their cultural traditions said they should do. Thwarted by well-armed colonial forces, natives resorted to magical leveling. They called on supernatural beings to intercede, to kill or otherwise deflate the European big men and redistribute their wealth.

The missionaries had taught that salvation (which natives interpreted to mean wealth or cargo) comes through hard work. However, Melanesians could plainly see that they, not the Europeans, were the ones doing the hard work on plantations and docks. They had to reject the explanation that hard work was the key. The only possible explanation for European material wealth was supernatural: Europeans, not natives, knew the magical secret of cargo.

Cargo cults are religious responses to an acculturative situation linked to the expansion of the world capitalist economy. However, this religious mobilization has often had political and economic results. Cult participation gave Melanesians a basis for common interests and activities and thus helped pave the way for political parties and economic interest organizations. Previously separated by geography, language, and customs, Melanesians started forming larger groups as members of the same cults and followers of the same prophets. Cargo cults eventually helped the Melanesians achieve nationhood. Therefore, although these cults began as magical solutions, they eventually helped Melanesians respond, in political terms that Europeans could understand, to their exploited condition.

Tribal Resistance and Cultural Survival

Cargo cults thus paved the way for political action through which indigenous peoples could attempt to regain their autonomy. Such nativistic movements express tribal resentment against colonialism, exploitation, and domination. However, the origins and leadership of tribal independence movements can be secular as well as religious. Areas of Africa, the Philippines, India, North America, Central America, Indonesia, and Australia have all witnessed forms of collective action for tribal autonomy. Tribal resistance has forced changes in government integration policies aimed at drawing tribes into the nation-state (often as underprivileged ethnic minorities). Some nations now admit the possibility of self-determination by tribal peoples. There is a growing recognition that native peoples have been denied basic rights to their traditional lands and cultural practices.

Ever since colonialism began, authorities in international law have argued that indigenous peoples have rights to political sovereignty and ancestral lands. Only conquest or treaty can end those rights. The United Nations is drafting a new declaration of basic human rights for indigenous peoples in the modern world (Bodley 1988), and many organizations have emerged to support native populations threatened by national development programs. One of the most prominent is Cultural Survival, founded in 1972 by Harvard anthropologist David Maybury-Lewis. Its goal is

to help native peoples maintain themselves as successful ethnic minorities within nation-states. There have also been national and international conferences of indigenous peoples, and the World Council of Indigenous Peoples was organized in 1975 (Bodley 1988).

However, although there is room for some optimism, states have not stopped assaulting tribes within their boundaries. Bodley (1988, p. 5) notes that "any degree of self-determination, particularly where control over valuable resources may be involved, is clearly an uphill struggle for indigenous peoples. . . . " Indigenous peoples have little real political or economic power, and they are likely to be at a distinct disadvantage in any struggle with the state for recognition of their rights. As I write this, I have just learned of a decree by the former Brazilian president restricting the rights of the Yanomami Indians to control their ancestral lands. The area reserved for the Yanomami has been cut, and miners and ranchers have won the right to travel in and exploit part of Yanomami territory. The sole restriction on Brazilian nationals in these lands (which the Indians still use) is that they may not bring in or use rifles. As one who knows that laws are rarely enforced in remote areas of Brazil, I doubt that this ban will be respected. The situation continues to change, but I fear that Yanomami genocide will intensify.

DEVELOPMENT

Change doesn't just happen; often it is planned. A strong current of thought during the early Industrial Revolution viewed industrialization as a beneficial process of organic development and progress. Still assuming that industrialization increases production and income, contemporary economists seek to create in Third World ("developing") countries a process like the one that first occurred spontaneously in eighteenth-century Great Britain.

Development plans usually are guided by some kind of **intervention philosophy,** an ideological justification for outsiders to guide native peoples in specific directions. Bodley (1988) argues that the basic belief behind intervention—whether by missionaries, governments, or modern development planners—has been the same for more than 100 years. This belief is that industrialization, modernization, westernization, and individualism are desirable evolutionary advances and that development schemes that promote them will bring long-term benefits to natives. In a more extreme form, intervention philosophy may contrast the assumed wisdom of enlightened planners with the conservatism, ignorance, or "obsolescence" of "inferior" natives.

Anthropologists dispute these views. We know that for thousands of years bands and tribes have done "a reasonable job of taking care of themselves" (Bodley 1988, p. 93) and—given their low energy adaptations—of managing their resources better than we manage our own. Many of the most severe problems that Third World people face today are due to their position within nation-states and their increasing dependence on the world cash economy.

Many Third World governments are reluctant to tamper with existing socioeconomic conditions in

Conflicts arise over resources on tribal lands as governments seek to wrest as much wealth as possible from their national territory. This goal helps explain the worldwide intrusion on indigenous peoples and their local ecosystems of highway construction, mining, hydroelectric projects, lumbering, and agribusiness. This highway will link Liberia and Sierra Leone.

their countries (Manners 1956/1973). The attempt to bring the "green revolution" to Java that is analyzed below illustrates this situation. Often, if natives are reluctant to change, it isn't because they have unduly conservative attitudes but because powerful interest groups oppose reform. Resistance by elites to land reform is a fact of life throughout the Third World. Millions of people in underdeveloped nations have learned from bitter experience that if they increase their incomes, their taxes and rents also rise.

Communities may be wary of innovation for many reasons. One anthropological study of a multimillion-dollar development project in Madagascar uncovered several reasons for its failure. The planners (all nonanthropologists) anticipated none of the problems that emerged. The project was aimed at draining and irrigating a large plain to increase rice production. The goal was to raise production through the use of machinery and double cropping—growing two crops annually on the same plot. However, the planners disregarded several things, including the unavailability of spare parts and fuel for the new machines. The designers also ignored the fact, well known to anthropologists, that cross-culturally, intensive cultivation is associated with dense populations. If there are no machines to do the work, there have to be people around to do it. However, population densities in the project area (fifteen per square kilometer) were much too low to support intensive cultivation without modern machinery.

The planners should have known that labor and machinery for the project were unavailable. Furthermore, many local people were understandably hostile toward the project because it gave their ancestral land away to outsiders. (Unfortunately, this is a common occurrence in development projects.) Many of the land-grant recipients were members of regional and national elites who used their influence to get fields that were intended for poor farmers. The project also suffered from technical problems. The foreign firm hired to dig the irrigation canals dug them lower than the land they had to irrigate, and so the water couldn't flow up into the fields.

Some of the most severe conflicts between governments and natives arise over exploitation by outside interests of resources on tribal lands. Driven by deficits and debts, governments seek to wrest as much wealth as possible from the national territory. This goal helps explain the worldwide intrusion on indigenous peoples and their local ecosystems by highway construction, mining, hydroelectric projects, lumbering, agribusiness, and planned colonization (Bodley 1988).

Collective resistance is sometimes an effective response. For example, tribes in Africa's Sudan and in the Philippines have used armed resistance to halt enormous development projects that would have destroyed traditional cultures, economies, and ecosystems. In 1974 the Sudanese government started building the Jonglei canal, which would have traversed the homelands of Nilotic peoples in the southern Sudan, including the Nuer and the Dinka. Construction was halted in 1984 after armed attacks on army units and construction camps. Calling themselves the Sudanese People's Liberation Army, the resisters were apparently disaffected Nilotes who considered the canal an invasion from the Muslim north. With a planned length of 360 kilometers (225 miles), the Jonglei canal was one of the world's most ambitious engineering projects. Its purpose was to bypass the great bend in the Nile in order to reduce ''water loss'' and to channel water northward for export crops such as cotton.

The native peoples resisted this project because the canal would have destroyed traditional cattle pastures, which depend on seasonal flooding. The national government had tried to justify the project with the claim that half the annual flood water was lost to evaporation and plants. However, the government ignored the fact that the Nuer, the Dinka, and their herds depended on that water and the pasture and plants it generated. An explicit government goal in building the canal was to increase tribalists' involvement with the national economy. The government cared little about the Nuer and Dinka cattle because they were ''merely'' the basis of a subsistence economy. Unlike the cash crops that the canal would have irrigated, cattle did not enter the marketplace (Lako 1988).

Something similar happened to the Igorots, a mountain people of Luzon in the Philippines. A giant hydroelectric project promoted by the Marcos government would have devastated the terraced irrigation-based native economy (Drucker 1988). Had Igorot political action and armed re-

sistance not stopped the project, the dams would have destroyed a highly productive, generations-old engineering system of water and soil management that supported 90,000 local people.

Development Anthropology

Studying people directly at the local level, ethnographers have a unique view of how national and international planning and aid affect the intended ''beneficiaries.'' Even when there is no threat of ethnocide or ecocide, local-level research often reveals inadequacies in the measures that economists and political scientists use to assess development and a nation's economic health. For example, per capita income and gross national product don't measure the distribution of wealth. These indices may show an increase in wealth, but because the first is an average and the second is a total, they may rise as the rich get richer and the poor get poorer.

In Chapter 17 we saw that applied anthropology uses anthropological findings, concepts, and methods to accomplish desired ends. The advocacy position states that anthropologists—as experts on human problems, social change, and cultural values—should make policy affecting people. In this view, proper roles for development anthropologists include (1) identifying needs for change that local people perceive, (2) designing socially appropriate intervention strategies, and (3) protecting local people from harmful development schemes.

Today, many government agencies, international organizations, and private foundations encourage attention to local-level social factors and the cultural dimension of development. Anthropological expertise is important because technical or social problems can doom projects to failure. A study of fifty development projects (Lance and McKenna 1975) judged only twenty-one to be successes. Social and cultural incompatibilities had doomed most of the failed projects. Hundreds of millions of dollars of development funds could have produced greater human benefits if anthropologists had helped plan, supervise, and evaluate the projects. Planners who are familiar with the language and customs of a country can make more accurate forecasts about project success than can those who are not. Accordingly, anthropologists increasingly work in organizations that promote, manage, and assess programs that influence human life in the United States and abroad.

However, ethical dilemmas often confront applied anthropologists. Our respect for cultural diversity is often offended because efforts to extend industry and technology may entail profound cultural changes. Foreign aid doesn't usually go where need and suffering are greatest. Rather, it is spent on political, economic, and strategic priorities as national leaders and powerful interest groups perceive them. Planner's interests don't always coincide with the best interests of the local people. According to Bodley (1988), although the stated aim of most development schemes is to improve the quality of life, the actual tendency of development is to lower living standards in the target area.

The Brazilian Sisal Scheme

A well-suited case in which development harmed the intended beneficiaries occurred in an arid area of Brazil's northeastern interior called the *sertão*. Here development increased dependence on the world capitalist economy, ruined the local subsistence economy, and worsened local health and income distribution. Until the 1950s the *sertão's* economy was based on corn, beans, manioc, and other subsistence crops. The *sertão* was also a grazing region for cattle, sheep, and goats. Most years peasants subsisted on their plots and crops. However, about once every decade there was a major drought, which drastically reduced yields and forced people to migrate to the coast to seek jobs. To develop the northeast and dampen the effects of drought, the Brazilian government began encouraging peasants in the *sertão* to plant **sisal**, a fibrous plant adapted to arid areas, on a large scale.

Sisal is a cash crop that cannot be eaten. Its fiber was exported mostly to the United States, where it was used to make rope. To ready sisal for export, preparation in the field was necessary. Throughout the *sertão* there arose local centers with decorticating machines, devices that strip water and residue from sisal leaf, leaving only the fiber. These machines were expensive. Small-scale farmers couldn't afford them and had to use machines owned by the elite.

Decorticating was done by a small team of workers with a marked division of labor. Two jobs were especially hard, both done by adult men. One was that of disfiberer, the person who fed the sisal leaf into the machine. This was a demanding and dangerous job because the machine exerted a strong pull, making it possible for the disfiberers to get their fingers caught in the press. The other job was that of residue man, who shoveled away the residue that fell under the machine and brought new leaves to the disfiberer.

In Petrolina, Bahia, Brazil, workers tie up bundles of decorticated sisal fiber. Since most sisal is grown for export, variation in its price on the world market has brought a boom and a bust to the Brazilian sertão.

Anthropologist Daniel Gross (1971a) studied the effects of sisal on the people of the *sertão*. Most sisal growers were people who had dedicated most of their land to the cash crop, completely abandoning subsistence cultivation. Because sisal takes four years to mature, peasants had to seek wage work, often as members of a decorticating team, until they could harvest their crop. When they did harvest, they often found that the price of sisal on the world market was less than it had been when they planted. Moreover, once sisal was planted, its strong root system made it almost impossible for the peasants to return to other crops. The land and people of the *sertão* became hooked on sisal.

A nutritionist, Barbara Underwood, collaborated with Gross in his field study of the effects of the new economy on nutrition. In order for people to subsist, calories expended in daily activity must be replaced by calories in the diet. We may determine whether energy intake and output are balanced by comparing calories consumed in the diet with those expended in activity. Gross calculated the energy expended in two of the jobs on the decorticating team: disfiberer and residue man. The former expended an average of 4,400 calories per day; the latter, 3,600 calories.

Gross then examined the diets of the households headed by each man. The disfiberer earned the equivalent of $3.65 per week, whereas the residue man made less—about $3.25. The disfiberer's household included just himself and his wife. The residue man had a pregnant wife and four children, aged three, five, six, and eight. By spending most of his income on food, the disfiberer was getting at least 7,100 calories a day for himself and his wife. This was ample to supply his daily needs of 4,400 calories and leave his wife a comfortable 2,700 calories.

However, the residue man's household was less fortunate. With more than 95 percent of his tiny income going for food, he could provide himself, his wife, and his four children with only 9,400 calories per day. Of this, he consumed 3,600 calories—enough to go on working. His wife ate 2,200 calories. His children, however, were nutritionally deprived. Table 18.1 compares the minimum daily requirements for his children with their actual intake.

Long-term malnutrition has physical and psychological results that are reflected in body weight.

Table 18.1 *Malnutrition among the children of a Brazilian sisal residue man.*

| Age of Child | CALORIES | | Percentage of Standard Body Weight |
	Minimum Daily Requirement	Actual Daily Allotment	
8 (M)	2,100	1,100	62
6 (F)	1,700	900	70
5 (M)	1,700	900	85
3 (M)	1,300	700	90

SOURCE: Gross and Underwood 1971, p. 733.

Table 18.1 shows that the weights of the residue man's malnourished children compared poorly with the standard weights for their ages. The longer malnutrition continues, the greater the gap is between children with poor diets and those with normal diets. Thus the residue man's oldest children, who had been malnourished longest, compared least favorably with the standard body weight.

The children of sisal workers were being malnourished to enable their fathers to go on working for wages that were too low to feed them. However, the children of business people and owners of decorticating machines were doing better; malnutrition was much less severe among them. Finally, the nutrition of sisal workers was also worse than that of traditional cultivators in the *sertão*. People who had reached adulthood before sisal cultivation began had more normal weights than did those who grew up after the shift.

The conclusions drawn from this study are important for understanding problems that beset many people today. A shift from a subsistence economy to a cash economy led neither to a better diet nor to more leisure time for the majority. Rather, the rich merely got richer and the poor got poorer. This is one among hundreds of examples of unforeseen and unfortunate consequences of poorly planned and socially insensitive economic development projects.

The Greening of Java

Like Gross in Brazil, anthropologist Richard Franke (1977) conducted an independent study of discrepancies between goals and results in a scheme to promote social and economic change.

Planners, experts, and government officials have assumed that as small-scale farmers get modern technology and more productive crop varieties, their lives improve. The media have publicized new, high-yielding varieties of wheat, maize, and rice. These new crops, along with chemical fertilizers, pesticides, and new cultivation techniques, have been hailed as the basis of a **green revolution.** This "revolution" will presumably increase the world's food supply and thus improve the diets and living conditions of victims of poverty, particularly in land-scarce, overcrowded regions.

A genetic cross between strains of rice from Taiwan and Indonesia produced a high-yielding "miracle" rice known as IR-8, which was capable of increasing the productivity of a given plot by at least half. Governments throughout southern Asia, including Indonesia, have encouraged the cultivation of IR-8, along with the use of chemical fertilizers and pesticides.

The Indonesian island of Java, one of the most densely populated places in the world (over 700 people per square kilometer), was a prime target for the green revolution. Java's total crop was insufficient to supply its people with minimal daily requirements of calories (2,150) and protein (55 grams). In 1960 the Javanese economy supplied 1,950 calories and 38 grams of protein per capita. By 1967 these already inadequate figures had fallen to 1,750 calories and 33 grams. Could miracle rice, by increasing agricultural yields 50 percent, reverse the trend?

Java shares with many other underdeveloped nations a history of socioeconomic stratification and colonialism. Precolonial contrasts in wealth and power were intensified by Dutch colonialism. Although Indonesia gained political independence from the Netherlands in 1949, internal stratification continued. Today, contrasts between the wealthy (government employees, business people, large landowners) and the poor (small-scale peasants) exist even in small farming communities. Stratification was one of the main reasons for the failure of Java's green revolution.

In 1963 the College of Agriculture of the University of Indonesia started a program in which students went to live in villages. They worked with peasants in the fields and shared their knowledge of new agricultural techniques while learning from the peasants. The program was a success.

Yields in the affected villages increased by half. The program, directed by the Department of Agriculture, was expanded in 1964; nine universities and 400 students joined. These intervention programs succeeded where others had failed because the outside agents recognized that economic development rests not only on technological change but on political change as well. Students could observe firsthand how interest groups resisted attempts by peasants to improve their lot. Once, when local officials stole fertilizer destined for peasant fields, students got it back by threatening in a letter to turn evidence of the crime over to higher-level officials.

The combination of new work patterns and political action was achieving promising results when, in 1965–1966, Indonesia had an antigovernment insurrection. In the eventual military takeover, Indonesia's President Sukarno was ousted and replaced by President Suharto. Efforts to increase agricultural production resumed soon after Suharto took control. However, the new government assigned the task to multinational corporations based in Japan, West Germany, and Switzerland rather than to students and peasants. These industrial firms were to supply miracle rice and other high-yielding seeds, fertilizers, and pesticides. Peasants adopting the whole green revolution kit were eligible for loans that would permit them to buy food and other essentials in the lean period just before harvesting.

Java's green revolution soon encountered problems. One of the pesticides, which had never been tested in Java, killed the fish in the irrigation canals and thus destroyed an important protein resource. One of the development agencies turned out to be a fraud, set up to benefit the military and government officials.

Java's green revolution was also failing at the village level because of entrenched interests. Traditionally, peasants had managed to feed their families by taking temporary jobs or by borrowing from wealthier villagers during the preharvest season. However, having accepted loans, the peasants were obliged to work for wages lower than those paid on the open market. The low-interest loans that were part of the green revolution program might have helped free peasants from their dependence on wealthy villagers, thus depriving the local patrons of cheap labor.

Governments throughout southern Asia, including Indonesia, have encouraged cultivation of new rice varieties and use of chemical fertilizers and pesticides. Shown here, experimental seedlings at Java's Rice Research Center.

Local officials were put in charge of spreading information about how the program worked, but they instead limited peasant participation by withholding information. Wealthy villagers discouraged peasant participation more subtly: They raised doubts about the effectiveness of the new techniques and about the wisdom of taking government loans when familiar patrons were at hand. Faced with the thought that starvation might follow if innovation failed, peasants were reluctant to take risks—an understandable reaction.

Wealthy villagers rather than small-scale farmers reaped the benefits of the green revolution. Only 20 percent of one village's 151 households participated in the program. However, because they were the wealthiest households, headed by people who owned the most land, 40 percent of the land was being cultivated by means of the new system. Some large-scale landowners systematically used their green revolution profits at the peasants' expense. They bought up peasants' small plots and purchased labor-saving machinery, including rice-milling machines and tractors. As a result, the poorest peasants lost both their means of subsistence—land—and local work opportunities. Their only recourse was to flock to cities, where a growing pool of unskilled laborers depressed already low wages.

In a complementary view of the local social ef-fects of the green revolution in Java, Ann Stoler (1977) focused on gender and stratification. She took issue with Esther Boserup's (1970) contention that colonialism and development inevitably hurt Third World women more than men by favoring commercial agriculture and excluding women from it. Stoler found that the green revolution had permitted some women to gain power over other women and men. Javanese women were not a homogeneous group but varied by class. Stoler found that whether the green revolution helped or harmed Javanese women depended on their position in the class structure. The status of land-holding women rose as they gained control over more land and the labor of more poor women. The new economy offered wealthier women higher profits, which they used in trading. However, poor women suffered along with poor men as traditional economic opportunities declined. Nevertheless, the poor women fared better than did the poor men, who had no access at all to off-farm work.

Like Gross's analysis of the Brazilian sisal scheme, these studies of the local implications of the green revolution reveal results very different from those foreseen by development agents and the media. Again we see the harmful effects of development programs that ignore traditional social, political, and economic divisions. Merely introducing new technology, no matter how promising, does not inevitably help the intended beneficiaries. It may very well hurt them if vested interests interfere. The Javanese student-peasant projects of the 1960s worked because peasants need not just technology but also political clout. The two ambitious development programs in Brazil and Java, although designed to alleviate poverty, actually increased it. Peasants stopped relying on their own subsistence production and started depending on a much more volatile and fickle economic pursuit—cash sale of labor. Agricultural production became profit-oriented, machine-based, and chemical-dependent. Local autonomy diminished as linkages with the world system increased. As a result, the rich got richer and the human implications of poverty became ever more tragic.

Equity

A common goal, in theory at least, of development policy is to promote equity. **Increased equity** entails a reduction in absolute poverty and a fairer (more even) distribution of wealth. However, a conflict between production goals and equity goals arises in many highly stratified nations. In such countries, if projects are to increase equity, they must have the full and forceful support of reform-minded governments. Peasants oppose projects that interfere too much with their basic economic activities. Similarly, wealthy and powerful people resist projects that threaten their vested interests, and their resistance is usually more difficult to combat.

Some types of projects, particularly irrigation schemes, are more likely than others are to widen wealth disparities, that is, to have a negative equity impact. An initial uneven distribution of resources (particularly land) often becomes the basis for greater skewing after the project. The social impact of new technology tends to be more severe, contributing negatively both to quality of life and to equity, when inputs are channeled to or through the rich, as in Java's green revolution.

Many fisheries projects have also had negative equity results. In Bahia, Brazil (Kottak 1983), sailboat owners (but not nonowners) got loans to buy motors for their boats. To repay the loans, the owners increased the percentage of the catch they took from the men who fished in their boats. Over the years, they used the rising profits to buy larger and more expensive boats. The result was stratification—the creation of a stratum of wealthy people within a formerly egalitarian community. These events hampered individual initiative and interfered with further development of the fishing industry. With new boats so expensive, ambitious young men who once would have sought careers in fishing no longer had any way to obtain their own boats. To avoid such results, credit-granting agencies must seek out enterprising young fishers rather than giving loans only to owners and established business people.

Development and Descent Groups

Many governments lack a genuine commitment to improving the lives of their citizens. Moreover, interference by major powers has also kept governments from enacting needed reforms. In many highly stratified societies, particularly in Latin America, the class structure is very rigid. Movement of individuals into the middle class is difficult, and it is equally hard to raise the living standards of the lower class as a whole. These nations have a long history of control of government by powerful interest groups which tend to oppose reform.

In some nations, however, the government acts more as an agent of the people. Madagascar provides an example. As in many areas of Africa, precolonial states had developed in Madagascar before its conquest by the French in 1896. The people of Madagascar, the Malagasy, had been organized into descent groups before the origin of the state. Imerina, the major precolonial state of Madagascar, wove descent groups into its structure, making members of important groups advisers to the king and thus giving them authority in government. Imerina made provisions for the people it ruled. It collected taxes and organized labor for public works projects. In return, it redistributed resources to peasants in need. It also granted them some protection against war and slave raids and allowed them to cultivate their rice fields in peace. The government supplied and maintained the water works necessary for rice cultivation. It opened to ambitious peasant boys the chance of becoming, through hard work and study, state bureaucrats.

Throughout the history of Imerina—and continuing in modern Madagascar—there have been strong relationships between the individual, the descent group, and the state. Local Malagasy communities, where residence is based on descent, are more cohesive and homogeneous than are communities in Java or Brazil. Madagascar gained political independence from France in 1960. Although it was still economically dependent on France when I first did research there in 1966–1967, the new government was committed to a form of socialist development. Its economic development schemes were increasing the ability of the Malagasy to feed themselves. Government policy emphasized increased production of rice, a subsistence crop, rather than cash crops. Furthermore, local communities, with their traditional cooperative patterns and solidarity based on kinship and descent, were treated as partners in, not obstacles to, the development process.

In a sense, the corporate descent group appears to be preadapted to equitable national development. In Madagascar, members of local descent groups have customarily pooled their resources to educate their ambitious members. Once educated, these men and women gain responsible and economically secure positions in the nation. They then share the advantages of their new positions with their kin. For example, they give room and board to rural cousins attending school and help them find jobs.

Malagasy administrations appear generally to have shared a commitment to democratic economic development. Perhaps this is because government officials are of the peasantry or have strong personal ties to it. This has more rarely been the case in Latin American countries, where the controllers and the lower class have different origins and no strong connections through kinship, descent, or marriage.

Furthermore, societies with descent-group organization contradict an assumption that many social scientists and economists seem to make. It is not inevitable that as nations become more tied to the world capitalist economy, native forms of social organization will break down into nuclear family organization, impersonality, and alienation. Descent groups, with their traditional communalism and corporate solidarity, have important roles to play in economic development.

SOCIOCULTURAL COMPATIBILITY AND INNOVATION

A few years ago, I did a comparative study of sixty-eight completed rural development projects all over the world (Kottak 1985). One of my most significant findings was that **culturally compatible economic development projects** were twice as successful financially as incompatible ones were. Regular use of anthropological expertise in development in order to ensure cultural compatibility is

To maximize social and economic benefits, development projects should: (1) be culturally compatible, (2) respond to locally perceived needs for change, (3) harness traditional organizations, and (4) have a proper (and flexible) social design for carrying out the project. This Zambian farm club, which draws on traditional social organization, plants cabbages.

therefore demonstrably cost-effective. To maximize social and economic benefits, projects must (1) be culturally compatible, (2) respond to locally perceived needs for change, (3) harness traditional organizations, and (4) have a proper (and flexible) social design for implementation. Applied anthropologists should not just *implement* development policies; they are as qualified as economists are to *make* policy as well.

Anthropological input is valuable during all the stages of a development project: identification, appraisal, design, implementation, and evaluation. Together these stages make up the **project cycle.** During identification, needs for potential projects in particular places are identified and discussed. At appraisal, background studies are done to determine project feasibility. If the project appears viable and funding is approved, design begins. Carrying out the project is known as implementation. After this comes evaluation, the final stage. Later, some projects receive ex post facto evaluation to assess their ongoing progress.

Too many true local needs cry out for a solution to waste money by funding projects that are inappropriate in area A but needed in area B or unnecessary anywhere. Social expertise is necessary to sort out the A's and B's and fit the projects accordingly. Culturally compatible projects, which put people first by responding to the needs for change that they perceive, must be identified. Thereafter social expertise is necessary to devise efficient and socially compatible ways of implementing the projects.

The Fallacy of Overinnovation

In my comparative study of sixty-eight development projects, I found that the compatible and successful ones avoided the fallacy of **overinnovation.** Instead, they applied Romer's rule, which was used in Chapter 9 to explain why the Industrial Revolution took place in England. Recall that Romer (1960) invented his rule to explain the evolution of land-dwelling vertebrates from fish. The ancestors of land animals lived in pools of water that dried up seasonally. Fins evolved into legs to enable these animals to get back to water when particular pools dried up. Thus an innovation (legs) that later proved essential to land life originated to maintain life in the water.

Romer's lesson is that an innovation that evolves to maintain a system can play a major role in changing that system. Evolution occurs in increments as gradually changing systems continue attempting to maintain themselves as they gradually change. Romer's rule seems applicable to economic development, which, after all, is a process of (planned) socioeconomic evolution. To apply Romer's rule to development is not to argue against change. The emergence of legs, which prompted Romer's rule, was a highly significant innovation which was to provide the vertebrates with multiple paths of diversification and development.

When we apply Romer's rule to development, we see that people are unlikely to cooperate with projects that require major changes in their daily lives, especially ones that interfere too much with customary subsistence pursuits. People usually wish to *change just enough to maintain what they have.* Although peasants want certain improvements, their motives for modifying their behavior come from their traditional culture and the small concerns of everyday existence. Their values are not such abstract ones as "learning a better way," "progressing," "increasing technical know-how," "improving efficiency," or "adopting modern techniques." (Those phrases exemplify intervention philosophy.) Instead, their objectives are down-to-earth and specific ones, such as improving yields in a rice field, amassing sufficient resources to host a ceremony, getting a child through junior high school, or paying the tax collector. The goals and values of subsistence producers differ from those of people who produce for cash, just as they differ from the intervention philosophy of development planners. These different value systems must be taken into account during planning.

By the way, a model of development following Romer's rule is in no way incompatible with government changes or social-reform movements that seek to reallocate land rights in highly stratified nations. If land reform permits peasants to go on farming their traditional fields and get more of the product, it can be very successful.

Appropriate and Inappropriate Innovation

Realistic development promotes change but not overinnovation. Many changes are possible if the aim is to preserve local systems while making them work better. Successful projects respect, or at least don't attack, local cultural patterns. Effective development usually incorporates indigenous cultural practices and social structures.

One example of appropriate innovation was an East African cattle project that has been judged to be one of the most successful livestock projects in Africa. It introduced cattle herding to a region that had recently been freed of tsetse fly infestation. (These flies transmit African sleeping sickness to people and animals.) The project made good use of local and regional conditions. Some examples:

1. Livestock came from a neighboring country, so that cattle were adapted to the regional ecology.
2. Cattle grazing was a culturally appropriate activity in the region. Previously, people in the project area had not herded only because of tsetse flies. With this barrier removed, people simply extended their traditional practice to fill in a new niche.
3. The project used a mixture of productive units: government ranches, a cooperative ranch, and private ranches.
4. Project aims were compatible with traditional land tenure, in which fences and small farms were customary and proved to be compatible with the project's private property and grazing goals.
5. The population was sufficiently dense for effective supervision, animal health care, marketing, and delivery.

Participants in a successful Papua–New Guinea palm oil resettlement project used their profits just as the ancestors of land vertebrates used their fin-like legs—not to forge a brand-new life style but to maintain their ties with home. Settlers constantly revisited their homelands and invested in their social life and ceremonies. This cash crop project was compatible with widespread Oceanian cultural values and customs involving competition for wealth and capital accumulation, such as big-man systems. The settlers came from different tribes, but interethnic and interlinguistic social mingling turned out to be compatible with local experience. Marriage between people who speak different languages or dialects is common in Papua–New Guinea, as is multitribal participation in common (religious) movements—cargo cults.

Sudan's Jonglei canal (the target of continuing tribal resistance) was planned to provide water for export crops such as cotton. The canal would have destroyed traditional cattle pastures, which depend on seasonal flooding. It is over-innovative—but not unusual—for development projects to try to convert nomadic pastoralists into sedentary cultivators.

Throughout the world, project incompatibilities have arisen from inadequate attention to, and consequent lack of fit with, local culture. A very naive and incompatible project was an overinnovative irrigation and settlement scheme in Ethiopia. Its major fallacy was to try to convert nomadic pastoralists into sedentary cultivators. It ignored traditional land rights. Outsiders—commercial farmers—were to get much of the herders' territory, and the pastoralists were expected to settle down and start farming. This project neglected social and cultural issues. It benefited wealthy outsiders instead of the natives. The planners naively expected free-ranging pastoralists to give up a generations-old way of life in order to work three times harder growing rice and picking cotton.

Another failure was a South Asian project that promoted the cultivation of onions and peppers, expecting this practice to fit into a preexisting labor-intensive system of rice growing. This project was the opposite of one guided by Romer's rule. Cultivation of these cash crops was not traditional in the area, and it conflicted with existing crop priorities and other interests of farmers. The labor peaks for pepper and onion production coincided with those for rice. Farmers gave priority to their traditional subsistence crop.

Sometimes development agencies ignore good preproject advice and go on with bad projects anyway. In one African cattle project, the planners ignored the appraisal team's advice not to establish ranches in the project area because they would conflict with established land-use patterns. The designers ignored the most basic (and easily available) government census and mapping data for the project area. During implementation, a few thousand local people, whose existence the planners had failed to notice, tore down fences, burned pasture, and rustled cattle. Local people continued guerrilla actions against the ranches built on their ancestral lands. These problems diminished when foreign managers were replaced with nationals, who used traditional pacts (blood brotherhood) between villages to end the rustling.

The Fallacy of Underdifferentiation

The fallacy of **underdifferentiation** refers to planners' tendency to see less-developed countries as an undifferentiated group. Development agencies have often ignored cultural diversity and adopted a uniform approach to deal with very different types of project beneficiaries. Neglecting cultural diversity, many projects have incorporated culturally biased and incompatible property notions and social units. Most often, faulty social design assumes either (1) individualistic productive units that are privately owned by an individual or couple and worked by a nuclear family or (2) cooperatives that are at least partially based on models from Eastern bloc and socialist countries.

Development often aims at exploiting resources for export in order to generate *individual* wealth. This goal contrasts with the tendency of bands and

tribes to share resources and depend on local ecosystems and renewable resources (Bodley 1988). Development planners commonly emphasize benefits that will accrue to individuals; more concern with the effects on total communities is needed (Bodley 1988).

One example of an inappropriate Euro-American model (based on the individual and the nuclear family) was a West African project designed for an area where the extended family was the basic social unit. The project succeeded despite its faulty social design because the participants used their traditional extended family networks to attract additional settlers. Eventually, twice as many people as planned benefited as extended family members flocked to the project area. This case illustrates the fact that local people are not helpless victims of the world system. Settlers modified the project design that had been imposed on them by using the principles of their traditional society.

The second dubious foreign social model that is common in development strategy is the cooperative. In my comparative study of development projects, new cooperatives fared badly. Cooperatives succeeded only when they harnessed preexisting local-level communal institutions. This is a corollary of a more general rule: participants' groups are most effective when they are based on traditional social organization or on a socioeconomic similarity among members.

Because neither foreign social model—the nuclear family farm or the cooperative—has an unblemished record in development, an alternative is needed: greater use of *Third World social models for Third World development*. These are traditional social units, such as the clans, lineages, and other extended kinship groups of Africa, Oceania, and many other nations, with their communally held estates and resources. The most humane and productive strategy for change is to base the social design for innovation on traditional social forms in each target area.

SUMMARY

Many changes have accompanied the incorporation of native populations into nation-states, colonial regimes, and the world capitalist economy. For decades anthro-

pologists have studied such social and cultural alterations. Acculturation refers to cultural changes that develop from continuous firsthand contact between cultures. Syncretisms are cultural blends or mixtures that emerge from acculturation, particularly under colonialism, such as the combination of African, Native American, and Roman Catholic saints and deities in Caribbean vodun, or "voodoo," cults.

Cargo cults developed in an acculturative context produced by expansion of the world capitalist economy and colonialism. These cults blend native expectations about tribal big men with magical explanations for the wealth of foreign overlords. Cargo cults have forged people into larger communities that have gained political and economic influence. The origins and leadership of tribal independence movements can be secular as well as religious. There is a growing recognition that native peoples have been denied basic rights to their traditional lands and cultural practices, but states have not stopped assaulting tribes within their boundaries.

Development plans are usually guided by some kind of intervention philosophy, an ideological justification for outsiders to direct native peoples toward particular goals. Development is usually justified by the belief that industrialization, modernization, westernization, and individualism are desirable and beneficial evolutionary advances. However, bands and tribes, with their low energy adaptations, usually manage resources better than industrial states do. Many of the most severe problems that Third World people face today are due to their position within nation-states and their increasing dependence on the world cash economy.

Some of the most severe conflicts between governments and natives arise over exploitation of resources on tribal lands by outside interests. There has been worldwide intrusion on indigenous peoples and their local ecosystems by highway construction, mining, hydroelectric projects, lumbering, agribusiness, and planned colonization. Collective resistance is sometimes an effective response, as in the Sudan and among the Igorots of the Philippines.

Increasingly, government agencies, international organizations, and private foundations are encouraging attention to local-level social factors and the cultural dimension of social change and economic development. Anthropologists work in organizations that promote, manage, and assess programs that affect human life in the United States and abroad.

Development projects that replace subsistence pursuits with economies dependent on the unpredictable ups and downs of the world capitalist economy can be especially damaging. Following a shift from subsistence to cash cropping in northeastern Brazil, local material conditions worsened. Research on the socioeconomic effects of sisal cultivation showed some of the unforeseen consequences (e.g., negative equity) that may accompany development. Similarly, research in Java found that the green revolution was failing because it stressed new technology rather than a combination of technology and peasant political organization. Java's green revolution was increasing poverty rather than ending it, although women were not as hard hit by the new economy as men were. Because many other projects have failed for social and political reasons, development organizations are increasingly using anthropologists in planning, supervision, and evaluation.

World governments are not equally committed to eradicating poverty and increasing equity. Local interest groups often oppose reform, and resistance by elites is especially hard to combat. Culturally compatible projects tend to be more financially successful than incompatible ones are. This means that the use of anthropological expertise in development not only promotes more humane changes but is also cost-effective. An anthropological perspective is valuable throughout the project cycle: identification, appraisal, design, implementation, and evaluation.

Compatible and successful projects avoid the fallacy of overinnovation and apply Romer's rule: an innovation that evolves to maintain a system can play a major role in changing that system. Natives are unlikely to cooperate with projects that require major changes in their daily lives, especially ones that interfere too much with customary subsistence pursuits. People usually want to change just enough to maintain what they have. Peasants' motives to change come from their traditional culture and the small concerns of everyday existence. Peasant values are not abstract and long-term and thus differ from those of development planners.

The fallacy of underdifferentiation refers to the tendency to see less-developed countries as an undifferentiated group. Neglecting cultural diversity and the local context, many projects impose culturally biased and incompatible property notions and social units on the intended beneficiaries. The most common flawed social models are the nuclear family farm and the cooperative, neither of which has an unblemished record in development. A more promising alternative is to harness Third World social units for purposes of development. These traditional social forms include the clans, lineages, and other extended kinship groups of Africa and Oceania, with their communally held resources. The most productive strategy for change is to base the social design for innovation on traditional social forms in each target area.

GLOSSARY

acculturation: Cultural changes that develop as a result of continuous firsthand contact between cultures.

candomblé: A syncretic "Afro-Brazilian" cult.

cargo cults: Postcolonial, acculturative religious movements, common in Melanesia, that attempt to explain European domination and wealth and to achieve similar success magically by mimicking European behavior.

charisma: Unusual qualities and talents, often perceived as superhuman or supernatural; attract and hold followers.

culturally compatible economic development projects: Projects that harness traditional organizations and locally perceived needs for change and that have a culturally appropriate design and implementation strategy.

equity, increased: A reduction in absolute poverty and a fairer (more even) distribution of wealth.

green revolution: Agricultural development based on chemical fertilizers, pesticides, twentieth-century cultivation techniques, and new crop varieties such as IR-8 ("miracle rice").

intervention philosophy: Guiding principle of colonialism, conquest, missionization, or development; an ideological justification for outsiders to guide native peoples in specific directions.

overinnovation: Characteristic of projects that require major changes in natives' daily lives, especially ones that interfere with customary subsistence pursuits.

project cycle: A development project through all its stages: identification, appraisal, design, implementation, and evaluation.

sertão: Arid interior of northeastern Brazil; backlands.

sisal: Plant adapted to arid areas; its fiber is used to make rope.

syncretisms: Cultural blends or mixtures that emerge from acculturation, particularly under colonialism, such as African, Native American, and Roman Catholic saints and deities in Caribbean vodun, or "voodoo," cults.

underdifferentiation: Planning fallacy of viewing less-developed countries as an undifferentiated group; ignoring cultural diversity and adopting a uniform approach (often ethnocentric) for very different types of project beneficiaries.

STUDY QUESTIONS

1. What is acculturation, and where can we study it?
2. How are cargo cults related both to traditional social structure and to the expansion of the world capitalist economy?
3. What are some common reasons for the failure of economic development programs?
4. What are equity goals, and what were the equity results of the Brazilian sisal scheme and Java's green revolution?
5. How did the equity results of Java's green revolution differ for men and for women?
6. What does it mean to say that an economic development project is culturally compatible? What are the advantages of ensuring that projects are culturally compatible?
7. What is Romer's rule, and how does it apply to development strategy?
8. What are some examples of the fallacy of overinnovation?
9. What is the fallacy of underdifferentiation? What are some possible alternatives to it?
10. How might descent-group organization contribute to economic development?
11. In your opinion, what criteria should be used to evaluate the success of an economic development program?

SUGGESTED ADDITIONAL READING

BARLETT, P. F., ED.
  1980 *Agricultural Decision Making: Anthropological Contribution to Rural Development.* New York: Academic Press. How farmers choose what to plant and decide how to plant it in various cultures.

BENNETT, J. W., AND J. R. BOWEN, EDS.
  1988 *Production and Autonomy: Anthropological Studies and Critiques of Development.* Monographs in Economic Anthropology, No. 5, Society for Economic Anthropology. New York: University Press of America. Twenty-three recent articles on many social aspects of economic development.

BODLEY, J. H.

1985   *Anthropology and Contemporary Human Problems,* 2nd ed. Mountain View, CA: Mayfield. Overview of major problems of today's industrial world: overconsumption, the environment, resource depletion, hunger, overpopulation, violence, and war.

1988   *Tribal Peoples and Development Issues: A Global Overview.* Mountain View, CA: Mayfield. Overview of case studies, policies, assessments, and recommendations concerning tribal peoples and development.

CERNEA, M., ED.

1990   *Putting People First: Sociological Variables in Rural Development,* 2nd ed. New York: Oxford University Press (published for the World Bank). First collection of articles by social scientists based on World Bank files and project experiences. Examines development successes and failures and the social and cultural reasons for them.

HART, K.

1982   *The Political Economy of West African Agriculture.* Cambridge: Cambridge University Press. Examines the origins of West African underdevelopment.

HUMAN ORGANIZATION

The quarterly journal of the Society for Applied Anthropology. An excellent source for articles on applied anthropology and development.

KORTEN, D. C.

1980   Community Organization and Rural Development: A Learning Process Approach. *Public Administration Review,* September-October, pp. 480–512. People-oriented development strategies as opposed to the "blueprint" approach used by most development agencies.

SELIGSON, M. A.

1984   *The Gap between Rich and Poor: Contending Perspectives on the Political Economy of Development.* Boulder, CO: Westview Press. Equity issues in development.

WALLMAN, S., ED.

1977   *Perceptions of Development.* New York: Cambridge University Press. Very readable original essays on the cultural context of development in Africa, Canada, Europe, and Hawaii.

WORSLEY, P.

1984   *The Three Worlds: Culture and World Development.* Chicago: University of Chicago Press. Examines the nature of development processes and critiques existing theories.

CHAPTER 19

THE FUTURE

Perhaps, though, there may come a day when some-one will work out the Laws of Humanics and then be able to predict the broad strokes of the future, and *know* what might be in store for humanity, instead of merely guessing as I do, and *know* what to do to make things better, instead of merely speculating. I dream sometimes of founding a mathematical science which I think of as "psychohistory," but I know I can't and I fear no one ever will. (Asimov 1983, p. 104)

Accurate predictions about the future aren't cen-turies away; people make them every day. Since Sir Isaac Newton, the movements of objects in the solar system have been predicted with great accu-racy. Since Albert Einstein, those predictions have been refined to account for the tiniest deviations. The weather, of course, can't be predicted as pre-cisely. Forecasters have to use statistical predic-tions, which indicate a certain probability (percent chance) of rain. In the social sciences, many de-velopments can be forecast with high probability, assuming continuation of current trends.

Probability prediction fits into today's world in many ways. We may change our plans to go to the beach after hearing a weather report. Economists issue annual and quarterly forecasts to aid in gov-ernment planning and private investment. Busi-nesses and governments consider demographic trends in charting new policies. Candidates use polls to plan their strategies. Predictions are based on the scientific assumption that current trends will continue, that regularities observed in the past and the present will also hold true in the future. This assumption is called *uniformitarianism*. In Chapter 16 we saw that linguists use it to explain changes in language. Thus, speech shifts and vari-ations like those we hear today (in regional dia-lects, for example), operating over a long enough time, result in major linguistic change.

We must distinguish between scientific and oc-cult predictions. Science is relatively recent, but **occult predictions** are thousands of years old. Probably dating back to Paleolithic foragers, occult predictions became more prominent during the Neolithic as people began to farm and herd. As-trology probably played a prominent role in sched-uling activities in the first agricultural societies, as it does among nonindustrial farmers today. As-trologers in Madagascar study patterns involving the sun, the moon, planets, stars, days, and months and consult configurations that form when they cast seeds, shells, and other small objects. Ancient Greeks used animal entrails to make pre-dictions. Canadian Indians chose where to hunt on a given day by examining the cracks that ap-peared in an animal's shoulder blade when it was heated. With occult prediction—unlike science—there is no empirical connection between the data or pattern and the events being predicted, regu-lated, or changed. The power of astrology and di-vination comes from the supernatural world, not the real one.

Astrology's most important historical role worldwide has probably been in scheduling agri-cultural activities. Astrology works differently, of course, in contemporary North America. Ameri-cans aren't hunters or peasants but participants in an industrial economy. Modern psychics are occult experts in a culture with experts on everything. Most of us know our astrological signs and some-times read astrology columns. However, most North Americans probably don't consider astrol-ogy an accurate predictive science, because they've seen the columns contradict personal experience too many times. Successful enterprises get their forecasts not from psychics but from established public-opinion and market research organizations. The organizations begun by George Gallup and Lou Harris are much more reliable forecasters than are any of the "top psychics."

The best predictions are based on the assump-tion of uniformitarianism. Of course, world de-struction, which cannot be accurately predicted, would prevent most predictions from coming true. However, assuming global survival, we can make several informed guesses about the future. The 30,000-member World Future Society consists of scientists who regularly make such predictions, some of which contribute to the discussion that follows.

GLOBAL TRENDS: THE POPULATION CRISIS

Current demographic facts and trends are the basis for predictions about future world population (see Figure 19.1). Ten thousand babies are born every hour (Reich 1989). Growing by an average of 92 million people annually in the 1990s, the global population will exceed 6 billion by the year 2000

WHY PSYCHICS CAN'T LOSE

Occult predictions figure in North American society not so much because we spend millions having our fortunes told but because stories about psychics and their predictions help sell publications. *The National Enquirer* and similar publications produce annual year-end issues in which "top psychics" make forecasts about the coming year. By year's end, most people have forgotten what was predicted the previous year and thus miss the chance to judge the psychics' accuracy. Since 1982, however, a group called the Bay Area Skeptics has been following the outcome of psychics' predictions and documenting a poor track record. Few of the predictions that prominent psychics made for 1985 had come true when I first wrote this box in 1986. (They still haven't as I revise it in 1990.) As far as I know, Mr. T hasn't been hit by lightning, Teddy Kennedy hasn't eloped with his secretary, and California hasn't fallen into the Pacific Ocean (*Ann Arbor News*, December 28, 1984).

To see how, in the United States as in other cultures, psychics hedge their bets, consider an interview with Jeane Dixon that appeared in *USA Today* (December 28, 1984). First, Dixon asserts that when her predictions fail, it's because the affected people change their plans or because someone stops the event from occurring. Asked about her faulty prediction of an attempt on President Nixon's life, Dixon explained that Arthur Bremer, who shot Governor George Wallace of Alabama, had also stalked Nixon but had failed to get him because of changes in "man-made plans." Dixon's prediction that World War III would begin in 1958 did not materialize, she explained, because world leaders changed their minds. (Anything that has to do with "man-made" plans can be changed, according to Dixon.) In other words, when predictions come to pass, she is right; when they don't, it's because someone changed his or her plans.

Other lessons for a successful psychic: Make predictions that anyone could make using public information. Make predictions based on current trends and known circumstances. Some of Dixon's predictions for 1985 illustrate this. Among her forecasts was one stating that neither Walter Mondale nor Jesse Jackson would ever be President of the United States. Evaluation: Given the magnitude of Mondale's 1984 defeat and the fact that Jackson's most loyal supporters belong to a minority group, it's hardly necessary to be a psychic to make such forecasts.

Dixon also predicted that 1984 Democratic VP candidate Geraldine Ferraro would have further political success but would separate from and eventually divorce her husband. Once again, the public information available in 1984 about the Ferraros' finances and marriage made this forecast anything but risky, especially given what is known about the strains that dual careers place on a marriage. If half of all contemporary American marriages end in divorce, chances are good that any given couple will split up. And if Ms. Dixon's predictions don't come true, she can always say that people changed their plans or life styles, thus removing the "man-made causes" on which the prediction was based.

Another 1984 Dixon prediction: "President Amin Gemayl of Lebanon will not make it. Either he will be assassinated or something will happen to him. It's not going to be way off. It's going to be soon" (*USA Today*, December 28, 1984).

From probabilities alone, what safer prediction could be made about the fate of a world leader? In 1984 Amin Gemayl was presiding over one of the world's most war-torn nations. His brother, the former president, had already been assassinated. Other Lebanese leaders were assassinated during Amin Gemayl's presidency; his successor as president was assassinated in 1989. However, Amin is still alive as I write this in 1990. Furthermore, the success of Dixon's prediction doesn't even require an actual assassination—only that "something will happen to him." The timing is also sufficiently vague so that several years may pass before the accuracy of the prediction can be known. How soon, after all, is "soon"? Continued good luck, Amin!

The final lesson about the psychic is this: An occasional well-publicized success renews the faith of the gullible. Despite Dixon's failed forecasts that the Soviet Union would put the first man on the moon, Fidel Castro would die in 1969, and World War III would begin in 1958, she claims to have predicted the assassinations of John and Robert Kennedy and Dr. Martin Luther King, Jr. She also took credit for foretelling Ferraro's inclusion on the 1984 Democratic ticket and Ronald Reagan's 1980 and 1984 election wins. The Reagan predictions hardly required a psychic.

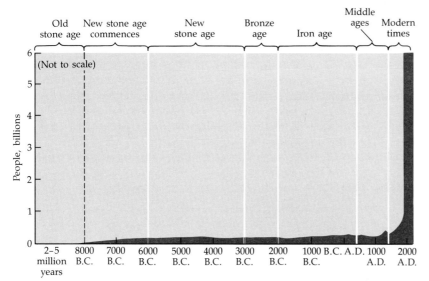

Figure 19.1 *The global human population, now approaching 6 billion, reached 1 billion only around A.D. 1800. Unless world population growth slows, more people will be born in the year A.D. 2050 than were born in the world between A.D. 1 and A.D. 1500. (Population Reference Bureau, reported in Murphy 1984, p. 1)*

(*Ann Arbor News*, September 10, 1989). Unless population growth slows, more people will be born in the single year 2050 than were born in the world between A.D. 1 and A.D. 1500.

Demographic Transitions

The current rate of human population increase reflects declining death rates resulting from medical advances. The **natural increase rate** is calculated from number of births minus number of deaths (per 1,000 population), plus or minus migration. In most countries migration has a minor effect on population, so that the rate of natural increase approximates births minus deaths.

The world has recently experienced two **demographic transitions** (changing patterns of population growth). The **old demographic transition** occurred in the developed countries. As the death rate declined, the birth rate didn't rise much, and so population increases were small. The **new demographic transition** applies to the Third World. In nations with a history of high birth rates, these rates have been maintained while the death rate has fallen. This has produced rates of natural increase never before experienced in human history. Provision of adequate resources for this expanding population and control of its increase are fundamental problems to be solved if humanity is to have a future.

As world population and human needs increase, other species are destroyed. Each year some 10,000 animal and plant species become extinct—mainly through destruction of tropical rain forests, which have existed for 60 million years and are particularly rich in species diversity. A century from now the habitat in which our primate ancestors developed probably won't exist (Bodley 1985; Richards 1973).

Global Population Shifts

By the twenty-first century, most people will be descendants of the non-Western groups that anthropologists have traditionally studied. It's easy to see that solutions to future problems will depend increasingly on understanding non-Western cultural backgrounds. The Southern Hemisphere is steadily increasing its share of world population, and the fastest population growth rates are in Third World cities. Rural migrants move to slums, where they live in hovels that lack utilities and public sanitation facilities. Growing by 12 to 20 percent each year, the world slum population will double in three to six years. If current demographic trends continue urban population increase and the concentration of city dwellers in slums will be accompanied by increasing rates of crime and water, air, and noise pollution. These problems will be most severe in the less-developed countries. However, they will also affect the United States, which shares a frontier with Mexico, one of the world's fastest growing nations.

As a result of petroleum- and chemical-dependent mechanized farming, the global food supply increased dramatically from the 1950s through the mid-1980s. Now, however, food production and food distribution are not keeping up with world population growth. The gap will surely widen if current trends continue. Children will go on dying as starvation substitutes for more humane means of limiting population growth. Today's African famine areas, including Ethiopia, provide a glimpse of things to come. From the global perspective, birth control and family planning are essential if resources are to be sufficient, if starvation, pestilence, and war are not to stalk the earth during the third millennium.

Energy Resources

The energy crisis isn't over. Energy and conservation are long-term global issues. The future will hold only occasional periods of low energy costs, resulting from short-term oil gluts and cost-lowering international disagreements on pricing. The Worldwatch Institute has estimated that world energy consumption will rise 225 percent by 2025. Careful projections suggest that the world supply of oil, natural gas, and coal will be exhausted in

67, 160, and 202 years, respectively, given current patterns of production and consumption (Bodley 1985). The United States remains the world's most wasteful nation, with more cars than any other country and an average fuel economy of only sixteen miles per gallon. The United States is the world's major consumer of nonrenewable resources, both absolutely and per capita. In 1970, with just 6 percent of the global population, Americans consumed 40 percent of the world's total annual production and 35 percent of its energy (Bodley 1985). Concerted global conservation measures *could* reduce the increase in energy use through 2025 from 225 percent to just 35 percent (*Ann Arbor News,* December 26, 1984). However, without conservation, the effects will be hardest on developing industrial nations such as Brazil, which imports half its huge energy needs.

Global Employment

Heavy-goods manufacture will shift increasingly to the Third World and to former "Iron Curtain" countries. This shift is well under way. Many of the parts used in American automobiles are manufactured in Brazil and Mexico. In 1990 General Motors negotiated auto-manufacturing operations in Hungary. Despite the global shift in manufacturing, unemployment will increasingly plague the less-developed countries because of their popula-

Heavy goods manufacture will shift increasingly to the Third World and to former "Iron Curtain" countries. Substantial parts of American automobiles are now manufactured in Brazil and Mexico.

tion growth, particularly in their urban areas. Forced off the land by rural development schemes and the lure of modern life, rural people are moving to cities at an alarming rate. China has taken severe measures to keep people on the farms and slow the population increase. Other governments will eventually adopt such measures, or they will tumble as a result of rising crime rates, urban riots, and other pressures toward social revolution.

AMERICA'S FUTURE

As unemployment mounts in the Third World, the job crunch will continue easing in the United States. For years Americans heard gloomy predictions about technological unemployment. Although machines *are* displacing people in traditional jobs, this has not stopped a huge increase in the number of Americans working outside the home. Between 1950 and 1980 the U.S. work force increased by 79 percent while the population grew less than 50 percent (*New York Times,* November 4, 1984). Between 1970 and 1989 the American economy added 38 million jobs, 17 million of them since 1982 (Morris 1989). The United States (but not the world) is on the brink of an era of full employment as the baby boom's pressure on the job market finally ends.

From Goods to Services and Information

At a growing rate, the American economy is shifting from the production of goods toward the provision of specialized services, including information processing. Third World countries with cheaper labor can produce steel, automobiles, and other heavy goods less expensively than the United States can. However, the United States excels at services. The American mass education system has many faults, but it does train millions of people for service- and information-oriented jobs, from sales clerks to computer operators.

Anthropology's systemic perspective recognizes that major economic changes have consequences throughout society—in politics, for example. Thus, many of the constituencies that once made the Democrats the undisputed majority party are disappearing because of economic shifts. During the 1950s a staggering 65 percent of American jobs were blue collar, compared with just 17 percent today. John Naisbitt, coauthor of *Megatrends 2000* (Naisbitt and Aburdene 1990), predicts that the proportion will fall to 4 percent by 2000. The American blue-collar worker will be almost as rare as the family farmer. Labor unions represent an ever smaller percentage of the work force. Republicans and yuppies have invaded the once "solid South." Because of social programs enacted by the Democrats, old people live longer and better than ever before. Women's work will continue to increase. The full-time housewife will join the family farmer and blue-collar worker as a museum piece.

Most Americans of your generation will eventually work in one of two employment categories: complex services and person-to-person services. **Complex services** involve information processing—the manipulation of data and abstract symbols. In this category are insurance, engineering, law, finance, computer programming, advertising, and scientific research. These activities now account for more than 25 percent of the American gross national product (GNP), compared with 13 percent in 1950. (Manufacturing now makes up just 20 percent of the GNP.) Examples of **person-to-person service** jobs include custodians, security guards, restaurant and retail workers, day-care providers, clerical workers, teachers, hotel workers, recreation directors, fitness teachers, bank tellers, salespersons, and health-care workers. With an aging population, health care (now accounting for 12 percent of our GNP) will grow especially (Reich 1989).

Mobility and the Suburbs

In our more rural past, children—especially sons—were encouraged to stay on the farm, eventually to replace their parents as farmers. Today, farmers make up less than 4 percent of the American work force. The decline of the family farm will continue. Today's economy favors mobility. Shunning the land, we leave home in search of cash employment. Successful professionals want to choose from among the best jobs in the nation even if it means living miles away from father, mother, sister, brother—or even spouse.

Unlike Third Worlders, Americans aren't flocking to big cities—just the opposite. Between 1970

Farmers make up less than 4 percent of the contemporary American work force. The decline of the family farm will continue, as Americans and Canadians leave the land to seek cash employment in an economy increasingly based on services and information.

and 1980, Americans' residence in small cities and towns increased 25 percent while the central-city population fell *below* the 1970 level (*New York Times*, November 4, 1984). Our increasing suburban population is the product of a highly developed culture of consumption based on highways, automobiles, and shopping malls, which make this living pattern possible for contemporary Americans.

The Culture of Consumption

More and more Americans must seek jobs in order to maintain the life styles promoted by our culture of consumption. We are all working harder to afford and maintain our possessions. The conclusion is inescapable: the trend is toward overwork rather than unemployment. Between 1973 and 1988 the average American's weekly work schedule increased from 41 to 47 hours as average leisure time fell from 26 to 17 hours (Yarrow 1988). One reason for these changes is that when women enter the work force, they spend more of their "free time" on housework. Another is that average Americans—male and female—must work longer hours to afford food, housing, clothing, automobiles, microwave ovens, videocassette recorders, home computers, and health care—and especially to meet the increasing costs of raising the children needed for our high-tech future. Debunking the

old, erroneous idea that leisure time increases with civilization, Marshall Sahlins (1968/1988) calls hunters and gatherers "the original affluent society." Table 19.1 shows that American women today (as in 1920) work more than twice as many hours as do Native Australian women. The contrast between stone-age hunters and modern American men would be just as striking.

The Decline of the Labor Union

Traditional American labor unions were concerned with guaranteeing their members' full-time (and even overtime) employment and benefits. This strategy was reasonable during the era of the one-earner household, but it is no longer viable. Union contracts will change to reflect an increasing proportion of women and part-time workers. Even if

Table 19.1 *Weekly work hours in various contexts.*

Group	Work Hours
Native Australian women (collecting and food preparation)	20
Rural American women, 1920s (housework)	52
Urban American "homemakers," 1970s (housework)	55

SOURCE: Bodley 1985, p. 69.

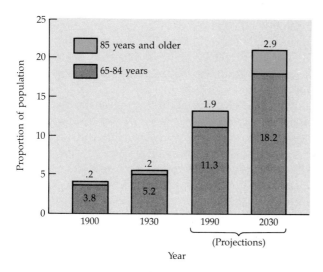

Figure 19.2 *The percentage of elderly Americans is increasing rapidly. As the baby boomers age, the population aged 65 and over will increase dramatically. By A.D. 2030 the oldest old (aged 85 and over) will comprise 3 percent of the national population—15 times the figure for 1930. (Bureau of the Census data in Gelman 1985, p. 62)*

unions attract more female members and leaders, they may never again be as powerful as they were during the 1950s or even in 1979 (the high of recent years), when 24 percent of the labor force was unionized. By 1989 the figure had fallen below 17 percent (*New York Times*, February 25, 1985; *Ann Arbor News*, September 4, 1989). Our corporations continue to shift production out of the United States, reducing American labor's competitive position and ability to organize.

An Aging Population

The baby boom (1946–1964) has ended, and the population of the United States is aging. In 1984 only 23 percent of Americans were sixteen and younger, compared with 29 percent a decade earlier. The population aged sixty-five and over grew from 9 percent to 13 percent in the same period. These trends will continue (Figure 19.2). Because the group aged 85 and older ("the oldest old") will grow faster than other segments of the population will, there will be 100,000 Americans over age 100 by A.D. 2000 (*Ann Arbor News*, December 26, 1984).

A new independence for the elderly, most of

whom now live in their own homes with adequate incomes, has a clear economic basis. The percentage of the elderly classified as poor declined from more than 30 percent in 1960 and 15 percent in 1980 to 12 percent in 1987. Other segments of the American population were not doing nearly as well (Tolchin 1988; *NASW News* 1985). One current trend (for men particularly) is early retirement, made possible in part by Social Security payments that increased 900 percent between 1950 and 1983 while wages and salaries were growing only 400 percent and prices were increasing only 300 percent (*Time*, February 18, 1985).

Despite these benefits, there are signs that the culture of consumption is enticing some elders to *re*enter the work force. Previewing a trend likely to intensify with the aging of the baby boomers, more older people are working part-time. Half of American men over sixty-five work part-time now, versus just a third in 1960 (*New York Times*, September 7, 1989). Even more of them might be working if Social Security weren't taxed above a certain amount. This increasing employment has accompanied a 46 percent real increase in Social Security benefits since 1970, a period during which wages and salaries were *decreasing*.

Social Alienation

It would appear that the elderly, like other segments of our population, are more socially isolated from their families than was the case thirty years ago. Although only 5 percent of American old people lived in nursing homes in 1980, a much smaller percentage (9 percent) lived with their families than was the case in 1950 (31 percent). Indeed, more Americans are living alone or with strangers, even at home. According to census data, only 73 percent of American households were made up of family members in 1980, versus 89 percent in 1950.

The average number of Americans per household has declined steadily from 4.8 in 1900 to 3.4 in 1960, 3.1 in 1970, 2.7 in 1980, and 2.6 in 1988 (*World Almanac and Book of Facts* 1985, p. 246; U.S. Census data). Compared with other cultures, our networks of personal ties are relatively restricted, and the trend is for this to continue. One-parent families more than doubled between 1970 and 1983 as two-parent households declined by 5 percent. Still, relationships with one's children and spouse

Illustrating a trend that will intensify with the aging of the baby boomers, more older Americans are working part-time.

continue to overshadow all other kin ties (e.g., to parents or siblings) for adult Americans. The American nuclear family must confront many problems that are dissipated within larger kin networks in nonindustrial cultures. Because it is expected to manage so many daily strains in this competitive society, the nuclear family experiences mounting tensions. Because marriage and children are so important, stresses are particularly obvious in these relationships.

As more American women work outside the home (52 percent in 1983, 67 percent in 1988, estimated to rise to 70 percent by 1992), parents have less time to lavish on large families. Among two-parent families, both husband and wife now work in 80 percent of American households (Schachter 1989). Day-care centers and preschools have increased in tandem with two-earner families. By the mid-1980s, some 40 percent of American parents sent their children to preschool, more than double the 1970 figure (Peebles 1985). Partly to meet day-care costs and partly because they can better afford it, full-time working parents spend an average of 23 percent more money on each child than do families with one employed parent (*Population Today* 1984). The current cost of a four-year Ivy League college education is more than $80,000—estimated to rise to $174,000 by the year 2000 (*Ann Arbor News*, September 5, 1989).

Given these work patterns, it's no surprise that fast food is proliferating. Franchise restaurant sales are increasing between 13 percent and 14 percent

annually. In 1990, 45.8 million Americans per day ate in a fast-food restaurant (Roberts 1990). There are far more McDonald's today than there were fast-food restaurants in the United States in 1945. With parents working to keep up their life styles and meet escalating child-rearing costs, who's at home to prepare lunch and dinner? No wonder microwaves sell like hotcakes and the franchise restaurant industry is expected to be one of the top ten economic advancers in the 1990s.

Economic forces such as the culture of consumption, the growth of the service-information economy, overwork, professionalism, and specialization contribute to the social issues we hear so much about today. These issues include problems of mental and physical health, alcohol and drug abuse, fragmenting marriages and families, and spouse and child abuse. American culture increasingly hands over to "experts" decisions that families once made. Intervention in personal and family matters by hospitals, police officers, court officials, social workers, physicians, and other experts is one of the most prominent trends in contemporary America, and there is no sign it will abate. This trend poses a major contrast between modern culture and the cultures that have existed throughout most of human history. The social alienation of today's America is rooted in its economic transformation: the change from an industrial economy specializing in the manufacture of goods to a high-tech economy oriented toward information processing and the provision of services.

Computer Technology and Information Processing

Although they reached the market only in 1976, 725,000 microcomputers were being sold annually by 1980. Since then they have proliferated faster than rats or lawyers. By 1989 there were 81 million computers worldwide, 40 million in the United States alone (Davis 1989). The trend toward information growth and automation will continue. The estimate is that scientific information, now growing by 15 percent annually, will be increasing at twice that rate by A.D. 2000. The robot labor force grows by 30 percent a year (*Ann Arbor News*, December 26, 1984) to do work that human blue-collar workers once did. Jobs of the future will require more technical knowledge and problem-solving abilities as robots and computers take over more of the rote tasks that people do today (*New York Times*, September 25, 1989). Educated people will be most likely to find jobs, get training from employers, earn more because of greater productivity, and change jobs less often. "The well educated face a future of expanded job opportunities and rising wages . . . while those not well educated face a future of contracting opportunities and poverty" (*New York Times*, September 25, 1989).

Despite the American ideology of equality and the self-identification of most Americans with the middle class, many disturbing, and lingering, aspects of our culture are based on socioeconomic stratification. The most affluent 20 percent of American households average twelve times the income of the poorest fifth (MacDouglas 1984). From case studies of development in Third World countries—Java's green revolution, for example—we know that an initially uneven distribution of resources often becomes the basis for greater inequality after a technological or economic shift. Java's experience teaches us that the social impact of an economic shift can be particularly severe, contributing negatively to equity, when the new technology is available mainly to the rich.

This lesson has an American application. If current stratification-based trends continue, we face results like Java's. The United States has a "persistent and substantial inequality in the access to new technology among both schools and school children. . . . The poorer a school is, the less likely that school is to have any of this new technology" (*Ann Arbor News*, February 10, 1985, p. A11). Math, science, and the computer are the strategic resources of a high-tech, statistical society, just as dams and irrigation canals are strategic resources among peasants. Microcomputers are concentrated in affluent school districts. Unless our schools provide widespread computer equipment and training, continuation of the current distribution pattern based on income and local property-tax support will ensure that we raise a differentially privileged generation of computer whizzes and dolts, the children of richer and poorer Americans.

Poverty and the Income Gap

U.S. Census Bureau figures for 1988 (Barringer 1989) showed that 32 million Americans live below the official poverty level ($12,091 per year for a family of four). The American poverty rate isn't shrinking but growing. From 1978 to 1988 it increased from 11.4 percent to 13.1 percent as the number of poor people rose from 24.5 million to 32 million. Over the past two decades middle- and lower-level American earners haven't made statistically significant income gains. The top fifth of Americans had a 16 percent income gain between 1979 and 1987, compared with a loss of 8 percent for the bottom fifth (Allen 1989).

One reason why the gap is widening is the combination of increasing female wage work and **homogamy**—the tendency to marry someone socially similar (of comparable socioeconomic and educational status). People tend to choose as a mate someone with a similar social background, education, job, outlook, and value system—someone on the "same rung of the social ladder." A growing number of American women, particularly the well educated, are working outside the home. Education is a key to social mobility in an open class system, particularly one based on services

Jobs of the future will require more technical knowledge and problem-solving abilities. Robots and computers will take over more of the rote tasks that people do today. The well-educated can anticipate expanded job opportunities and rising wages, but the poorly educated face a future of shrinking opportunities.

and information. As people marry homoga-
mously, the combined income of better-educated,
wealthier couples mounts geometrically, and this
trend will continue.

Race and Ethnicity

Race and ethnicity (Figure 19.3) are obvious features of stratification in the United States. The 1988
poverty rate was 10.1 percent for whites, 31.6 percent for blacks, and 26.8 percent for Hispanics.
Census data confirm the inequality that continues
to deny African-Americans and Hispanics full access to advantages that most other Americans enjoy. In 1983, 47 percent of American black children
and 38 percent of Hispanic children lived in households with subpoverty incomes. This was true for
just 15 percent of American white children. Inequality shows up consistently in unemployment
figures (*Ann Arbor News,* May 23, 1985).

Although the health of Americans is improving,
disparity in the death and illness rates of blacks
and whites persists. African-Americans tend to die
younger and have higher infant mortality rates
than do whites. In 1987 life expectancy for American whites was 75.6 years, versus 69.4 years for
blacks. Infant mortality rates that year were 8.6

(per 1,000) for whites and 17.9 for blacks. Black
males aged fifteen to nineteen die by homicide,
execution, or police actions at a rate of 52 per 1,000,
versus 9 per 1,000 for white males of the same age
(Johnson 1989). The drug-related death rate for
African-Americans in 1987 was more than twice
the rate for whites, and the black homicide death
rate was six times that of whites (*New York Times,*
September 27, 1989).

Homelessness

Much of the poverty in industrial nations is caused
by unemployment, which is unknown in nonstates, where people derive their subsistence from
land, livestock, and natural resources. In modern
society, the shift to a service economy requires a
better-educated and more skillful work force, and
this discriminates against people who lack access
to quality education. In the United States and
throughout the world, members of the **underclass**
(the abjectly poor) lack jobs, adequate food, medical care, and even shelter. Poverty and homelessness are particularly obvious on the streets of big
cities. Millions of rural Brazilians have settled in
burgeoning urban shanty towns (*favelas*). Poorer
Brazilians, including abandoned children, camp in

Figure 19.3 *The proportion of the American population that is white and non-
Hispanic is declining. Consider two projections of the ethnic composition of the
United States in A.D. 2080. The first assumes an annual immigration rate of
500,000; the second assumes 1 million immigrants per year. With either projection
the Hispanic and Asian segments of the population grow dramatically (much more
so than do Blacks and non-Hispanic whites). (From Bouvier and Davis 1982,
p. 40)*

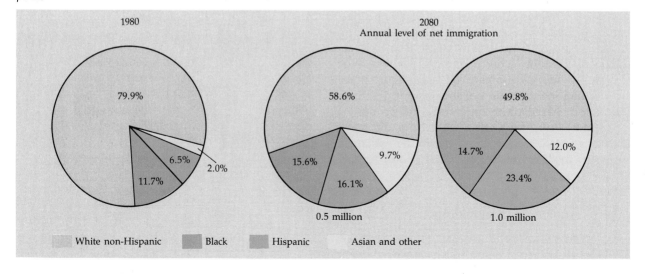

Poverty is particularly obvious in big cities throughout the world. Millions of rural Brazilians have settled in burgeoning urban shanty towns (favelas), such as this one in Rio de Janeiro.

the streets, bathe in fountains, beg, rob, and scavenge like their homeless counterparts in North America.

If these trends continue, the underclass will fall even further as the gap between rich (educated) and poor (uneducated) increases. Homelessness in the United States is an extreme form of downward mobility, which may follow job loss, layoffs, or situations in which women and children flee from domestic abuse. The causes of homelessness are varied—psychological, economic, and social. They include inability to pay rent, eviction, sale of urban real estate to developers, and mental illness. In New York City today many of the urban poor sleep in cardboard cartons and at train stations, on sidewalks and near warm-air gratings. They feed themselves by begging, scavenging, and raiding garbage (particularly that of restaurants) for food. The homeless are the foragers of modern society. They are poorly clad urban nomads, shaggy men and bag ladies who carry their meager possessions with them as they move.

Today's most extreme socioeconomic contrasts within the world capitalist economy are between the richest people in core nations and the poorest people on the periphery. However, as the gap between rich and poor widens in North America, the social distance between the underclasses of core and periphery shrinks. The road to Bangladesh passes through Times Square.

THE CONTINUANCE OF DIVERSITY

Anthropology has a crucial role to play in promoting a more humanistic vision of social change, one that respects the value of cultural diversity. The existence of anthropology is itself a tribute to the continuing need to understand social and cultural differences. Anthropology teaches us that the adaptive responses of humans can be more flexible than can those of other species because our main adaptive means are sociocultural. However, the cultural forms, institutions, values, and customs of the past always influence subsequent adaptation, producing continued diversity and giving a certain uniqueness to responses by different groups.

Anthropology focuses on similarities and differences in cultures and human adaptive strategies. Evolution, cultural or biological, must always accommodate itself to, and proceed by using, the material at hand. People with different cultural backgrounds react differently to modern trends, including the spread of the world system. Because of this, among populations that manage to adapt to the twenty-first century, the diversity that has intrigued students of anthropology since its beginning should endure. Let us hope that vigorous cultural differences will prevent what some social scientists see as a bland convergence in the future, so that free and open investigation of human diversity can continue. With our knowledge and our awareness of our professional responsibilities, let us work to keep anthropology, the study of humankind, the most humanistic of all the disciplines.

SUMMARY

Social scientists predict the probability of future developments by assuming that regularities observed in the past and the present will continue to hold true, an assumption called uniformitarianism. Scientific predictions contrast with occult predictions, which date back to the Paleolithic. Astrology, based on nonscientific procedures, is widely used by nonindustrial farmers in scheduling the cycle of agricultural activities. Unlike science, the power of astrology and divination comes from the supernatural world, not the real one. Successful organizations get their forecasts not from physics but from established public-opinion and market-research organizations. The best predictions are based on the probability that social forces operating today will work the same way in the future.

Current demographic trends are the basis for predictions about future world population. The world has recently experienced two demographic transitions (changing patterns of population growth). The new demographic transition is going on now in Third World nations. Birth rates stay high while death rates have fallen because of medical advances. This has produced rates of natural increase never before experienced in human history. Provision of adequate resources for the expanding global population and control of its increase are fundamental problems that must be solved if humanity is to have a future.

Because descendants of the non-Westerners whom anthropologists have traditionally studied are increasing their share of the world's population, understanding diverse cultural backgrounds is of growing importance. The fastest current population growth rates are in Third World cities. The slum growth rate will lead to a doubling of slum populations in three to six years. Rates of Third World crime and pollution will also increase.

Growth in the world food supply since the 1950s has been based mainly on petroleum- and chemical-dependent mechanized farming. However, food production is no longer keeping up with population growth. Energy resources and conservation are long-term global issues, and the energy crunch will return. The United States is the world's most wasteful nation. Without massive global conservation measures, the effects of energy shortages will be hardest on developing industrial nations such as Brazil, which imports half its huge energy needs.

Goods manufacture is shifting to Third World countries. However, unemployment will continue to plague those nations because of population growth, particularly urban growth. As unemployment mounts in the Third World, the job crunch will ease in the United States. Although machines are displacing people in traditional jobs, this hasn't prevented a huge increase in the number of Americans working outside the home. More and more Americans must work for wages to maintain our consumer life style. The trend is toward overwork rather than unemployment. In order to maintain the culture of consumption, Americans are working longer hours outside the home than they were a decade ago.

At an increasing rate, the American economy is shifting from heavy-goods production toward the provision of specialized services, including information processing. As a result, blue-collar workers, family farmers, labor unions, and homemakers all represent declining segments of the American population. There is increasing geographical mobility, but Americans are residing more and more in small cities and suburbs rather than cities. This growing suburban population is made possible by a highly developed consumer economy, highways, affordable automobiles, and shopping malls.

The population of the United States is aging. A new economic independence for the elderly, most of whom now live in their own homes and have adequate incomes, is based partly on Social Security benefits that have increased faster than have wages, salaries, and prices. However, the elderly, like other segments of the population, are more isolated from their families than they were thirty years ago. More Americans are living by themselves or with strangers. Compared with other cultures, our networks of personal and family ties are restricted, and the trend is for this to continue. The American nuclear family must confront many problems that are dissipated within larger kin networks in nonindustrial cultures.

Such economic forces as the culture of consumption, the rise of the service-oriented economy, increasing employment, professionalism, and specialization have given rise to issues we hear much about today. These issues include problems of mental and physical health, the family, marriage, divorce, and spouse and child abuse. Decisions that once belonged to families have been handed over to such "experts" as hospitals, court officials, social workers, and physicians. This trend provides a major contrast between contemporary American culture and the cultures that have existed throughout most of human history.

The trend toward information and automation will continue. Despite the American ideology of equality and the fact that most Americans identify with the middle class, many lingering problems are based on socioeconomic stratification. An uneven distribution of resources can become the basis for even greater inequality after a technological or economic shift. Math, science, and the computer are the strategic resources of a high-tech society. Current access to quality education, including computer technology, is based on income and local property-tax support. Today's America offers its school-children unequal access to training and technology.

Much of the poverty in industrial nations is caused by unemployment, which is unknown in nonstates. The American poverty rate is not shrinking but growing. One reason why the gap between rich and poor is widening is the combination of female wage work (particularly by educated women) and homogamy—the tendency to marry someone socially similar. Race and ethnicity are obvious features of stratification in the United States. As the gap between rich and poor widens in North America, the social distance between the underclasses of core and periphery shrinks.

GLOSSARY

complex services: Jobs in information processing—the manipulation of data and abstract symbols—including insurance, engineering, law, finance, computer programming, advertising, and scientific research.

demographic transition: A changing pattern of population growth.

homogamy: Tendency to marry someone socially similar (of comparable socioeconomic and educational status).

natural increase rate: Number of births minus number of deaths (per 1,000 population), plus or minus migration.

new demographic transition: Going on currently in Third World nations; in areas that historically have had high birth rates, these rates have been maintained while the death rate has fallen, producing rates of natural increase never before experienced in human history.

occult predictions: In contrast to scientific predictions, those based on the supernatural world rather than the real one, such as astrology, divination, and psychic forecasts.

old demographic transition: Occurred in the developed countries; as the death rate declined, the birth rate did not increase significantly; population increases were small.

person-to-person services: Personal-contact service jobs, such as custodians, security guards, restaurant and retail workers, day-care providers, clerical workers, teachers, hotel workers, recreation directors, fitness teachers, bank tellers, salespersons, and health-care workers.

probability prediction: One based on the likelihood (percent chance) of future events or developments.

underclass: The abjectly poor of modern society; those who lack jobs, adequate food, medical care, and shelter.

STUDY QUESTIONS

1. What is the difference between scientific and occult predictions?
2. On what basis do social scientists predict the future?
3. Why does occult prediction continue in modern society?
4. What is the difference between the old and the new demographic transitions?
5. Where is the population increasing most rapidly?
6. Are there likely to be food and energy shortages in the future? If so, what can be done to avoid or solve them?
7. How do employment trends in the United States contrast with those in less-developed countries?
8. What is the significance of the shift from a manufacturing economy to a service and information economy?
9. Which segments of the American work force are currently increasing, and which are declining?
10. What are the political implications of these increases and declines?
11. What age group within the American population is increasing most rapidly, and why?
12. Will the spread of a world system end cultural diversity? Why or why not?

SUGGESTED ADDITIONAL READING

DOUGLAS, M., AND A. WILDAVSKY

    1982   *Risk and Culture: An Essay on the Selection of Technological and Environmental Dangers.* Berkeley: University of California Press. Controversial analysis and comparison of ideologies concerning pollution in tribal and industrial societies.

MARGOLIS, M. L.

    1984   *Mothers and Such: American Views of Women and How They Changed.* Berkeley: University of California Press. Changing views on women, their employment, and their role in the family.

NAISBITT, J., AND P. ABURDENE

    1990   *Megatrends 2000: Ten New Directions for the 1990's.* New York: William Morrow. Forecasts: a booming global economy, a renaissance in the arts, free-market socialism, global life styles and cultural nationalism, privatization of the welfare state, the rise of the Pacific Rim (including California), female leadership, the age of biology, and the triumph of the individual.

NEWMAN, K. S.

    1988   *Falling from Grace: The Experience of Downward Mobility in the American Middle Class.* New York: Free Press. An anthropologist provides personal accounts by middle-class Americans who have lost their jobs and experienced downward mobility; supplemented by statistics and insightful analysis.

TOFFLER, A.

    1980   *The Third Wave.* New York: William Morrow. The author of the best-selling *Future Shock* speculates about the twenty-first century.

CONTEMPORARY AMERICAN POPULAR CULTURE

Although culture is shared, all cultures have divisive as well as unifying forces. Tribes are divided by residence in different villages and membership in different descent groups. Nations, though united by government, are divided by class, region, ethnicity, religion, and political party. Unifying forces in tribal cultures include marriage, trade, and segmentary lineage structure. In any society, of course, a common cultural tradition also provides a basis for uniformity.

Whatever unity contemporary American culture has doesn't rest on a particularly strong central government. Nor is our national unity based on segmentary lineage structure or marital exchange networks. In fact, many of the commonalities of behavior, belief, and activity that enable us to speak of "contemporary American culture" are relatively new. They are founded on and perpetuated by twentieth-century developments, particularly in business, transportation, and the mass media.

ANTHROPOLOGISTS AND AMERICAN CULTURE

When anthropologists study urban ethnic groups or relationships between class and household or-

ganization, they focus on variation, a very important topic. However, anthropology is concerned as much with uniformity as with variation. "National character" studies of the 1940s and 1950s foreshadowed anthropology's growing interest in unifying themes in modern nations. Unfortunately, those studies, of such countries as Japan and Russia, focused too much on the psychological characteristics of individuals. Contemporary anthropologists interested in national culture realize that culture is an attribute of groups. Shared cultural themes (beliefs, values, ways of thinking and acting) override differences between individuals. This appendix focuses on unifying factors, on common experiences, actions, and beliefs in contemporary American culture.

Anthropologists should study American society and culture. Anthropology, after all, deals with universals, generalities, and uniqueness. American culture is a particular cultural variant, as interesting as any other. Techniques developed in smaller-scale societies, where sociocultural uniformity is more marked, can contribute to an understanding of American life.

Native anthropologists are those who study their own cultures—for example, American anthropologists working in the United States, French ones working in France, and Nigerians working in Nigeria. Anthropological training and field work abroad provide an anthropologist with a certain degree of detachment and objectivity that most natives lack. However, life experience as a native gives an advantage to anthropologists who wish to study their own cultures. Nevertheless, more than when working abroad, the native anthropologist is both participant and observer, often emotionally and intellectually involved in the events and beliefs being studied. Native anthropologists must be particularly careful to resist their own emic biases (their prejudices as natives). They must strive to be as objective in describing their own cultures as they are in analyzing others.

Natives often see and explain their behavior very differently than anthropologists do. For example, most Americans have probably never considered the possibility that apparently secular, commercial, and recreational institutions such as sports, movies, Walt Disney enterprises, and fast-food restaurants have things in common with religious beliefs, symbols, and behavior. However, these similarities can be demonstrated anthropologically. Anthropology helps us understand ourselves. By studying other cultures, we learn both to appreciate and to question aspects of our own. Furthermore, the same techniques that anthropologists use in describing and analyzing other cultures can be applied to American culture.

American readers may not find this section convincing. In part this is because you are natives, who know much more about your own culture than you do about any other. However, it is also because I am trying to extract culture (widely *shared* aspects of behavior) from varied individual opinions, activities, and experiences, which may contradict parts of the argument. The following analyses depart from areas that can be quantified, such as population density and socioeconomic variation. We are entering a more impressionistic domain, one in which analysis sometimes seems as akin to philosophy or the humanities as to science. Certainly you will be right in questioning some of the conclusions that follow. Some are surely debatable, and some may be plain wrong. However, if they illustrate how anthropology can be used to shed light on aspects of your own life and experience and to revise and broaden your understanding of your own culture, they will have served a worthwhile function.

A reminder about culture, ethnocentrism, and native anthropologists is needed here. For anthropologists, culture means much more than refinement, cultivation, education, and appreciation of the fine arts—its popular usage. Curiously, however, when some anthropologists confront their own culture, they forget this. They carry an image of themselves as adventurous and broad-minded specialists in the unusual, the ethnic, and the exotic. Like other academics and intellectuals, they may regard American "pop" culture as trivial and unworthy of serious study. In doing so, they demonstrate ethnocentrism and reveal a bias that comes with being members of an academic-intellectual subculture.

In examining American culture, native anthropologists must be careful to overcome the bias associated with the academic subculture. Although some academics discourage their children from watching television, the fact that TVs outnumber toilets in American households is a significant cultural fact that anthropologists can't afford to ignore. My own research on Michigan college students may be generalizable to other young Americans. They visit McDonald's more often than they visit houses of worship. I found that almost all had seen a Walt Disney movie and had attended rock concerts or football games. If they are true of young Americans generally, as I suspect they are, these experiences reveal major features of American enculturation patterns. Certainly any extraterrestrial anthropologist doing field work in the United States would stress them. The mass media and the culture of consumption have created major, perhaps dominant, themes in contemporary American culture. These themes merit anthropological study.

FOOTBALL

Football, we say, is only a game, yet is has become a popular spectator sport. On fall Saturdays millions of people travel to and from college football games. Smaller congregations meet in high school stadiums. Millions of Americans watch televised football. Indeed, more than half the adult population of the United States watches the Super Bowl. Because football is of general interest to Americans, it is a unifying cultural institution that merits anthropological attention. Our most popular sports manage to attract people of diverse ethnic backgrounds, regions, religions, political parties, jobs, social statuses, wealth levels, and genders.

The popularity of football, particularly professional football, depends directly on the mass media, especially television. Is football, with its territorial incursion, hard hitting, and violence—occasionally resulting in injury—popular because Americans are violent people? Are football spectators vicariously realizing their own hostile, violent, and aggressive tendencies? Anthropologist W. Arens (1981) discounts this interpretation. He points out that football is a peculiarly American pastime. Although a similar game is played in Canada, it is considerably less popular there. Baseball has become a popular sport in the Caribbean, parts of Latin America, and Japan. Basketball and volleyball are also spreading. However, throughout most of the world, soccer is the most popular sport. Arens argues that if football were a particularly effective channel for expressing aggression, it would have spread (like soccer and baseball) to many other countries, where people have as many aggressive tendencies and hostile feelings as Americans do. Furthermore, he suggests that if a sport's popularity rested simply on a bloodthirsty temperament, boxing, a far bloodier sport, would be America's national pastime. Arens concludes that the explanation for the sport's popularity lies elsewhere, and I agree.

He contends that football is popular because it symbolizes certain key features of American life. In particular, it is characterized by teamwork based on elaborate specialization and division of labor, which are pervasive features of modern life. Susan Montague and Robert Morais (1981) take the analysis a step further. They argue that Americans appreciate football because it presents a miniaturized and simplified version of modern organizations. People have trouble understanding organizational bureaucracies, whether in business, universities, or government. Football, the anthropologists argue, helps us understand how decisions are made and rewards are allocated in organizations.

Montague and Morais link football's values, particularly teamwork, to those associated with business. Like corporate workers, ideal players are diligent and dedicated to the team. Within corporations, however, decision making is complicated

and workers aren't always rewarded for their dedication and good job performance. Decisions are simpler and rewards are more consistent in football, these anthropologists contend, and this helps explain its popularity. Even if we can't figure out how Citibank and IBM run, any fan can become an expert on football's rules, teams, scores, statistics, and patterns of play. Even more important, football suggests that the values stressed by business really do pay off. Teams whose members work hardest, show the most spirit, and best develop and coordinate their talents can be expected to win more often than other teams do.

STAR TREK AS A SUMMATION OF DOMINANT CULTURAL THEMES*

Star Trek, a familiar, powerful, and enduring force in American popular culture, can be used to illustrate the idea that popular media content often is derived from prominent values expressed in many other domains of culture. Americans first encountered the Starship *Enterprise* on NBC in 1966. *Star Trek* was shown in prime time for just three seasons. However, the series not only survives but thrives today in reruns, books, cassettes, and theatrical films. Revived as a regular weekly series with an entirely new cast in 1987, *Star Trek: The Next Generation* became the third most popular syndicated program in the United States (after *Wheel of Fortune* and *Jeopardy*).

What does the enduring mass appeal of *Star Trek* tell us about American culture? I believe the answer to be this: *Star Trek* is a transformation of a fundamental American origin myth. The same myth shows up in the image and celebration of Thanksgiving, a distinctively American holiday. Thanksgiving sets the myth in the past, and *Star Trek* sets it in the future.

When they encounter the word *myth*, most Americans probably think of stories about Greek, Roman, or Norse gods and heroes. However, all societies have myths. Their central characters need not be unreal, superhuman, or physically immor-

*This section is adapted from *Prime-Time Society: An Anthropological Analysis of Television and Culture* by Conrad Phillip Kottak. © 1990 by Wadsworth, Inc. Used by permission of the publisher.

tal. Such tales may be rooted in actual historical events.

> The popular notion that a "myth" is . . . "untrue"— indeed that its untruth is its defining characteristic— is not only naive but shows misunderstanding of its very nature. Its "scientific truth" or otherwise is irrelevant. A myth is a statement about society and man's place in it and the surrounding universe (Middleton 1967a, p. x).

Myths are hallowed stories that express fundamental cultural values. They are widely and recurrently told among, and have special meaning to, people who grow up in a particular culture. Myths may be set in the past, present, or future or in "fantasyland." Whether set in "real time" or fictional time, myths are always at least partly fictionalized.

The myths of contemporary America are drawn from a variety of sources, including such popular-culture fantasies as *Star Wars, The Wizard of Oz* (see below), and *Star Trek.* Our myths also include real people, particularly national ancestors, whose lives have been reinterpreted and endowed with special meaning over the generations. The media, schools, churches, communities, and parents teach the national origin myths to American children. The story of Thanksgiving, for example, continues to be important. It recounts the origin of a national holiday celebrated by Protestants, Catholics, and Jews. All those denominations share a belief in the Old Testament God, and they find it appropriate to thank God for their blessings.

Again and again Americans have heard idealized retellings of that epochal early harvest. We have learned how Indians taught the Pilgrims to farm in the New World. Grateful Pilgrims then invited the Indians to share their first Thanksgiving. Native American and European labor, techniques, and customs thus blended in that initial biethnic celebration. Annually reenacting the origin myth, American public schools commemorate "the first Thanksgiving" as children dress up as Pilgrims, Indians, and pumpkins.

More rapidly and pervasively as the mass media grow, each generation of Americans writes its own revisionist history. Our culture constantly reinterprets the origin, nature, and meaning of national holidays. The collective consciousness of contemporary Americans includes TV-saturated memories of "the first Thanksgiving" and "the first Christmas." Our mass culture has instilled widely shared images of a *Peanuts*-peopled Pilgrim-Indian "love-in."

We also conjure up a fictionalized Nativity with Mary, Joseph, Jesus, manger animals, shepherds, three oriental kings, a little drummer boy, and, in some versions, Rudolph the Red-Nosed Reindeer. Note that the interpretation of the Nativity that American culture perpetuates is yet another variation on the same dominant myth. We remember the Nativity as a Thanksgiving involving interethnic contacts (e.g., the three kings) and gift giving. It is set in Bethlehem rather than Massachusetts.

We impose our present on the past as we reinterpret quasi-historic and actual events. For the future we do it in our science-fiction and fantasy creations. *Star Trek* places in the future what the Thanksgiving story locates in the past—*the myth of the assimilationist, incorporating, melting-pot society.* The myth says that America is distinctive not just because it is assimilationist but because it is *founded* on unity in diversity. (Our *origin* is unity in diversity. After all, we call ourselves "the United States.") Thanksgiving and *Star Trek* illustrate the credo that unity through diversity is essential for survival (whether of a harsh winter or of the perils of outer space). Americans survive by sharing the fruits of specialization.

Star Trek proclaims that the sacred principles that validate American society, because they lie at its foundation, will ensure across the generations and even the centuries. The Starship *Enterprise* crew is a melting pot. Captain James Tiberius Kirk is symbolic of real history. His clearest historical prototype is Captain James Cook, whose ship, the *Endeavor,* also sought out new life and civilizations. Kirk's infrequently mentioned middle name, from the Roman general and eventual emperor, links the captain to the earth's imperial history. Kirk is also symbolic of the original Anglo-American. He runs the *Enterprise* (America is founded on free enterprise), just as laws, values, and institutions derived from England continue to run the United States.

McCoy's Irish (or at least Gaelic) name represents the next wave, the established immigrant. Sulu is the successfully assimilated Asian-American. The African-American female character Uhura, "whose name means freedom," indicates that blacks will become full partners with all other

Americans. However, Uhura was the only major female character in the original crew. This reflects the fact that female extradomestic employment was less characteristic of American society in 1966 than it is now.

One of *Star Trek*'s constant messages is that strangers, even enemies, can become friends. Less obviously, this message is about cultural imperialism, the assumed irresistibility of American culture and institutions. Communist nationals (Chekhov) can be seduced and captured by an expansive American culture. Spock, although from Vulcan, is half human, with human qualities. We learn, therefore, that our assimilationist values will eventually not just rule the earth but extend to other planets as well. By "the next generation," Klingon culture, even more alien than Vulcan culture, personified by Bridge Officer Worf, has joined the melting pot.

Even God is harnessed to serve American culture, in the person of Scotty. His role is that of the ancient Greek *deus ex machina*. He is a stage controller who "beams" people up and down, back and forth, from earth to the heavens. Scotty, who keeps society going, is also a servant-employee who does his engineering for management—illustrating loyalty and technical skill.

The Next Generation contains many analogues of the original characters. Several "partial people" are single-character personifications of particular human qualities represented in more complex form by the original *Star Trek* crew members. Kirk, Spock, and McCoy have all been split into multiple characters. Captain Jean-Luc Picard has the intellectual and managerial attributes of James T. Kirk. With his English accent and French name, Picard, like Kirk, draws his legitimacy from symbolic association with historic Western European empires. First Officer Riker replaces Kirk as a romantic man of action.

Spock, an alien (strange ears) who represents science, reason, and intellect, has been split in two. One half is Worf, a Klingon bridge officer whose cranial protuberances are analogous to Spock's ears. The other is Data, an android whose brain contains the sum of human wisdom. Two female characters, an empath and the ship's doctor, have replaced Dr. McCoy as the repository of healing, emotion, and feeling.

Mirroring contemporary American culture, *The Next Generation* features prominent black, female,

and physically handicapped characters. An African-American actor plays the Klingon Mr. Worf. Another, LeVar Burton, appears as Geordi La Forge. Although blind, Geordi manages, through a vision-enhancing visor, to see things that other people cannot. His mechanical vision expresses the characteristic American faith in technology. So does the android, Data.

During its first year, *The Next Generation* had three prominent female characters. One was the ship's doctor, a working professional with a teenage son. Another was an empath, the ultimate "helping professional." The third was the ship's security officer.

America is more specialized, differentiated, and professional than it was in the sixties. The greater role specificity and diversity of *Next Generation* characters reflect this. Nevertheless, both series convey the central *Star Trek* message, one that dominates the culture that created them: Americans have varied backgrounds. Individual qualities, talents, and specialties divide us. However, we make our livings and survive as members of cohesive, efficient groups. We explore and advance as members of a crew, a team, an enterprise, or, most generally, a society. Our nation is founded on and endures through assimilation—effective subordination of individual differences within a smoothly functioning multiethnic team. The team is American culture. It worked in the past. It works today. It will go on working across the generations. Orderly and progressive democracy based on mutual respect is best. Inevitably, American culture will triumph over all others—by convincing and assimilating rather than conquering them. Unity in diversity guarantees human survival, and for this we should be thankful.

FANTASY FILMS AS MYTH

Techniques that anthropologists use to analyze myths can be extended to two fantasy films that most students have seen. *The Wizard of Oz* has been telecast annually for decades. *Star Wars* is one of the most popular films of all time. Both are familiar and significant cultural products with obvious mythic qualities. The contributions of French structuralist anthropologist Claude Lévi-Strauss and neo-Freudian psychoanalyst Bruno Bettelheim (Chapter 14) permit the following analysis of visual fairy tales that contemporary Americans know well. I will show that *Star Wars* is a systematic structural transformation of *The Wizard of Oz*. I cannot say how many of the resemblances were conscious and how many merely express a collective unconscious that *Star Wars* writer and director George Lucas shares with other Americans through common enculturation.

The Wizard of Oz and *Star Wars* both begin in arid country, the first in Kansas and the second on the desert planet Tatooine (Table A.1). *Star Wars* changes *The Wizard*'s female hero into a boy, Luke Skywalker. Fairy tale heroes usually have short, common first names and second names that describe their origin or activity. Thus Luke, who travels aboard spaceships, is a Skywalker, while Dorothy Gale is swept off to Oz by a cyclone (a gale of wind). Dorothy leaves home with her dog, Toto,

who is pursued by and has managed to escape from a woman who in Oz becomes the Wicked Witch of the West. Luke follows his "Two-Two" (R2D2), who is fleeing Darth Vader, the witch's structural equivalent.

Dorothy and Luke both live with an uncle and an aunt. However, because of the gender change of the hero, the primary relationship is reversed and inverted. Thus Dorothy's relationship with her aunt is primary, warm, and loving, whereas Luke's relationship with his uncle, though primary, is strained and distant. Aunt and uncle are in the tales for the same reason. They represent home (the nuclear family of orientation), which children (according to American culture norms) must eventually leave to make it on their own. As Bettelheim (1975) points out, fairy tales often disguise parents as uncle and aunt, and this estab-

Table A.1 Star Wars *as a structural transformation of* The Wizard of Oz.

Star Wars	*The Wizard of Oz*
Male hero (Luke Skywalker)	Female hero (Dorothy Gale)
Arid Tatooine	Arid Kansas
Luke follows R2D2 R2D2 flees Vader	Dorothy follows Toto Toto flees witch
Luke lives with uncle and aunt Primary relationship with uncle (same sex as hero) Strained, distant relationship with uncle	Dorothy lives with uncle and aunt Primary relationship with aunt (same sex as hero) Warm, close relationship with aunt
Tripartite division of same-sex parent: 2 parts good, 1 part bad father Good father dead at beginning Good father dead (?) at end Bad father survives	Tripartite division of same-sex parent: 2 parts bad, 1 part good mother Bad mother dead at beginning Bad mother dead at end Good mother survives
Relationship with parent of opposite sex (Princess Leia Organa): Princess is unwilling captive Needle Princess is freed	Relationship with parent of opposite sex (Wizard of Oz): Wizard makes impossible demands Broomstick Wizard turns out to be sham
Trio of companions: Han Solo, C3PO, Chewbacca	Trio of companions: Scarecrow, Tin Woodman, Cowardly Lion
Minor characters: Jawas Sand People Stormtroopers	Minor characters: Munchkins Apple Trees Flying Monkeys
Settings: Death Star Verdant Tikal (rebel base)	Settings: Witch's castle Emerald City
Conclusion: Luke uses magic to accomplish goal (destroy Death Star)	Conclusion: Dorothy uses magic to accomplish goal (return to Kansas)

lishes social distance. The child can deal with the hero's separation (in *The Wizard of Oz*) or the aunt's and uncle's death (in *Star Wars*) more easily than with the death of or separation from real parents. Furthermore, this permits the child's strong feelings toward his or her real parents to be represented in different, more central characters, such as the Wicked Witch of the West and Darth Vader.

Both films focus on the child's relationship with the parent of the same sex, dividing that parent into three parts. In *The Wizard,* the mother is split into two parts bad and one part good. They are the Wicked Witch of the East, dead at the beginning of the movie; the Wicked Witch of the West, dead at the end; and Glinda, the good mother, who survives. The first *Star Wars* film reversed the proportion of good and bad, giving Luke a good father (his own), the Jedi knight who is proclaimed dead at the film's beginning. There is another good father, Ben Kenobi, who is ambiguously dead when the movie ends. Third is a father figure of total evil, Darth Vader. As the good-mother third survives *The Wizard of Oz,* the bad-father third lives on after *Star Wars,* to strike back in the sequel.

The child's relationship with the parent of the opposite sex is also represented in the two films. Dorothy's father figure is the Wizard of Oz, an initially terrifying figure who later is proved to be a fake. Bettelheim notes that the typical fairy tale father is disguised as a monster or giant or else (when preserved as a human) is weak, distant, or ineffective. Children wonder why Cinderella's father lets her be treated badly by her stepmother and stepsisters, why the father of Hansel and Gretel does not throw out his new wife instead of his children, and why Snow White's father doesn't tell the queen she's narcissistic. Dorothy counts on the wizard to save her but finds that he makes seemingly impossible demands and in the end is just an ordinary man. She succeeds on her own, no longer relying on a father who offers no more than she herself possesses.

In *Star Wars* (although not in the later films in the trilogy), Luke's mother figure is Princess Leia Organa. Bettelheim notes that boys commonly fantasize their mothers to be unwilling captives of their fathers, and fairy tales often disguise mothers as princesses whose freedom the boy-hero must obtain. In graphic Freudian imagery, Darth Vader

threatens Princess Leia with a needle the size of the witch's broomstick. By the end of the film, Luke has freed Leia and defeated Vader.

There are other striking parallels in the structure of the two films. Fairy tale heroes are often accompanied on their adventures by secondary characters who personify the virtues needed in a successful quest. Dorothy takes along wisdom (the Scarecrow), love (the Tin Woodman), and courage (the Cowardly Lion). *Star Wars* includes a structurally equivalent trio—Han Solo, C3PO, and Chewbacca—but their association with particular qualities is not as precise. The minor characters are also structurally parallel: Munchkins and Jawas, Apple Trees and Sand People, Flying Monkeys and Stormtroopers. And compare settings—the witch's castle and the Death Star, the Emerald City and the rebel base. The endings are also parallel. Luke accomplishes his objective on his own, using the Force (Oceanian mana, magical power). Dorothy's aim is to return to Kansas. She does that by tapping her shoes together and drawing on the Force in her ruby slippers.

All successful cultural products blend old and new, drawing on familiar themes. They rearrange them in novel ways and thus win a lasting place in the imaginations of the culture that creates or accepts them. *Star Wars* successfully used old cultural themes in novel ways, and it drew on *the American fairy tale,* one that had been available in book form since the turn of the century.

DISNEY MYTH AND RITUAL

Just as anthropological techniques developed to analyze myths also fit fantasy films, anthropology can show how an ostensibly secular activity, a visit to Walt Disney World, takes on some of the attributes of a religious pilgrimage. The Disney "shrines"—Disneyland in California and Walt Disney World in Florida—owe their success not just to the amusement they offer but to years of preprogramming that have influenced Americans for over half a century. Disney's creations—films, television programs, a cable channel, cartoons, comics, toys, and amusement parks—have been important forces in American enculturation. I will examine the Disney mythology and then look at what happens during a visit to Walt Disney World. We shall see that certain observations about religion also apply to this quasi-religious dimension of contemporary American culture.

Walt Disney, who died in 1966, was a highly successful businessman whose commercial empire was built on movies, television programs, and amusement parks. Disney products have cultural as well as commercial significance. Specifically, exposure to Disney creations (just as to *Star Wars* and *The Wizard of Oz*) has been part of Americans' common enculturation, particularly since 1937, when *Snow White and the Seven Dwarfs,* Disney's first full-length cartoon, was released. Disney products, transmitted through the mass media, provide a set of quasi-mythological symbols. Diffused worldwide, they have affected enculturation in many nations. Particularly important are the images of childhood fantasy, the cartoon characters—unusual humans and humanlike animals—that continue to be part of the mythology of American childhood.

Disney mythology shows similarities with myths of other cultures and can be analyzed in the same terms. In myths, binary oppositions (polar contrasts) are often resolved by mediating figures, entities that somehow link opposites. Consider the binary opposition between nature and culture, which is a concern of people everywhere. We know scientifically that many differences between humans and other animals are differences of degree rather than kind. However, religions and myths, for thousands of years and throughout the world, have been concerned with demonstrating just the opposite—that people stand apart from nature, that humans are unique. The opposition between people and nature has been symbolized by major attributes of culture, such as speech ("In the beginning was the word"), technology (Prometheus stole fire from the gods), thought (the soul), and knowledge (the Fall of Adam and Eve). Human knowledge of good and evil is opposed to animal innocence.

Myths often use mediating figures to resolve oppositions. Animals, for example, are given human abilities, thus bridging the opposition between culture and nature. In Genesis, a humanlike animal (a bipedal, talking, lying snake) brings culture and nature closer together. In the beginning, Adam and Eve are innocent parts of nature, yet they are

unique because of their creation in God's image. The snake encourages Original Sin, which keeps humans unique, but in a far less exalted way. The punishment for eating forbidden fruit is a destiny of physical labor, a struggle with nature. That humans are a part of nature while also being different from other animals is explained by the serpent-mediator's role in the Fall. The fall of humanity is paralleled in the fall of the serpent—from culture-bearing creature to belly-crawling animal.

According to Lévi-Strauss (1967), myths often resolve an apparent contradiction. Mediating figures and events may resolve such oppositions as culture versus nature by showing that just as mythical animals can have human abilities and thus be cultural, people, while different from nature, are also part of nature. People are like animals in many ways, dependent on natural resources and participants in natural systems.

Disney creations address the culture-nature opposition. Disney conferred human attributes on his animated (from *anima*, Latin for "soul") characters. These qualities include talking, laughing, tricking, bumbling, lying, singing, making friends, and participating in family life. In most of his movies, the animals—and witches, dwarfs, fairies, mermaids, and other not-quite-human characters—deny the opposition of culture and nature by having more human qualities than the stereotypically perfect heroes and heroines do.

In "Cinderella," for example, the nature-culture opposition is inverted (turned over, reversed). Mice—natural (undomesticated) animals that are ordinarily considered pests—are endowed with speech and other cultural attributes and become Cinderella's loyal friends. The cat, ordinarily a part of culture (domesticated), becomes a dark creature of evil who almost blocks Cinderella's transformation from domestic servant into princess. The reversal of the normal opposition—that is, cat-culture-good versus mouse-nature-bad—shows how Disney characterization overcomes the opposition between culture and nature. Similarly, just as natural animals in Disney films are depicted as cultural creatures, people are often represented as being closer to nature than they normally are. In several Disney films human actors are used to portray close relationships between children and undomesticated animals such as raccoons, foxes, bears, and wolves. Disney's choice of Kipling's *The*

Jungle Book as the subject matter for a cartoon feature also illustrates this second means of dealing with the nature-culture opposition.

A Pilgrimage to Walt Disney World

With Disney as creator and myth maker for so many Americans, his shrines could hardly fail. In many cultures, religion focuses on sacred sites. Infertile women in Madagascar seek fecundity by spilling the blood of a rooster in front of phallic stones. Australian totems are associated with holy sites where, in mythology, totemic beings first emerged from the ground. Sacred groves provide symbolic unity for dispersed clans among the Jie of Uganda (Gulliver 1965/1974). A visit to Mecca (*haj*) is an obligation of Islam. Pilgrims seek miraculous cures at shrines such as Lourdes and Fátima, which are associated with Roman Catholicism. In the arid *sertão* of northeastern Brazil, thousands of pilgrims journey each August 6 to fulfill their vows to a wooden statue in a cave— Bom Jesus da Lapa. Similarly, but virtually every day of the year, thousands of American families travel long distances and invest significant amounts of money to experience Disneyland and Walt Disney World.

A conversation with anthropologist Alexander Moore, then of the University of Florida, first prompted me to think of Walt Disney World as analogous to religious pilgrimage centers. The behavior of the millions of Americans who visit it is comparable to that of religious pilgrims. Moore pointed out that like other shrines, Walt Disney World has an inner, sacred center and an outer, more secular domain. At Walt Disney World, appropriately enough, the inner, sacred area is known as "the Magic Kingdom."

Motels, restaurants, and campgrounds dot the approach to Disney World, becoming increasingly concentrated near the park. You enter Walt Disney World on "World Drive." You can choose between the Magic Kingdom or turnoffs to Epcot Center and the MGM Theme Park. The following analysis applies only to the Magic Kingdom. A sign on World Drive instructs you to turn to a specified radio station. A recording played continuously throughout the day gives information about where and how to park and how to proceed on the journey to the Magic Kingdom. It also promotes new Magic Kingdom activities and special attractions, such as "America on Parade" and "Senior American Days."

Travelers enter the mammoth parking lot by driving through a structure like a turnpike toll booth. As they pay the parking fee, they receive a brochure describing attractions both inside and outside the central area. (Campgrounds, lakes, islands, and an "international shopping village" are in the park's outlying areas.) Sections of the parking lot have totemlike designations—Minnie, Goofy, Pluto, and Chip 'n' Dale—each with several numbered rows. Uniformed attendants direct motorists to parking places. They make sure that cars park within the marked spaces and that every space is filled in order. As visitors emerge from their cars, they are directed to open-air trainlike buses called trams. Lest they forget where their cars are parked, they are told as they board the tram to "remember" Minnie, Pluto, or whichever mythological figure has become the temporary guardian of their vehicle. Many travelers spend the first minute of the tram ride reciting "Minnie 30, Minnie 30," memorizing the automobile's row number. Leaving the tram, visitors hurry to booths where they purchase entrance to the Magic Kingdom and its attractions ("adventures"). They then pass through turnstiles behind the ticket sales booths and prepare to be transported, by "express" monorail or ferryboat, to the Magic Kingdom itself.

Because the approach to the central area occurs in gradual stages, the division of Walt Disney World into outer, secular space and inner, sacred space is not clear-cut. Moving concentrically inward, the zones become gradually rather than abruptly more sacred. Even after one passes the parking lot and turnstiles, a zone that is still secular, with hotels, beaches, and boating areas, comes before the Magic Kingdom. This is the obviously more ordinary part of Walt Disney World, where visitors can check into hotels and eat in restaurants that recall similar places throughout the United States. The "Polynesian" architecture and decor of one of the hotel complexes aren't unusual for Sun Belt condominium communities. Nor do the white beaches, paddle boats, and water sports visible in this peripheral area suggest anything other than a typical vacationland. Although visitors have the option of taking a "local" monorail to one of the hotels, most pilgrims board the express monorail directly to the Magic Kingdom. The alternative to this futuristic mode of transportation is a more sedate ferryboat.

On the express monorail, which bridges the opposition between the secular areas and the Magic Kingdom, similarities between Disney pilgrims and participants in rites of passage are especially obvious. (Rites of passage may be transitions in space, age, or social status.) Disney pilgrims who ride the express monorail exhibit, as one might expect in a transition from secular to sacred space (a magic kingdom), many of the attributes associated with liminal states, as discussed in Chapter 14. Like liminal periods in other passage rites, aboard the monorail all prohibitions that apply everywhere else in Disney World are intensified. In the secular areas and in the Magic Kingdom itself people may smoke and eat, and in the secular areas they can consume alcohol and go shoeless, but all these things are taboo on the monorail. Like ritual passengers, monorail riders temporarily relinquish control over their destinies. Herded like cattle into the monorail, passengers move out of ordinary space and into a time out of time in which social distinctions disappear and everyone is reduced to a common level. As the monorail departs, a disembodied voice prepares the pilgrims for what is to come, enculturating them in the lore and standards of Walt Disney World.

Symbols of rebirth at the end of liminality are typical of liminal periods. Rebirth symbolism is an aspect of the monorail ride. As the monorail speeds through the Contemporary Resort Hotel, travelers facing forward observe and pass through an enormous tiled mural that covers an entire wall. Just before the monorail reaches the hotel, but much more clearly after it emerges, travelers see Walt Disney World's primary symbol—Cinderella's castle. The sudden emergence from the mural into full view of the Magic Kingdom is a simulation of rebirth.

Within the Magic Kingdom

Once the monorail pulls into the Magic Kingdom station, the transition is complete. Passengers are on their own. Attendants, so prominent at the other end of the line, are conspicuously absent. Walking down a ramp, travelers pass through another turnstile; a transit building where lockers,

phones, rest rooms, strollers, and wheelchairs are available; and a circular open area. Soon they are in the Magic Kingdom, walking down "Main Street, U.S.A."

The Magic Kingdom itself invites comparison with shrines and rites. Pilgrims agree implicitly to constitute a temporary community, to spend a few hours or days observing the same rules, sharing experiences, and behaving alike. They share a common social status as pilgrims, waiting for hours in line and partaking in the same "adventures." Several anthropologists have argued that the major social function of rituals is to reaffirm, and thus to maintain, solidarity among members of a congregation. Victor Turner (1974) suggested that certain rituals among the Ndembu of Zambia serve a mnemonic function (they make people remember). Women's belief that they can be made ill by the spirits of their deceased matrilineal kinswomen leads them to take part in rites that remind them of their ancestors.

Similar observations can be made about Walt Disney World. Frontierland, Liberty Square, Main Street, U.S.A., Tomorrowland, Fantasyland, and Mickey's Birthdayland—the major sections of the Magic Kingdom—make us remember departed presidents (our national ancestors) and American history. They also juxtapose and link together the past, present, and future; childhood and adulthood; the real and the unreal. Many of the adventures, or rides, particularly the roller coasters, can be compared to anxiety-producing rites. Anxiety is dispelled when the pilgrims realize that they have survived simulated speeds of ninety miles an hour.

Detaching oneself from American culture, one might ask how a visitor from Madagascar would view Disney World adventures, particularly those based on fantasy. In Madagascar, as in many nonindustrial societies, witches are actual people—part of reality rather than fantasy. Peasants in Brazil and elsewhere believe in witches, werewolves, and nefarious creatures of the night. A villager from Madagascar would find it hard to understand why Americans voluntarily take rides designed to produce uncertainty and fright.

Yet the structure and attractions of the Magic Kingdom also relate to higher levels of sanctity. They represent, recall, and reaffirm not only Walt Disney's creative acts but the values of American society at large. In Liberty Square's Hall of Presidents, pilgrims silently and reverently view moving, talking lifelike dummies. Like Tanzanian rites, the Magic Kingdom makes us remember not just presidents and history but characters in children's literature such as Tom Sawyer. And, of course, we meet the cartoon characters who, in the person of costumed humans, walk around the Magic Kingdom, posing for photographs with children.

The juxtaposition of past, present, future, and fantasy symbolizes eternity. It argues that our nation, our people, our technological expertise, our beliefs, myths, and values will endure. Dress codes for employees reaffirm the stereotype of the clean-cut American. Disney propaganda uses Walt Disney World itself to illustrate what American creativity joined with technical know-how can accomplish. Students in American history are told how our ancestors carved a new land out of wilderness. Similarly, Walt Disney is presented as a mythic figure, creator of cosmos out of chaos— a structured world from the undeveloped chaos of Florida's central interior.

A few other links between Walt Disney World and religious and quasi-religious symbols and shrines should be examined. Disney World's most potent symbol is Cinderella's castle, complete with a moat where pilgrims throw coins and make wishes. On my first visit I was surprised to discover that the castle has a largely symbolic function as a trademark or logo for Walt Disney World. The castle has little utilitarian value. A few shops on the ground floor were open to the public, but the rest of the building was off limits. In interpreting Cinderella's castle, I recalled a lecture given in 1976 by British anthropologist Sir Edmund Leach. In describing the ritual surrounding his dubbing as a knight, Leach noted that Queen Elizabeth stood in front of the British throne and did not, in accordance with our stereotype of monarchs, sit on it. Leach surmised that the primary value of the throne is to represent, to make concrete, something enduring but abstract—the British sovereign's right to rule. Similarly, the most important thing about Cinderella's castle is its symbolism. It offers concrete testimony to the eternal aspects of Disney creations.

A Pilgrimage to a "Religious" Shrine

A comparison of Walt Disney World to a shrine in Brazil reveals further similarities between Disney

World and "religious" pilgrimage sites. As described by Daniel Gross (1971*b*), the Brazilian shrine Bom Jesus da Lapa is also located in the interior of a state. It receives an annual influx of more than 20,000 pilgrims, mostly on August 6. The patron saint, Bom ("Good") Jesus, is a wooden statue atop an altar in a cave. Like Cinderella's castle, a well-known landmark—a gray limestone outcrop pitted with caves—identifies Bom Jesus to pilgrims.

Most pilgrims go to Bom Jesus to fulfill vows, usually vows concerned with health. They promise to make the pilgrimage if a prayer is answered. Bom Jesus may be asked to help cure a specific malady, guarantee a safe journey, or help lovers stop quarreling. To fulfill their vows, pilgrims make offerings at the altar. If the prayer concerned a successful marriage, a photograph of the happy couple may be offered. People who have prayed for a broken leg to heal may leave an X-ray or cast at the altar.

The reasons why people make pilgrimages vary from shrine to shrine. Brazilians go to Bom Jesus to fulfill vows. Miraculous cures are sought and reported at Lourdes in France. Visitors to Disney World have various motives for the trip. "Pleasing the children" is a frequent reason. Also, parents offer a trip to Disney World as a reward for children's good behavior and achievements or perhaps as an incentive to help them recover from an illness.

Most Americans probably visit Walt Disney World for amusement, recreation, and vacation. In this sense, they differ from pilgrims to religious shrines. Americans don't appear to believe that a Disney visit has curative properties, although they may feel that vacations promote health. Nonetheless, television news programs occasionally run stories about communities pooling their resources to send terminally ill children to Disneyland. Thus, even though a visit to a Disney park is not regarded as curative, it is an appropriate last wish.

Furthermore, even when people undertake "religious" pilgrimages, their motives may not be exclusively or even primarily "religious" as the Bom Jesus da Lapa pilgrimage illustrates. Because there are so many pilgrims, most have no chance to worship the wooden statue. Chapel attendants rapidly herd them past the altar, just as Disney visitors are corralled into tram and monorail. Many Bom Jesus pilgrims must make way for others before they have a chance to kneel.

Bom Jesus da Lapa and Disney World also have similar commercial and recreational aspects. A variety of souvenirs, not limited to church-related icons, are sold to Bom Jesus pilgrims, just as in Disney World. In fact, the Bom Jesus pilgrim spends little time in religious contemplation. Several kinds of entertainment come to Bom Jesus along with the pilgrims, including traveling circuses, trained boa constrictors, vaudeville acts, gambling devices, and singing troubadours. During the height of the pilgrimage, Bom Jesus also has more than a dozen brothels. Most Americans would probably find Walt Disney World purer than Bom Jesus da Lapa. Similar nonreligious activities and a similar representation of other-than-religious motives characterize popular shrines and pilgrims elsewhere.

RECOGNIZING RELIGION

Some anthropologists think that rituals are distinguished from other behavior by special emotions, nonutilitarian intentions, and supernatural entities. However, other anthropologists define ritual more broadly. Writing about football, Arens (1981) pointed out that behavior can simultaneously have sacred and secular aspects. On one level, football is "simply a sport"; on another, it is a public ritual. Similarly, Walt Disney World, an amusement park, is on one level a mundane, secular place, but on another it assumes some of the attributes of a sacred place.

In the context of comparative religion, this isn't surprising. The French sociologist/anthropologist Émile Durkheim (1912/1961) pointed out long ago that almost everything from the sublime to the ridiculous has in some societies been treated as sacred. The distinction between sacred and profane doesn't depend on the intrinsic qualities of the sacred symbol. In Australian totemism, for example, sacred beings include such humble creatures as ducks, frogs, rabbits, and grubs, whose inherent qualities could hardly have given rise to the religious sentiment they inspire. If frogs and grubs can be elevated to a sacred level, why not Disney creations?

Many Americans believe that recreation and re-ligion are separate domains. From my field work in Brazil and Madagascar and my reading about other societies, I believe that this separation is both ethnocentric and false. Madagascar's tomb-centered ceremonies are times when the living and the dead are joyously reunited, when people get drunk, gorge themselves, and enjoy sexual license. Perhaps the gray, sober, ascetic, and moralistic aspects of many religious events in the United States, in taking the "fun" out of religion, force us to find our religion in fun. Many Americans seek in such apparently secular contexts as amusement parks, rock concerts, and sports what other people find in religious rites, beliefs, and ceremonies.

Standing back from the native explanations provided by my culture, I perceive Walt Disney not merely as a commercial figure and view his amusement parks not simply as recreational domains. There is a deeper level of attachment between Americans and Disney creations. The implication is not that this constitutes a religion, although there are parallels with passage rites and religious pilgrimages. There is no doubt, however, that Disney, his parks, and his creations do constitute powerful enculturative forces in the contemporary United States.

RITUALS AT McDONALD'S

Each day, on the average, a new McDonald's restaurant opens somewhere in the world. The number of McDonald's outlets today surpasses the total number of fast-food restaurants in the United States in 1945. McDonald's has grown from a single hamburger stand in San Bernardino, California, into today's international web of thousands of outlets. Have factors less obvious to American natives than relatively low cost, fast service, and taste contributed to McDonald's success? Could it be that natives—in consuming the products and propaganda of McDonald's—are not just eating but experiencing something comparable in certain respects to participation in religious rituals? To answer this question we must briefly review the nature of ritual.

Rituals, we know, are formal—stylized, repetitive, and stereotyped. They are performed in special places at set times. Rituals include liturgical orders—set sequences of words and actions laid down by someone other than the current performers. Rituals also convey information about participants and their cultural traditions. Performed year after year, generation after generation, rituals translate messages, values, and sentiments into action. Rituals are social acts. Inevitably, some participants are more strongly committed than others are to the beliefs on which the rituals are founded. However, just by taking part in a joint public act, people signal that they accept an order that transcends their status as mere individuals.

For several years, like many other Americans, I have occasionally eaten at McDonald's. Eventually I began to notice certain rituallike aspects of Americans' behavior at these fast-food restaurants. Tell your fellow Americans that going to McDonald's is similar in some ways to going to church and their bias as natives will reveal itself in laughter, denial, or questions about your sanity. Just as football is a game, *Star Wars* a movie, and Walt Disney World an amusement park, McDonald's, for natives, is just a place to eat. However, an analysis of what natives do at McDonald's will reveal a very high degree of formal, uniform behavior by staff members and customers alike. It is particularly interesting that this invariance in word and deed has developed without any theological doctrine. McDonald's ritual aspect is founded on twentieth-century technology, particularly automobiles, television, work away from home, and the short lunch break. It is striking nevertheless that one commercial organization should be so much more successful than other businesses, the schools, the military, and even many religions in producing behavioral invariance. Factors other than low cost, fast service, and the taste of the food—all of which are approximated by other chains—have contributed to our acceptance of McDonald's and adherence to its rules.

Remarkably, when Americans travel abroad, even in countries noted for good food, many visit the local McDonald's outlet. The same factors that lead us to frequent McDonald's at home are responsible. Because Americans are thoroughly familiar with how to eat and more or less what they will pay at McDonald's, in its outlets overseas they have a home away from home. In Paris, whose people aren't known for making tourists, particularly Americans, feel at home, McDonald's offers

sanctuary. It is, after all, an American institution, where natives, programmed by years of prior experience, can feel completely at home. Americans, if they wish, can temporarily reverse roles with their hosts. If American tourists can't be expected to act like the French, neither can the French be expected to act in a culturally appropriate manner at McDonald's.

This devotion to McDonald's rests in part on uniformities associated with its outlets, at least in the United States: food, setting, architecture, ambience, acts, and utterances. The McDonald's symbol, the golden arches, is an almost universal landmark, as familiar to Americans as Mickey Mouse, E.T., and the flag. The McDonald's nearest my university is a brick structure whose stained-glass windows have golden arches as their central theme. Sunlight floods in through a skylight that is like the clerestory of a church.

Americans enter a McDonald's restaurant for an ordinary, secular act—eating. However, the surroundings tell us that we are somehow apart from the variability of the world outside. We know what we are going to see, what we are going to say, and what will be said to us. We know what we will eat, how it will taste, and how much it will cost. Behind the counter, agents wear similar attire. Permissible utterances by customer and worker are written above the counter. Throughout the United States, with only minor variation, the menu is in the same place, contains the same items, and has the same prices. The food, again with only minor regional variation, is prepared according to plan and varies little in taste. Obviously, customers are limited in what they can choose. Less obviously, they are limited in what they can say. Each item has its appropriate designation: "large fry," "quarter pounder with cheese." The novice who innocently asks, "What kind of hamburgers do you have?" or "What's a Big Mac?" is out of place.

Other ritual phrases are uttered by the person behind the counter. After the customer has completed his order, if no potatoes are requested, the agent ritually asks, "Any fries?" Once food is presented and picked up, the agent conventionally says, "Have a nice day." Nonverbal behavior is also programmed. As customers request food, agents look back to see if the desired sandwich item is available. If not, they tell you, "That'll be a few minutes," and prepare your drink. After this a proper agent will take the order of the next customer in line. McDonald's lore and customs are even taught at a "seminary" called Hamburger University in Illinois. Managers who attend the program pass on what they learn to the people who work in their restaurants.

It isn't simply the formality and regularity of behavior at McDonald's but its total ambience that invites comparison with sacred places. Like the Disney organization, McDonald's image makers stress clean living and draw on an order of values—"traditional American values"—that transcends McDonald's itself. Agents submit to dress codes. Kitchens, grills, and counters sparkle. Styrofoam food containers that promise to haunt the world's garbage dumps for ages (banned now in some places) are used only once. Understandably, the chain's contributions to worldwide product pollution (along with labor practices that have been questioned) evoke considerable hostility. In 1975 the Ann Arbor campus McDonald's was the scene of a ritual rebellion—desecration by the Radical Vegetarian League, which held a "puke-in." Standing on the second-story balcony just below the clerestory, a dozen vegetarians gorged themselves on mustard and water and vomited down on the customer waiting area. McDonald's, defiled, lost many customers that day.

The formality and invariance of behavior in a demarcated setting thus suggest analogies between McDonald's and the sacred. Furthermore, as in a ritual, participation in McDonald's occurs at specified times. In American culture our daily food consumption is supposed to occur as three meals: breakfast, lunch, and dinner. Americans who have traveled abroad are aware that cultures differ in which meal they emphasize. In many countries, the midday meal is primary. Americans are away from home at lunchtime because of their jobs and usually take less than an hour for lunch. They view dinner as the main meal. Lunch is a lighter meal symbolized by the sandwich. McDonald's provides relatively hot and fresh sandwiches and a variety of subsidiary fare that many American palates can tolerate.

The ritual of eating at McDonald's is confined to ordinary, everyday life. Eating at McDonald's and religious feasts are in complementary distribution in American life. That is, when one occurs, the other doesn't. Most Americans would consider it inappropriate to eat at a fast-food restaurant on Christmas, Thanksgiving, Easter, or Passover. Our culture regards these as family days, occasions when relatives and close friends get together. However, although Americans neglect McDonald's on holidays, television reminds us that McDonald's still endures, that it will welcome us back once our holiday is over. The television presence of McDonald's is particularly obvious on such occasions—whether through a float in the Macy's Thanksgiving Day parade or through sponsorship of special programs, particularly "family entertainment."

Although Burger King, Wendy's, and Arby's compete with McDonald's for the fast-food business, none rivals McDonald's success. The explanation may lie in the particularly skillful ways in which McDonald's advertising plays up the features just discussed. Its commercials are varied to appeal to different audiences. On Saturday morning television, with its steady stream of cartoons, McDonald's is a ubiquitous sponsor. The commercials for children's shows usually differ from the ones adults see in the evening and on sports programs. Children are reminded of McDonald's through fantasy characters, headed by clown Ronald McDonald. Children can meet "McDonaldland" characters again at outlets. Their pictures appear on cookie boxes and plastic cups. Children also have a chance to meet Ronald McDonald as actors scatter visits throughout the country. One can even rent a Ronald for a birthday party.

Adult advertising has different but equally effective themes. Breakfast at McDonald's has been promoted by a fresh-faced, sincere, happy, clean-cut young woman. Healthy, clean-living Americans gambol on ski slopes or in mountain pastures. The single theme, however, that for years has run through the commercials is personalism. McDonald's, the commercials drone on, is something other than a fast-food restaurant. It's a warm, friendly place where you are graciously welcomed and feel at home, where your children won't get into trouble. McDonald's commercials tell you that you aren't simply an anonymous face in an amorphous crowd. You find respite from a hectic and impersonal society, the break you deserve. Your individuality and dignity are respected at McDonald's.

McDonald's advertising tries to deemphasize

the fact that the chain is a commercial organization. One jingle proclaimed "You, you're the one; we're fixin' breakfast for ya"—not "We're making millions off ya." Commercials make McDonald's seem like a charitable organization by stressing its program of community good works. "Family" television entertainment such as the film *The Sound of Music* is "brought to you by McDonald's." McDonald's commercials regularly tell us that it supports and works to maintain the values of American family life.

As with the Disney organization, the argument here is not that McDonald's has become a religion. Rather, I am suggesting that specific ways in which Americans participate in McDonald's bear analogies to religious systems involving myth, symbol, and ritual. Just as in rituals, participation in McDonald's requires temporary subordination of individual differences in a social and cultural collectivity. In a land of ethnic, social, economic, and religious diversity, we demonstrate that we share something with millions of other Americans. Furthermore, as in rituals, participation in McDonald's is linked to a cultural system that transcends the chain itself. By eating there we say something about ourselves as Americans, about our acceptance of certain collective values and ways of living. By returning to McDonald's, we affirm that certain values and life styles, developed through the collective experience of Americans before us, will continue.

ANTHROPOLOGY AND AMERICAN "POP" CULTURE

In Chapter 14 we saw that ritual pig slaughter in New Guinea and taboos on beef eating in India have material causes and effects. Correspondingly, we see here that consumption of the propaganda and products of commercial organizations can entail ritual behavior and mythological and symbolic components that go unrecognized by native participants. Just as rituals can have material consequences, businesses can share features with rituals and myths.

This appendix has stressed not variation but experiences and enculturative forces that are common to most Americans, particularly the young. I have emphasized several points. Techniques developed for studying other cultures can be used in interpreting our own. Studying their own cultures, native anthropologists can contribute uniquely by coupling professional detachment and objectivity with personal experience and understanding.

Anthropology's structural and symbolic analyses share as much with the humanities as with science. These approaches seek primarily to discover, interpret, and illuminate otherwise hidden dimensions of phenomena rather than to explain them. Structural and symbolic analyses are therefore difficult to confirm or disprove. They can be evaluated emically: Do natives accept them or prefer them to other interpretations? Do they enable natives to make more sense of familiar phenomena? They can also be evaluated etically: Do they fit within a comparative framework provided by data and analyses from other societies? In previous chapters we have discussed correlations between, say, population density and political organization. Such relationships, which can be evaluated statistically, can be confirmed by researchers who independently examine the same data. However, structural and symbolic hypotheses, although relying more on impressions, can be revealing as well. They may enlighten us about otherwise unsuspected coherence and contradictions in cultural forms.

The examples considered in this appendix are shared cultural forms that have appeared and spread rapidly during the twentieth century because of major changes in the material conditions of American life—particularly work organization, communication, and transportation. Most contemporary Americans deem at least one automobile a necessity. Televisions outnumber toilets in American households. Through the mass media, institutions such as sports, movies, TV shows, amusement parks, and fast-food restaurants have become powerful elements of American national culture. They provide a framework of common expectations, experiences, and behavior overriding differences in region, class, formal religious affiliation, political sentiments, gender, ethnic group, and place of residence. Although some of us may not like these changes, it's difficult to deny their significance.

The rise of these institutions is linked not just to the mass media but also to decreasing participation in traditional religion and the weakening of ties based on kinship, marriage, and community within industrial society. Neither a single church, a strong central government, nor segmentary lineage organization unites most Americans. Unification through the mass media and consumerism opens a new chapter in the exploration of cultural diversity.

These dimensions of contemporary culture are dismissed as passing, trivial, or "pop" by some. However, because millions of people share them, they deserve and are receiving scholarly attention. Such studies help fulfill the promise that by studying anthropology we can learn more about ourselves. Americans can view themselves not just as members of a varied and complex nation but also as a population united by distinctive shared symbols, customs, and experiences. American culture takes its place within the realm of cultural diversity. That, after all, is the subject matter of anthropology.

BIBLIOGRAPHY

AGAR, M.H.
  1980   *The Professional Stranger: An Informal Introduction to Ethnography*. New York: Academic Press.

ALBEE, G.W.
  1985   The Answer Is Prevention, the Question: If More than 40 Million of Us Need Help for Mental and Emotional Problems, What Can Be Done? *Psychology Today*, February, pp. 60–62, 64.

ALBERT, B.
  1989   Yanomami 'Violence': Inclusive Fitness or Ethnographer's Representation? *Current Anthropology* 30: 637–640.

ALLEN, H.
  1989   The Mystery of the '80s. *Washington Post*, November 14, 1989, pp. C1, C4.

AMADIUME, I.
  1987   *Male Daughters, Female Husbands*. Atlantic Highlands, N.J.: Zed.

AMERICAN ANTHROPOLOGICAL ASSOCIATION
        AAA Guide: A Guide to Departments, a Directory of Members. (Formerly *Guide to Departments of Anthropology*). Published annually by the American Anthropological Association, Washington, D.C.
        Anthropology Newsletter. Published nine times annually by the American Anthropological Association, Washington, D.C.

AMERICAN PSYCHIATRIC ASSOCIATION
  1987   *Diagnostic and Statistical Manual of Mental Disorders*, 3d ed., rev. Washington, D.C.: American Psychiatric Press.

ANN ARBOR NEWS
  1984   More People Will Reach Age 100 as Plants Disappear, Futurists Predict. December 26, 1984, p. B1.
  1984   1984, Predictably a Bad Year for Predictions, Skeptic Says. December 28, 1984, p. B4.
  1985   Testimony of Linda Tarr-Whelan of the National Education Association to the House Committee on Science, Research and Technology; quoted in Karen Grassmuck, Local Educators Join Push for "A Computer in Every Classroom." February 10, 1985, p. A11.
  1985   Poverty Affecting More Children, Government Study Finds. May 23, 1985, p. C5.
  1985   More Young Adults Are Postponing Marriage, Living with Their Parents (from UPI). November 10, 1985.
  1989   Organized Labor Forces Uncertain Future. September 4, 1989, p. B6.
  1989   Census Shows Big Change in Families. September 5, 1989, p. C2.
  1989   College Costs for Year 2000: Save Up Now. September 5, 1989, p. D2.
  1989   Population Control Key to World Hunger, Economist Says. September 10, 1989, p. C1.

ANN ARBOR OBSERVER
  1985   Surveys of Black Americans: Most Feel Oppressed. May 1985, pp. 42–43.

APPEL, R., AND MUYSKEN, P.
 1987 *Language Contact and Bilingualism.* London: Edward Arnold.

APPELL, G. N.
 1978 *Ethical Dilemmas in Anthropological Inquiry: A Case Book.* Waltham, Mass.: Crossroads Press.

ARDREY, R.
 1961 *African Genesis.* New York: Atheneum.
 1966 *The Territorial Imperative.* New York: Atheneum.

ARENS, W.
 1981 Professional Football: An American Symbol and Ritual. In *The American Dimension: Cultural Myths and Social Realities,* 2d ed., ed. W. Arens and S. B. Montague, pp. 1–10. Sherman Oaks, Calif.: Alfred.

ARENS, W., AND S. P. MONTAGUE
 1981 *The American Dimension: Cultural Myths and Social Realities,* 2d ed. Sherman Oaks, Calif.: Alfred.

ARENSBERG, C.
 1978 Theoretical Contributions of Industrial and Development Studies. In *Applied Anthropology in America,* ed. E. M. Eddy and W. L. Partridge, pp. 49–78. New York: Columbia University Press.

ASIMOV, I.
 1983 *The Robots of Dawn.* New York: Ballantine.

BANTON, M.
 1957 *West African City. A Study in Tribal Life in Freetown.* London: Oxford University Press.

BARASH, D.P.
 1977 *Sociobiology and Behavior.* Amsterdam: Elsevier.

BARLETT, P. F., ED.
 1980 *Agricultural Decision Making: Anthropological Contribution to Rural Development.* New York: Academic Press.

BARNABY, F.
 1988 *The Gaia Peace Atlas: Survival into the Third Millennium.* New York: Doubleday.

BARNES, J.A.
 1954 Class and Committees in a Norwegian Island Parish. *Human Relations* 7: 39–58.

BARNOUW, V.
 1985 *Culture and Personality,* 4th ed. Belmont, Calif.: Wadsworth.

BARRINGER, F.
 1989 32 Million Lived in Poverty in '88, a Figure Unchanged. *The New York Times,* October 19, p. 18.

BARRY, H., M. K. BACON, AND I. L. CHILD
 1959 Relation of Child Training to Subsistence Economy. *American Anthropologist* 61: 51–63.

BATALLA, G. B.
 1966 Conservative Thought in Applied Anthropology: A Critique. *Human Organization* 25: 89–92.

BATESON, M.
 1984 *With a Daughter's Eye: A Memoir of Margaret Mead and Gregory Bateson.* New York: William Morrow.

BELLAH, R. N.
 1978 Religious Evolution. In *Reader in Comparative Religion: An Anthropological Approach,* 4th ed., ed. W. A. Lessa and E. Z. Vogt, pp. 36–50. New York: Harper & Row.

BELSHAW, C. S.
 1978 The Significance of Modern Cults in Melanesian Development. In *Reader in Comparative Religion: An Anthropological Approach,* 4th ed., ed. W. A. Lessa and E. Z. Vogt, pp. 523–527. New York: Harper & Row.

BENEDICT, R.
 1946 *The Chrysanthemum and the Sword.* Boston: Houghton Mifflin.
 1959 (orig. 1934). *Patterns of Culture.* New York: New American Library.

BENNETT, J. W.
 1969 *Northern Plainsmen: Adaptive Strategy and Agrarian Life.* Chicago: Aldine Publishing Company.

BENNETT, J. W., AND J. R. BOWEN, EDS.
 1988 *Production and Autonomy: Anthropological Studies and Critiques of Development.* Monographs in Economic Anthropology, no. 5, Society for Economic Anthropology. New York: University Press of America.

BERLIN, B. D., E. BREEDLOVE, AND P. H. RAVEN
 1974 *Principles of Tzeltal Plant Classification: An Introduction to the Botanical Ethnography of a Mayan-Speaking People of Highland Chiapas.* New York: Academic Press.

BERLIN, B., AND P. KAY
 1969 *Basic Color Terms: Their Universality and Evolution.* Berkeley: University of California Press.

BERNARD, H. R.
 1988 *Research Methods in Cultural Anthropology.* Newbury Park, Calif.: Sage.

BERNARD, H. R., AND W. E. SIBLEY
 1975 *Anthropology and Jobs: A Guide for Undergraduates.* A Special Publication of the American Anthropological Association. Washington, D.C.: American Anthropological Association.

BERNOR, R. L.
 1983 Geochronology and Zoogeographic Relation-

ships of Miocene Hominoidea. In *New Interpretations of Ape and Human Ancestry,* ed. R. L. Ciochon and R. S. Corruccini, pp. 21–64. New York: Plenum.

BERREMAN, G. D.
1962 Pahari Polyandry: A Comparison. *American Anthropologist* 64: 60–75.
1973 (orig. 1969). Academic Colonialism: Not So Innocent Abroad. In *To See Ourselves: Anthropology and Modern Social Issues,* gen. ed. T. Weaver, pp. 152–156. Glenview, Ill.: Scott, Foresman.
1975 Himalayan Polyandry and the Domestic Cycle. *American Ethnologist* 2: 127–138.

BETTELHEIM, B.
1975 *The Uses of Enchantment: The Meaning and Importance of Fairy Tales.* New York: Vintage.

BLOCH, M.
1971 *Placing the Dead: Tombs, Ancestral Villages, and Kinship in Madagascar.* New York: Seminar Press.

BLOCH, M., ED.
1975 *Political Language and Oratory in Traditional Societies.* London: Academic.

BLUM, H. F.
1961 Does the Melanin Pigment of Human Skin Have Adaptive Value? *Quarterly Review of Biology* 36: 50–63.

BOAS, F.
1966 (orig. 1940). *Race, Language, and Culture.* New York: Free Press.

BOCK, P. K.
1980 *Continuities in Psychological Anthropology.* San Francisco: W. H. Freeman.

BODLEY, J. H.
1985 *Anthropology and Contemporary Human Problems,* 2d ed. Palo Alto, Calif.: Mayfield.

BODLEY, J. H., ED.
1988 *Tribal Peoples and Development Issues: A Global Overview.* Palo Alto, Calif.: Mayfield.

BOGORAS, W.
1904 The Chukchee. In *The Jesup North Pacific Expedition,* ed. F. Boas. New York: Memoir of the American Museum of Natural History.

BOHANNAN, P.
1955 Some Principles of Exchange and Investment among the Tiv. *American Anthropologist* 57: 60–70.
1963 *Social Anthropology.* New York: Holt, Rinehart & Winston.

BOHANNAN, P., AND J. MIDDLETON, EDS.
1968 *Marriage, Family, and Residence.* Garden City, N.Y.: Natural History Press.

BOSERUP, E.
1965 *The Conditions of Agricultural Growth.* Chicago: Aldine.
1970 *Women's Role in Economic Development.* London: Allen and Unwin.

BOTT, E.
1957 *Family and Social Network.* London: Tavistock.

BOURDIEU, P.
1982 *Ce Que Parler Veut Dire.* Paris: Fayard.
1984 *Distinction: A Social Critique of the Judgment of Taste,* trans. R. Nice. Cambridge: Harvard University Press.

BOURGUIGNON, E.
1979 *Psychological Anthropology: An Introduction to Human Nature and Cultural Differences.* New York: Holt, Rinehart & Winston.

BOURQUE, S. C., AND KAY B. WARREN
1981 *Women of the Andes: Patriarchy and Social Change in Two Peruvian Villages.* Ann Arbor: University of Michigan Press.
1987 Technology, Gender and Development. *Daedalus* 116(4): 173–197.

BOUVIER, L. F., AND C. B. DAVIS
1980 *The Future Racial Composition of the United States.* Washington: Demographic Information Services Center of the Population Reference Bureau.

BOYD, R., AND P. J. RICHERSON
1985 *Culture and the Evolutionary Process.* Chicago: University of Chicago Press.

BRACE, C. L., AND F. B. LIVINGSTONE
1971 On Creeping Jensenism. In *Race and Intelligence,* ed. C. L. Brace, G. R. Gamble, and J. T. Bond, pp. 64–75. Anthropological Studies, no. 8. Washington: American Anthropological Association.

BRADY, I., ED.
1983 Special Section: Speaking in the Name of the Real: Freeman and Mead on Samoa. *American Anthropologist* 85 (1983): 908–947.

BRAUDEL, FERNAND
1973 *Capitalism and Material Life, 1400–1800,* trans. M. Kochan. London: Weidenfeld and Nicolson.
1977 *Afterthoughts on Material Civilization and Capitalism.* Baltimore: Johns Hopkins University Press.
1981 *Civilization and Capitalism, 15th–18th Century. Vol. I: The Structure of Everyday Life: The Limits,* trans. S. Reynolds. New York: Harper & Row.
1982 *Civilization and Capitalism, 15th–18th Century. Vol. II: The Wheels of Commerce.* New York: Harper & Row.

1984   *Civilization and Capitalism, 15th–18th Century. Vol. III: The Perspective of the World.* New York: Harper & Row.

BRIM, J. A., AND D. H. SPAIN
1974   *Research Design in Anthropology.* New York: Holt, Rinehart, and Winston.

BRITANNICA BOOK OF THE YEAR
1990   Chicago: Encyclopedia Britannica.

BRONFENBRENNER, U.
1975   Nature with Nurture: A Reinterpretation of the Evidence. In *Race and IQ,* ed. A. Montagu, pp. 114–144. New York: Oxford University Press.

BROWN, J. K.
1975   Iroquois Women: An Ethnohistoric Note. In *Toward an Anthropology of Women,* ed. R. Reiter, pp. 235–251. New York: Monthly Review Press.

BROWN, R. W.
1958   *Words and Things.* Glencoe, Ill.: Free Press.

BUCHLER, I. R., AND H. A. SELBY
1968   *Kinship and Social Organization: An Introduction to Theory and Method.* New York: Macmillan.

BUNZEL, R.
1952   *Chichicastenango: A Guatemalan Village.* New York: J. J. Augustin.

BURKE, P., AND R. PORTER
1987   *The Social History of Language.* Cambridge: Cambridge University Press.

BURLING, R.
1970   *Man's Many Voices: Language in Its Cultural Context.* New York: Holt, Rinehart & Winston.

CARNEIRO, R. L.
1956   Slash-and-Burn Agriculture: A Closer Look at Its Implications for Settlement Patterns. In *Men and Cultures,* Selected Papers of the Fifth International Congress of Anthropological and Ethnological Sciences, pp. 229–234. Philadelphia: University of Pennsylvania Press.
1968   (orig. 1961). Slash-and-Burn Cultivation among the Kuikuru and Its Implications for Cultural Development in the Amazon Basin. In *Man in Adaptation: The Cultural Present,* ed. Y. A. Cohen, pp. 131–145. Chicago: Aldine.
1970   A Theory of the Origin of the State. *Science* 69: 733–738.
1990   Chiefdom-Level Warfare as Exemplified in Figi and the Cauca Valley. In *The Anthropology of War,* ed. J. Haas, pp. 190–211. Cambridge: Cambridge University Press.

CARTER, J.
1988   Freed from Keepers and Cages, Chimps Come of Age on Baboon Island. *Smithsonian,* June, pp. 36–48.

CASSON, R.
1983   Schemata in Cognitive Anthropology. *Annual Review of Anthropology* 12: 429–462.

CERNEA, M., ED.
1990   *Putting People First: Sociological Variables in Rural Development,* 2d ed. New York: Oxford University Press (published for The World Bank).

CHAGNON, N.
1974   *Studying the Yanomamo.* New York: Holt, Rinehart & Winston.
1983   *Yanomamo: The Fierce People,* 3d ed. New York: Holt, Rinehart & Winston.
1988   Life Histories, Blood Revenge and Warfare in a Tribal Population. *Science* 239: 985–991.

CHAGNON, N. A., AND W. IRONS, EDS.
1979   *Evolutionary Biology and Human Social Behavior: An Anthropological Perspective.* North Scituate, Mass.: Duxbury.

CHOMSKY, N.
1957   *Syntactic Structures.* The Hague: Mouton.

CLAMMER, J., ED.
1976   *The New Economic Anthropology.* New York: St. Martin's Press.

CLIFFORD, J.
1982   *Person and Myth: Maurice Leenhardt in the Melanesian World.* Berkeley: University of California Press.
1988   *The Predicament of Culture: Twentieth-Century Ethnography, Literature and Art.* Cambridge: Harvard University Press.

CLIFTON, J. A.
1970   *Applied Anthropology: Readings in the Uses of the Science of Man.* Boston: Houghton Mifflin.

COE, M.
1962   *Mexico.* New York: Praeger.

COHEN, R.
1967   *The Kanuri of Bornu.* New York: Holt, Rinehart & Winston.

COHEN, R., AND E. R. SERVICE, EDS.
1978   *Origins of the State: The Anthropology of Political Evolution.* Philadelphia: Institute for the Study of Human Issues.

COHEN, Y.
1974   *Man in Adaptation: The Cultural Present.* 2d ed. Chicago: Aldine.
1974   Culture as Adaptation. In *Man and Adaptation: The Cultural Present,* 2d ed., ed. Y. A. Cohen, pp. 45–68. Chicago: Aldine.

COLLIER, J. F. ED.
1988   *Marriage and Inequality in Classless Societies.* Stanford: Stanford University Press.

COLLIER, J. F., AND S. J. YANAGISAKO, EDS.
1987 *Gender and Kinship: Essays toward a Unified Analysis.* Stanford: Stanford University Press.

COLLINS, T. W.
1989 Rural Economic Development in Two Tennessee Counties: A Racial Dimension. Paper presented at the annual meetings of the American Anthropological Association, Washington, D.C.

COMAROFF, J.
1982 Dialectical Systems, History and Anthropology: Units of Study and Questions of Theory. *The Journal of Southern African Studies* 8: 143–172.

COMAROFF, J., ED.
1980 *The Meaning of Marriage Payments.* New York: Academic Press.

CONKLIN, H. C.
1954 The Relation of Hanunóo Culture to the Plant World. Ph.D. dissertation, Yale University.

COOK-GUMPERZ, J.
1986 *The Social Construction of Literacy.* Cambridge: Cambridge University Press.

COOPER, F., AND A. L. STOLER
1989 Introduction, Tensions of Empire: Colonial Control and Visions of Rule. *American Ethnologist* 16: 609–621.

COWAN, A. L.
1989 Poll Finds Women's Gains Have Taken Personal Toll. *The New York Times,* August 21, pp. 1, 8.

COX, V.
1976 Jane Goodall: Learning from the Chimpanzee. *Human Behavior,* March, pp. 25–30.

CRANE, L. B., E. YEAGER, AND R. L. WHITMAN
1981 *An Introduction to Linguistics.* Boston: Little, Brown.

CROSBY, A. W., JR.
1972 *The Columbian Exchange: Biological and Cultural Consequences of 1492.* Westport, Conn.: Greenwood Press.

CULTURAL SURVIVAL QUARTERLY
Quarterly Journal. Cambridge, Mass.: Cultural Survival, Inc.

DAHLBERG, F., ED.
1981 *Woman the Gatherer.* New Haven: Yale University Press.

DALTON, G., ED.
1967 *Tribal and Peasant Economies.* Garden City, N.Y.: The Natural History Press.

DAMATTA, R.
1981 *Carnavais, Malandros, e Heróis.* Rio de Janeiro: Zahar.

D'ANDRADE, R.
1984 Cultural Meaning Systems. In *Culture Theory: Essays on Mind, Self, and Emotion,* ed. R. A. Shweder and R. A. Levine, pp. 88–119. Cambridge: Cambridge University Press.

DAVIS, D. L., AND R. G. WHITTEN
1987 The Cross-Cultural Study of Human Sexuality. *Annual Review of Anthropology* 16: 69–98.

DAVIS, S. E.
1989 Twilight Zone of the Tech World. *Washington Post,* August 22, 1989, pp. 8–9.

DENICH, B. S.
1974 Sex and Power in the Balkans. In *Woman, Culture, and Society,* ed. M. Z. Rosaldo and L. Lamphere, pp. 243–262. Stanford, Calif.: Stanford University Press.

DENTAN, R. K.
1968 *The Semai: A Nonviolent People of Malaya.* New York: Holt, Rinehart & Winston.

DI LEONARDO, M., ED.
1990 *Toward a New Anthropology of Gender.* Berkeley: University of California Press.

DIVALE, W. T., AND M. HARRIS
1976 Population, Warfare, and the Male Supremacist Complex. *American Anthropologist* 78: 521–538.

DOUGLAS, M., AND A. WILDAVSKY
1982 *Risk and Culture: An Essay on the Selection of Technological and Environmental Dangers.* Berkeley: University of California Press.

DRAPER, P.
1975 !Kung Women: Contrasts in Sexual Egalitarianism in Foraging and Sedentary Contexts. In *Toward an Anthropology of Women,* ed. R. Reiter, pp. 77–109. New York: Monthly Review Press.

DRENNAN, R. D., AND C. A. URIBE, EDS.
1987 *Chiefdoms in the Americas.* Landon, Md.: University Press of America.

DRUCKER, C.
1988 (orig. 1985) Dam the Chico: Hydropower, Development and Tribal Resistance. In *Tribal Peoples and Development Issues: A Global Overview,* ed. J. H. Bodley, pp. 151–165. Palo Alto, Calif.: Mayfield.

DURKHEIM, E.
1951 (orig. 1897). *Suicide: A Study in Sociology.* Glencoe, Ill.: Free Press.
1961 (orig. 1912). *The Elementary Forms of the Religious Life.* New York: Collier Books.

DWYER, K.
1982 *Moroccan Dialogues: Anthropology in Question.* Baltimore: Johns Hopkins University Press.

EARLE, T.
  1987   Chiefdoms in Archaeological and Ethnohistorical Perspective. *Annual Review of Anthropology* 16: 279–308.
EASTMAN, C. M.
  1975   *Aspects of Language and Culture.* San Francisco: Chandler and Sharp.
ECKERT, P.
  1989   *Jocks and Burnouts: Social Categories and Identity in the High School.* New York: Teachers College Press, Columbia University.
EDDY, E. M., AND W. L. PARTRIDGE, EDS.
  1978   *Applied Anthropology in America.* New York: Columbia University Press.
EDGERTON, R.
  1965   "Cultural" versus "Ecological" Factors in the Expression of Values, Attitudes and Personality Characteristics. *American Anthropologist* 67: 442–447.
EDWARDS, J.
  1985   *Language, Society and Identity.* London: Basil Blackwell.
EISELEIN, E. B., AND M. TOPPER
  1976   Media Anthropology: A Symposium. *Human Organization* 35: 111–192.
ERRINGTON, F., AND D. GEWERTZ
  1987   *Cultural Alternatives and a Feminist Anthropology: An Analysis of Culturally Constructed Gender Interests in Papua New Guinea.* New York: Cambridge University Press.
ETIENNE, M., AND E. LEACOCK, EDS.
  1980   *Women and Colonization: Anthropological Perspectives.* New York: Praeger and J. F. Bergin.
EVANS-PRITCHARD, E. E.
  1940   *The Nuer: A Description of the Modes of Livelihood and Political Institutions of a Nilotic People.* Oxford: Clarendon Press.
  1970   Sexual Inversion among the Azande. *American Anthropologist* 72:1428–1433.
FAGAN, B. M.
  1988   *Archeology: A Brief Introduction,* 2d ed. Glenview, Ill.: Scott, Foresman.
  1989   *People of the Earth: An Introduction to World Prehistory,* 6th ed. Glenview, Ill.: Scott, Foresman.
FEDIGAN, L.
  1982   *Primate Paradigms: Sex Roles and Social Bonds.* Montreal: Eden Press.
FERGUSON, C. A., AND S. B. HEATH, EDS.
  1981   *Language in the U.S.A.* New York: Cambridge University Press.
FERGUSON, R. B.
  1989a   Game Wars?: Ecology and Conflict in Amazonia. *Journal of Anthropological Research* 45(2): 179–207.
  1989b   Ecological Consequences of Amazonian Warfare. *Ethnology* 28(3): 249–264.
  1989c   Do Yanomamo Killers Have More Kids? *American Ethnologist* 16: 564–565.
FERRARO, G. P.
  1990   *The Cultural Dimension of International Business.* Englewood Cliffs, N.J.: Prentice-Hall.
FLANNERY, K.
  1972   The Cultural Evolution of Civilizations. *Annual Review of Ecology and Systematics* 3: 399–426.
FORD, C. S., AND F. A. BEACH
  1951   *Patterns of Sexual Behavior.* New York: Harper Torchbooks.
FOSTER, G. M.
  1965   Peasant Society and the Image of Limited Good. *American Anthropologist* 67: 293–315.
FOSTER, G. M., AND B. G. ANDERSON
  1978   *Medical Anthropology.* New York: Wiley.
FOUTS, R. S., D. H. FOUTS, AND T. E. VAN CANTFORT
  1989   The Infant Loulis Learns Signs from Cross-Fostered Chimpanzees. In *Teaching Sign Language to Chimpanzees,* ed. R. A. Gardner, B. T. Gardner, and T. E. Van Cantfort, pp. 280–292. Albany, N.Y.: State University of New York Press.
FOX, J.
  1989   On the Rise and Fall of *Tuláns* and Maya Segmentary States. *American Anthropologist* 91: 656–681.
FOX, R.
  1985   *Kinship and Marriage.* New York: Viking Penguin.
FRAKE, C. O.
  1961   The Diagnosis of Disease among the Subanun of Mindanao. *American Anthropologist* 63: 113–132.
FRANKE, R.
  1977   Miracle Seeds and Shattered Dreams in Java. In *Readings in Anthropology,* pp. 197–201. Guilford, Conn.: Dushkin.
FRASER, D.
  1980   Industrial Revolution. *Academic American Encyclopedia,* pp. 158–160. Princeton, N.J.: Arête.
FREEMAN, D.
  1983   *Margaret Mead and Samoa: The Making and Unmaking of an Anthropological Myth.* Cambridge, Mass.: Harvard University Press.
FREUD, S.
  1950   (orig. 1918). *Totem and Taboo,* trans. J. Strachey. New York: W. W. Norton.

FRICKE, T.
1986 *Himalayan Households: Tamang Demography and Domestic Processes.* Ames, Iowa: Iowa State University Press.

FRIED, M. H.
1960 On the Evolution of Social Stratification and the State. In *Culture in History,* ed. S. Diamond, pp. 713–731. New York: Columbia University Press.
1967 *The Evolution of Political Society: An Essay in Political Anthropology.* New York: Random House.

FRIED, M. N., AND M. H. FRIED
1980 *Transitions: Four Rituals in Eight Cultures.* New York: W. W. Norton.

FRIEDL, E.
1975 *Women and Men: An Anthropologist's View.* New York: Holt, Rinehart & Winston.

FRIEDMAN, J., AND M. J. ROWLANDS, EDS.
1978 *The Evolution of Social Systems.* Pittsburgh: University of Pittsburgh Press.

GAL, S.
1989 Language and Political Economy. *Annual Review of Anthropology* 18: 345–367.

GAMST, F. C., AND E. NORBECK, EDS.
1976 *Ideas of Culture: Sources and Uses.* New York: Holt, Rinehart and Winston.

GARDNER, R. A., B. T. GARDNER, AND T. E. VAN CANTFORT, EDS.
1989 *Teaching Sign Language to Chimpanzees.* Albany, N.Y.: State University of New York Press.

GEERTZ, C.
1973 *The Interpretation of Cultures.* New York: Basic Books.
1980 Blurred Genres: The Refiguration of Social Thought. *American Scholar* 29(2): 165–179.
1983 *Local Knowledge.* New York: Basic Books.

GELMAN, D.
1985 Who's Taking Care of Our Parents? *Newsweek,* May 6, 1989, pp. 60–64, 68.

GIBBS, N.
1989 How America Has Run Out of Time, *Time,* April 24, 1989, pp. 59–67.

GIDDENS, A.
1973 *The Class Structure of the Advanced Societies.* New York: Cambridge University Press.

GOLDSCHMIDT, W.
1965 Theory and Strategy in the Study of Cultural Adaptability. *American Anthropologist* 67: 402–407.

GOLDSCHMIDT, W., ED.
1979 *The Uses of Anthropology.* Washington, D.C.: American Anthropological Association.

GOLEMAN, D.
1989 New Measure Finds Growing Hardship for Youth. *The New York Times,* October 19, p. 26.

GOODALL, J.
1968a A Preliminary Report on Expressive Movements and Communication in Gombe Stream Chimpanzees. In *Primates: Studies in Adaptation and Variability,* ed. P. C. Jay, pp. 313–374. New York: Holt, Rinehart & Winston.
1968b The Behavior of Free Living Chimpanzees in the Gombe Stream Reserve. *Animal Behavior Monographs* 1: 161–311.
1971 *In the Shadow of Man.* Boston: Houghton Mifflin.
1986 *The Chimpanzees of Gombe: Patterns of Behavior.* Cambridge, Mass.: Belknap Press of Harvard University Press.
1988 *In the Shadow of Man,* rev. ed. Boston: Houghton Mifflin.

GOODENOUGH, W. H.
1953 *Native Astronomy in the Central Carolines.* Philadelphia: University of Pennsylvania Press.

GOODY, J.
1977 *Production and Reproduction: A Comparative Study of the Domestic Domain.* New York: Cambridge University Press.

GOODY, J., AND S. T. TAMBIAH
1973 *Bridewealth and Dowry.* Cambridge: Cambridge University Press.

GORER, G.
1943 Themes in Japanese Culture. *Transactions of the New York Academy of Sciences* (Series II) 5: 106–124.

GOUGH, K.
1973 (orig. 1968). World Revolution and the Science of Man. In *To See Ourselves: Anthropology and Modern Social Issues,* gen. ed. T. Weaver, pp. 156–165. Glenview, Ill.: Scott, Foresman.

GRABURN, N., ED.
1971 *Readings in Kinship and Social Structure.* New York: Harper & Row.

GRAY, J. P.
1985 *Primate Sociobiology.* New Haven, Conn.: HRAF Press.

GROSS, D.
1971a The Great Sisal Scheme. *Natural History,* March, pp. 49–55.
1971b Ritual and Conformity: A Religious Pilgrimage to Northeastern Brazil. *Ethnology* 10: 129–148.

GROSS, D., AND B. UNDERWOOD
1971 Technological Change and Caloric Costs:

Sisal Agriculture in Northeastern Brazil. *American Anthropologist* 73: 725–740.

GULLIVER, P. H.
1955 *The Family Herds: A Study of Two Pastoral Peoples in East Africa, the Jie and Turkana.* New York: Humanities Press.
1974 (orig. 1965). The Jie of Uganda. In *Man in Adaptation: The Cultural Present,* 2d ed., ed. Y. A. Cohen, pp. 323–345.

GUMPERZ, J. J.
1982 *Language and Social Identity.* Cambridge: Cambridge University Press.

HALL, E. T.
1966 *The Hidden Dimension.* Garden City, N.Y.: Doubleday.

HAMBURG, D. A., AND E. R. McCOWN, EDS.
1979 *The Great Apes.* Menlo Park, Calif.: Benjamin Cummings.

HARDING, S.
1975 Women and Words in a Spanish Village. In *Toward an Anthropology of Women,* ed. R. Reiter, pp. 283–308. New York: Monthly Review Press.

HARGROVE, E. C.
1986 *Religion and Environmental Crisis.* Athens, Ga.: University of Georgia Press.

HARNER, M.
1977 The Ecological Basis for Aztec Sacrifice. *American Ethnologist* 4: 117–135.

HARRIS, M.
1964 *Patterns of Race in the Americas.* New York: Walker.
1968 *The Rise of Anthropological Theory.* New York: Crowell.
1974 *Cows, Pigs, Wars, and Witches: The Riddles of Culture.* New York: Random House.
1978 *Cannibals and Kings.* New York: Vintage.
1979 *Cultural Materialism: The Struggle for a Science of Culture.* New York: Random House.
1987 *Why Nothing Works: The Anthropology of Daily Life.* New York: Simon and Schuster.
1989 *Our Kind: Who We Are, Where We Came from, Where We Are Going.* New York: Harper and Row.

HARRIS, M., AND C. P. KOTTAK
1963 The Structural Significance of Brazilian Racial Categories. *Sociologia* 25: 203–209.

HARRISON, G. G., W. L. RATHJE, AND W. W. HUGHES
1989 Food Waste Behavior in an Urban Population. In *Applying Anthropology: An Introductory Reader,* ed. A. Podolefsky and P. J. Brown. Mountain View, Calif.: Mayfield, pp. 99–104.

HART, C. W. M., AND A. R. PILLING
1960 *The Tiwi of North Australia.* New York: Holt, Rinehart & Winston.

HART, K.
1982 *The Political Economy of West African Agriculture.* Cambridge: Cambridge University Press.

HAUSFATER, G., AND S. HRDY, EDS.
1984 *Infanticide: Comparative and Evolutionary Perspectives.* Hawthorne, N.Y.: Aldine.

HEIDER, K.
1988 The Rashomon Effect: When Ethnographers Disagree. *American Anthropologist* 90: 73–81.

HELLER, M.
1988 *Codeswitching: Anthropological and Sociolinguistic Perspectives.* Berlin: Mouton deGruyter.

HENDRY, J.
1981 *Marriage in Changing Japan.* London: Croom Helm Ltd.

HENRY, J.
1955 Docility, or Giving Teacher What She Wants. *Journal of Social Issues* 2: 33–41.

HERRNSTEIN, R. J.
1971 I.Q. *The Atlantic* 228(3): 43–64.

HEWITT, R.
1986 *White Talk, Black Talk.* Cambridge: Cambridge University Press.

HILL, C. E., ED.
1986 *Current Health Policy Issues and Alternatives: An Applied Social Science Perspective.* Southern Anthropological Society Proceedings. Athens, Ga.: University of Georgia Press.

HILL, J. H.
1978 Apes and Language. *Annual Review of Anthropology* 7: 89–112.

HILL-BURNETT, J.
1978 Developing Anthropological Knowledge through Application. In *Applied Anthropology in America,* ed. E. M. Eddy and W. L. Partridge, pp. 112–128. New York: Columbia University Press.

HINDE, R. A.
1974 *Biological Bases of Human Social Behavior.* New York: McGraw-Hill.
1983 *Primate Social Relationships: An Integrated Approach.* Sunderland: Sinaeur Associates.

HOBHOUSE, L. T.
1915 *Morals in Evolution,* rev. ed. New York: Holt.

HOEBEL, E. A.
1954 *The Law of Primitive Man.* Cambridge, Mass.: Harvard University Press.
1968 (orig. 1954). The Eskimo: Rudimentary Law in a Primitive Anarchy. In *Studies in Social and*

Cultural Anthropology, ed. J. Middleton, pp. 93–127. New York: Crowell.

HOLLAND, D., AND N. QUINN, EDS.
1987   *Cultural Models in Language and Thought.* Cambridge: Cambridge University Press.

HOPKINS, T., AND I. WALLERSTEIN
1982   Patterns of Development of the Modern World System. In *World System Analysis: Theory and Methodology,* by T. Hopkins, I. Wallerstein, R. Bach, C. Chase-Dunn, and R. Mukherjee, pp. 121–141. Beverly Hills, Calif.: Sage.

HRDY, S. B.
1981   *The Woman That Never Evolved.* Cambridge, Mass.: Harvard University Press.

HUGHES, J. D.
1983   *American Indian Ecology.* El Paso: Texas Western Press.

HUMAN ORGANIZATION
Quarterly Journal. Oklahoma City: Society for Applied Anthropology.

HYMES, D., ED.
1964   *Language in Culture and Society: A Reader in Linguistics and Anthropology.* New York: Harper & Row.

IANNI, F.
1977   New Mafia: Black, Hispanic and Italian Styles. In *Readings in Anthropology,* pp. 66–78. Guilford, Conn.: Dushkin.

JAMESON, F.
1984   Postmodernism, or the Cultural Logic of Late Capitalism. *New Left Review* 146: 53–93.
1988   *The Ideologies of Theory: Essays 1971–1986.* Minneapolis: University of Minnesota Press.

JANSON, C. H.
1986   Capuchin Counterpoint: Divergent Mating and Feeding Habits Distinguish Two Closely Related Monkey Species of the Peruvian Forest, *Natural History* 95: 44–52.

JENSEN, A.
1969   How much Can We Boost I.Q. and Scholastic Achievement? *Harvard Educational Review* 29: 1–123.

JOHNSON, A. W., AND T. EARLE
1987   *The Evolution of Human Societies: From Foraging Group to Agrarian State.* Stanford, Calif.: Stanford University Press.

JOHNSON, J.
1989   Childhood Is Not Safe for Most Children, Congress Is Warned. *The New York Times,* October 2, pp. 1, 10.

JONES, G., AND R. KRAUTZ
1981   *The Transition to Statehood in the New World.* Cambridge: Cambridge University Press.

KAGAN, J.
1975   The Magical Aura of I.Q. In *Race and IQ,* ed. A. Montagu, pp. 55–58. New York: Oxford University Press.

KAN, S.
1986   The 19th-Century Tlingit Potlatch: A New Perspective. *American Ethnologist* 13: 191–212.

KARDINER, A., ED.
1939   *The Individual and His Society.* New York: Columbia University Press.

KELLY, R. C.
1976   Witchcraft and Sexual Relations: An Exploration in the Social and Semantic Implications of the Structure of Belief. In *Man and Woman in the New Guinea Highlands,* ed. P. Brown and G. Buchbinder, pp. 36–53. Special Publication, no. 8. Washington, D.C.: American Anthropological Association.

KIMBALL, S. T.
1978   Anthropology as a Policy Science. In *Applied Anthropology in America,* ed. E. M. Eddy and W. L. Partridge, pp. 277–291. New York: Columbia University Press.

KINSEY, A. C., W. B. POMEROY, AND C. E. MARTIN
1948   *Sexual Behavior in the Human Male.* Philadelphia: W. B. Saunders.

KIRSCH, P. V.
1984   *The Evolution of the Polynesian Chiefdoms.* Cambridge: Cambridge University Press.

KLEINFELD, J.
1975   Positive Stereotyping: The Cultural Relativist in the Classroom. *Human Organization* 34: 269–274.

KLINEBERG, O.
1951   Race and Psychology. In *The Race Question in Modern Science.* Paris: UNESCO.

KORTEN, D. C.
1980   Community Organization and Rural Development: A Learning Process Approach. *Public Administration Review,* September–October, pp. 480–512.

KOTTAK, C. P.
1971   Social Groups and Kinship Calculation among the Southern Betsileo. *American Anthropologist* 73: 178–193.
1972   Ecological Variables in the Origin and Evolution of African States: The Buganda Example. *Comparative Studies in Society and History* 14: 351–380
1980   *The Past in the Present: History, Ecology, and Social Organization in Highland Madagascar.* Ann Arbor: University of Michigan Press.
1983   *Assault on Paradise: Social Change in a Brazilian Village.* New York: McGraw-Hill.

1985   When People Don't Come First: Some Sociological Lessons from Completed Projects. In *Putting People First: Sociological Variables in Rural Development*, ed. M. Cernea, pp. 325–356. New York: Oxford University Press.

1990   *Prime-Time Society: An Anthropological Analysis of Television and Culture*. Belmont, Calif.: Wadsworth.

KOTTAK, C. P., ED.
1982   *Researching American Culture: A Guide for Student Anthropologists*. Ann Arbor: University of Michigan Press.

KRAMARAE, R., M. SHULZ, AND M. O'BARR, EDS.
1984   *Language and Power*. Beverly Hills, Calif.: Sage.

KRETCHMER, N.
1975   (orig. 1972). Lactose and Lactase. In *Biological Anthropology, Readings from Scientific American*, ed. S. H. Katz, pp. 310–318. San Francisco: W. H. Freeman.

KROEBER, A. L., AND C. KLUCKHOLN
1963   *Culture: A Critical Review of Concepts and Definitions*. New York: Vintage.

LABARRE, W.
1945   Some Observations of Character Structure in the Orient: The Japanese. *Psychiatry* 8: 326–342.

LABOV, W.
1972a   *Language in the Inner City: Studies in the Black English Vernacular*. Philadelphia: University of Pennsylvania Press.

1972b   *Sociolinguistic Patterns*. Philadelphia: University of Pennsylvania Press.

LAKO, G. T.
1988   (orig. 1985). The Impact of the Jonglei Scheme on the Economy of the Dinka. In *Tribal Peoples and Development Issues: A Global Overview*, ed. J. H. Bodley, pp. 135–150. Palo Alto, Calif.: Mayfield.

LAKOFF, R.
1975   *Language and Woman's Place*. New York: Harper & Row.

LANCE, L. M., AND E. E. McKENNA
1975   Analysis of Cases Pertaining to the Impact of Western Technology on the Non-Western World. *Human Organization* 34: 87–94.

LAWRENCE, P.
1964   *Road Belong Cargo*. Manchester: Manchester University Press.

LEACH, E. R.
1955   Polyandry, Inheritance and the Definition of Marriage. *Man* 55: 182–186.

1961   *Rethinking Anthropology*. London: Athlone Press.

1985   *Social Anthropology*. New York: Oxford University Press.

LeCLAIR, E. E., AND H. K. SCHNEIDER, EDS.
1968   (orig. 1961). *Economic Anthropology: Readings in Theory and Analysis*. New York: Holt, Rinehart and Winston.

LEE, R. B.
1974   (orig. 1968). What Hunters Do for a Living, or, How to Make Out on Scarce Resources. In *Man in Adaptation: The Cultural Present*, 2d ed., ed. Y. A. Cohen, pp. 87–100. Chicago: Aldine.

LEE, R. B., AND I. DeVORE, EDS.
1977   *Kalahari Hunter-Gatherers: Studies of the !Kung San and Their Neighbors*. Cambridge, Mass.: Harvard University Press.

LENSKI, G.
1966   *Power and Privilege: A Theory of Social Stratification*. New York: McGraw-Hill.

LESSA, W. A., AND E. Z. VOGT, EDS.
1978   *Reader in Comparative Religion: An Anthropological Approach*, 4th ed. New York: Harper & Row.

LEVINE, N.
1988   *The Dynamics of Polyandry: Kinship, Domesticity, and Population in the Tibetan Border*. Chicago: University of Chicago Press.

LEVINE, R. A.
1982   *Culture, Behavior, and Personality: An Introduction to the Comparative Study of Psychosocial Adaptation*, 2d ed. Chicago: Aldine.

LEVINE, R. A., ED.
1974   *Culture and Personality: Contemporary Readings*.

LEWIS, O.
1959   *Five Families*. New York: Basic Books.

LEVI-STRAUSS, C.
1963   *Totemism*, trans. R. Needham. Boston: Beacon Press.

1967   *Structural Anthropology*. New York: Doubleday.

1969   (orig. 1949). *The Elementary Structures of Kinship*. Boston: Beacon Press.

LIEBAN, R. W.
1977   The Field of Medical Anthropology. In *Culture, Disease, and Healing: Studies in Medical Anthropology*, ed. D. Landy, pp. 13–31. New York: Macmillan.

LIGHT, D., S. KELLER, AND C. CALHOUN
1989   *Sociology*, 5th ed. New York: McGraw-Hill.

LINDENBAUM, S.
1972   Sorcerers, Ghosts, and Polluting Women: An Analysis of Religious Belief and Population Control. *Ethnology* 11: 241–253.

LINTON, R.
1927 Report on Work of Field Museum Expedition in Madagascar. *American Anthropologist* 29: 292–307.
1943 Nativistic Movements. *American Anthropologist* 45: 230–240.

LITTLE, K.
1965 *West African Urbanization: A Study of Voluntary Associations in Social Change.* Cambridge: Cambridge University Press.
1971 *Some Aspects of African Urbanization South of the Sahara.* Reading, Mass.: Addison-Wesley, McCaleb Modules in Anthropology.

LIZOT, J.
1985 *Tales of the Yanomami: Daily Life in the Venezuelan Forest.* New York: Cambridge University Press.

LOOMIS, W. F.
1967 Skin-pigmented Regulation of Vitamin-D Biosynthesis in Man. *Science* 157: 501–506.

LOWIE, R. H.
1935 *The Crow Indians.* New York: Farrar and Rinehart.
1961 (orig. 1920). *Primitive Society.* New York: Harper & Brothers.

MACDOUGLAS, A. K.
1984 Yawning Chasms between Classes Widen in the Third World. *Ann Arbor News,* November 4, 1984, p. B14.

MACKINNON, J.
1974 *In Search of the Red Ape.* New York: Ballantine.

MAIR, L.
1969 *Witchcraft.* New York: McGraw-Hill.

MALINOWSKI, B.
1927 *Sex and Repression in Savage Society.* London and New York: International Library of Psychology, Philosophy and Scientific Method.
1929a Practical Anthropology. *Africa* 2: 23–38.
1929b *The Sexual Life of Savages in North-Western Melanesia.* New York: Harcourt, Brace, and World.
1948 *Magic, Science and Religion, and Other Essays.* Boston: Beacon Press.
1961 (orig. 1922). *Argonauts of the Western Pacific.* New York: Dutton.
1978 (orig. 1931). The Role of Magic and Religion. In *Reader in Comparative Religion: An Anthropological Approach,* 4th ed., ed. W. A. Lessa and E. Z. Vogt, pp. 37–46. New York: Harper & Row.

MANNERS, R.
1973 (orig. 1956). Functionalism, Realpolitik and Anthropology in Underdeveloped Areas. *America Indigena* 16. In *To See Ourselves: Anthropology and Modern Social Issues,* gen. ed. T. Weaver. Glenview, Ill.: Scott, Foresman, pp. 113–126.

MAQUET, J.
1964 Objectivity in Anthropology. *Current Anthropology* 5: 47–55 (also in Clifton, ed., 1970).

MARCUS, G. E., AND CUSHMAN, D.
1982 Ethnographies as Texts. *Annual Review of Anthropology* 11: 25–69.

MARCUS, G. E., AND FISCHER, M. M. J.
1986 *Anthropology as Cultural Critique: An Experimental Moment in the Human Sciences.* Chicago: University of Chicago Press.

MARGOLIS, M.
1984 *Mothers and Such: American Views of Women and How They Changed.* Berkeley: University of California Press.

MARTIN, K., AND B. VOORHIES
1975 *Female of the Species.* New York: Columbia University Press.

MARX, K., AND F. ENGELS
1976 (orig. 1948). *Communist Manifesto.* New York: Pantheon.

MAUSS, M.
1954 *The Gift: Forms and Functions of Exchange in Archaic Societies.* New York: Free Press.

MAYESKE, G. W.
1971 *On the Explanation of Racial-Ethnic Group Differences in Achievement Test Scores.* Washington, D.C.: U.S. Government Printing Office, Office of Education.

MCDONALD, G.
1984 *Carioca Fletch.* New York: Warner Books.

MCGRAW, T. K., ED.
1986 *America versus Japan.* Boston: Harvard Business School Press.

MCGREW, W. C.
1979 Evolutionary Implications of Sex Differences in Chimpanzee Predation and Tool Use. In *The Great Apes,* ed. D. A. Hamburg and E. R. McCown, pp. 441–463. Menlo Park, Calif.: Benjamin Cummings.

MEAD, M.
1930 *Growing up in New Guinea.* New York: Blue Ribbon.
1950 (orig. 1935). *Sex and Temperament in Three Primitive Societies.* New York: New American Library.
1961 (orig. 1928). *Coming of Age in Samoa.* New York: Morrow Quill.
1972 *Blackberry Winter; My Earlier Years.* New York: Simon and Schuster.

MERCER, J. R.
1971 Pluralistic Diagnosis in the Evaluation of

Black and Chicano Children: A Procedure for Taking Sociocultural Variables into Account as Clinical Assessment. Paper presented at the meetings of the American Psychological Association, Washington, D.C.

MIDDLETON, J.
1967 Introduction. In *Myth and Cosmos: Readings in Mythology and Symbolism,* ed. John Middleton, pp. ix–xi. Garden City, N.Y.: The Natural History Press.

MIDDLETON, J., ED.
1967a *Gods and Rituals.* Garden City, N.Y.: The Natural History Press.

MILES, H. L.
1983 Apes and Language: The Search for Communicative Competence. In *Language in Primates,* ed. J. de Luce and H. T. Wilder, pp. 43–62. New York: Springer Verlag.

MINTZ, S.
1985 *Sweetness and Power: The Place of Sugar in Modern History.* New York: Viking Penguin.

MITCHELL, J. C.
1966 Theoretical Orientations in African Urban Studies. In *The Social Anthropology of Complex Societies,* ed. M. Banton, pp. 37–68. London: Tavistock.

MITTERMEIER, R. A., AND M. J. POLTKIN, EDS.
1982 *Primates and the Tropical Forest.* Washington, D.C.: World Wildlife Fund.

MONTAGU, A.
1975 *The Nature of Human Aggression.* New York: Oxford University Press.

MONTAGU, A., ED.
1975 *Race and IQ.* New York: Oxford University Press.

MONTAGUE, S., AND R. MORAIS
1981 Football Games and Rock Concerts: The Ritual Enactment. In *The American Dimension: Cultural Myths and Social Realities,* 2d ed., ed. W. Arens and S. B. Montague, pp. 33–52. Sherman Oaks, Calif.: Alfred.

MOORE, S. F.
1986 *Social Facts and Fabrications.* Cambridge, Mass.: Cambridge University Press.

MOORE, S. F., AND B. G. MYERHOFF, EDS.
1978 *Secular Ritual.* Atlantic Highlands, N.J.: Humanities Press.

MORAN, E.
1979 *Human Adaptability: An Introduction to Ecological Anthropology.* North Scituate, Mass.: Duxbury.

MORGAN, L. H.
1963 (orig. 1877). *Ancient Society.* Cleveland: World Publishing.

MORGEN, S., ED.
1989 *Gender and Anthropology: Critical Reviews for Research and Teaching.* Washington, D.C.: American Anthropological Association.

MORRIS, B.
1987 *Anthropological Studies of Religion: An Introductory Text.* New York: Cambridge University Press.

MORRIS, C. R.
1989 The Coming Global Boom. *Atlantic Monthly,* October, pp. 51–64.

MOWAT, F.
1987 *Woman in the Mists: The Story of Dian Fossey and the Mountain Gorillas of Africa.* New York: Warner Books.

MUHLHAUSLER, P.
1986 *Pidgin and Creole Linguistics.* London: Basil Blackwell.

MUKHOPADHYAY, C., AND P. HIGGINS
1988 Anthropological Studies of Women's Status Revisited: 1977–1987. *Annual Review of Anthropology* 17: 461–495.

MULLINGS, L., ED.
1987 *Cities of the United States: Studies in Urban Anthropology.* New York: Columbia University Press.

MURDOCK, G. P.
1949 *Social Structure.* New York: Macmillan.
1957 World Ethnographic Sample. *American Anthropologist* 59: 664–687.

MURPHY, E. M.
1984 *Food and Population: A Global Concern.* Washington, D.C.: U.S. Government Printing Office, Office of Education.

MURPHY, R. F., AND L. KASDAN
1959 The Structure of Parallel Cousin Marriage. *American Anthropologist* 61: 17–29.

NAISBITT, J.
1982 *Megatrends: Ten New Directions Transforming Our Lives.* New York: Warner Books.

NAISBITT, J., AND P. ABURDENE
1990 *Megatrends 2000: Ten New Directions for the 1990's.* New York: William Morrow.

NASH, D.
1988 *A Little Anthropology.* Englewood Cliffs, N.J.: Prentice-Hall.

NASH, J.
1981 Ethnographic Aspects of the World Capitalist System. *Annual Review of Anthropology* 10: 393–423.

NASH, J., AND P. FERNANDEZ-KELLY, EDS.
1983 *Women, Men and the International Division of Labor.* Albany: State University of New York Press.

NASH, J., AND H. SAFA, EDS.
1986 *Women and Change in Latin America.* South Hadley, Mass.: Bergin and Garvey.

NASW NEWS
1985 Editorial Note. 30(10):4. Silver Springs, Md. National Association of Social Workers.

NELSON, H., AND R. JURMAIN
1988 *Introduction to Physical Anthropology,* 4th ed. St. Paul, Minn.: West.

NETTING, R. M. C., R. R. WILK, AND E. J. ARNOULD, EDS.
1984 *Households: Comparative and Historical Studies of the Domestic Group.* Berkeley: University of California Press.

NEWMAN, K.
1983 *Law and Economic Organization: A Comparative Study of Pre-Industrial Societies.* New York: Cambridge University Press.
1988 *Falling from Grace: The Experience of Downward Mobility in the American Middle Class.* New York: The Free Press.

NEW YORK TIMES
1984 Work Force Increases. November 4, pp. E4-5.
1985 The Union Movement Looks in the Mirror. February 25, p. E5.
1989 More Retirees on the Job. September 7, p. 20.
1989 U.S. Businesses Brace for a "Disaster": A Work Force Unqualified to Work. September 25, pp. A1, 12.
1989 Black and White Death Rates Continue to Differ, Study Says. September 27, p. 11.
1990 Tropical Diseases on March, Hitting 1 in 10. March 28, pp. A3.

NIETSCHMANN, B.
1987 *Cultural Survival Quarterly* 11(3): 1–16.

ONG, A.
1987 *Spirits of Resistance and Capitalist Discipline: Factory Women in Malaysia.* Albany: State University of New York Press.
1989 Center, Periphery, and Hierarchy: Gender in Southeast Asia. In *Gender and Anthropology: Critical Reviews for Research and Teaching,* ed. S. Morgen, pp. 294–312. Washington: American Anthropological Association.

OTTERBEIN, K. F.
1968 (orig. 1963). Marquesan Polyandry. In *Marriage, Family and Residence,* ed. P. Bohannan and J. Middleton, pp. 287–296. Garden City, N.Y.: Natural History Press.

PARACHINI, A.
1988 Study Shows Mental Illness Much More Common Than Thought, *Ann Arbor News,* November 13, 1988, p. G6.

PARKER, S., AND R. KLEINER
1970 The Culture of Poverty: An Adjustive Dimension. *American Anthropologist* 72: 516–527.

PARKIN, D.
1969 *Neighbours and Nationals in an African City Ward.* London: Routledge and Kegan Paul.

PATTERSON, F.
1978 Conversations with a Gorilla. *National Geographic,* October, pp. 438–465.

PAUL, R.
1989 Psychoanalytic Anthropology. *Annual Review of Anthropology* 18: 177–202.

PEEBLES, S.
1985 Preschool: A Headstart toward Academic Success? *Ann Arbor News,* May 5, 1985, p. H4.

PELETZ, M.
1988 *A Share of the Harvest: Kinship, Property, and Social History among the Malays of Rembau.* Berkeley: University of California Press.

PELTO, P. J., AND G. H. PELTO
1978 *Anthropological Research: The Structure of Inquiry,* 2d ed. New York: Cambridge University Press.

PFEIFFER, J.
1977 *The Emergence of Society.* New York: McGraw-Hill.
1985 *The Emergence of Humankind,* 4th ed. New York: Harper and Row.

PIDDOCKE, S.
1969 The Potlatch System of the Southern Kwakiutl: A New Perspective. In *Environment and Cultural Behavior,* ed. A. P. Vayda, pp. 130–156. Garden City, N.Y.: Natural History Press.

PLATTNER, S., ED.
1989 *Economic Anthropology.* Stanford, Calif.: Stanford University Press.

PODOLEFSKY, A., AND P. J. BROWN, EDS.
1989 *Applying Anthropology: An Introductory Reader.* Mountain View, Calif.: Mayfield.

POPULATION TODAY
1984 Now it Costs $98,000 to Raise a Child, September 1984, p. 3.

POSPISIL, L.
1963 *The Kapauku Papuans of West New Guinea.* New York: Holt, Rinehart & Winston.

POTASH, B., ED.
1986 *Widows in African Societies: Choices and Constraints.* Stanford, Calif.: Stanford University Press.

QUINN, N., AND C. STRAUSS
1989 A Cognitive Cultural Anthropology. Paper presented at the Invited Session "Assessing

Developments in Anthropology," American Anthropological Association 88th Annual Meeting, November 15–19, 1989, Washington, D.C.

RADCLIFFE-BROWN, A. R.
1950 Introduction to *African Systems of Kinship and Marriage,* ed. A. R. Radcliffe-Brown and D. Forde, pp. 1–85. London: Oxford University Press.
1965 (orig. 1962). *Structure and Function in Primitive Society.* New York: Free Press.

RAMOS, A.
1987 Reflecting on the Yanomami: Ethnographic Images and the Pursuit of the Exotic. *Cultural Anthropology* 2: 284–304.

RAPPAPORT, R. A.
1974 Obvious Aspects of Ritual. *Cambridge Anthropology* 2: 2–60.
1979 *Ecology, Meaning, and Religion.* Richmond, Calif.: North Atlantic Books.
1984 *Pigs for the Ancestors: Ritual in the Ecology of a New Guinea People,* 2d ed. New Haven: Yale University Press.

REDFIELD, R.
1941 *The Folk Culture of Yucatan.* Chicago: University of Chicago Press.

REDFIELD, R., R. LINTON, AND M. HERSKOVITS
1936 Memorandum on the Study of Acculturation. *American Anthropologist* 38: 149–152.

REICH, R.
1989 Memorandum: The Future of Work. *Harper's,* April, pp. 26–32.

REITER, R.
1975 Men and Women in the South of France: Public and Private Domains. In *Toward an Anthropology of Women,* ed. R. Reiter, pp. 252–282. New York: Monthly Review Press.

RICHARDS, P.
1973 The Tropical Rain Forest. *Scientific American* 229(6): 58–67.

RICOEUR, P.
1971 The Model of the Text: Meaningful Action Considered as a Text. *Social Research* 38: 529–562.

ROBERTS, C.
1990 The Terrible Truth about Fast Food. *Bottom Line Personal* 11(2): 8.

ROBERTS, S.
1979 *Order and Dispute: An Introduction to Legal Anthropology.* New York: Penguin Books.

ROMER, A. S.
1960 *Man and the Vertebrates,* 3d ed., vol. 1. Harmondsworth, England: Penguin.

ROSALDO, M. Z.
1980a *Knowledge and Passion: Notions of Self and Social Life.* Stanford, Calif.: Stanford University Press.
1980b The Use and Abuse of Anthropology: Reflections on Feminism and Cross-Cultural Understanding. *Signs* 5(3): 389–417.

ROSALDO, M. Z., AND L. LAMPHERE
1974 Introduction to *Woman, Culture, and Society,* ed. M. Z. Rosaldo and L. Lamphere, pp. 1–16. Stanford, Calif.: Stanford University Press.

ROSEBERRY, WILLIAM
1988 Political Economy. *Annual Review of Anthropology* 17: 161–185.

ROWAN, H.
1985 The Slowdown and the Summit. *The Washington Post Weekly,* May 6, 1985, p. 5.

ROYAL ANTHROPOLOGICAL INSTITUTE
1951 *Notes and Queries on Anthropology,* 6th ed. London: Routledge and Kegan Paul.

SAHLINS, M. D.
1961 The Segmentary Lineage: An Organization of Predatory Expansion. *American Anthropologist* 63: 322–345.
1968 *Tribesmen.* Englewood Cliffs, N.J.: Prentice-Hall.
1972 *Stone Age Economics.* Chicago: Aldine.
1978 Culture for Protein and Profit. *New York Review of Books,* November 23, 1978, pp. 45–53.
1988 (orig. 1968). Notes on the Original Affluent Society. In *Tribal Peoples and Development Issues: A Global Overview,* ed. J. H. Bodley, pp. 15–21. Palo Alto, Calif.: Mayfield.

SAHLINS, M. D., AND E. R. SERVICE
1960 *Evolution and Culture.* Ann Arbor: University of Michigan Press.

SALZMAN, P. C.
1974 Political Organization among Nomadic Peoples. In *Man in Adaptation: The Cultural Present,* 2d ed., ed. Y. A. Cohen, pp. 267–284. Chicago: Aldine.

SANDAY, P. R.
1974 Female Status in the Public Domain. In *Woman, Culture, and Society,* ed. M. Z. Rosaldo and L. Lamphere, pp. 189–206. Stanford, Calif.: Stanford University Press.

SANDERS, W. T., AND B. J. PRICE
1968 *Mesoamerica: The Evolution of a Civilization.* New York: Random House.

SANDERS, W. T., J. R. PARSONS, AND R. S. SANTLEY
1979 *The Basin of Mexico: Ecological Processes in the Evolution of a Civilization.* New York: Academic Press, 1979.

SANKOFF, G.
    1980   *The Social Life of Language.* Philadelphia: University of Pennsylvania Press.

SANTINO, J.
    1983   Night of the Wandering Souls, *Natural History* 92(10): 42.

SAPIR, E.
    1931   Conceptual Categories in Primitive Languages. *Science* 74: 578–584.

SCHACHTER, J.
    1989   Life in the Daddy Track. *Ann Arbor News,* November 28, 1989, pp. B1–B2.

SCHAEFER, R.
    1989   *Sociology,* 3d ed. New York: McGraw-Hill.

SCHEPER-HUGHES, N.
    1987   Culture, Scarcity, and Maternal Thinking: Mother Love and Child Death in Northeast Brazil. In *Child Survival,* ed. N. Scheper-Hughes, pp. 187–208. Boston: D. Reidel.

SCHIEFFELIN, E.
    1976   *The Sorrow of the Lonely and the Burning of the Dancers.* New York: St. Martin's.

SCHNEIDER, J.
    1977   Was There a Pre-capitalist World System? *Peasant Societies* 6: 20–28.

SEBEOK, T. A., AND J. UMIKER-SEBEOK, EDS.
    1980   *Speaking of Apes: A Critical Anthropology of Two-Way Communication with Man.* New York: Plenum.

SELIGSON, M. A.
    1984   *The Gap between Rich and Poor: Contending Perspectives on the Political Economy of Development.* Boulder: Westview.

SERRIE, H., ED.
    1986   *Anthropology and International Business.* Studies in Third World Societies, no. 28. Williamsburg, Va.: Department of Anthropology, College of William and Mary.

SERVICE, E. R.
    1962   *Primitive Social Organization: An Evolutionary Perspective.* New York: Random House.
    1966   *The Hunters.* Englewood Cliffs, N.J.: Prentice-Hall.
    1971   *Primitive Social Organization: An Evolutionary Perspective,* 2d ed. New York: Random House.
    1975   *Origins of the State and Civilization: The Process of Cultural Evolution.* New York: W. W. Norton.

SEYFARTH, R. M., D. L. CHENEY, AND P. MARLER
    1980   Monkey Responses to Three Different Alarm Calls. *Science* 210: 801–803.

SHABECOFF, P.
    1989a   Ivory Imports Banned to Aid Elephant. *The New York Times,* June 7, p. 15.
    1989b   New Lobby Is Helping Wildlife of Africa. *The New York Times,* June 9, p. 14.

SHANNON, T. R.
    1989   *An Introduction to the World System Perspective.* Boulder: Westview.

SHWEDER, R., AND H. LeVINE, EDS.
    1984   *Culture Theory: Essays on Mind, Self, and Emotion.* Cambridge: Cambridge University Press.

SILVERBLATT, I.
    1988   Women in States. *Annual Review of Anthropology* 17: 427–460.

SIPES, R. G.
    1973   War, Sports, and Aggression: An Empirical Test of Two Rival Theories. *American Anthropologist* 75: 64–86.

SKODAK, M., AND H. M. SKEELS
    1949   A Final Follow-up Study of One Hundred Adopted Children. *Journal of Genetic Psychology* 75: 85–125.

SLADE, M.
    1984   Displaying Affection in Public. *The New York Times,* December 17, p. B14.

SMALL, M., ED.
    1984   *Female Primates: Studies by Women Primatologists.* New York: Alan R. Liss.

SMUTS, B. B.
    1985   *Sex and Friendship in Baboons.* New York: Aldine.

SPINDLER, G. D., ED.
    1978   *The Making of Psychological Anthropology.* Berkeley: University of California Press.
    1982   *Doing the Ethnography of Schooling: Educational Anthropology in Action.* New York: Holt, Rinehart and Winston.

SPRADLEY, J. P.
    1979   *The Ethnographic Interview.* New York: Holt, Rinehart and Winston.

STACK, C. B.
    1975   *All Our Kin: Strategies for Survival in a Black Community.* New York: Harper Torchbooks.

STEEDMAN, C., URWIN, C., AND V. WALKERDINE, EDS.
    1985   *Language, Gender and Childhood.* London: Routledge and Kegan Paul.

STEPONAITIS, V.
    1986   Prehistoric Archaeology in the Southeastern United States. *Annual Review of Anthropology* 15: 363–404.

STEVENSON, R. F.
    1968   *Population and Political Systems in Tropical Africa.* New York: Columbia University Press.

STEWARD, J. H.
    1949   Cultural Causality and Law: A Trial Formu-

lation of the Development of Early Civilizations. *American Anthropologist* 51: 1–27.

1955 *Theory of Culture Change.* Urbana: University
of Illinois Press.

STOCKING, G. W., ED.

1986 *Malinowski, Rivers, Benedict and Others: Essays
on Culture and Personality.* Madison, Wis.:
University of Wisconsin Press.

STOLER A.

1977 Class Structure and Female Autonomy in Rural Java. *Signs* 3: 74–89.

SWANSON, G. E.

1960 *The Birth of the Gods: The Origin of Primitive
Beliefs.* Ann Arbor: University of Michigan
Press.

SWIFT, M.

1963 Men and Women in Malay Society. In *Women
in the New Asia,* ed. B. Ward, pp. 268–286.
Paris: UNESCO.

TANNER, N.

1974 Matrifocality in Indonesia and Africa and
among Black Americans. In *Women, Culture,
and Society,* ed. M. Z. Rosaldo and L. Lamphere, pp. 129–156. Stanford, Calif.: Stanford
University Press.

TAYLOR, C.

1978 Anthropologist-in-Residence. In *Applied Anthropology in America,* ed. E. M. Eddy and
W. L. Partridge, pp. 229–244. New York: Columbia University Press.

TELEKI, G.

1973 *The Predatory Behavior of Wild Chimpanzees.*
Lewisburg, Pa.: Bucknell University Press.

TERRACE, H. S.

1979 *Nim.* New York: Knopf.

THOMASON, S. G., AND KAUFMAN, T.

1988 *Language Contact, Creolization and Genetic Linguistics.* Berkeley: University of California
Press.

THOMPSON, W.

1983 Introduction: World System with and without the Hyphen. In *Contending Approaches to
World System Analysis,* ed. W. Thompson, pp.
7–26. Beverly Hills, Calif.: Sage.

TIME

1985 New Look at the Elderly: A White House Report Seeks to Dispel Some Myths. February
18, 1985, p. 81.

TOFFLER, A.

1980 *The Third Wave.* New York: William Morrow.

TOLCHIN, M.

1988 What's Fair to the Young and the Taxed?
The New York Times, November 27, sec. 4,
p. 5.

TRUDGILL, P.

1983 *Sociolinguistics: An Introduction to Language
and Society,* rev. ed. Baltimore: Penguin.

TURNER, V. W.

1974 *The Ritual Process.* Harmondsworth, England:
Penguin.

TYLOR, E. B.

1958 (orig. 1871). *Primitive Culture.* New York:
Harper Torchbooks.

USA TODAY

1984 If I Err, It's because People Change Plans,
Interview with Jeane Dixon, December 28,
1984, p. 11A.

1985 [Boxed Statistics]. February 14, 1985, p. B1.

VALENTINE, C.

1968 *Culture and Poverty.* Chicago: University of
Chicago Press.

VAN BAAL, J.

1966 *Dema, Description and Analysis of Marindanim
Culture (South New Guinea).* The Hague:
M. Nijhoff.

VAN CANTFORT, T. E., AND J. B. RIMPAU

1982 Sign Language Studies with Children and
Chimpanzees. *Sign Language Studies* 34: 15–
72.

VAN SCHAIK, C. P., AND G.A.R.A.M. VAN HOOFF

1983 On the Ultimate Causes of Primate Social
Systems. *Behaviour* 85: 91–117.

VAN WILLINGEN, J.

1986 *Applied Anthropology: An Introduction.* South
Hadley, Mass.: Bergin and Garvey.

1987 *Becoming a Practicing Anthropologist: A Guide
to Careers and Training Programs in Applied Anthropology.* NAPA Bulletin 3. Washington,
D.C. American Anthropological Association/
National Association for the Practice of Anthropology.

VAYDA, A. P.

1968 (orig. 1961). Economic Systems in Ecological
Perspective: The Case of the Northwest
Coast. In *Readings in Anthropology,* 2d ed.,
vol. 2, ed. M. H. Fried, pp. 172–178. New
York: Crowell.

WAGLEY, C. W.

1968 *The Latin American Tradition.* New York: Columbia University Press.

1977 *Welcome of Tears: The Tapirapé Indians of Central
Brazil.* New York: Oxford University Press.

WAGNER, R.

1981 *The Invention of Culture,* rev. ed. Chicago:
University of Chicago Press.

WALLACE, A. F. C.

1956 Revitalization Movements. *American Anthropologist* 58: 264–281.

1966   *Religion: An Anthropological View.* New York: Random House.

1970a *Culture and Personality,* 2d ed. New York: Random House.

1970b *The Death and Rebirth of the Seneca.* New York: Knopf.

WALLERSTEIN, I.

1974   *The Modern World-System: Capitalist Agriculture and the Origins of the European World-Economy in the Sixteenth Century.* New York: Academic Press.

1980   *The Modern World System II: Mercantilism and the Consolidation of the European World-Economy, 1600–1750.* New York: Academic Press.

1982   The Rise and Future Demise of the World Capitalist System: Concepts for Comparative Analysis. In *Introduction to the Sociology of "Developing Societies,"* ed. H. Alavi and T. Shanin, pp. 29–53. New York: Monthly Review Press.

WALLMAN, S., ED.

1977   *Perceptions of Development.* New York: Cambridge University Press.

WAX, M. L., AND J. CASSELL, EDS.

1979   *Federal Regulations: Ethical Issues and Social Research.* Boulder: Westview Press.

WEAVER, T., GEN. ED.

1973   *To See Ourselves: Anthropology and Modern Social Issues.* Glenview, Ill.: Scott, Foresman.

WEBER, M.

1947   *The Theory of Social and Economic Organization.* London: Hodge.

1958   (orig. 1904). *The Protestant Ethic and the Spirit of Capitalism.* New York: Scribner's.

1968   (orig. 1922). *Economy and Society,* trans. E. Fischoff et al. New York: Bedminster Press.

WEBER, W.

1976   *Peasants into Frenchman.* Stanford, Calif.: Stanford University Press.

WEISS, M. L., AND A. E. MANN

1989   *Human Biology and Behavior: An Anthropological Perspective,* 5th ed. Glenview, Ill.: Scott, Foresman.

WESTERMARCK, E.

1894   *The History of Human Marriage,* 2d ed. London: Macmillan.

WHITE, D., ET AL.

n.d.   Effects of World-System Linkages: Consequences of Nomothetic Patterns in History. In *Comparative Research: Theory, Method and Synthesis,* ed. Melvin Ember and Douglas White. New Haven, Conn.: HRAF Press (in press).

WHITE, L. A.

1959   *The Evolution of Culture: The Development of Civilization to the Fall of Rome.* New York: McGraw-Hill.

WHITING, B. E., ED.

1963   *Six Cultures: Studies of Child Rearing.* New York: Wiley.

WHO OWNS WHOM

Annual directories of parent, associate and subsidiary companies, by region. London: O. W. Roskill.

WHO OWNS WHOM IN NORTH AMERICA

1984   16th ed. Philadelphia: International Publications Service.

WHORF, B. L.

1956   A Linguistic Consideration of Thinking in Primitive Communities. In *Language, Thought, and Reality: Selected Writings of Benjamin Lee Whorf,* ed. J. B. Carroll, pp. 65–86. Cambridge, Mass.: MIT Press.

WILLIAMS, J.

1985   What They Say, Home? English Dialects are Adding to Racial Misunderstandings. *The Washington Post National Weekly Edition,* May 6, 1985, p. 10.

WITTFOGEL, K. A.

1957   *Oriental Despotism: A Comparative Study of Total Power.* New Haven, Conn.: Yale University Press.

WOLCOTT, H. F.

1977   *Teachers versus Technocrats: An Educational Innovation in Anthropological Perspective.* Eugene: Center for Educational Policy and Management, University of Oregon.

WOLF, E. R.

1955   Types of Latin American Peasantry. *American Anthropologist* 57: 452–471.

1966   *Peasants.* Englewood Cliffs, N.J.: Prentice-Hall.

1982   *Europe and the People without History.* Berkeley: University of California Press.

WOLF, M.

1985   *Revolution Postponed: Women in Contemporary China.* Stanford, Calif.: Stanford University Press.

WOOLARD, K. A.

1989   *Double Talk: Bilingualism and the Politics of Ethnicity in Catalonia.* Stanford, Calif.: Stanford University Press.

WORLD ALMANAC & BOOK OF FACTS

Published annually. New York: Newspaper Enterprise Association.

WORLD ALMANAC & BOOK OF FACTS

1985   New York: Newspaper Enterprise Association.

WORSLEY, P.

    1970   *The Trumpet Shall Sound: A Study of Cargo Cults in Melanesia.* New York: Schocken.

    1984   *The Three Worlds: Culture and World Development.* Chicago: University of Chicago Press.

    1985   (orig. 1959). Cargo Cults. In *Readings in Anthropology,* Guilford, Conn.: Dushkin.

WRANGHAM, R.

    1980   An Ecological Model of Female-Bonded Primate Groups. *Behavior* 75: 262–300.

    1987   The Significance of African Apes for Reconstructing Human Social Evolution. In *The Evolution of Human Behavior: Primate Models,* ed. W. G. Kinzey, pp. 51–71. Albany: State University of New York Press.

WRIGHT, H. T., AND G. A. JOHNSON

    1975   Population, Exchange, and Early State Formation in Southwestern Iran. *American Anthropologist* 77: 267–289.

WULFF, R. M., AND S. J. FISKE, EDS.

    1987   *Anthropological Praxis: Translating Knowledge into Action.* Boulder, Colo.: Westview Press.

YARROW, A. L.

    1988   Harris Poll Finds Arts Attendance Has Declined. *The New York Times,* March 16, p. 24.

PHOTO CREDITS

INDEX